Symbol	Chapter where introduced	Definition
e	5	Real foreign exchange rate, defined as units of foreign currency per unit of domestic currency (e.g., 2.2 deutsche marks per dollar) adjusted for differences in inflation rates
e'	5, 14	Nominal foreign exchange rate
e	7	Superscript e means "expected"
e	8	Efficiency factor
e	17	Fraction of deposits that banks hold as reserves
E	2	Real expenditures ($E = C + I + G$)
E_p	3	Planned real expenditures ($E_p = C + I_p + G$)
f	5-appendix	Response of money demand to a 1 percent change in the interest rate
F	2	Real government transfer payments
F_G	2	Real government transfer payments
FOMC	17	Federal Open Market Committee
F_p	2	Real interest paid by consumers to business
F	6	Production function
g	10-appendix	Slope of the short-run Phillips curve (SP)
G	2	Real government purchases of goods and services
GNP	1	Gross national product, either nominal or real
GRH	13	Gramm–Rudman–Hollings Act
h	5-appendix	Response of money demand to a \$1 change in income at a fixed interest rate
h	7	Response of output to a price surprise in the Lucas–Friedman supply function
h	11	Response of unemployment to the output ratio (Q/Q^N)
h	13	Growth rate of high-powered money
H	13, 17	High-powered money
i	11	Nominal or market interest rate
I	2	Real gross private investment
I_n	12,19	Net investment
I_p	3	Planned real gross private investment
I_u	3	Real unintended inventory investment, $I_u = E - E_p$
IS	4	Commodity-market equilibrium curve
j	9	Coefficient of adjustment of expectations
k	3	Spending multiplier
k_1	5-appendix	Multiplier for autonomous spending
k_2	5-appendix	Multiplier for real money supply
k	12	Growth rate of capital input
k	18	Marginal propensity to consume for permanent income
K	12,19	Capital stock
K^*	19	Desired capital stock
L	18	Age at death in life-cycle hypothesis
LCH	18	Life-cycle hypothesis
LM	4	Money-market equilibrium curve
LP	9	Long-run Phillips curve

(continued on inside back cover)

Fifth Edition

Macroeconomics

Fifth Edition

Macroeconomics

Robert J. Gordon

Stanley G. Harris Professor in the Social Sciences
Northwestern University

SCOTT, FORESMAN / LITTLE, BROWN HIGHER EDUCATION
A Division of Scott, Foresman and Company
Glenview, Illinois   London, England

About the Cover: The two curved lines represent the U.S. "twin deficits" in the 1970s and 1980s, expressed as a share of real GNP. The upper curved line represents the foreign trade deficit, which shifted from surplus in the 1970s to deficit in the 1980s. The lower curved line represents the U.S. federal budget deficit, which shifted from small deficits in the 1970s to larger deficits in the 1980s.

Library of Congress Cataloging-in-Publication Data

Gordon, Robert J. (Robert James)
    Macroeconomics/Robert J. Gordon.—5th ed.
        p.   cm.
    Includes bibliographical references.
    ISBN 0-673-52052-8
    1. Macroeconomics.   I. Title.
HB172.5.G67   1989   89-39456
339—dc20   CIP

with love, for Julie

Contents

Summary, Concepts, Questions and Problems, and Self-Test Answers appear at the end of each chapter. Boxed features appear in color.

PART III Aggregate Demand, Aggregate Supply, and Stabilization Policy 155

6 The *IS-LM* Model, and the Aggregate Demand and Supply Curves 156

7 The Keynesian Revolution and the New Classical Economics 179

PART V   Macroeconomics in the Long Run: Growth, the Public Debt, and the Foreign Debt   *355*

Preface:
To the Instructor

A characteristic of the development of macroeconomics, at least since Keynes, is the response of ideas to the evolution of events. Reflecting the record-breaking U. S. business expansion (1982–89 and still counting), the deepening concern over slow productivity growth, and the growing debate about the twin deficits—fiscal and foreign trade—there is a growing consensus that a major shift should occur in the teaching of macroeconomics.

As has often occurred before, this shift in consensus has raced ahead of the textbooks. The fifth edition of *Macroeconomics* takes the lead in reorienting the instruction of intermediate macroeconomics courses for the 1990s in response to the major events and theoretical developments of the 1980s. These developments include the emergence of the twin deficits and the debate over their importance, ranging from the view that they are benign to the view that they represent a catastrophe; the implications of the record-breaking post-1982 economic expansion for economic theory and policy; intensified concern about the long-running productivity growth slowdown and about future growth in the U. S. standard of living; the reorientation of new classical macroeconomics from policy ineffectiveness to the real-business-cycle approach; the emergence of a better-developed new Keynesian theory of wage and price stickiness; and the internationalization of the U. S. economy. These issues, either new or of greater importance in the 1980s, set the agenda for the major innovations introduced in the fifth edition.

Major Changes in Organization and Emphasis

Economic Growth and the Twin Deficits

Macroeconomics brings to the forefront a greatly increased emphasis on long-run growth and the long-run effects of fiscal and foreign trade deficits. At the same time, it retains intact the time-tested organization of the first eleven chapters of the book. Most important, this new emphasis is achieved by introducing a new three-chapter Part V "Macroeconomics in the Long Run: Growth, the Public Debt, and the Foreign Debt," immediately after the core chapters on unemployment and inflation.

The three chapters in this section discuss economic growth and the productivity slowdown (12), long-run fiscal policy issues (13), and foreign trade and debt (14). Each is an expanded and rewritten version of previous chapters on these topics, with more emphasis on long-run issues and less on issues related to stabilization policy. The growth chapter now incorporates a simplified graphic treatment of the Solow growth model, which adds insight to the current debate over whether a reduction in the fiscal deficit and an increase in the national saving rate is necessary for an increase in the rate of economic growth. The treatment of the productivity growth slowdown incorporates the latest research findings. The new Chapter 13 on long-run fiscal policy issues concentrates on the government budget constraint, the burden of the debt, the government's solvency condition, and the Barro–Ricardo equivalence theory. Material on fiscal stabilization policy, such as fiscal policy lags, is moved into a unified treatment of monetary and fiscal stabilization policy in the new Chapter 17.

The emphasis on the twin deficits is also reflected elsewhere. The twin deficits are added to the list of major macroeconomic concepts and puzzles in Chapter 1. And the traditional issues of strong and weak effects of monetary and fiscal policy, and of fiscal crowding out, have been moved to the end of Chapter 4, so that Chapter 5 can be reserved for interactions between the twin deficits and the central issue of the monetary-fiscal policy mix.

New Classical and New Keynesian Theory

The second major change in the text reflects the direction of macroeconomic research in the late 1980s. Two new developments in the theory of business cycles have come to the fore in the past five years. On the new classical side, research on the Lucas "information barriers" approach has been discontinued in favor of the real business cycle model and the related issues of distinguishing economic growth from business fluctuations. On the other side there has been an outpouring of research on the new Keynesian approach, based on building microeconomic foundations for wage and price stickiness.

The treatment of new classical economics has been greatly expanded. A longer section on the original Lucas model provides more detail on the local-aggregate distinction that is basic to his deduction that the slope of the Phillips curve will vary, depending on the source of the shocks. A completely new section on real business cycles explains how these models work and notes some of their limitations that have surfaced in recent critiques. The text not only gives a full treatment of the real business cycle model, but presents it in the proper context of its chronological development as an outgrowth of the earlier new classical model. Chapter 7 is organized to present the intellectual transition from the new classical "Mark I" (policy-ineffectiveness proposition) approach to the "Mark II" approach (real business cycle analysis). Other textbooks, if they treat real business cycle analysis at all, do so in isolation from its relation to the original Friedman and Lucas innovations.

Developments on the new Keynesian side are reflected in a greatly expanded Chapter 8, entirely devoted to new Keynesian economics. This provides a unique presentation, simplified for undergraduate students, of the latest developments in the research of Blanchard, Ball, Romer, Summers,

Mankiw, and others, including the topics of small menu costs versus large social costs, macroeconomic externalities, coordination failures, the absence of complete indexation, implicit contracts, the efficiency wage model, and the input-output approach. Long-term labor contracts and the differences between the United States and Japan are treated as just one of the new Keynesian explanations of wage and price rigidity.

Financial Markets, the Demand for Money, and the Stock Market

The deregulation of the financial system has introduced far more substitutes for money than is recognized by the conventional textbook treatment of the demand for money. A new Chapter 16, "Financial Markets and the Demand for Money," provides a unique setting and context for the traditional money demand theory by starting with an introduction to financial intermediaries and financial markets. The role of money within the financial system is clearly illustrated with a new table and graph, that places the $M1$ and $M2$ definitions of monetary aggregates within the context of financial markets as a whole.

The new broader treatment of financial markets is carried over into the chapters on consumption (18) and investment (19). A new case study examines the connections between the stock market and consumption spending and asks why the 1987 stock market crash did not have a major impact on consumption. The role of the stock market is examined again in a new box in Chapter 19 on the q-theory of investment, which contrasts the attractive theoretical properties of the theory with its poor empirical performance.

Monetarism, Activism, and Stabilization Policy

There is a growing consensus that, in view of a political stalemate over the fiscal deficit, the task of stabilizing the economy's business cycle swings in demand falls primarily on monetary policy, while the effects of fiscal policy are now more closely related to long-run concerns over growth, the public debt, and the foreign debt. Reflecting this consensus, the former chapter on fiscal stabilization policy has been completely recast in a long-run growth setting (Chapter 13), and previous topics on fiscal stabilization have been placed in the same section as the related material on monetary stabilization in Chapter 17. New case studies in this chapter (Sections 17-8 and 17-9) provide a unified treatment of monetary and fiscal actions in the major postwar episodes.

Internationalization of Macroeconomics: Further Integrated in the Text

This edition continues the process of converting the traditional closed-economy treatment of macroeconomics into a consistent open-economy treatment from beginning to end. This emphasis begins with the selection of the foreign trade deficit as one of the six core macroeconomic concepts in Chapter 1 and with the new Section 1-8, "The Internationalization of Macroeconomics," which illustrates key differences in macroeconomic performance among the United States, Europe and Japan.

Chapter 2 is improved by adding a separate foreign sector to the theoretical circular flow diagram (2-4) and to the plumbing diagram (2-6). The leakage and injection equations in Chapters 2 and 3, and the illustration of the leakage-injection balance in Figure 2-5, also include foreign trade. The section on international crowding out in Chapter 5 is now consistent with the Appendix to Chapter 5. An open economy with fixed exchange rates has a smaller fiscal multiplier as a result of its higher marginal leakage rate. However, in an open economy a shift from a fixed exchange rate system to a flexible exchange rate system results in a higher fiscal multiplier, since flexible rates add the extra channel of crowding out through the relation of the exchange rate to the interest rate.

An international focus is added to Chapter 10, previously concerned exclusively with supply shocks. Both a new case study and a new theoretical section highlight the differing behavior of U. S. and European unemployment in the 1980s, and introduce the new structuralist and hysteresis theories that attempt to explain the difference.

The international chapter (14) maintains the simple, straightforward introduction to the balance of payments, the theory of exchange rate adjustment, purchasing-power parity, and problems of international adjustment. There is a new emphasis on the long lag in the economy's adjustment to the 1985–88 depreciation of the dollar, and on the growing debate over the desirability of international policy coordination.

Finally, in keeping with the role of previous editions in developing and presenting a unique array of macroeconomic data, Appendix B now includes data for major macro variables for the other six major industrial nations—Canada, France, Germany, Italy, Japan, and the United Kingdom.

Core Analytical Treatment Maintained

Despite changes, the strengths of the treatment of core macroeconomic theory, the emphasis on applications and case studies, and the full array of pedagogical tools are all retained.

1. The traditional Keynesian and *IS-LM* models are presented concisely, with the *IS* and *LM* curves crossing by page 107 in the text.

2. The core material on the twin deficits, fiscal and foreign trade, is introduced before the development of the *AS-AD* diagrams. This allows us to link clearly the twin deficits to the *IS-LM* model and the issue of the monetary-fiscal mix.

3. By far the most important feature of the organization is the presentation of wage and price adjustment in an *early* and *unified* series of chapters. The presentation of the *AS-AD* model in Chapter 6 begins a unique five-chapter unit that takes the student through the development of macroeconomics and shows how each theory developed in response to the inadequacies of its predecessors: classical self-correction, the original Keynesian model, Friedman's fooling model and its successor, new classical Mark I (Lucas), then the real business cycle model (Mark II), and

the new Keynesian model. Next is a treatment of inflation dynamics that is explicitly derived from the *AS-AD* diagram and treats demand and supply disturbances symmetrically.

4. The early treatment of wage and price adjustment is achieved by moving the detailed theory of consumption and investment behavior to the back of the book. In any other position, the presentation of these topics interrupts the flow, and they are clearly less important than growth and the two debt chapters for instructors who can only teach the book through Chapter 15.

5. The new organization is designed so that those instructors who can only go through Chapter 15 will conclude with the chapter on activism, leaving the last four chapters to cover the details of financial markets, policy implementation, consumption, and investment.

Real-World Focus and Case Studies

The fifth edition retains not just the treatment of core macro theory, but also the unique emphasis on case studies. Rather than describing historical events in a separate chapter long after the relevant theory has been introduced, the case studies appear in the middle of chapters adjacent to the relevant theoretical sections. The case studies continually remind the student that the theory helps explain real-world episodes. And, as in previous editions, many of the case studies use consistent series developed in my research for natural real GNP, the natural unemployment rate, and the natural employment deficit.

New or substantially expanded case studies include "International Crowding Out and Crowding In, 1981–89" (Section 5-9), "Disinflation in the 1980s" (9-9), "The Divergence of Unemployment Rates in the United States and Europe" (10-9), "Monetary Policy in the Longest Peacetime Expansion" (17-9), "Main Features of the U. S. Consumption Data" (18-2), and "The Historical Instability of Investment" (19-2). New topic boxes include one on the thrift institution debacle (in Chapter 16) and on Tobin's *q*-theory of investment (in Chapter 19).

The Fifth Edition: Presentation and Pedagogy

Clarity of Presentation

As in the fourth edition, the integrated algebraic and graphical presentation of the *DG-SP* inflation-output model is treated in full in the Appendix to Chapter 10. The algebra is simplified by using a single symbol for the percent log output ratio. Instructors can either assign the appendix or limit their presentation to the simplified treatment of the text in Chapters 9 and 10, which does not introduce the *DG* line.

Continuing the emphasis of the last edition, the text has been carefully combed for overly mechanical explanations, and for unnecessary digressions, in order to stress intuitive explanations of substantive economic principles.

Design and Organizational Changes

Users will immediately notice the new design format of the book, which gives this edition a more spacious look and allows for more of the explanation of each graph to appear on the same spread as the graph itself.

The data graphs use the available space fully, and many use unique "blow-up" magnified sections to show the details of the recent past in the context of a longer span of history. Shading is used liberally in both theoretical and data diagrams. Photos of major macroeconomists appear in the margins, and most topic boxes are illustrated with photos to maintain student interest.

The organization of the book is similar to the fourth edition through Chapter 11, except that the material on strong and weak effects of fiscal policy has been moved to the end of Chapter 4 from the middle of Chapter 5. The new section on growth and the twin deficits (Chapters 12–14) incorporates some sections of the previous Chapters 19, 15, and 18, respectively. The final group of chapters (15–19) is in the same order as the previous unit consisting of Chapters 12–17.

Teaching Aids

Self-test questions.   A new and unique feature of this textbook is the set of "Self-Test" questions interspersed through each chapter. These promote more active student learning than simple mid-chapter summaries. Each self-test asks the student a simple question about the preceding material, allowing the student to test his or her comprehension of the material. Answers appear at the end of each chapter.

End-of-chapter questions and problems.   The end-of-chapter questions and problems have been completely revised for the fifth edition. Answers are provided in the Instructor's Manual/Test Bank.

Glossary and marginal definitions.   The glossary contains a cross-reference to the section where each term is first introduced. Terms with glossary definitions are identified in boldface type when they are first introduced. Definitions are also set in the margin adjacent to the point where each boldface term appears. The marginal definitions are in some cases shorter than, but otherwise identical to, the definitions in the glossary.

Expanded data appendix.   Since its beginning, this book has been unique in developing its own set of data on core concepts such as natural output and unemployment, based on my research. Testimony to the usefulness of these data series comes from the number of economic principles textbooks that include them. This edition now includes Tables A-1 (U. S. annual data since 1875), A-2 (U. S. quarterly data since 1947), and B (postwar annual data for the six other industrialized countries). Appendix C provides sources and methods for the appendix tables and for graphs containing data created specially for the text.

Features retained. The fifth edition contains many additional teaching aids to facilitate student understanding, and most of these remain intact from previous editions. Third-level headings and summary paragraphs break up long sections and provide a running commentary on the main points. Color is used consistently in diagrams, with red lines identifying demand curves and black lines identifying supply curves. Diagrams use labels to help the student distinguish between the sources of shifts in curves and movements along curves. Each chapter ends with a summary, a list of new concepts, and a set of questions and problems. Each equation in the text and appendixes is presented twice, in its general form and in a numerical example. A single running numerical example links the text figures in Chapters 3–6.

Ancillary Material

Instructor's Manual/Test Bank. The fifth edition provides a completely new test bank of multiple-choice exam questions, with more than twice as many questions as before. New questions are based on graphs provided as part of the test bank. The Instructor's Manual, also completely rewritten, provides suggestions on how to use the book and how to teach each chapter, how to use the various text appendixes, answers to discussion questions and problems in the text, and additional essay and discussion questions.

Computerized Test Bank. The expanded test bank contains over 1000 multiple-choice questions and is provided both in the Instructor's Manual/ Test Bank and on PC diskettes. Numerous questions are based on graphs provided with the test bank.

Student Workbook. An unusually complete student workbook is available. It contains both short objective questions and longer numerical exercises. Blank grids are included to encourage students to work out graphic solutions to numerical problems.

The Gordon software package: Data analysis and modeling programs. This greatly expanded and improved software package now features both problem sets and "what if" scenarios in which students explore how changes in variables produce different macroeconomic effects depending on the model used. Data analysis programs allow students to test macroeconomic theories by running regressions and graphing variables, all by using the data in the test's data appendixes and additional data. Throughout, students can easily change inputs and see their effects with graphs that show both the original and new curves over time.

The *Gordon Update*. The *Gordon Update* will be issued each spring and fall semester, just as it has been since the spring of 1981, to provide a review of recent events in the context of the theory developed in the text. The *Update* also provides updates on key data series used in the text.

Acknowledgments

I remain grateful to all those who were thanked in the preface of the first four editions. Space limitations prevent me from repeating all of these acknowledgments.

My greatest debt in preparing the fifth edition goes to questionnaire respondents, who helped steer me toward the major substantive improvements described above, and to the reviewers. Several reviewers went far beyond the call of duty by providing extremely detailed and insightful comments, and I have incorporated as many as possible of the reviewers' suggestions and corrections into the final text. The reviewers were: Francis W. Ahking, University of Connecticut; Stuart Allen, University of North Carolina, Greensboro; Richard J. Cebula, Emory University; A. Edward Day, University of Central Florida; David W. Findlay, Colby College; Daniel Himarios, University of Texas at Arlington; Nancy Jianakoplos, Michigan State University; Stephen A. McCafferty, Ohio State University; Anne Mayhew, University of Tennessee; Jerry Miner, Syracuse University; Khan A. Mohabbat, Northern Illinois University; Douglas V. Orr, California State University, Hayward; William Shingleton, Valparaiso University; John M. Veitch, University of Southern California; and Herbert D. Werner, University of Missouri, St. Louis.

Over the past three years a number of instructors have written to me with questions and protests about the fourth edition. Some of the most valuable suggestions came from those who were later asked to be reviewers. Others making helpful comments were Richard M. Alston, Weber State College; John Cownie, Northeastern Illinois University; Martyn Duffy, University of Manchester (U.K.); Robert Eisner, Northwestern University; Shahrukh R. Khan, State University of New York, College at Oneonta; Sun M. Kahng, University of Minnesota, Morris; Lisa Lipowski, Rutgers University; Paul L. Morgan, Westmont College; James J. Rakowski, University of Notre Dame; J. Kirker Stephens, University of Oklahoma; and Jack H. Stone, Spelman College.

This book contains a great deal of data, some of it originally created for this book, both in the data appendix and in individual case studies. George Williams developed data and graphs for the fifth edition, with help from Dan Shiman, Ronald Rats, Donald Dell, and Sam Sweetpea. Richard M. Alston developed the new end-of-chapter questions and problems. Tim Schmidt compiled the glossary and endpaper text and checked the end-of-chapter questions and answers.

Thanks go to the Scott, Foresman/Little Brown staff. Reviewing, project coordination, and nagging were efficiently and graciously handled by the developmental editor, Kathy Richmond. Carrie Dierks, the project editor, effectively and consistently rephrased the author's English to make it intelligible to students, and managed with aplomb the production of the book.

Finally, thanks go to my wife Julie for putting up with the overwhelming litter of manuscript and proofs that often spilled off the desks and tables onto the floor. As always, her unfailing encouragement and welcome diversions made the book possible.

Robert J. Gordon

Preface:
To the Student

Macroeconomics is one of the most important topics for college students, because the health of the economy will have an influence on your whole life. The overall level of employment and unemployment will determine the ease with which you find a job after college and with which you will be able to change jobs or obtain promotions in the future. The inflation rate will influence the interest rate you receive on your savings and pay when you borrow money, and also the extent to which the purchasing power of your savings will be eroded by higher prices.

This macroeconomics text will equip you with the principles you need to make sense out of the conflicting and contradictory discussions of economic conditions and policies in newspapers and news magazines. You will be better able to appraise the performance of the President and Congress, and to predict the impact of their policy actions on your family and business.

Who Should Read This Book?

Most college students taking this course will have taken a course in economic principles. But this book has been written to be read by *all* students, even those who have not previously enrolled in an economics course. How is this possible? In Chapters 1–3 we review material covered in every principles course. By the end of Chapter 3, all students will have learned the essential concepts they need to understand the material to be developed.

This book has been carefully designed to look and read like a principles book. The entire presentation is graphic, with simple ninth-grade algebra used only in the review of elementary ideas in Chapter 3. Examples are used frequently. Most chapters have one or more case studies to give you a breather from the analysis and to show how the ideas of the chapter can be applied to real-world episodes. New words are set off in boldface type and defined both in the margins and in the Glossary in the back of the book, thus easing vocabulary problems. The diagrams in the first part of the book as well as the text description itself use numerical examples instead of mathematical symbols to show movement of the economy from one situation to another.

And, finally, a major innovation in this edition is the set of "Self-Test" questions. These questions, which appear three or four times in each chapter, test your understanding of the main point of the preceding section. Write down your answers on a sheet of paper and compare them with those provided at the end of each chapter. You will quickly see whether you have understood what you have been reading, or whether you need to review the material again.

How to Read This Book

Each chapter begins with an introduction, linking it to previous chapters, and ends with a Summary. When you begin a chapter, first read the introduction to make sure you understand how the chapter differs from the previous ones. Then plan to read each chapter twice. On the first reading, use the Self-Test questions and answers to check whether you understand what you have been reading. Then, after completing your first reading of the chapter, study the Summary and try to answer the end-of-chapter questions, marking those points you do not understand. Finally, go back for a second reading, paying attention to the discussion of issues you may not have grasped fully at first.

Always try to write out answers to the questions and problems. Another aid to comprehension is to work through the chapter and substitute a different numerical example for the one used in the text. Those who have purchased the accompanying *Student Workbook* will find that the path to greater comprehension has been laid out for you in detail.

If you should get lost in the course of reading the text, remember that there are built-in study aids to help, in addition to the Self-Test questions. If you don't understand a particular section, turn to the Summary at the end of the chapter. If you forget the meaning of a word, turn to the Glossary. (The Glossary will also help you tackle assigned outside readings.) A Guide to Symbols on the inside covers of the book will help you with the alphabetical symbols that are used in equations or in diagrams as labels.

Optional Material

Footnotes and chapter appendixes have been provided as a place to put more difficult or less important material. Your instructor will decide whether an appendix is to be assigned, but even if not assigned, tackle it on your own when you have mastered the ideas in the chapter. Footnotes contain qualifications, bibliographical references (valuable if you ever need to write a term paper on these topics), and cross-references to related material and diagrams in the book.

Finally, notice that tables in the appendix contain historical data starting with 1875 and updated to mid-1989. These figures can help you determine what was going on in periods not covered by the case studies or can be used in outside assignments and term papers. Don't forget possible applications in history, political science, and sociology courses.

Fifth Edition

Macroeconomics

PART I
Introduction and Measurement

CHAPTER ONE

What Is Macroeconomics?

Business will be better or worse.

— *Calvin Coolidge, 1928*

1-1 How Macroeconomics Affects Everyday Lives

Macroeconomics is the study of the major economic totals or aggregates.

Macroeconomics is concerned with the big economic issues that determine your own economic well-being as well as that of your family and everyone you know. Each of these issues involves the overall economic performance of the nation, rather than that of particular individuals.

For instance, do citizens find it easy or difficult to find jobs? On average, are prices rising rapidly, slowly, or not at all? How much total income is the nation producing, and how rapidly is total income growing year after year? Is the interest rate charged to borrow money high or low? Is the government spending more than it collects in tax revenue? Is the nation as a whole accumulating assets in other countries or is it becoming more indebted to them?

Each of these six questions involves a central macroeconomic concept to which you will be introduced in this chapter. The basic task of macroeconomics is to study the behavior of each of the six concepts, why each matters to individual citizens, and what the government can do (if anything) to improve macroeconomic performance. Of course, there are many additional concepts in macroeconomics beyond the six selected here as the most central. But for now it helps to start slowly by focusing just on the six, so let us take each one in turn and see how it affects everyday life:

The **unemployment rate** is the number of jobless individuals who are actively looking for work (or are on temporary layoff), divided by the total of those employed and unemployed.

1. The **unemployment rate.** The higher the overall unemployment rate, the harder it is for each individual who wants a job to find work. College seniors who want permanent jobs after graduation are likely to have more job offers if the national unemployment rate is low than high. All adults fear a high unemployment rate, which raises the chances that they will be laid off, will be unable to pay their bills, will have their cars repossessed, or even will lose their homes through a mortgage foreclosure. In "bad times," when the unemployment rate is high, crime, mental illness, and suicide also increase. It is no wonder that many people consider unemployment to be the single most important macroeconomic issue. And this is nothing new. Robert Burton, an English clergyman, wrote in 1621 that "employment is so essential to human happiness that indolence is justly considered the mother of misery."

The inflation rate is the percentage rate of increase in the economy's average level of prices.

2. **The inflation rate.** A high inflation rate means that prices on average are rising rapidly, while a low inflation rate means that prices on average are rising slowly. An inflation rate of zero means that prices on average remain the same, month after month. Many people are affected when the economy shifts from a low to a high inflation rate, as it did in the United States in the 1970s and might again in the 1990s. Retired people, or those about to retire, are the biggest losers since their hard-earned savings buy less and less as prices go up. Even college students may lose as the rising prices of room, board, and textbooks erode their savings accounts from past summer and after-school jobs. While a high inflation rate harms those who have saved in the past, it helps those who have borrowed. It is this capricious aspect of inflation, taking from some and giving to others, that makes people dislike inflation.

Productivity is the average amount of output produced per employee or per hour.

3. **Productivity** growth. "Productivity" is the average amount per worker that a nation produces in total goods and services, about $44,000 per worker in the United States in 1989. The higher a nation's average productivity, the more there is to go around. The faster average productivity grows, the easier it is for each member of society to improve his or her standard of living. If productivity were to grow at 3 percent from 1989 to the year 2000, U.S. productivity would rise from $44,000 to $61,000. This extra $17,000 for each employee would make it possible for the nation to have more houses, cars, hospitals, roads, airplane trips, and defense weapons, without the need for cutting spending elsewhere. But if the growth rate of productivity were zero instead of 3 percent, U.S. productivity would remain at $44,000 in the year 2000. The extra $17,000 would not be available. To have more houses and cars, we would have to sacrifice and build fewer hospitals or schools. Such an economy, with no productivity growth, has been called "the zero-sum society" because any additional good or service enjoyed by one person requires that something be taken away from someone else. Such a society, with constant sacrifice and strife, is not likely to be a very pleasant place to live.

The interest rate is the percentage rate that is paid by borrowers to lenders.

4. **The interest rate.** When interest rates are high, as they were in the United States during the early 1980s, borrowing is expensive. The biggest losers are those who would like to become homeowners, since high interest rates boost the monthly payments on mortgages enough to make homeownership unaffordable for many people. College students and recent college graduates find that monthly payments on the new car of their dreams become too high, and they are forced to buy a smaller car, a used car, or perhaps no car at all. *Changes* in interest rates, whether up or down, disrupt financial planning for everyone, and create windfall gains and losses for savers, investors, and borrowers.

The government budget deficit is the excess of government expenditures (on goods, services, and transfer payments) over the government's tax revenues.

5. **The government budget deficit.** When the government spends more money than it takes in as tax revenue, it runs a deficit. People benefit from a budget deficit at the time it occurs, since they gain from the higher level of government spending (or lower taxes) than would occur if the budget were balanced. This is not a "free lunch," however, because eventually someone must pay the bill. Today's deficit will be paid, directly or indirectly, by citizens in the future, including college students now reading this book. Citizens will eventually "pay the bill" for today's

government deficit through lower government spending than would have occurred otherwise, through higher taxes, or through lower income.

The **foreign trade deficit** is the excess of the nation's imports of goods and services over its exports of goods and services.

6. **The foreign trade deficit.** During the 1980s Americans purchased far more imports from foreign nations than we sold as exports. To pay for all these imports, Americans sold many assets to foreigners, including most of the hotels in Honolulu and the Burger King hamburger chain. By the end of the decade the United States had run up a debt to foreigners of hundreds of billions of dollars. The net result is to make tomorrow's citizens poorer by making foreign goods more expensive and by requiring that they pay a fraction of their future income as interest payments to foreigners.

1-2 Defining Macroeconomics

How Macroeconomics Differs from Microeconomics

An **aggregate** is the total amount of an economic magnitude for the economy as a whole.

Most topics in economics can be placed in one of two categories: macroeconomics and microeconomics. *Macro* comes from a Greek word meaning "large"; *micro* comes from a Greek word meaning "small." Put another way, macroeconomics deals with the "totals" or **aggregates** of the economy and microeconomics deals with the "parts." Among these crucial economic aggregates are the six central concepts introduced in the last section. Other related aggregates that play a prominent role in macroeconomics are total wealth, money, income, and business investment. Microeconomics is devoted to the relationships among the different *parts* of the economy. For example, in macro we study fluctuations in the national income of all U.S. citizens, while in micro we try to explain the wage or salary of one type of worker in relation to another. For example, why is a professor's salary more than that of a secretary but less than that of a university president?

Economic Theory: A Process of Simplification

Economic theory achieves its understanding of the economy by a process of simplification. Ignoring the detailed differences among the millions of individuals, firms, and products in the economy, theory throws a spotlight on just a few key relations. There is no conflict between macroeconomics and microeconomics. Instead, they differ by spotlighting different relationships. Microeconomics examines the behavior of individual households and firms by making the simplifying assumption that aggregates like national income and the unemployment rate remain constant. In contrast, macroeconomics examines the behavior of aggregates like national income and the unemployment rate while ignoring differences among individual households.

It is this process of simplification that makes the study of economics so exciting. Macroeconomics is important and interesting because it affects us all. Discussions of macroeconomic issues appear in newspapers, magazines, radio, and television every day. By learning a few basic macroeconomic relations, you can quickly learn how to sift out the hundreds of irrelevant details in the news in order to focus on the few key items that foretell where the economy is going. You also can begin to understand which national and personal economic goals can be attained, and which are "pie-in-the-sky."

1-3   Nominal GNP, Real GNP, and the GNP Deflator

What Is Gross National Product?

Gross national product is the value of all currently produced goods and services sold on the market during a particular time interval.

To understand the behavior of the six key macroeconomic aggregates we need a measure of the size of the economy as a whole. Probably the most frequently used abbreviation in macroeconomics is GNP, which stands for **gross national product.** This measure of the economy's overall size is defined as the value of all currently produced goods and services sold on the market during a particular time interval.

Gross national product, or GNP, includes consumer purchases of food, clothing, gasoline, new automobiles, and haircuts and other commodities and services; it includes purchases of machinery and equipment by business firms; it includes residential structures bought by households and firms as well as nonresidential structures; and it also includes purchases of goods and services by government as well as the excess of exports over imports. GNP can be most easily thought of as the *total amount of current production.*

Economists compute GNP by a process of adding up all the different types of current production. The market value of the actual amount of production is called **nominal GNP.** The word **nominal** means the actual amount produced at current prices.

Nominal GNP is the value of gross national product in current (actual) prices.

Nominal is an adjective that modifies any economic magnitude measured in current prices.

Real and nominal magnitudes.   Nominal amounts are not very useful for economic analysis because they can increase either when people buy more physical goods and services—more cars, steaks, and haircuts—or when prices rise. An increase in my nominal spending on consumption goods from $20,000 in 1990 to $25,000 in 1991 might indicate that I became able to buy more items, or it could simply mean that I had to pay more for the same items purchased in 1990.

Are we better off if we spend more money? Or have price increases chewed up all our higher spending, leaving us no better off than before? Changes in nominal magnitudes cannot answer these questions; they hide more than they reveal. So economists concentrate on changes in real magnitudes, which eliminate the influence of year-to-year changes in prices and reflect true changes in the number, size, and quality of items purchased.

Real GNP and Real Output

Real GNP is the value of gross national product in constant prices.

Nominal GNP suffers the defects of any nominal magnitude, since its increases could reflect either increases in real production or in prices. To focus on changes in production and eliminate the influence of changing prices, we need a measure of real gross national product, or **real GNP.** Like any real magnitude, real GNP is expressed in the prices of an arbitrarily chosen "base year." The official measures of GNP in the United States use 1982 as the base year. Real GNP for every year, whether 1929 or 1990, is measured by taking the production of that particular year expressed at the constant prices of 1982.

For instance, 1990 real GNP measured "in 1982 prices" represents the amount that the actual 1990 production of goods and services would have cost if each item *had been sold at its 1982 price.* Similarly, 1929 real GNP measured in 1982 prices represents the amount that the actual 1929 production of goods and services would have cost if each item had been sold at its 1982 price.

Is real GNP in a particular year larger or smaller than nominal GNP? The answer depends on whether prices in that particular year on average were higher or lower than in 1982. Since prices usually increase each year, nominal GNP is higher than real GNP for years after 1982. Similarly, nominal GNP is lower than real GNP for years before 1982. You can see this regular pattern in Figure 1-1, which displays nominal and real GNP for each year since 1870. Notice that in every year before 1982, the thin black nominal GNP line is below the thick black real GNP line. After 1982 the nominal GNP line is above the real GNP line. Only in 1982 do the two lines cross.

Later on we will consider other real magnitudes, such as real consumption and the real money supply. An alternative label for real magnitudes is "constant-dollar," in contrast to nominal magnitudes, which are usually called "current-dollar." In other words:

	Alternative labels for magnitudes		
Items measured in prices of a single year; for instance, 1982	Constant-dollar	or	Real
Items measured in actual prices paid in each separate year	Current-dollar	or	Nominal

The GNP Deflator

The **implicit GNP deflator** is the economy's aggregate price index and is defined as the ratio of nominal GNP to real GNP.

The ratio of nominal to real GNP is called the **implicit GNP deflator.** The deflator tells us the ratio of prices actually charged in any single year (say, 1929) to the prices charged in the base year 1982. For instance, the implicit GNP deflator in 1929 was 0.146, the ratio of actual nominal GNP ($103.9 billion) to spending for the same year measured in 1982 prices ($709.6 billion):

$$\text{implicit GNP deflator for 1929} = 0.146 = \frac{\$103.9 \text{ billion}}{\$709.6 \text{ billion}} = \frac{\text{nominal GNP}}{\text{real GNP}}$$

In words, this equation states that the implicit GNP deflator in 1929 was 0.146 because 1929 nominal GNP was 14.6 percent of the value of the 1929 real GNP. This in turn reflects the fact that the average level of prices in 1929 was about one seventh the level of the base year 1982.

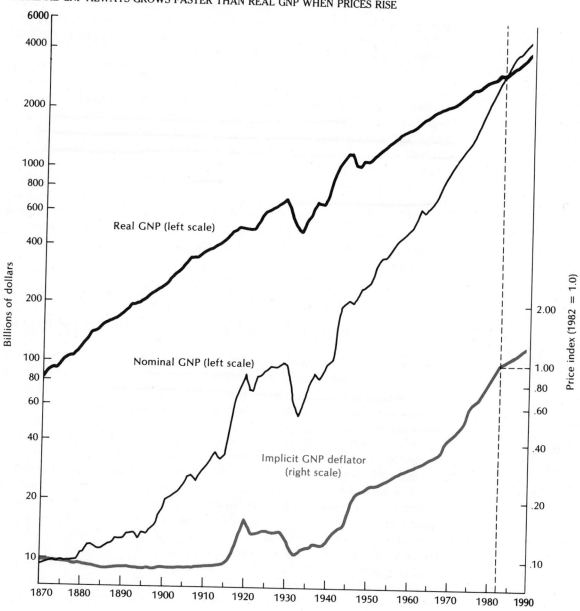

NOMINAL GNP ALWAYS GROWS FASTER THAN REAL GNP WHEN PRICES RISE

Figure 1-1 **Nominal GNP, Real GNP, and the Implicit GNP Deflator, 1870–1989**

Notice how the nominal GNP line lies below the real GNP line before 1982 but lies above the real GNP line after 1982. This reflects the fact that the current prices used to measure nominal GNP were lower before 1982 than the 1982 prices used to measure real GNP. After 1982 the current prices used to measure nominal GNP were higher than the 1982 prices used to measure real GNP. Notice how the nominal GNP line crosses the real GNP line in 1982, the same year that the GNP deflator attains the value of 1.00. This occurs because in 1982 (and no other year) the prices used to measure nominal GNP and real GNP are the same.

Without looking at Figure 1-1, you should now be able to answer the following: Is the implicit GNP deflator greater or less than 1.000 in every year before 1982? In every year after 1982? In what year is the implicit GNP deflator equal to exactly 1.000?

Relation between inflation and the implicit GNP deflator. We have now learned that the implicit GNP deflator is the average price level in the economy, defined as nominal GNP divided by real GNP, or, equivalently, the ratio of prices actually charged in each year to those charged in 1982. How is the implicit GNP deflator related to the "inflation rate," the second of the six central macroeconomic concepts? The inflation rate is the rate of change of the implicit GNP deflator.

To calculate the inflation rate, we simply compute the percentage rate of change of the implicit GNP deflator. For instance, the GNP deflator was 1.00 in 1982 and 1.04 in 1983, and its change (the inflation rate) between 1982 and 1983 was:

$$\frac{\text{1983 GNP deflator} - \text{1982 GNP deflator}}{\text{1982 GNP deflator}} = \frac{1.04 - 1.00}{1.00} = 0.04$$

To convert the answer (0.04) into a percentage, just multiply by 100 to obtain 4 percent.

The relationship between the implicit GNP deflator and the inflation rate can be remembered easily. When the implicit GNP deflator is rising, the inflation rate is positive. When the implicit GNP deflator is unchanged, the inflation rate is zero. And when the implicit GNP deflator is falling (a rarity), the inflation rate is negative.

An inflation is said to occur when the inflation rate is positive for a sustained period, that is, when there is a sustained upward movement in the implicit GNP deflator. A deflation is said to occur when the inflation rate is negative for a sustained period, that is, when there is a sustained downward movement in the implicit GNP deflator. The period since World War II in the United States has been one of inflation, as is evident from the sustained upward movement in the red implicit GNP deflator line in Figure 1-1. The last deflation occurred in the Great Depression of 1929–33, when the average level of prices fell by 23 percent over a four-year interval. The last deflation spanning a period of several decades occurred in the final third of the nineteenth century, when prices fell almost continuously from 1865 to 1896.

1-4 Business Cycles, Inflation, and "Natural Real GNP"

Recurring Business Cycles

Business cycles consist of expansions occurring at about the same time in many economic activities, followed by similarly general recessions and revivals that merge into the expansion phase of the next cycle.

Throughout history the economy has experienced **business cycles,** alternating periods of good times and bad times. Look again at Figure 1-1 and find the thick black real GNP line. Notice that real GNP becomes larger over time, but also exhibits up-and-down wiggles. These wiggles represent the business cycles that have recurred throughout history, culminating in the

Figure 1-2
Basic Business Cycle Concepts
The red real GNP line exhibits a typical succession of business cycles. The highest point reached by real GNP in each cycle is called the "peak" and the lowest point the "trough." The "recession" is the period between peak and trough, the "expansion" the period between the trough and the next peak.

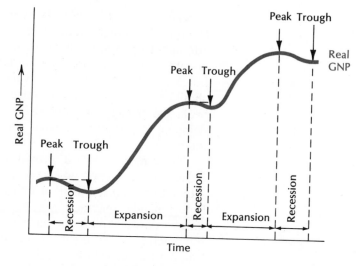

A SUCCESSION OF CYCLES

The **peak** is the highest point reached by real GNP in each business cycle.

The **trough** is the lowest point reached by real GNP in each business cycle.

The **recession** is the interval in the business cycle between the peak and the trough.

The **expansion** is the period in the business cycle between the trough and the peak.

most extreme business cycle of all, the Great Depression of 1929–33 when real GNP declined by 30 percent in one continuous and catastrophic downward movement.

The distinguishing characteristic of business cycles is their pervasive character, which affects many different types of economic activity at the same time. Business cycles are recurrent but not periodic. This means that they recur again and again but are not always the same length. Business cycles in the past have ranged in length from one to twelve years.[1]

Figure 1-2 illustrates two successive business cycles in real GNP. The high point in real GNP in each cycle is called the business-cycle **peak.** The low point is called the **trough.** The period between peak and trough is called a **recession.** After the recession comes the **expansion,** which continues until the following peak.

Although a simplification, Figure 1-2 contains two realistic elements that have been common to most real-world business cycles. First, the expansions last longer than the recessions. This occurs because on average real GNP is growing over time, so each successive peak is higher than the last peak. Second, the two business cycles illustrated in the figure differ in length. Since World War II, business-cycle expansions have been as short as one year (July 1980 to July 1981) and as long as nine years (February 1961 to December 1969).[2]

---

[1] A comprehensive source for the chronology of and data on historical business cycles, as well as research papers by distinguished economists, is Robert J. Gordon, ed., *The American Business Cycle: Continuity and Change* (University of Chicago Press, 1986).

[2] The economic expansion of the 1980s began in the trough quarter, November 1982. It will set the record for the longest U.S. expansion of all time in October 1991, if there is no recession before then.

Why Too Much or Too Little Real GNP Is Undesirable

Although business cycles have recurred for centuries, they are not desirable. Much of the subject of macroeconomics is concerned with the feasibility of attempts by government to "dampen" business cycles—that is, to make the growth of real GNP smoother and the up-and-down fluctuations less severe. But we cannot tell just by looking at Figure 1-2 what a government's goal should be. Should a nation's government aim at maintaining real GNP at the peak, the trough, or somewhere in between? Nor can we tell how much damping is possible, or what the costs of damping real GNP fluctuations might be.

Since more real GNP provides more goods and services for the average citizen, a first answer would seem to be that a nation's government should attempt to keep real GNP at its peak level all the time. This is wrong. Why? Unfortunately, maximum production tends to make inflation worse. When business firms are producing "flat out," they find it easy to raise prices. Thus too much real GNP is inflationary and must be avoided if the overall inflation rate is to be kept from accelerating.

Too little real GNP is undesirable as well. Low levels of real GNP mean layoffs, unemployment, and a decline in the overall standard of living. These harmful effects of low real GNP are only partly balanced by the tendency of the inflation rate to slow down in such a situation.

Real GNP: Actual and Natural

Between a high production level that causes the inflation rate to speed up, and a low production level that causes the inflation rate to slow down, there is some desirable compromise level that keeps the inflation rate constant. This intermediate level of real GNP has been called "natural," a situation in which there is no tendency for inflation to accelerate or decelerate.

Figure 1-3 illustrates the relationship between actual real GNP, natural real GNP, and the rate of inflation. In the upper frame the red line is actual real GNP, exhibiting exactly the same business cycles as in Figure 1-2. In the lower frame is shown the inflation rate. The thin dashed vertical lines connect the two frames. The first dashed vertical line marks time period t_0. Notice in the bottom frame that the inflation rate is constant at t_0.

Natural real GNP designates the level of real GNP at which the inflation rate is constant, with no tendency to accelerate or decelerate.

By definition, **natural real GNP** is equal to actual real GNP when the inflation rate is constant. Thus in the upper frame at t_0 the red actual real GNP line is crossed by a black natural real GNP line. To the right of t_0 actual real GNP falls below natural real GNP, and we see in the bottom frame that inflation slows down. This continues until time period t_1, when actual real GNP recovers to once again equal natural real GNP. Here the inflation rate stops falling and is constant for a moment before it begins to rise.

This cycle repeats again and again. Only when actual real GNP is equal to natural real GNP is the inflation rate constant. For this reason, natural real GNP is a natural or compromise level to be singled out for special attention. During a period of low actual real GNP, designated by the gray area, the inflation rate slows down. During a period of high actual real GNP,

Figure 1-3
The Relation between Actual and Natural Real GNP and the Inflation Rate

In the upper frame the solid black line shows the steady growth of natural real GNP—the amount the economy can produce at a constant inflation rate. The red line shows the path of actual real GNP, the same as that in Figure 1-2. In the region designated by the gray area in the top frame, actual real GNP is below natural real GNP, so inflation slows down in the bottom frame. In the region designated by the pink area, actual real GNP is above natural real GNP, so inflation speeds up in the bottom frame.

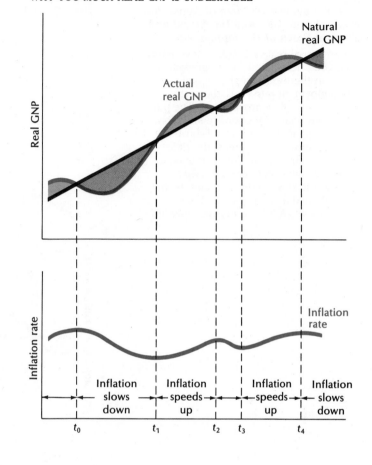

designated by the pink area, the inflation rate accelerates. Sometimes the condition of excessive actual real GNP is called "an overheated economy," a designation that you can link to the pink area on the diagram.

SELF-TEST   There is a natural level of output, defined in this section. There is a natural rate of unemployment, defined in the next section. Is there a *natural rate of inflation?*

Unemployment: Actual and Natural

When actual real GNP is low, many people lose their jobs, and the unemployment rate is high, as shown in Figure 1-4. The top frame duplicates Figure 1-3 exactly, comparing actual real GNP with natural real GNP. The red line in the bottom frame is the actual percentage unemployment rate,

Figure 1-4

The Behavior over Time of Actual and Natural Real GNP and the Actual and Natural Rates of Unemployment

When actual real GNP falls below natural real GNP, designated by the gray shaded areas in the top frame, the actual unemployment rate rises above the natural rate of unemployment. The pink areas designate the opposite situation. Comparing Figures 1-3 and 1-4, we see that the gray shaded areas, the time intervals when unemployment is high, also represent time intervals when inflation is slowing down. Similarly, the pink shaded areas represent time intervals when inflation is speeding up.

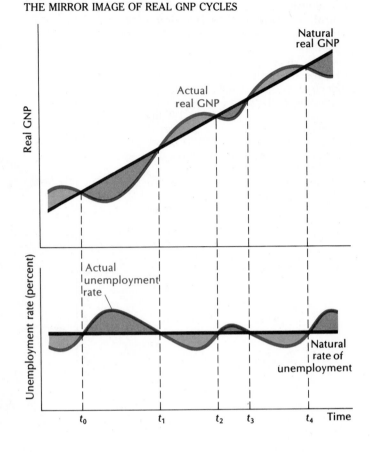

UNEMPLOYMENT CYCLES ARE
THE MIRROR IMAGE OF REAL GNP CYCLES

The **natural rate of unemployment** designates the level of the unemployment rate at which the inflation rate is constant, with no tendency to accelerate or decelerate.

the first of the six central concepts of macroeconomics. The unemployment rate is defined as the number of jobless individuals who are actively looking for work (or are on temporary layoff), divided by the total of those employed and unemployed. The thin vertical dashed lines connect the upper frame and lower frame; they show that whenever actual and natural real GNP are equal in the top frame, the actual unemployment rate is equal to the **natural rate of unemployment** in the bottom frame.

The definition of the natural rate of unemployment corresponds exactly to natural real GNP, describing a situation when there is no tendency for the inflation rate to change. When the actual unemployment rate is high, actual real GNP is low (shown by gray shading in both frames) and the inflation rate slows down. In periods when actual real GNP is high and the economy prospers, the actual unemployment rate is low (shown by pink shading in both frames) and the inflation rate speeds up. Notice that in Figures 1-3 and 1-4 the peak of the business cycle occurs when actual real GNP is high, and the trough occurs when actual real GNP is low. But this is not always the case. The short 1980–81 business-cycle expansion was incomplete, and at the peak in August 1981, actual real GNP was still below natural real GNP.

The natural rate of unemployment in the bottom frame of Figure 1-4 is illustrated as a horizontal line just for convenience. In the real world the natural rate of unemployment is not necessarily constant; in fact it appears to have risen moderately between the mid-1950s and the mid-1970s and to have remained constant since then. This means that a higher unemployment rate is required now to keep inflation from accelerating than was required in the 1950s. Possible causes of this increase in the natural rate of unemployment are a matter of debate and are discussed later in Chapter 10.

Figures 1-3 and 1-4 summarize a basic dilemma faced by government policymakers who are attempting to achieve a low unemployment rate and a low inflation rate at the same time. If the inflation rate is high, lowering it requires a decline in actual real GNP and an increase in the actual unemployment rate. If, on the contrary, the policymaker attempts to provide jobs for everyone and keep the actual unemployment rate low, then the inflation rate will speed up. America made the transition from roughly a 9 percent inflation rate in 1981 to a 3 percent inflation rate in 1986 only at the cost of very high unemployment during much of the intervening five years. And the low unemployment rate in 1988–89 caused an increase in the inflation rate well above 3 percent.

1-5 CASE STUDY: Business Cycles in This Century

This section examines U.S. macroeconomic history since the late nineteenth century. You will see that unemployment, as bad as it was in the early 1980s, did not reach the extreme crisis levels of the 1930s. You will also see that inflation was worse in several previous periods.

Real GNP

Figure 1-5 is arranged just like Figure 1-4. But whereas Figure 1-4 shows hypothetical relationships, Figure 1-5 shows the actual historical record. In the top frame the solid black line is natural real GNP, an estimate of the amount the economy could have produced each year without causing an acceleration or deceleration of inflation.

The red line in the top frame plots actual real GNP, the total production of goods and services each year measured in the constant prices of 1982. The red actual real GNP line in Figure 1-5 is identical to the real GNP line in Figure 1-1. See if you can pick out those years when actual and natural real GNP are roughly equal. Some of these years were 1891, 1900, 1910, 1924, 1964, 1972, 1979, and 1987.

In years marked by gray shading, actual real GNP fell below natural real GNP. A maximum deficiency occurred in 1933, when actual real GNP was only 64 percent of natural and about 36 percent of natural real GNP was wasted. Before 1929 and since 1950 these intervals of substantial out-

A HISTORICAL REPORT CARD ON REAL GNP AND UNEMPLOYMENT

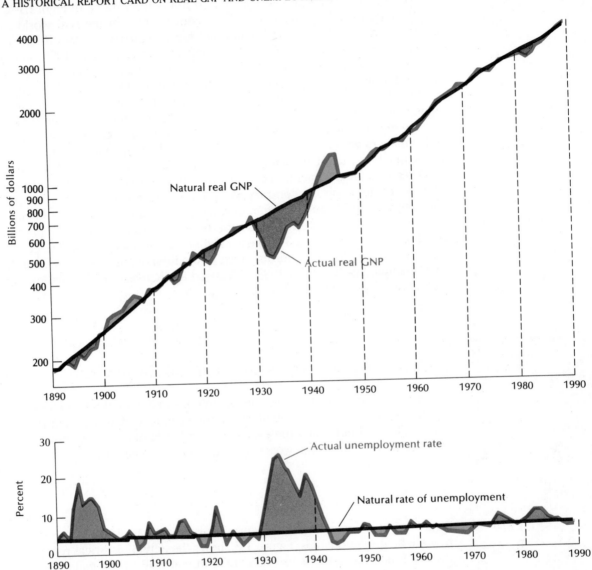

Figure 1-5 **Actual and Natural Real GNP and Unemployment, 1890–1989**

A historical report card for two important economic magnitudes. In the top frame the black line indicates natural real GNP. The red line shows actual real GNP, which was well below natural real GNP during the Great Depression of the 1930s and well above it during World War II. In the bottom frame the black line indicates the natural rate of unemployment, and the red line indicates the actual unemployment rate. Actual unemployment was much higher during the Great Depression of the 1930s than at any other time during the century. Notice how periods of high actual unemployment like the 1930s are designated by gray areas in the bottom frame that occur simultaneously with periods of low actual real GNP in the top frame. Pink areas indicate times when the economy was "overheated," with high actual real GNP and low unemployment.

put deficiency, shown by gray shading, have been much less serious than in the Great Depression but nevertheless have added up to billions in lost output.

In some years actual real GNP exceeded natural real GNP, as marked off by the shaded pink areas. This occurred mainly in wartime periods, particularly during World War I (1917–18), World War II (1942–45), the Korean War (1951–53), and the first half of the U.S. involvement in the Vietnam War (1965–69).

Unemployment

In the bottom frame of Figure 1-5 the red line plots the actual unemployment rate. By far the most extreme episode was the Great Depression, when the actual unemployment rate remained above 10 percent for ten straight years, 1931–1940. It is not surprising that the Depression left a profound mark on economic theory, government policy, and political alignments; the masses of unemployed of the 1930s had no welfare programs or unemployment insurance to ease their misery.

The black line in the bottom frame of Figure 1-5 estimates the natural rate of unemployment, the minimum attainable level of unemployment that is compatible with avoiding an acceleration of inflation. The natural unemployment rate sets a lower limit on the level of actual unemployment that can be attained without accelerating inflation. The pink shaded areas mark years when unemployment fell below the natural rate, as in 1917–19 and 1966–69. The gray shaded areas mark years when unemployment exceeded the natural rate.

Notice now the relationship between the top and bottom frames of Figure 1-5. The gray areas in both frames designate periods of low production and real GNP, and high unemployment, such as the Great Depression of the 1930s and the "Great Recessions" of 1975 and 1981–82. The pink areas in both frames designate periods of high production and real GNP, and low unemployment, such as World War II and other wartime periods.

Inflation

Figure 1-6 illustrates the year-to-year change in the implicit GNP deflator since 1900—that is, the percentage inflation rate. The red inflation rate line in Figure 1-6 shows the percentage rate of change in the red implicit GNP deflator line in Figure 1-1. When the deflator rises rapidly, as in 1917–18 or 1973–74 (Figure 1-1), its rate of change is high (Figure 1-6). The inflation rate has fluctuated widely. Some periods have been marked by nearly stable prices—an inflation rate close to zero—as in 1900–14, 1923–29, and 1958–63. Other periods have exhibited short, sharp extremes of price movement, especially during and after World War I (1916–19), before and after World War II (1941–42 and 1946–48), at the outbreak of the Korean War (1951), and, more recently, in 1973–74 and 1979–81.

Let us now compare the historical record of inflation displayed in Figure 1-6 with that for unemployment and real GNP in Figure 1-5. We would

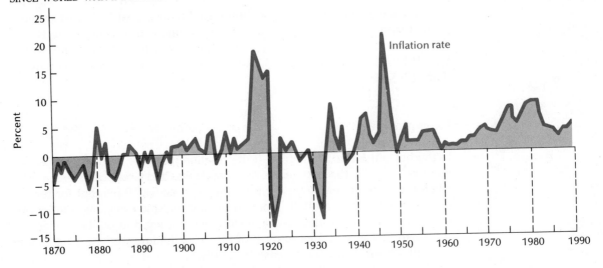

Figure 1-6   The Inflation Rate 1870–1989
A historical report card on the rate of change of the GNP deflator. During the
periods designated by the pink areas, the inflation rate was positive, and the GNP
deflator rose. During the periods designated by the gray areas, the inflation rate was
negative, and the GNP deflator fell. Before World War II prices both rose and fell,
with no clear tendency to go in one direction or another. But since World War II
the inflation rate has been positive every year but one (1949). Inflation has clearly
become a much more serious problem since 1966. But in 1986 the inflation rate was
lower than in any year since 1972.

expect that when real GNP was high and unemployment low (in those periods designated by pink shading in Figure 1-5) inflation would speed up. If
you look closely, you will find that the period between 1965 and 1969 (the
peak years of spending on the Vietnam War) is characterized by pink shading on the real output and unemployment diagrams, and an acceleration of
inflation from about 2 percent to 5 percent per year. Similarly, real output
was relatively low from 1981 to 1983, as shown by the gray shading on the
output diagram, and inflation slowed down from about 9 percent to 4 percent per year over the same period. However, in 1988–89, when unemployment fell below the national rate, inflation began to speed up once again.

But there are other years when the relationship between inflation and
real output is different. In 1973–74, for instance, inflation worsened while
real output fell. The same thing happened again in 1979–80. One of the
most important questions to be explained in this book is why in the 1970s
both inflation and unemployment became worse at the same time, while
during 1982–86 both improved.

1-6 The Six Macroeconomic Puzzles

Now that we have examined the behavior of real GNP, the unemployment rate, and the inflation rate over the past 100 years, we are ready to take a closer look at the past 30 years. Corresponding to each of the six key macroeconomic aggregates—the unemployment rate, inflation rate, productivity growth, interest rate, government budget deficit, and foreign trade deficit—is a puzzle concerning the recent behavior of the economy. A basic task of the book is to develop the tools that will help us solve these puzzles.

You may have noticed by now that real GNP is not included among the six central concepts and you may notice in this section that the behavior of real GNP is not included among the six puzzles. The reason for the omission of real GNP is contained in Figure 1-4, where the gray and pink areas in the top frame are *mirror images* of the gray and pink areas in the bottom frame. When actual real GNP falls below natural real GNP, the actual unemployment rate rises above the natural rate of unemployment. Therefore, the first puzzle concerning fluctuations in the unemployment rate simultaneously involves fluctuations in real GNP around the rising level of natural real GNP—in other words, business cycles. Real GNP receives ample attention in this book, but as a "means" to the "end" of understanding the six central aggregates that impinge more directly on everyday life.

Puzzle 1: Why Has the Unemployment Rate Been So High and So Variable?

We have seen that the unemployment rate is the mirror image of real GNP, rising when real GNP falls and vice versa. As shown in Figures 1-5 and 1-7, a graph of the unemployment rate looks like a roller coaster, moving up and down every few years. The unemployment rate is just one of many macro-

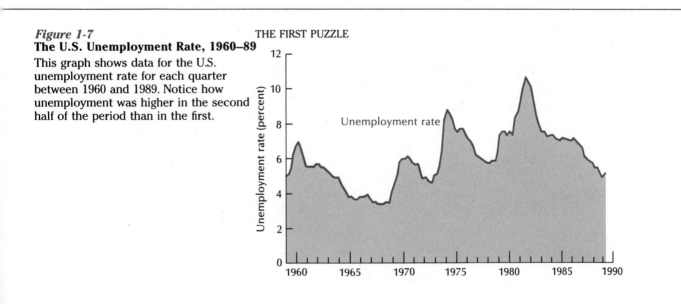

Figure 1-7
The U.S. Unemployment Rate, 1960–89
This graph shows data for the U.S. unemployment rate for each quarter between 1960 and 1989. Notice how unemployment was higher in the second half of the period than in the first.

THE FIRST PUZZLE

economic aggregates exhibiting cyclical movements. We focus on unemployment in the first puzzle because of its obvious importance to the great majority of people, who want to be able to find jobs easily.

Puzzle 1 has two parts. The first is why the unemployment rate is so "volatile"—that is, why it moves up and down so much. Why can't the economy be managed so as to keep the unemployment rate at a stable level? This question can be stated even more basically: Why can't business cycles be prevented?

The second part of the puzzle is why there has been a tendency recently for the peaks in each unemployment cycle to become higher and higher. The business-cycle recession of 1969–70 brought unemployment to a peak rate of 6.1 percent; at the trough of the 1973–75 recession the unemployment rate soared to 9.1 percent; and in the most recent recession, 1981–82, the unemployment rate rose to an even higher 10.8 percent. Even in 1989, a good year by recent standards, unemployment was higher than the *average* achieved in 1962–74.

Puzzle 2: Why Has the Inflation Rate Been So High and So Variable?

The behavior of the inflation rate since 1960 is shown in Figure 1-8. The inflation rate was much higher between 1973 and 1982 than before or after. The inflation rate soared to a peak rate of 14.3 percent in the fourth quarter of 1974. The high rates of inflation reached in 1974–75 and 1979–80 indirectly caused the high rates of unemployment shown in the previous figure for the years 1974–76 and 1980–82. The reason is that policymakers in

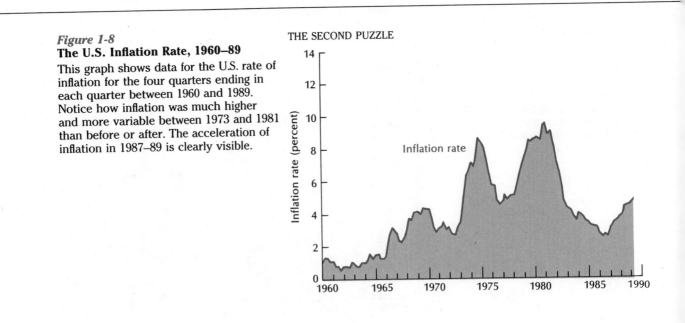

Figure 1-8
The U.S. Inflation Rate, 1960–89
This graph shows data for the U.S. rate of inflation for the four quarters ending in each quarter between 1960 and 1989. Notice how inflation was much higher and more variable between 1973 and 1981 than before or after. The acceleration of inflation in 1987–89 is clearly visible.

THE SECOND PUZZLE

Washington believed that the primary economic problem was inflation, which called for restrictive economic policies designed to depress real GNP and raise the unemployment rate. In short, policymakers deliberately created recessions and caused an upsurge of unemployment in those years.

The second puzzle is why the inflation rate has been so high and so variable, particularly after 1973. Since inflation affects people directly and also indirectly causes unemployment through the reaction of policymakers in Washington, a central task of this book is to explain what causes inflation and how to cure it. Is it possible to maintain a low rate of inflation? Can the inflation rate be kept at a stable rate year after year without the wild swings that have occurred during 1973–82? Will a continued relatively low unemployment rate, as in 1988–89, cause inflation to accelerate?

Puzzle 3: Why Has Productivity Grown So Slowly?

Productivity is formally defined as real GNP divided by the total number of hours spent on the job by the nation's workers. The rate of productivity growth determines how rapidly the well-being of the average citizen increases. Will today's college students belong to the first generation in U.S. history that fails to exceed the living standards of its parents? The answer will depend in part on whether productivity growth remains as slow as it has since 1973, or whether it picks up speed.

Figure 1-9 shows the percentage growth rate of productivity on an annual basis since 1948. The line zigzags but reveals a disturbing downward trend, averaging 0.9 percent per year since 1973, compared to the 2.4 percent average rate achieved during 1948–73.

Figure 1-9
Labor Productivity Growth, 1948–89
The zigzag line shows data for the annual percentage change in output per hour (productivity) in the U.S. between 1948 and 1989. The average growth rate of productivity between 1974 and 1989 was only 0.9 percent per year, much less than the 2.4 percent average rate between 1948 and 1973.

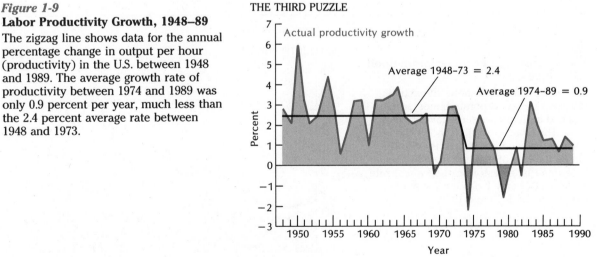

THE THIRD PUZZLE

Actual productivity growth

Average 1948–73 = 2.4

Average 1974–89 = 0.9

The slowdown in productivity growth is one of the most mysterious puzzles in macroeconomics. The American economy no longer increases its annual average output per worker as quickly as it used to. Nor does it match the increases in productivity still being achieved by such countries as Japan, Germany, or France. Because the productivity puzzle remains over several successive business cycles, its causes require a different analysis than the basic treatment of cycles in the unemployment and inflation rates (the first two puzzles). For this reason, full treatment of the productivity puzzle is postponed until Chapter 12.

Puzzle 4: Why Were Interest Rates in the 1980s Higher Than Ever Before?

Despite the seriousness of the unemployment and inflation problems in recent years, the numbers recorded in Figures 1-7 and 1-8 did not set historical records. Unemployment was worse in the Great Depression of the 1930s. Inflation was worse in several previous episodes, particularly during the Civil War and World War I, and immediately after World War II. But the behavior of interest rates in the early 1980s was novel, with no historical precedent in the past century.

The **nominal interest rate** is the market interest rate actually charged by financial institutions and earned by bondholders.

After being below 5 percent in the early 1960s and below 10 percent in 1979, the **nominal interest rate** (depicted as the black upper line in Figure 1-10) surged up, reaching 16 percent in 1981. Then in 1982 the interest rate dropped, and by early 1986 it was again back down to 9 percent. However, even in 1986 the rate was higher than in any year before 1979, and in 1987–88 the rate began to increase again.

A high interest rate is a boon to those who have substantial savings. But it is a disaster for many business firms, large and small, which have to bor-

Figure 1-10
The Nominal and Real Corporate Bond Rate, 1980–89

The upper black line shows the actual interest rate on corporate bonds, which reached an unprecedented level during 1981. The lower (red) line shows the real interest rate and is equal to the top line minus the rate of inflation from Figure 1-8. Notice that investors earned a real rate of interest of only 1 percent for brief periods in 1974–75 and 1979.

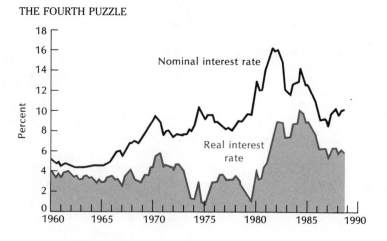

THE FOURTH PUZZLE

row money regularly. The high interest rate in the 1980s also contributed to a massive federal government budget deficit, since the federal government had to make interest payments on its outstanding debt. The effect on business firms contributed to the record business bankruptcy rate, which in 1982 was the highest since 1933.

Notice the similarity between the inflation rate in Figure 1-8 and the interest rate in Figure 1-10. Both were low in the early 1960s and rose sharply in the 1970s. So it might appear that inflation contributed to higher interest rates. The lower red line in Figure 1-10 is the **real interest rate**, which is simply the nominal interest rate, plotted as the upper line in Figure 1-10, minus the rate of inflation (from Figure 1-8). Even with adjustment for inflation, the real interest rate is highly variable and also reached an unprecedented level in the 1980s.

The puzzle of the high real interest rate is one of the first that we tackle in the book. Chapters 3, 4, and 5 develop a simple model that helps explain the movements of both interest rates and real GNP. The distinction between the nominal and real interest rate is explored further in Chapter 11, where we inquire into the effects of inflation on savers and borrowers.

The **real interest rate** is the nominal interest rate minus the inflation rate.

Puzzle 5: Why Has the Government Budget Deficit Persisted in the 1980s?

The government budget deficit is closely related to three of our other puzzles. When the government spends more than it takes in, it must borrow from households and business firms, who then have less remaining for consumption and investment spending. A government deficit may therefore cut private investment; this may lead to slower growth in capital per worker and hence lower productivity growth (Puzzle 3). A government deficit may also account in part for higher interest rates in the 1980s (Puzzle 4), since to borrow funds to pay its bills, the government may have to pay a higher interest rate. Finally, a government deficit can lead to a trade deficit (Puzzle 6).

As shown in Figure 1-11, the government's budget has been in deficit (shown by pink shading) in most years since 1960. In fact, the deficit in 1975 (defined as a percent of natural GNP) was larger than in any year in the 1980s. What is unusual about the 1980s is the *persistence* of the deficit, continuing year after year instead of going away promptly as in previous episodes. When the government runs a deficit, it adds to the national debt. The federal government's outstanding debt held by private investors more than tripled between 1980 and 1989, from $600 to $1800 billion.

The ongoing government deficits of the 1980s created an ongoing debate among politicians and economists. Politicians argued about the underlying cause of the deficits—was it higher expenditures or lower taxes? Economists argued about whether the deficit was harmful or not. But few economists denied that the deficits had allowed Americans in the 1980s to consume more than they produced, and that at some point in the future Americans would have to tighten their belts, consuming less than they produced.

Figure 1-11
The U.S. Government Budget Surplus as a Percent of GNP, 1960–89

Shown is the total U.S. government budget surplus, including the budgets of the Federal government, as well as all state and local governments. As shown by the pink shading, the government has operated in "red ink," running a budget deficit, in almost every year. What is unusual about the 1980s is that the budget deficit remained so large, year after year, in contrast to the short-lived deficits of 1967, 1971, and 1975–76.

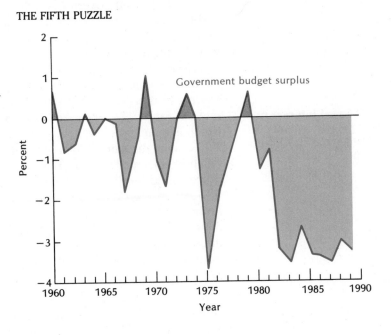

THE FIFTH PUZZLE

Puzzle 6: Why Has America's Trade Dropped into Persistent Deficit After Years of Surplus?

How can a nation buy more imports from foreigners than it sells to them in the form of exports? Just as a government deficit requires the issuance of debt, so a trade deficit requires that the nation goes into debt to foreigners. This debt can consist of pieces of paper, as when a Japanese investor holds a U.S. government bond. Or it can consist of foreign ownership of American factories, office buildings, and hotels. In the 1980s the United States financed its foreign trade deficit in both ways, through sales of securities to foreigners, and through foreign purchases of U.S. assets. One of the largest of these sales occurred in 1988, when the Pillsbury company (owner of, among other things, Burger King), was sold to a British corporation for $5.7 billion.

The collapse of the U.S. trade balance in the 1980s was even more sudden and dramatic than that of the government budget, as shown in Figure 1-12. After years of substantial surplus, starting in 1983 the trade balance plunged into a deficit that lasted for the rest of the decade. Each year's deficit required that more and more U.S. assets be sold to foreigners. By the late 1980s the U.S. was by far the world's largest "debtor nation."

The implications of the trade deficit are not happy ones for today's college students. The only way to cure the trade deficit is through further declines in the **foreign exchange rate** of the U.S. dollar. This means that anything produced abroad is likely to become gradually more expensive relative to goods produced at home, including German beer, Japanese cameras,

The **foreign exchange rate** is the amount of another nation's money that residents of a country can obtain in exchange for a unit of their own money.

Figure 1-12

The U.S. Foreign Trade Surplus as a Percent of GNP, 1960–89

Shown is the U.S. trade surplus, defined as exports of goods and services minus imports of goods and services. After running a persistent trade surplus before 1983, the U.S. ran a persistent trade deficit in every year starting in 1983. In comparing the government budget surplus in Figure 1-11 with the trade surplus in Figure 1-12, notice a difference: there were budget deficits before the 1980s, but not trade deficits.

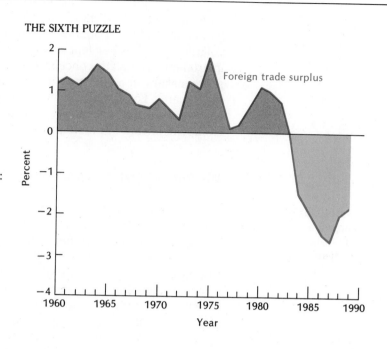

THE SIXTH PUZZLE

and summer vacations to Europe. It is not far-fetched to predict that summer trips to Europe, enjoyed by millions of young Americans in the mid-1980s, may soon become a thing of the past.

1-7 Taming Business Cycles: Stabilization Policy

Target variables are aggregates whose values society cares about.

Policy instruments are elements that government policymakers can manipulate directly to influence target variables.

Monetary policy tries to influence target variables by changing the money supply or interest rates or both.

Fiscal policy tries to influence target variables by manipulating government expenditures and tax rates.

Macroeconomic analysts have two tasks: to analyze the causes of changes in important aggregates and to predict the consequences of alternative policy changes. In policy discussions the group of aggregates that society cares most about—inflation, unemployment, the long-term growth rate of productivity—are called "goals" or **target variables.** When the target variables deviate from desired values, alternative **policy instruments** can be used in an attempt to achieve needed changes. Instruments fall into three broad categories: **monetary polices,** which include control of the money supply and interest rates; **fiscal policies,** which include changes in government expenditures and tax rates; and a third, miscellaneous group, which includes wage and price controls and employment policy.

How are target variables and policy instruments related to the six central macroeconomic concepts introduced at the beginning of this chapter? The first three of the concepts—the unemployment rate, inflation rate, and productivity growth—are the key target variables of economic policy, the goals society cares most about. The next two are policy instruments. The fourth concept, the interest rate, is one of the policy instruments of monetary policy. Since people also care about interest rates, the effectiveness of monetary policy in dealing with the three target variables can sometimes be inhibited if required actions would require interest rates to be too high or volatile. The fifth concept, the government budget deficit, is also a policy instrument. The sixth concept, the foreign trade deficit, can "constrain" the policymakers in achieving their target variables with their available policy instruments. For instance, to avoid a large trade deficit and the indebtedness to foreigners that it implies, policymakers may have to sacrifice a low unemployment rate or stable prices.

The Role of Stabilization Policy

A **stabilization policy** is any policy that seeks to influence the level of aggregate demand.

Macroeconomic analysis begins with a simple message: either type of **stabilization policy,** monetary or fiscal, can be used to offset undesired changes in private spending. The effects of monetary and fiscal policy on the price level and on real GNP are the main subject of Parts II and III of this book. Fiscal policy can raise output and employment by increasing government spending that creates jobs through government hiring. Or fiscal policy can stimulate private spending by cutting tax rates, thus inducing a higher level of private purchases, production, and employment. A monetary policy stimulus to output and employment takes the form of a reduction in interest rates and may in turn boost stock prices and make lending institutions more willing to grant credit.

This initial message of macroeconomics, that stabilization policy can smooth undesired fluctuations in aggregate demand, is only part of the story. We can assume that policy stimulus should be applied in a recession when unemployment is high and inflation is absent. And policy restraint is required when inflation is raging and unemployment is low. But we must go further. What is to be done when *both* unemployment and inflation are excessive? In the midst of such **stagflation,** should stabilization policy adopt a stance of stimulus to fight unemployment or restraint to fight inflation? Why inflation and unemployment coexist and some possible solutions are discussed in Part IV.

Stagflation is a situation combining stagnation (zero or negative output growth) with inflation.

Can today's college students look forward to a higher standard of living than their parents? This depends on large part on achieving a revival of America's lagging growth rate of productivity (Puzzle 3), which many consider to be America's greatest economic problem. In Part V we consider the possible causes of the slowdown in productivity growth and its relation to the "twin deficits," that is, the government budget deficit and the foreign trade deficit. Should the government abandon using fiscal policy as one of the tools of stabilization policy and focus on the implications of fiscal policy for the long-term growth of productivity?

There are further problems in applying stabilization policy. It may not be possible to control aggregate demand instantly and precisely. A policy stimulus intended to fight current unemployment might boost aggregate demand only after a long and uncertain delay, by which time the stimulus might not be needed. The impact of different policy changes may also be highly uncertain. These and other limitations of policy "fine tuning" or "activism" are central themes in the consideration of monetary and fiscal policy in Part VI.

Relation Between Theory and Policy

The first third of this book uses economic theory to examine the causes of changes in real GNP, unemployment, and the price level. Instead of just describing a collection of unrelated economic facts, theory isolates the important economic variables that help explain inflation and unemployment. Theory also creates useful generalizations to describe the relationships among groups of variables, such as consumption and income or money and interest rates. We can then look at the facts to test whether the generalizations of theory have predictive power.

Positive economics is the attempt scientifically to describe and explain the behavior of the economy.

Economists use theory for two quite separate purposes: for **"positive" economics,** *explaining* the behavior of important variables, and for **"normative" economics,** *recommending* changes in economic policy. Economists have developed theories that explain most of the changes observed in the unemployment rate or the rate of inflation and why interest rates are now higher than they were twenty years ago. Most disagreements among economists no longer focus on different explanations of these major phenomena; rather they center on the proper conduct of economic policy, a normative issue.

Normative economics involves recommendations for changes in economic policy to achieve an optimal or desirable state of affairs.

Most policy disagreements stem from the incompatibility of worthy economic goals. Most people would like the price level to be stable and the unemployment rate to be close to zero. But this state of nirvana cannot be achieved instantly, if ever. Macroeconomics, like economics in general, is the science of *choice* in the face of limitations for each of the possible alternatives. Choices emphasized in this book include whether to reduce the inflation rate at the cost of higher unemployment during a transition period that may last five years or longer, and whether to boost investment and economic growth at the cost of higher federal tax rates.

SELF-TEST Is it the task of stabilization policy to set the unemployment rate to zero? Why or why not? Is it the task of stabilization policy to set the inflation rate to zero? Why or why not? What are the two big problems in applying stabilization policy to control aggregate demand?

1-8 The "Internationalization" of Macroeconomics

A **closed economy** has no trade in goods, services, or financial assets with any other nation.

More than ever before, macroeconomics is an international subject. The days are gone in which the effects of U.S. stabilization policy could be analyzed in isolation, without consideration for their repercussions abroad. This old view of the United States as a **closed economy** described reality in the first decade or so after World War II. In the 1940s and 1950s, trade accounted for only about 5 percent of the U.S. economy, exchange rates were fixed, and financial flows to and from other nations were restricted.

An **open economy** exports goods and services to other nations, imports from them, and has financial flows to and from foreign nations.

The United States has increasingly become an **open economy.** Imports now exceed 12 percent of U.S. GNP. The exchange rate of the dollar has been flexible since 1973 and has fluctuated far more widely than anyone had predicted prior to that time. International financial flows are massive and often instantaneous, with computers sending messages to buy or sell stocks and bonds at the speed of light among the major financial centers of Tokyo, London, New York, and Chicago.

As the economy has become "internationalized," so has macroeconomic analysis. This textbook reflects this trend by including the foreign trade balance among the six major macroeconomic concepts and its sharp turn from surplus to deficit as one of the six macroeconomic puzzles. We find the influence of international flows of goods, services, and finance affecting many topics. No longer can we assume that a large government budget deficit automatically depresses or "crowds out" private investment spending. Instead, the economy may get the capital it needs to finance *both* private investment and the government deficit from abroad through foreign purchases of U.S. stocks, bonds, factories, and hotels. The availability of foreign capital has this good side, but also a bad side. By financing the government budget deficit through capital flows from abroad, Americans have run up a massive foreign debt which will require a sacrifice by future generations to pay the interest bill.

Just as budget deficits are financed differently in an open economy, different as well is the operation of the Federal Reserve Board's monetary policy. If the Fed pushes down interest rates to stimulate the economy, it may also push down the exchange rate of the dollar and worsen inflation. We can no longer analyze U.S. inflation without considering the effects of foreign trade. Here also there is a good and bad side. It was bad when higher prices of imported oil jolted inflation upward in the 1970s but good when falling oil prices facilitated the disinflation of the 1980s. It is good when the availability of cheap foreign goods helps keep the lid on prices of products made inside the United States, but bad when U.S. workers find their employers unable to afford pay increases. And it is bad when the falling dollar boosts the prices of imports, as well as domestic goods competing with imports.

Along with a new analysis of fiscal and monetary policy and of the determinants of inflation, the internationalization brings new concerns about American efficiency and competitiveness. Why, Americans wondered in 1989, was the U.S. foreign trade deficit still greater than $100 billion when the dollar had already fallen so far? Should not the falling dollar have made U.S. goods cheaper and sufficiently attractive to foreign purchasers for the foreign trade deficit to have disappeared? Were Americans "hooked" on foreign goods, because they were superior in actual or perceived quality, or because some products like VCRs were not made by American manufacturers?

How Does U.S. Economic Performance Stack Up?

One result of the internationalization of macroeconomics is an increased attention to the comparative economic performance of the United States. Figure 1-13 shows how the United States compares with Japan and the major European nations in its unemployment, inflation, and productivity growth rates (the first three of our "big six" macroeconomic concepts). The data are presented as a set of bar graphs, with the unemployment performance displayed in the top frame, inflation in the middle frame, and productivity growth in the bottom frame. Three bars are grouped together in each frame

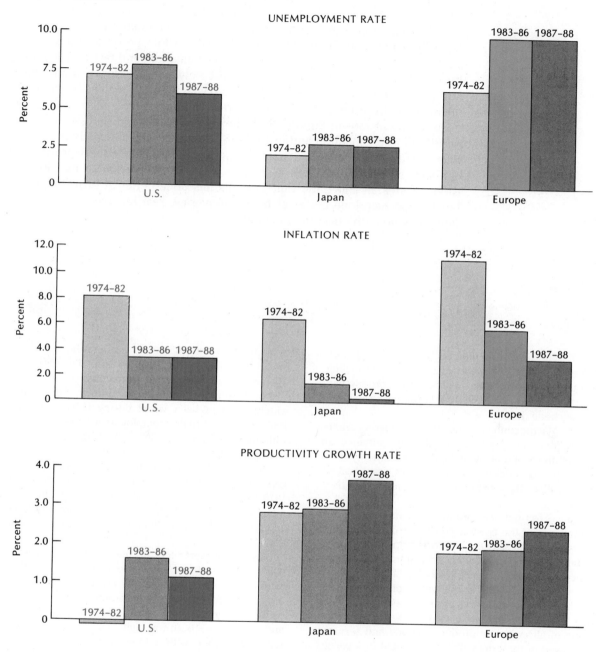

Figure 1-13 **Unemployment, Inflation, and Productivity Growth in the U.S., Japan, and Four European Countries, 1974–88**

The recent economic performance of the U.S. is compared to that of Japan and "Europe," which is the average of four large European countries (France, Italy, United Kingdom, and West Germany). Japan has the lowest unemployment rate throughout, while the U.S. unemployment rate has improved as Europe's has worsened. Inflation in all three areas has improved, so that in 1987–88 inflation was the same in the U.S. and Europe, but lower in Japan. The U.S. is the laggard in productivity growth, behind both Japan and Europe.

for each country, showing performance during the years 1974–82, then 1983–86, and finally 1987–88.

Above all, one startling fact stands out. The economic performance of Japan is superior to both the United States and Europe by all three measures: Japan has lower unemployment, lower inflation, and faster productivity growth. Who is leading in the contest between the United States and Europe is not so clear. The United States has achieved a major reduction in unemployment in recent years, in contrast to an extremely high and stable unemployment rate in Europe. Both the United States and Europe have experienced lower inflation and in 1987–88 registered almost exactly the same inflation rate. But the United States is the laggard on productivity growth; in 1987–88 productivity growth in Europe was more than double that in the United States. In short, the United States has done better at providing jobs but Europe has done better at boosting average real income per job. And Japan has done the best on all counts.

SUMMARY

1. The six central macroeconomic concepts are those that most affect everyday lives. They include the unemployment rate, inflation rate, productivity growth, interest rate, government budget deficit, and foreign trade deficit.

2. Macroeconomics differs from microeconomics by focusing on aggregates that are summed up over all the economic activities in the economy. Theory in macroeconomics is a process of simplification that identifies the most important economic relationships.

3. Gross national product is a measure of the overall size of the economy. While it does not affect everyday life directly, its behavior helps us to understand the behavior of the six central macroeconomic concepts that do influence everyday life.

4. Nominal GNP is the value of all currently produced goods and services expressed in the prices that people actually pay each year. Real GNP is the value of all currently produced goods and services expressed in the prices that people paid in a particular base year, for instance, 1982. Real GNP measures changes in output at constant prices and, unlike nominal GNP, is not influenced by price changes. Recurrent fluctuations in real GNP are called business cycles.

5. Neither too much or nor too little real GNP is desirable. The best compromise level is called natural real GNP and is consistent with a constant inflation rate. When the economy is operating at its natural level of real GNP, it is also by definition operating at its natural rate of unemployment.

6. In this century, U.S. inflation has fluctuated widely but has been worst during wars and after 1965. Periods of high unemployment have coincided with those of low real GNP. The Great Depression clearly scored worst on both counts.

7. Each of the six central macroeconomic concepts has exhibited puzzling behavior since the early 1970s. The unemployment rate, inflation rate, interest rate, and twin deficits have all been unusually high and variable, while productivity growth has slowed down.

8. Of the six central macroeconomic aggregates, the first three (unemployment rate, inflation rate, and productivity growth) are the main targets of stabilization policy. Stabilization policy may not be effective in improving well-being if unemployment and inflation are both too high, and stabilization policy may operate with a long delay or have effects that are highly uncertain.

9. Macroeconomics is now an international subject. International repercussions influence the way fiscal and monetary policy work and how the inflation process operates. The foreign trade deficit raises new concerns about American competitiveness.

macroeconomics
unemployment rate
inflation rate
productivity
interest rate
government budget deficit
foreign trade deficit
aggregate
gross national product
nominal GNP
nominal
real GNP
implicit GNP deflator
business cycles
peak
trough
recession

expansion
natural real GNP
natural rate of unemployment
nominal interest rate
real interest rate
foreign exchange rate
target variables
policy instruments
monetary policy
fiscal policy
stabilization policy
stagflation
positive economics
normative economics
closed economy
open economy

QUESTIONS AND PROBLEMS

Questions

1. If the official measure of GNP in the U.S. used, say, 1992 rather than 1982 as the base year, what adjustments would have to be made in Figure 1-1 to reflect the change in the base year?

2. Using the quarterly data in Table A-2 (Appendix A), attempt to identify the peak, recession, trough, and expansion phases of the basic business cycle depicted in Figure 1-2 for the periods 1947–1989. (Assume that an expansion or recession must be two or more consecutive quarters long.)

3. Why might two economists share a common economic theory but disagree on their policy recommendations?

4. The inflation performance of the U.S. economy in the 1980s was in part attributable to the fact that America's trade balance dropped into persistent deficit. Explain.

5. Some individuals benefit from inflation while others suffer. Is the same true with respect to the rising foreign trade deficit and an overvalued dollar on the foreign exchange market? Who gains? Who loses?

6. Which of the following statements are the subject of positive economics? Which are the subject of normative economics?
   (a) A decrease in the interest rate causes an increase in GNP
   (b) The foreign trade deficit should be decreased
   (c) The United States should increase its economic growth rate
   (d) The growth rate in Japan is higher than in the United States because the Japanese save a larger percentage of their income
   (e) The current natural rate of unemployment is too high

7. Is the level of real GNP a target variable? Why or why not?

8. If you learn that nominal GNP for 1990 is greater than nominal GNP for 1989, what do you know about changes in the level of output during this period? Changes in prices during this period?
   Would your answer change if it were real GNP that had increased in 1990?

1. If the level of nominal GNP (Y) is 6000 and the level of real GNP (Q) is 4500, what is the value of the real GNP deflator?

2. If the GNP deflator in year 1 is 1.20 and in year 2 it is 1.26, what was the rate of inflation (p) in year 2?

3. Using the GNP deflators in problem 2, if the level of real GNP in year 1 was 4000 and in year 2 it was 4120, what was the level of nominal GNP in each year? What was the growth rate of nominal GNP (y)? What was the growth rate of real GNP (q)? What is the relationship between y, p, and q?

SELF-TEST ANSWERS

p. 8 Notice in Figure 1-1 that the nominal GNP lines lies below the real GNP line before 1982, but lies above the real GNP line after 1982. This reflects the fact that before 1982 the current prices used to measure nominal GNP were lower than the 1982 prices used in measuring real GNP. The implicit GNP deflator is nominal GNP divided by real GNP, and thus the deflator is less than 1.000 when nominal GNP is less than real GNP. This occurs in each year before 1982. The deflator is greater than 1.000 in each year after 1982 because nominal GNP is greater than real GNP. In order to be exactly 1.000, the prices used in measuring nominal and real GNP must be identical. This occurs only in 1982.

p. 11 There is no such thing as the natural rate of inflation. At the natural rate of unemployment, when the economy is producing the natural level of real GNP, we know only that the inflation rate is constant, *but not what that inflation rate will be*. This depends on the history of inflation, and on how long and how far unemployment has differed from the natural rate of unemployment. (Notice in the bottom frame of Figure 1-3 that there are no numbers for the inflation rate on the vertical axis).

p. 25 Stabilization policy cannot set the unemployment rate to zero or any other rate below the natural rate of unemployment without causing accelerating inflation. Stabilization policy can set the inflation rate to zero only at the cost of a recession and a substantial cost in terms of lost output. The two big problems are lags and uncertainty. A policy change may affect aggregate demand only after a long and uncertain delay, and the impact of difference policy changes may also be highly uncertain.

The Measurement of Income and Prices

It has been said that figures rule the world; maybe. I am quite sure that it is figures which show us whether it is being ruled well or badly.

—*Johann Wolfgang Goethe, 1830*

Our first task is to develop a simple theoretical model to explain real output (GNP) and the price level. Before we can turn to theory in Chapter 3, however, we must stop in Chapter 2 for a few definitions. What are GNP and the price level? How are they measured? What goods and services are included in or excluded from GNP? How are private saving, private investment, the government deficit, and the foreign trade deficit related to each other?

2-1 Why We Care About Income

A basic lesson of Figure 1-5 is that movements in the unemployment rate are closely related to the parallel movements of the gap between actual and natural real GNP. When production drops off, people are laid off and put out of work. When production is very high relative to natural output, job openings will be plentiful and unemployment will be low. So the key to understanding changes in unemployment is the total real *product,* which is equal to total real *income.*

Measures of total real income serve a second purpose. If the total amount of real income is divided by the number of people or the number of families in a nation, we obtain a measure of the relative income of one nation compared to another. For example, how well off is the average American compared to the average German or Mexican? Further, we can chart the growth of income per person over long periods and determine whether the rate of increase of the U.S. real national product has been accelerating or decelerating and whether other nations are growing faster than the United States.

The subject of this chapter, the definition and measurement of national income—what is included and excluded and why—is an essential prelude to study of the determinants of changes in real income and output. We will see that many of the rules governing the calculation of national income are arbitrary, that controversial choices must be made as to the proper set of ingredients in the official measure of income, and that the size of any nation's gross national product is to some degree at the discretion of the economists and government officials who mark off the dividing lines between the included and excluded items.

2-2 The Circular Flow of Income and Expenditure

Let us begin with a very simple economy, consisting of households and business firms. We will assume that households spend their entire income, saving nothing, and that there is no government.[1] Figure 2-1 depicts the operation of our simple economy, with households represented by the box on the left and business firms by the box on the right. There are two kinds of transactions between the households and the firms.

First, the firms sell goods and services (product) to the households—for instance, bread and shoes—represented in Figure 2-1 by the lower dashed line labeled "product." The bread and shoes are not a gift but are paid for by a flow of money (C), say \$1,000,000 per year, represented by the solid line labeled **"consumer expenditures."**

Consumer expenditures are purchases of goods and services by households for their own use.

Second, households must work to earn the income to pay for the consumption goods. They work for the firms, selling their skills as represented by the upper dashed line labeled "labor services." Household members are willing to work only if they receive a flow of money, usually called "wages," from the firms for each hour of work. Wages are the main component of income (Q), shown by the upper solid line.

Since households are assumed to consume all of their income, and since firms are assumed to pay out all of their sales in the form of income to households, it follows that income (Q) and consumption expenditures (C) are equal. For the same reason, the labor services provided in return for income are equal to the goods and services (product) sold by the firms to households in return for the money flow of consumer expenditures:

$$
\begin{aligned}
\text{income } (Q) &= \text{labor services} \\
&= \text{consumption expenditure } (C) \qquad (2.1) \\
&= \text{product}
\end{aligned}
$$

SELF-TEST

Imagine that a student purchases a haircut, priced at \$10, with a \$10 bill. Describe in words how the student's haircut will be included in each of the four flows of Figure 2-1.

A **flow magnitude** is an economic magnitude that moves from one economic unit to another at a specified rate per unit of time.

Each of the four magnitudes in equation (2.1) is a **flow magnitude**—any money payment or physical good or service that flows from one economic unit to another. A flow of expenditure, just like a flow of water through a pipe, can be measured only if we first specify the length of time over which the flow is measured. Thus U.S. gross national product (= income = expenditure = factor services) in 1988 was nearly \$5000 billion *per year*. Most flow magnitudes in the United States are measured at annual

---

[1]Because households do no saving, there is no capital or wealth, and all household income is in the form of wages for labor services.

Figure 2-1

The Circular Flow of Income and Consumer Expenditure

Circular flow of income and expenditure in a simple imaginary economy in which households consume their entire income. There are no taxes, no government spending, no saving, no investment, and no foreign sector.

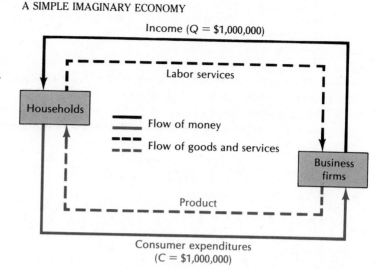

A SIMPLE IMAGINARY ECONOMY

Income (Q = $1,000,000)

Labor services

Households

—— Flow of money

- - - Flow of goods and services

Business firms

Product

Consumer expenditures
(C = $1,000,000)

rates. If the flow of GNP in a quarter-year ("quarter") is $1250 billion, this amounts to $5000 billion at an annual rate.

A flow is distinguished from a **stock,** which is an economic magnitude in the possession of a single unit at a particular moment of time. The stock of money, savings accounts, business equipment, or government debt can be measured by adding up its value at a given point in time, for instance, midnight on December 31, 1989. Measuring a stock is like taking a flash snapshot. It requires specifying a specific date but not a time interval.

A **stock** is an economic magnitude in the possession of a given economic unit at a particular point in time.

2-3 What Transactions Should Be Included in Income and Expenditure?

National Income and Product Accounts is the official U. S. government economic accounting system which keeps track of GNP and its subcomponents.

The **National Income and Product Accounts** (NIPA) is the official U.S. government accounting of all the millions of flows of income and expenditure in the United States. The basic ideas and methods used in the NIPA were originally developed in the 1930s by economists working at the National Bureau of Economic Research, including Simon Kuznets (one of the first winners of the Nobel Prize in economics). During World War II, the U.S. Department of Commerce took over the task of computing the NIPA, and it has gradually refined and updated the procedures.[2] Historical data for GNP and other macro concepts are listed in Appendix A for the United States and in Appendix B for other major nations. A guide to government data sources is provided in the box in this section. Those responsible for counting up gross national income and product do not mindlessly add up every figure

[2]The latest methodological and data revisions are described in "Revised Estimates of the National Income and Product Accounts of the United States, 1929–85: An Introduction," *Survey of Current Business,* vol. 65 (December 1985), pp. 1–19.

Where to Find the Numbers: A Guide to the Data

The first place to start in finding macroeconomic data is the appendix in the back of this textbook. There you will find annual data for major macroeconomic concepts for the United States covering more than a century, back to 1870, and quarterly data since 1947. Also included are several important annual data series for Japan, Canada, and the major European nations for the period since 1960.

Time Passes and Revisions Occur: How to Cope

The appendix is unlikely to satisfy all of your data needs for any of three reasons: (1) you may want to find a data series that does not appear in the appendix, (2) you may need data for quarters and years not included in the appendix (which is current through mid-1989), or (3) some of the data in the appendix may have been revised. Whether you are curious about more recent developments or need to complete a class assignment, you need to know where to look.

You are unlikely to find what you need at the newsstand or college bookstore; instead head to the library. There you can find these sources of economic data (ask the reference librarian for assistance).

• *The Economic Report of the President (ERP).* Published annually in early February, the back half of this paperback book is a wonderful treasure chest of current and comprehensive data. Every number presented is current, to within a few days of publication, and data revisions are incorporated in all the data series presented. The book packs a huge amount of information into a small space,

with about 100 full-page tables each containing about 10 columns giving different series, most covering the entire postwar era.

• *Economic Indicators.* A slim monthly supplement to the *ERP,* this is the place to look for the latest values of many series during the months between the publication dates of the ERP.

• *Business Conditions Digest (BCD).* This monthly source contains a different selection of series than *Economic Indicators,* and many of them are "processed" (turned into growth rates and ratios). The strong point of *BCD* is the extensive set of charts that plot the most important macro variables at the greatest available frequency (monthly or quarterly) over a period of 25 to 35 years. Also unique to *BCD* is the availability of historical monthly and quarterly data, in contrast to the *ERP,* which only lists annual data prior to the last few years. An index in the back of each *BCD* issue indicates where to find the historical monthly or quarterly data you need.

The "Big Three" Agency Publications

Often an economist needs data at a more detailed level than is available in the general sources listed above—for instance, data on the unemployment rate for blacks aged 20–24, or productivity in the electric utility industry, or how much American consumers spend on funerals. For these and many other series, turn to one of the data periodicals published by the specialized government statistical agencies that actually produce the data. The three most important of these agencies are the Bureau of Economic Analysis (BEA—a branch of the Commerce

on every piece of paper mailed to the government by private households and business firms. Instead, they have a set of rules to determine which items to include.

Defining GNP

In our free-market economy, the fact that a good or service is sold is usually a sign that it is capable of satisfying certain human wants and needs; otherwise people would not be willing to pay a price for it. So by including in the gross national product only things that are sold through the market for

Department), the Bureau of Labor Statistics (BLS—a branch of the Labor Department), and the Federal Reserve Board (usually called by its nickname, the Fed).

National income data. All the data on GNP and related income and product series are produced by the BEA in an organized system of tables called the National Income and Product Accounts, or "national accounts" for short. These extend back to 1929 for annual data and to 1947 for quarterly data and are published for the most recent quarters in the BEA's monthly publication, *The Survey of Current Business.* Each year figures for the last three years are revised and are published in the July issue of the *Survey.* The BEA publishes a full set of national accounts from 1929 to 1982 in a paperback supplement volume. The *Survey* also contains a back section of blue pages containing data for the last few months on a wide range of data series that are not part of the national accounts; these are presented at a more detailed level than in *Economic Indicators* or *BCD.* Historical data for these "blue page" series are published in a biennial publication called *Business Statistics.*

Labor market, price, and wage data. While the BEA mainly reprocesses data originally produced by other agencies, the BLS is a primary producer of data on employment, unemployment, consumer and producer prices, and wage rates. The BLS runs large surveys, contacting thousands of families each month to learn about their employment and unemployment experience, and thousands of retail outlets to track price changes. While the BLS data series at the most aggregated level are published in the general data sources listed above, users needing more detailed figures consult the BLS monthly publications *Monthly Labor Review, Employment and Earnings,* and *Producer Prices and Price Indexes.*

Financial market data. The Fed compiles data on interest rates, the money supply, and other figures describing the banking and financial system. Its major publication is the monthly *Federal Reserve Bulletin.* One of the regional Feds, the Federal Reserve Bank of St. Louis, publishes several monthly and quarterly publications containing data on financial and general economic variables. Numerous economists obtain their numbers, where possible, from the St. Louis Fed publications because these are available by mail without charge.

Overall, the federal government's many statistics-gathering activities cost the taxpayer $1.6 billion per year. And the list above does not even include the grandfather of all statistics agencies, the Bureau of the Census, which conducts the decennial Census of Population and, every five years, economic censuses of business establishments. The Census data form the raw material for much of the BEA's work in creating the national accounts, not to mention much research by economists on both macro and micro topics.

a price, we can be fairly sure that most of the components of GNP do contribute to human satisfaction. There are three major requirements in the rule for including items in the total **final product,** or GNP:

Final product includes all currently produced goods and services that are sold through the market but are not re-sold.

> *Final product consists of all* currently produced *goods and services that are* sold through the market *but* not resold during the current time period.

Currently produced. The first part of the rule—*to be included in final product, a good must be currently produced*—obviously excludes sales of any used items such as houses and cars, since they are not currently produced. It also excludes any transaction in which money is transferred with-

Transfer payments are those made for which no goods or services are produced in return.

out any accompanying good or service in return. Among the **transfer payments** excluded from national income in the United States are gifts from one person to another and "gifts" from the government to persons, such as social security, unemployment, and welfare benefits. Also excluded are capital gains accruing to persons as the prices of their assets increase.

Sold on the market. The second part of the rule—*goods included in the final product must be sold on the market and are valued at market prices*—means that we measure the value of final product by the market prices that people are willing to pay for goods and services. We assume that a Cadillac gives 10,000 times as much satisfaction as a package of razor blades for the simple reason that it costs about 10,000 times as much. Excluded from GNP by this criterion is the value of personal time engaged in activities that are not sold on the market (time spent commuting, baking a cake, and so on). Also excluded is any allowance for the costs of air pollution, water pollution, acid rain, or other by-products of the production process for which no explicit charge is made.

But not resold. The third part of the rule—*to be included in final product, a good must not be resold in the current time period*—further limits the acceptability of items. The many different goods and services produced in the economy are used in two different ways. Some goods, like wheat, are mainly used as ingredients in the making of other goods, in this case, bread. Any good resold by its purchaser, rather than used as is, goes by the name **intermediate good.**

A **final good** is part of final product, whereas an **intermediate good** is resold by its purchaser either in its present form or in an altered form.

The opposite of an intermediate good is a **final good,** one that is not resold. Bread sold at the grocery is a final good, used by consumers, as are shoes, clothes, haircuts, and everything else the consumer buys directly.

Why Intermediate Goods Are Excluded from GNP

Why can't we just add up all transactions in the economy and call that total GNP? Why must we take the trouble to exclude intermediate goods? The answer is simple: many sales transactions amount to much more than the income created by the seller. To include all of these transactions in GNP would "double count" materials created at an early stage of production and resold in later stages.

Look at Figure 2-2, which shows how the $.50 that a consumer spends for a loaf of bread is divided among the four firms that produce the bread. The bars on the left side of the diagram show the receipts of each of the firms involved in making and selling the bread, and those on the right side show the income of the firms' workers, managers, and stockholders *after* the purchase of the intermediate goods.

For instance, the baker adds $.19 of income to the $.21 he pays to the miller for the flour, and the grocer adds $.10 to the $.40 he pays to the baker for the bread. The total paid by the consumer to the grocer, $.50, exactly equals the total income created by all four firms (.09 + .12 + .19 + .10 = .50). By excluding from final product all goods that are resold (the intermediate goods) and including only the final purchase of $.50 by the consumer who actually uses the bread, we automatically guarantee that final product ($C = \$.50$) equals total income created or **value added** ($Q = \$.50$).

Value added is the value of the labor and capital services that take place at a particular stage of the production process.

FINAL PRODUCT EQUALS TOTAL INCOME CREATED

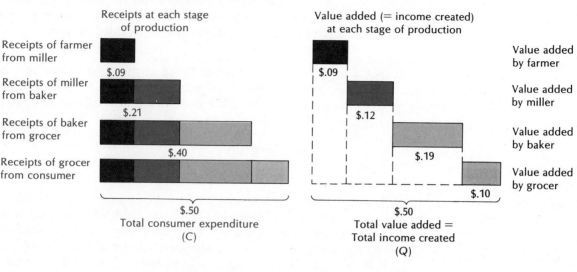

Figure 2-2 **The Contribution of One Loaf of Bread to Consumer Expenditure and Income Created**

The bar graph on the left shows the amount that each firm—farmer, miller, baker, and grocer—receives in the process of producing one loaf of bread. These total receipts are used for two purposes. First, part of the receipts of each firm are used to pay for the intermediate goods purchased from the firm listed directly above (for instance, the miller pays $.09 to the farmer for the wheat). Second, what is left over, shown on the right side of the diagram, is the income created or value added (such as wages, salaries, profits; $.12 in the case of the miller).

The $.50 paid by the consumer for the bread is an ingredient in the lower loop of consumer expenditure *(C)* in Figure 2-1. The $.50 of income created is part of the upper loop of income *(Q)* in Figure 2-1. Now we can see why, by definition, the two loops are equal in size.

2-4 Investment and Saving

Investment is the portion of final product that adds to the nation's stock of income-yielding physical assets or that replaces old, worn-out physical assets.

Inventory investment includes all changes in the stock of raw materials, parts, and finished goods held by business.

Types of Investment

The goods and services produced by business firms that are not resold as intermediate goods to other firms or consumers during the current period qualify by our rule as final product. But the business firm does not consume them. Final goods that business firms keep for themselves are called "private investment" or private capital formation. They add to the nation's stock of income-yielding assets. Private investment consists of

Inventory investment. Bread purchased by the grocer but not resold to consumers in the current period stays on the shelves, raising the level of the grocer's inventories. Inventories of raw materials, parts, and finished goods are an essential form of income-yielding assets for businesses, since goods immediately available "on the shelf" help satisfy customers and make sales. The *change* in inventories between the beginning and end of the current time period is included in GNP.

SELF-TEST
Imagine that a grocer has ten loaves of bread at the close of business on December 31, 1989. Valued at the wholesale baker's price of $.40, the value of the grocer's inventory is $4.00. At the close of business on March 31, 1990, the grocer has 15 loaves or $6.00 of bread on the shelves. What is the implication of these numbers for the contribution of the grocer's inventories to GNP in the first quarter of 1990?

Fixed investment includes all final goods purchased by business that are not intended for resale.

Fixed investment. This includes all final goods purchased by business other than additions to inventory. The main types of fixed investment are structures (factories, office buildings, shopping centers, apartments, houses) and equipment (cash registers, computers, trucks). Newly produced houses and condominiums sold to individuals are also counted as fixed investment—a homeowner is treated in the national accounts as a business firm that owns the house as an asset and rents the house to itself.[3]

Relation of Investment and Saving

Figure 2-1 described a simple imaginary economy in which households consumed their total income. Figure 2-3 introduces investment into that economy. Total expenditures on final product are once again $1,000,000, but this time they are divided into $800,000 for household purchases of consumption goods (*C*) and $200,000 for business purchases of investment goods (*I*). The $1,000,000 of total expenditures flowing to the business firms from the lower loops generates $1,000,000 in income for households shown in the top loop, just as before. Households take their $1,000,000 in income and spend $800,000 on purchases of consumption goods. Where does the remaining $200,000 go?

Personal saving is that part of personal income that is neither consumed nor paid out in taxes.

The portion of household income that is not consumed is called **personal saving.** What happens to income that is saved? The funds are channeled to business firms in two basic ways:

1. Households buy bonds and stocks issued by the firms, and the firms then use the money to buy investment goods.

2. Households leave the unused income (saving) in banks. The banks then lend the money to the firms, which use it to buy investment goods.

---

[3] An individual who owns a house is treated as a schizophrenic in the national accounts: as a business firm *and* as a consuming household. My left side is a businessman who owns my house and receives imaginary rent payments from my right side, the consumer who lives in my house. The NIPA identifies these imaginary rent payments as "imputed rent on owner-occupied dwellings," and they are the most important exception to the rule that a good must be sold on the market to be counted in GNP. See Table 2-1, line E.2.

Figure 2-3

Introduction of Saving and Investment to the Circular Flow Diagram

Our simple imaginary economy (Figure 2-1) when households save 20 percent of their income. Business firms' investment accounts for 20 percent of total expenditure. Again, we are assuming that there are no taxes, no government spending, and no foreign sector.

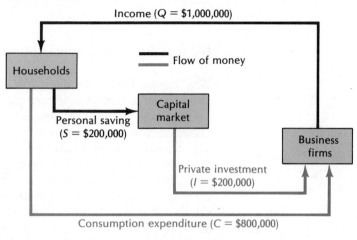

SAVING LEAKS OUT OF THE SPENDING STREAM BUT REAPPEARS AS INVESTMENT

Income (Q = $1,000,000)

Flow of money

Households

Capital market

Personal saving
(S = $200,000)

Business firms

Private investment
(I = $200,000)

Consumption expenditure (C = $800,000)

Whether households channel their saving to firms directly (through purchases of bonds and stock) or indirectly (through banks), the effect is the same: business firms obtain funds to purchase investment goods. The box labeled "capital market" in Figure 2-3 symbolizes the transfer of personal savings to business firms for the purpose of investment. Just as total expenditure on final product is equal by definition to income created, investment purchases must be equal to saving. Why? This conclusion follows from the definitions of three concepts just introduced:[4]

$$\text{income } (Q) \equiv \text{expenditure } (E) \tag{2.2}$$

$$\text{expenditure } (E) \equiv \text{consumption } (C) + \text{investment } (I) \tag{2.3}$$

$$\text{saving } (S) \equiv \text{income } (Q) - \text{consumption } (C) \tag{2.4}$$

It is customary in economics to eliminate unnecessary words by writing equations like these using alphabetical symbols only:

$$Q \equiv E \tag{2.2}$$

$$Q \equiv C + I \tag{2.3}$$

$$S \equiv Q - C \quad \text{or rearranging,} \quad Q \equiv C + S \tag{2.4}$$

Now we can see why saving and investment must be equal. Substitute equation (2.3) for E on the right side of equation (2.2) and substitute equation (2.4) for Q on the left side of equation (2.2). The result:

$$
\begin{aligned}
C + S &\equiv \quad C + I \\
-C & \qquad\quad -C \\
\hline
S &\equiv \qquad I
\end{aligned}
\quad \text{(subtracting } C \text{ from both sides)} \tag{2.5}
$$

---

[4]A three-bar equality sign is an "identity" and means that the relationship is true by definition.

In other words, saving is a "leakage" from the income spent on consumption goods. This leakage from the spending stream must be balanced by an "injection" of nonconsumption spending in the form of private investment.

Investment Versus Consumption

Why do we bother to distinguish between consumption and investment? One reason is that expenditure plans for the two are made by different economic units. Households decide how much of their incomes they want to consume and save; business firms decide how much they want to invest. The mismatch between household saving plans and business investment plans has been a major source of instability in U.S. output and income.

A second reason for distinguishing between consumption and investment is the different implication of the two types of spending for the economy's ability to produce output in the future. An economy that consumes a small portion of its income has a large portion left over for saving and investment—that is, for the formation of capital assets. It can build a relatively large number of factories, office buildings, computers, or other business equipment, and those capital assets add to the nation's "natural" real GNP for next year and the years to follow. For instance, Japan devotes a very high proportion of its income to investment, and its productivity (output per hour) growth rate has been correspondingly high.

2-5 Net Exports

Exports are goods produced within one country and shipped to another.

Imports are goods consumed within one country that are produced in another country.

Net exports and **net foreign investment** are both equal to exports minus imports.

Exports are expenditures for goods and services produced in the United States and sent to other countries. Such expenditures create income in the United States but are not part of the consumption or investment spending of U.S. residents. **Imports** are expenditures by U.S. residents for goods and services produced elsewhere, which thus do *not* create domestic income. For instance, an American-made Chevrolet exported to Canada is part of U.S. production and income but is Canadian consumption. A German-made Mercedes imported to the United States is part of German production and income but is U.S. consumption. If income created from exports is greater than income spent on imported goods, the net effect is a higher level of domestic production and income. Thus the difference between exports and imports, **net exports,** is a component of final product and GNP.[5]

SELF-TEST Chapter 1 introduced "foreign trade deficit" as one of the six major macroeconomic concepts. How is the foreign trade deficit related to net exports?

---

[5]Thus equation (2.3) can be rewritten

$$E = C + I + X$$

where X equals net exports.

Another name for net exports is **net foreign investment,** which can be given the same economic interpretation as domestic investment. Why? Both domestic and foreign investment are components of domestic production and income created. Domestic investment creates domestic capital assets; foreign investment creates U.S. claims on foreigners that likewise yield us future flows of income. An American export to Japan is paid for with Japanese yen, which can be used to buy a Japanese bank account or part of a Japanese factory.[6] The opposite occurs as well. When the United States imports more than it exports, net foreign investment is negative. U.S. payments for imports provide dollars for Japanese investors to use in buying American factories and hotels.

2-6 The Government Sector

Up to this point we have been examining an economy consisting only of private households and business firms. Now we consider the government, which collects taxes from the private sector and makes two kinds of expenditures. Government purchases of goods and services (tanks, fighter planes, schoolbooks) generate production and create income. The government can also make payments directly to households. Social security, unemployment compensation, and welfare benefits are examples of these transfer payments, given the name "transfer" because they are gifts from the government to the recipient without any obligation for the recipient to provide any services in return. As we learned in Section 2-3, transfer payments are not included in GNP.

Spending, Taxes, and Transfers

Figure 2-4 adds the government (federal, state, and local) to our imaginary economy of Figures 2-1 and 2-3. A flow of tax revenue (R = $100,000) passes from the households to the government.[7] The government buys $100,000 of goods and services (G), raising total expenditures on GNP and income created from the $1,000,000 of Figure 2-3 to $1,100,000. So far the government's budget is balanced. But in addition the government sends $100,000 back to the households in the form of transfer payments (F), such as welfare payments, leaving a deficit of $100,000 that must be financed. The government sells $100,000 of bonds to private households through the capital market, just as business firms sell bonds and stock to households to finance their investment projects.

---

[6]There is an additional alternative. American exporters may not want a Japanese asset but may want payment in U.S. dollars. They can obtain dollars from the U.S. government in trade for yen. The increased U.S. government holdings of yen and other currencies can be kept, thus counting as foreign capital asset, or can be used to pay off U.S. debts, reducing U.S. liabilities to foreigners.

[7]In the "real world' that will be described in Figure 2-6, both households and business firms pay taxes. Here we keep things simple by limiting tax payments to personal income taxes.

Figure 2-4
Introduction of Taxation, Government Spending, and the Foreign Sector to the Circular Flow Diagram

Our simple imaginary economy with the addition of a government collecting $100,000 in tax revenue, paying households $100,000 in transfer payments, and purchasing $100,000 of goods and services. Its total expenditures ($200,000) exceed its tax revenues ($100,000), leaving a $100,000 deficit that is financed by selling government bonds to the households.

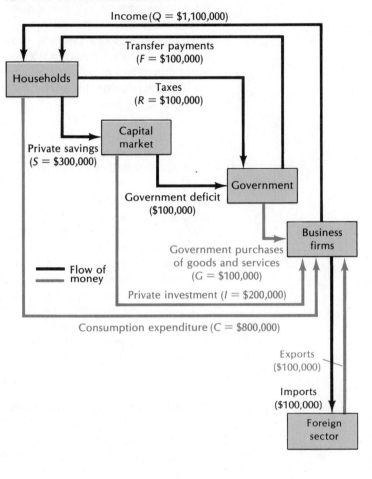

THE GOVERNMENT SURPLUS OR DEFICIT BALANCES THE REQUIREMENTS OF THE CAPITAL MARKET AND THE GOVERNMENT SECTOR

Income (Q = $1,100,000)

Transfer payments (F = $100,000)

Households

Taxes (R = $100,000)

Capital market

Private savings (S = $300,000)

Government deficit ($100,000)

Government

Business firms

Government purchases of goods and services (G = $100,000)

— Flow of money

Private investment (I = $200,000)

Consumption expenditure (C = $800,000)

Exports ($100,000)

Imports ($100,000)

Foreign sector

Including the Foreign Sector

Also shown in the bottom right corner of Figure 2-4 is the foreign sector. Imports are already included in consumption and investment spending, so imports are shown as a leakage by the black arrow pointing down toward the foreign sector box. Exports are spending on domestic production, as shown by the red arrow going from the foreign sector to the business firms. To keep the diagram simple, exports equal imports.[8]

---

[8]If imports exceed exports, there is a flow equal to the difference going from the foreign sector box to the capital market box. This is the inflow of foreign capital available to finance private investment or the government deficit.

As before, total income created (Q) is equal to total expenditure on final product (E):

$$Q \equiv E$$

Now there are four types of expenditure on final product: consumption (C); private domestic investment (I); government purchase of goods and services (G), and net exports (X):

$$E \equiv C + I + G + X \tag{2.6}$$

The total personal income that households receive consists of the income created from production (Q) and transfer payments from the government (F). This total ($Q + F$) is available for the purchase of consumption goods (C), saving (S), and the payment of taxes (R):

$$Q + F \equiv C + S + R$$

An equivalent expression is obtained if we subtract F from both sides:

$$Q \equiv C + S + R - F \tag{2.7}$$

Transfer payments (F) can be treated as negative taxes. Thus there is no reason to distinguish tax revenues from transfers. Instead, we define net tax revenue (T) as taxes (R) minus transfer (F), converting equation (2.7) into the simpler expression:

$$Q \equiv C + S + T \qquad R - F = T \tag{2.8}$$

Leakages, Injections, and the Government Budget Deficit

Since $Q \equiv E$, the right side of equation (2.8) is equal to the right side of equation (2.6), and we obtain:

$$
\begin{array}{r}
C + S + T \equiv \quad C + I + G + X \\
-C \qquad\qquad -C \\
\hline
S + T \equiv \quad\quad I + G + X
\end{array}
\qquad \text{(subtracting } C \text{ from both sides)} \quad (2.9)
$$

Now we can see that saving and investment do not always have to be equal, as they were in equation (2.5). Instead, we have a more general rule:

Since income is equal to expenditure, the portion of income not consumed (saving plus net taxes) must be equal to the nonconsumption portion of expenditure on final product (investment plus government spending plus net exports).

In other words, **leakages** out of the income available for consumption goods ($S + T$) must be exactly balanced by **injections** of nonconsumption spending ($I + G + X$).

This rule helps explain how the economy finances the **government budget deficit.** Subtracting S and G from both sides of equation (2.9), we have:

$$T - G \equiv I - S + X \tag{2.10}$$

Leakages describe the portion of total income that flows to taxes or saving rather than into purchase of consumer goods.

Injections is a term for nonconsumption expenditures.

The **government budget deficit** is the excess of government spending on goods and services over net tax revenue.

The left side of the equation is the government budget surplus—net tax revenues (T) minus expenditures by the government on goods and services (G). Whenever the government runs a surplus, the private economy must adjust to make private investment plus net exports exceed private saving. When the left side of (2.10) is negative, the government is running a deficit and the private economy must adjust to make private saving exceed private investment plus net exports.

2-7   *CASE STUDY:*   Saving, Investment, and Government
                        Deficits

Figure 2-5 illustrates the workings of equation (2.10) for the postwar period 1947–88. The top section of the illustration shows the annual values of real private investment, including both domestic investment (I) and net foreign investment (X), as well as saving (S). The bottom section shows the government surplus ($T - G$). All values are displayed as percentages of natural GNP. As required by equation (2.10), years in which $I + X$ fell short of saving were also years in which the government ran a deficit.

Deficits imply an excess of saving over $I + X$. In 1967, U.S. government spending for the Vietnam War was high. As a consequence the private economy had to adjust to reduce private investment below private saving, as indicated by the pink shading for 1967. In this instance, the behavior of government caused private investment to fall below private saving.

More recently, in 1982–88, an excess of government spending over tax receipts occurred, due in part to the Reagan administration's tax rate reductions that began in 1981. The resulting government budget deficit required the private economy to reduce $I + X$ below saving. In this episode, it was *net foreign investment* (X) that fell, as imports skyrocketed. Since net foreign investment became negative after 1982 and is included in the $I + X$ line in Figure 2-5, the growing imbalance between U.S. exports and imports shows up as a drop in that line.

But exactly the same situation (low $I + X$ with a government deficit) can occur for a different reason. In 1949, 1954, 1958, 1961, 1970, 1975–76, and again in 1982, a marked drop in private investment caused the government to run a deficit, by weakening the economy and causing net tax revenue (T) to fall below government expenditure (G). There is no way to tell from Figure 2-5 whether a government deficit is caused by high government spending, as in the Vietnam War in 1967, by negative foreign investment as in 1983–88, or by a weak economy, as in 1982. The economy influences the government budget, and vice versa.

Figure 2-5 can also be viewed as summarizing the relation between household saving and business spending. In years designated by pink shading, business firms did not invest all the funds that the households saved, leaving a remainder available to finance the government deficit. In years designated by gray shading, on the other hand, business firms invested more than households saved, requiring that the government run a surplus

PRIVATE INVESTMENT MINUS PRIVATE SAVING EQUALS THE GOVERNMENT SURPLUS

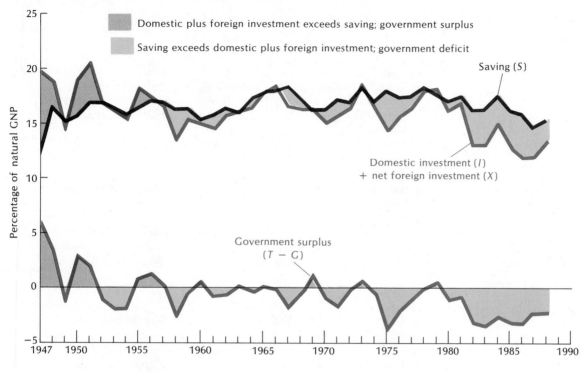

Figure 2-5   **Private Saving and Investment and the Government Surplus, 1947–88**
In the top of the diagram, the pink shaded area indicates that S exceeds I. In the bottom part, the pink area shows that G exceeds T and that the government is running a deficit. By definition—equation (2.10)—the top and bottom pink areas are equal. The same goes for the gray areas: in the top part I exceeds S, in the bottom part T exceeds G, and the government is running a surplus. *Source: Economic Report of the President,* January 1989.

to provide the extra funds needed by business. James Tobin sums up the relation this way:

> The moral is inescapable, if startling. If you would like the federal deficit to be smaller, the deficits of business must be bigger. Would you like the federal government to run a surplus and reduce its debt? Then business deficits must be big enough to absorb that surplus as well as the funds available from households and financial institutions.[9]

[9]James Tobin, "Deficit, Deficit, Who's Got the Deficit," *National Economic Policy* (New Haven: Yale University Press, 1966), p. 52.

Table 2-1   Items Included in and Excluded from GNP

Type of expenditure	Included in GNP?	1988 spending, $ billions	Examples
A. Final goods and services (GNP)	Yes	4864.3	
1. Consumption	Yes	3227.5	
a. Durable goods	Yes	451.1	Autos, TV sets
b. Nondurable goods	Yes	1046.9	Food, clothes, shoes
c. Services	Yes	1729.6	Haircuts, airline trips
2. Private investment (I)	Yes	766.5	
a. Change in business inventories	Yes	48.4	
b. Producers' durable equipment	Yes	345.6	Computers, tractors
c. Structures	Yes	372.5	
i. Nonresidential	Yes	142.8	Factories, office buildings, shopping centers
ii. Residential	Yes	229.7	Houses, condominiums
3. Government purchases of goods and services (G)	Yes	964.9	
a. Consumption	Yes	—	Fire fighters, police officers, city parks, street cleaners
b. Investment	Yes	—	Airports, university dormitories, hospitals
4. Net exports (exports minus imports)	Yes	−94.6	*Exports:* tractors, computers *Imports:* coffee, bananas, wine
B. Government interest and transfer payments	No	689.1	Social security, welfare, unemployment benefits
C. Private intermediate goods	No	—	Wheat, iron ore
D. Private purchases of used assets	No	—	Purchases of used houses, used cars
E. Nonmarket activities			
1. Value of leisure time	No	—	Watching television, playing tennis
2. Services from existing durables			
a. Housing	Yes	—	Estimated value of services from housing stock, included above on line A.1.c.
b. Other durables	No	—	Value of use of auto, dishwasher
3. Costs of pollution	No	—	Costs of smog, water pollution
4. Illegal activities	No	—	Earnings from theft, drugs, illegal betting

Source: Survey of Current Business, March 1989. For government interest and transfer payments, see Appendix C, notes to Figure 2-6.

2-8 A Summary of Types of Spending

Table 2-1 summarizes the NIPA treatment of the different types of expenditures. The top part of the table splits total expenditures on final goods and services (GNP) into four basic components: private consumption, private investment, government spending, and net exports. Private consumption and investment exclude purchases of intermediate goods, which are listed separately on line C.

The treatment of government spending is different. All government purchases of goods and services, whether intermediate or final, and whether consumption or investment, are included in the GNP and on line A.3.

Which items are excluded from GNP, and why? These items are shown at the bottom of Table 2-1, on lines B through E. Recall that GNP includes *currently produced* goods and services, thus ruling out items that do not represent current production. These include government interest and transfer payments (line B), because the recipient does not have to provide a good or service in return. Also excluded are purchases of used assets on line D (houses, cars), since they do not involve current production (except for sales commissions).

Intermediate goods on line C are excluded, as we have learned previously, to avoid double-counting. Finally, the goods and services included in GNP must be *sold on the market.* This rules out a number of "nonmarket activities" listed on line E. The single largest excluded item is the value of leisure time—that is, the value people place on the time spent in all activities other than work. We know that people value their leisure time because many could obtain additional part-time jobs but willingly give up the extra wages to avoid working too much. Additional nonmarket items excluded are the value people receive from their consumer durables (in contrast to the value of housing services, which are included as explained in footnote 3 of this chapter). Costs of air and water pollution (illness, dirty clothes) are excluded, because they are not charged for on the market. Illegal activities are excluded, even though there is a market for illegal drugs and other activities, because of obvious difficulties in obtaining data.

2-9 The Circular Flow in 1988: A Tour of the "Plumbing Diagram"

Figure 2-6 is a more realistic version of Figure 2-4, showing the relation of the spending streams between households, business firms, the capital market, and the government, using actual data on spending and income from 1988. The width of the "pipes" flowing among the sectors is proportional to the actual 1988 flows of spending, income, taxes, and so on.

Start in the lower right corner, where business firms produce three types of final product: consumption goods, investment goods, and government purchases. Expenditures (E) are shown as wide red pipes flowing to the right from households, the capital market, and the government to the business firms box. Business firms also produce exports, shown as a red pipe, but this is more than offset by a leakage into imports, shown flowing down to the foreign sector box.

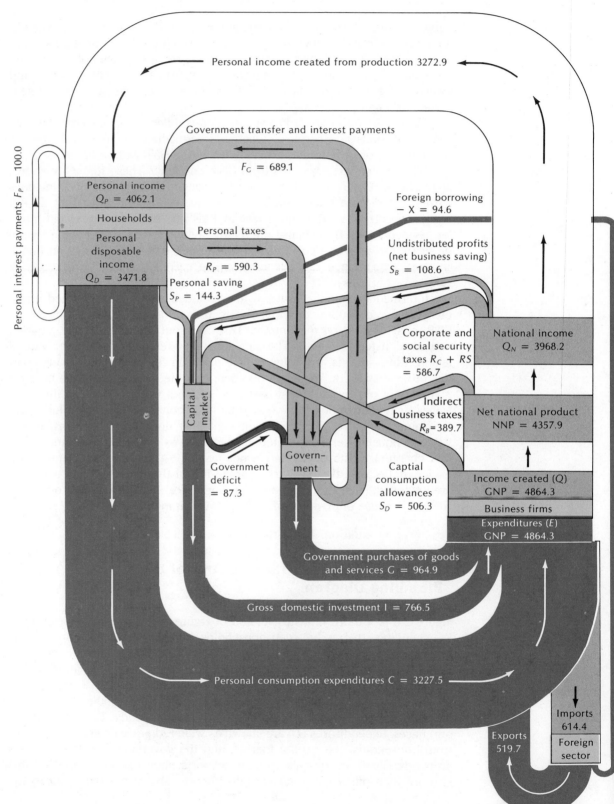

Personal income created from production 3272.9

Government transfer and interest payments

$F_G = 689.1$

Personal income
$Q_P = 4062.1$

Households

Personal disposable income
$Q_D = 3471.8$

Personal taxes

$R_P = 590.3$

Personal saving
$S_P = 144.3$

Personal interest payments $F_P = 100.0$

Foreign borrowing
$- X = 94.6$

Undistributed profits
(net business saving)
$S_B = 108.6$

Corporate and social security taxes $R_C + RS = 586.7$

National income
$Q_N = 3968.2$

Indirect business taxes
$R_B = 389.7$

Net national product
NNP = 4357.9

Capital market

Government deficit
$= 87.3$

Govern-ment

Captial consumption allowances
$S_D = 506.3$

Income created (Q)
GNP = 4864.3

Business firms

Expenditures (E)
GNP = 4864.3

Government purchases of goods and services $G = 964.9$

Gross domestic investment I = 766.5

Personal consumption expenditures C = 3227.5

Imports
614.4

Exports
519.7

Foreign sector

Leakages from the Spending Stream

Depreciation or **capital consumption allowances** are for the part of the capital stock used up due to obsolescence and physical wear.

Let us look at how the income created from the sale of final output is distributed. The first deduction is for **depreciation (capital consumption allowances)** charged by business firms (*saving for depreciation, thus S_D*). This S_D is shown flowing through a gray pipe from the business firms to the capital market box at the left.

A part of the nation's capital equipment wears out each year, and business firms deduct a capital consumption allowance from their income to provide funds to replace worn-out equipment. To this extent a part of total output and spending does not represent net income paid to factors of production but is used to *replace* capital goods used up in the process of production. This portion of output, capital consumption allowances, must be included in GNP if we are to show the expenditures of final users on the national output. But at the same time, capital consumption allowances must be excluded from **net national product (NNP)** if we are to show the incomes actually earned by the factors of production.

Net national product is equal to GNP minus capital consumption allowances.

A **gross** magnitude includes capital consumption allowances, whereas a **net** magnitude excludes them.

*The terms **gross** and **net** in economics usually refer to the inclusion or exclusion of capital consumption allowances. Thus the difference between "gross investment" and "net investment," or between "gross saving" and "net saving," is exactly the same as that between GNP and NNP.*

The next leakage is the collection by the government (federal, state, and local) of **indirect business taxes** (taxes on business, hence R_B). These taxes—for instance, state or city excise and sales taxes—are included in the prices paid by the consumer but are not available for payment as income to workers or firms. Indirect business taxes are shown flowing from the NNP box to the government sector. With the deduction of R_B we move up above NNP to **national income** (Q_N), the sum of all net incomes earned by the factors of production (labor and capital) in producing current output.

National income is the earnings of factors of production, computed as net national product, minus **indirect business taxes,** which in turn are taxes levied on business sales.

Not all of the national income is paid out to individuals. Corporations withhold part of their income as undistributed corporate profits (also called "retained earnings"), shown in Figure 2-6 as a leakage flowing from the national income box to the capital market. This is saving by incorporated business (S_B). In addition, a substantial amount "leaks out" to the government as corporate income taxes (R_C) and social security taxes (R_S). Finally, what remains of national income after deducting undistributed corporate profits, corporation income taxes, and social security taxes is paid out to persons

Figure 2-6 **Income, Product, and Transfer Flows in the 1988 U.S. Economy**
An elaboration of Figure 2-4 showing that much of the income created in producing GNP (lower right corner) "leaks out" of the white income flow through the gray pipes into saving $(S_D + S_B + S_P)$, into taxes $(R_B + R_C + R_S + R_P)$, and into imports. Government transfer payments (F_G) are a negative leakage adding to personal income. Only the remaining portion of GNP net of all the leakages is available for the red consumption pipe. In addition, total expenditures on GNP include the red expenditure pipes representing private investment and government spending, which are financed by the gray tax and saving leakages, and exports, which are more than offset by imports. *Source and method:* See Appendix C.

in the form of wages, salaries, rent, interest dividends, and the profits of unincorporated enterprises (for example, the income of small shopkeepers and farmers).

Transfers and Personal Income

Some individuals receive incomes that are not earned as a payment for any productive service and therefore are not included in GNP, NNP, or the national income. Part of these payments are government transfers and interest payments on the government debt (F_G), shown flowing from the government sector in the middle of Figure 2-6 to the personal income box at the upper left, bypassing GNP, NNP, and national income on the way. Interest payments by consumers (F_P) are shown flowing away from the household sector and then back again.[10]

Personal income is the income received by households from all sources, including earnings and transfer payments.

Personal disposable income is personal income minus personal income tax payments.

The total we now arrive at is **personal income** (Q_P), the sum of all income payments to individuals. This represents the current flow of purchasing power to individuals through the workings of the productive system plus the transfers from the government and personal sectors. If we now deduct personal tax payments (R_P), we obtain one of the most important totals in national income accounting. This remainder is **personal disposable income** (Q_D), which is the amount of income that individuals as consumers have available to spend or save.

We see three different flows emerging below the personal sector box: personal consumption expenditure (C), which flows around to the right to be spent on GNP; interest paid by consumers (F_P), which is a transfer payment and flows back to households; and the final leakage from the spending stream, personal savings (S_P).[11] The flow of consumption expenditure to the business firms brings us full circle.

Leakages Equal Investment Again

An overall view of Figure 2-6 shows a series of leakages flowing through gray pipes (taxes and saving of various types minus transfer payments) that reduces the amount spent on GNP ($4864.3 billion) to the total disposable income of persons, $3471.8 billion. A further diversion, in the form of personal saving and interest payments, results in consumer expenditures of $3227.5 billion. The total of the leakages, after the necessary adjustments, is exactly equal to the sum of investment (including net exports) and govern-

---

[10]Why does the pipe for personal interest payments flow away from households and then back to households? Households make interest payments to banks and other financial institutions. Banks use their income from these interest payments to pay interest to households on their bank accounts. The pipe shown in the figure omits the banks to simplify the diagram. Households on balance receive much more interest income than they pay in personal interest payments. The remainder of their interest income is hiding in the large white pipe "Personal income created from production" and in the gray pipe labeled "government transfer and interest payments."

[11]The Department of Commerce has labeled consumer expenditures plus interest payments ($C + F_p$) as "personal outlays." In practice, disposable income and personal outlays are directly estimated, and personal saving is obtained as a residual.

ment spending. We can now rewrite equation (2.9) using the specific symbols of the actual U.S. economy as described in Figure 2-6:

$$\underbrace{(S_D + S_B + S_P)}_{\text{Saving}} + \underbrace{(R_B + R_C + R_S + R_P)}_{\text{Taxes}} - \underbrace{F_G}_{\text{Transfers}} \equiv \underbrace{I + G + X}_{\text{Injections}} \qquad (2.11)$$

or, once again, the more general form (2.9) that combines all the saving terms into one symbol (S) and lets T stand for all tax receipts minus transfers:

$$S + T \equiv I + G + X$$

Equations (2.11) and (2.9) both summarize the main lesson of Figure 2-6: *leakages must be equal to injections, by definition.*

2-10 Measuring Prices

For most problems in economic analysis, we are interested in comparing measurements of income and expenditures at different times. Hence we must measure these magnitudes in "real terms"—that is, terms adjusted for the effects of price changes. The illustration of actual and natural GNP in Figure 1-5 shows these magnitudes in real terms. How do the national income accountants take the recorded nominal income and expenditure (Y) of two years in which prices were different (say, 1982 and 1990) and compute real GNP (Q) adjusted for all effects of price changes?

Implicit GNP Deflator

Real GNP (Q) is the value of expenditures for *each year* (say, 1990) when each separate good or service is measured in the prices of a selected base year (say, 1982). The implicit GNP deflator, in turn, is the ratio of nominal to real GNP:

$$P \equiv \frac{Y}{Q}$$

The implicit GNP deflator (P) is the ratio of nominal GNP (Y) to real GNP (Q).

Table 2-2 works through an example of the calculation of nominal GNP, real GNP, and the GNP deflator for a hypothetical economy in 1982 and 1990 producing only steak and eggs. Nominal GNP (line 3c) is the sum of expenditures on the two products in the two years at the actual prices paid. Real GNP (line 4c) is the sum of expenditures on the two products in the two years in both cases measured at 1982 prices. The GNP deflator (line 5) is the ratio of nominal to real GNP (1.36 for 1990), which indicates that the average price level in 1990 was 136 percent of the 1982 price level.

SELF-TEST   To see whether you understand price indexes, recalculate nominal GNP, real GNP, and the GNP deflator for 1982 and 1990 from the data in Table 2-2, if we now assume that 1990 (not 1982) is the base year.

Table 2-2 Calculation of Nominal GNP, Real GNP, and the Implicit GNP Deflator in an Imaginary Economy Producing Only Steak and Eggs

	1982	1990
1. Prices		
a. Steak, pound	$ 2.25	$ 3.50
b. Eggs, dozen	.75	.80
2. Production in physical units		
a. Steak, pounds	10	8
b. Eggs, dozens	10	16
3. Production in current prices of each year		
a. Steak (1a times 2a)	22.50	$28.00
b. Eggs (1b times 2b)	7.50	12.80
c. Nominal GNP (3a plus 3b)	30.00	40.80
4. Real production in constant 1982 prices		
a. Steak (1a for 1982 times 2a for each year)	$22.50	$18.00
b. Eggs (1b for 1982 times 2b for each year)	7.50	12.00
c. Real GNP (4a plus 4b)	30.00	30.00
5. GNP deflator, 1982 base (3c/4c)	1.00	1.36

The calculation of the GNP deflator in the imaginary world of Table 2-2 is mere child's play compared to the real world with its thousands of individual products. This complex job requires not only the use of a large computer for all the arithmetic but also diligent legwork and many difficult choices. The GNP deflator is just one **price index** among the several published by the U.S. government. Of the others, the most important is the Consumer Price Index.

A **price index** is a weighted average of prices at any given time, divided by the prices of the same goods in a base year.

The Consumer Price Index (CPI)

How the CPI is measured. The Department of Commerce, which compiles and publishes the quarterly figures on nominal GNP, real GNP, and the implicit GNP deflator, does not actually collect the individual prices of steak, eggs, and other products. This job of collection is performed by the U.S. Bureau of Labor Statistics (BLS), which also publishes two price indexes of its own, the Consumer Price Index (CPI) and the Producer Price Index (PPI).

The CPI, which is published monthly, is based on the prices of several thousand products, grouped into 224 sets of items. Prices paid by consumers are recorded by hundreds of price collectors who call or visit thousands of stores monthly in 85 geographical areas, obtaining more than 100,000 prices each month. Then the average prices for individual products, say steak and eggs, are combined by the BLS into group indexes—for instance, "food and beverages." Then the group indexes are combined into the "all-items CPI." The weights used to combine the different product prices into group indexes and to arrive at the all-items index are based on the proportions of these items in consumer expenditures as recorded in a survey.

The CPI Measurement Error

The government publishes two alternative price indexes for consumption goods and services. One is the CPI. The other is the personal consumption component of the GNP deflator, the so-called **personal consumption deflator.**[12] Since 1983 these have indicated about the same rate of inflation. But for the decade before 1983, the increase in the CPI is seriously misleading and overstates the rise in prices by more than 10 percent. Figure 2-7, which plots the CPI, the consumption deflator, and the ratio between the two, shows this miscalculation. The pink shading indicates the excessive price increase registered by the CPI. Starting at zero in 1970, the excess price increase reached 12 percent by 1982.

> The **personal consumption deflator** is the price deflator for the personal consumption expenditures component of GNP.

Reasons for the CPI measurement error. The main reason for the CPI measurement error is that, until 1983, it placed excessive weight on changes in mortgage interest rates, which rose rapidly in the 1970s. Most homeowners held 20- or 30-year mortgages with fixed interest rates. However, the CPI assumed that every mortgage holder had to take out a new mortgage every four months and pay higher interest rates in periods when interest rates increased. Furthermore, until 1986 the CPI used 1972–73 expenditure weights for averaging the various product prices. This tended to exaggerate the impact of higher oil prices on inflation in 1979–81 and of lower oil prices on inflation during 1981–86, since these weights ignore energy-saving conservation that lowered fuel use in 1979–86 compared to the 1972–73 period used for the weights.

Why the measurement error still matters. The CPI fixed the erroneous treatment of mortgage interest rates in 1983, and it shifted to more up-to-date weights in 1987. But all of the *historical errors* depicted in Figure 2-7 still remain. Why? Unlike the GNP deflator, the CPI *is never revised to correct mistakes,* because the CPI is used to escalate wages, social security increases, and other payments. Many workers and recipients of social security benefits received increases based on the CPI's exaggerated measure of inflation in the 1970s. Historical revision of the CPI could lead to lawsuits and turmoil if firms that had paid excessive wages attempted to cut wages or otherwise regain these past overpayments.

Because the CPI is never revised, any comparison of historical growth in real wages or real incomes is incorrect if it uses the CPI as a measure of

---

[12]Every component of the GNP deflator, including the personal consumption deflator, is published with three alternative weighting systems for adding up its components: the implicit deflator (ratio of nominal to real GNP for that component), fixed 1982 weights, and chain weights that change each quarter. All comparisons between the CPI and the personal consumption deflator in this section and in Figure 2-7 use the fixed 1982 weight version of the deflator, which is closest in weighting method to that of the CPI.

THE CPI DISPLAYS A FALSE BULGE

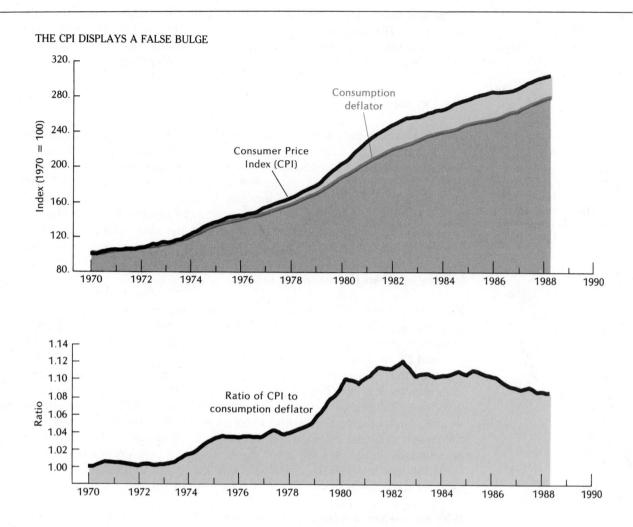

Figure 2-7 **The CPI and the Consumption Deflator, 1970–89**
The upper frame plots the CPI against the price deflator for consumption goods
("Consumption Deflator") over the period since 1970. The CPI rises faster than the
Consumption Deflator, shown by the upward bulge of the CPI line above the
Consumption Deflator line. The bottom frame shows the ratio of the CPI to the
Consumption Deflator, which reached a maximum of 1.12 in 1982.

inflation. For instance, the CPI erroneously implies that real wages *were unchanged* between 1973 and 1982, while the more accurate consumption deflator implies that real wages *rose* over the same period by 10.9 percent.
Between 1982 and 1988 the relationship is reversed: the CPI implies an increase of 4.3 percent and the consumption deflator only 1.3 percent. Thus
one could conclude incorrectly from the CPI figures that workers' real earnings grew *faster* in 1982–88 than 1973–82, while the more accurate consumption deflator implies that they grew *slower*. In 1988 political candidates de-

bated whether workers had become better off or worse off, and they could come up with either answer, depending on whether they used the CPI or the more accurate consumption deflator. Because misleading historical comparisons can be made when the CPI is used to calculate changes in real variables like real wages or the real money supply, we make *no use whatsoever* of the CPI in this book, and historical CPI data are excluded from the appendix in the back of the book.

Policy mistakes caused by the CPI error.   Unfortunately, the CPI is used widely as a cost-of-living escalator in wage contracts as well as for many government transfer programs, including food stamps and social security benefits. In the 1979–81 period, the exaggeration of inflation by the CPI caused social security benefits to go up too fast, and thus contributed directly to the financial crisis of the social security system, which was fixed by raising social security taxes. Everyone today is paying higher social security taxes, in part because of the CPI measurement error!

By making wage rates rise too rapidly as a result of cost-of-living escalation, the CPI error prolonged the inflation of the late 1970s and worsened the 1981–82 recession. Finally, the erroneous 17 percent inflation rate registered in the first quarter of 1980 by the CPI (compared with 12 percent for the deflator) created panic within the Carter administration. Ill-advised credit controls were introduced, causing instability in production, employment, interest rates, and the money supply throughout 1980 and early 1981.[13]

SELF-TEST   Which price index will imply a faster increase in real wages between 1972 and 1982? The CPI or the deflator for personal consumption expenditures?

The Producer Price Index (PPI)

Another BLS price index, the Producer Price Index (PPI), collects prices on a large number of commodities that are not purchased directly by consumers. These include raw materials such as coal and crude oil, intermediate products such as flour and steel, and many types of machinery purchased by businesses (cash registers, tractors). The actual price data are recorded on mail questionnaires submitted monthly by thousands of firms that sell these goods. Just as the group indexes of the CPI are used for the consumption part of the GNP deflator by the Department of Commerce, so product and group indexes of the PPI are used to create other components of the implicit GNP deflator, including producers' durable equipment and inventory investment.

Even after using the available information in the individual and group indexes in the CPI and PPI, the Department of Commerce still must make many difficult choices to obtain estimates of price change for goods not included in the BLS price-collection program, including electronic comput-

---

[13]For more on the CPI measurement error, see Robert J. Gordon, "The Consumer Price Index: Measuring Inflation and Causing It," *The Public Interest,* no. 63 (Spring 1981), pp. 112–134.

ers, jet aircraft, ships, and buildings. We return to measurement issues involving official data on prices and real output in Chapter 12, when we discuss the puzzle of slow U.S. productivity growth since 1973.

SUMMARY

1. This chapter is concerned with the definition and measurement of national income—what is included and excluded and why. Since many of the rules governing the calculation of national income are arbitrary, the size of any nation's GNP is at the discretion of its economists and government officials who mark off the dividing lines between the included and excluded items.

2. A flow magnitude is any money payment, physical good, or service that flows from one economic unit to another per unit of time. A flow is distinguished from a stock, which is an economic magnitude in the possession of an individual or firm at a moment of time.

3. Final product (GNP) consists of all currently produced goods and services sold through the market but not resold during the current time period. By counting intermediate goods only once, and by including only final purchases, we avoid double counting and ensure that the value of final product and total income created (value added) are equal.

4. Leakages out of income available for consumption goods are by definition exactly balanced by injections of nonconsumption spending. This equality of leakages and injections is guaranteed by the accounting methods used.

5. In the same way, by definition total income (consumption plus leakages) equals total expenditure (consumption plus injections). Injections of nonconsumption spending fall into three categories—private domestic investment (on business equipment and structures, residential housing, and inventory accumulation); foreign investment or net exports; and government spending on goods and services. The definitions require private investment (including domestic and foreign) to exceed private saving by the amount of the government surplus.

6. Net national product (NNP) is obtained by deducting depreciation from GNP. Deduction of indirect business taxes from NNP yields national income, the sum of all net incomes earned by factors of production in producing current output. If we deduct corporate undistributed profits, corporate income taxes, and social security taxes, and add in transfer payments, we arrive at personal income, the sum of all income payments to individuals. Personal disposable income is simply personal income after the deduction of personal income taxes.

7. The implicit GNP deflator, the economy's aggregate price index (P), is defined as nominal GNP in actual current prices (Y) divided by real GNP measured in prices of a base year (Q). Other price indexes are the CPI and PPI.

8. Measurement errors make the CPI inaccurate for historical comparisons of real wages and other real variables.

CONCEPTS

consumer expenditures
flow and stock magnitudes
final product
transfer payments
final and intermediate goods
value added
inventory and fixed investment
personal saving
exports, imports, and net exports
net foreign investment

leakages and injections
capital consumption allowances
net national product and national income
gross versus net
indirect business taxes
personal income
personal disposable income
price index
personal consumption deflator

Questions

1. Explain the difference between a stock magnitude and a flow magnitude. Label each of the following as either a stock or a flow:
   (a) depreciation (S_D)
   (b) real saving (S)
   (c) wealth
   (d) government debt
   (e) government deficit
   (f) foreign trade deficit
   (g) savings
   (h) nominal money supply
   (i) labor force
   (j) labor services
   (k) real net exports (X)
   (l) net tax revenue (T)

2. What are the major drawbacks in the attempt to use nominal GNP as a measure of social welfare?

3. Assume that the GNP for the United States is eight times as large as the GNP for China. Can you conclude, based on this information, that the average individual in the United States is eight times as well off as the average individual in China? Why or why not?

4. One way to calculate the production taking place within a country would be to sum all value added during the production process. Yet, in the United States this is not done. Why not? What technique is used to calculate production taking place in the United States? Do we get the same answer as the value added approach? Why or why not?

5. Assuming that all other things remain equal in the current time period (GNP, G, T, S, C, etc.), what do you predict will happen to the level of domestic investment if the exchange rate between the dollar and the yen appreciates? Explain how it is possible for consumption (C) to remain constant in this situation. What do you predict will happen to GNP in the next time period?

6. Saving and taxes are referred to as leakages. From what do they leak? To where do they go? Imports are also a leakage. From what do they leak? To where do they go?

7. What are the sources of money flows in the capital market? How are these funds used?

8. Explain why the *change* in the level of inventories and not the *level* of inventories are included in the calculation of GNP.

9. In the national income and product accounts, personal income (*PI*) can be calculated by subtracting from national income (*NI*) income earned but not received and adding back in income received but not earned. Explain.

10. Four hundred tires are produced by a tire producer and sold to General Motors in December 1989 for $50 each. In February 1990, General Motors puts the tires on one hundred newly produced cars and sells each car for $20,000. What is the contribution made to GNP in 1989 and 1990 by the transactions described? (Assume all other components of the cars are produced in 1990.)

11. Starting from the situation depicted in Figure 2-3, assume that business firms produce an additional $500,000 worth of goods, of which only $450,000 are bought during the current year. What are the new values for the following:
    (a) income
    (b) consumption expenditures
    (c) personal saving
    (d) investment

12. Prior to 1983, the government often had a budget deficit, but the economy as a whole experienced a foreign trade surplus. After 1983, both the government budget and foreign trade account were running deficits. What does this imply about the relationship that existed between private saving and private domestic investment in the period before and after 1983?

13. The Consumer Price Index is an attempt to measure the cost of a fixed "basket of goods and services" in different years. An alternative measure of inflation would estimate the value of a changing basket of goods at fixed, base year prices. Which is the better measure of the impact of inflation on household well-being? Explain.

Problems

1. Assume that a country produces only two goods, compact disc players and compact discs. Infor-

mation regarding the levels of output and prices for two years is given below:

	1985	1989
Compact disc players		
Output	500	1,000
Price	$4,000	$2,000
Compact discs		
Output	80,000	160,000
Price	$10.00	$20.00

Fill in the following table based on the above data:

	1985	1989
Nominal GNP		
Real GNP (1985 Dollars)		
Real GNP (1989 Dollars)		
GNP Deflator (1985 Dollars)		
GNP Deflator (1989 Dollars)		

2. Use the following data to answer the questions below:

Item	Amount
Government Purchases of Goods and Services (G)	815.3
Exports	370.0
Capital Consumption Allowance (SD)	438.5
Net Fixed Investment	200.1

Corporate Income Taxes (R_C)	90.1
Personal Consumption (C)	2582.1
Indirect Business Taxes (R_B)	338.6
Imports	446.9
Inventory Change	30.0
Social Security Contributions (R_S)	300.3
Undistributed Corporate Profits (S_B)	75.0
Government Transfer and Interest Payments (F_G)	546.7
Personal Interest Payments (F_P)	87.4
Personal Taxes (R_P)	492.7

(a) What is the level of Gross National Product?
(b) What is the level of National Income?
(c) What is the level of Disposable Personal Income? (Hint: Include personal interest payments (F_P) in personal income, then calculate personal saving as Q_D less personal outlays [see footnote 11]).
(d) What is the level of Personal Saving?
(e) Prove that the level of leakages in this economy is equal to the level of injections.

3. Assume that gross private domestic investment is $800 billion and that the government (state, local, and federal combined) is currently running a $400 billion dollar deficit. If households and businesses are saving $1000 billion, what is the value of net exports? Use equation (2.9) to explain your answer.

SELF-TEST ANSWERS

p. 32 The payment of the $10 bill to the barber is a flow of money shown by the solid red "consumer expenditures" line. The provision of the haircut by the barber for the student is shown by the dashed red "product" line. The barber's income of $10 is shown by the solid black "income" line, and the barber's provision of labor services to perform the haircut is shown by the dashed black "labor services" line.

p. 38 Included in GNP for the first quarter of 1990 is the *change* in the value of the grocer's inventories between December 31, 1989, and March 31, 1990. This is $6.00 minus $4.00, or $2.00. If the level of inventories had fallen, instead of rising as in the example, inventory investment would have been negative.

p. 40 The foreign trade deficit and net exports are the same concept, but with the sign reversed. For instance, if exports are 90 and imports are 100, we say that there is a foreign trade deficit of 10, and that net exports are −10.

p. 51 With a base year of 1990, then of course nominal and real GNP are the same in 1990, and the GNP deflator for 1990 is 1.0. For 1982 nominal GNP is 30.0, real GNP is 43.0, and the GNP deflator is 0.7.

p. 55 Because the CPI grew faster between 1972 and 1982, it implies a slower increase in real wages and the deflator for personal consumption expenditures implies a faster increase in real wages.

PART II

Output, Interest Rates, Money, and the Government Budget

CHAPTER THREE The Simple Keynesian Theory of Income Determination

An honest man is one who knows that he can't consume more than he has produced.
—*Ayn Rand, 1966*

The book began with six central macroeconomic aggregates and their puzzling behavior since the early 1970s. The first and second of these aggregates are the unemployment and inflation rates. Unemployment and inflation behavior is explained in Part IV of the book, Chapters 9 and 10. The explanation provided there requires that beginning with this chapter, and continuing throughout Parts II and III, business cycles in real GNP first be explained.

In Chapter 2 we examined the methods used by the government to *measure* real income and product, that is, real GNP. Now we begin to develop the theory of how real GNP is *determined.* In this chapter the theory is exceedingly simple, showing only how unexplained changes in investment spending are transmitted to consumption spending and to real GNP as a whole. But soon, in subsequent chapters, the theory becomes more realistic and allows us to make predictions about the effects of monetary and fiscal policy on real GNP. The theory also sheds light on the behavior of other central macroeconomic aggregates, the interest rate, the government budget deficit, and the foreign trade deficit.

3-1 Income Determination as an Explanation of Unemployment

Endogenous variables are explained by an economic theory.

Exogenous variables are those that are relevant but whose behavior the theory does not attempt to explain; their values are taken as given.

Chapter 1 introduced the fact that throughout history, as far back as economists' measures extend, the unemployment rate has exhibited the recurrent fluctuations known as business cycles. We learned that business cycles in unemployment have as their mirror image business cycles in the gap between actual real GNP and natural real GNP. When actual real GNP falls below natural real GNP, the unemployment rate rises. Thus *understanding the causes of business cycles in real GNP is the key to understanding business cycles in the unemployment rate.*

The theory of income determination takes major macroeconomic aggregates (or variables) and divides them into two groups, **endogenous** variables whose movements the theory explains, and **exogenous** variables whose movements are not explained but just taken as given. At the beginning of this chapter most important economic aggregates are treated as exogenous, or unexplained, and the list of endogenous aggregates is very short. As we progress we will gradually shift variables from the exogenous to the endogenous category.

In this chapter we make two important simplifying assumptions that are later abandoned. First, the interest rate (and thus monetary policy) is not allowed to influence desired spending. The interest rate thus falls into the category of economic aggregates (variables) that are assumed to be both exogenous and constant. Second, the price level is also assumed to be exogenous and constant. Thus, because the price level is fixed, all changes in real GNP are also changes in nominal GNP of the same amount.

The assumption of an exogenous and constant interest rate is maintained only in this chapter; in the next chapter we will convert the interest rate into an endogenous variable explained by our economic theory. The assumption of a fixed or "rigid" price level is maintained throughout Chapters 3–5; then in Chapters 6 and 7 we will examine the effects of private spending decisions and government policy on the price level.

When our theory is finally developed, all the important economic aggregates will be treated as endogenous, explained by the theory. What will remain in the exogenous category? The disturbances that can aggravate business cycles and that government policy attempts to offset. Examples of exogenous disturbances are unpredictable changes in consumption and investment spending by private individuals and firms, changes in government spending caused by wars and other political events, and changes in the price of oil and other important raw materials.

3-2 The Division of Disposable Income Between Consumption and Saving

To determine real income (which is the same as real GNP) we naturally start with the most important component of aggregate demand: personal consumption expenditures. By definition household disposable income (Q_D) is divided between consumption expenditures (C) and saving (S).[1]

The Consumption Function and the Marginal Propensity to Consume

How do households divide their disposable income between consumption and saving? Let us imagine that households always spend $250 billion on consumption spending at every level of income, an amount we shall call **autonomous** consumption. *Autonomous* consumption is completely independent of income. If autonomous consumption were the only form of consumption, then consumption expenditures (C) would simply be:

An **autonomous** magnitude is independent of the level of income.

$$C = 250 \qquad (3.1)$$

---

[1]For the rest of the chapter we consider only personal saving and ignore business saving. Thus personal saving is labeled S in this chapter instead of S_P as in Figure 2-6.

But we know that people tend to consume more as their disposable income increases. The amount by which consumption expenditures increase for each extra dollar of disposable income is a fraction called the **marginal propensity to consume.** For instance, we shall assume in our example that households consume 75 cents more for each extra dollar of disposable income they receive. This component of consumption is called **induced consumption.** If induced consumption were the only form of consumption, then consumption expenditures *(C)* would simply be the marginal propensity to consume (0.75) times disposable income (Q_D):

$$C = 0.75Q_D \tag{3.2}$$

Both equations (3.1) and (3.2) are unrealistic. It is more realistic to combine them, allowing consumption to consist both of an autonomous component and an induced component. In our numerical example, the autonomous component is 250 and the induced component is $0.75Q_D$. This combined relationship is called the "consumption function" and shows the amount of total consumption spending for each level of disposable income:

Numerical Example

$$C = 250 + 0.75Q_D \tag{3.3}$$

A more general way of writing the consumption function, which does not require us to specify particular numbers, uses letters of the alphabet as symbols for autonomous consumption *(a)*, the marginal propensity to consume *(c)*, and induced consumption (cQ_D):

General Linear Form

$$C = a + cQ_D \tag{3.4}$$

Either way of writing the consumption functions states that total consumption is the sum of autonomous and induced consumption.

The consumption function described by the numerical example in equation (3.3) is also illustrated in Table 3-1. Along the left-hand side of the table

---

Table 3-1   **A Hypothetical Schedule of Consumption and Saving Behavior**

Point in Figure 3-1	Disposable income ($ billions) (Q_D)	Marginal propensity to consume (c)	Induced consumption (cQ_D) (2) × (1)	Autonomous consumption (a)	Total consumption $a + cQ_D$ (4) + (3)	Marginal propensity to save (s)	Induced saving (sQ_D) (6) × (1)	Total saving $-a + sQ_D$ $-(4) + (7)$
	(1)	(2)	(3)	(4)	(5)	(6)	(7)	(8)
	0	0.75	0	250	250	0.25	0	−250
F	1000	0.75	750	250	1000	0.25	250	0
	2000	0.75	1500	250	1750	0.25	500	250
	3000	0.75	2250	250	2500	0.25	750	500
D	4000	0.75	3000	250	3250	0.25	1000	750
	5000	0.75	3750	250	4000	0.25	1250	1000

---

are listed six different values of disposable income, ranging from zero to $5000 billion. Next, column (2) shows that the marginal propensity to consume is always 0.75. This fraction times each level of disposable income is equal to induced consumption, shown in column (3). Total consumption, listed in column (5), includes not just the induced portion in column (3), but also the autonomous portion (always equal to 250) listed in column (4). Column (5), showing total consumption at different levels of disposable income, is just another way of exhibiting the consumption function.

The consumption function can also be shown graphically, as in Figure 3-1. The thick red line goes through the same numbers as shown in column (5) of Table 3-1. When disposable income is zero, total consumption consists just of the autonomous component ($250 billion). For each extra $1000 billion of disposable income, as we move to the right on the graph, the red consumption function line rises by $750 billion, since its slope (the marginal propensity to consume) is 0.75. For instance, at point D disposable income is $4000 billion and total consumption is $3250 billion (consisting of $3000 billion of induced consumption and $250 billion of autonomous consumption).

Figure 3-1
A Simple Hypothesis Regarding Consumption Behavior
The red line passing through F and D illustrates the consumption function, showing that consumption is 75 percent of disposable income plus an "autonomous" component of $250 billion that is spent regardless of the level of disposable income. The pink area shows the amount of positive saving that occurs when income exceeds consumption; the gray area shows the amount of negative saving ("dissaving") that occurs when consumption exceeds income.

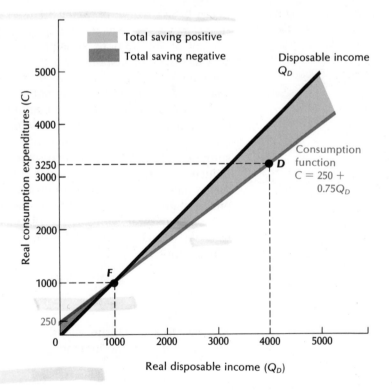

HOW DISPOSABLE INCOME IS DIVIDED BETWEEN CONSUMPTION AND SAVING

The Saving Function and Induced Saving

The simplest way to show the amount of saving is to use a graph like Figure 3-1. The thick black line shows the amount of disposable income in both a horizontal and a vertical direction. Since the thick red line shows the consumption function, the distance between the two lines indicates the total amount of saving. To the right of point F total saving is positive because disposable income exceeds consumption; this is indicated by the pink shading. To the left of point F total saving is negative because consumption exceeds disposable income; this is indicated by the gray shading. How can saving be negative? Individuals can consume more than they earn, at least for a while, by withdrawing funds from a savings account, by selling stocks and bonds, or by borrowing. Negative saving is quite typical for many students who borrow to finance their education.

Marginal propensity to save is the change in personal saving induced by a $1 change in personal disposable income.

Table 3-1 also illustrates the determination of saving. The fraction of an extra dollar of disposable income that is not consumed is the **marginal propensity to save,** for which we use the abbreviation s. By definition each extra dollar of income must be consumed or saved, so the marginal propensities to consume and to save must add up to unity:

General Linear Form	Numerical Example	
$c + s = 1.0$	$0.75 + 0.25 = 1.0$	(3.5)

Induced saving is the portion of saving that responds to changes in income.

In column (6) of Table 3-1 we find that the marginal propensity to save is always the fraction 0.25 at every level of disposable income. **Induced saving** is the marginal propensity to save times disposable income, as shown in column (7). Total saving in column (8) is induced saving *minus* the amount of autonomous consumption, $250 billion at every level of disposable income. For instance, when disposable income is zero, induced saving must also be zero, and total saving is equal to minus $250 billion, the amount of autonomous consumption.

Figure 3-2 illustrates the relationship between induced saving, autonomous consumption, and total saving. The top frame duplicates Figure 3-1 but emphasizes the division of disposable income between induced consumption ($0.75Q_D$) and induced saving ($0.25Q_D$). The bottom frame subtracts induced consumption from the top frame and isolates the relationship between autonomous consumption and induced saving. As in Figure 3-1, the pink and gray shaded areas show the amount of total saving.

The *saving function* is just disposable income minus the consumption function. It is also equal to the amount of induced saving minus autonomous consumption:

General Linear Form	Numerical Example
$S = -a + sQ_D$	$S = -250 + 0.25Q_D$

It is easy to see that the saving function plus the consumption function must add up to disposable income:

$$S + C = -a + sQ_D + a + cQ_D$$
$$= (s + c)Q_D$$
$$= Q_D$$

Figure 3-2

The Relation between Induced Consumption, Induced Saving, and the Consumption Function

The upper frame duplicates Figure 3-1. The thin black line shows the dividing line between induced saving and induced consumption. Starting at zero disposable income, each dollar of disposable income is divided between 75 cents of induced consumption and 25 cents of induced saving. The lower frame subtracts induced consumption from the upper frame. It shows the relation between induced saving and autonomous consumption. Total saving in both parts of the diagram is shown by the pink and gray shading and equals induced saving minus autonomous consumption.

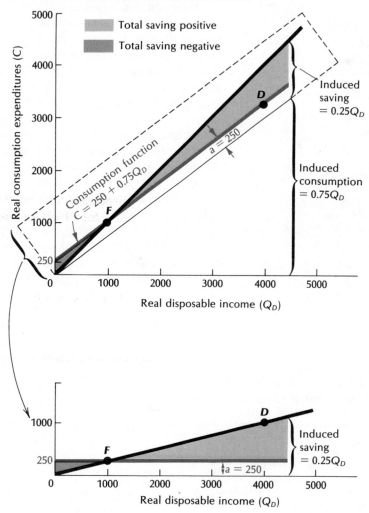

ANY CHANGE IN DISPOSABLE INCOME IS DIVIDED BETWEEN INDUCED CONSUMPTION AND INDUCED SAVING

3-3 CASE STUDY: Actual U.S. Consumption and Saving Behavior

When disposable income falls very low, as it did during the Great Depression, households take money out of their savings accounts or borrow in order to buy the basic necessities of life.[2] Saving is negative (dissaving)

---

[2]Be careful to distinguish between "savings" (with a terminal "s"), which is the stock of assets that households have in savings accounts or under the mattress, from "saving" (without a terminal "s"), which is the *flow* per unit of time that leaks out of disposable income (see Figure 2-6) and is unavailable for purchases of consumption goods. It is the flow of *saving* that is designated by the symbol S.

because consumers must draw on their savings accounts and other assets in order to purchase the consumption goods that their disposable income alone can no longer purchase.

How can this happen, you may ask, when many people have no jobs? Indeed, people who have exhausted their savings accounts and cannot borrow are incapable of consuming more than their income. But even in the Great Depression many households still held jobs and still had funds in their savings accounts that could be drawn down to allow consumption spending to exceed income. After all, when the Depression began, people held financial assets equal to at least one year's GNP, and this provided ample opportunity for some people to draw on their savings accounts, bonds, and stocks in those perilous times.

Figure 3-3, arranged exactly like Figure 3-1, shows the actual values of disposable income, consumption, and saving in the United States during the years 1929–88. Three major conclusions can be drawn from the evidence. First, both consumption and saving have increased as disposable income has grown during the years since World War II. Second, in the worst years of the Great Depression, households consumed more than their incomes, so that saving was negative in 1932 and 1933 (about −3.5 percent of disposable income in 1933). Third, these usual peacetime relationships were interrupted during World War II (1942–45), when consumer goods

Figure 3-3
Consumption, Saving, and Disposable Income, 1929–85

Notice that in 1933 U.S. saving was negative. In 1988 saving was positive and amounted to 4.2 percent of disposable income, leaving the remaining 93.0 percent for consumption and 2.8 percent for interest payments. Saving was unusually high during World War II because consumer goods were rationed. *(Source: National Income and Product accounts.)*

HOW ACTUAL U.S. DISPOSABLE INCOME HAS BEEN SPLIT BETWEEN CONSUMPTION AND SAVING

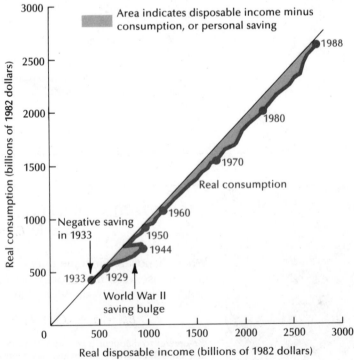

were unavailable or rationed. In that period households were forced to consume much less and save much more than is normal in peacetime, fully 25 percent of disposable income in 1944. After the war, consumers rushed out to spend their accumulated savings accounts, helping to maintain prosperity in spite of the drastic drop in government spending that occurred in 1945–46.

3-4 Determination of Equilibrium Income

Planned Investment Spending

In addition to our neglect of interest rates and monetary policy, and our assumption that the price level is fixed, we also assume temporarily that there is no foreign trade and that both government expenditures and tax revenues are equal to zero. Thus total expenditures on GNP include only consumption and private domestic investment.

Our task in this chapter is not to explain the causes of fluctuations in private investment (we turn to this question in Chapter 4). Instead, we treat investment as an exogenous variable and attempt to answer a more limited question: *Given* the level of planned investment, what determines the total level of real GNP?

Throughout the chapter, the level of planned investment will be an assumed **parameter,** taken as given or known within a given analysis. For instance, initially we shall assume that planned autonomous investment (I_p) is \$500 billion:

A **parameter** is a value taken as given or known within a particular analysis.

$$I_p = 500 \qquad (3.6)$$

So far we have encountered two other parameters in our analysis, the level of autonomous consumption (a = \$250 billion) and the marginal propensity to consume (c = 0.75). As in the case of planned investment, these values are assumed to be given within a particular analysis and not to respond to changes in income.

$$E_p = C + I_p.$$

Total Planned Expenditures

The total of household and business purchases, or planned expenditures (E_p), is the amount of household consumption (C) plus business planned investment (I_p):

$$E_p = C + I_p \qquad (3.7)$$

Substituting the consumption function from (3.3) and (3.4) for C, (3.7) becomes:[3]

General Linear Form	Numerical Example	
$E_p = a + cQ + I_p$	$E_p = 250 + 0.75Q + 500$	(3.8)

---

[3]The consumption function depends on disposable income (Q_D) in Figure 3-1 and equations (3.3) and (3.4). But in Figure 3-4 and equation (3.8) the consumption function depends on total real income (Q). This makes no difference because $Q = Q_D$ under our current assumption that there is no business saving and no tax collections by the government.

In Figure 3-4 the red planned expenditure (E_p) line plots the numerical example in equation (3.8). The E_p line lies above the red consumption function line by exactly $500 billion, the amount of planned investment.

When Is the Economy in Equilibrium?

Equilibrium is a state in which there exists no pressure for change.

A basic lesson of Chapter 2 was that *actual* expenditures (E) and total income (Q) are always equal by definition. But there is no reason for income (Q) always to equal *planned* expenditures (E_p.) The main principle of this chapter is that the economy is in **equilibrium** when income is equal to planned expenditures. Only then do households and business firms want to

---

Figure 3-4
Planned Autonomous Investment and the Level of Total Planned Expenditures

The lower red line repeats the red consumption function from Figure 3-1. When we add $500 billion of planned autonomous investment we obtain total planned expenditures as illustrated by the upper red line.

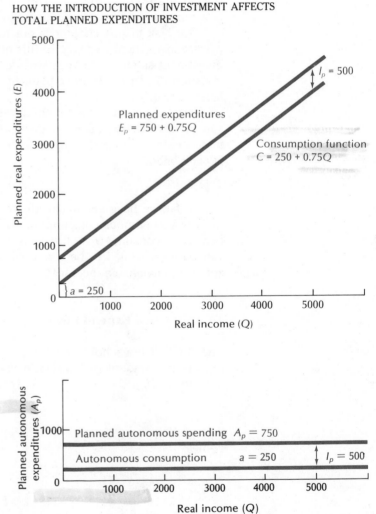

HOW THE INTRODUCTION OF INVESTMENT AFFECTS TOTAL PLANNED EXPENDITURES

Planned expenditures
$E_p = 750 + 0.75Q$

Consumption function
$C = 250 + 0.75Q$

$I_p = 500$

$a = 250$

Planned real expenditures (E)

Real income (Q)

Planned autonomous spending $A_p = 750$

Autonomous consumption $a = 250$ $I_p = 500$

Planned autonomous expenditures (A_p)

Real income (Q)

---

spend exactly the amount of income that is being generated by the current level of production, all of which can be sold to households and firms.

Equilibrium is a *situation in which there is no pressure for change.* When the economy is *out of equilibrium,* production and income are out of line with planned expenditures, and business firms will be forced to raise or lower production. When the economy is *in equilibrium,* production and income equal planned expenditures, and on the average, business firms are happy to continue the current level of production.

This idea is illustrated in Figure 3-5. The thick black line in the top frame has a slope of 45 degrees; everywhere along it the level of income plotted on the horizontal axis is equal to the level of expenditures plotted on the vertical axis. Hence the black line is labeled $E = Q$. The red line is

Figure 3-5
How Equilibrium Income is Determined

The economy is in equilibrium in the top frame at point B, where the red planned expenditures (E_p) line crosses the 45-degree income line. At any other level of income, the economy is out of equilibrium, causing pressure on business firms to increase or reduce production and income. For instance, at point H, E_p falls $250 billion short of production, so $250 billion of output piles up on the shelves unsold $(I_u = 250)$. In the lower frame equilibrium occurs at point B, where induced saving (sQ) equals planned autonomous spending (A_p).

THE ECONOMY IS IN EQUILIBRIUM ONLY WHERE THE RED AND BLACK LINES CROSS

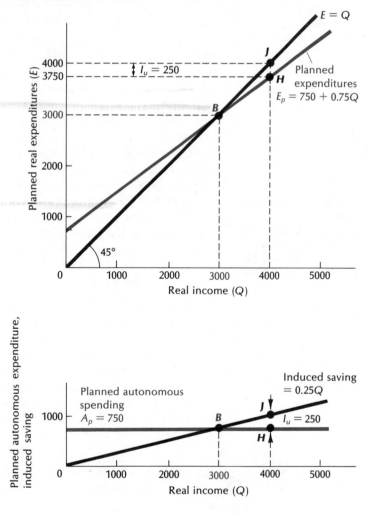

the total level of planned expenditures (E_p) and is copied directly from Figure 3-4. Only where the black and red lines cross at point B is income equal to planned expenditure, with no pressure for change. Households and business firms want to spend $3000 billion when income is $3000 billion. And this amount of income is created by the $3000 billion of production of the goods and services that households and business firms want to buy.

What Happens Out of Equilibrium?

The economy is out of equilibrium at all points other than B along the 45-degree income line (labeled $E = Q$). For instance, at point J, income is $4000 billion. How much do households and business firms want to spend? The three components of planned expenditures are:

$$
\begin{array}{rl}
\text{planned autonomous investment } (I_p) = & 500 \\
\text{induced consumption } (0.75Q) = & 3000 \\
\underline{\text{autonomous consumption } (a) = } & \underline{250} \\
\text{planned expenditures } (E_p) = & 3750
\end{array}
$$

Thus at an income level of $4000 billion, planned expenditures (E_p) are only $3750 billion (point H on the E_p line), leaving business firms with $250 billion of merchandise that nobody wants to purchase.

The $250 billion of unsold production is counted as inventory investment in the official national income accounts. But businesses do not desire this inventory buildup (if they did, they would have included it in their planned investment, I_p). To bring inventories back to the original desired level, businesses react to the situation at J by cutting production and income, which moves the economy left toward point B. In the diagram, the distance between points J and H, amounting to $250 billion, is labeled I_u, which stands for **unintended inventory investment.**

Unintended inventory investment is the amount business firms are forced to accumulate when planned expenditures are less than income.

The distance JH measures the excess of income over planned expenditures—that is, the positive value of I_u. Production and income will be cut until this discrepancy disappears and the unwanted inventory buildup ceases $(I_u = 0)$. This occurs only when the economy arrives back at B. Only at B are businesses producing exactly the amount that is demanded.

> **Example:** In late 1981, consumer purchases of automobiles declined, and industry found itself producing more cars than consumers wanted to buy. The Chrysler Corporation had so many unsold cars in stock that it barely had room to store them. Since Chrysler neither planned nor desired this inventory accumulation, the company reacted by drastically cutting production, which caused a drop in Chrysler's contribution to national income and national product. The whole automobile industry's contribution to real GNP fell from $85.1 billion in the third quarter of 1981 to $58.7 billion in the first quarter of 1982, a decline of 31 percent.

SELF-TEST   What happens in the top frame of Figure 3-5 when income is only $2000 billion? Describe the forces that move the economy back to equilibrium at B.

At point *J*, as in every situation, income and actual expenditures are equal by definition:

$$\text{income } (Q) \equiv \text{expenditures } (E)$$
$$\equiv \text{planned spending } (E_p = C + I_p) + \qquad (3.9)$$
$$\text{unintended inventory accumulation } (I_u)$$

By contrast, the economy is in equilibrium only when unintended inventory accumulation or decumulation is equal to zero ($I_u = 0$) (see Table 3-2). Equation (3.9) can be rewritten to describe the economy's equilibrium situation:

$$Q = E_p \qquad (3.10)$$

Autonomous Planned Spending Equals Induced Saving

The lower frame of Figure 3-5 illustrates the determination of equilibrium income in an equivalent but slightly different way. It subtracts induced consumption from both income and planned expenditure. The red horizontal line is total planned autonomous spending (A_p), which includes the $250 billion of autonomous consumption *(a)*, plus the $500 billion in planned autonomous investment (I_p).

Take the definition of equilibrium in equation (3.10) and subtract induced consumption *(cQ)* from both sides of that equation:

$$Q - cQ = E_p - cQ$$

Table 3-2 **Comparison of the Economy's "Always True" and Equilibrium Situations**

	Always true by definition	*True only in equilibrium*
1. What concept of expenditures is equal to income?	Actual expenditures including unintended inventory accumulation	Planned expenditures
2. Amount of unintended inventory accumulation (I_u)?	Can be any amount, positive or negative	Must be zero
3. Which equation is valid, (3.9) or (3.10)?	(3.9) $Q = E = E_p + I_u$	(3.10) $Q = E_p$
4. How does equilibrium differ from other points in top frame of Figure 3-5?	Any point on 45-degree income line (example: point *J*)	Only at point where E_p line crosses 45-degree income line
5. Numerical example in Figure 3-5?	At point *J*, $Q(4000) = E(4000)$ $= E_p(3750) + I_u(250)$	At point B,

We can replace $E_p - cQ$ on the right-hand side by its equivalent, A_p, which is simply total planned expenditures (E_p) minus consumption (cQ).[4]

$$(1 - c)Q = A_p \qquad (3.11)$$

Because the marginal propensity to save equals 1.0 minus the marginal propensity to consume $(s = 1 - c)$, we can rewrite (3.11) as

General Linear Form	Numerical Example	
$sQ = A_p$	$0.25Q = 750$	(3.12)

Thus equilibrium can occur only if induced saving (sQ) equals planned autonomous spending (A_p). The black sloped induced saving line in the lower frame of Figure 3-5 rises by \$0.25 per \$1.00 of income and crosses the red A_p line at point B, which is at an income level of \$3000 billion and lies directly beneath the top frame's point B. The economy is in equilibrium at B in the top frame because production (Q) equals planned spending (E_p). When this occurs, point B in the lower frame shows that the induced leakage into saving (sQ) just balances planned autonomous spending (A_p) injected back into the spending stream.

The equilibrium level of income in this simple model is always equal to planned autonomous spending (A_p) divided by the marginal propensity to save (s), as we can see when both sides of (3.12) are divided by s:

General Linear Form	Numerical Example	
$Q = \dfrac{A_p}{s}$	$Q = \dfrac{750}{0.25} = 3000$	(3.13)

Equilibrium income adjusts to generate enough induced saving to balance planned autonomous spending. In our numerical example, \$3000 billion of income is required to generate the \$750 billion of induced saving needed to balance \$750 billion of planned autonomous spending.

General Method for Determining Equilibrium Income

The lower frame of Figure 3-5 and equation (3.13) both illustrate the two-step method used throughout the chapter for determining equilibrium income. To represent this in a graph, first draw a horizontal line at a height equal to planned autonomous spending (A_p). Then plot a line with a slope equal to the marginal propensity to save (s). The point where the horizontal A_p line crosses the sloped sQ line indicates the equilibrium level of income. At any other point, for instance, J, sQ does not balance A_p, indicating a discrepancy between E_p and Q and hence an unplanned increase or decrease in inventories.

Income equilibrium can be determined using the same technique with the symbols in equation (3.13). The numerator is A_p and corresponds to the

---

[4]Because $E_p = a + cQ + I_p$ in equation (3.8), it follows that $E_p - cQ = a + I_p$. When we define total planned autonomous spending (A_p) as equal to $a + I_p$, we obtain the righthand side of (3.11).

horizontal A_p line in the figure. The denominator is the fraction of income that leaks out of the spending stream into saving (s), corresponding to the slope of the induced saving line in the figure.

3-5 The Multiplier Effect

The conclusion of Section 3-4, that equilibrium income equals $3000 billion, is absolutely dependent on the assumption that planned autonomous spending (A_p) equals $750 billion. A change in planned autonomous spending will cause a change in equilibrium income. To illustrate the consequences of a change in A_p, assume that business people become more optimistic, raising their guess as to the likely profitability of new investment projects. They increase their investment spending by $250 billion, boosting A_p from $750 billion to $1000 billion. In each situation where a change is described, a numbered subscript is used to distinguish the original from the new situation. Thus A_{p0} denotes the original level of A_p ($750 billion), and A_{p1} denotes the new level ($1000 billion).

Calculating the Multiplier

Economic theorists typically examine the effects of a change in one parameter on the assumption that all other things are equal. In equation (3.13) where the only "other thing" besides A_p determining income is s, we assume that s is constant. We use (3.13) to calculate the equilibrium level of income in the new and old situations:

	General Linear Form	Numerical Example	
Take new situation	$Q_1 = \dfrac{A_{p1}}{s}$	$Q_1 = \dfrac{1000}{0.25} = 4000$	
Subtract old situation	$Q_0 = \dfrac{A_{p0}}{s}$	$Q_0 = \dfrac{750}{0.25} = 3000$	(3.14)
Equals change in income	$\Delta Q = \dfrac{\Delta A_p}{s}$	$\Delta Q = \dfrac{250}{0.25} = 1000$	

The top line of the table calculates the new level of income when $A_{p1} = 1000$. The second line calculates the original level of income when $A_{p0} = 750$. The change in income, abbreviated ΔQ, is simply the first line minus the second. The multiplier (k) is defined as the ratio of the change in income (ΔQ) to the change in planned autonomous spending (ΔA_p) that causes it:

General Linear Form	Numerical Example
multiplier $(k) = \dfrac{\Delta Q}{\Delta A_p} = \dfrac{1}{s}$	$\dfrac{\Delta Q}{\Delta A_p} = \dfrac{1}{0.25} = 4.0$

In Figure 3-6 we can see why the multiplier (k) is $1/s$, or 4.0. Figure 3-6 reproduces from Figure 3-5 the "original situation," with A_p at its original value of $750 billion.

Figure 3-6

The Change in Equilibrium Income Caused by a $250 Billion Increase in Autonomous Planned Spending

Increasing planned autonomous spending (A_p) by $250 billion raises the horizontal red A_p line by $250 billion, moving the equilibrium position from B to J. Thus a change in A_p has a multiplier effect, raising income by $1000 billion.

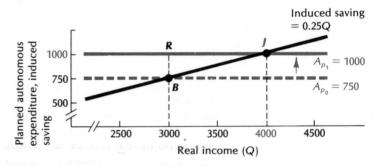

HOW HIGHER AUTONOMOUS PLANNED SPENDING RAISES INCOME

The $250 billion increase in A_p causes the A_p line to shift upward by $250 billion and to intersect the fixed induced saving line at point J. Because only 25 percent of extra income is saved, income must rise by $1000 billion to generate the required $250 billion increase in induced saving. In terms of the line segments:

$$\text{multiplier } (k) = \frac{\Delta Q}{\Delta A_p} = \frac{RJ}{RB} = \frac{1}{s} \quad (\text{since } s = \frac{RB}{RJ})$$

Example of the Multiplier Effect in Action

How does the magic of the multiplier work? One answer is given by Figure 3-6, which is based on the idea that the economy can be in equilibrium only when induced saving (sQ) is equal to planned autonomous spending (A_p). If A_p rises, so sQ must rise by exactly the same amount, and this can happen only if income (Q) rises by $1/s$ times the increase in A_p.

A real-life example provides another answer. An example of an increase in planned investment is the decision by American Airlines in 1988 to purchase $2 billion of Boeing 757 aircraft. Initially the $2 billion of new investment spending would raise income by the $2 billion earned by Boeing workers in Seattle, where the aircraft plant is located. But, using our example of a marginal propensity to consume (c) of 0.75, the Boeing workers would soon spend 0.75 of the $2 billion, or $1.5 billion, on goods and services at Seattle stores. The stores would have to reorder $1.5 billion of additional goods, causing production to rise at plants all over the country that supply the goods to the stores in Seattle. Workers at these supplying plants also have a marginal propensity to consume of 0.75, adding another $1.125 billion of income. So far in the first three "rounds of spending" income has gone up by $2.0 plus $1.5 plus $1.125 billion, or $4.625 billion. But the process continues, as induced consumption is increased in each successive round of spending. Eventually, the total increase in income will be four times the initial increase in planned investment, or \$8 billion (= \$2 billion times 1/.25), just as in Figure 3-6.[5]

3-6 Recessions and Fiscal Policy

Is a multiplier expansion or contraction of output following a change in planned autonomous spending desirable or not? The answer depends on the desired level of total real income. In Section 1-4 we defined the most desirable level of real income as "natural real GNP," that is, the level of real GNP consistent with a constant inflation rate. A multiplier expansion or contraction of output is desirable if it moves the economy closer to its natural real GNP.

Assume that the level of natural real GNP is \$4000 billion. In Figure 3-6 a level of planned autonomous spending (A_p) of \$1000 billion would be perfect, for it would bring about an equilibrium level of actual real GNP of \$4000 billion at point J, the desired level. On the other hand, a decline in A_p by \$250 billion would cut equilibrium income to \$3000 billion at B and would open up a gap of \$1000 billion between actual and natural GNP.

What might cause actual real GNP to decline below natural real GNP? A drop in planned investment (I_p), a major component of A_p, can be and has been a major cause of actual real-world recessions and depressions. In the Great Depression, for instance, fixed investment dropped by 74 percent, and this contributed to the 29 percent decline in actual real GNP between 1929 and 1933. But the changing plans of business firms are not the only possible cause of a change in planned autonomous spending. Changes in household autonomous consumption (a) can cause exactly the same kinds of effects on income as changes in the level of planned investment.

---

[5]It is possible to use an algebraic trick to prove that the sum of ΔA_p plus the induced consumption at each round of spending is exactly equal to the multiplier $(1/s)$ times ΔA_p. The first round of consumption is $c\Delta A_p$. The second is c times the first, $c(c\Delta A_p)$, or $c^2 A_p$. Thus the total ΔQ is the series:

$$\Delta Q = \Delta A_p \qquad + c\Delta A_p \ + c^2 \Delta A_p \ + \cdots + c^n \Delta A_p \qquad \text{[a]}$$

"Factor out" the common element ΔA_p on the right-hand side of equation (a):

$$\Delta Q = \Delta A_p(1.0 \quad + c \quad + c^2 \quad + \cdots + c^n \quad) \qquad \text{[b]}$$

Multiply both sides of equation (b) by $-c$:

$$-c\Delta Q = \Delta A_p(\quad - c \quad - c^2 \quad - \cdots - c^n - c^{n+1}) \qquad \text{[c]}$$

The difference between lines (b) and (c) is

$$(1 - c)\Delta Q = \Delta A_p(1.0 \qquad\qquad\qquad - c^{n+1}) \qquad \text{[d]}$$

Since c^{n+1} is almost zero (because c is a fraction and $n + 1$ is large), we can neglect it. Dividing both sides of equation (d) by $(1 - c)$, we obtain the familiar

$$\Delta Q = \frac{\Delta A_p}{1 - c} = \frac{\Delta A_p}{s}$$

Government Spending and Taxation

The government can adjust its expenditures on goods and services as well as its tax revenues in an attempt to offset fluctuations in autonomous investment and consumption. Thus far the simple economic model in this chapter has excluded any consideration of the government sector. Now it is time to introduce government spending and taxation, which alter the economy in two ways. An increase in government spending can raise total income through the multiplier effect, and an increase in tax revenue has the opposite impact.

First, government spending on goods and services (G) is part of planned expenditures. Thus equation (3.7) is modified:

$$E_p = C + I_p + G \tag{3.15}$$

Second, a positive level of tax revenues (T) reduces disposable income (Q_D) below total actual income (Q):

$$Q_D = Q - T \tag{3.16}$$

Inserting (3.16) into the consumption function makes the level of consumption spending depend on tax revenues:

$$C = a + cQ_D = a + c(Q - T) \tag{3.17}$$

We have previously developed a simple theory stating that equilibrium income equals planned autonomous spending (A_p) divided by the marginal propensity to save (s). What is A_p in an economy influenced by the government? Substituting the consumption function given in (3.17) into the definition of planned spending in (3.15), we have:

$$E_p = a + cQ - cT + I_p + G \tag{3.18}$$

Planned autonomous spending (A_p) is simply E_p minus induced consumption (cQ):

$$A_p = a - c\overline{T} + I_p + G \tag{3.19}$$

We have converted (3.18) to (3.19) by subtracting cQ and by writing a "bar" on top of T. The bar indicates that tax revenues are assumed to be *autonomous*—that is, they do not change automatically with income. Examples of autonomous taxes are local dog licenses and property taxes.

SELF-TEST   Why is I_p written with a "p" subscript, but the other components of autonomous planned spending—a, $-c\overline{T}$, and G—are not?

Now we are equipped with a complete theory of income determination that takes into account government spending (G) and autonomous tax revenue ($\overline{T}$). Equation (3.19) implies that the change in planned autonomous spending equals the change in four components. If we insert the "change in" symbol Δ in front of each element in equation (3.19), we have four different events that can cause a change in planned autonomous spending. The only remaining element is the marginal propensity to consume (c), which we are assuming to be fixed throughout this discussion:

$$\Delta A_p = \Delta a - c\Delta\overline{T} + \Delta I_p + \Delta G \tag{3.20}$$

In sum, the four causes of changes in A_p are

1. A \$1 change in autonomous consumption (a) changes A_p by \$1 in the same direction.
2. A \$1 change in autonomous tax revenue ($\overline{T}$) changes A_p by c (the marginal propensity to consume) times \$1 in the opposite direction. For example, a \$100 billion increase in $\overline{T}$ would reduce A_p by \$75 billion if c were 0.75. Households pay for the other \$25 billion in higher tax revenue by reducing their saving.
3. A \$1 change in planned investment (I_p) changes A_p by \$1 in the same direction.
4. A \$1 change in government spending (G) changes A_p by \$1 in the same direction.

Once the change in A_p has been calculated from this list, our basic multiplier expression from (3.14) determines the resulting change in equilibrium income:

$$\Delta Q = \frac{\Delta A_p}{s} \tag{3.14}$$

Notice that the addition of government spending and tax revenue to our theory makes *absolutely no difference* to the multiplier formula. It remains just the same as before.

SELF-TEST Notice that there is no "Δ" in front of the s in equation (3.14). Why?

Fiscal Expansion

To provide an example of a situation in which higher government spending can expand real income, let us assume that initially the level of autonomous planned spending (A_p) is 750. This means that the level of real income will be 3000, as shown at point B in the top frame of Figure 3-7. This is unsatisfactory, because natural real GNP is at the higher level of \$4000 billion. Thus point B represents a situation in which actual real GNP and real income are \$1000 billion too low, and in which many members of the labor force are jobless. How can government fiscal policy correct this situation through its control over the level of government expenditures?

It is clear from our basic income-determination formula (3.14) that the required \$1000 billion increase in real income and real GNP can be achieved by any action that raises autonomous spending (A_p) by \$250 billion. Two possibilities are (1) a \$250 billion increase in G (government spending on goods and services) and (2) a \$333 billion reduction in autonomous tax revenue.[6]

---

[6]Why \$333 billion? Because according to equation (3.20), a reduction in taxes raises A_p by c times the reduction, where c is the marginal propensity to consume. If $c = 0.75$, as in our numerical example, then

$$\Delta A_p = -c\Delta\overline{T} = -0.75(-333) = 250$$

Recall that transfer payments (welfare, social security, and unemployment benefits) are equivalent to negative taxes, so that a \$333 billion *reduction* in taxes has the same impact on A_p as a \$333 billion *increase* in transfer payments.

Figure 3-7

Effect on Income of a $250 Billion Increase in Government Spending Followed by a $250 Billion Increase in Autonomous Tax Revenue

The top frame is identical to Figure 3-6. It shows that a $250 billion increase in government spending moves the economy from B to J, having the same multiplier impact on equilibrium income as a $250 billion increase in A_p caused by alterations in private spending decisions. In the lower frame the $250 billion tax increase only reduces A_p by $187.5 billion, since the remaining $62.5 billion of tax revenue is paid for by lower saving. The economy moves from point J down to point K.

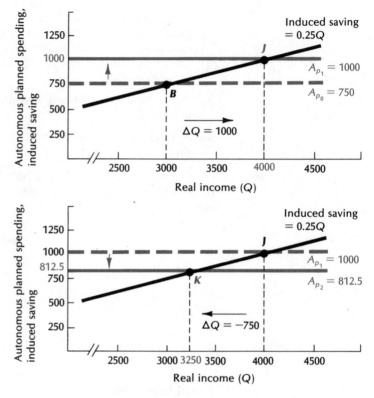

GOVERNMENT SPENDING AND TAXES ALSO HAVE MULTIPLIER EFFECTS

The $250 billion change in government spending ($\Delta G = 250$) in Figure 3-7 has exactly the same effect on income as any other $250 billion increase in A_p. The economy reaches a new equilibrium at point J, just as it did in Figure 3-6. The multiplier (k) for ΔG is also the same. As before, we calculate the multiplier by taking the change in income (ΔQ) and dividing it by the factor that is changing (ΔG in this case):

General Linear Form

$$k = \frac{\Delta Q}{\Delta G} = \frac{\Delta Q}{\Delta A_p} = \frac{1}{s}$$

Numerical Example

$$k = \frac{\Delta Q}{\Delta G} = \frac{1}{0.25} = 4.0 \qquad (3.21)$$

In the top frame of Figure 3-7 the government manages to push total income up from $3000 billion at point B to $4000 billion at point J by making $250 billion of purchases.

The Government Budget Deficit and Its Financing

Any change in government expenditures or tax revenues has consequences for the government's budget. The government budget surplus has already been defined in Section 2-6 as tax revenues minus government expenditures ($T - G$). The government budget deficit is simply a negative value of the surplus. In the example illustrated in Figure 3-7, the government starts with a balanced budget, having no expenditures and no tax revenues:

$$\text{government budget deficit at } B = G - T = \$0$$

Then, the government begins spending $250 billion, moving the economy from B to J. Since its tax revenues remain at zero, the government's purchases cause a government budget deficit of $250 billion:

$$\text{government budget deficit at } J = G - T = \$250 \text{ billion}$$

How is this budget deficit financed? Recall from Chapter 2 (see Figure 2-5) that government surplus equals the difference between private investment and saving plus net exports.

$$S - I - X \equiv G - T$$

Similarly, the change in the left side of the equation must balance the change in the right side:

$$\Delta S - \Delta I - \Delta X \equiv \Delta G - \Delta T \qquad (3.22)$$

The movement in the top frame of Figure 3-7 from point B to point J assumes that investment and net exports are fixed ($\Delta I = \Delta X = 0$) and that tax revenue remains at zero ($\Delta T = 0$). Thus the only elements of (3.22) that are changing are ΔS and ΔG:

$$\Delta S - \Delta I - \Delta X \equiv \Delta G - \Delta T$$

$$s\Delta Q - 0 - 0 \equiv 250 - 0$$

$$0.25(1000) \equiv 250$$

The $1000 billion increase in output induces $250 billion of extra saving, but there is no extra private investment or net exports for the extra saving to finance ($\Delta I = \Delta X = 0$). Thus each extra dollar of saving is available for households to purchase the $250 billion of government bonds that the government must sell when it runs its $250 billion budget deficit.

3-7 Tax Changes and the Multiplier

Effect of Autonomous Taxes

The government may prefer not to run a budget deficit. If equilibrium were at point J in Figure 3-7 with $G = \$250$ billion, what would happen if autonomous tax revenues ($\overline{T}$) were raised from zero to $250 billion ($\Delta \overline{T} = 250$)? Once again we assume everything else remains the same (*ceteris paribus*) so we can use our basic two-step method to calculate the change in income. First, the change in A_p in equation (3.20) is:

$$\Delta A_p = \Delta a - c\Delta \overline{T} + \Delta I_p + \Delta G$$

$$= 0 - c\Delta \overline{T} + 0 + 0 \qquad (3.20)$$

$$= -0.75(250)$$

$$= -187.5$$

A $250 billion increase in autonomous tax revenues ($\Delta \overline{T} = 250$) reduces autonomous planned spending by only $187.5 billion because households "pay" the remaining $62.5 billion of higher taxation by saving less than they otherwise would.

The lower frame of Figure 3-7 illustrates the effect of tax increase on income. Autonomous spending drops by $187.5 billion from $1000 billion to $812.5 billion, and equilibrium income drops from $4000 billion to $3250 billion (point K).

What multiplier expression corresponds to the change from J to K? The only component of autonomous spending that is changing is tax revenues. Thus we can take our general expression used to calculate income change (3.14) and substitute for ΔA_p the expression $-c\Delta \overline{T}$ that indicates the response of A_p to the tax change:

General Linear Form   Numerical Example

$$\Delta Q = \frac{\Delta A_p}{s} = \frac{-c\Delta \overline{T}}{s} \qquad \Delta Q = \frac{-(0.75)250}{0.25} = -750 \qquad (3.23)$$

The multiplier for an increase in taxes is the income change in equation (3.23) divided by $\Delta \overline{T}$.

General Linear Form   Numerical Example

$$\frac{\Delta Q}{\Delta \overline{T}} = \frac{\Delta A_p}{s\Delta \overline{T}} = \frac{-c\Delta \overline{T}}{s\Delta \overline{T}} = \frac{-c}{s} \qquad \frac{\Delta Q}{\Delta \overline{T}} = \frac{-0.75}{0.25} = -3.0 \qquad (3.24)$$

SELF-TEST   What is the multiplier for a "balanced budget" fiscal policy operation that raises both government spending and autonomous taxes by $250 billion?

Effect of Income Taxes

When the government raises some of its tax revenue (T) with an income tax, in addition to the autonomous tax ($\overline{T}$), its total tax revenue is:

$$T = \overline{T} + \overline{t}Q \qquad (3.25)$$

The first component, as before, is the autonomous tax. The second component is income tax revenue, the tax rate ($\overline{t}$) times income (Q). Disposable income (Q_D) is total income minus tax revenue:

$$Q_D = Q - T = Q - \overline{T} - \overline{t}Q = (1 - \overline{t})Q - \overline{T} \qquad (3.26)$$

Leakages from the spending stream. Following any change in total income (Q), disposable income changes by only a fraction ($1 - \overline{t}$) as much. For instance, if the tax rate ($\overline{t}$) is 0.2, then disposable income changes by 80 percent of the change in total income. Any change in total income (ΔQ) is now divided into induced consumption, induced saving, and induced income tax revenue. The fraction of ΔQ going into consumption is the marginal propensity to consume disposable income (c) times the fraction of income going into disposable income ($1 - \overline{t}$). Thus the change in total income is divided up as shown in the following table.

Fraction going to:	General Linear Form	Numerical Example
1. Induced consumption	$c(1 - \bar{t})$	$0.75(1 - 0.2) = 0.6$
2. Induced saving	$s(1 - \bar{t})$	$0.25(1 - 0.2) = 0.2$
3. Induced tax revenue	$\bar{t}$	0.2
Total	$(c + s)(1 - \bar{t}) + \bar{t}$ $= 1 - \bar{t} + \bar{t} = 1.0$	1.0

As in (3.10), the economy is in equilibrium when income equals planned expenditures:

$$Q = E_p \qquad (3.10)$$

As before, we can subtract induced consumption from both sides of the equilibrium condition. According to the table above, income (Q) minus induced consumption is the total of induced saving plus induced tax revenue. Planned expenditures (E_p) minus induced consumption is planned autonomous spending (A_p). Thus the equilibrium condition is

induced saving + induced tax revenue

$$= \text{planned autonomous spending } (A_p) \quad (3.27)$$

From the table just given, (3.27) can be written in symbols as:

$$[s(1 - \bar{t}) + \bar{t}]Q = A_p \qquad (3.28)$$

The term in brackets on the left-hand side is the fraction of a change in income that does not go into induced consumption—that is, the sum of the fraction going to induced saving $s(1 - \bar{t})$ and the fraction going to the government as income tax revenue ($\bar{t}$). The sum of these two fractions within the brackets is called the **marginal leakage rate.** The equilibrium value for Q can be calculated when we divide both sides of (3.28) by the term in brackets:

The **marginal leakage rate** is the fraction of income that is taxed or saved rather than being spent on consumption.

General Linear Form · Numerical Example

$$Q = \frac{A_p}{s(1 - \bar{t}) + \bar{t}} \qquad Q = \frac{1000}{0.25(0.8) + 0.2} = \frac{1000}{0.4} = 2500 \quad (3.29)$$

The numerical example shows that if planned autonomous spending (A_p) is $1000 billion, income will be only $2500 billion, rather than $4000 billion. Why? A greater fraction of each dollar of income now leaks out of the spending stream—0.4 in this numerical example—than occurred due to the saving rate of 0.25 by itself. This allows the injection of planned autonomous spending ($A_p = 1000$) to be balanced by leakages out of the spending stream at a lower level of income.

Income Taxes and the Multiplier

The change in income (ΔQ) is simply the change in autonomous spending (ΔA_p) divided by the marginal leakage rate:

$$\Delta Q = \frac{\Delta A_p}{s(1 - \bar{t}) + \bar{t}} \qquad (3.30)$$

The multiplier ($\Delta Q/\Delta A_p$) is simply 1.0 divided by the marginal leakage rate. Earlier in the chapter, the multiplier was $1/s$ when there was no income tax. Now, with an income tax:

$$\text{multiplier} = \frac{1}{\text{marginal leakage rate}} = \frac{1}{s(1 - \bar{t}) + \bar{t}} \qquad (3.31)$$

Earlier in the chapter, when the income tax rate was zero, the numerical example of the multiplier was 4. Now that we have introduced an income tax rate of 0.2, the marginal leakage rate is 0.4 (see equation 3.29) and the multiplier is 1/0.4 or 2.5. Thus, raising the income tax rate reduces the multiplier and vice versa. This gives the government a new tool for stabilizing income. When the government wants to stimulate the economy and raise income, it can raise income in (3.29) and the multiplier in (3.31) by cutting income tax rates. This actually occurred in 1975. And, when the government wants to restrain the economy, it can raise income tax rates, as occurred in 1968.

The Government Budget Deficit

The government budget deficit is defined as before; it equals government expenditure minus tax revenue, $G - T$. Substituting the definition in (3.25) which expresses tax revenue (T) as the sum of autonomous and induced tax revenue, we can write the government deficit as:

$$\text{government budget deficit} = G - T = G - \bar{T} - \bar{t}Q \qquad (3.32)$$

Thus the government budget deficit automatically shrinks when the level of income expands. This consequence of the income tax is sometimes called **automatic stabilization.** This name reflects the automatic rise and fall of income tax revenues as income rises and falls. When income rises, income tax revenues rise and siphon off some of the income before households have a chance to spend it. Similarly, when income falls, income tax revenues fall and help minimize the drop in disposable income. This is why the presence of an income tax makes the multiplier smaller.

Automatic stabilization is the effect of income taxes in lowering the multiplier effect of changes in autonomous planned spending.

SELF-TEST Does the government budget deficit grow or shrink in an economic expansion? In a recession?

3-8 Foreign Trade, Net Exports, and the Multiplier

The theory of income determination in equation (3.29) states that equilibrium income equals planned autonomous spending (A_p) divided by the marginal leakage rate. When the United States trades with nations abroad, U.S. producers sell part of domestic output as exports. Households and business firms purchase imports from abroad, so part of U.S. expenditures does not generate U.S. production.

How do exports and imports affect the determination of income? We learned in Chapter 2 that the difference between exports and imports is called net exports and is part of GNP. When exports increase, net exports increase. When imports increase, net exports decrease. Designating net exports by X, we can write the relationship between net exports and income (Q) as:

$$X = \bar{X} - xQ \qquad (3.33)$$

Net exports contains an autonomous component ($\bar{X}$), reflecting the fact that the level of exports depends mainly on income in foreign countries (which is exogenous, not explained by our theory) rather than on domestic income (Q). Net exports also contains an induced component ($-xQ$), reflecting the fact that imports rise if domestic income (Q) rises, thus reducing net exports.

Because we now have a new component of autonomous expenditure, the autonomous component of net exports ($\bar{X}$), we can rewrite our definition of A_p as the following in place of equation (3.19):

$$A_p = a - c\bar{T} + I_p + G + \bar{X} \qquad (3.34)$$

Because imports depend on income (Q), the induced component of net exports ($-xQ$) has exactly the same effect on equilibrium income and the multiplier as does the income tax. Imports represent a leakage from the spending stream, a portion of a change in income that is not part of the disposable income of U.S. citizens and thus not available for consumption. The fraction of a change in income that is spent on net exports (x) is part of the economy's marginal leakage rate.

Types of leakages	Marginal leakage rate
Saving only	s
Saving and income tax	$s(1 - \bar{t}) + \bar{t}$
Saving, income tax, and imports	$s(1 - \bar{t}) + \bar{t} + x$

When we combine (3.29), (3.34), and the table, equilibrium income becomes:

$$Q = \frac{A_p}{\text{marginal leakage rate}} = \frac{a - c\bar{T} + I_p + G + \bar{X}}{s(1 - \bar{t}) + \bar{t} + x} \qquad (3.35)$$

SELF-TEST   In Belgium both exports and imports are a much higher fraction of income than in the United States. Which country has the higher multiplier for changes in government spending, Belgium or the United States?

This completes our analysis of the simple Keynesian model of income determination. As explained at the beginning of the chapter, we have maintained two crucial assumptions, that both the interest rate and the price level are fixed. We now turn in Chapter 4 to a more realistic model that builds on what we have learned but allows the interest rate to vary and to influence the level of planned autonomous spending. We retain the assumption of a fixed price level throughout Chapters 4 and 5 before allowing the price level to be flexible, starting in Chapter 6.

1. This chapter presents a simple theory for determining real income. Important simplifying assumptions include the constancy of the interest rate and the price level.

2. Disposable income is divided between consumption and saving. Throughout the chapter consumption is assumed to be a fixed autonomous amount, $250 billion in the numerical example, plus 0.75 of disposable income. Saving is the remaining 0.25 of disposable income minus the $250 billion of autonomous consumption.

3. During the 1929–85 period, U.S. consumption was a roughly constant fraction of disposable income. Exceptions were during the worst year of the Great Depression, when consumption exceeded income, and during World War II, when rationing prevented households from obtaining the goods they desired and forced them to save an abnormal fraction of their income.

4. Output and income (Q) are equal by definition to total expenditures (E), which in turn can be divided up between planned expenditures (E_p) and unintended inventory accumulation (I_u). We convert this definition into a theory by assuming that business firms adjust production whenever I_u is not zero. The economy is in equilibrium, with no pressure for production to change, only when there is no unintended inventory accumulation or decumulation ($I_u = 0$).

5. Planned autonomous spending (A_p) equals total planned expenditures minus induced consumption. The four components of planned autonomous expenditures are autonomous consumption (a), planned investment (I_p), government spending (G), and the effect on consumption of autonomous tax revenue ($-c\overline{T}$).

6. Any change in planned autonomous spending (ΔA_p) has a multiplier effect: an increase raises income and induced consumption over and above the initial boost in A_p. Income must increase until enough extra saving has been induced ($s\Delta Q$) to balance the injection of extra planned autonomous spending (ΔA_p). For this reason the multiplier, the ratio of the change in income to the change in planned autonomous spending ($\Delta Q/\Delta A_p$), is the inverse of the marginal propensity to save ($1/s$).

7. The same multiplier is valid for a change in any component in A_p. Thus if private spending components of A_p are weak, the government can raise its spending (G) or cut taxes ($\overline{T}$) to maintain stability in A_p and thus in real output.

8. The multiplier is the inverse of the marginal propensity to save only if there is no income tax and no foreign trade. More generally, the multiplier is the inverse of the marginal leakage rate, which consists of the fraction of GNP that "leaks out" of the spending stream into saving, income tax revenue, and imports.

9. Reductions in the income tax rate raise income and the multiplier, while increases in the income tax rate reduce income and the multiplier.

CONCEPTS

endogenous versus exogenous variables
autonomous magnitudes
marginal propensity to consume and save
induced consumption and saving
parameter

equilibrium
unintended inventory investment
multiplier
marginal leakage rate
automatic stabilization

QUESTIONS AND PROBLEMS

Questions

1. Explain the distinction between exogenous variables and endogenous variables. Explain the distinction, if any, between a parameter and an exogenous variable. For the most complete model used in this chapter, which of the following variables are endogenous? Which are exogenous?
   (a) autonomous taxes
   (b) marginal leakage rate
   (c) consumption

(d) marginal propensity to consume
(e) exports
(f) net exports
(g) GNP
(h) price level
(i) interest rate
(j) tax rate
(k) investment
(l) tax revenue
(m) disposable income
(n) saving
(o) foreign trade surplus (deficit)
(p) government budget surplus (deficit)

2. Given a consumption function of the form $C = a + c(Q_D)$ where $Q_D = Q - T$ and $T = \overline{T} + \overline{t}Q$, write the formula for the expanded consumption function. Write the formula for the expanded saving function that is implied by the stated consumption function.

3. Why do we distinguish between autonomous consumption and induced consumption?

4. Does the existence of positive inventory change imply that the economy is out of equilibrium? Why or why not?

5. Assume that there is an increase in autonomous investment of $100 billion. Under which circumstance will the ultimate impact on the level of equilibrium GNP be greater: a) with a relatively high marginal propensity to consume, or b) a relative low marginal propensity to consume? Explain.

6. How would your answer in question 5 change if the alternatives read: a) with a relatively high marginal leakage rate, or b) with a relatively low marginal leakage rate? Explain.

7. Is it more desirable for an economy to have a large multiplier or a small multiplier?

8. What is the effect on the multiplier of including induced taxes in the model of income determination presented in this chapter?

9. Explain why government action which increases the deficit is expansionary fiscal policy. What about action which decreases the surplus?

10. Why are imports considered to be a leakage in the economy? How are imports included in the model presented in this chapter?

Problems

1. Consider an economy in which all taxes are autonomous and the following values of autonomous consumption, planned investment, government expenditures, taxes and the marginal propensity to consume are given:
$a = 400 \quad I_p = 450 \quad G = 300 \quad \overline{T} = 400 \quad c = .75$

(a) What is the level of consumption when the level of income (Q) equals $4200?
(b) What is the level of saving when the level of income (Q) equals $4200?
(c) What is the level of planned investment when the level of income (Q) equals $4200? What is the level of actual investment? What is the level of unintended inventory investment?
(d) Show that injections equal leakages when income (Q) equals $4200.
(e) Is the economy in equilibrium when income $(Q) = 4200? If not, what is the equilibrium level of income for the economy described in this question?

2. $C = a + cQ_D$
   $T = \overline{T} + \overline{t}Q$
   $X = \overline{X} - xQ$

where:
$a = 300 \quad I_p = 400 \quad \overline{T} = 200 \quad \overline{X} = 400$
$c = 0.5 \quad \overline{t} = 0.3 \quad x = 0.1 \quad G = 500$

(a) Determine the equilibrium levels of GNP, consumption, saving, and taxes.
(b) What is the value of the marginal propensity to save? What is the value of the marginal leakage rate? Why are these two magnitudes not equal?
(c) At the equilibrium level of GNP, is there a surplus or deficit in the government budget? How much?
(d) What is the balance of trade in the foreign sector at the equilibrium level of income?
(e) What is the new equilibrium level of GNP if government spending increases by $30 billion?

3. Given a consumption function of the form $C = a + c(Q_D)$, where $Q_D = Q - T$ and $T = \overline{T} + \overline{t}Q$, and given the following values,
   $a = 300 \quad c = 0.8 \quad \overline{T} = 100 \quad \overline{t} = 0.25$
(a) What is the level of tax revenue when $Q = 5000$ billion?
(b) What is the level of disposable income (Q_D) when $Q = 5000$ billion?
(c) What is the level of consumption when $Q = 5000$ billion?
(d) Assuming that saving and taxes are the only leakages in this economy, what is the value of the marginal leakage rate?
(e) Assuming that the only other source of spending in the economy is government spending, what must the value of G be in order to generate an equilibrium value of $Q = 5000$?
(f) What is the value of the government budget surplus or deficit in this example?

4. Assume that in addition to strictly autonomous investment and government spending, the economy has the following behavioral equations for consumption (C), net tax revenue (T) and net exports (X):

$$C = a + cQ_D$$
$$T = T + tQ$$
$$X = X - xQ$$

where:

$a = 170$ $I_p = 600$ $T = 800$ $X = 800$
$c = t$ $t = .25$ $x = 0.175$ $G = 1650$

(a) What is the value of planned autonomous expenditures?
(b) What is the value of the marginal leakage rate?
(c) What is the equilibrium value of income (Q)?
(d) What is the size of the government surplus or deficit? The foreign trade surplus or deficit?
(e) At equilibrium, how is the level of invest- ment being *financed*? (Hint: Show that leakages equal injections in this situation.)

5. Assume that the marginal propensity to consume equals 0.6 for every consumer in the economy. You have just been paid $20,000 to produce a research report for the Commerce Department. How will this action by the government affect your spending plans? What would be the total effect on the economy of this action? (Assume that $t = 0$ and $x = 0$). What would be the total effect if $t = 0.2$ and $x = 0.08$.?

6. Assume that the marginal propensity to consume equals 0.6 for every consumer in the economy. You have just received a tax cut of $20,000. How will this action by the government affect your spending plans? What would be the total effect on the economy of this action? (Assume that $t = 0$ and $x = 0$). What would be the total effect if $t = 0.2$ and $x = 0.08$? Are your answers the same for problems 5 and 6? Why or why not?

SELF-TEST ANSWERS

p. 70 When income is only $2000, planned expenditures are equal to autonomous spending (500 + 250) plus induced consumption (0.75 times 2000 = 1500), for a total of 2250. Thus planned expenditures exceed income, forcing firms to reduce their inventories in order to meet demand. Unintended inventory investment is −250, and firms raise production in order to provide goods to meet planned expenditures; this increase in production moves the economy toward the equilibrium income level of 3000.

p. 76 We write planned investment as I_p with a "p" subscript, to reflect our assumption that *consumers and the government are always able to realize their plans*, so that there is no such thing as unplanned autonomous consumption, autonomous tax revenues, or government spednding. Only business firms can find that they are forced to make unplanned expenditures, as occurs when investment (I) is not equal to what they plan (I_p) but also includes unplanned inventory accumulation (I_u).

p. 77 The absence of a "Δ" in front of the s in equation (3.14) reflects the fact that we are interested in the effects of a change in autonomous spending, *while holding constant the marginal propensity to consume (c) and to save (s = 1 − c)*. To keep the formula simple, it assumes there is no change in s^7.

p. 80 The "balanced budget multiplier" is the multiplier for a change in government spending (1/s) from equation (3.21) plus the multiplier for a change in autonomous taxes ($-c/s$) from equation (3.24). Adding (1/s) and ($-c/s$), we obtain (1 − c)/s = 1. Thus the balanced budget multiplier is unity whenever there is no income tax or leakage from spending into imports. See if you can work out the value of the balanced-budget multiplier for the more general case based on equation (3.35).

p. 82 Because government tax revenues grow in an economic expansion, the government budget deficit shrinks in an expansion and grows in a recession.

p. 83 Because Belgium has a much higher x in equation (3.35), it will have a lower multiplier for any change in autonomous spending, including a change in government spending.

---

[7]Using the calculus formula for the change in a ratio, the change in income when both A_p and s are allowed to change is:

$$\Delta Q = \Delta A_p/s - A_p\Delta s/s^2$$

Formula (3.14) in the text simply sets Δs equal to zero in this expression.

CHAPTER FOUR

Spending, the Interest Rate, and Money

It may be laid down as a maxim, that wherever a great deal can be made by the use of money, a great deal will commonly be given for the use of it.

—Adam Smith, 1776

4-1 Introduction

The basic theme of the last chapter was that income and real GNP change by a *multiple* of any change in planned autonomous spending. But changes in planned autonomous spending (ΔA_p) were assumed to be already known, that is, *exogenous,* and were not explained. In this chapter we accept everything in Chapter 3 as valid. But we go further by relating the level of private planned investment and autonomous consumption ($I_p + a$) to the level of the interest rate.

If private planned spending depends partly on the interest rate, what determines the interest rate? First we will explore the connection between the interest rate and the supply of money. Then we will see how the government uses its control over the money supply to influence the interest rate, and thus the equilibrium level of income.

This chapter adds to our understanding of the process of income determination, and begins our investigation of the key questions at the heart of recent economic debates:

PUZZLE 4: WHY WERE INTEREST RATES IN THE 1980s HIGHER THAN EVER BEFORE?

1. What factors make the interest rate for borrowing higher in some periods than in others? This is Puzzle 4 identified at the beginning of the book. Why, for instance, did the interest rate on short-term loans reach 19.1 percent in June 1981? Why was the same rate as low as 0.5 percent in early 1958?[1]

2. What have been the effects of unprecedented federal budget deficits in the years since 1981? Once we allow for an increase in the interest rate, does an expansion in government spending or a tax cut (a "fiscal policy stimulus") have the full multiplier effect of Chapter 3?

---

[1]Figures refer to the federal funds rate, the rate on overnight loans of bank reserves between one bank and another.

3. If an increase in the interest rate reduces the size of the multiplier, which components of spending are affected? Will planned private domestic investment be "crowded out," or will the main effect of the fiscal stimulus be to reduce net exports and net foreign investment?

4. If a stimulus to the economy is needed when actual real GNP is below natural real GNP, should that stimulus be provided by monetary or fiscal policy?

In this chapter, as in Chapter 3, we will assume that the price level is fixed. All changes in real income and real GNP are accompanied by the same change in nominal income and nominal GNP. All effects of spending on inflation, and of inflation on the interest rate, are postponed for treatment later.

4-2 Interest Rates and Rates of Return

Functions of Interest Rates

Interest rates help the economy allocate saving among alternative uses. For savers, the interest rate is a reward for abstaining from consumption and waiting to consume at some future time. The higher the interest rate, the greater the incentive to save. For borrowers, the interest rate is the cost of borrowing funds to invest or buy consumption goods. At a higher interest rate people will borrow fewer funds and purchase fewer goods. Thus if the desire to borrow exceeds the willingness to save sufficient funds, the interest rate tends to rise.

Business borrowers decide how much to invest by comparing the interest rate charged on borrowed funds with the earnings of investment projects. The projects—for example, structures like office buildings and durable goods like airplanes and computers—would not be undertaken unless the investor expected earnings to remain after paying expenses like wages and rent. These earnings provide the funds needed to pay the interest charged for borrowed funds. Clearly, any increase in the interest rate will reduce the likelihood that earnings will be large enough to cover interest payments, and as a result investment is likely to fall. The same reasoning applies to consumer borrowing. Consumers compare the interest payments on a loan with the desirability of having a good like a house or car sooner rather than later. Higher interest rates will cause some consumers to wait rather than buy now, and autonomous consumption will fall.

Interest rates are central to the role of monetary policy. Because currency does not pay interest while most types of bank deposits do, individuals give up interest by holding currency. Since the government, through the Federal Reserve Board (the "Fed"), can control the supply of currency, it can influence the interest rate and thus indirectly affect the cost of borrowed funds to private borrowers.

Types of Interest Rates

Banks offer a variety of interest rates on checking and saving accounts. Some types of accounts allow customers to obtain funds instantly, and others require customers to leave funds on deposit for a year or more. The phrase "short-term interest rate" refers to funds that can be obtained within

Interest Rates and Bond and Stock Prices

Any increase in the demand for stocks and bonds drives up their prices. This simultaneously reduces the interest rate. Why? The interest rate on a stock is its dividend yield, the dollar dividend divided by the stock's price. Let us assume that initially the price of a stock paying a $5 dividend is $50, so that the dividend yield is 0.10, or 10 percent (= 5/50). If, however, an increase in the demand for stocks drives the stock price up to $100, the dividend yield drops from 10 percent (= 5/50) to 5 percent (= 5/100), because the $5 dividend payment in this example is unaffected by movements in stock prices.

Similarly, the annual dollar payment of interest on a long-term bond, say $5 per year, is unaffected by movements in bond prices. If the bond's price is initially $50, the bond pays a 10 percent interest "yield" or interest "rate." When the bond price is driven up to $100, the interest yield or rate drops from 10 percent (5/50) to 5 percent (5/100).

In short, stock prices and long-term interest rates tend to move in opposite directions. In exactly the same way, bond prices and long-term interest rates move in opposite directions. Journalists for daily newspapers frequently write that stock prices move up because interest rates on long-term bonds have decreased. As shown in this chapter, The Federal Reserve Board can influence the level of interest rates and thus, indirectly, the level of stock market prices.

three months or less; "long-term interest rate" refers to funds that cannot be obtained for a year or more.

Besides short-term interest rates on bank deposits, there are short-term interest rates that apply to funds borrowed by the government (the "Treasury bill rate"), businesses (the "commercial paper rate"), and banks (the "federal funds rate"). Besides long-term rates on bank deposits, there are long-term interest rates that apply to funds borrowed by the government (the "Treasury bond rate"), businesses (the "corporate bond rate"), and households (the "mortgage rate"). The business sections of most local newspapers and the *Wall Street Journal* publish the daily values of these rates.

This chapter examines the determination of real income and "the" interest rate. The hallmark of a good theory is its ability to spotlight important relationships and to ignore unnecessary details. For most purposes, the differences between alternative interest rates fall into that category of detail, in contrast to the important overall *average* level of interest rates. Thus "the" interest rate discussed in this chapter can be regarded as an average of all the different interest rates listed in the previous paragraph.

4-3 The Relation of Private Autonomous Planned Spending to the Interest Rate

Why should private planned investment and autonomous consumption $(I_p + a)$ depend on the interest rate? Business firms attempt to profit by borrowing funds to buy investment goods—office buildings, shopping centers, factories, machine tools, computers, airplanes. Obviously, firms can stay in business only if the earnings of investment goods are at least enough to pay the interest on the borrowed funds (or to attract enough investors to warrant a new issue of stocks).

Example of an Airline's Investment Decision

American Airlines calculates that it can earn $8 million per year from one additional Boeing 757 jet airliner after paying all expenses for employee salaries, fuel, food, and airplane maintenance—that is, all expenses besides interest payments on borrowed funds. If the 757 costs $40 million that level of earnings represents a 20 percent **rate of return** ($8,000,000/$40,000,000), defined as annual earnings divided by the cost of the airplane. If American must pay 10 percent interest to obtain the funds for the airplane, the 20 percent rate of return is more than sufficient to pay the interest expense.

In the top frame of Figure 4-1, point *A* shows that the 20 percent rate of return on the first 757 exceeds the 10 percent interest rate on borrowed funds. The steplike red line in the top frame of Figure 4-1 shows the rate of return on the first through fifth planes. The gray area between point *A* and the 10 percent interest rate represents the annual profit rate made on the

The **rate of return** on an investment project is its annual earnings divided by its total cost.

Figure 4-1
The Payoff to Investment for an Airline and the Economy

The red steplike line in the top frame shows the rate of return to American Airlines for purchases of additional 757s. If the interest rate is 10 percent, a profit is made by purchasing the first two planes, and the company breaks even by buying the third plane. Purchase of a fourth or fifth plane would be a mistake, because the planes would not generate enough profit to pay for the cost of borrowing the money to buy them. The bottom frame shows the same phenomenon for the economy as a whole.

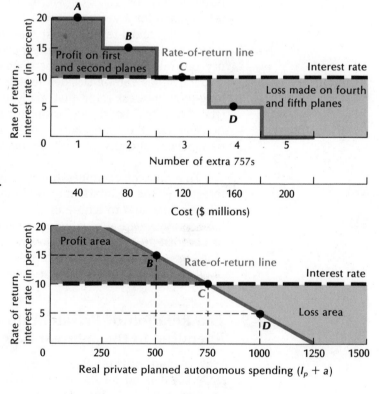

AN INCREASE IN PLANNED PRIVATE SPENDING REDUCES THE RATE OF RETURN

Can Families Afford Housing?

Textbooks traditionally emphasize the effect of changes in the interest rate on investment by business firms. But changes in interest rates also have a profound effect on the ability of ordinary people to purchase houses and consumer durable goods like automobiles.

Most people who buy houses must obtain a mortgage loan from a financial institution. In judging an individual's ability to qualify for a mortgage, the loan officer compares income with the annual mortgage payment (including interest and principal). One common rule of thumb is that the mortgage payment should be no more than 25 percent of income. When interest rates go up, the mortgage payment increases, so that some people who formerly qualified for mortgages no longer qualify. These people are thus prevented from buying houses, and the demand for housing decreases. This is an additional reason for the negative relationship between planned autonomous spending and the interest rate developed in Section 4-3.

As an example of how higher mortgage rates influence the ability of people to buy houses, the following table shows how the annual mortgage payment more than doubled between 1978 and 1982, far exceeding the growth in median family income. As a result, median family income fell as a percentage of qualifying income (four times the

mortgage payment) from 111.4 percent in 1978 to 69.5 percent in 1982. By 1985 interest rates had fallen sufficiently to reverse this process, bring the percentage back from 69.5 in 1982 to 94.9 in 1985, with a further improvement to 113.6 in 1988.

The annual number of houses constructed ("housing starts") corresponded to the sharp decline in the ability of people to afford mortgage payments, from 2.0 million in 1978 to 1.1 million in 1982, and then recovered to 1.7 million in 1985 and 1.5 million in 1988.[a]

	Median home price	Mortgage interest rate	Annual mortgage payment	Qualifying income— four times mortgage payment	Median family income	(5) as percentage of (4)
	(1)	(2)	(3)	(4)	(5)	(6)
1978	$48,700	9.58%	$3,960	$15,840	$17,640	111.4%
1982	67,800	15.38	8,424	33,696	23,433	69.5
1985	75,500	11.74	7,308	29,232	27,735	94.9
1988	89,100	9.31	7,080	28,320	32,172	113.6

[a]All data in the table are from the National Association of Realtors, except for median family income from the Census Bureau (1988 estimated). Housing starts are from the *Economic Report of the President.*

first plane. Point *B* for the second plane also indicates a profit. Point *C* shows that purchase of a third extra 757 earns only a 10 percent rate of return or $4 million in extra earnings after payment of all noninterest expenses.

Why do the second and third planes earn less than the first? The first plane is operated on the most profitable routes; the second and third must fly on routes that are less likely to yield full passenger loads. A fourth plane (at point *D*) would have an even lower rate of return, insufficient to pay the interest cost of borrowed funds. How many planes will be purchased? The third can pay its interest expense and will be purchased, but the fourth will not. If the interest cost of borrowed funds were to rise above 10 percent, purchases would be cut from three planes to two, but if the interest rate were to fall to or below 5 percent, then four planes would be purchased.

The Interest Rate and the Rate-of-Return Line

The interest rate not only influences the level of business investment but also affects the level of household consumption. For instance, households deciding whether to purchase a dishwasher or a second automobile will consider the size of the monthly payment, which depends on the interest rate. In the bottom frame of Figure 4-1 the rate-of-return line shows that the return on planned investment and autonomous consumption spending $(I_p + a)$ declines as the level of spending increases. As for American Airlines, each successive investment good purchased by business firms is less profitable than the last. Similarly, each successive consumption good purchased by households provides fewer services than the last (for instance, a family's second car is less important and useful than its first car).

The rates of return for three alternative quantities of $I_p + a$ are plotted along the rate-of-return line in the bottom frame of Figure 4-1. They are

Point	$I_p + a$	Rate of return	Interest rate	Profit
B	500	15	10	5
C	750	10	10	0
D	1000	5	10	−5

The gray area shows that if the interest rate is 10 percent, a profit will be made on the first $750 billion of $I_p + a$. However, the rate of return of further spending is below the interest rate and creates the losses indicated by the pink area.

Thus, determination of the level of $I_p + a$ is a two-step process. First we plot the rate-of-return line representing firms' and consumers' expectations of the benefit of additional purchases. Second, we find the level of $I_p + a$ at the point where the rate-of-return line crosses the interest-rate level.

When the interest rate is 10 percent, as in Figure 4-1, autonomous planned spending $(I_p + a)$ will be $750 billion at point C, as long as the level of business and consumer optimism remains constant. A decrease in the interest rate will increase purchases $(I_p + a)$; for instance, a decrease from 10 percent to 5 percent moves autonomous planned spending from $750 billion at C to $1000 billion at D.

Business and Consumer Optimism

Can purchases ever change when the interest rate is held constant at 10 percent? Certainly—an increase in business and consumer optimism about the expected payoff of additional purchases can shift the entire rate-of-return line to the right, as indicated by the red "new rate-of-return line" in Figure 4-2. This shifts to the right (to point F) the intersection of the rate-of-return line with the fixed horizontal interest-rate line.

Figure 4-2
Effect on Planned Autonomous Spending of an Increase in Business and Consumer Confidence

The dashed red "Original rate-of-return line" is an exact copy of the solid red "Rate-of-return line" in Figure 4-1. If the level of business and consumer confidence were to increase, the spending schedule would shift rightward to the solid red "New rate-of-return line." If the interest rate were to stay constant at 10 percent, then planned autonomous spending (A_p) would increase from $750 billion at point C to $1000 billion at point F.

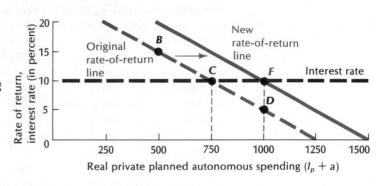

Summarizing, we can show the amount of $I_p + a$ spending that would occur at different interest rates and different levels of confidence.

	Demand for $I_p + a$	
Interest rate	Original rate-of-return line (expectations pessimistic)	new higher rate-of-return line (expectations optimistic)
15	500 (at B)	750
10	750 (at C)	1000 (at F)
5	1000 (at D)	1250

The left-hand column (expectations pessimistic) is plotted as the "original rate-of-return line" (red dashes) in Figure 4-2. The right-hand column (expectations optimistic) is plotted as the solid red "new rate-of-return line."

4-4 The *IS* Curve

The ***IS* curve** is the schedule that identifies the combinations of income and the interest rate at which the commodity market is in equilibrium; everywhere along the *IS* curve, the demand for commodities equals the supply.

You have now learned that total planned autonomous spending (A_p) depends on the interest rate. And in Chapter 3 you learned that the total level of real GNP and real income depend on the total level of planned autonomous spending. Now, if we put these two relations together, we conclude that total real GNP and real income must depend on the interest rate. In this section we derive a graphical schedule that shows the different possible combinations of the interest rate and real income that are compatible with a given state of business and consumer confidence and a given marginal propensity to save. This schedule is the *IS* **curve.**

How to Derive the *IS* Curve

The lower left-hand corner of Figure 4-3 shows the first ingredient in the derivation of the *IS* curve. This "A_p line" shows the demand for planned autonomous spending at different levels of the interest rate and is copied from the "Original rate-of-return line" in Figure 4-2. Notice that at a 10 percent interest rate (point C), A_p will be $750 billion, just the same as in Figure 4-2 at point C. Initially we assume that there is no government spending, tax revenue, or net exports, so total autonomous spending consists simply of the two components, $I_p + a$.

What will be the equilibrium level of real income if A_p equals $750 billion? We answer this question just as in Chapter 3 by plotting the level of A_p in the upper right-hand corner of Figure 4-3 as the horizontal red line (with a height of $750 billion). Where the $A_p = 750$ line crosses the upward-sloping "Induced saving" line at point C, equilibrium real income is $3000 billion. In the lower right-hand side of Figure 4-3 is plotted the equilibrium level of real income of $3000 billion against the assumed 10 percent level of the interest rate.

The figure also shows other possibilities, for instance point B. At point B in the lower right-hand frame the assumed 15 percent interest rate is plotted against the $2000 billion level of real income that is compatible with it. Point B in the other figures shows the determination of autonomous spending and induced saving.

SELF-TEST What interest rate is compatible with a $4000 billion level of equilibrium real income? At what point does this equilibrium recur in the lower right-hand frame of Figure 4-3?

Because A_p depends on the interest rate, equilibrium income does also. The "*IS* curve" in Figure 4-3 plots the values of equilibrium real income when the marginal propensity to save is 0.25 and the multiplier is 4.0, as in the last chapter. Notice that points B, C, and D along the *IS* curve are all plotted at a horizontal distance exactly 4.0 times the value of the A_p line in the lower left-hand frame.

What the *IS* Curve Shows

The *IS* curve shows all the different combinations of the interest rate (r) and income (Q) at which the economy's market for commodities (goods and services) is in equilibrium, which occurs only when income equals planned expenditures. At any point off the *IS* curve the economy is out of equilibrium.

It will be convenient to have a label for the horizontal position of the A_p line, since this will in turn affect the horizontal position of the *IS* curve.[2] *Let*

---

[2]We call the *IS* schedule a "curve," even though we have drawn it as a straight line because in the real world the relationship might be a curve. Also, "*IS* curve" has been familiar terminology to generations of economists since its invention by the late Sir John Hicks in a classic article, "Mr. Keynes and the 'Classics': A Suggested Interpretation," *Econometrica*, vol. 5 (April 1937), pp. 147–159.

94   *Chapter 4 / Spending, the Interest Rate, and Money*

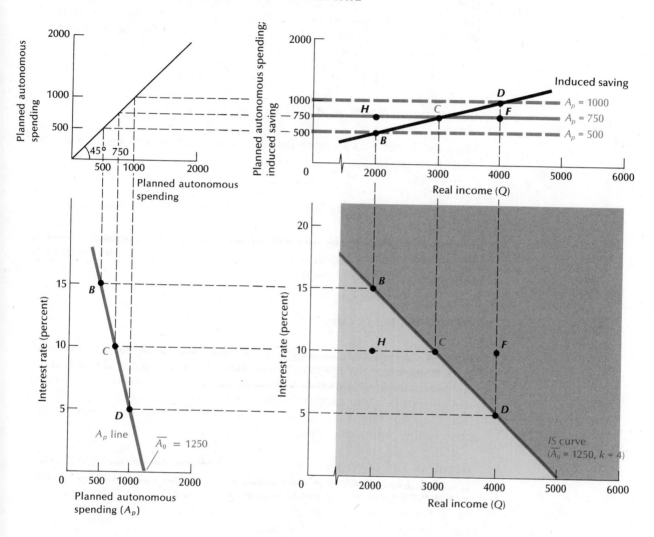

Figure 4-3   **Relation of the *IS* Curve to the Demand for Autonomous Spending and the Amount of Induced Saving**

In the lower left frame the "A_p line" is copied from Figure 4-2. It shows that the demand for autonomous planned spending depends on the interest rate. For instance, at a 10 percent interest rate the level of A_p is $750 billion at point C. Following the thin dashed black line up above point C and over to the upper right frame, we see that the economy is in equilibrium at point C, where both A_p and induced saving are equal. This equilibrium level of income is $3000 billion and is plotted directly below in the lower right-hand frame, opposite the 10 percent interest rate that we assumed at the beginning.

us define $\bar{A}$ as the value of planned autonomous spending that would take place at an interest rate of zero. In Figure 4-3 the A_p line intersects the horizontal axis at \$1250 billion, so our label for this A_p line will be $\bar{A}_0 = 1250$. The IS curve always lies at a horizontal distance 4.0 times the A_p line, because the multiplier (k) is 4.0. Notice in Figure 4-3 that the IS curve intersects the horizontal axis at \$5000 billion, exactly 4.0 times the level of $\bar{A}_0 = 1250$.

4-5   Learning to Shift and Tilt the IS Curve

Since the IS curve is so important and useful, we need to pause here and study it more closely.[3]

Why Does the IS Curve Slant Down to the Right?

A lower interest rate raises A_p, and a higher level of A_p raises equilibrium Q by k times as much. The fact that the level of A_p is sensitive to the interest rate makes the IS curve interest sensitive.

What Shifts the IS Curve?

Figure 4-3 demonstrates that the horizontal intercept of the IS curve is always equal to the multiplier (k) times $\bar{A}$, the amount of planned autonomous spending that would occur at a zero interest rate. For instance, the IS_0 curve has a horizontal intercept at \$5000 billion, equal to 4.0 (k) times \$1250 billion $(\bar{A}_0)$. Anything that changes $\bar{A}$ will shift the IS curve. Anything that charges the multiplier (k) will rotate the IS curve.

Business and consumer confidence.   Both the A_p line and the IS curve will shift if businesses and consumers become more optimistic and desire to spend more at any given interest rate. For instance, bank failures in the Great Depression may have created pessimism, shifting the IS curve to the left, and the inauguration of President Roosevelt in March 1933 may have helped restore confidence and shift the IS curve to the right.

In Figure 4-4 the left-hand frame shows two A_p lines. Along the left-hand "old A_p line" confidence is relatively low, but the "new A_p line" reflects a higher level of confidence and lies everywhere exactly \$250 billion farther to the right. Since the multiplier is 4.0 the "new IS curve" lies \$1000 billion to the right, so that with an interest rate of 10 percent equilibrium real income is \$4000 billion at point F.

---

[3]Despite its name, the IS curve has no unique connection with investment (I) or saving (S). It shifts whenever $\bar{A}$ changes, which can be caused by a change in government spending, in tax rates, or in net exports, as well as by changes in business and consumer confidence.

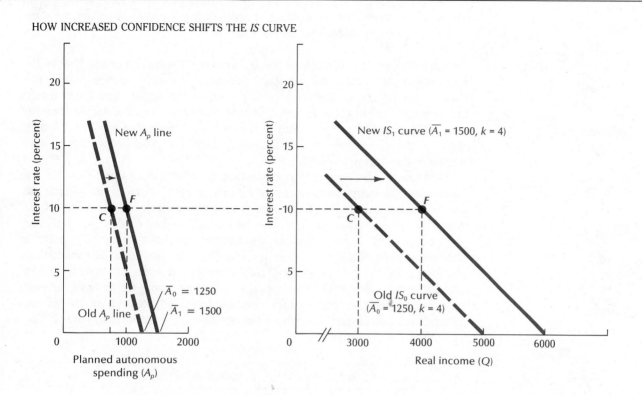

Figure 4-4 **Effect on the *IS* Curve of a Rightward Shift in the Demand for Planned Autonomous Spending**

The "old" A_p line and *IS* curve are copied from Figure 4-3. Now we assume that an increase in the level of business and consumer confidence shifts the A_p line \$250 billion to the right, just as occurred in Figure 4-2. The *IS* curve shifts to the right by four times as much. Notice that the horizontal intercept of the new *IS* curve at 6000 is four times the horizontal intercept of the A_p line—that is, $\overline{A}_1 = 1500$.

Once again, it is convenient to label each *IS* curve by the amount of autonomous planned spending that would occur at an interest rate of zero—that is, $\overline{A}_0 = 1250$ along the "old A_p line" and $\overline{A}_1 = 1500$ along the "new A_p line."

Government actions. So far we have assumed that there is no government spending or tax revenue. Now consider a \$250 billion increase in government spending. This raises planned autonomous spending by \$250 billion. Starting from the "old A_p line," the addition of \$250 billion of government spending would move us to the "new A_p line" and would cause the *IS* curve to shift in just the way depicted in Figure 4-4.

The rightward shift in Figure 4-4 of \$250 billion in the A_p line and of \$1000 billion in the *IS* curve can be caused by any event that raises by \$250 billion the amount of autonomous spending desired at a given interest rate,

$\overline{A}$. These events include an increase in business or consumer confidence, an increase in government spending, a reduction in autonomous tax revenue, and an increase in autonomous net exports.

The multiplier.   The slope of the IS curve will rotate relative to that of the A_p line in Figure 4-3 if the marginal propensity to save changes, since this will rotate the black "induced saving" line in the upper right-hand frame. For instance, an increase in the marginal propensity to save will reduce the multiplier ($k = 1/s$), thus rotating the IS curve clockwise for any given A_p line and any given level of $\overline{A}$. A decrease in the marginal propensity to save will have the opposite effect.

We saw at the end of Chapter 3 that the multiplier is equal to $1/s$, the inverse of the marginal propensity to save, only if there is no income tax and no foreign trade. More generally, the multiplier (k) is equal to 1.0 divided by the marginal leakage rate, which is the sum of the after-tax marginal propensity to save, the income tax rate, and the share of imports in GNP (multiplier $= 1/(s(1 - \overline{t}) + \overline{t} + x)$. Thus the multiplier is reduced not just by an increase in the marginal propensity to save, but also by an increase in the income tax rate or in the share of imports in GNP, in each case rotating the IS curve clockwise. Because the position of the IS line depends on both k and $\overline{A}$, both values are always given next to each IS line, as in Figure 4-4.

SELF-TEST   Does a change in the interest rate (r) cause IS to shift?

What Is True of Points That Are off the IS Curve?

The entire area to the left of each IS curve, for example, point H in Figure 4-3, is characterized by too low a level of production for the economy to be in equilibrium. There is undesired inventory decumulation and an *excess demand for commodities*. All points in the region to the right of an IS curve are characterized by purchases below production, which means undesired inventory accumulation and an *excess supply of commodities*. Thus at any point off the IS curve, there is pressure for production to adjust until the economy returns to the IS curve.

What Changes the Slope of the IS Curve?

How is the responsiveness of spending related to changes in the interest rate? **Spending responsiveness** or "A_p responsiveness" refers to the change in autonomous spending (ΔA_p) divided by the change in the interest rate (Δr) that causes it. Along the original A_p line in the left frame of Figure 4-4, for instance, a $250 billion increase in planned autonomous spending (ΔA_p) is caused by a 5 percent drop in the interest rate (Δr). Thus A_p responsiveness is 250/5, a $50 billion increase in A_p per 1 percentage point drop in r.

The dollar change in planned autonomous spending divided by the percentage point change on the interest rate which causes it is termed **spending responsiveness.**

The IS curve becomes flatter either when the multiplier (k) becomes larger (as, for instance, when the marginal propensity to save declines) or when A_p responsiveness increases. The IS curve becomes steeper if either the multiplier or A_p responsiveness is small. When businesses and households fail to raise spending in response to a lower interest rate, then the *IS* curve is vertical.

Value of A_p responsiveness for a given multiplier	Slope of IS curve
0	Vertical
Small	Steep
Large	Flat
Infinity	Horizontal

The Scope for Government Action

Our study of the *IS* curve leaves two major questions unanswered. First, will $\bar{A}$ be at the right level to set actual real GNP equal to its desired level (natural real GNP)? If not, can $\bar{A}$ be controlled by the government? Second, will the interest rate (r) be at the right level to achieve the desired level of income and, if not, can r be controlled by the government? To answer these questions we now turn to a second relationship between real income and the interest rate.

4-6   The Money Market and the *LM* Curve

This second relationship between real income and the interest rate occurs in the "money market," a general expression for the financial sector of the economy. We learn in this section how the "Fed" (Federal Reserve Board) can operate its monetary policy to change the interest rate and, indirectly, planned autonomous spending and the level of real income.

The **money supply** (M^s) consists of two parts, currency and checking accounts at banks and thrift institutions. In the United States the money supply is controlled by the Fed. The Fed controls the total of the reserves that banks hold at each regional Federal Reserve bank through its ability to purchase or sell government bonds. This allows the Fed to control the total money supply by setting the fraction of total deposits that must be kept in the form of bank reserves at the Fed.

At this stage in the book, the money supply may be considered as a policy instrument that the Fed can set exactly at any desired value, just as we have been assuming that the government can precisely set the level of its fiscal policy instruments—that is, purchases of goods and services and tax rates. Later in Chapter 17 we learn how the Fed actually achieves its control over the money supply.

*The **money supply** consists of currency and transactions accounts, including checking accounts at banks and thrift institutions.*

Income and the Demand for Money

The hypothesis that links the money supply, income, and the interest rate states that *the amount of money that people demand in real terms depends both on income and on the interest rate.* Why do households give up consumption goods to hold money balances that pay no interest? The main reason is that at least *some* holding of money is necessary to facilitate transactions.

Funds held in the form of stocks or bonds pay interest but cannot be used for transactions. People have to carry currency in their pockets or have money in their bank accounts to back up a check before they can buy anything. (Even if they use credit cards, they need money in their bank accounts to keep up with their credit card bills). Because rich people make more purchases, they generally need a larger amount of currency and larger bank deposits. Thus the demand for **real money balances** increases when everyone becomes richer—that is, when the total of real income increases.

Real money balances equal the total money supply divided by the price level.

Changes in real income alter the demand for money in real terms—that is, adjusted for changes in the price level. Let us assume that the demand for real money balances (M/P) equals half of real income (Q):

$$\left(\frac{M}{P}\right)^d = 0.5Q$$

The superscript d means "the demand for."

If real income (Q) is $4000 billion, the demand for real money balances $(M/P)^d$ will be $2000 billion, as shown in Figure 4-5 by the vertical line (L') drawn at $2000 billion. The line is vertical because we are assuming initially that the demand for real balances $(M/P)^d$ does not depend on the interest rate (r).

Figure 4-5
The Demand for Money, the Interest Rate, and Real Income

The vertical line L' is drawn on the unrealistic assumption that the demand for real balances is equal to half of real income ($4000 billion in this case), but does not depend on the interest rate. The L_0 curve maintains income at $4000, but it allows the demand for real balances to decrease by $500 billion for each 5 percent increase in the interest rate. The gray area shows the amount shifted into other assets, an amount that grows as the interest rate rises, leaving a smaller and smaller amount to be held as money.

HOW INCOME AND THE INTEREST RATE SHIFT
THE DEMAND FOR REAL BALANCES

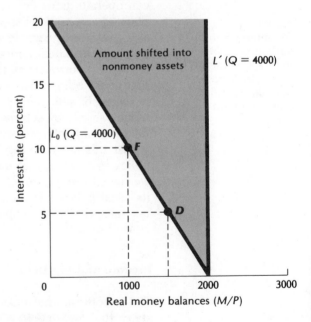

Financial Deregulation and the Demand for Money

The theory developed in this chapter assumes for simplicity that the supply of money, defined as currency and demand deposits, does not pay interest. Thus people want to hold less money when there is an increase in the interest rate paid on alternatives to money. However, in the late 1970s and early 1980s, changes in the regulations controlling U.S. financial institutions have introduced several new types of accounts that individuals could use for transactions while at the same time earning interest. Is our theory in the text still valid, now that interest is paid on part of the money supply?

The first change in regulations was the nationwide legalization in November 1978 of automatic transfer services (ATS) that allowed checks to be written on deposits held in savings accounts. In January 1981, negotiable order of withdrawal (NOW) accounts also became legal. Then, in 1982–83 new accounts were introduced that pay interest equivalent to that of money-market mutual funds and allow holders to write checks.

The nation's basic money-supply measure ("$M1$") includes these new accounts, as well as regular checking accounts and currency. Thus interest is paid on part but not all of the basic $M1$ money

supply. When the interest rate (r) on bonds or savings certificates increases by one percentage point, the interest rate paid on $M1$ goes up by less than one percentage point. This occurs because the interest paid on $M1$ is an *average* of the interest rates on accounts which adjust promptly, on accounts paying a roughly constant interest rate, and the interest rate on regular checking accounts and currency holdings, which remains at zero. Thus, whenever there is an increase in the interest rate paid on bonds and other alternatives to $M1$, relative to the average interest rate paid on $M1$, people will want to hold a smaller quantity of $M1$. And this is just what is assumed along the L_0 line in Figure 4-5.

The Interest Rate and the Demand for Money

The L' line is unrealistic, however, because individuals will not hold as much money at a 10 percent interest rate as at a zero interest rate. Why? Because the interest rate plotted on the vertical axis is paid on *assets other than money,* such as bonds and savings certificates. The higher the reward (r) for holding interest-earning financial assets (that are not money), the less money will be held. (This assumes that an increase in r raises the return on bonds and savings instruments *more* than any increase in the interest rate paid on checking accounts—see box on this page).

If the interest rate (r) paid on nonmoney assets were less than the interest paid on money, there would be no point in holding them. Individuals would hold all of their financial assets in the form of money to take advantage of its convenience. But if the interest rate on them were higher than the interest paid on money, individuals would cut down on their average money holding in order to earn the higher interest available on alternative assets. They would consider these higher interest earnings sufficient compensation for the nuisance of periodically converting these assets into money.

In Figure 4-5 the downward slope of L_0 through points F and D indicates that when real income is $4000 billion and the interest rate is zero, the demand for real balances is $2000 billion. But when the interest rate rises from zero to 5 percent, people suffer inconvenience to cut down their money holdings from $2000 billion to $1500 billion (point D). When the interest rate is 10 percent, only $1000 billion is demanded (point F). The new L_0 line can be summarized as showing that the real demand for money $(M/P)^d$ is half of income minus $100 billion times the interest rate:

$$\left(\frac{M}{P}\right)^d = 0.5Q - 100r$$

A change in the interest rate moves the economy up and down its real money demand schedule, whereas a change in real output (Q) shifts that schedule to the left or right, as shown in Figure 4-6.

SELF-TEST   What are the two determinants of the real demand for money? What is the effect of each determinant on the real demand for money? Does a change in either determinant shift the IS curve?

The LM schedule.   To have equilibrium in the money market the real supply of money (M^s/P) must equal the demand for real money $(M/P)^d$:

$$\left(\frac{M^s}{P}\right) = \left(\frac{M}{P}\right)^d = 0.5Q - 100r \qquad (4.1)$$

Figure 4-6

Effect on the Money Demand Schedule of a Decline in Real Income from $4000 to $3000 Billion

The L_0 line is copied from Figure 4-5 and shows the demand for real balances at different interest rates on the assumption that real income is $4000 billion. A $1000 billion drop in the level of income to $3000 billion causes the demand for real balances to drop by half as much, or $500 billion, at each interest rate. For instance, at a 10 percent interest rate the demand for real balances falls from $1000 billion at point F to $500 billion at point C.

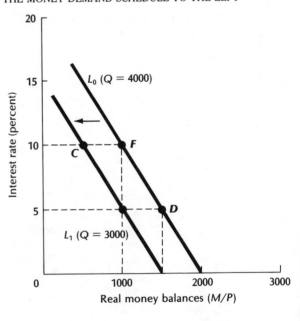

A DROP IN THE LEVEL OF INCOME SHIFTS THE MONEY DEMAND SCHEDULE TO THE LEFT

If the amount of money supplied by the government is $1000 billion and the price index (P) is set at a constant value of 1.0, then (M^s/P) equals $1000 billion. To simplify the analysis, we assume that the supply of money does not depend on the interest rate, so (M^s/P) is drawn in the left frame of Figure 4-7 as a vertical line at a level of $1000 billion for every interest rate. The two money demand schedules, L_0 and L_1, are copied from Figure 4-6.

How to derive the *LM* curve. The sloped money demand line L_0, drawn for an income of $4000 billion, crosses the M^s/P line at point F, where the interest rate is 10 percent. The demand for money at F is $1000 billion, and the supply of money is also $1000 billion. Because the two are equal, the money market is in equilibrium when $Q = 4000$ (assumed in drawing the L_0

A FIXED MONEY SUPPLY IS CONSISTENT WITH MANY DIFFERENT LEVELS OF INCOME

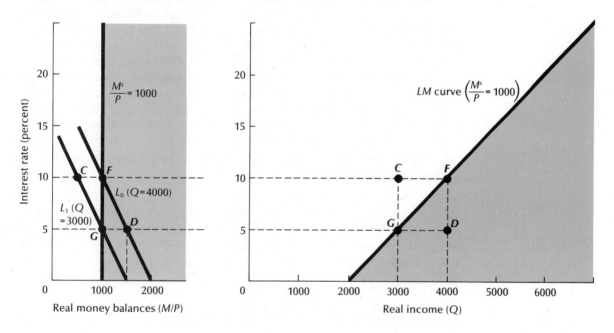

Figure 4-7 **Derivation of the *LM* Curve**
In the left frame the L_0 and L_1 schedules are copied from the previous figure. The vertical M^s/P line shows the available supply of money provided by the government. The money market is in equilibrium where the supply line (M^s/P) crosses the demand line (L_0 or L_1). When income is $4000 billion, equilibrium occurs at point F, plotted again in the right frame. When income is $3000 billion, equilibrium occurs where L_1 crosses M^s/P at point G, also plotted in the right frame. The *LM* curve or schedule shows all combinations of Q and r consistent with equilibrium in the money market.

line) and $r = 10$ percent. This equilibrium combination of values is plotted at point F in the right frame of Figure 4-7.[4]

If income is $3000 billion instead of $4000 billion, the demand for money is shown by schedule L_1 passing through points C and G. Now the demand for real money balances can be equal to the fixed real supply of money only at point G, where the interest rate is 5 percent. Thus $Q = 3000$ and $r = 5$ is another combination consistent with equilibrium in the money market, and it is plotted at point G in the right frame of Figure 4-7.[5]

What the *LM* curve shows. The line connecting points G and F in the right-hand frame of Figure 4-7 is called the **LM curve.** The *LM* curve represents all combinations of income (Q) and interest rate (r) where the money market is in equilibrium—that is, where the real supply of money equals the real demand for money.

At any point off the *LM* curve, say point D, the money market is not in equilibrium. The problem at D and all other points in the pink area is that the demand for real money exceeds the available supply. At point C and all other points in the white area there is an excess supply of money that exceeds the demand.

How does the economy adjust to guarantee that the given supply of money created by the government is exactly equal to the demand when the money market is out of equilibrium, as at point D? One possible adjustment, a reduction in the price level, will be considered later. In this chapter we assume the price index (P) to be equal to 1.0. Without changing prices, the economy might achieve money-market equilibrium from point D by increasing the interest rate from 5 to 10 percent. This would move it to point F, cutting the demand for money. Or, instead, income might fall from $4000 billion to $3000 billion while the interest rate remains fixed. This would cause a movement to point G and would also cut the demand for money. Or some other combination might occur, with a partial drop in income and partial increase in the interest rate.

The **LM curve** is the schedule that identifies the combinations of income and the interest rate at which the money market is in equilibrium; on the *LM* curve the demand for money equals the supply of money.

SELF-TEST   By how much does the demand for money change when the economy moves from point D to point F in Figure 4-7? From point D to point G? If you are stumped, you need to review the money demand equation (4.1) and footnotes 4 and 5, which show how to use it in specific examples.

4-7   Learning to Shift and Tilt the *LM* Curve

We shall learn later in this chapter, and in the next, that the effects of monetary and fiscal policy differ, depending on the slopes of the *IS* and *LM*

---

[4]Thus in equation (4.1)

$$1000 = 0.5(4000) - 100(10)$$
$$= 2000 - 1000$$
$$= 1000$$

[5]Thus in equation (4.1)

$$1000 = 0.5(3000) - 100(5)$$
$$= 1500 - 500$$
$$= 1000$$

curves. Thus it is important for us to learn what factors determine the slope of the *LM* curve, and what makes it shift.

Why Does the *LM* Curve Slope Up?

When the real money supply (M^s/P) is fixed, an increase in the interest rate leads people to put up with the inconvenience of carrying less money per dollar of income. The higher interest rate has the effect of "stretching" the available real money supply to support a higher level of real income. For instance, along the *LM* line in Figure 4-7 the real money supply is assumed to be $1000 billion. If the interest rate is zero, real income is only $2000 billion. But each percentage point increase in the interest rate stretches the available money and makes possible an extra $200 billion of income. Thus an increase in the interest rate from zero to 5 percent at point *G* makes possible an increase in real income by $1000 billion, from $2000 to $3000 billion.

Along any given *LM* curve the level of real money balances (M^s/P) is fixed, but real income (Q) varies. The ratio of real income to real balances is called the **velocity** of money (V):

The **velocity** of money is the ratio of nominal income (PQ) to the money supply (M); it is the average number of times per year that the money stock is used in making payments for final goods and services.

$$\text{velocity } (V) \equiv \frac{Q}{M^s/P} \equiv \frac{PQ}{M^s}$$

The right-hand expression states that velocity is also equal to nominal income (PQ) divided by the nominal supply M^s. The higher the interest rate, the higher is velocity. Why? If r increases, people wish to hold less money. But the money supply is fixed. To maintain equilibrium in the money market, there *must be an increase in income* to induce households to hold the fixed existing quantity of money. Anything that can cause the economy to move up and down along a fixed *LM* curve achieves a change of velocity by altering Q while M^s/P is fixed.

What Makes the *LM* Curve Shift?

The Fed can decide to alter M^s, the nominal money supply. If the price level P is fixed, this will alter the real money supply (M^s/P). In Figure 4-8, for instance, a $500 billion increase in the money supply from $1000 to $1500 billion shifts the *LM* curve from the left-hand dashed line LM_0 to the right-hand solid line LM_1. Since each dollar of extra available money makes possible 2.0 extra dollars of income, the *LM* curve shifts horizontally by $1000 billion.

What Alters the Slope of *LM*?

The slope of *LM* measures the extra dollars of income made possible by a higher interest rate, $200 billion for each 1 percent increase in the interest rate in our example. This is the product of two components, the money-demand responsiveness to a higher interest rate ($100 billion per percentage point), and the number of dollars of extra income needed to absorb each dollar of money released by the higher interest rate (2.0). Thus a

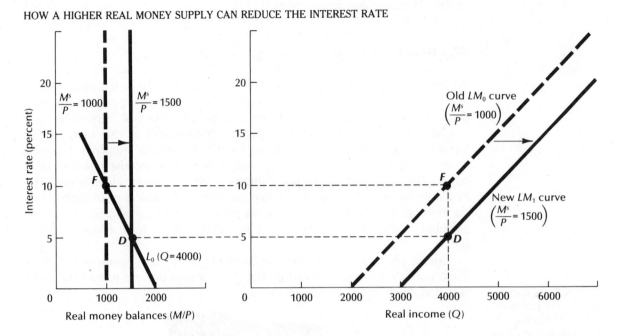

Figure 4-8   **The Effect on the *LM* Curve of an Increase in the Real Money Supply from $1000 Billion to $1500 Billion**
The dashed LM_0 line in the figure is identical to *LM* in Figure 4-7. When the money supply is increased, the money available to support output increases, and the *LM* curve shifts rightward by 2.0 dollars per dollar of extra money to the new line LM_1.

change in either factor will alter the slope of the *LM* curve. The slope of *LM* depends on the responsiveness of money demand to a higher interest rate in the following way:

Responsiveness of money demand to a higher interest rate	Slope of LM schedule
0	Vertical
Small	Steep
Large	Flat
Infinity	Horizontal

4-8   Simultaneous Equilibrium in the Commodity and Money Markets

Equilibrium in the commodity market occurs only at points on the *IS* curve. Figure 4-9 copies the IS_0 schedule from Figure 4-4, drawn for a value of $\overline{A} = 1250$. At any point off the IS_0 curve, for instance, *G* and *F*, the commodity market is out of equilibrium. *C*, *D*, and E_0 all represent different combinations of income and the interest rate that are compatible with commodity-

Figure 4-9
The IS and LM Schedules Cross at Last

The IS_0 schedule is copied from Figure 4-4; the LM_0 schedule from Figure 4-8. Only at the red point E_0 is the economy in a "general" equilibrium, with the conditions for equilibrium attained in both the commodity market (along *IS*) and the money market (along *LM*). At points $U, V, G,$ and F the commodity market is out of equilibrium. At points $U, V, C,$ and D the money market is out of equilibrium.

THE ECONOMY'S "GENERAL" EQUILIBRIUM

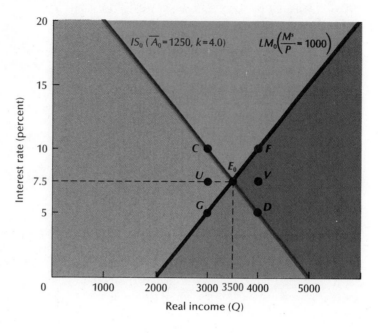

General equilibrium is a situation of simultaneous equilibrium in all the markets of the economy.

market equilibrium. At which equilibrium point will the economy come to rest? The single IS_0 schedule does not provide enough information to determine *both* income and the interest rate. *Two* schedules are needed to pin down the equilibrium values of *two* unknown variables.

The *LM* curve provides the necessary additional information showing all combinations of income and the interest rate at which the money market is in equilibrium for a given real money supply—in this case, $1000 billion. Figure 4-9 copies the LM_0 schedule from Figure 4-8 drawn for a value of $M_0^s/P = 1000$. At any point off the LM_0 curve—for instance, points C and D—the money market is out of equilibrium. At D income is too high and the real demand for money exceeds the real supply. At C income is too low and the real demand for money is below the real supply. Equilibrium in the money market occurs only at points such as $G, F,$ and E_0, each representing combinations of income and the interest rate at which the real demand for money is equal to a real money supply of $1000 billion.

How does the economy arrive at its **general equilibrium** at point E_0 if it starts out at the wrong place, as at points U or V? If the commodity market is out of equilibrium and involuntary inventory decumulation or accumulation occurs, firms will step up or cut production, pushing the economy in the direction needed to reach E_0. If the money market is out of equilibrium, there will be pressure to adjust interest rates, since people will have to sell stocks and bonds if they cannot otherwise satisfy their demand for money. Either way the economy arrives at E_0.

Finding a Solution in Economics

The *LM* curve by itself cannot tell us the level of both income and the interest rate. Why? You cannot find a city like Des Moines on a map if you are given only the number of a road passing through it, say Interstate 80. The city could be anywhere between New York and San Francisco! Instead, you need to know two roads that intersect at Des Moines, say Interstate 80 and Interstate 35. In exactly the same way, the *LM* curve is a single line, like a highway, and is not enough by itself to determine the two unknown magnitudes (*Q* and *r*).

The other line relating the interest rate and income is the *IS* curve of Section 4-4. Together, the *IS* and *LM* curves can determine both income and the interest rate, just as two crossing highways can determine a location on a two-dimensional map. In more formal language, it takes two schedules—the *IS* curve and the *LM* curve—to determine two un-

knowns (*Q* and *r*). If there were three unknowns, three schedules on a three-dimensional graph would be necessary, just as it is necessary to know latitude, longitude, and altitude to find an airplane in a three-dimensional sky.

4-9 Strong and Weak Effects of Monetary Policy

The model thus far developed shows how real income (or GNP) and the interest rate are determined. The exogenous variables, which the model does not explain, are the level of business and consumer optimism, the single instrument of monetary policy (the money supply), the two instruments of fiscal policy (government spending and tax rates), and net exports. In this section we examine the effects of monetary policy.

What level of real GNP does the monetary policymaker (the Fed) desire? We shall assume that the desired level of income, "natural real GNP," is $4000 billion. In Figure 4-9 the equilibrium level of real income (GNP) is only $3500 billion. Thus there is a $500 billion "gap" between actual and natural real GNP that needs to be filled. What should the Fed do?

To raise real GNP by the required $500 billion, the Fed must increase the money supply. By how much depends on the effect of changes in the money supply on real income. This effect may be strong, weak, or anything between, depending on the slopes of the *IS* and *LM* curves.

Strong Effects of an Increase in the Real Money Supply

The top frame of Figure 4-10 repeats the LM_0 curve of Figure 4-9, drawn on the assumption that the real money supply is $1000 billion. Also repeated is the IS_0 curve of Figure 4-9, which assumes that $\overline{A} = 1250$ and $k = 4.0$. The economy's general equilibrium, the point where both the money and commodity markets are in equilibrium, occurs at point E_0.

Figure 4-10
The Effect of a $500 Billion Increase in the Money Supply with a Normal *LM* Curve and a Vertical *LM* Curve

The top frame repeats the $500 billion increase in the money supply that was shown in Figure 4-8. In order to maintain equilibrium in both the commodity and money markets here, two effects occur: equilibrium income rises and the interest rate declines, as indicated by the movement from E_0 to E_1. In the bottom frame, the *LM* curve is vertical and the same $500 billion increase in the money supply shifts the *LM* curve to the right by $1000 billion, leading to a greater drop in the interest rate and a greater increase in equilibrium income.

WHY A VERTICAL *LM* CURVE MAKES MONETARY POLICY MORE POTENT

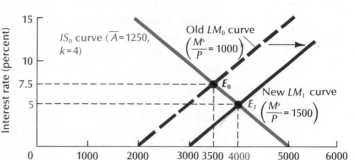

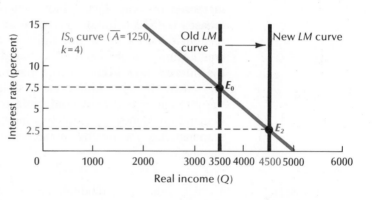

Assume that the Fed raises the nominal money supply from $1000 billion to $1500 billion. As long as the price level stays fixed at 1.0, the real money supply increases by the same amount. The *LM* curve shifts horizontally to the right by $1000 billion. Now, with the new higher real money supply of $1500 billion, there is an "excess supply of money" of $500 billion. How can the economy generate the $500 billion increase in the real demand for money needed to balance the new higher supply?

Finding themselves with more money than they need, individuals transfer some money into savings accounts and use some to buy stocks, bonds, and commodities. This raises the prices of bonds and stocks and reduces the interest rate. The initial decline in interest rates is sometimes called the "liquidity effect" of a monetary expansion. The lower interest rate raises the desired level of autonomous consumption and investment spending, requiring an increase in production. This is the "income effect" of a monetary expansion. Only at point E_1, with an income level of $4000 billion and interest rate of 5 percent, are both the money and commodity markets in equilibrium. Compared to the starting point E_0, the increase in the real money supply has caused both an increase in real income and a reduction in the interest rate, due to the combined impact of the liquidity and income effects.

Interest response of money demand. The size of the drop in the interest rate depends on the interest responsiveness of the demand for money. For instance, if demand is unresponsive, then it takes a very large drop in the interest rate to induce individuals voluntarily to hold the higher money supply. An extreme case is illustrated in the bottom frame of Figure 4-10, where we assume that the demand for money depends only on real income and does not depend on the interest rate at all (as signified by the vertical *LM* curve). Here no interest rate will raise the demand for money even one cent above its initial level at E_0 in response to a $500 billion increase in the real money supply. Because the demand for money depends only on income, then the only way for the demand for money to rise by the necessary $500 billion is for real income to rise by $1000 billion (recall that the demand for money increases by half of the increase in real income). We move down the *IS* curve to a new equilibrium at point E_2.

Now compare the top and bottom frames of Figure 4-10. In both, the real money supply increases by $500 billion. Yet in the top frame income increases by only $500 billion, whereas in the bottom frame income increases by $1000 billion, or twice as much. Why? In the top diagram the responsibility for increasing the demand for money by $500 billion between equilibrium points E_0 and E_1 is shared—half is accomplished by the drop in the interest rate from 7.5 to 5 percent, and the remaining half is accomplished by the $500 billion increase in income. But in the bottom diagram the interest rate cannot contribute to raising money demand because the demand for money is completely independent of the interest rate. The entire responsibility for raising money demand is shouldered by an increase in income.

SELF-TEST   To test your understanding, ask yourself: If the demand for money is independent of the interest rate, is the *LM* curve vertical or horizontal? Does an increase in the money supply have strong or weak effects when the *LM* curve is steeper than normal? Flatter than normal?

Weak Effects of Monetary Policy

Unresponsive expenditures. In some hypothetical circumstances, the Fed is *impotent*. Its control over the money supply does no good, for changes in the money supply do not raise real GNP. One such circumstance, shown in the top frame of Figure 4-11, occurs if the *IS* curve is vertical, that is, if the interest responsiveness of autonomous planned spending (A_p) is zero. This might occur in a severe depression as a result of extreme pessimism about the future privatility of investment. Since income is independent of the interest rate, changes in the interest rate caused by changes in the money supply have no impact on real income. In Figure 4-11 income remains "stuck" at $3500 billion. If such a situation were ever to occur in the United States, the Fed would be impotent, and all eyes would be on the president and Congress, the makers of fiscal policy through their control over government spending and tax rates.

Figure 4-11
Effect of a $500 Billion Increase in the Real Money Supply with a Zero A_p Responsiveness and with a Liquidity Trap

In the top frame the higher money supply does not stimulate expenditures, because expenditures are assumed to be independent of the interest rate, that is, the *IS* curve is vertical. Real income remains "stuck" at $3500 billion. In the lower frame the interest rate is fixed at a minimum level of 2.5 percent, because of a liquidity trap. The increase in the money supply has no impact in lowering the interest rate, and for this reason real income remains stuck at $3500 billion, just as in the top frame.

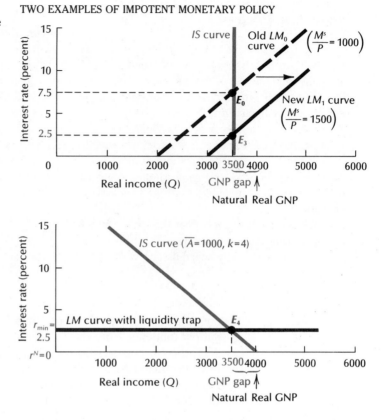

TWO EXAMPLES OF IMPOTENT MONETARY POLICY

Horizontal *LM* curve. Even with the normal, negatively sloped *IS* curve, the Federal Reserve may be unable to push real income as high as natural real GNP. This case of monetary impotence may occur if there is a lower limit to the interest rate. The Fed does not control the interest rate directly; it influences only the money supply. An increase in the money supply usually reduces the interest rate because people try to get rid of their excess money by purchasing stocks and bonds.

But under special conditions, if people are convinced that stock and bond prices are about to fall, they will refuse to purchase stocks and bonds. Instead they just hold their money. In this case, the Fed loses its power over the interest rate, which becomes independent of the money supply. This hypothetical circumstance is called a **liquidity trap.** The *LM* curve becomes a horizontal line, as in the bottom frame of Figure 4-11. With the *IS* curve shown, the economy is "stuck" at point E_4, and real income is $3500 billion instead of the desired level of $4000 billion.

The **liquidity trap** is a situation in which the interest rate does not respond to an expansion of the money supply, making the *LM* curve horizontal.

Only if something occurred to push the *IS* curve sufficiently to the right could the economy attain the desired income level of $4000 billion. One possibility would be a direct effect of the money supply on the *IS* curve, something we have ruled out. Thus far in our analysis, changes in the money supply influence only the *LM* curve, unless as in the bottom frame of Figure 4-11, the *LM* curve is horizontal, meaning that changes in the money supply have no influence. We shall return to the possibility of a direct effect of the money supply on the *IS* curve, sometimes called a "real balance effect," in Chapter 7.

4-10 Crowding Out: The Normal Effect of Fiscal Expansion

In the last section we examined the effects on real income and the interest rate of changes in monetary policy by shifting the *LM* curve along a fixed *IS* curve. Now we shall do the reverse and shift the *IS* curve along a fixed *LM* curve. The original *IS* curve is copied from Figure 4-9 and is labeled in Figure 4-12 as the "old IS_0 curve"; it is drawn on the assumption that the amount of autonomous planned spending that would occur at a zero interest rate ($\overline{A}$) is equal to $1250 billion.

Expansionary Fiscal Policy Shifts the *IS* Curve

Since planned autonomous spending includes government spending, an expansionary fiscal policy taking the form of a $250 billion increase in government purchases raises $\overline{A}$ by the same amount and shifts the *IS* curve to the right. The new *IS* curve is labeled "New IS_1 curve" in Figure 4-12; the $250 billion increase in government spending has boosted $\overline{A}$ from $1250 to $1500 billion. Note that the horizontal distance between the old and new *IS* curves is not $250 billion but $1000 billion, since the horizontal position of *IS* is $\overline{A}$ times the multiplier, still assumed to be 4.0.

Figure 4-12

The Effect on Real Income and the Interest Rate of a $250 Billion Increase in Government Spending

Along the original IS_0 curve autonomous spending desired at a zero interest rate ($\overline{A}$) is 1250, and the economy's equilibrium occurs at point E_0. A $250 billion increase in government spending boosts $\overline{A}$ from 1250 to 1500, and shifts the IS curve rightward to IS_1. The economy's equilibrium slides up the LM curve from point E_0 to point E_5. In contrast to Chapter 3's multiplier of 4.0, now the government spending multiplier is only 2.0. But, since income does increase from E_0 to E_5, crowding out is partial, not complete.

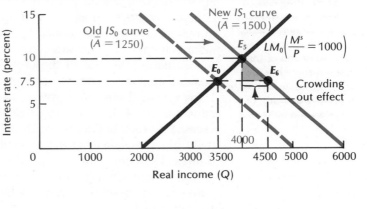

THE CROWDING OUT EFFECT CUTS THE FISCAL MULTIPLIER

Figure 4-12 demonstrates that the effect of an expansionary fiscal policy on real income is not indicated by our original Chapter 3 multiplier ($k = 4.0$) once the money market is taken into consideration. The full fiscal multiplier of $k = 4.0$ would move the economy horizontally from the initial equilibrium position at E_0 to point E_6, where income is $1000 billion higher. At E_6, however, the money market is not in equilibrium, because E_6 is off of the LM_0 curve. Income is higher than at E_0, raising the demand for money, but the real supply of money remains unchanged at the original assumed value $M^s/P = 1000$). There is an excess demand for money. To cut the demand for money back to the level of the fixed supply, the interest rate must rise. But an increase in the interest rate makes point E_6 untenable by reducing planned consumption and investment expenditures. *Only at point E_5 are both the commodity and money markets in equilibrium.* Real income does not increase by the full $1000 billion, but only by half as much, $500 billion.

The higher interest rate accounts for the fact that the fiscal policy multiplier is 2.0, rather than 4.0, when the requirement for money-market equilibrium is taken into account. The increase in the interest rate from 7.5 to 10 percent cuts private autonomous planned consumption and investment spending by $125 billion, fully half of the $250 billion increase in government spending. Thus fully half of the original multiplier of 4.0 is "crowded out."

Comparison of equilibrium positions E_0 and E_5

	Initial E_0	New E_5
Interest rate (r)	7.5	10.0
Private autonomous spending $(I_p + a = 1250 - 50r)$	875	750
Government spending (G)	0	250
Total autonomous spending $(A_p = I_p + a + G)$	875	1000
Income ($Q = 4.0A_p$)	3500	4000

The Crowding Out Effect

The **crowding out effect** describes the effect of an increase in government spending or a reduction of tax rates in reducing the amount of one or more other components of private expenditures.

Some economists and journalists use the phrase **crowding out effect** to compare points such as E_6 and E_5 in Figure 4-12. The $500 billion difference in real income between points E_6 and E_5 represents the investment and consumption spending "crowded out" by the higher interest rate. Point E_6, used in calculating the size of the crowding out effect, is a purely hypothetical position that the economy cannot and does not reach. Actually, far from being crowded out, total private spending is higher in the new equilibrium situation at E_5 than at the original situation at E_0—real income has increased by $500 billion, of which only $250 billion represents higher government purchases, leaving the remaining $250 billion for extra private expenditures. The composition of private spending changes, however, as a result of the higher interest rate. Induced consumption spending increases, but autonomous spending decreases. Expenditures are divided up as follows in the two situations:

	At E_0	At E_5
Government purchases	0	250
Autonomous private spending ($I_p + a$)	875	750
Induced consumption	2625	3000
Total real expenditures	3500	4000

4-11   CASE STUDY: Interest Rates and the Expansion of Vietnam Spending

The 1965–67 period, during which U.S. government spending expanded rapidly as our involvement in the Vietnam War deepened, provides an unusual case study of the consequences of fiscal expansion while the real money supply remains fixed. In the fourth quarter of 1966 (October through December), written as 1966:Q4, the real money supply was almost exactly the same as five quarters earlier, in 1965:Q3. An *LM* curve corresponding to this fixed level of M^s/P is drawn in Figure 4-13. During this five-quarter interval the level of real government purchases grew by 12.2 percent, represented in Figure 4-13 by the rightward shift in the *IS* curve from IS_0 to IS_1.

How did real income and the interest rate behave over the five-quarter interval? Real income increased by $129.9 billion, more than the $60.2 billion increase in government spending, because of the multiplier effect. And the higher demand for money forced an increase in the interest rate from 4.7 to 6.0 percent to keep the total demand for money equal to the fixed real money supply.

The immediate victim of the higher interest rates was investment in residential housing. By 1966:Q4 this component of investment had declined 17.9 percent from the level reached in 1965:Q3. As shown in the table under Figure 4-13, nonresidential investment—including inventory change and expenditures on plant and equipment—continued to grow despite the increase in interest rates through 1966:Q4. The reason for this growth, rather than the "crowding out" that our theory predicts, stems from the *delay* between the increase in the interest rate and the subsequent decline

Figure 4-13

Real Income and the Interest Rate during a Period of Expanding Government Expenditures, 1965:Q3 to 1966:Q4

In both 1965:Q3 and 1966:Q4 the economy was on the same *LM* curve because the real money supply was identical in both periods. But government spending was much higher in the second period, so that the *IS* curve was much farther to the right. One consequence of the rightward shift of the *IS* curve was to raise the interest rate in order to release extra money to support the higher level of transactions in 1966:Q4.

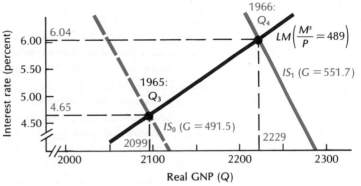

THE CROWDING OUT EFFECT IN ACTION

	Real income	Real government expenditures	Real residential investment	Real nonresidential investment	Real money supply	Interest rate, Moody's Aaa (%)
1965:Q3	2099.3	491.5	113.3	256.5	489.0	4.65
1966:Q4	2229.2	551.7	91.4	293.7	488.4	6.04
1967:Q2	2255.2	573.1	99.3	262.4	497.7	5.85

Note: All real magnitudes in 1982 prices.

Source: The National Income and Product Accounts of the United States, 1985 revision.

in nonresidential investment, a factor our *IS-LM* model does not take into account. The table shows that in the subsequent two quarters, between 1966:Q4 and 1967:Q2, nonresidential investment dropped back almost to its original level of 1965:Q3, despite the fact that the real money supply began to grow again and the interest rate declined a bit from its peak level.

A basic principle of economics holds that a wartime economy cannot boost military spending without decreasing civilian expenditures; that is, the economy "cannot have both guns and butter." In this case the economy could not have both "guns and houses." The principle is not true in a recession or depression. But it is true when the economy is fully utilizing its resources, as in 1965–66. Through the end of 1966 this age-old rule was enforced by the tightness of monetary policy through high interest rates and the stable level of the real money supply. An increase in tax rates to pay for wartime expenditures would have achieved the same results.

In 1967 and early 1968 the economy tried to have *both* "guns and butter." President Lyndon Johnson delayed proposing a tax increase, which was not finally approved by Congress until July 1968. Consequently, the money supply began to grow rapidly, and this allowed private spending as well as defense spending to grow. The excessive spending growth of 1967–68 in an economy that was straining at the limit of its productive capacity unleashed a serious inflation. Many analysts think that an underlying cause of the inflation suffered by the United States since the late 1960s dates back to President Johnson's refusal to "pay for" the Vietnam War in 1966.

4-12 Strong and Weak Effects of Fiscal Policy

The effect of a fiscal policy stimulus on real income may be either greater or less than in the numerical example of Figure 4-12, depending on the slopes of the *IS* and *LM* curves. Fiscal policy is strong when the demand for money is highly interest-responsive, as illustrated in the top frame of Figure 4-14, were we choose the largest possible responsiveness, infinity. This makes the *LM* curve horizontal, so that the multiplier becomes just the simple multiplier (4.0) of Chapter 3.

The opposite situation occurs when the interest responsiveness of money demand is zero, which makes the *LM* curve vertical. An increase in government spending by $250 billion shifts the *IS* curve to the right in the bottom frame of Figure 4-12 exactly as in the top frame, but real income cannot increase without throwing the money market out of equilibrium. Even $1 of extra income above $3500 billion raises money demand, but because of the zero interest responsiveness of money demand, there is no increase in the interest rate that can bring money demand back into balance

Figure 4-14
Effect of a $250 Billion Fiscal Stimulus When Money Demand Has an Infinite and a Zero Interest Responsiveness

In the top frame an increase in government spending has exactly the same effect as in Figure 3-7 with the full multiplier effect of 4.0. An infinite interest responsiveness means only that the interest rate is fixed, and no crowding out can occur. In contrast, the same fiscal stimulus has no effect on income when the interest responsiveness is zero (bottom frame), because then a higher interest rate releases no extra money to support higher income, and the income level is completely determined by the size of the real money supply. Since the fiscal stimulus causes no growth at all in income from E_0 to E_7, crowding out is complete.

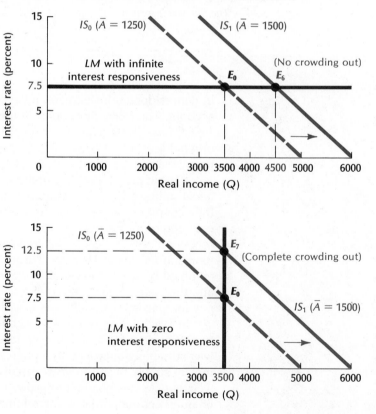

WHY THE INTEREST RESPONSIVENESS OF MONEY DEMAND MATTERS SO MUCH FOR THE POTENCY OF FISCAL POLICY

with the fixed money supply. In this case, the only effect of a fiscal stimulus is to raise the interest rate. The crowding out effect is complete, with the higher interest rate cutting autonomous private spending by exactly the amount by which government spending increases.

Which diagram is the most accurate depiction of the effects of expansionary fiscal policy with a fixed real money supply: Figure 4-12, the top frame of Figure 4-14, or the bottom frame of Figure 4-14? The case study of the Vietnam War period suggests that the original analysis of Figure 4-12 is accurate—that the crowding out effect is partial rather than complete or nonexistent. Further, statistical evidence shows that the interest responsiveness of the demand for money is neither zero nor infinity. For this reason we should regard Figure 4-12 as giving a reliable example of the effects of expansionary fiscal policy, while Figure 4-14 is a depiction of two artificial extreme cases rather than a realistic possibility.

Summary of crowding out. The fundamental cause of crowding out is an increase in the interest rate caused by a fiscal policy stimulus. Crowding out can be avoided only if there is no upward pressure on the interest rate when the IS curve shifts rightward, and this requires a horizontal LM curve as in the top frame of Figure 4-14. In this frame, there is zero crowding out.

Crowding out can be either partial or complete. If there is any increase in real income in response to the fiscal policy stimulus, crowding out is partial. This is shown in Figure 4-12, where the economy's equilibrium level of income increases from point E_0 to E_5. If there is no increase in income at all in response to the fiscal policy stimulus, then crowding out is complete. This occurs in the bottom frame of Figure 4-14, where there is absolutely no increase in income at the new point E_7 as compared with the initial point E_0.

SUMMARY

1. Interest rates allocate the supply of funds available from savers to alternative borrowers. Not only do private households and firms borrow in order to buy consumption and investment goods, but the government also borrows to finance its budget deficit.

2. Private planned autonomous spending (A_p) depends partly on the interest rate. The higher the interest rate, the lower is A_p.

3. Private planned autonomous spending (A_p) also depends on the optimism or pessimism of investors and consumers about the future. An increase in optimism tends to raise A_p for any given level of the interest rate.

4. The IS curve indicates all the combinations of the interest rate and real income at which the economy's commodity market is in equilibrium. At any point off the IS curve the economy is out of equilibrium.

5. The real quantity of money that people demand depends both on real income and on the interest rate. Equilibrium in the money market requires that the real supply of money equal the demand for real money.

6. The LM curve represents all the combinations of real income and of the interest rate where the money market is in equilibrium.

7. Normally an increase in the money supply raises real income and reduces the interest rate. Monetary policy has a stronger effect on real income when the interest responsiveness of the demand for money is zero. Monetary policy is impotent either when the interest responsiveness of autonomous spending is zero, or when a liquidity trap makes the LM curve horizontal.

8. Normally a fiscal expansion raises real income and the interest rate, causing "crowding out." Fiscal policy is strongest when the LM curve is horizontal and impotent when the LM curve is vertical.

rate of return
IS curve
spending responsiveness
money supply
LM curve

real money balances
velocity
general equilibrium
liquidity trap
crowding out effect

QUESTIONS AND PROBLEMS

Questions

1. Which among the exogenous variables listed in question 1 at the end of Chapter 3 have become endogenous given the most complete model used in Chapter 4? Is this true as well for autonomous consumption expenditures? Velocity? Have any other endogenous variables been introduced in this Chapter? Exogenous variables?

2. In early 1989, many economists and economic forecasters predicted that a major recession would occur sometime in late 1989 or early 1990. How might these forecasts have affected the actual performance of the economy?

3. During the 1980s, the size of the federal government debt became so large that servicing the interest payments became a significant portion of total federal expenditures. In response, many congressmen felt that the federal deficit needed to be reduced. If government spending (*G*) became (negatively) sensitive to changes in the interest rate, what effect would this have on the slope of the *IS* curve? If autonomous taxes ($\overline{T}$) became (positively) sensitive to changes in the interest rate, what effect would this have on the slope of the *IS* curve?

4. A change in which of the following would cause the *IS* curve to shift? The *IS* curve to rotate? The *IS* curve to both shift and rotate? Which have no effect on the position or slope of the *IS* curve?
   (a) Planned autonomous expenditures ($\overline{A}$)
   (b) Marginal tax rate ($\overline{t}$)
   (c) Marginal propensity to save (s)
   (d) Share of imports in GNP (x)
   (e) Interest rate
   (f) Money supply
   (g) Money demand
   (h) Marginal leakage rate (MLR)
   (i) Multiplier (k)

   (j) Interest sensitivity of autonomous planned expenditures
   (k) Business and consumer confidence

5. Describe the automatic adjustment that will take place in the economy when the current position of the economy is "off" the *IS* curve.

6. Describe the automatic adjustment that will take place in the economy when the current position of the economy is "off" the *LM* curve.

7. Why is the distinction between autonomous expenditures and induced expenditures crucial to the understanding of the crowding out effect?

8. Under what circumstances would it be possible for government spending (federal, state, local, etc.) to be "crowded out"? Do you think this is likely to be the case?

9. What is the velocity of money? What happens to the velocity of money when the economy moves along the *LM* curve? Calculate the velocity for 1965:Q3 and 1966:Q4 implied in Figure 4-13.

10. Describe the situation in the commodity market and the money market at point *V* in Figure 4-9. What will happen to the economy if the current position is at point *V* in Figure 4-9?

11. The effectiveness of fiscal policy may be limited if the demand for money is insensitive to the interest rate. The effectiveness of monetary policy may be limited if planned autonomous spending is insensitive to the interest rate. Explain.

12. If the *LM* curve is vertical can there be any crowding out? If the *IS* curve is vertical can there be any crowding out? Considering the slopes of both the *IS* and *LM* curves, under what circumstances is the crowding out effect the largest?

Problems

1. The equation of the *IS* curve is given by the following formula: $Q = k\bar{A} - (b/\text{MLR})\, r$, where
   $\underline{k}$ = the multiplier
   $\bar{A}$ = planned autonomous spending at a zero interest rate
   b = interest responsiveness of planned autonomous expenditures
   $\underline{\text{MLR}}$ = the marginal leakage rate $[s(1 - \bar{t}) + \bar{t} + x]$
   r = the interest rate
   Using the information above, and given that the following equations summarize the structure of the commodity market:
   $C = a + .75Q_D$; $a = 50 - 10r$;
   $T = 200 + .2Q$; $I_p = 300 - 30r$; $G = 400$
   (a) What is the value of the multiplier (k)?
   (b) What is the coefficient for the interest sensitivity of planned autonomous spending?
   (c) What is the equation for planned autonomous spending (A_p)?
   (d) What is the equation for the *IS* curve?
   (e) What is the slope of the *IS* curve?
   (f) If government spending increases by 50, at what value on the horizontal axis does the new *IS* curve intersect it? What happens to the slope of the *IS* curve?

2. The equation of the *LM* curve is given by the following formula: $Q = (M^s/P)/h + (f/h)\, r$, where:
   M^s/P = real money supply
   h = response of money demanded to a $1 change in income at a fixed interest rate
   f = response of money demand to a one percentage point change in the interest rate
   Using the information above, and given that the following equations summarize the structure of the money market:
   $M^s/P = 300$; $h = 0.4$; $f = 50$
   (a) What is the horizontal intercept of the *LM* curve?
   (b) What is the slope of the *LM* curve?
   (c) What is the equation of the *LM* curve?
   (d) If the Fed increased the money supply by 100, at what value on the horizontal axis would the *LM* curve intersect it? What happens to the slope of the *LM* curve?

3. Using the information contained in questions 1 and 2 concerning the structure of the economy, what is the equilibrium level of income and the equilibrium rate of interest
   (a) in the initial situation (i.e., $G = 400, M^s/P = 300$)?

   (b) if G increases to 450? What is the amount of autonomous spending that is "crowded out" in this situation? What happens to velocity?
   (c) if M^s/P increases to 400?
   (d) if both G and M^s/P increase (i.e., $G = 450$, $M^s/P = 400$)?

4. Assume that the economy is initially in equilibrium at a level of real output (Q) of $5,000 and an interest rate (r) of 5%. If as a result of an increase in government spending of $500, the economy moves to a new equilibrium at $Q = $5,750$, $r = 6.5\%$ (and given that the multiplier, k, is 3), how much autonomous spending was "crowded out" due to the increase in interest rates? What is the value of the coefficient for interest rate responsiveness of planned autonomous spending?

5. Assume that the following equations summarize the structure of the economy:

   $C = a + 0.8Q$ $(M/P)^d = .2Q - 20r$
   $a = 160 - 10r$ $M^s = 160$
   $I_p = 240 - 10r$ $P = 1$

   (a) What is the equation for the *IS* curve for this economy?
   (b) What is the equation for the *LM* curve for this economy?
   (c) What is the equilibrium level of output for the economy?
   (d) What is the equilibrium interest rate for the economy?
   (e) What is the level of consumption at equilibrium?
   (f) What is the level of investment at equilibrium?
   (g) Assume that the economy is at the following point:

   $$r = 4, \quad Q = 1200$$

   Is there excess demand for money or excess supply of money in this situation? How much?
   Are there unintended inventory changes taking place? If so, what is the value of the unintended inventory changes?
   (h) Assume that the economy is at the following point:

   $$r = 4, \quad Q = 1600$$

   Is there excess demand for money or excess supply of money in this situation? How much?
   Are there unintended inventory changes taking place? If so, what is the value of the unintended inventory changes?

p. 94 An interest rate of 5 percent generates $1000 billion in autonomous planned spending in the lower left-hand frame at point D. When multiplied by the multiplier ($k = 4$) and interest rate of 5 percent generates $4000 billion in output in the lower right-hand frame at point D.

p. 98 No, a change in the interest rate (r) does not cause the IS curve to shift. When there is a change in a variable already plotted on the axes, Q and r in this case, we move along a schedule like the IS curve. If a change occurs in an element relevant to the graph, but *not* on the axes, the line shifts. This is true of any graphic line or curve.[6]

p. 102 The evel of income (Q) and of the interest rate on assets other than money (r) are the two determinants of the real demand for money ($M/P)^d$. An increase in Q raises the real demand for money and an increase in the interest rate reduces the real demand for money. Neither determinant shifts the IS curve, because the axes of the IS curve diagram are these very determinants, Q and r.

p. 104 In going from D to F, the interest rate rises form 5 to 10 percent, and the demand for money decreases by the interest resonsiveness (100) times the change in the interest rate (5), that is, by 500. In going from D to G, the level of real income falls from 4000 to 3000. The demand for money decreases by the income responsiveness (0.5) times the change in real income (1000), that is, by 500.

p. 110 Check the box on p. 112. If the demand for money is independent of the interest rate, the variable on the vertical axis, then the LM curve is vertical. An increase in the money supply has strong effect when the LM curve is steeper than normal, as occurs in the bottom frame of Figure 4-10. An increase in the money supply hs weak effects when the LM curve is flatter than normal, as occurs in the bottom frame of Figure 4-11.

---

[6]The line shifts only if the change is in a variable not on the axes that matters for the relationship being plotted. Here, for instance, a change in $\bar{A}$ or k will shift IS, but a change in the money supply will not.

CHAPTER FIVE

The Twin Deficits:
The Government Budget and
Foreign Trade in the *IS-LM* Model

Virtually everything is under federal control nowadays except the federal budget.
—Herman Talmadge, 1975

5-1 The New Importance of the "Twin Deficits"

The book began by defining six central macroeconomic concepts, two of which are the government budget deficit and the foreign trade deficit. Prior to the 1980s budget deficits mainly occurred during recession years, and the U.S. trade balance was normally in surplus. The 1980s, however, were the decade of persistent budget and trade deficits. Alternative proposals to bring the "twin deficits" into balance dominated the discussion of economic policy in the late 1980s. And economists had begun a heated debate whether the twin deficits were a large problem, small problem, or no problem at all.

Our central task in this chapter is to understand the basic economics of the twin deficits. We begin with the budget deficit and learn to distinguish between two basic causes of changes in the deficit—the effects of the business cycle and of discretionary fiscal policy, that is, changes in government spending and tax rates. We then study which of these two main causes can account for the persistence of budget deficits in the 1980s. Turning to the trade deficit, we trace the interactions between the budget and trade deficits, working through interest rates and the **foreign exchange rate.** We examine the effects of fiscal policy in an economy that trades with other nations and find that the impact of foreign trade augments the crowding out effect studied at the end of the last chapter.

The **foreign exchange rate** is the amount of another nation's money that residents of a country can obtain in exchange for a unit of their own money.

In Chapter 3 the economic theory explained the level of real income—the main endogenous variable. The development of the *IS-LM* model in Chapter 4 introduced the interest rate as an additional endogenous variable, determined by the model. The price level was still held fixed and exogenous, as it is in this chapter. The new endogenous variable added in this chapter is the foreign exchange rate, which in turn helps (along with income) determine net exports. The monetary and fiscal policy variables—the real money supply, real government expenditures, and tax rates—continue to be exogenous parameters that can be set at any desired value by the government.

121

5-2 The Government Budget and Its Pervasive Effects

The **government budget deficit** is the excess of government spending on goods and services over net tax revenue, and the **government budget surplus** is the reverse.

Each year the government sets its budget. If revenue exceeds expenditures, there is a **government budget surplus.** If expenditures exceed revenue, there is a **government budget deficit.** In the United States in the 1980s, rising expenditures combined with reductions in some tax rates created a substantial increase in the federal government's budget deficit. This episode stands as a prominent example that illustrates the effects of an expansionary fiscal policy.

Crowding Out of Net Exports

Crowding out of net exports by expansionary fiscal policy was perhaps the leading macroeconomic issue of the 1980s—not just in the United States but in the rest of the world. For the United States, the crowding out of net exports occurred when higher interest rates pushed up the value of the foreign exchange rate between 1980 and 1985. As the dollar become more valuable, foreigners had to pay more of their own currencies in order to buy U.S. exports. American consumers and business firms had to pay fewer dollars to purchase imported goods.

American firms attempting to sell exports abroad, or attempting to compete with imports, saw customers vanish and sales plummet. This in turn meant a shrinkage of employment in American manufacturing firms. Many firms went out of business, creating job losses not just for manufacturing workers but also for executives and middle managers, and creating financial losses for stockholders as well. The "strong" (that is, valuable) dollar also hurt U.S. farmers, because goods sold overseas yielded smaller profits.

A **protectionist** measure raises tariffs or quotas on foreign goods in an attempt to reduce imports.

The plight of American manufacturers and farmers brought forth numerous **protectionist** proposals to stem the import tide by raising tariffs on foreign goods or by imposing quotas to limit the quantity of imported goods. The desire to avert the protectionist sentiment and maintain free trade in the United States led to renewed interest in reducing the federal government's budget deficit, which was the original cause of the strong dollar and the foreign trade problem.

The U.S. government budget deficit not only had profound effects on the American manufacturing and farm sectors, but also influenced economic activity in many foreign nations. Expansionary fiscal policy raised interest rates and the value of the dollar. While foreigners experienced higher export sales as U.S. imports soared in response to the strong dollar, domestic sales in some foreign economies were depressed by the effects of higher U.S. interest rates. In less-developed countries with heavy debts to banks in the industrialized world, high interest rates raised the burden of repayment and brought several nations close to default.

Why Did the Falling Dollar Fail to Cure the Foreign Trade Deficit?

Between 1985 and 1988 the value of the dollar fell dramatically, entirely reversing its previous rise from 1980 to 1985. Since America's foreign trade had been balanced in 1980, many economists expected that the reversal of the dollar's rise would return the foreign trade balance from a large deficit to a modest deficit or even a surplus. Yet the deficit remained high, raising new questions for economic analysis. Some economists suggested that in addition to a decline in the exchange rate, a decline in the government budget deficit was also necessary to correct the trade deficit. To understand the interrelations between the twin deficits, we start with the government budget deficit, and subsequently analyze the connections between that deficit and interest rates, the foreign exchange rate, and the foreign trade deficit.

5-3   CASE STUDY: The U.S. Government Budget Deficit in Historical Perspective

The government budget deficit is defined as government expenditures minus government revenue. Throughout history the largest deficits have been incurred as a result of wars, when government expenditures tend to increase more than government tax revenue. Governments choose not to pay the full cost of wars through taxation, for fear that heavy taxes will demoralize citizens when their utmost efforts are needed for war production.

The top frame of Figure 5-1 plots U.S. government real expenditures (including transfer payments) and revenues, both as a percentage of natural real GNP, for this century. The difference between expenditures and revenue is shaded, with pink shading indicating a government budget deficit and gray shading indicating a government budget surplus. Included is not just the federal government budget, but also the budgets of the state and local governments.

Wars and the Increasing Size of Government

Four facts stand out in the top frame. First, government expenditures exhibit a marked "spike" in war years, with World War II having a much greater impact than World War I. Second, tax revenues also exhibit a spike in wartime, but a smaller spike than expenditures so that deficits increase in wartime. Third, the size of government has increased in the years since World War II, as compared with the years before 1930, with real expenditures averaging about 30 percent of natural real GNP and edging up to about 35 percent in the 1980s. Fourth, most of the shading is pink, indicating that the government budget has been in deficit in many more years than it has been in surplus.

The middle frame shows the government budget deficit and surplus. The areas in pink and gray shading in the middle frame are identical to the corresponding areas in the top frame. Here the tendency of wars to create deficits is even more evident. If the graph extended back to the eighteenth century, we would see that substantial deficits also occurred during the Revolutionary War, the War of 1812, and the Civil War. Graphs for other nations would also show increased government spending during wars, for instance, the Napoleonic wars for Britain and France.

The deficits after 1955 pale in comparison with the gigantic deficit of World War II. To compare more clearly the deficits that have occurred since 1955, the period 1955–88 is magnified in the bottom frame. Here we

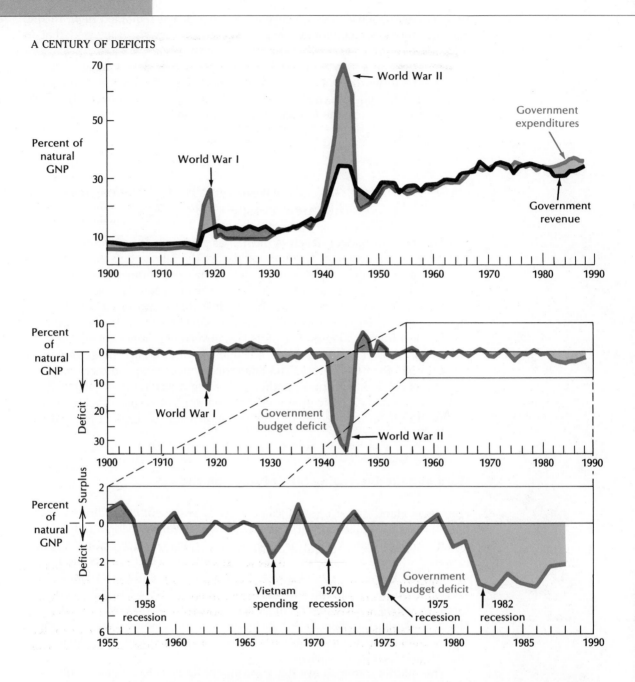

Figure 5-1 **Real Government Expenditures, Real Government Revenues, and the Real Government Budget Deficit, 1900–88**

The top frame compares real government expenditures and revenues as a share of natural GNP, showing the dramatic effects of wars and also the gradual increase in the expenditure share in the 1970s and 1980s. The middle frame shows the government budget deficit for the century, and the bottom frame magnifies the deficit experience of the 1955–88 period, which calls attention to the unusual post-1982 deficits that involve neither war nor recession.

see three relatively small deficits in 1958, 1967, and 1970–72, and two substantially larger deficits incurred in 1975–77 and 1980–88. Only the 1967 deficit resulted from a war-related spending increase—in this case the Vietnam War.

The Effect of Recessions

What caused the other post-1955 episodes when the government budget plunged sharply into deficit? The most important factor was recession. Recession is defined in Chapter 1 as the interval between the "peak" of real GNP in a business cycle and the subsequent "trough" of real GNP. In a recession, when real GNP is falling, government revenues decline and transfer payments increase. Sales decline, reducing government revenue from the sales tax. Incomes decline, reducing government revenue from the income tax. Corporate profits decline, reducing government revenue from the corporate income tax, and government transfer payments, especially unemployment benefits, increase. Notice in the bottom frame how deficits occurred during the recessions of 1958, 1970, 1975, and 1982.

If government deficits had frequently been associated with recessions in the past, why did the deficits of the 1980s create so much controversy? The answer is visible in the bottom frame of Figure 5-1. Each of the previous recession deficit episodes has a sharp "V" shape, and the government budget deficit quickly dropped to zero as the economy recovered after each previous recession. But 1983–88 was different. As the economy recovered after the 1982 recession, the *government budget deficit became larger, not smaller,* reaching a peak in mid-1986. After 1986 the deficit fell but remained large by historical standards. These large 1983–88 deficits occurred in peacetime, not in wartime, and in a situation of economic recovery and expansion rather than recession. We shall see later why the 1983–88 deficits occurred.

5-4   Structural and Cyclical Budget Deficits

The **cyclical deficit** is the amount by which the actual government budget deficit exceeds the **structural deficit,** which in turn is defined as what the deficit *would be* if the economy were operating at natural real GNP.

In this section we distinguish between two types of change in the government budget deficit. The first type is called a **cyclical deficit** and occurs *automatically* as a result of the business cycle: recessions cause government revenues to shrink and the cyclical deficit to grow; this condition is followed by recoveries and expansions that cause government revenues to grow and the cyclical deficit to shrink. The second type is called a **structural deficit;** this is the deficit that remains after the effect of the business cycle is separated out. The structural deficit is calculated by assuming that current levels of government spending and tax rates remain in effect but that the economy is operating at natural real GNP rather than the actual observed level of real GNP.

Automatic Stabilization

In Chapter 3 we learned to define the government budget surplus in the presence of an income tax as follows:

$$\text{budget surplus} = T - G = \overline{T} + tQ - G \qquad (3.32)$$

where T is real tax revenue net of transfer payments, $\overline{T}$ is autonomous tax revenue, t is the income tax rate, and G is real government spending on goods and services. Since autonomous tax revenue plays no role in the analysis of this chapter, it is convenient to rewrite (3.32) by assuming that T is simply proportional to Q as follows:

$$\text{budget surplus} = T - G = tQ - G \qquad (5.1)$$

The government budget deficit is simply a negative value of the surplus, as defined in (5.1). The purpose of writing the government budget surplus or deficit in this way is to distinguish two main sources of change in the surplus or deficit, (1) **automatic stabilization** through changes in Q and (2) **discretionary fiscal policy** through changes in G and t (where t is the ratio of T to Q).

Automatic stabilization occurs because government tax revenues depend on income, causing the economy to be stabilized by the leakage of tax revenues from the spending stream when income rises or falls.

Discretionary fiscal policy alters tax rates and/or government expenditure in a deliberate attempt to influence real output and the unemployment rate.

When real GNP increases in an economic expansion, the government surplus automatically rises as more tax revenues are generated. The higher surplus (or lower deficit) helps to stabilize the economy, since the extra tax revenues that are generated by rising incomes leak out of the spending stream and help restrain the boom. Similarly, tax revenues drop in a recession, cutting the leakages out of the spending stream and helping dampen the recession.

The **automatic stabilization** effect of real income or GNP (Q) on the government surplus or deficit is illustrated in Figure 5-2. The horizontal axis is real income and the vertical axis is the government budget surplus and deficit. In the gray area above the zero level on the vertical axis, the government runs a surplus with tax revenues exceeding expenditures. In the pink area below zero, the government runs a deficit with expenditures exceeding tax revenues. Along the horizontal line separating the gray and pink areas, the government budget is balanced with expenditures exactly equal to tax revenues. To simplify the exposition, we have not included specific numerical values along the vertical axis. What is important is the *direction* of move-

---

Figure 5-2
The Relation between the Government Budget Surplus or Deficit and Real Income

In the gray area the government budget is in surplus, while in the pink area the government budget is in deficit. The budget line BB_0 shows all the levels of the government budget surplus or deficit that are compatible with a given level of government expenditures (G_0) and tax rate (t_0). The BB line slopes upward to the right, because as we move rightward the higher real income (Q) raises tax revenues (t_0Q), thus increasing the surplus or reducing the deficit.

HOW THE ECONOMY INFLUENCES THE BUDGET

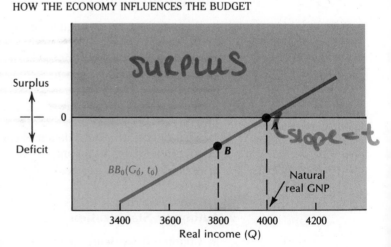

ment, with the government budget surplus rising as we move in an upward direction on the diagram and declining as we move downward.

The **budget line** shows the government budget surplus or deficit at different levels of real income.

The red upward-sloping BB_0 schedule is the **budget line,** which illustrates the automatic stabilization relationship between the government budget and real income when the other determinants of the budget in equation (5.1) are constant, that is, G and t. The budget line BB_0 has a slope equal to the tax rate t. In Figure 5-2 the budget line BB_0 is drawn so that the government runs a balanced budget at point A, when real income is equal to natural real GNP, assumed to be \$4000 billion. If the economy were to fall from \$4000 billion to \$3800 billion, the economy would move from point A to point B, where the government is running a deficit because its tax revenues have fallen by the tax rate t times the \$200 billion drop in real income.

Discretionary Fiscal Policy

The second source of change in the government budget deficit comes from alterations in government spending (G) and in the tax rate (t). It is evident from equation (5.1) that a decline in government spending (G) reduces the budget deficit while a decrease in the tax rate (t) raises the deficit. How do such discretionary changes affect the budget line? Figure 5-3 copies the budget line BB_0 from Figure 5-2. The initial budget line BB_0 is drawn on the assumption that government spending is G_0. An increase in government spending from G_0 to G_1 shifts the red budget line downward for any given level of real income, since at a given level of income the government spends more and has a higher deficit at G_1 compared to the original spending level G_0. The new budget line is shown in the position BB_1.

↓G, ↓deficit

↓t, ↑deficit

Figure 5-3
Effect on the Budget Line of an Increase in Government Expenditures

The upper budget line BB_0 is copied from Figure 5-2 and assumes a value for government spending of G_0. The lower budget line BB_1 assumes that the level of government spending has increased to G_1, an amount larger than G_0, thus reducing the government budget surplus or increasing the government budget deficit at every level of real income.

Slope shows "automatic stabilization"

reduce G

DOES THE BUDGET INFLUENCE THE ECONOMY, OR DOES THE ECONOMY INFLUENCE THE BUDGET?

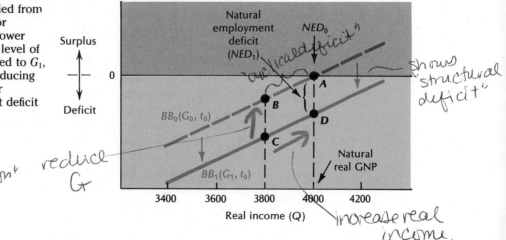

shows structural deficit

increase real income.

Find point C along the new budget line BB_1. This shows that at the new higher level of government spending G_1 the budget would have a large deficit at a real income level of $3800 billion. There are three ways to reduce the deficit. One way, shown by a movement from C to D, would be to increase real income. The second way, shown by a movement from C to B, would be to reduce government spending. A third way, not shown separately, would be to increase the tax rate (t), which would also shift the budget line up.[1] Clearly, changes in the actual budget deficit provide no measure of discretionary fiscal policy actions (that is, changes in government spending and the tax rate), since the actual budget deficit can also change as real income increases or decreases with no change in tax rates or government expenditures.

The Natural Employment Surplus or Deficit

The **natural employment deficit** is government expenditures minus a hypothetical figure for government revenue, calculated by applying current tax rates to natural real GNP rather than actual real GNP.

Since the actual budget surplus or deficit cannot identify discretionary fiscal policy changes, how can we determine a single number that can summarize the effect of fiscal policy on the economy? In the diagram the fact that the budget line BB_1 represents a more expansionary fiscal policy is evident from the fact that its vertical position is *lower* than that of the original budget line BB_0. Thus its expansionary effect can be summarized by describing the vertical position of the budget line at some standard agreed-upon level of real income, for instance, when real income is equal to natural real GNP.

The budget surplus or deficit at the natural level of real GNP is called the natural employment surplus or the **natural employment deficit** (NED). It is defined as the government budget deficit that *would* occur *if* actual real GNP (Q) were equal to natural real GNP (Q^N). If we substitute natural real GNP (Q^N) for actual real GNP in equation (5.1), we can define the natural employment surplus as:

$$\text{natural employment surplus} = tQ^N - G \tag{5.2}$$

The natural employment deficit is simply a negative value of the surplus in (5.2) and changes when there is a change in government spending (G), the tax rate (t), or natural real GNP itself (Q^N).

In Figure 5-3 there is a different natural employment deficit for each of the two budget lines shown. For the original budget line BB_0, the natural employment deficit is abbreviated NED_0. The value of NED_0 is zero, since along BB_0 the government budget is in balance when the economy is operating at natural real GNP—assumed to be $4000 billion. For the new budget line BB_1, the natural employment deficit is NED_1 and is shown by the distance AD, since along BB_1 the government deficit is the amount AD when the economy is operating at natural real GNP.

We can now review the major budget concepts with the help of Figure 5-3. The "actual budget deficit" is shown by the economy's actual position along the appropriate BB line in Figure 5-3, for instance at points like B or C. The "natural employment deficit" is the deficit along each budget line

---

[1] An increase in the tax rate *rotates* the budget line, shifting it upward while making it steeper. A reduction in the tax rate shifts the budget line down while making it flatter.

measured at the natural level of real GNP. The "structural deficit" is another name for the natural employment deficit and changes whenever there is a change in government expenditures or tax rates. The "cyclical deficit" is the difference between the actual deficit and the natural employment deficit, the vertical distance between A and B along budget line BB_0, and the vertical distance between D and C along budget line BB_1. "Automatic stabilization" is represented by the slope of the budget line, since higher tax rates make the budget line steeper and cause a greater percentage of real income to leak out of the spending stream whenever real income expands.

SELF-TEST How would the following be shown in Figure 5-3? More spending for "Star Wars"? An increase in the social security tax rate? An increase in social security benefits? A recession that increases the unemployment rate from 5 to 10 percent? What effect would each of these have on the natural employment deficit?

The Actual and Natural Employment Deficits: Historical Behavior

We are now prepared to take another look at the history of fiscal policy in the last thirty years. The red line in Figure 5-4 is copied from the bottom frame of Figure 5-1 and displays the actual government budget outcome. Pink shading indicates the size of the government budget deficit. The new element in Figure 5-4 is the natural employment surplus or deficit, shown by the black line.

The black line isolates the structural component of the budget deficit. The distance between the red and black lines represents the cyclical component of the deficit. When the red line is underneath the black line, as in 1958, 1975–77, and 1980–86, the economy was weak, with actual real GNP falling below natural real GNP. Recessions occurred in 1958, 1960–61, 1970, 1975, and 1982. In addition, the red line remains beneath the black line for several years after the 1975 and 1982 recessions because the economic expansions that followed those recessions were not strong enough to bring actual real GNP back to the level of natural real GNP. When the red line is above the black line the economy was prosperous, with actual real GNP greater than natural real GNP. Primary examples of periods with a high level of actual real GNP are 1955–56, 1965–69, 1973, and 1988–89.

The black natural employment deficit line highlights two periods when there was a large structural budget deficit. The first occurred in 1966–68 as the result of an expansion in defense spending for the Vietnam War. The Vietnam structural deficit was mostly eliminated after 1968 by a surcharge on the federal income tax. A surcharge, like any increase in the tax rate, shifts up the budget line and reduces the natural employment deficit (Figure 5-3); the corresponding fact in Figure 5-4 is the marked upward movement in the natural employment deficit line that occurred in 1968–69.

A second and even greater structural deficit occurred after 1982, as is indicated in Figure 5-4 by the label "Reagan Era Deficits." In 1981 Congress approved a Reagan administration plan to reduce income tax rates in several stages between 1982 and 1984. As this plan was put into action and

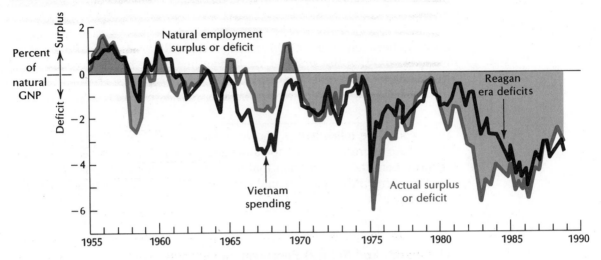

Figure 5-4   **A Comparison of the Actual Budget and Natural Employment Budget, 1955–88**

The black "Natural Employment Surplus or Deficit" line lies above the red "Actual Surplus or Deficit" line in years when the economy was weak and lies below when the economy was strong. The two main periods exhibiting a natural employment deficit were 1966–68, due to Vietnam spending, and 1983–88, due to the Reagan administration's program of combining a defense buildup with tax cuts.

tax rates declined, government revenues fell (as a percentage of GNP) and the structural budget deficit widened. In the late 1980s the structural deficit declined slightly but still persisted at a high level by historical standards.

5-5   The Government Budget, Monetary Policy, and the Policy Mix

A crucial step in understanding the links between the government budget deficit and foreign trade deficit is to determine the impact of discretionary fiscal policy actions on the interest rate. Will tax cuts and spending increases, like those instituted by the Reagan Administration in 1981–86, raise the interest rate or leave it unchanged? Recall from Section 4-10 that higher interest rates and the crowding out effect are the "normal" effects of a fiscal stimulus. In turn, the crowding out effect reduces the fiscal policy multiplier in comparison with the multiplier of Chapter 3, which assumed a constant interest rate. But this analysis of the crowding out effect *assumed that the real money supply remained constant.* In this section we examine two other possibilities. The first is that the main objective of the Fed is to fix the interest rate, in which case fiscal policymakers gain indirect control of the money supply. ~~The second is that monetary and fiscal policy are coordinated, lead-~~ ing to a policy "menu" of alternative interest rates that are compatible with maintaining actual output at the level of natural output (Q^N).

Fiscal Expansion with an Accommodating Money Supply

In Chapter 4 we considered the effects of a discretionary fiscal expansion that involved no change in the money supply. Because both the money supply and the price level were held fixed, the LM curve in Figures 4-12 and 4-14 remained stationary as the IS curve shifted rightward. Figure 5-5 illustrates again the same rightward shift in the IS curve caused by a $250 billion increase in real government purchases. If the goal of the monetary authority is not to keep the money supply fixed but to keep the interest rate fixed, the money supply must be allowed to change passively whenever there is a shift in the IS curve.

~~The result of any fiscal change when the monetary authority stabilizes the interest rate is exactly the same as the result of the same fiscal change when the interest responsiveness equals infinity.~~ No increase in the interest rate occurs, so there is no crowding out; the economy's equilibrium moves directly to the right from point E_0 to point E_6. The multiplier for the fiscal change in this case of monetary accommodation is the simple multiplier of Chapter 3, $k = 4.0$.

The Monetary-Fiscal Policy Mix

Recall that the primary objective of government stabilization policy is to dampen business cycles by maintaining the level of actual real GNP (real income) equal to natural real GNP, which in our numerical example is $4000 billion. The original intersection of the IS and LM curves occurred at an

[Handwritten margin note: $F_1 \Rightarrow \Delta G$ has no effect]

Figure 5-5

Effect on Real Income of a $250 Billion Fiscal Stimulus When the Fed Acts to Keep the Interest Rate Constant

If the money supply were to remain constant in the face of the $250 billion fiscal stimulus, the economy would move from E_0 to E_5, just as in Figure 4-12. Now, however, the Fed attempts to keep the interest rate constant. The money supply must be increased by exactly enough to support the higher level of income. Because $1 of extra money is needed for each $2 of extra income, the money supply must be raised $500 billion to allow income to grow $1000 billion in response to the fiscal stimulus.

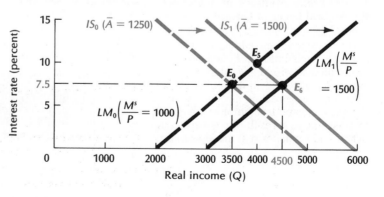

FISCAL POLICY GAINS CONTROL OF THE MONEY SUPPLY IF THE MONETARY AUTHORITIES ATTEMPT TO STABILIZE INTEREST RATES

unsatisfactory level of real income, $3500 billion, and we have seen how expansionary monetary and fiscal policy can raise real income from $3500 to $4000. An example for monetary policy was shown in Figure 4-10, where an increase in the real money supply by $500 billion shifted the *IS-LM* intersection from point E_0 at $3500 billion to point E_1 at $4000 billion. An example for fiscal policy was shown in Figure 4-12, where an increase in government spending by $250 billion shifted the *IS-LM* intersection from point E_0 at $3500 billion to point E_5 at $4000 billion. If government policy has these two options for creating an economic expansion sufficient to bring real income to the level of natural real GNP, $4000 billion, which option is preferable?

Figure 5-6 compares points E_1 and E_5. In both cases the total level of real income is identical and equal to natural real GNP, $4000 billion. We can assume that the total level of employment and unemployment would also be identical. What are the differences? Point E_5 has a lower real money supply and, in order to keep money demand equal to money supply, also has a higher interest rate. This can be described as the "tight money, easy fiscal" position.

Point E_1, on the other hand, is the "easy money, tight fiscal" position, with a higher real money supply and a lower interest rate to stimulate a demand for money equal to the supply. The higher interest rate at point E_5 cuts planned private autonomous spending, both investment and consumption, below that at point E_1, to make room for the government spending. Induced consumption is the same at both E_1 and E_5.

Which position, E_1 or E_5, should society prefer? At point E_1 investment is higher; thus the economy's rate of productivity growth is likely to be higher. This growth will benefit us in future years. At point E_5, government spending is higher than at point E_1. The government purchases may be currently consumed government services (national defense, police and fire protection, education, or health) or government investment (school buildings, highways). Should society prefer the faster output growth of point E_1 to the

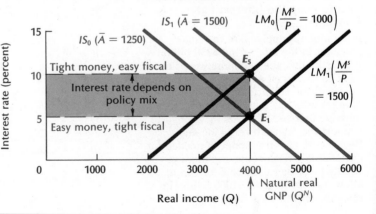

Figure 5-6
Two Alternate Methods of Achieving the Natural Level of Output

The IS_0, IS_1, LM_0, and LM_1 curves are the same as we have encountered in Figure 5-5. The combination at E_1 achieves target income with a low interest rate by avoiding a government deficit and allowing a large real money supply. At E_5 the same income level implies a higher interest rate as a result of a government deficit and a smaller real money supply.

POLICYMAKERS CAN ALTER THE INTEREST RATE WITHOUT CHANGING INCOME BY CHOOSING THE POLICY MIX

higher level of public services of point E_5? This is a difficult problem to which we will return in Chapters 12 and 13. Its solution depends partly on society's preference for public versus private goods and partly on its taste for present goods and services versus those deferred to the future.

The fiscal stimulus that takes the economy to the tight money, easy fiscal point E_5 takes the form of an increase in government expenditures. A tax rate reduction is another type of expansionary fiscal policy that could, in combination with tight monetary policy, achieve the high interest rate outcome at point E_5. Such a policy mix, with tax cuts and tight money, would stimulate private consumption (as higher disposable income made possible by the tax cuts raises consumption) but would cut private investment (through the crowding out effect).

5-6 The Foreign Exchange Rate and the Determination of Net Exports

The **international crowding out effect** occurs when an expansionary fiscal policy reduces net exports.

An **appreciation** is a rise in the value of one nation's currency relative to another nation's currency. When the dollar can buy more units of a foreign currency, say the German mark, the dollar is said to appreciate relative to that foreign currency.

A **depreciation** is a decline in the value of one nation's currency relative to another nation's currency. When the dollar can buy fewer units of a foreign currency, say the British pound, the dollar is said to depreciate relative to that foreign currency.

To this point we have examined the effects of fiscal policy in a closed economy without foreign trade. In the absence of accommodating monetary policy, expansionary fiscal policy raises the interest rate and "crowds out" domestic spending that is interest-sensitive, particularly private domestic investment. This traditional analysis is no longer adequate because the major impact of the large structural budget deficit that occurred in the United States after 1982 was to crowd out not domestic investment, but net exports. This **international crowding out effect** occurs when an economy is open and operates under a system of flexible exchange rates.

The Flexible Exchange Rate System and the Exchange Rate of the Dollar

One of the major determinants of the foreign trade deficit is the foreign exchange rate of the dollar. As we learned in Section 2-5, the foreign exchange rate is said to "appreciate" when the dollar becomes worth more, that is, can purchase more foreign currency. The dollar appreciated against the German deutschemark (DM) between February 1980, when one dollar could purchase only 1.73 DMs and March 1985, when the dollar was worth almost twice as much, 3.40 DMs. An **appreciation** hurts American exports by making U.S. goods more expensive in terms of DMs and other foreign currencies and by making imports cheaper. The opposite of an appreciation is a **depreciation** of the exchange rate, as occurred after March 1985, when the dollar plunged from 3.40 to as low as 1.5 DMs in early 1988. A depreciation makes U.S. goods cheaper, benefitting exporters and cutting the demand for imports. Thus an appreciation cuts net exports while a depreciation tends to boost net exports.

SELF-TEST   As a college student planning a trip to Europe this summer, do you hope for an appreciation or depreciation of the dollar? Looking ahead to the plot of the exchange rate in Figure 5-7, if you had the choice would you have preferred to travel to Europe in 1985 or 1988?

Until the early 1970s the foreign exchange rate of the dollar was fixed against most foreign currencies. For instance, $2.80 was sufficient to purchase one British pound for the entire period between 1949 and 1967, and the exchange rate of the German deutschemark was $0.25 between 1948 and 1969. However, after 1970 the **fixed exchange rate system,** often called the "Bretton Woods" system (after the New Hampshire conference site where the system was established in 1944), collapsed. The main culprit in the collapse was U.S. inflation caused by the Vietnam War, which led to persistent U.S. foreign trade deficits. Using the language of supply and demand, the supply of dollars greatly exceeded the demand. As a result, only massive purchases of dollars by other countries, particularly Germany and Japan, could maintain the fixed exchange rate of the dollar. Germany became alarmed at the inflated money supply and prices that resulted from this influx of dollars. Speculators made the safe bet that the fixed exchange rate between the dollar and other currencies could not be maintained, and added to the excess supply of dollars by selling them to the governments of Germany and Japan. Finally, governments of the major nations abandoned the attempt to support the dollar's value, and on March 19, 1973 adopted the **flexible exchange rate system.**

> In a **fixed exchange rate system** the foreign exchange rate is fixed for long periods of time.

The history of the dollar's exchange rate since 1960 is shown in Figure 5-7. Displayed is the "effective" exchange rate of the dollar, which weights the exchange rate of the dollar against an average of the DM, British pound, Japanese yen, and other currencies, in proportion to the importance of each country in American foreign trade. After a decade of stability, the dollar's effective exchange rate plunged in the early 1970s. The world's central bankers made several futile attempts to save the Bretton Woods system by "devaluing" the dollar, that is, reducing its fixed value from one level to another. They failed, however, and the flexible rate era began in 1973. The dollar fluctuated within a range of about 10 percent between 1973 and 1980 but then began its rapid ascent to a peak value in 1985:Q1, fully 60 percent

> In a **flexible exchange rate system** the foreign exchange rate is free to change every day.

Figure 5-7
Nominal Effective Exchange Rate of the Dollar, 1961–89

The dollar depreciated substantially in the early 1970s when the flexible exchange rate system began, and again in 1977–79 as U.S. inflation accelerated relative to that in Germany and Japan. The most dramatic movements came in the 1980s, when a 60 percent increase between late 1980 and early 1985 was followed by an equal decline in an even shorter time.

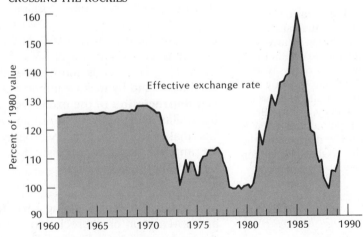

THE DOLLAR IN THE 1980s WAS LIKE A MOUNTAIN CLIMBER CROSSING THE ROCKIES

above the 1980 average level. Then by 1988–89 the dollar had declined back to roughly its 1980 value. An important theme of the rest of this chapter is the role of fiscal and monetary policy in causing the soaring and collapsing dollar in the 1980s and the effect of the dollar's appreciation and subsequent depreciation on net exports and the foreign trade deficit.

The Foreign Trade Surplus and Deficit

Net exports (X), as we learned in Chapter 2, is an aggregate that equals exports minus imports and is a component of total expenditure on GNP, along with consumption (C), investment (I), and government spending (G):

$$E = C + I + G + X$$

A $100 billion increase in net exports provides just as much of a stimulus to income and employment as a $100 billion increase in consumption, investment, or government spending. More important for understanding the U.S. economy in the 1980s, a $100 billion *decrease* in net exports can offset much of the stimulus to expenditures provided by expansionary monetary and fiscal policy.

The **foreign trade surplus** is the same as net exports; the **foreign trade deficit** is net exports with the sign reversed.

A **foreign trade surplus** is an excess of exports over imports, that is, a positive quantity of net exports. A **foreign trade deficit** is an excess of imports over exports, that is, a negative quantity of net exports. The fluctuations in net exports are illustrated in Figure 5-8, which plots data on real exports, real imports, and real net exports from 1955 to 1988. Exports and imports have both risen in real terms over the past thirty years, but not at an even pace.

During most years until the late 1960s there was a fairly even balance between exports and imports. However, in the late 1960s an excess of imports over exports (a trade deficit) developed as a result of the inflation that occurred in the United States at that time; inflation tends to raise the price of exports and also to make imports from foreign countries more attractive.

In the 1970s and 1980s the United States experienced an alternation of trade surpluses, in 1975 and 1979–82, with trade deficits in other years. This alternation is directly related to fluctuations in the real exchange rate of the dollar. The depreciation of the dollar in the early 1970s and again in the late 1970s helps to explain the two periods of trade surplus, while the sharp appreciation of the dollar in 1980–85 helps explain why the trade deficit reached unprecedented proportions in the mid-1980s. A puzzle, however, is why the 1985–88 depreciation in the dollar caused such a small improvement in the trade deficit.

Net Exports and the Foreign Exchange Rate

Clearly the fluctuations of net exports, illustrated in Figure 5-8, play an important part in fluctuations of total real expenditures. Determining the ups and downs of net exports are real income and the foreign exchange rate.

The effect of real income. We have already discovered, at the end of Chapter 3, that net exports depend on real income. There we wrote the determination of net exports (X) as

$$X = \overline{X} - xQ, \tag{3.33}$$

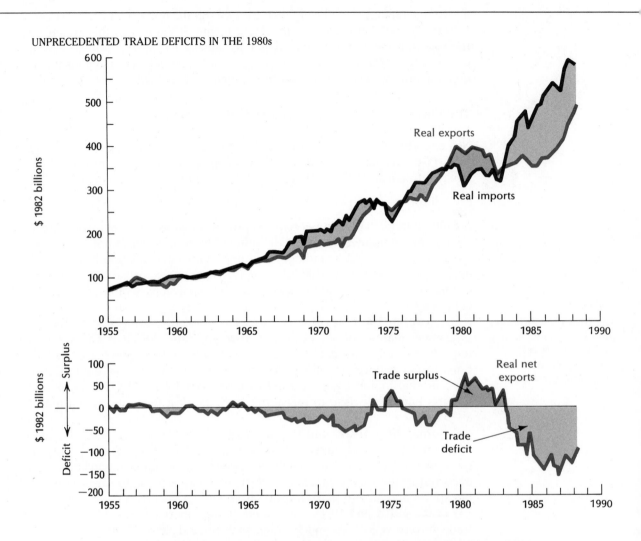

Figure 5-8 **U.S. Real Exports, Real Imports, and Real Net Exports, 1955–88**
The top frame shows real exports and imports, and the bottom frame shows real net exports. In each frame a trade surplus is indicated by gray shading and a trade deficit by pink shading. After a period of positive net exports in 1979–81, the 1980s were characterized by a growing and unprecedented trade deficit.

where $\overline{X}$ is the autonomous component of net exports (determined mainly by foreign income), x is the fraction of a change in income that is spent on imports, and Q is real income. If we ignored changes in the foreign exchange rate, (3.33) would adequately explain net exports. Given the behavior of foreign incomes that determines the autonomous component $(\overline{X})$, net exports would be low in economic expansions when income is high, causing a large volume of imports, and net exports would be high in recessions when income is low, causing a small volume of imports.

The **real exchange rate** is equal to the average nominal foreign exchange rate between a country and its trading partners, with an adjustment for the difference in inflation rates between that country and its trading partners.

Effect of the foreign exchange rate. When the exchange rate rises in value (or appreciates) against foreign currencies, U.S. exports become more expensive in terms of foreign currencies, and exports tend to decline. Also, lower dollar prices of imports attract American customers, and the quantity of goods imported into the United States rises. With exports down and imports up, the appreciation of the foreign exchange rate causes a drop in net exports. This is just what happened in the United States in the 1980s. The appreciation of the dollar was already shown in Figure 5-7, and the collapse of net exports in Figure 5-8. In Figure 5-9 these two phenomena are brought together. The red net export line is copied from Figure 5-8. The black foreign exchange rate line plots the **real exchange rate** of the dollar. Any *real*

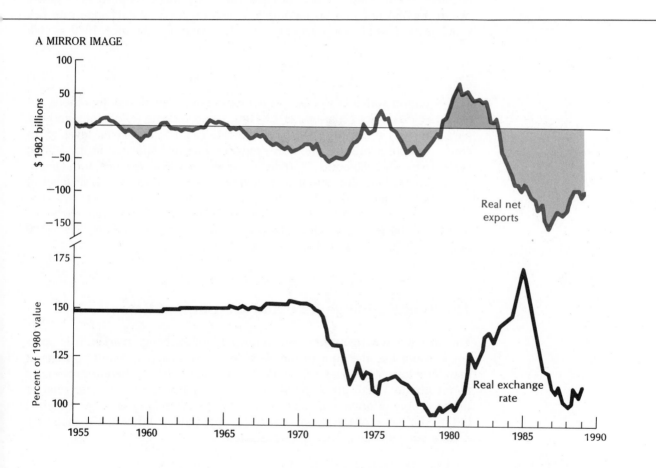

Figure 5-9   **U.S. Real Net Exports and the Real Exchange Rate of the Dollar, 1955–89**
The real net export line is copied from Figure 5-10. The real exchange rate line shows that the dollar depreciated in the 1970s, appreciated from 1980 to 1985, and then depreciated again after 1985. The two lines display a striking mirror image relationship, indicating that an appreciating dollar tends to reduce net exports, and vice versa.

variable, like real GNP, is adjusted for the effects of inflation. The real exchange rate is the nominal exchange rate from Figure 5-7 adjusted for differences between the inflation rates of the United States and foreign nations with which it engages in foreign trade.[2]

Two facts stand out in Figure 5-9. First, movements in both net exports and the real exchange rate were much smaller before 1970 than afterward. The second striking fact is the strong negative relationship between net exports and the real exchange rate. When the real exchange rate was low in the late 1970s, U.S. net exports rose and peaked in 1980. The rise in the real exchange rate between 1980 and 1985 was accompanied by a continuous decline in net exports. Following the 1985–88 depreciation of the dollar, net exports began to improve in 1988 (although not by much). To reflect this negative relationship, we amend equation (3.33) above to allow net exports (X) to depend not just on income but also on the real exchange rate (e), which is expressed as a percentage of a base year, for instance, 1980 = 100:

General Linear Form	Numerical Example	
$X = \overline{X} - xQ - ue$	$X = 600 - .1Q - 2e$	(5.3)

This equation states in words that net exports are equal to autonomous net exports ($\overline{X}$), minus a parameter (x) times real income (Q), minus another parameter (u) times the real exchange rate (e). For any given level of income, an appreciation of the real exchange rate as happened in the United States between 1980 and 1985 reduces net exports. For instance, if the economy is operating with actual real income at the natural real GNP level of $4000 billion, and the real exchange rate is 100 then net exports are zero $[= 600 - (0.1 \times 4000) - (2 \times 100)]$. An appreciation in the real exchange rate from 100 to 150 would reduce net exports in this example to $-\$100$ billion $= [600 - (0.1 \times 4000) - (2 \times 150)]$.

5-7 The Real Exchange Rate and the Interest Rate

The foreign exchange rate is set in the foreign exchange market. It is not a single room like the floor of the New York Stock Exchange, but consists of bank employees all over the world buying and selling different currencies by telephone. When the demand for a currency like the dollar rises relative to the supply of dollars, these bank employees ("foreign exchange traders") bid up the value of the dollar, so that it appreciates. When the demand for dollars falls, its value falls, or depreciates.

---

[2]The real exchange rate (e) shown in Figure 5-9 is defined as the nominal effective exchange rate (e') times the ratio of the U.S. price level (P) to the average foreign price level (P^f):

$$e = e'(P/P^f)$$

Thus if the nominal exchange rate (e') doubled, but foreign prices doubled while U.S. prices remained the same (halving the P/P^f ratio), the real exchange rate would remain fixed. In the term "nominal effective exchange rate," the adjective "effective" refers to the calculation of the actual exchange rate as a weighted average of the exchange rate of the United States with each of its trading partners, using the share of each nation in U.S. foreign trade as weights.

The Demand for Dollars and the "Fundamentals"

The demand for dollars stems from two sources, the desire to buy American products and the desire to buy securities denominated in dollars (like U.S. government bonds and the bonds issued by U.S. corporations). Changes in the worldwide desire to buy American products tend to occur gradually. Among the factors, sometimes called the "fundamentals," that might create such changes are the invention of new American products like personal computers. A fundamental factor that might *reduce* the desire to hold dollars might be the development of new products in other countries, like Japanese VCRs or Korean automobiles. Higher expected inflation in the United States than in other countries would also reduce the desire to hold dollars.

Because the fundamental factors tend to change slowly, they cannot account for much of the highly volatile movements in the dollar's real exchange rate evident in Figure 5-9. Instead, these sharp up and down movements can be attributed to the second main source of the demand for dollars, the desire by foreigners to buy securities denominated in dollars. When U.S. securities become more attractive, the demand for dollars increases and the foreign exchange traders bid up the dollar's value. Similarly, when foreign securities become more attractive to Americans, U.S. residents supply extra dollars to the foreign exchange traders to obtain the foreign currencies they need to buy foreign securities and the dollar's value goes down.

The interest rate differential is the average U.S. interest rate minus the average foreign interest rate.

The relative attractiveness of U.S. and foreign securities depends on the **interest rate differential,** defined as the average U.S. interest rate minus the average foreign interest rate. When the U.S. interest rate increases and the foreign interest rate remains unchanged, the interest rate differential increases. Foreigners find U.S. securities attractive; they demand additional dollars to buy them, and the foreign exchange rate of the dollar is bid up by the foreign exchange traders.

The Real Exchange Rate and the Monetary-Fiscal Policy Mix

This connection between the U.S. interest rate and the real exchange rate of the dollar establishes a link between U.S. fiscal policy and the value of the dollar. When the Fed holds the real money supply constant, as in Figure 4-12, a fiscal policy stimulus (for instance, an increase in government spending) raises both real income and the interest rate. Foreigners attempt to buy U.S. securities, and the dollar appreciates.

Another factor causing an appreciation of the dollar would be a restrictive monetary policy that shifts the *LM* curve to the left as the Fed reduces the real money supply. A particularly sharp appreciation of the dollar would be likely to accompany a shift in the policy mix from tight fiscal and easy money, as at point E_1 in Figure 5-6, to easy fiscal and tight money, as at point E_5 in the same figure.

This section has suggested that an increase in the U.S. interest rate should cause an appreciation of the dollar, and a decrease in the U.S. interest rate should cause a depreciation of the dollar. The close positive rela-

PUZZLE 4: WHY WERE INTEREST RATES IN THE 1980S HIGHER THAN EVER BEFORE?

PUZZLE 6: WHY HAS AMERICA'S TRADE DROPPED INTO PERSISTENT DEFICIT AFTER YEARS OF SURPLUS?

tionship between the U.S. interest rate and the value of the dollar is demonstrated in Figure 5-10, which plots the two together for the period since 1970. The real interest rate is copied from Figure 1-10, where the puzzle of high interest rates was first introduced. The real exchange rate of the dollar is copied from Figure 5-9. The periods of the lowest real interest rates in the 1970s coincided with periods when the dollar was low. The period of high interest rates after 1980 was accompanied by an appreciation of the dollar. The 1984 peak in the real interest rate matches the 1984 peak in the real exchange rate. Finally, the turnaround in the exchange rate in 1989 followed that of the interest rate in 1988. While changes in the interest rate cannot predict every wiggle in the dollar, they capture the most important changes.

SELF-TEST   Assuming that they pay cash for their summer vacation trips to Europe, would college students prefer a policy mix of tight monetary and easy fiscal, or easy monetary and tight fiscal, during the summer that they are planning to go to Europe?

Exchange Rate Expectations

More advanced treatments of the relationship between the interest rate and exchange rate introduce an additional element—expectations about future exchange rate changes. Imagine a situation in which the U.S. and German real interest rates are both 3 percent. If no future change is expected in the exchange rate of the dollar relative to the German mark (the "dollar-mark rate"), investors will be happy to hold either U.S. or German securities.

Figure 5-10
The U.S. Real Corporate Bond Rate and the Real Exchange Rate of the Dollar, 1970–89
The real exchange rate is copied from Figure 5-9 but is displayed over the shorter 1970–89 period. The real corporate bond rate is copied from Figure 1-10. A positive relationship between the two lines is evident, with movements in the interest rate appearing to occur prior to movements in the exchange rate.

A HIGH INTEREST RATE MAKES THE DOLLAR STRONG

Now imagine that a shift toward an easy fiscal and tight monetary policy mix in the United States boosts the U.S. real interest rate to 6 percent, while the German rate remains at 3 percent. Why would anyone hold German securities? These would be held only if the dollar-mark rate *were expected to fall in the future by 3 percent a year,* so that a German investor holding dollar securities would earn the 6 percent rate on dollar securities minus the 3 percent annual decline in the value of the dollar. If such a 3 percent decline in the dollar-mark rate were expected to persist for ten years, this reasoning could explain a 30 percent *increase* in the dollar-mark rate at the time of the initial shift in the policy mix.

Since investors tend to form expectations by following the old saying "What goes up must come down," they are likely to react to a 30 percent *appreciation* of the dollar-mark rate by expecting a *depreciation* in the future, 3 percent per year for ten years in this example. This expectation of a future depreciation is what makes people willing to hold German bonds at 3 percent rather than U.S. bonds at 6 percent, since they believe that the 3 percent loss in value of the dollar relative to the mark will erode fully half of the 6 percent return of the U.S. bonds. After taking the depreciation into account, then, people expect the return *expressed in marks* of both German bonds and U.S. bonds to be 3 percent.

This analysis is consistent with the previous discussion and with Figure 5-10, which indicate a positive relationship between the interest rate and the exchange rate. The analysis adds an extra element by explaining why investors would be willing to continue to hold German securities when the U.S. interest rate increases.

5-8 International Crowding Out in the *IS-LM* Model

We have now established that expansionary fiscal policy raises the interest rate, an increase in the interest rate raises the real exchange rate, and an increase in the real exchange rate causes a decline in net exports. In short, expansionary fiscal policy reduces net exports. How can our *IS-LM* model illustrate this effect of fiscal policy?

Is the effect of a monetary or fiscal stimulus stronger or weaker in an open economy than a closed economy? And does the answer depend on whether or not the foreign exchange rate is flexible? Several conclusions are possible. Here we focus on the effects of a fiscal stimulus, since this is the dramatic policy shift with international repercussions in the 1980s. In Chapter 14 we will provide a more complete review of policy effects in an open economy.

The Open Economy, the Multiplier, and the *IS* Curve

Here we distinguish two different issues, whether the economy is closed or open, and the exchange rate "regime," that is, whether exchange rates are fixed or flexible. We are interested in effects on the slope of the *IS* curve, which in turn will influence the fiscal policy multiplier. We assume that the

LM curve is unaffected by the openness of the economy and by the exchange rate regime. To review, we learned in Chapter 4 that the slope of the *IS* curve depends on the multiplier (*k*—the inverse of the marginal leakage rate) and on the interest responsiveness of planned autonomous spending.

There can be no doubt that an open economy with fixed exchange rates will have a steeper *IS* curve than a closed economy, simply because its marginal leakage rate must be higher and hence its multiplier (*k*) must be lower. In a closed economy the marginal leakage rate is the after-tax marginal propensity to save $[s(1 - \bar{t})]$ plus the income-tax rate $(\bar{t})$. In an open economy the marginal leakage rate adds an additional fraction (x), which is the response of imports to GNP. Thus we have, using the numerical example of the appendix to this chapter:

	Marginal leakage rate	Multiplier
Closed economy	$1/k = s(1 - \bar{t}) + \bar{t} = 0.25(0.8) + 0.8 = 0.4$	$k = 2.5$
Open economy	$1/k = s(1 - t) + t + x$	
	$= 0.25(0.8) + 0.8 + 0.1 = 0.5$	$k = 2.0$

Our original analysis of the crowding-out effect showed that a flat *IS* curve leads to a reduction in private spending in response to a higher interest rate. Thus crowding out increases and the fiscal policy multiplier decreases. In an open economy with fixed exchange rates, however, the marginal leakage rate must be higher than in a closed economy, since there is an added leakage from the circular flow into imports. Hence in an open economy with fixed exchange rates the *IS* curve is steeper, the crowding-out effect is smaller, and the fiscal policy multiplier is larger than in a closed economy. This is shown in the top frame of Figure 5-11.

The Crowding-Out Effect with Flexible Exchange Rates

However, the opposite effect occurs when an open economy shifts from a fixed exchange rate system to a flexible exchange rate system, as shown in the bottom frame of Figure 5-11. We start with an assumed increase in interest rates and examine the crowding-out effect along the *new IS* curve. The distance *BC* denotes the crowding-out effect resulting from an increase in the interest rate from r_0 to r_1, with a fixed exchange rate. *BC* indicates the response of private autonomous spending $(a + I_p)$ to the higher interest rate. But with flexible exchange rates, higher interest rates also cause an appreciation of the foreign exchange rate and a reduction in net exports. This impact on net exports (X) is shown by the distance between *A* and *B*.

In short, a fiscal policy stimulus creates both a domestic and international crowding-out effect in an open economy with flexible exchange rates. The international crowding-out effect is the distance *AB*, the domestic effect is *BC*. The sharp deterioration of the U.S. foreign trade balance in the 1980s reflects partly the international crowding-out effect depicted in Figure 5-11, and partly the extra impact of tight money in raising the real interest rate beyond the amount explained by the fiscal policy stimulus.

Figure 5-11
The IS Curve in an Open Economy with Fixed and Flexible Exchange Rates

Both frames have the same LM curve. The top frame shows that the IS curve is steeper in an open economy with fixed exchange rates than in a closed economy. The bottom frame shows that the IS curve is flatter in an open economy with flexible exchange rates than an open economy with fixed exchange rates. In such an economy, the crowding out effect consists of two parts, international (line AB) and domestic (BC).

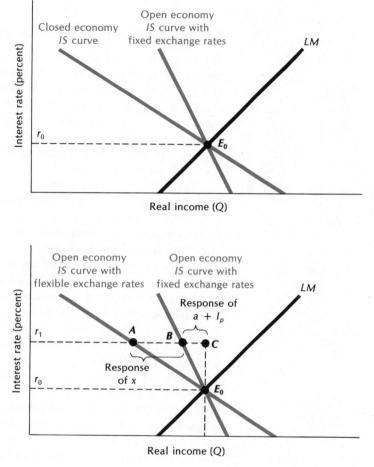

THE OPEN ECONOMY TILTS THE IS CURVE

Finally, comparing the top and bottom frames of Figure 5-11, we cannot tell whether the crowding-out effect in the open economy with flexible exchange rates (bottom frame) is larger or smaller than in the closed economy (top frame). Although we have drawn the flexible exchange rate IS curve in the bottom frame flatter than the closed economy IS curve in the top frame, this is an arbitrary choice. However, our uncertainty about the overall effect of the open economy is of no great importance, since the U.S. and other industrialized economies are open economies, and it seems clear that the switch from fixed to flexible exchange rates has led to a flatter IS curve, a reduced fiscal policy multiplier, and an increased importance of the crowding-out effect.

CASE STUDY: International Crowding Out and
Crowding In, 1981–89

The Interest Rate and the Dollar Rise, 1981–85

The theoretical analysis in this chapter helps to explain several important aspects of macroeconomic performance in the United States during the first half of the 1980s. We have seen that a shift in the policy mix toward an easier fiscal policy and a tighter monetary policy (as shown by a movement from E_1 to E_5 in Figure 5-6) can raise the interest rate without changing real income. The higher interest rate causes an appreciation of the exchange rate and leads to crowding out of net exports as well as private domestic spending.

The shift in the policy mix in the United States differed from the textbook diagram because it did not happen simultaneously. The tight money came first, and the easy fiscal policy followed several years later. First, monetary policy was shifted in a more restrictive direction, beginning in late 1979. By the spring of 1981 the real interest rate (Figure 5-10) was higher than it had been at any previous time in the postwar era. The economy plunged into a recession that lasted from July 1981 to November 1982.

Expansionary fiscal policy consisted of two main parts. One part was an expansion of defense spending, which occurred gradually beginning in 1982; the second part took the form of income tax cuts. Although legislated in August 1981, the tax cuts were introduced in three stages between 1982 and 1984. Thus the main thrust of the fiscal expansion occurred in 1983 and 1984, accounting for the fact that the natural employment deficit (the black line in Figure 5-4) does not become large until 1983.

At first the growth of the natural employment deficit caused real income to grow, and the economy enjoyed a vigorous recovery from the 1981–82 recession over the eighteen months between early 1983 and mid-1984. But then the international crowding out effect came into play as the expansion of real income was dampened by a decline in net exports (shown in Figures 5-8 and 5-9). The slow growth in real income continued throughout the rest of 1984 and 1985. This performance is consistent with the theoretical explanation in Figure 5-10, which shows that international crowding out reduces the multiplier effect of a fiscal expansion but does not eliminate it.

The main discrepancy between the theoretical analysis and the actual behavior of the U.S. economy during this period involves domestic investment. Instead of declining, as implied by the crowding out effect, investment was relatively strong as a percentage of total GNP. The absence of a decline in investment can be attributed to the Reagan administration's tax cuts, some of which amounted to subsidies for investment and stimulated investment spending. As a result, virtually all of the crowding out effect fell on net exports, and there was little crowding out of domestic investment.

The Interest Rate and the Dollar Fall, 1985–87

As is evident in Figure 5-10, both the real interest rate and real exchange rate declined sharply and dramatically during 1985 and 1986. Most of this chapter has emphasized the role of the policy mix (easy fiscal and tight monetary policy) in both raising the real interest rate and in causing the dollar to appreciate. What happened to cause the decline in the interest rate and exchange rate?

The answer lies partly in a change in the policy mix. The slow growth of the economy between mid-1984 and early 1986, due mainly to the enormous trade deficit, caused the Federal Reserve to make monetary policy progressively easier. The growth of the money supply was very rapid in 1985–86 and exceeded the Fed's own stated goals; this helped to bring interest rates down. In turn, lower interest rates helped to reduce the exchange rate of the dollar.

The shift toward lower interest rates became particularly rapid in the first few months of 1986 in response to a collapse in the worldwide price of oil. This brought the inflation rate almost to zero, at least temporarily, and allowed the Fed to shift from fighting inflation to promoting economic recovery and growth. The decline in interest rates, prompted by the Fed's concern about slow economic growth and by the effect of collapsing oil prices in creating a lower inflation rate, was the main cause of the 1985–87 depreciation of the dollar evident in Figure 5-10. But other factors also contributed. The trade deficit had become so large that the United States was forced to borrow heavily from foreigners each year. The prospect for the future was that the year-by-year buildup of debt by the United States was unsustainable, because at some point foreign investors would lose confidence in the dollar and withdraw their funds and cause it to depreciate. The dollar declined more promptly and sharply between mid-1985 and late 1987 than most analysts had thought possible, as doubts about the sustainability of the dollar's high value began to spread. Further, the dollar was pushed down by the stated agreement of the five major industrial countries in September 1985, that the dollar had become too high.

The final element in the turnaround of interest rates and the dollar was a shift in fiscal policy. In 1985 Congress passed and the president signed the Gramm-Rudman-Hollings legislation that required a gradual elimination of the federal budget deficit by 1991, which was subsequently postponed to 1993. Even though there were doubts about the constitutionality of the legislation, Congress responded by making substantial cuts in government expenditures. Forecasters began to predict that the budget deficit would shrink, and financial markets responded by reducing interest rates.

In response to lower interest rates and easy monetary policy, the economy began to grow more rapidly in early 1987. Finally, in response to the sharp drop in the dollar, the foreign trade deficit began to decline somewhat, as shown in Figure 5-9, further stimulating the economy. By late 1987 the unemployment rate had fallen below the natural unemployment rate of 6 percent and was close to 5 percent in mid-1989. Concerned that inflation was beginning to speed up, the Fed allowed interest rates to rise in 1988–89, thus bringing the depreciation of the dollar to a halt.

The Falling Dollar and the Persistent Trade Deficit

The budget deficit, interest rates, exchange rate, and trade deficit seem to interconnect neatly—except for one problem. As of 1988–89, the dollar had reached its 1980 level and had remained there for more than a year, yet (as in Figure 5-9) the trade deficit had recovered only about 20 percent of the ground lost since 1980. Why did the falling dollar in 1985–88 do so little to stimulate net exports in contrast to the enormous damage done by the rising dollar in 1980–85?

For a while, economists excused their incorrect predictions of a rapid recovery of the trade deficit with statements like "Oh, it looks like the lags in the response of net exports to changes in the exchange rate are longer than we thought." They pointed out that in the short run a falling dollar makes U.S. imports more expensive and may actually make the trade deficit *worse* (this is the "J-curve" effect discussed in Chapter 14). But, as time went on with only a small recovery in the trade deficit, it became necessary to look elsewhere to explain the changing relationship of the exchange rate and net exports. The answer had to be a simple fact: The world had changed since 1980 in ways that reduced the world's demand for U.S. exports while raising the U.S. demand for imported foreign goods and services.

Between 1980 and mid-1988 there was little net change in the dollar. But the share of imports in GNP had risen from 11.7 to 12.5 percent, while the share of exports in GNP had fallen from 12.8 to 10.9 percent. Net exports as a percentage of GNP had fallen from $+1.1$ to -1.6 percent (these figures are in current dollars; the net export percentage is higher in constant 1982 dollars). Thus exports were too low *and* imports were too high. Factors that had changed since 1980 include the following:

Different growth rates. The U.S. economy grew faster than most European economies in the 1980s. As we saw in Figure 1-13, in 1987–88 European unemployment was close to 10 percent, while U.S. unemployment had fallen below 6 percent. More rapid growth in the United States gave consumers the income to purchase added imports, while slow growth in Europe reduced the demand for U.S. exports.

Latin America. A closely related problem was the economic disaster area of Latin America (including Mexico), where the United States had been the dominant supplier. In the late 1970s and early 1980s several major Latin American nations financed imports from the United States by accumulating massive amounts of debt. Since then they have drastically reduced imports as a condition of debt restructuring and repayment. For this reason, the U.S. trade surplus in 1980 was unsustainable.

The farm problem. U.S. farmers have been undermined by subsidies to foreign farmers, restrictions on the sale of American farm products to foreign countries, and increasing farm production abroad. Of these three elements, the first two have existed for a long time. But the growing list of nations that can feed themselves, with something left over for export, attests to the success of the "Green Revolution" and is a bad omen for the revival of U.S. farm exports.

All those new factories in Japan and the NICs. When newly industrialized countries ("NICs"—South Korea, Taiwan, Hong Kong, and Singapore) discovered in the 1980s how to make many products that Americans wanted but could not obtain at home, U.S. imports from Asia increased. Americans have been eagerly buying VCRs, compact disc players, fax machines, computer equipment, and many other products that are not manufactured in the United States at all, or only in limited quantities. Other products assembled in America, like the Hewlett-Packard laser printer for personal computers, rely on imported components.

Import prices have not increased enough.   One reason Americans buy so many imports is that import prices have not increased nearly as much as the dollar has fallen. This has happened in part because Japanese firms have been willing to accept a squeeze on profit margins from the excessively high levels of 1984–85, and because the currencies of the NICs have not risen nearly as much as the dollar has fallen. Also, American automakers and other firms competing with imports have responded to the falling dollar by raising prices in tandem with import prices, thus missing the chance to gain a larger market share at the expense of imported goods.

Implications for the Dollar and for Policy

If the U.S. trade position deteriorated permanently between 1980 and 1989, the dollar would have to fall even further below 1989 levels to achieve a recovery in the trade deficit. As year after year of trade deficits continued, the United States was forced to borrow from foreigners to pay for all those imports, and the interest payments on the borrowing added further to the U.S. deficit. Most economists estimated that the "equilibrium value of the dollar," that is, the value of the dollar necessary to achieve balanced trade, was far below the 1989 level.

What response of fiscal and monetary policy was appropriate? This question is best addressed in the context of our basic definition from Chapter 2:

$$T - G \equiv I - S + X - M \qquad (2.10)$$

In words, this states that the government budget surplus is equal to the difference between private domestic investment and private saving, plus net exports. In the 1980s the United States experienced rough equality of I and S, so that the twin deficits (negative $T - G$ and negative X) balanced each other.

One possible policy response would be to do nothing, allowing $T - G$ and X to remain negative. Another would be to allow the dollar to fall, hopefully bringing X up to zero. This, however, would throw equation (2.10) out of balance unless the government budget deficit (negative $T - G$) were also eliminated; otherwise $I - S$ would have to become negative, requiring sufficiently high interest rates to dampen domestic investment on the assumption that a revival in the saving rate did not occur.

A third possibility, supported by many economists, would be for both of the twin deficits to shrink gradually toward zero. This would allow $S - I$ to remain close to zero and would prevent a possible collapse in investment. In terms of the *IS-LM* model, the solution creates a shift toward fiscal tightness and monetary ease, which would allow real interest rates to decline, as from point E_5 to E_1 in Figure 5-6. We return to the debate over the twin deficits, whether they are harmful, and what should be done to eliminate them, in Chapters 13 and 14.

1. The government has run a budget deficit in most years of this century. The most common reasons for the government to run a budget deficit are wars and recessions.

2. The natural employment deficit (NED) can be distinguished from the actual budget deficit. The actual deficit can change either through discretionary fiscal policy actions or because of business-cycle movements in real income. The NED is defined for a particular level of real income, the natural level of real GNP, so that its movements can be caused only by discretionary fiscal policy changes or by growth in natural real GNP.

3. Large natural employment deficits occurred in two periods of the postwar era, in 1966–68 when Vietnam War spending was high and there was a delay in raising tax rates to pay for the war, and in 1983–85 when defense spending was increasing while tax rates were reduced.

4. The size of the fiscal policy multipliers depends on whether the Fed holds the real money supply constant or accommodates the fiscal changes by holding the interest rate constant. When the real money supply is held constant, a fiscal expansion increases the interest rate and causes a crowding out effect. When the Fed allows the real money supply to increase enough to prevent any increase in the interest rate, the crowding out effect does not occur.

5. The composition of total expenditures depends on the mix of monetary and fiscal policy. An easy fiscal, tight monetary policy mix tends to cut back on domestic investment and net exports while raising government spending and, if personal income tax cuts are part of the fiscal stimulus, private consumption.

6. Net exports, the difference between exports and imports, is a component of spending on GNP. Under a system of flexible exchange rates, net exports depend not just on real income but also on the real exchange rate.

7. An increase in the real interest rate causes an appreciation of the real exchange rate, as foreign investors find domestic securities more attractive and bid up the exchange rate in order to buy them.

8. In an open economy under the flexible exchange rate system, a fiscal expansion raises the interest rate, which in turn raises the exchange rate, which then reduces net exports. This international crowding out effect supplements the domestic crowding out effect and makes the multiplier for a fiscal policy expansion smaller than in an open economy with fixed exchange rates.

foreign exchange rate
government budget surplus and deficit
protectionist measure
cyclical vs. structural deficits
automatic stabilization
discretionary fiscal policy
budget line
natural employment deficit
international crowding out effect

appreciation
depreciation
fixed exchange rate system
flexible exchange rate system
foreign trade surplus and deficit
real exchange rate
interest rate differential
monetary-fiscal policy mix

Questions

1. You have heard that the actual government deficit for the current year is going to be $30 billion greater than in the past year. Based on this projection, what conclusions can you make regarding the government's fiscal policy?

2. Explain the distinction among the following concepts:
   (a) cyclical deficit
   (b) structural deficit
   (c) natural employment deficit
   (d) actual deficit
   (e) government budget deficit

(f) foreign trade deficit

(g) twin deficits

3. Explain the connection between the federal government budget deficit in the early 1980s and the accompanying "twin" foreign trade deficit.

4. During the 1983–85 period, the behavior of the government budget deficit was quite different than in the other recent post-recession periods. Explain in what way the budget deficit differed and why this difference occurred.

5. Explain why you would expect the actual government deficit to be larger than the natural employment deficit when the economy is weak.

6. Assume that in a closed economy the Federal Reserve Board has decided to maintain the interest rate at the current level. If Congress passes a $50 billion decrease in personal income taxes, what action, if any, would the Fed have to take? What would be the effect of Congress's actions on real output? What would be the effect of the Fed's action on real output? How would your answer change in an open economy with flexible exchange rates?

7. Assume that in a closed economy the Federal Reserve Board has decided to maintain the level of real GNP at the current level. If Congress passes a $50 billion decrease in personal income taxes, what action, if any, would the Fed have to take? Describe the effect of the actions of Congress and the Fed on: (a) the interest rate; (b) the composition of output in the economy; (c) the future growth rate of GNP. How would your answer change in an open economy with flexible exchange rates?

8. "If the Fed seeks to fix the interest rate, fiscal policymakers gain indirect control of the money supply." Explain.

9. What is the impact of including foreign trade on the slope of the IS curve, assuming fixed exchange rates? In an open economy, what is the impact on the slope of the IS curve of moving from fixed to flexible exchange rates? How does the slope of a closed economy IS curve compare to that of an open economy with flexible exchange rates (all other things being equal)?

Problems

1. Assume $Q^N = 3,000$, $t = .15$, and $G = 500$.
   (a) What is the level of the natural employment deficit (NED)?
   (b) If there is an increase in G to 650, what happens to the NED?
   (c) Assume that G has the original value (500) and that there is a decrease in t so that now $t = .10$. What is the new value of the NED?

2. Assume the following equations summarize the structure of the economy:

$$C = a + .75Q_D \qquad G = 400$$
$$a = 50 - 10r \qquad M^s/P = 300$$
$$T = 200 + 0.2Q \qquad h = 0.4$$
$$I_p = 300 - 30r \qquad f = 50$$
$$X = 400 - 0.2Q - 5e, \text{ where the exchange}$$
rate $e = dr = 10r$

Using the information above, answer the following.
   (a) What is the equation of the IS curve?
   (b) What is the equation of the LM curve?
   (c) What is the equilibrium level of income (Q)?
   (d) How do your answers to (a), (b), and (c) above compare with your answers to questions 1(d), 2(c), and 3(a) at the end of Chapter 4?
   (e) If G increases to 450, what is the new level of income and interest rate?
   (f) How does your answer to (d) above compare with your answer to question 3(b) at the end of Chapter 4? Explain.

---

p. 129 More spending for Star Wars shifts the budget line *BB* down (raises the natural employment deficit, NED). An increase in the social security tax rate moves *BB* up (reduces NED), an increase in social security benefits moves *BB* down (raises NED), while a recession moves the economy leftward down a fixed *BB* schedule (no change in NED).

p. 133 College students hope for an appreciation of the dollar. If a hotel room in Germany costs 90 German DM, a student would have to pay $50 for the hotel room if the exchange rate is $1 to 1.8 DM, but if the dollar appreciates to 2.5 DM, the hotel room costs only $36, that is, 90/2.5. You would have preferred to travel in 1985, when the dollar was much stronger than in 1988.

p. 140 We assume that students pay cash for their summer trip, do not borrow, and so are not affected by interest rates. Then students would prefer a mix of easy fiscal and tight monetary policy, since this would cause the dollar to appreciate and make their trip to Europe cheaper.

The Elementary Algebra of Equilibrium Income

When you see an *IS* curve crossing an *LM* curve, as in Chapters 4 and 5, you know that the equilibrium level of income (Q) and the interest rate (r) occur at the point of crossing, as at point E_0 in Figure 4-9. But how can the equilibrium level of income and the interest rate be calculated numerically without going to the trouble of making careful drawings of the *IS* and *LM* curves? Wherever you see two lines crossing to determine the values of two variables, such as Q and r, exactly the same solution can be obtained by solving together the two equations describing the two lines.

The *IS-LM* Model in a Closed Economy

In Section 3-7 we found that equilibrium income is equal to autonomous planned spending (A_p) divided by the marginal leakage rate (MLR), so that the autonomous spending multiplier (k) is equal to the inverse of the marginal leakage rate ($k = 1/\text{MLR}$). Combining this with the definition of the marginal leakage rate as the fraction that leaks out of income into saving [$s(1 - \bar{t})$, tax revenues ($\bar{t}$), and imports (x)], we can write the multiplier as:

$$\text{multiplier} = k = \frac{1}{\text{marginal leakage rate}} \\ = \frac{1}{s(1 - \bar{t}) + \bar{t} + x} \quad (1)$$

The numerical example chosen for the *IS-LM* diagrams in Chapters 4 and 5 assumes that the tax rate ($\bar{t}$) is zero. Also, because a closed economy is assumed, there are no imports, and no dependence of net exports on income ($x = 0$). In this special case, the marginal leakage rate is just the marginal propensity to save, and the multiplier is the inverse of the marginal propensity to save. With a marginal propensity to save assumed to be 0.25, the multiplier is $k = 1/s = 1/0.25 = 4.0$ in the numerical example of Chapters 4 and 5.

Once we have determined the multiplier from equation (1) above, we can write real income simply as:

General Linear Form

$$Q = kA_p \quad (2)$$

Numerical Example

$$Q = 4.0A_p$$

At the beginning of Chapter 4 (Figures 4-1 and 4-2), the assumption was introduced that autonomous planned spending (A_p) declines when there is an increase in the interest rate (r). If the amount of A_p at a zero interest rate is written as $\bar{A}$, then the value of A_p can be written:

General Linear Form

$$A_p = \bar{A} - br \quad (3)$$

Numerical Example

$$A_p = \bar{A} - 50r$$

where b is the interest responsiveness of A_p, in our example $50 billion of decline in A_p per one percentage point increase in the interest rate. Substituting (2) into (1), we obtain the equation for the *IS* schedule:

General Linear Form

$$Q = k(\bar{A} - br) \quad (4)$$

Numerical Example

$$Q = 4.0(\bar{A} - 50r)$$

Thus if $\bar{A}$ is 1250 and $r = 0$, the IS_0 curve intersects the horizontal axis at 5000, as in Chapters 4 and 5.

The *LM* curve shows all combinations of income (*Q*) and the interest rate (*r*) where the real money supply (M^s/P) equals the real demand for money ($(M/P)^d$), which in turn depends on *Q* and *r*. This situation of equilibrium in the money market was previously written as equation (4.1) in the text:

General Linear Form

$$\left(\frac{M^s}{P}\right) = \left(\frac{M}{P}\right)^d = hQ - fr \qquad (5)$$

Numerical Example

$$\left(\frac{M^s}{p}\right) = 0.5Q - 100r$$

where *h* is the responsiveness of real money demand to higher real income, 0.5 in our example, and *f* is the interest responsiveness of real money demand, in the example of $100 billion decline in real money demand per one percentage point increase in the interest rate. Adding *fr* (or 100*r*) to both sides of (5), and then dividing by *h* (or 0.5), we obtain the equation for the *LM* schedule when M^s/P is 1000:

General Linear Form

$$Q = \frac{\dfrac{M^s}{P} + fr}{h} \qquad (6)$$

Numerical Example

$$Q = \frac{1000 + 100r}{0.5}$$

We are assured that the commodity market is in equilibrium whenever *Q* is related to *r* by equation (4) and that the money market is in equilibrium whenever *Q* is related to *r* by equation (6). To make sure that both markets are in equilibrium, both equations must be satisfied at once.

Equations (4) and (6) together constitute an **economic model.** Finding the value of two unknown variables in economics is very much like baking a cake. One starts with a list of ingredients, the **parameters,** or knowns, of the model: $\overline{A}$, M^s/P, *b*, *f*, *h*, and *k*. Then one stirs the ingredients together using the "instructions of the recipe," in this case equations (4) and (6). The outcome is the value of the unknown variables, *Q* and *r*. The main rule in economic cake-baking is that the number of equations, the instructions of the recipe, must be equal to the number of unknowns to be determined. In this ex-

ample there are two equations and two unknowns (*Q* and *r*). There is no limit on the number of ingredients known in advance, the parameters. Here we have six parameters, but we could have seven, ten, or any number.

To convert the two equations of the model into one equation specifying the value of unknown *Q* in terms of the six known parameters, we simply substitute (6) into (4). To do this, we rearrange (6) to place the interest rate on the left side of the equation, and then we substitute the resulting expression for *r* in (4). First, rearrange (6) to move *r* to the left side:[1]

$$r = \frac{hQ - \dfrac{M^s}{P}}{f} \qquad (6a)$$

Second, substitute the right side of (6a) for *r* in (4):

$$Q = k(\overline{A} - br) = k\left[\overline{A} - \frac{bhQ}{f} + \frac{b}{f}\left(\frac{M^s}{P}\right)\right] \qquad (7)$$

Now (7) can be solved for *Q* by adding *kbhQ/f* to both sides and dividing both sides by *k*:

$$Q\left(\frac{1}{k} + \frac{bh}{f}\right) = \overline{A} + \frac{b}{f}\left(\frac{M^s}{P}\right)$$

Finally, both sides are divided by the left term in parentheses:

$$Q = \frac{\overline{A} + \dfrac{b}{f}\left(\dfrac{M^s}{P}\right)}{\dfrac{1}{k} + \dfrac{bh}{f}} \qquad (8)$$

---

[1]First multiply both sides of (6) by *h*:

$$hQ = \frac{M^s}{P} + fr$$

then subtract M^s/P from both sides:

$$hQ - \frac{M^s}{P} = fr$$

Now divide both sides by *f*:

$$\frac{hQ - \dfrac{M^s}{P}}{f} = r$$

Equation (6a) is then obtained by reversing the two sides of this equation.

Equation (8) is our master general equilibrium income equation and combines all the information in the *IS* and *LM* curves together; when (8) is satisfied, both the commodity market and money market are in equilibrium. It can be used in any situation to calculate the level of real income by simply substituting into (8) the particular values of the six known right-hand parameters in order to calculate unknown income.[2] Note that $1/k$ is the marginal leakage rate (MLR) from equation (1), and so the denominator of (8) can be rewritten MLR + (bh/f).

Because we are interested primarily in the effect on income of a change in $\overline{A}$ or M^s/P, we can simplify (8):

$$Q = k_1\overline{A} + k_2\left(\frac{M^s}{P}\right) \qquad (9)$$

All we have done in converting (8) into (9) is to give new names, k_1 and k_2, to the multiplier effects of $\overline{A}$ and M^s/P on income. The definitions and numerical values of k_1 and k_2 are:

General Linear Form

$$k_1 = \frac{1}{\dfrac{1}{k} + \dfrac{bh}{f}} \qquad (10)$$

$$k_2 = \frac{b/f}{\dfrac{1}{k} + \dfrac{bh}{f}} = \left(\frac{b}{f}\right)k_1 \qquad (11)$$

Numerical Example

$$k_1 = \frac{1}{\dfrac{1}{4.0} + \dfrac{50(0.5)}{100}} = 2.0$$

$$k_2 = \frac{50(2.0)}{100} = 1.0$$

Using the numerical values in (10) and (11), the simplified equation (9) can be used to calculate the value of real income illustrated by E_0 in Figure 4-9.

$$Q = k_1\overline{A} + k_2\left(\frac{M^s}{P}\right)$$
$$= 2.0(1250) + 1.0(1000) \qquad (12)$$
$$= 3500$$

With this equation it extremely easy to calculate the new value of Q when there is a change in $\overline{A}$ caused by government fiscal policy, or by a change in business and consumer confidence, and when there is a change in M^s/P caused by a change in the nominal money supply.[3] Remember, however, that the definitions of k_1 and k_2 in (10) and (11) do depend on particular assumptions about the value of parameters b, f, h, and k.

The main point of Sections 4-9 and 4-12 is that changes in fiscal and monetary policy may have either strong or weak effects on income, depending on the answers to these questions.

1. How does the effect of a change in $\overline{A}$ on income, the multiplier k_1, depend on the values of b and f (the interest responsiveness of the demand for commodities and money)?

2. How does the effect of a change in M^s/P on income, the multiplier k_2, depend on the values of b and f?

You should work through these sections to see if you can derive each of the diagrammatic results by substituting the appropriate definition of k_1 and k_2 into the simplified general equilibrium equation (9).

Example: If we work through Figure 4-10, the value of k_1 is 2.0, using (10). The value of k_2 is 1.0, using (11). Thus income in the new situation at point E_1 in the top frame of Figure 4-10, using equation (9), is:

$$Q = k_1\overline{A} + k_2\left(\frac{M^s}{P}\right)$$
$$= 2.0(1250) + 1.0(1500)$$
$$= 4000$$

In the bottom frame, $f = 0$, and so

$$k_1 = \frac{1}{\dfrac{1}{k} + \dfrac{bh}{f}} = \frac{1}{\dfrac{1}{4} + \dfrac{50(0.5)}{0}} = 0$$

$$k_2 = \frac{b}{\dfrac{f}{k} + bh} = \frac{50}{0(0.25) + 50(0.5)} = 2.0$$

Thus in the bottom frame of Figure 4-10, the new equilibrium situation at point E_2 is as follows when

[2]A parameter is taken as given or known within a given exercise. Parameters include not just the small letters denoting the multiplier (k), and the interest and income responsiveness of planned autonomous expenditures and money demand (b, h, and f), but also planned autonomous expenditures at a zero interest rate ($\overline{A}$) and the real money supply (M^s/P). Most exercises involve examining the effects of a change in a single parameter, as in $\overline{A}$ or in M^s/P.

[3]The equilibrium interest rate illustrated in Figure 4-9 can be calculated in the same way by substituting the numerical values into equation (6a):

$$r = \frac{0.5(3500) - 1000}{100} = \frac{750}{100} = 7.5 \text{ percent}$$

the real money supply rises from 1750 along the left-hand LM line to 2250 along the right-hand LM line.[4]

$$Q = k_1\overline{A} + k_2\left(\frac{M^s}{P}\right) = 0(500) + 2.0(2250) = 4500$$

The *IS-LM* Model in an Open Economy with Flexible Exchange Rates

Now we may adapt the *IS-LM* model so that it can deal with changes in monetary and fiscal policy in an open economy. This involves two changes. First, allowing for a dependence of net exports on income alters the numerical value of the multiplier. We shall assume that a change in income induces a change in imports 10 percent as large, so the x ("the marginal propensity to import") is 0.1. At this stage we shall also make the model more general by introducing an income tax rate of 0.2—the same numerical example used in Section 3-7. These two additions change the value of the marginal leakage rate (MLR). Instead of MLR $= s = 0.25$, as in the numerical example in the earlier part of this appendix, we now have MLR $= s(1 - \overline{t}) + \overline{t} + x = 0.25(.8) + 0.2 + 0.1 = 0.5$. The multiplier is now:

General Linear Form

$$k = \frac{1}{s(1 - \overline{t}) + \overline{t} + x} \qquad (13)$$

Numerical Example

$$k = \frac{1}{0.25(.8) + 0.2 + 0.1} = 2.0$$

For an open economy with fixed exchange rates, where there is no dependence of net exports on the foreign exchange rate, we could stop here. The new value of k ($= 2.0$) could be substituted into (10) and (11), and our new monetary and fiscal policy multipliers would be $k_1 = 1/(0.5 + 0.25) = 1.333$ and $k_2 = 0.5(1.333) = 0.667$.

In an open economy with flexible exchange rates, however, there is an additional element that

must be taken into consideration. Repeating from Chapter 5 equation (5.3) for net exports, we have:

General Linear Form

$$X = \overline{X} - xQ - ue \qquad (5.3)$$

Numerical Example

$$X = 600 - 0.1Q - 2e$$

Here the final term ($-ue$) reflects the dependence of net exports on the real exchange rate in a flexible exchange rate system.

In Chapter 5 we learned that the real exchange rate was positively related to the interest rate. This can be expressed in the following simple way:

General Linear Form   Numerical Example

$$e = dr \qquad\qquad e = 25r \qquad (14)$$

For instance, the numerical example states that at a real interest rate of 4 percent, the real exchange rate would be 100 ($= 25 \times 4$), and at a real interest rate of 6 percent would be 150 ($= 25 \times 6$). (**Caution:** (14) is highly over-simplified and intended to represent the behavior of the exchange rate only in the short run when other more fundamental factors remain fixed.)

Once we substitute (14) into the expression for net exports, we obtain:

General Linear Form

$$X = \overline{X} - xQ - udr \qquad (15)$$

Numerical Example

$$X = 600 - .1Q - 2(25)r$$

Since X is a component of total expenditure, our new equation (15) changes the equation for commodity market equilibrium, the IS curve equation, from (4) to:

General Linear Form

$$Q = k(\overline{A} - [b + ud]r) \qquad (16)$$
$$= k(\overline{A} - b'r)$$

Numerical Example

$$Q = 2.0\overline{A} - 2.0[50 + 2(25)]r$$
$$Q = 2.0\overline{A} - 2.0(100)r$$

Comparing (15) and (16), we note that the dependence of net exports on the interest rate, the term

---

[4]These assumed numerical values for the real money supply were not used as labels for the bottom frame of Figure 4-10 to avoid complicating the exposition in the text.

	Closed economy, no income tax ($t = 0, x = 0, d = 0$)	Closed economy with income tax ($t = .2, x = 0, d = 0$)	Open economy with income tax, fixed exchange rate ($t = .2, x = .1, d = 0$)	Open economy with income tax, flexible exchange rate ($t = .2, x = .1, d = 25$)
MLR	0.25	0.4	0.5	0.5
k	4.0	2.5	2.0	2.0
k_1	2.0	1.54	1.33	1.0
k_2	1.0	0.77	0.67	1.0
IS slope (Change in Q for each point increase in r)	-200	-125	-100	-200

udr in (15), makes the IS curve slope depend on the term $[b + ud]$ times the interest rate (r). The first element in the brackets, b, is the interest responsiveness of domestic spending ($a + I_p$), while the second element, ud, is the interest responsiveness of net exports. To simplify the equations that come below, in the second line of (16) we relabel $[b + ud]$ as b'. What happened to the other terms, $\overline{X} - xQ$, in (15)? The autonomous component of net exports ($\overline{X}$) is included in $\overline{A}$, which is the total amount of autonomous spending that occurs at zero interest rate. It includes not just the autonomous component of net exports, but also private planned spending ($a + I_p$), government spending (G), and the effect of autonomous tax revenue on consumption ($-c\overline{T}$). And the xQ term alters the Chapter 3 multiplier (k) as in equation (3.25).

Thus the effect of the interest rate on net exports in a flexible exchange rate system can be introduced into the IS-LM model by the simple device of replacing the interest responsiveness term b (50 in our numerical example) by b' (100 in our numerical example). Substituting b' for b in equations (10) and (11) for multiplier effects of $\overline{A}$ and M^s/P on income, and using our new numerical example for the Chapter 3 multiplier ($k = 1/\text{MLR} = 2.0$), we obtain:

General Linear Form

$$k_1 = \frac{1}{\frac{1}{k} + \frac{b'h}{f}} \quad (17)$$

Numerical Example

$$k_1 = \frac{1}{\frac{1}{2.0} + \frac{100(.5)}{100}} = 1.0$$

Similarly, $k_2 = (b'/f)k_1 = (100/100)1.0 = 1.0$.

Using these multipliers, a real income level of 3500 could be obtained with $\overline{A} = 2500$ and $M^s/P = 1000$, using equation (9):

$$Q = k_1\overline{A} + k_2 (M^s/P) \quad (18)$$
$$= 1.0(2500) + 1.0(1000) = 3500$$

Note in (18) that because the autonomous spending multiplier is now 1.0 instead of 2.0 (as in the earlier numerical example of equation [12]), it takes 2500 rather than 1250 of autonomous spending to reach a real income of 3500. Where does this extra autonomous spending come from? Recall from (13) that the Chapter 3 multiplier (k) is lower in this section not just because of the dependence of imports on income, but also because of the introduction of an income tax. Assuming that the income tax finances extra government expenditures, we can explain the higher level of autonomous spending in our example in the following comparison:

	Assumed in equation (12)	In equation (18)
Autonomous consumption	250	
Autonomous consumption after tax at 0.2 rate		200
Planned investment (untaxed)	1000	1000
Government spending	0	700
Autonomous component of net exports	0	600
Total of $\overline{A}$	1250	2500

The table at the top of this page provides a comparison showing the difference made by the income tax, and by introducing the open economy with fixed and flexible exchange rates. Each example continues to assume $s = .25$, $b = 50$, $h = 0.5$, $f = 100$, and $u = 2$.

PART III

Aggregate Demand, Aggregate Supply, and Stabilization Policy

The *IS-LM* Model, and the Aggregate Demand and Supply Curves

The price of commodities in the market is formed by means of a certain struggle which takes place between the buyers and the sellers.

—Henry Thornton, 1802

Until now we have assumed that the level of prices is fixed. We have shown how real income (or GNP) and the interest rate are shifted about by changes in "exogenous disturbances." Some of these disturbances originate in the private sector, including changes in business and consumer confidence and in foreign trade (that is, in the autonomous component of net exports). Others originate in the government sector, sometimes because government policymakers are trying to stabilize the economy through changes in government spending, tax rates, or the money supply, and sometimes because wars or other political events cause sharp changes in government spending.

6-1 The Role of Aggregate Demand and Supply

Now it is time to add the price level to the list of endogenous variables which, like real income and the real interest rate, our economic theory can explain. Recall that the price level is measured by an aggregate price index like the implicit GNP deflator, which is simply an economywide weighted average of the prices of goods today compared to the prices of the same goods in a base year like 1982. When the prices of most goods are rising, the aggregate deflator (P) increases, and we have inflation. When the prices of most goods are falling, P decreases, and we have deflation. During a period of aggregate price stability, the prices of some goods increase, some decrease, but the average of all prices (P) stays approximately the same.

The **aggregate de- mand curve shows dif- ferent combinations of the price level and real output at which the money and commodity markets are both in equilibrium.**

The purpose of this chapter is to show how exogenous disturbances originating either in the private sector or in the government can cause *simultaneous* changes in real income and the price level. We begin by showing that the *IS-LM* model developed in Chapters 4 and 5 implies a negatively sloped schedule, the **aggregate demand curve,** relating real income to the price level. If the price level for some reason becomes higher, real income tends to decrease, when we hold constant the nominal money supply and planned autonomous spending.

But the aggregate demand curve is just one relationship between real income and the price level and is inadequate to determine both variables, just as the *IS* curve by itself cannot determine real income and the interest rate without the help of a second schedule, the *LM* curve. Similarly, in this chapter we need a second schedule, the **aggregate supply curve,** in order to determine real income and the price level. Both variables are determined at the point where the aggregate demand and supply curves intersect.

This chapter concentrates on deriving the aggregate demand and supply curves and explaining their position and the factors underlying their slopes. Then the next two chapters *use* both curves to examine the differing views of various groups of economists regarding the effectiveness and desirability of stabilization policy.

The **aggregate supply curve** shows the amount of output that business firms are willing to produce at different price levels.

6-2 Flexible Prices and the *DD* Curve

In this section we develop a new tool, the aggregate demand (*DD*) curve, which summarizes the effect of changing income. It is derived directly from the *IS-LM* model developed in the last two chapters.

Effect of Changing Prices on the *LM* Curve

We already know that the *LM* curve shifts its position whenever there is a change in the real money supply. Until now every *LM* shift has resulted from a change in the nominal money supply, while the price level has been held at a constant level. The price level has been treated as a parameter, or a known variable, allowing us to concentrate on the determination of the two unknowns, real income (Q) and the interest rate (r).

However, the *LM* curve can shift in exactly the same way when a change in the real money supply M^s/P is caused by a change in the price level P, while the nominal money supply M^s remains fixed at a single value, say $1000 billion. The top frame of Figure 6-1 illustrates three *LM* curves drawn for three values of P and M^s/P, each assuming the same nominal money supply, $M^s = 1000$. For instance, the middle curve LM_0 is identical to LM_0 in the previous chapter. The price index is 1.0, and because $M^s = 1000$, M^s/P also equals 1000.

A doubling of the price level to $P = 2.0$ would cut the real money supply in half to $M^s/P = 1000/2.0 = 500$. For the real demand for money to be equal to the smaller real supply of money, some combination of lower real income and a higher interest rate is needed, as along the left-hand curve LM_1. Similarly, if the price level is very low, only 0.5, the real money supply is a large $M^s/P = 1000/0.5 = 2000$, and equilibrium in the money market occurs at combinations of r and Q along the right-hand curve LM_2.

What is the level of real income if the nominal money supply remains fixed at $1000 billion? The answer depends on which price level and *LM* curve is valid and on the position of the *IS* curve. When $\overline{A} = 1500$, the commodity market is in equilibrium anywhere along the IS_1 curve copied

Figure 6-1
Effect on Real Income of Different Values of the Price Index

In the top frame three different *LM* curves are drawn for three different hypothetical values of the price index. Corresponding to the three levels of the price index are three positions of equilibrium, J, E_0, and H. These three points are drawn again in the lower frame with the same horizontal axis (real output), but the price index for the vertical axis. A drop in the price index from point J to E_0 and then to H raises the *real* money supply and stimulates real output along the aggregate demand curve DD_0.

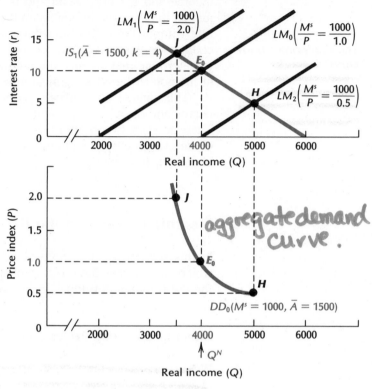

THE AGGREGATE DEMAND CURVE SHOWS THAT A DECLINE IN THE PRICE LEVEL STIMULATES REAL OUTPUT

aggregate demand curve.

from Chapters 4 and 5.[1] When $P = 1.0$ and the LM_0 curve describes money-market equilibrium, the economy's general equilibrium occurs at point E_0, where LM_0 crosses IS_1 and equilibrium real output (Q) is \$4000 billion.[2]

Characteristics of the *DD* Curve

To show the relationship between equilibrium Q and the assumed price index P, a new diagram is drawn in the bottom frame of Figure 6-1. The horizontal dimension once again is real output, and so point E_0 in the bottom frame lies just below E_0 in the upper frame. The vertical dimension in the bottom frame measures the price index P, so E_0 is plotted at the assumed value $P = 1.0$.

Other values of real income would occur if the price level were higher or lower than 1.0. A price level of 2.0 cuts the real money supply in half, as shown along LM_1 in the top frame, and it reduces real output to \$3500 billion at point J. Point J is plotted in the lower frame again at a vertical height

---

[1] Recall that the definition of $\bar{A}$ is the level of autonomous planned real spending that would occur if the interest rate were zero.

[2] E_0 is the same as E_5 in Chapters 4 and 5. We now take the opportunity to renumber the equilibrium points.

$P = 2.0$. Similarly, a lower price index of $P = 0.5$ boosts the real money supply, shifts the LM curve to LM_2, and raises output to $5000 billion, as plotted at point H.

The curved line in the bottom frame connecting points J, E_0, and H shows all the possible combinations of P and Q consistent with a nominal money supply of $1000 billion and a value of $\bar{A}$ of $1500 billion. If the assumed value of P is high, then Q is low, and vice versa. The curved line is called the aggregate demand curve and is abbreviated DD. The main characteristics of DD are

1. The DD curve shows all the possible crossing points of a single IS commodity-market equilibrium curve with the various LM money-market equilibrium curves drawn for each possible price level. Everywhere along the DD curve *both* the commodity and money markets are in equilibrium.

2. The DD curve slopes downward because a lower price index (P) raises the real money supply, thereby lowering the interest rate and stimulating planned expenditures, requiring an increase in actual real GNP (Q) to keep the commodity market in equilibrium. The steeper the IS curve, the steeper the DD curve.

SELF-TEST Try to determine whether a steeper LM curve would make the DD curve steeper or flatter.

3. Because it describes the economy's general equilibrium, the position of the DD curve depends on all the factors that can shift the IS and LM curves except the price level.[3] Since a shift in either M^s or $\bar{A}$ will shift DD, the assumed values of both M^s and $\bar{A}$ are always written next to each DD curve.

4. An increase in either M^s or $\bar{A}$ will shift the DD curve to the right, and a decrease in either will shift the curve to the left.

6-3 Shifting the Aggregate Demand Curve with Monetary and Fiscal Policy

Effects of a Change in the Nominal Money Supply

We begin by showing how an increase in M^s, the nominal money supply, shifts the DD curve to the right. Begin at point E_0 in the upper frame of Figure 6-2 and assume that the price level equals 1.0. If the nominal money supply were raised from $1000 to $2000 billion, then M^s/P would rise to 2000 and the money market would be in equilibrium along LM_2, not LM_0. General equilibrium would occur at point H in the top frame, where LM_2 crosses the fixed IS curve, at $Q = 5000 billion.

---

[3]The equation of the DD curve is the income equation (9) in the appendix to Chapter 5:

$$Q = k_1 \bar{A} + k_2 \frac{M^s}{P}$$

Figure 6-2

The Effect on the *DD* Curve of an Increase in the Nominal Money Supply from $1000 to $2000 Billion

In the top frame a doubling of the nominal money supply from $1000 to $2000 billion moves the *LM* curve rightward from LM_0 to LM_2 and the economy's general equilibrium (where *IS* crosses *LM*) from point E_0 to point H. In the lower frame we remain at a vertical distance of $P = 1.0$, since nothing has happened to change the price level. The higher money supply raises real output and causes the economy's equilibrium position to be at point H' rather than at point E_0. Notice that the new DD_1 curve running through point H' lies everywhere twice as high as the old DD_0 curve.

HOW A BOOST IN MONEY PUSHES THE *DD* CURVE TO THE RIGHT

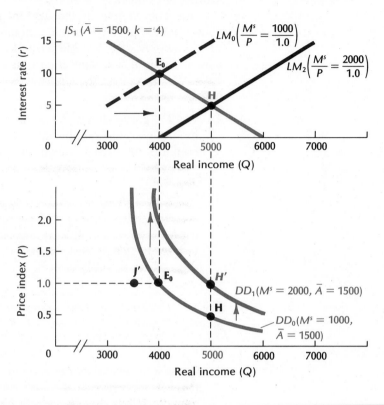

Looking directly below, point H' is plotted for $Q = \$5000$ billion and $P = 1.0$, the assumed value. Thus H' lies on a higher aggregate demand curve DD_1, which shows the various possible combinations of real output with various assumed price levels when $M^s = \$2000$ billion. Curve DD_1 lies above the original DD_0 curve drawn for $M^s = \$1000$ billion. By the same reasoning, a low assumed nominal money supply value of $500 billion would shift the *DD* curve downward to a new curve (not drawn) running through point J'.

Notice that the aggregate demand schedule *DD* shifts up vertically in Figure 6-2 by exactly the same proportion as the nominal money supply. Along DD_1 the nominal money supply ($2000 billion) is exactly double its value along DD_0 ($1000 billion), and at H' the DD_1 curve is exactly twice as high (where $P = 1.0$) as the DD_0 curve at H (where $P = 0.5$). This occurs because a doubling of money and a doubling of prices from point H to H' leads to the same real money supply, hence the same *LM* curve, the same interest rate, and the same real GNP.[4]

---

[4]As a technical matter, the proportional vertical movement in the *DD* schedule described in the text requires that all forms of real wealth double when the money supply doubles. Thus, for instance, 1) outstanding government bonds must double, or 2) there can be no outstanding government bonds, or 3) individuals must discount fully the future tax liabilities made necessary to pay the interest on the bonds, implying that government bonds are not part of wealth. See Don Patinkin, *Money, Interest, and Prices,* 2nd ed. (New York: Harper & Row, 1965), pp. 288–310.

Effects of a Change in Autonomous Spending

Until now, in both Figures 6-1 and 6-2, the IS curve has remained fixed at its original position given by the multiplier ($k = 4.0$) and the value of autonomous spending that occurs at a zero interest rate ($\bar{A} = 1500$). Note in both of those figures that the assumed value of $\bar{A}$ is indicated in parentheses, along with the assumed value of the nominal money supply, next to the DD_0 and DD_1 curves. What happens if we change the assumed value of $\bar{A}$, while leaving M^s at its original value of $1000 billion?

Figure 6-3 shows the effect on the DD curve of an assumed *decline in $\bar{A}$* from $1500 to $1250 billion. We learned in Figure 4-12 that a $250 billion change in $\bar{A}$ would cause a $500 billion change in real income, for a multiplier of 2.0, once the requirement for equilibrium in the money market is taken into account. Similarly, in Figure 6-3 the assumed $250 billion drop in autonomous spending shifts the DD_0 curve leftward by $500 billion at each point to the new position DD_2. Among the reasons that autonomous spending might decline, causing such a leftward DD shift, are a decline in business and consumer confidence, a decline in government spending, an increase in tax rates, or a decrease in the autonomous component of net exports.

Comparing Figures 6-2 and 6-3, we note that the directions of the shifts in DD are different. A change in the money supply as in Figure 6-2 shifts the DD curve up or down *vertically*. Since in Figure 6-2 the nominal money supply is assumed to double, curve DD_1 lies everywhere at double the vertical position of curve DD_0. However, a change in autonomous spending as in Figure 6-3 shifts the DD curve left or right *horizontally*. The $250 billion reduction in autonomous spending shifts the DD curve leftward by exactly $500 billion at each price level.

Will the reduction in autonomous spending reduce real income and leave the price level unchanged? If so, the economy will move from point E_0 to point F, and real income will fall from $4000 billion to $3500 billion. Or, will the reduction in autonomous spending reduce the price level and leave real income unchanged? If so, the economy will move from point E_0 to point G, and the price level will fall from 1.0 to 0.67. Which outcome will occur?

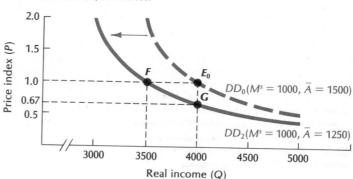

Figure 6-3

The Effect on the DD Curve of a $250 Billion Decline in Planned Autonomous Spending

Starting from point E_0, the equilibrium position when $\bar{A}$ = $1500 billion, a drop in $\bar{A}$ to $1250 billion would move the economy to point F if the price index were to remain constant, as in earlier chapters. But now at any point to the left of 4000 the price index declines. A drop in the price index from 1.0 to 0.67 raises the real money supply from the initial $1000 billion to $1500 billion, enough to push the economy's real output equilibrium to point G.

WILL A DECLINE IN AUTONOMOUS SPENDING CUT REAL INCOME, THE PRICE LEVEL, OR BOTH?

Figure 6-3 cannot tell us, because the *DD* curve by itself does not contain enough information to pin down both the price level and real income. To ascertain where the economy will come to rest along the numerous possible positions along the *DD* curve, we must find another schedule to intersect the *DD* curve. We now turn to the possible shapes of this additional schedule, called the aggregate supply curve, and to its derivation.

6-4 Possible Shapes of the Aggregate Supply Curve

The aggregate supply schedule shows how much business firms are willing to produce at different hypothetical price levels. Such a schedule of business firms' behavior can have several possible shapes. Depending on the shape, the implications of a shift in the aggregate demand curve (whether caused by an increase in the money supply or in autonomous spending) are quite different. In Figure 6-4 we show a rightward shift from aggregate demand curve DD_0 to DD_1. Note that there are no numbers on the axes, since what is important is whether the aggregate supply curve is vertical, horizontal, or positively sloped. The precise value of the slope, if positive, does not matter for the analysis of this chapter.

How will the increase in aggregate demand be divided between a higher level of real GNP and a higher price level? Three hypothetical answers, corresponding to three hypothetical aggregate supply curves, are shown in Figure 6-4. In Chapters 3–5 we assumed that the price level always remains fixed; thus we assumed that the economy moved from its initial position E_0 directly rightward to a higher level of real GNP at point E_1 along the "horizontal aggregate supply curve." A second possibility is that real GNP is al-

---

Figure 6-4
Effect of a Rightward Shift in the *DD* Curve with Three Alternative Aggregate Supply Curves

The horizontal supply curve at the price level P_0 reflects the "fixed price" assumption of Chapters 3–5. An increase in aggregate demand that shifts the DD_0 curve to DD_1 will move the economy from its initial position E_0 to new position E_1. In contrast, if the supply curve is vertical, higher aggregate demand pushes the economy from point E_0 to E_3. An intermediate possibility is that both output and prices rise *in the short run* to a point such as E_2, and that *in the long run* the *boost* in real GNP gradually disappears until we arrive at E_3.

THE REACTION OF REAL GNP AND THE PRICE LEVEL TO HIGHER AGGREGATE DEMAND DEPENDS ON THE SHAPE OF THE AGGREGATE SUPPLY CURVE

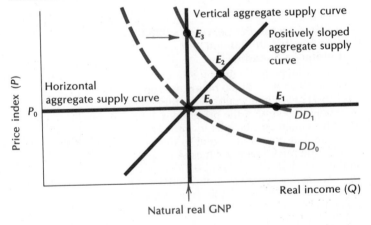

ways fixed at the level of natural real GNP. If so, the same increase in aggregate demand would have no effect at all on real GNP. Instead, business firms would simply raise the price level from P_0 to a higher price level at point E_3 along the "vertical aggregate supply curve" in Figure 6-4, leaving their level of production (Q) unchanged.

A third possibility is shown by the positively sloped curve labeled "Positively sloped aggregate supply curve." If this curve were valid, then the rightward shift in aggregate demand would cause business firms to raise *both* their prices and their level of production, moving the economy to a point like E_2. As we shall see, a point like E_2 is likely to be achieved only temporarily. In succeeding periods the positively sloped aggregate supply curve is likely to shift its position, so that eventually the economy winds up at a point like E_3, with real GNP back where it started but with a higher price level.

This analysis shares with previous chapters the approach of **comparative statics.** Our basic diagram measures the level, not the rate of change, of real output and the price level. Our analysis is just like a show of photographic slides. We show one slide in the form of a single static equilibrium position, we turn out the lights, and, when the lights come back on, the economy has moved to a new static equilibrium position such as point E_2 in Figure 6-4. Our comparative static slide-show method of analysis cannot tell us anything about economic dynamics. How long does it take output and the price level to change? What is the rate of price change (the inflation rate) per year or per month? We will examine the dynamic relationship between the rate of inflation and real GNP in Chapter 9.

Comparative statics is a technique of economic analysis in which a comparison is made between two equilibrium positions, ignoring the behavior of the economy between the two equilibrium positions, either the length of time required or the route followed during the transition between the initial and final positions.

6-5 The Aggregate Supply Curve When the Wage Rate Is Constant

Supply Curve for the Individual Firm

A basic tool introduced in every elementary economics course is the supply curve for the individual business firm. We will briefly examine the factors that account for the positive slope of the firm's supply curve, and will then assume that the economy's aggregate supply curve has the same positive slope.

The firm makes production decisions by comparing the price of a good with its marginal cost—that is, the extra cost the firm incurs by producing an extra unit of output. Because firms are in business to make a profit, they will not produce extra output unless the extra revenue they receive from selling an extra unit is *at least as high* as the extra cost they incur in producing that unit.

The **production function** is a relationship, usually written in algebra, that shows how much output can be produced by a given quantity of factor inputs.

The firm's production function. We analyze the firm's production decision in the short run during which its capital stock (machines and factories), its usage of land and natural resources like energy, and its technological knowledge are all assumed to be fixed. The firm's **production function** shows how its output is related to its inputs of labor, capital, natural re-

Table 6-1   Derivation of the Supply Curve for an Individual Firm

Point in Figures 6-5 and 6-6	Workers hired	Total output	Extra units of output per extra worker (marginal product)	Marginal labor cost per extra worker	Marginal labor cost per extra unit of output	Required selling price
(1)	(2)	(3)	(4)	(5)	(6)	(7)
A	1	10	10	$80	$ 8.00	$ 8.00
B	2	18	8	$80	$10.00	$10.00
C	3	24	6	$80	$13.33	$13.33
D	4	28	4	$80	$20.00	$20.00

sources, and technology. Because we assume that in the short run all of the inputs other than labor are fixed, we are concerned only with the extra amount the firm can produce by hiring more labor. In Table 6-1 each of the four lines shows how much the firm can produce as its number of employees is increased from one to four.

The first worker can produce ten units, but adding the second worker produces only eight extra units, bringing total output to eighteen. Why is the second worker less productive than the first? The available machinery, factory, energy, and land now have to be "stretched" over two workers, rather than just one, so each worker has less of the other inputs to work with. The same principle of the diminishing **marginal product of labor** is evident when the third and fourth workers are added. Thus the third worker adds only six units of output, and the fourth adds only four units.

Figure 6-5 illustrates the relationships shown in Table 6-1. The top frame is the production function itself, plotting output against the number of workers hired. The production function is a curved line, reflecting the diminishing marginal product of extra workers. In the bottom frame is the marginal product line that slopes downward, reflecting labor's diminishing marginal product.[5]

Marginal cost equals price.   We do not yet know how much the firm will choose to produce. The production function is like a menu, showing alternative possibilities, and just as a diner wants to know the price of each item, so the firm needs similar information. In particular, the firm must know (1) what wage each worker earns and (2) what price can be charged for the product. Column (5) in Table 6-1 shows the assumption that every worker is paid the same wage, $80 per day. The first worker costs the firm $80, and

The **marginal product of labor** is the extra output that a firm can produce by adding an extra unit of labor input.

---

[5] In the language of calculus the marginal product line shows the derivative of the production function with respect to changes in labor input. In terms of the diagrams, the lower portion of Figure 6-5 represents the slope of the production function plotted in the upper frame of Figure 6-5.

Figure 6-5
The Relation between the Number of Workers Hired, Total Output, and the Marginal Product of Labor

This figure shows how hiring additional workers will raise output and that the extra amount each new worker can produce is less than the output of the last worker hired. The top frame illustrates the production function, which is a relation between labor input and output. The bottom frame illustrates the diminishing marginal product of labor itself.

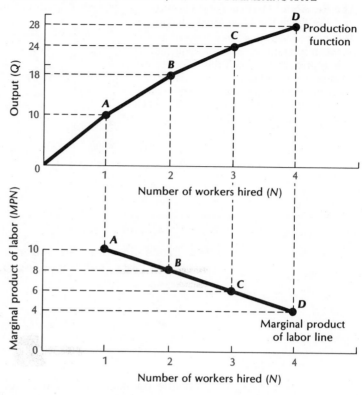

he produces ten units, so the "marginal labor cost" incurred for the first ten units is $80/10, or $8.00 apiece. Similarly, the second worker is paid $80 and produces eight units, which cost the firm $80/8, or $10 apiece. The marginal costs of the output produced by the third and fourth workers are $13.33 and $20, respectively.

Once we know the firm's marginal cost schedule as written in column (6) of Table 6-1, we know its supply schedule, because the firm will be willing to produce only up to the point where *the price of the product equals its marginal cost.* To produce more than this would mean expanding into the region where marginal cost exceeds price and the extra units raise total cost more than total revenue. To produce less than this would mean giving up additional profit because the marginal cost is less than the price. In the classic agricultural example often used to illustrate this idea, farmers decide how much wheat to plant on the basis of the market price they expect to receive for the wheat. The firm's supply curve can be drawn as in Figure 6-6, which simply plots the total level of output in column (3) of Table 6-1 against the price the firm must receive to be willing to produce this amount from column (7).

Figure 6-6

The Relation between Total Output and the Price the Firm Must Charge

This figure illustrates the relationship between total output and the required selling price derived in Table 6-1. Because each additional worker is paid the same daily wage but produces less and less output, the marginal cost of each additional unit of output rises.

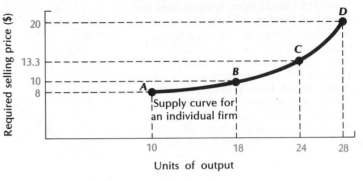

DIMINISHING MARGINAL LABOR PRODUCTIVITY MAKES THE FIRM'S SUPPLY CURVE SLOPE UP EVEN WHEN THE WAGE RATE IS FIXED

The firm's demand for labor. The connection between the marginal product of labor (*MPN*), marginal cost (*MC*), and the wage rate (*W*) can be written:

General Form / Numerical Example for First Worker

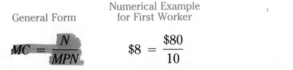

$$MC = \frac{N}{MPN} \qquad \$8 = \frac{\$80}{10} \tag{6.1}$$

From the point of view of the individual firm, the wage rate is given. This implies that marginal cost changes inversely with marginal product. Thus the hiring of additional workers brings with it a *rising* marginal cost corresponding to a *diminishing* marginal product. Marginal cost can be defined solely in terms of labor cost because all other factors of production (for example, capital, energy) are being held fixed. This relation in (6.1) can be combined with the condition that a competitive firm maximizes profits when it selects its output level where price (*P*) is equal to marginal cost:

$$P = MC \tag{6.2}$$

For instance, in Table 6-1 the "required selling price" (*P*) in column (7) is equal to marginal cost (*MC*) in column (6).

Combining the two equations by substituting (6.1) into (6.2), we obtain a relation among price, wage rate, and marginal product:

$$P = \frac{W}{MPN} \tag{6.3}$$

By interchanging the position of the *P* and *MPN* terms, we can also use (6.3) to show another implication of profit maximizing behavior by an individual firm: the real wage rate (*W/P*) must be equal to the marginal product of labor.

General Form / Numerical Example for First Worker

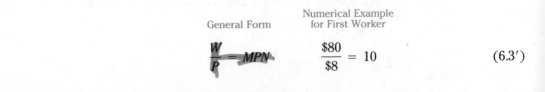

$$\frac{W}{P} = MPN \qquad \frac{\$80}{\$8} = 10 \tag{6.3'}$$

Now we see that there are two equivalent ways of stating that the firm maximizes profit. First, in equation (6.2), the firm must choose the number of workers to make price equal to marginal cost ($P = MC$). Second, in equation (6.3'), the firm must hire until the real wage (W/P) is equal to the marginal product of labor. For a competitive firm (for example, a farmer), both the wage rate and the price level (and hence the real wage) are given, set by the large market of which the individual firm is one very small part. This means that the only choice the firm must make is how much labor to hire. Thus equation (6.3') says, in essence, that the *quantity of labor demanded by the firm depends on the real wage that is set for the firm by the market*.

The Aggregate Supply Curve

If all business firms in the economy are identical, and if all maximize their profits, then equation (6.3') is just as valid for the whole economy as for a single firm, as long as we continue to assume that the nominal wage rate is given. The derivation of the economy-wide aggregate supply curve is shown in Figure 6-7.

Notice that in Figures 6-4 and 6-7, we have discontinued writing specific numerical values on the axes. We do not indicate the exact level of real GNP but label points only by general designations; for instance, P_0, N_0, and Q_0. Why? From here on, with only a few exceptions, specific numbers on the axes would add unnecessary arithmetic without contributing anything essential to understanding. The main thing to notice about a diagram such as Figure 6-7 is the direction of the relation being discussed.

The labor demand curve.   Now let us look more closely at the derivation of the aggregate supply curve in Figure 6-7. The aggregate "labor demand curve" in the lower left frame of Figure 6-7 is just the same as the "marginal product of labor line" in Figure 6-5, but it has been horizontally added across all firms. All firms in the economy choose the level of employment by looking along the labor demand curve to the point where the real wage (W/P) equals labor's marginal product (MPN). Because the marginal product of labor (MPN) is always set equal to the real wage (W/P), in Figure 6-7 the vertical axis in the lower left frame has been labeled W/P rather than MPN as in Figure 6-5.

For instance, if the wage rate is W_0 and the price level is P_0, then the real wage is W_0/P_0. The labor demand curve shows the number of workers to be hired at point B, and this number, N_0, is marked on the horizontal axis. If the price level happened to be higher at P_1, but the wage rate remained fixed at W_0, then the real wage rate (W_0/P_1) would be lower. Workers would be cheaper to hire, and firms would raise employment to N_1, as shown by point C along the labor demand curve. Similarly, at the lower price level P_2, the real wage would be higher, and the number of workers hired would be N_2 at point A.

The labor demand curve simply states that a decrease in the real wage will induce firms to hire more workers, and vice versa. Its position depends on the slope of the production function. The labor demand curve in Figure 6-7 is labeled N_0^d, to remind us that the position of the labor demand schedule would shift up if something happened to raise the marginal product of labor, and it would shift down in the opposite case. Anything that shifts the production function will shift the labor demand curve.

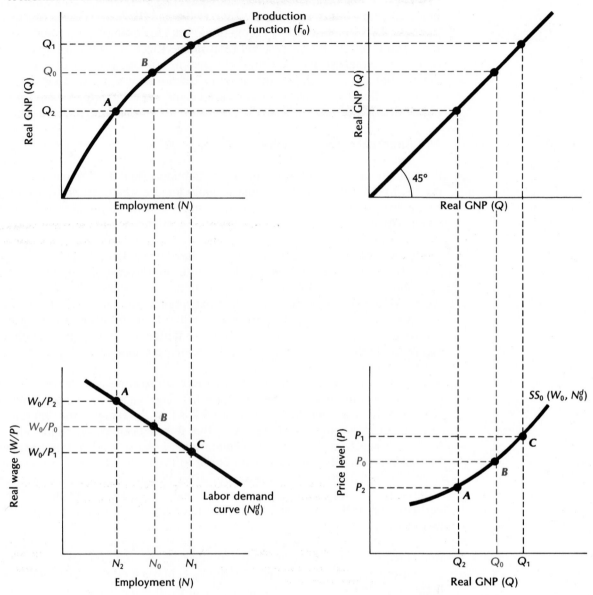

Figure 6-7 **The Labor Demand Curve, the Production Function, and the Aggregate Supply Curve for the Whole Economy**

The production function and the labor demand curve are derived by horizontally summing up all of the individual firm production functions and marginal product lines from Figure 6-5. Similarly, the aggregate supply curve is derived by horizontally summing up all the individual firm supply curves from Figure 6-6. Notice that in this diagram there are no numbers on the axes. Also, we have switched terminology from "output" to "real GNP," and from "number of workers" to "employment" in order to make this diagram correspond with the official concepts used to describe the entire economy.

The production function and the aggregate supply curve. Now we can examine the relationship between employment and real GNP at different price levels. For instance, point B shows that N_0 workers will be hired if the price level is P_0 and real wage is W_0/P_0. Looking directly above point B to the top left frame of Figure 6-7, we see another point B that lies on the production function and shows the amount of real GNP (Q_0) that can be produced by N_0 workers. Then, following the dashed line to the right and down, we come to a third point B in the lower right frame. This shows that the price level P_0 induces firms to produce Q_0, as long as the wage rate is W_0. Similarly, we can trace around the diagram and find the amount of output that will be produced if the price level is higher at P_1, and lower at P_2.

The line connecting the points A, B, and C in the lower right frame is the aggregate supply curve, labeled with the symbol "SS". It slopes upward for the same reason as the individual firm's supply curve in Figure 6-6. Notice that all three points A, B, and C, share exactly the same nominal wage rate (W_0). For this reason, the SS curve is labeled with the wage rate assumed in drawing it, W_0. Only the price level differs among the three points. Because a change in the price level also changes the real wage, it changes employment and real GNP.

Distinguishing Features of the SS Curve

Elementary economics textbooks describe the determination of price and quantity for an individual product by examining the intersection of demand and supply curves for that product. In the same way, in this chapter we describe the determination of the aggregate price level and real GNP by examining the intersection of the aggregate demand (DD) and aggregate supply (SS) curves. The main characteristics of the DD curve were enumerated in Section 6-2. Now we are prepared to enumerate the main characteristics of the SS curve.

1. The SS curve shows the profit-maximizing level of real GNP for different levels of an aggregate price index like the GNP deflator. Everywhere along the SS curve business firms are content to continue producing the same amount of output.

2. The SS curve slopes upward because a higher price index (P) reduces the real wage and makes an increase in production more profitable, given the fixed wage rate. Firms can raise their profits if they hire more workers, thus raising employment. Higher employment moves the economy out along its production function, raising real GNP. The steeper the economy's labor demand curve—that is, the more steeply the marginal product of labor falls when added workers are hired—the steeper will be the positively sloped SS curve.

3. The position of the SS curve depends on the assumed level of the nominal wage rate (W). In Figure 6-7 this assumed level is W_0. Anything that raises the wage rate will shift the SS curve upward. For instance, if the wage rate were to rise to W_1, Figure 6-8 shows that the SS curve would shift upward from SS_0 to SS_1.

4. The position of the SS curve also depends on the productivity of labor. For this reason we have written the label of the labor demand curve,

A HIGHER NOMINAL WAGE RATE SHIFTS THE *SS* CURVE UP

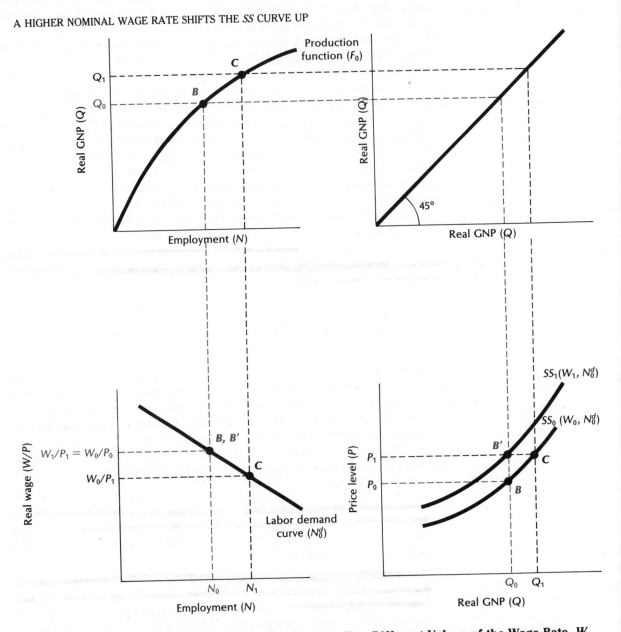

Figure 6-8   **The Aggregate Supply Curve for Two Different Values of the Wage Rate, W_0 and W_1**

The labor demand curve, production function, and aggregate supply curve SS_0 are identical to those drawn in Figure 6-7. So also are points B and C, the quantities N_0 and Q_0, and the price levels P_0 and P_1. The new ingredient here is a higher wage rate W_1, which shifts the aggregate supply curve up from SS_0 to SS_1. The higher wage rate shifts the *SS* curve because at a given price level, workers are more costly, and so firms hire fewer workers and produce less output. Points B and B' in the lower left-hand frame are identical, because we assume that the percentage difference between W_1 and W_0 is the same as between P_1 and P_0. Thus point B' lies directly above point B in the lower right-hand frame.

N_0^d, also as part of the label of the SS_0 curve in Figures 6-7 and 6-8. Recall that the amount of output that each extra worker could produce in Table 6-1 was derived on the assumption that all other inputs, including capital, natural resources, and technology, were fixed. If any of the other inputs were to increase, then each extra worker could produce more, and the labor demand curve would shift up. The production function would shift up as well, and the aggregate supply curve would shift to the right. In the opposite direction, an adverse event like the sharp jump in world energy prices of 1973–74 and 1979–80 can cut the quantity of energy that each firm uses. This will shift the labor demand curve down, the production function down, and the aggregate supply curve to the left.

SELF-TEST   Which of the following causes a movement *along* the aggregate supply curve, and which causes a shift in the curve? If the curve shifts, does it shift up or down? (1) A union concession that reduces the wage rate to help a firm survive foreign competition. (2) A discovery of a giant oil field in Missouri that reduces the price of oil. (3) An increase in the money supply.

6-6   How the Wage Rate Is Set

So far we have seen that the aggregate supply curve slopes upward for any *given* nominal wage rate. But surely the wage rate will not stay at the same level forever. If the wage rate increases, the SS curve will shift up, and its intersection point with the economy's aggregate demand curve (DD) will shift as well.

Thus the determinants of the actual wage rate paid have a crucial effect on the nature of the economy's response to a change in aggregate demand.

The Equilibrium Real Wage Rate

Distinguishing the nominal and real wage rates.   We first encountered the distinction between nominal and real variables in Chapter 1, where we introduced nominal and real GNP. The nominal wage rate is simply the actual wage rate paid. This is assumed to be a fixed amount (for example, $80 per day) in the derivation of supply curve SS_0 of Figure 6-7. The real wage rate (W/P) is the nominal wage rate (W) divided by an aggregate price index like the GNP deflator. For instance, if the GNP deflator for a 1982 base year were 2.0, and the nominal wage rate were $80 per day, then the real wage rate would be $40 per day in 1982 dollars.

In Figure 6-8 we can see in operation the distinction between the nominal and real wage rates. As long as the labor demand curve is at the fixed position N_0^d, then an increase in employment from N_0 to N_1 requires a decrease in the real wage rate from W_0/P_0 to W_0/P_1. If the nominal wage rate W_0 remains fixed, then this required decline in the real wage rate *must* be accomplished by an increase in the price level. This increase in labor employed, and hence in real output, when P increases and W remains fixed, is why the aggregate supply curve slopes up in the right side of Figure 6-8.

But the nominal wage rate is unlikely to stay fixed forever. If it shifts up to W_1, then the aggregate supply curve will shift up from SS_0 to SS_1. In Figure 6-8 we assume that W_1 exceeds W_0 by the same percentage as P_1 exceeds P_0, so

$$\frac{W_1}{P_1} = \frac{W_0}{P_0}$$

Thus the real wage rate W_1/P_1 at point B' along the new SS_1 line is exactly the same as the real wage rate W_0/P_0 at point B. Hence the level of employment and real GNP (N_0 and Q_0) must be identical at points B and B'. Indeed we see in the lower left frame of Figure 6-8 that points B and B' coincide.

Determinants of the equilibrium real wage rate. In Chapter 3 we defined equilibrium as a situation in which there is no pressure for change. The key insight into understanding aggregate supply behavior is the concept of the **equilibrium real wage rate.** Just like the equilibrium price for a product in an elementary demand and supply diagram, the equilibrium real wage rate is determined by the intersection of labor demand and supply curves. In Figure 6-9 we have copied our previous labor demand curve (N_0^d), which shows the marginal product of additional labor input.

The supply of labor is also assumed to depend on the real wage, and in Figure 6-9 it is represented by a "labor supply curve" that slopes upward. This indicates that a higher real wage rate would induce a higher quantity of labor supplied. For instance, a higher real wage rate might induce homemakers to take outside jobs by increasing their willingness to put up with

The **equilibrium real wage rate** is the real wage rate at which the labor supply and demand curves intersect, so there is no pressure for change.

Figure 6-9
Determination of the Equilibrium Real Wage Rate

Here the labor demand curve (N_0^d) is just the same as in Figures 6-7 and 6-8. But now we add a labor supply curve (N_0^s). This slopes upward, indicating that more people will be willing to take jobs at a higher real wage rate. Whenever an event pushes the economy away from point B, there is pressure for the real wage rate to change, as shown by the arrows.

ANYWHERE AWAY FROM POINT B THERE IS PRESSURE FOR CHANGE

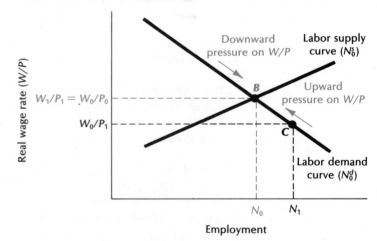

the inconvenience of commuting and arranging day care for their children. A higher real wage rate might also make people more willing to "moonlight," sacrificing leisure and sleep to take second jobs.

The position of the labor supply curve can shift if anything occurs that makes people more or less willing to take jobs at a given real wage rate. For instance, an increase in the working-age population, resulting from immigration or a high birth rate, will tend to shift the labor supply curve to the right. Factors that make jobs less attractive—for instance, the availability of generous unemployment or welfare benefits for those not working—will tend to shift the labor supply curve to the left.

The equilibrium real wage rate is simply the real wage rate where the labor demand curve crosses the labor supply curve. This occurs at point B in Figure 6-9, with an equilibrium level of employment (N_0) and an equilibrium real wage (W_0/P_0). The diagram poses a dilemma for firms, however. If firms are to raise employment from N_0 to N_1, the real wage rate must be reduced, as shown at point C. Put point C does not lie on the labor supply curve.

Employers need to find some factor that will make workers willing to provide more work than shown by their labor supply curve. Otherwise, we would never observe changes in employment, nor changes in real GNP, over the business cycle.

Pressure for change at point C.   At the equilibrium real wage rate, point B in Figure 6-9, by definition there is no pressure for W or N to change. But at point C, a real wage below equilibrium, there is pressure for the real wage rate to rise. This is the essence of our simple theory of how the nominal wage rate is set. We start at point B, with the economy in equilibrium. Then an increase in aggregate demand pushes up the price level, say from P_0 to P_1. The real wage falls, and the economy moves from B to C in Figures 6-8 and 6-9. Because the real wage has dropped below its equilibrium value, there is upward pressure for change. Workers are unhappy about being asked to work more when they are paid less in real terms. They demand real wage increases. As soon as the real wage increases are granted, the nominal wage rate rises from W_0 to W_1, and the real wage returns to its initial value, $W_1/P_1 = W_0/P_0$.

6-7   Short-Run Output and Price Effects of Fiscal and Monetary Expansion

We have previously examined the effect of fiscal stimulus, such as a $250 billion increase in planned autonomous spending caused by higher government purchases. In Chapter 5 we assumed that the price level was fixed, and that the fiscal stimulus raised real output. Now we find that the fiscal stimulus causes both output and the price level to increase simultaneously in the short run.

In Figure 6-10, we begin in equilibrium at point B with an actual price level equal to P_0. This is exactly the same as point B in Figures 6-7 and 6-8.

Figure 6-10

Effects on the Price Index and Real Income of an Increase in Planned Autonomous Spending from $\overline{A}_0$ to $\overline{A}_1$

Higher planned autonomous spending shifts the economy's equilibrium position from the initial point B to C, where both the price level and the real output have increased. Point C is not a sustainable position, however, because the real wage rate has fallen below the equilibrium real wage rate. Only at point E does the actual real wage rate return to its initial equilibrium value.

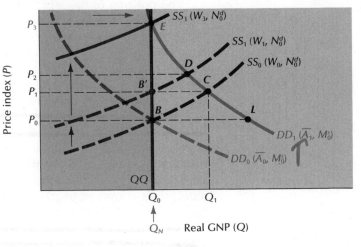

A FISCAL EXPANSION RAISES BOTH THE PRICE INDEX AND REAL GNP IN THE SHORT RUN

Initial Short-Run Effect of a Fiscal Expansion

Now a fiscal stimulus is introduced, in the form of an increase in government purchases that raises autonomous planned spending from $\overline{A}_0$ to $\overline{A}_1$. Where do we find the new equilibrium levels of output and the price index? If the price level were to remain constant, we would move straight to the right in Figure 6-10 from point B to point L. But the price level cannot remain fixed because firms will insist on an increase in the price level to cover the increasing marginal cost of additional production. In short, point L is off the short-run supply curve SS_0 and is not a point at which firms will be willing to produce.

Point C is the intersection of the new DD_1 schedule with the SS_0 schedule, which shows combinations of the price level and real output that are compatible with profit maximization by business firms. The increase in government purchases has simultaneously raised the price level to P_1 and increased output to Q_1. This has occurred because higher aggregate demand has raised prices, stimulating business firms to produce more, at least as long as the wage rate fails to adjust in full proportion to the increased price level.

Note that output has not increased by the full Chapter 5 multiplier based on a fixed price level, the horizontal distance between B and L. Instead, point C lies northwest of the constant price point L, because the higher price level at C reduces the real money supply and hence the demand for commodities. The situation illustrated in Figure 6-10 at point C would result from any stimulative factor that raises aggregate demand—not only an increase in government purchases, but also cuts in tax rates or increases in transfer payments, business and consumer confidence, net exports, or the money supply. As long as the short-run supply curve SS slopes upward to the right, any of these changes will shift the DD curve rightward and raise both output and prices simultaneously to point C.

The Rising Nominal Wage Rate and the Arrival at Long-Run Equilibrium

Point C is not the end of the adjustment of the economy to the higher level of government purchases, however, because business firms are satisfied but workers are not. The price level has risen from P_0 at point B to P_1 at point C. But for business firms to continue producing at point C would require a drop in the real wage rate from the equilibrium level W_0/P_0 to the new lower level W_0/P_1, just as in Figure 6-9.

Each SS (short-run supply) curve assumes that the nominal wage rate is fixed at a particular value, which is W_0 for the supply curve SS_0. Once workers learn that the actual price index has risen, they will discover to their dismay that the real wage rate has fallen. To achieve a return of their real wage to the original level at the next round of wage bargaining, workers will insist on an increase in the nominal wage rate to W_1. This would make the real wage rate W_1/P_1 equal to the original W_0/P_0 *if the price index remained at* P_1. Just as in Figure 6-8, the new aggregate supply schedule SS_1 shows the consequences of an increase in the nominal wage rate from W_0 to W_1.

Clearly the economy moves to point D, with a higher price level P_2. The price level could stay at P_1, with the nominal wage rate at W_1, only at point B' in the diagram. But B' is not on the aggregate demand curve DD_1. At point B' real GNP would be too low to keep the commodity and money markets in equilibrium. Inventories would be reduced, production would rise to restock inventories, and the economy would move to point D. This is why the economy always moves to the intersection of the DD and SS lines.

Now at point D once again workers are upset. The real wage rate is W_1/P_2, lower than the equilibrium real wage rate. Again they insist on an increase in the nominal wage rate. Eventually the economy must move up the DD_1 line to point E. Why? Because only at the initial level of real GNP (Q_0) and employment (N_0) is the real wage rate at its equilibrium value (W_0/P_0). Anytime the economy is operating in the pink area to the right of Q_0, there is upward pressure on the nominal wage rate, and SS will shift up.

Thus only at the original real GNP level Q_0 is there is no upward pressure on the real wage rate. For that reason, the red label and red arrow show that this is the natural level of real GNP, Q^N. A vertical QQ line has been drawn above Q_0 to show the different price levels consistent with a long-run equilibrium, defined as a situation with no pressure for change in the real wage rate. The only place where the economy can be on its DD curve and simultaneously at its equilibrium real wage level is at the point of crossing of DD and QQ. Only then are business firms willing to produce output level Q_0 at the same time the labor market is in equilibrium—that is, workers are content with the equilibrium real wage.

Thus at the natural level of real GNP (Q^N) the actual real wage rate is equal to the equilibrium real wage rate. The vertical QQ line shows all the possible combinations of the price index (P) and natural real GNP (Q^N).

Short-Run and Long-Run Equilibrium

Short-run equilibrium occurs at the point where the aggregate demand curve crosses the short-run aggregate supply curve.

The economy is in **short-run equilibrium** when two conditions are satisfied. First, the level of output produced must be enough to balance the demand for commodities without any involuntary accumulation or decumulation of inventory. This first condition is satisfied at any point along the appropriate *DD* curve. Second, the price level *P* must be sufficient to make firms both able and willing to produce the level of output specified along the *DD* curve. This can happen only along a short-run supply curve (*SS*) specified for a particular nominal wage rate (W_0).

Long-run equilibrium is a situation in which labor input is the amount voluntarily supplied and demanded at the equilibrium real wage rate.

The economy is in **long-run equilibrium** only when all the conditions for a short-run equilibrium are satisfied, and, in addition, the real wage rate is at its equilibrium value. In Figure 6-10, long-run equilibrium occurs only where all three schedules (*DD*, *SS*, and *QQ*) intersect. The reason that the economy does not move immediately to its new long-run equilibrium following a *DD* shift is that adjustment takes time, and that there are time lags in the response of wages and prices.

SELF-TEST

If the economy is to remain in long-run equilibrium, what must happen to the price level, the wage level, and the level of real GNP when the following events occur: Increase in government-financed highway construction? Increase in Japanese GNP that boosts U.S. net exports? Increase in the U.S. money supply?

Interpretations of the Business Cycle

The preceding theory of price and output adjustment contains two troubling elements that have perplexed students and teachers for decades. First, it does not identify what factors make workers willing to provide more or less employment than indicated along their labor supply curve. Second, the theory requires a **countercyclical** movement of the real wage, that is, a movement in the real wage in the opposite direction from the movement in real GNP. But numerous statistical studies have failed to find the required countercyclical fluctuations in the real wage rate, thus raising a basic question about the validity of the theory.

A **countercyclical** variable moves over the business cycle in the opposite direction as real GNP.

These two issues raise several questions about the sources of business cycles. Is it rational for workers to agree to work more in a business cycle expansion in order for output to increase? Will output increase as workers *know* that the source of the increase in aggregate demand is a deliberate attempt by the government to stimulate demand by conducting expansionary monetary or fiscal policy? Is a monetary or fiscal expansion perceived to be occurring by workers and firms "effective" in raising output, or is it "ineffective," leaving no trace of an effect on output but rather just causing the price level in Figure 6-10 to jump? Macroeconomics offers several schools of thought on these issues, and the next chapter introduces some of the conflicting views.

1. The aggregate demand curve shows the different combinations of real output and the price level consistent with equilibrium in the commodity and money markets (where the economy is on both the *IS* and *LM* curves). The position of the aggregate demand curve depends on autonomous planned spending and on the money supply.

2. A shift in aggregate demand may change the level of real output, the price level, or both. With a horizontal aggregate supply curve, only real output changes. With a vertical aggregate supply curve, only the price level changes. With a positively sloped aggregate supply curve, both real output and the price level change.

3. The supply curve for the individual firm slopes up because the marginal product of labor decreases as extra workers are added; this makes the firm's marginal cost of producing extra output increase.

4. The equilibrium real wage rate is that where the labor supply and demand curves cross. If a shift in demand changes the price level, and hence pushes the real wage rate away from the equilibrium real wage rate, there is pressure for change in the nominal wage rate.

5. The short-run aggregate supply curve for the economy has a position that depends on the nominal wage rate. When changing demand conditions raise the nominal wage rate, the short-run aggregate supply curve shifts up.

6. A fiscal or monetary expansion raises both real output and the price level in the short run. However, the short-run change in real output puts pressure for change on the nominal wage rate and causes the short-run aggregate supply curve to shift. This pressure for change is eliminated only when real output returns to the value that occurred prior to the fiscal or monetary expansion.

7. The economy is in long-run equilibrium only at a single level of natural real GNP, where there is no upward or downward pressure on the nominal wage rate. In the long run, any change in aggregate demand changes the price level without causing a change in real GNP.

CONCEPTS

aggregate demand curve
aggregate supply curve
comparative statics
production function
marginal product of labor

equilibrium real wage rate
short-run equilibrium
long-run equilibrium
countercyclical

QUESTIONS AND PROBLEMS

Questions

1. Explain the difference between the aggregate demand curve developed in this chapter and the demand curve for a product (e.g. movies) used in microeconomics.

2. How will the *DD* curve be affected if, all other things remaining equal, (a) the interest responsiveness of the demand for money becomes larger? (b) the income responsiveness of the demand for money becomes larger?

3. All other things remaining equal, which of the following changes would cause the *DD* curve to shift to the right? To the left? Make it flatter? Make it steeper? Leave it unchanged (that is, cause a movement along the *DD* curve)? (Hint: Explain how each change affects the *IS* or *LM* curves that lay behind the *DD* curve.)
   (a) An increase in the nominal money supply
   (b) An increase in autonomous exports
   (c) An increase in the marginal tax rate (*t*)
   (d) An increase in the marginal propensity to consume
   (e) An increase in the responsiveness of net exports to a change in the exchange rate
   (f) A decrease in the responsiveness of investment to changes in the interest rate
   (g) An increase in the price level
   (h) An increase in government spending
   (i) A decrease in the exchange rate

4. Explain the importance of the assumption of fixed *nominal* wages in the determination of the aggregate supply curve.

5. Explain why it is that every point on the *SS* curve is a profit maximizing point for the firm(s).

6. Describe whether the following variables increase or decrease when real GNP increases above the natural real GNP (Q^N) in Figure 6-7:
   (a) The price level (P)
   (b) The nominal wage rate (W)
   (c) The actual real wage rate (W/P)
   (d) The equilibrium real wage rate
   (e) The level of employment
   (f) The demand for labor
   (g) The quantity of labor demanded

7. Do the following events increase or decrease the equilibrium real wage?
   (a) An increase in worker productivity due to the introduction of new computerized machinery.
   (b) A decrease in worker productivity in response to higher oil prices as firms "retire" machinery which is very energy intensive.
   (c) An increase in unemployment benefits for individuals who are not working.
   (d) An increase in immigration of workers who are willing to work for less than present American workers.

8. Is the actual real wage equal to the equilibrium real wage at every point on the *SS* curve?

9. Assume that the aggregate demand curve shifts to the right by an equal amount through *either* increased government spending or an increase in the nominal money supply. Assuming that only the position and not the shape of the *DD* curve changes, compare the effects on the economy of the two expansionary policies. How does each action affect the twin deficits discussed in Chapter 5?

10. Is a sustainable long-run equilibrium always reached when the *DD* and *SS* curves intersect? Why or why not?

Problems

1. The *IS* and *LM* curves for the economy have the following equations:

$$IS: Q = k\,(\bar{A} - 50\,r)$$
$$LM: Q = 3\,(M^s/P) + 300\,r$$

   where k $= 4, \bar{A} = 1200, M^s = 600, P = 1.00$. For the purpose of this question, which aims solely at deriving the *DD* curve, assume away the *SS* curve and *QQ* (Q^N) line.
   (a) Find the equilibrium level of real output and the equilibrium interest rate.
   (b) What is the equilibrium real output when the price level equals 0.8? When it is 1.2? When it is 1.5? Plot the aggregate demand curve based on your answer to (*b*).
   (c) Assume that $\bar{A}$ is now 1000. What is the equilibrium real output when the price level equals 0.8, 1.0, 1.2, and 1.5? Plot the aggregate demand curve.

2. Using the information in question 1(a), and assuming that an upward sloping *SS* curve intersects the *DD* curve at $Q = 3600, P = 1.00$, explain what will happen in the economy if the natural level of output is $3600.

3. Using the information in question 1(c), and assuming that an upward sloping *SS* curve intersects the original *DD* curve at $Q = 3600, P = 1.00$, explain what will happen in the short run to output (Q), the price level (P), and the real wage (W/P). What do you predict will happen to those variables in the long run if the natural level of output is $3600.

The Keynesian Revolution and the New Classical Macroeconomics

Take not from the mouth of labor the bread it has earned.
— *Thomas Jefferson, 1801*

The aggregate demand and supply curves developed in the last chapter equip us with the graphical tools that we need to analyze changes in real income and the price level. The theory of income determination developed in Chapters 3–5 identifies those factors that can shift the aggregate demand curve—business and consumer optimism, net exports, the nominal money supply, government expenditures, and tax rates—but the curves by themselves do not provide us with an adequate theory of the business cycle. Even if we were to identify the sources of the exogenous changes that shift the aggregate demand curve, we do not know whether these demand shifts raise real income, raise the price level, or a combination of the two.

It is not enough to know the slope of the aggregate supply curve, that is, whether it is vertical, horizontal, or positively sloped (the three alternatives shown in Figure 6-4). Even if the aggregate supply curve is positively sloped, nothing rules out the possibility that *following a change in aggregate demand, nominal wages may change in proportion, causing the aggregate supply curve to shift vertically by the same amount as the demand shift.* If every demand shift were mimicked by a simultaneous supply shift by the same amount in the same direction, real income would never deviate from natural real GNP, and *there would be no business cycles.* Indeed, this was the view of the classical economists, who wrote prior to the 1936 publication of John Maynard Keynes's *General Theory.* With few exceptions, these classical economists had no theory of cyclical unemployment or of the business cycle in real GNP.

This chapter and the next examine several alternative theories of the business cycle in real income, real GNP, and the unemployment rate. Economists have developed these alternative theories to explain the slope of the aggregate demand and supply curves, and the circumstances and speed with which the supply curve would shift following a change in aggregate demand. We begin with the classical economists who predated Keynes, and their views about the business cycle. We then learn what Keynes criticized about their approach. Weaknesses of the Keynesian model are examined by studying two modern attempts to revive classical economics in the form of Milton Friedman's "fooling model" and the "new classical macroeconomics" of Robert Lucas that followed from Friedman's work. Inadequacies of Lucas's model have in turn led to an alternative new classical model called the theory of "real business cycles." Then in Chapter 8 we develop the modern Keynesian approach built around the institutional realities of long-term labor contracts and other impediments to perfect price flexibility.

Each of these alternative explanations of the business cycle implies a corresponding view of the role of stabilization policy, both monetary and fiscal. At one extreme, the original Keynesian approach stresses activist fiscal policy as necessary to stabilize the business cycle. At the other extreme, the new classical macroeconomics of Robert Lucas stresses the ineffectiveness of policy, particularly systematic monetary policy strategies that respond to economic events in a predictable way. By learning about the alternative explanations of the business cycle, we will also begin to understand why economists hold differing views about the role of stabilization policy.

7-1 The Self-Correcting Economy: Deflation as a Cure for Recession

The economy's **self-correcting forces** refer to the role of flexible prices in stabilizing real GNP under some conditions.

The classical economists who predated Keynes's *General Theory,* including Adam Smith, David Ricardo, John Stuart Mill, Alfred Marshall, and Arthur C. Pigou, believed that the economy possessed powerful **self-correcting forces** that guaranteed full employment and prevented actual real GNP (Q) from falling below natural real GNP (Q^N) for more than a short time. These forces consisted of flexible wages and prices, which would adjust rapidly to absorb the impact of shifts in aggregate demand. Because the classical economists did not believe that business cycles in real output or in unemployment were problems, they saw no need for the government to engage in stabilization policy.

Pressure on the Price Level Away from Q^N

The flexibility of the price level was the automatic mechanism that was believed capable of regulating real output without help from government policymakers. In Figure 7-1 the vertical line marked QQ has the same meaning as in Figure 6-10; it is plotted at the position of the economy's long-run equilibrium, or natural real GNP (Q^N). Note that there are no specific numbers on the vertical axis for the price level or on the horizontal axis for actual real GNP. Any vertical line is independent of the variable plotted on the vertical axis, so that the vertical QQ schedule represents the assumption that the economy's natural real GNP (Q^N) does not depend on the price level (P).

The classical economists assumed that the economy would not operate to the left or right of the vertical QQ line for more than a brief time. The reason was that with actual real GNP (Q) below natural real GNP (Q^N), firms would be producing less than the capacity of their factories and would tend to cut nominal wage rates and prices. Wage and price cuts would continue

Figure 7-1

Effect of a Decline in Planned Autonomous Spending When the Price Level is Perfectly Flexible

The classical economists assumed that the price level would decline whenever a drop in aggregate demand occurred. Starting from point E_0, the equilibrium position with $\bar{A}_0$, a drop in planned autonomous spending to $\bar{A}_1$ would move the economy straight down to point E_1. The level of real GNP remains at Q^N, because the lower price level raises the level of real balances (M_0^s/P) by exactly enough to offset the decline in autonomous spending from $\bar{A}_0$ to $\bar{A}_1$. A shift back to DD_0 would raise the price level and return the economy to the original position E_0.

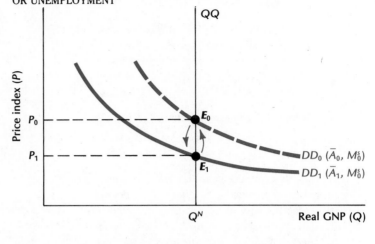

A BUSINESS CYCLE IN PRICES, NOT IN REAL GNP OR UNEMPLOYMENT

until production once again reached the natural level of real GNP. For instance, if a decline in demand caused the aggregate demand curve to shift leftward from DD_0 to DD_1 in Figure 7-1, the classical economists would predict that the economy would move from the initial point E_0 to the new point E_1 with only a brief interval (shown by the arrow pointing downward from E_0 to E_1) during which actual real GNP (Q) remains below natural real GNP (Q^N). The price level would fall from its initial level at P_0 to the new level P_1.

The classical economists took the same view of the economy's behavior in response to an increase in aggregate demand. With Q above Q^N, firms would be producing more than the capacity of their factories and would be able to raise nominal wage rates and prices. Wage and price increases would continue until production fell back to the Q^N level.

Because the downward and upward movement of the economy from E_0 to E_1 and back again would not involve any significant movement of real GNP (Q) away from natural real GNP (Q^N), *no business cycle in real GNP would occur.* Yet there would be a business cycle in the price level, from P_0 down to P_1 and back to P_0, and it was this movement in the price level that the classical economists attempted to explain in their early theories of the business cycle. However, price movements were not viewed by classical economists as sufficiently undesirable to warrant the intervention of government stabilization policy.

Classical View of Unemployment and Output Fluctuations

We have seen that classical economists did not believe that real GNP could remain for more than a short period below natural real GNP (Q^N). How, then, did they explain the unemployment that occurs in real-world modern economies when people are laid off and production is cut back? Jobless individ-

The Quantity Equation and the Quantity Theory of Money

The most important model developed by classical economists to analyze macroeconomic behavior is the famous "quantity equation" relating the money supply (M^s) and velocity (V) to the price level (P) and real GNP (Q):

Money supply (M^s) times velocity (V)
$$\equiv \text{Price level } (P) \text{ times real GNP } (Q)$$
or $M^s V \equiv PQ$

The quantity equation is true by definition, simply because velocity (Section 4-7) is *defined* as $V \equiv PQ/M^s$. The inverse of velocity ($1/V = M^s/(PQ)$) can also be regarded as the fraction of nominal GNP (PQ) that people want to hold in the form of their stock of money (M^s).

In the *IS-LM* model developed in Chapter 4, velocity (V) changes when a change in planned autonomous spending causes the *IS* curve to shift along a fixed *LM* curve (due to a change in business and consumer confidence, fiscal policy, or net exports). Velocity also changes when a change in the real money supply (M^s/P) shifts the *LM* curve along a fixed *IS* curve, because the resulting change in the interest rate changes the amount people want to hold as money instead of as interest-bearing assets.

To convert the quantity equation into a theory, classical economists assumed that any change in M^s or V on the left-hand side of the equation would be balanced by a proportional change in P on the right-hand side of the quantity equation, with no change in Q. Primary emphasis in this theory, called the **quantity theory of money**[a], was placed on changes in the money supply (M^s) causing proportional changes in the price level P. For instance,

the classical economists who adhered to the quantity theory would have predicted that a shift in the *DD* curve of Figure 7-1 would have caused only a vertical movement in the price level, with no horizontal movement in real output, regardless of whether the *DD* shift was caused by a change in M^s or in V.[b]

Further, primary emphasis in the quantity theory was placed on changes in M^s rather than in changes in V. Velocity (V) was regarded as being relatively stable and primarily determined by changes in payment methods (for instance, cash vs. checks) that evolved gradually over time. Over shorter periods of two-to-five years, business cycles were attributed mainly to fluctuations in M^s.

[a]The **quantity theory of money** in its strong version assumes that real output is fixed, so that price changes are proportional to changes in the money supply.

[b]Less attention was given to the possibility of changes in V. In fact, another version of the quantity theory took no position on price flexibility but held that velocity (V) was a constant, determined by technological factors influencing the amount of money that people wanted to hold.

uals were sometimes written off as irresponsible, having an insufficient desire to work. Any normal person would be compelled by hunger to seek work, some classical economists thought. And most believed that if there were not enough jobs to go around, competition among workers would reduce the real wage rate until an equilibrium was obtained in the labor market.

Although some journalists and a few isolated economists (including Karl Marx and Friedrich Engels) began to suggest that unemployment was an inevitable by-product of the newly emerging industrial society of England in the mid-nineteenth century, most classical economists dismissed unemployment as a transitory, self-correcting condition of only minor social importance. In fact, the term "unemployment" did not exist until the early twentieth century.

Ironically, some governments outside the United States developed unemployment insurance before classical economists were willing to recognize the existence of prolonged unemployment. The world's first unemployment insurance system was introduced in the United Kingdom by Winston Churchill in 1911; only afterward, in 1913, was the first important book by a classical economist (Arthur C. Pigou) written on the subject of unemployment.[1] The book attributed such unemployment as existed to the failure of wages to adjust fast enough to maintain equilibrium in the labor market. Suggested cures for unemployment involved remedies for wage stickiness rather than any suggestion that there was a role for the government to intervene and stimulate aggregate demand through expansionary monetary or fiscal policy.

7-2 The Keynesian Revolution: The Failure of Self-Correction

John Maynard Keynes (1883–1946) His The General Theory of Employment, Interest, and Money *(1936) is one of the most influential works in economics in this century.*

The Great Depression began with the stock market crash in late 1929 and by 1932 real GNP had declined by one third, while unemployment spiraled upward beyond 20 percent. Classical economists were caught flat-footed, without any explanation for the severe and prolonged unemployment beyond the claim that real wages were for some reason too high. Yet the calamity of the Great Depression could not be ignored. Every part of the economy of every country felt its impact. Not only did the relentless decline in real GNP continue for the three and one half years between October 1929 and March 1933, but the recovery failed fully to make up the lost ground. In most countries unemployment never fell close to the 1929 level until after World War II broke out in 1939. In the United States, 10 million persons were still unemployed as late as 1940, fully eleven years after the start of the Great Depression.

The existence of unprecedented unemployment in the Depression discredited classical economists, who had no convincing explanation for a reality too obvious to be ignored. Economics had lost its intellectual moorings, and it was time for a new diagnosis. In this atmosphere, it was perhaps not surprising that the 1936 publication of Keynes's *The General Theory of Employment, Interest, and Money* was eagerly awaited. Its publication transformed macroeconomics, and only one year later John R. Hicks published an article in which he set out the *IS-LM* model of Chapters 4 and 5 as an interpretation of what Keynes had written.

---

[1]This was Arthur C. Pigou's *Unemployment.* The description of the views of the classical economists in this section is taken from the much more detailed and fully documented treatment in John A. Garraty, *Unemployment in History: Economic Thought and Public Policy* (New York: Harper & Row, 1978), pp. 70–145.

Monetary Impotence and the Failure of Deflation in Extreme Cases

We can use the aggregate demand and supply curves to illustrate Keynes's analysis of the high unemployment that bedeviled the world's economy in the 1930s. For Keynes, the economic problem could be divided into two categories, one concerning demand and one concerning supply. The demand problem was the possibility of **monetary impotence,** while the supply problem was that of **rigid wages.**

Unresponsive expenditures: The vertical *IS* curve. As we learned in Section 4-9, increases in the real money supply (M^s/P) can have either strong or weak effects, depending on the shapes of the *IS* and *LM* curves. One case of monetary impotence occurs when the *IS* curve is vertical. Any change in the nominal money supply shifts the *LM* curve up and down along the vertical and unchanging *IS* curve, leaving real GNP unaffected. Just as important, any decline in the price level (P) that raises the real money supply (M^s/P) leaves real GNP unaffected. Thus "monetary impotence," the inability of changes in M^s to raise Q implies **deflation impotence,** the inability of a decline in P to raise Q.

When spending responsiveness is zero along the vertical *IS* curve, actual real GNP is "stuck" at the spot where the vertical *IS* curve happens to be. If this location of the *IS* curve lies to the left of natural real GNP (Q^N), then Q is below Q^N, and the economy suffers from a **GNP gap.** And when there is a GNP gap, with Q below Q^N, the unemployment rate is above the natural rate of unemployment.

We examined a vertical *IS* curve in Figure 4-11; now, in Figure 7-2, we observe its implications for the aggregate demand curve. If *IS* is vertical at an income level like Q', then a decline in P has no power to raise real GNP

Monetary impotence is the failure of real GNP to respond to an increase in the real money supply.

Rigid wages refers to the failure of the nominal wage rate to adjust by the amount needed to maintain equilibrium in the labor market.

Deflation impotence refers to the failure of real GNP to respond to an increase in the real money supply caused by falling prices.

The **GNP gap** is the amount by which actual real GNP falls short of natural real GNP.

Figure 7-2
The Lack of Effect of a Drop in the Price Index When There Is Deflation Impotence

The conditions for deflation impotence are either 1) a vertical *IS* curve that lies to the left of Q^N or 2) a normal *IS* curve that intersects a horizontal *LM* curve to the left of Q^N. With deflation impotence the aggregate demand schedule is a vertical line like DD', in contrast to the normally sloped DD_0 curve. Because of the inability of a higher real money supply to stimulate the economy with deflation impotence, a decline in the price level just moves the economy down from F to F' to F''.

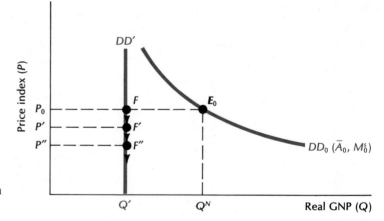

DEFLATION IMPOTENCE IMPLIES A VERTICAL DD LINE

above Q', so the aggregate demand curve is the vertical line DD' in Figure 7-2. Shown for contrast in Figure 7-2 is a normally sloped DD_0 curve from Figure 7-1.

The liquidity trap: A horizontal *LM* curve.   The same problem of a vertical DD' curve that fails to intersect the QQ line may occur even with a normally sloped *IS* curve, if there is a liquidity trap that makes the *LM* curve horizontal and *if the IS curve intersects this horizontal LM curve to the left of Q^N* (as illustrated in the bottom frame of Figure 4-11). In this case an increase in M^s/P does not shift the *LM* curve down, because the interest rate is already at its lowest possible level due to the refusal of individuals to purchase bonds. Such purchases would raise bond prices and push interest rates down further, but individuals refuse to buy bonds because they fear that bond prices are higher than normal and may fall, leading to capital losses. In this case real GNP is "stuck" at the point, for example Q', where the horizontal *LM* curve crosses the normally sloped *IS* curve. There is monetary impotence and deflation impotence, and the aggregate demand curve is vertical, as in Figure 7-2.

Monetary impotence and deflation impotence arise when there is a vertical *IS* or horizontal *LM* curve.[2] In either case, the aggregate demand curve is vertical, like DD' in Figure 7-2. And, in either case, the classical "cure-all" of deflation cannot remedy a cyclical recession or depression. The classical economists, as we have seen, believed that the price level would fall continuously whenever real GNP moved even slightly to the left of natural real GNP (Q^N). But in Figure 7-2 the price level can fall continuously, from P_0 to P' to P'', yet real GNP remains "stuck" at Q'. The economy just moves downward vertically from point F to F' to F'', without any rightward motion.

Fiscal Policy and the Real Balance Effect

The crucial problem that makes the DD' curve in Figure 7-2 lie to the left of natural real GNP (Q^N) *is not the liquidity trap, but the position of the IS curve* caused by low business and consumer confidence. How can confidence be revived? All problems disappear if autonomous planned spending (A_p) can be raised by enough to make the *IS* curve intersect *LM* at or to the right of Q^N. For this reason Keynes believed that fiscal policy, which can shift the *IS* curve, is the obvious antidepression tool to use.

In theory, however, government action may not be necessary. A. C. Pigou originally pointed out that the Keynesian dilemma illustrated by the

---

[2]A more precise definition of the conditions necessary for monetary impotence and deflation impotence is as follows: there must be (1) no effect of a change in M^s/P on the *IS* curve, and (2) the interest rate where the *IS* curve crosses natural real GNP (Q^N), which we can call r^N, lies below the minimum attainable interest rate along the *LM* curve, which we can call r_{min}. When there is no liquidity trap, r_{min} is zero, and (2) is satisfied whenever r^N is negative or whenever *IS* is vertical and lies left of Q^N (as in the top frame of Figure 4-11). When there is a liquidity trap, the *LM* curve is horizontal at the level of r_{min}, and (2) is satisfied even with a normally sloped *IS* curve, as long as r^N is less than r_{min}. For instance, in the lower frame of Figure 4-11 r^N is zero (this is the interest rate where the *IS* curve crosses $4000 billion, the assumed value of Q^N) and is less than the r_{min} of 2.5 percent along the horizontal *LM* curve.

vertical DD' curve in Figure 7-2 may not be a dilemma at all. Why? The demand for commodities may depend directly on the level of real money balances (M^s/P). This would make the IS curve shift rightward whenever P falls, thus raising M^s/P and *guaranteeing a negative slope for the DD curve*. The **Pigou effect** or **real balance effect** occurs when an increase in M^s/P influences the demand for commodities *directly* without requiring a reduction in interest rates. With the real balance effect the DD curve is *always* negatively sloped like DD_0, and a price deflation can achieve any desired real GNP level if prices fall far enough. The DD curve *cannot be vertical* in the presence of a real balance effect.

The **Pigou** or **real balance effect** is the direct stimulus to aggregate demand caused by an increase in the real money supply and does not require a decline in the interest rate.

Why is the real balance effect so powerful when the price level is flexible? Imagine yourself owning only a $10 bill. You would not be able to consider purchasing a $70,000 Mercedes. But there is some price level at which your money would have more impressive buying power. If the price index were to decline from 1.0 to 0.0001, the price of the Mercedes would fall from $70,000 to $7.00, and your $10 would be more than ample to buy the Mercedes, leaving $3.00 in change! Although the numbers in this illustration are extreme, they forcefully illustrate the logic of the real balance effect. A fixed nominal amount of money buys more when the price level falls, so that individuals are bound to find some portion of their previous money balances excessive and to spend more on real commodities.

When the price level is perfectly flexible and the real balance effect is in operation, no monetary or fiscal policy is necessary. The Federal Reserve governors and the President's Council of Economic Advisers can "go fishing," confident that the DD curve crosses the QQ curve, as in Figure 7-1.

We have now identified two stimulative effects of price deflation:

The **Keynes effect** is the stimulus to aggregate demand caused by a decline in the interest rate.

1. The **Keynes effect** is the stimulus to aggregate demand (both consumption and investment) due to a decline in the interest rate, which in turn is brought about by an increase in the nominal money supply (M^s) or decrease in the price level (P), both of which increase the real money supply (M^s/P). It is the Keynes effect that can be thwarted by monetary and deflation impotence, as summarized by a vertical DD curve as in Figure 7-2.

2. The Pigou (or real balance) effect is the direct stimulus to consumption spending that occurs when a price deflation causes an increase in the real money supply; this stimulus does not require a reduction in the interest rate.

The **expectations effect** is the decline in aggregate demand caused by the postponement of purchases when consumers expect prices to decline in the future.

The **redistribution effect** is the decline in aggregate demand caused by the effect of falling prices in redistributing income from high-spending debtors to low-spending savers.

Destabilizing effects of falling prices.   Unfortunately, the stimulative effects of price deflation are not always favorable, even when the Pigou or real balance effect is in operation. There are two major unfavorable effects of deflation.

1. The **expectations effect.** When people expect prices to continue to fall, they tend to postpone purchases as much as possible to take advantage of lower prices in the future. This decline in the demand for commodities may be strong enough to offset the stimulus of the Pigou effect.

2. The **redistribution effect** may be more important. An unexpected deflation causes a redistribution of income from debtors to creditors.

Why? Debt repayments are usually fixed in dollar value so that a uniform deflation in all prices, which was not expected when the debts were incurred, causes an increase in the real value of mortgage and installment repayments from debtors to creditors (banks and, ultimately, savers).[3] This redistribution reduces aggregate demand, since creditors tend to spend only a relatively small share of their added income, while debtors have nothing to fall back on and are forced to reduce their consumption to meet their higher real interest payments.

During the Great Depression deflation of 1929–33, for instance, the GNP price deflator fell from an initial 14.6 to 11.2 in 1933 (1982 = 100), a decline of 24 percent. Yet the interest income of creditors hardly fell at all, from $4.7 to $4.1 billion (current dollars). Farmers were hit worst by falling prices—their current-dollar income fell by two thirds, from $6.2 to $2.6 billion—and many lost their farms through foreclosures as a result of this heavy debt burden. Although many factors were at work in the collapse of real autonomous spending during the Great Depression, it appears that the negative expectations and redistribution effects of the 1929–33 deflation may have dominated the stimulative Keynes and Pigou effects.

The expectations and redistribution effects are not just ancient fossils relevant only to the 1930s. In the 1980s falling prices of farm products, farm land, and oil reduced the income of farmers, oil producers, and employees of farms and oil companies. Many of these people were severely hurt by falling prices, especially since in the 1970s some (especially farmers) had incurred a heavy burden of debt to buy high-priced farm land.

SELF-TEST   Not only do falling prices and a depressed economy affect aggregate demand, but so do rising prices in prosperity. Explain whether the Pigou (or real balance) effect stabilizes or destabilizes the economy when aggregate demand is high. How does this effect occur? Similarly, explain whether the expectations and redistribution effects stabilize or destabilize the economy when prices are rising, and describe how these effects occur.

Nominal Wage Rigidity

Keynes attacked the classical economists on two fronts. As we have seen, his first line of attack was the possibility of a vertical *DD'* line that fails to intersect the *QQ* line, creating deflation impotence. His second line of attack was simply that deflation would not occur in the necessary amount because of rigid nominal wages. And if little or no deflation occurred, *the debate about the relative potency of the Keynes, Pigou, expectations, and distribution effects would become irrelevant.*

---

[3]A relatively advanced discussion of the consequences of these effects on the economy's self-correcting mechanism is contained in James Tobin, "Keynesian Models of Recession and Depression," *American Economic Review,* vol. 65 (May 1975), pp. 195–202. See also Axel Leijonhufvud. *On Keynesian Economics and the Economics of Keynes* (New York: Oxford University Press, 1968), pp. 315–331.

Figure 7-3 shows the effects of rigid nominal wages. In the right-hand frame the two aggregate demand curves, DD_0 and DD_1, are copied from Figure 7-1. They have the normal negative slopes. DD_1 lies to the left of DD_0 because consumer and business pessimism lowers the assumed amount of planned autonomous spending. The short-run aggregate supply curve SS_0 is fixed in position by the fixed nominal wage rate (W_0). Starting at point E_0, the leftward shift in aggregate demand moves the economy to point A, where the new DD_1 curve intersects the aggregate supply curve SS_0.

Keynes pointed out that the economy would remain "stuck" at point A even with the normally sloped aggregate demand curve DD_1. Why? If the nominal wage is completely rigid and never changes from the value W_0, then the supply curve is fixed as well at the position SS_0. There would be no more deflation. Hence the economy would not move from point A to point E_1 in Figure 7-3, as required in the analysis of the classical economists.

UNEMPLOYMENT IN THE ORIGINAL KEYNESIAN MODEL

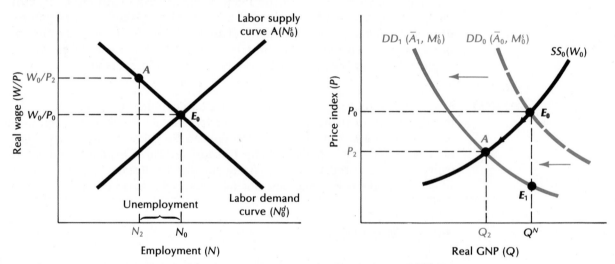

Figure 7-3 **Effect of a Decline in Autonomous Spending from $\bar{A}_0$ to $\bar{A}_1$ When the Nominal Rate Is Fixed at W_0**

The aggregate supply curve SS_0 in the right frame is fixed in position by the assumption of a rigid nominal wage rate W_0. The decline in autonomous spending shifts the aggregate demand curve in the right frame leftward from DD_0 to DD_1, and the economy moves southwest from point E_0 to point A. In the left frame the reduction in the price level raises the real wage from the original W_0/P_0 to the new W_0/P_2, and the economy moves from point E_0 to point A. Unemployment is represented by the distance between N_2 and N_0.

Failure to attain equilibrium in the labor market. Keynes's assumption of a rigid *nominal* wage differs from the description of the economy's adjustment toward long-run equilibrium in Sections 6-6 and 6-7, which assumed that there is an equilibrium *real* wage rate that equates demand and supply in the labor market. For instance, in the left-hand frame of Figure 7-3, the employment level N_0 shows the number of jobs when the economy is operating at Q^N in the right-hand frame. In order for firms to demand N_0 workers along the labor demand curve N^d, and for N_0 individuals to be willing to work along the labor supply curve N^s, the real wage rate must be at the equilibrium level W_0/P_0.

However, the decline in aggregate demand in the right-hand frame of Figure 7-3 has pushed the economy to point A. In the left-hand frame point A is at the intersection of the employment level N_2 and real wage W_0/P_2, higher than the equilibrium real wage W_0/P_0. In Chapter 6, our analysis stated that at any real wage level other than the equilibrium real wage rate (W_0/P_0), there would be "pressure for change." To be consistent with this story there must also be "pressure for change" at point A. Won't unemployed workers compete with employed workers by offering to work for less?

Keynes's assumption of nominal wage rigidity fails to explain how or why the wage remains rigid. Its only virtue is that it provides an explanation of **persistent unemployment,** as at point A in Figure 7-3, without requiring any special shape for the aggregate demand curve. But the arbitrariness of the assumption raises four important questions that will concern us throughout the rest of this chapter and the next:

Persistent unemployment is a situation in which a high level of unemployment can last for many years, as in the United States from 1929 to 1941 and from 1980 to 1985.

1. Is the nominal wage rigidity assumption realistic? Did the aggregate supply curve in the Great Depression remain at a fixed position like SS_0, or did it steadily shift downward and bring the economy to long-run equilibrium, as the classical economists would have predicted? This question is the subject of the case study in the next section.

2. Is it possible to devise a convincing theory of business cycles without relying on either deflation impotence or rigid nominal wages? The Keynesian rigid nominal wage "story" raises a basic puzzle: Why do markets "fail to clear"? That is, why does the economy not operate continuously at the intersection of the labor supply and demand curves? Several prominent economists, particularly Milton Friedman, Robert Lucas, and Edward Prescott, have attempted to revive classical economics in a way that is consistent with observed business cycles yet allows for **market-clearing,** in contrast to the Keynesian tradition of **non-market-clearing.** We turn to these models in the last half of this chapter.

A **market-clearing** model or theory holds that the economy is always in equilibrium, at the intersection of supply and demand curves, particularly in the labor market.

A **non-market-clearing** model holds that the economy can be pushed off its supply and demand curves in the labor market and sometimes in other markets.

3. How do labor unions and current practices of wage negotiation relate to the Keynesian assumption of wage rigidity? Do they justify his assumption of non-market-clearing and support his explanation of persistent unemployment? This question is addressed in Chapter 8.

4. In a recession the real wage in the left-hand frame of Figure 7-3 rises from point E_0 to point A when real GNP declines from Q^N to Q_2. Does an adequate theory of the business cycle require such a *countercyclical*

movement in the real wage? This issue has troubled many analysts in light of the limited or nonexistent countercyclical movements in the real wage evident in historical data and is also addressed in Chapter 8.

7-3 CASE STUDY: Interest Rates, Output, and Prices During the Great Depression

This case study investigates several important aspects of the Great Depression years of 1929 to 1941. Three topics are given primary emphasis. First, why was aggregate demand so low? Is there evidence to support monetary or deflation impotence? Second, did the economy's aggregate supply curve shift downward to provide self-correction, or did it remain stationary as it does in the right-hand frame of Figure 7-3 when the nominal wage is rigid? Third, was the nominal wage rigid, and did real wages fluctuate counter-cyclically?

Table 7-1 exhibits several important features of the period between 1929 and 1941. This twelve-year period is distinguished most by the unemployment figures shown in column (7), especially by the extraordinarily

Table 7-1 **Money, Output, Unemployment, Prices, and Wages in the Great Depression, 1929–41**

Year	Money Supply ($ Billions)	Real Money Supply	Real GNP	Real Fixed Investment	Output Ratio (Q/Q^N) (percent)	GNP Deflator (1982 = 100)	Unemployment Rate (percent)	Long-term Interest Rate	Average Hourly Earnings (dollars)	Avg. Real Hourly Earnings (1982 dollars)
		($ Billions, 1982 Prices)								
	(1)	(2)	(3)	(4)	(5)	(6)	(7)	(8)	(9)	(10)
1929	26.6	182.2	709.6	128.4	102.6	14.6	3.2	3.6	0.563	3.86
1930	25.8	181.7	643.5	98.4	90.5	14.2	8.9	3.3	0.560	3.94
1931	24.1	185.4	588.1	67.3	80.8	13.0	16.3	3.3	0.532	4.09
1932	21.1	183.5	509.2	39.0	68.3	11.5	24.1	3.7	0.485	4.21
1933	19.9	177.7	498.5	33.5	65.6	11.2	25.2	3.3	0.457	4.08
1934	21.9	179.5	536.7	42.9	68.9	12.2	22.0	3.1	0.512	4.20
1935	25.9	207.2	580.2	54.7	72.8	12.5	20.3	2.8	0.524	4.19
1936	29.5	236.0	662.2	63.1	81.2	12.5	17.0	2.7	0.534	4.27
1937	30.9	235.9	695.3	85.7	83.1	13.1	14.3	2.7	0.566	4.32
1938	30.5	236.4	664.2	69.2	77.1	12.9	19.1	2.6	0.576	4.47
1939	34.2	269.3	716.6	82.1	81.7	12.7	17.2	2.4	0.583	4.59
1940	39.7	305.4	772.9	97.5	85.8	13.0	14.6	2.2	0.597	4.59
1941	46.5	337.0	909.4	111.0	98.6	13.8	9.9	2.0	0.655	4.74

Sources: See Appendix A. The interest rate is series B–72 in *Long-term Economic Growth* (U.S. Department of Commerce, 1973). Average hourly earnings from Martin N. Baily, "The Labor Market in the 1930s," in James Tobin, ed., *Macroeconomics, Prices, and Quantities* (Brookings Institution, 1983), Table 1, p. 23.

high level the unemployment rate reached (25.2 percent in 1933), and the long duration of high unemployment (ten straight years in 1931–40 with unemployment above 10 percent). An obvious puzzle is why the economy was so weak, especially between 1934 and 1939. In 1939 *the real money supply* (column 2) *was 50 percent higher than in 1934 and 48 percent higher than in 1929.* Yet in 1939 real GNP (column 3) *was only 1.0 percent higher than in 1929.* In 1939 the output ratio (Q/Q^N) (column 5) was only 81.7 percent (much lower than in 1929 because Q^N had grown between 1929 and 1939), and the unemployment rate was still 17.2 percent.

Explanations of Weak Aggregate Demand

The inability of the rapidly rising real money supply in the late 1930s to bring the economy back to full employment raises the possibility of monetary impotence and deflation impotence, as emphasized in our discussion above of the Keynesian revolution. Monetary and deflation impotence can occur either with a vertical *IS* curve or horizontal *LM* curve *as long as the IS curve has shifted sufficiently far to the left.*

The Keynesian view that the *IS* curve shifted far to the left is supported in Table 7-1 by column (4), which shows the collapse of fixed real investment from $128.4 billion in 1982 prices in 1929 to $33.5 billion in 1933, *a decline of 74 percent.* Also shown is the incomplete recovery of real fixed investment, with a value in 1939 of only $82.1 billion, 36 percent below the 1929 level. The failure of investment to recover fully to the 1929 level, despite a 48 percent increase in the real money supply since 1929, is consistent with either a vertical *IS* curve or a horizontal *LM* curve. Which diagnosis is more realistic?

For the *IS* curve to be vertical, a decline in the interest rate must fail to stimulate autonomous planned spending, which chiefly consists of fixed investment. As shown in Table 7-1, the interest rate declined substantially from 1934 to 1941 and yet real fixed investment in 1939, 1940, and even 1941 was far below its 1929 level. The *IS* curve was sufficiently steep, and far to the left, so that even the 2.0 percent long-term interest rate of 1941 did not stimulate as much investment as had occurred in 1929 with a 3.6 percent long-term interest rate.

For the *LM* curve to be horizontal, the case of the liquidity trap, an increase in the real money supply must fail to reduce the interest rate. Yet the long-term interest rate displayed in Table 7-1, column (8), fell fairly steadily from 3.7 percent in 1933 to 2.0 percent in 1941. Thus the observations between 1934 and 1941 seem consistent with the hypothesis that the demand for money depends inversely on the interest rate. There is no sign at all that the interest rate hit a minimum level at any time during the latter half of the Great Depression decade.

The verdict taken from these data would not have surprised Keynes, who was not an apostle of the liquidity trap. As of the publication of his book in 1936, Keynes knew "no example of it hitherto," although he was willing to concede that the trap "might become important in the future."[4]

---

[4] J. M. Keynes, *The General Theory of Employment, Interest, and Money* (London: Macmillan, 1936), p. 207.

He recognized that the logical assumptions necessary for the liquidity trap were unlikely to occur, primarily because the "normal" expected interest rate was likely to drift downward in a continuing state of depression.

Monetary versus nonmonetary factors.   In recent years there has been a lively debate regarding the relative role of monetary and nonmonetary factors in causing the Great Depression, particularly the collapse of nominal and real GNP between 1929 and 1933. In an extensive statistical study of the data with James A. Wilcox, I have concluded that both monetary and nonmonetary factors were important, but at different times.[5] For instance, in the first two years of the contraction (1929–31) the decline in the nominal money supply (Table 7-1, column 1) was much too small to account for the drop in spending, which must be attributed mainly to nonmonetary factors (including overbuilding in the 1920s and the impact of the 1929 stock market crash on consumption). But after September 1931 the contraction was caused mainly by monetary factors, including the enormous loss of lifetime savings in bank failures.

Prices and the Output Ratio in the Great Depression

Does the behavior of output and the price level in the Great Depression support the Keynesian assumption of rigid nominal wages or the classical interpretation of a self-correcting economy? If the classics are correct we should find evidence of the economy's self-correcting forces at work through price deflation. Turning back to the right frame of Figure 7-3, we would expect that when price deflation works in a stabilizing direction, the economy would slide down a DD curve to the southeast as from point A to point E_1.

Now compare this theoretical diagram to a graph of the actual data plotted in the top frame of Figure 7-4. The horizontal axis is measured as the ratio of actual to natural real GNP (Q/Q^N). Starting on the vertical QQ schedule at natural real GNP in 1929, with a price index of 100 (on a 1929 base), the economy moved rapidly to the southwest until 1933. Then a recovery to the northeast began, interrupted briefly in 1938.

Absence of self-correction.   The story of the Great Depression appears to lie in shifts in the DD curve to the left and then back to the right. There is no evidence at all of a movement southeast along a given DD curve, as would have occurred had price deflation played a major role in stimulating the recovery. Particularly important is the fact that there was no deflation between 1936 and 1940, even though Q/Q^N remained at or below 86 percent throughout that five-year interval. Thus the evidence appears quite conclusive that the government cannot rely on rapid and massive price deflation to revive the economy, at least if the price level today is as sluggish as it was in the late 1930s.

Despite the absence of perfect price flexibility, the price level was not rigid during the Great Depression and did drop 24 percent between 1929

---

[5]Robert J. Gordon and James A. Wilcox, "Monetarist Interpretations of the Great Depression: An Evaluation and Critique," in Karl Brunner (ed.), *Contemporary Views of the Great Depression* (Hingham, Mass.: Martinus Nijhoff, 1981), pp. 49–107.

Figure 7-4

The Price Level (*P*) and the Ratio of Actual to Natural Output (Q/Q^N) during the Great Depression, 1929–42

The upper frame illustrates the actual values of the implicit GNP deflator (*P*) and an estimate of the ratio of actual to natural output during the Great Depression era, 1929–42. The remarkable fact in the top frame is that the economy returned to natural output in 1942 with a price level that was actually higher than in 1929, despite the intervening decade that should have pushed the price level down. The bottom frame illustrates a hypothetical interpretation of what happened. (*Source:* Appendix A.)

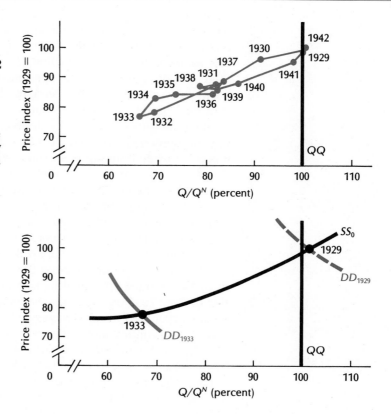

and 1933. The path from northeast to southwest to northeast reflects a regularity, as if the *DD* curve were following a well-marked highway. The bottom frame of Figure 7-4 represents a hypothetical interpretation of what happened. The *DD* curve in 1929 was close to the vertical *QQ* schedule, but by 1933 it had moved well to the left as business and consumer confidence collapsed. The actual location of the economy in 1933 suggests that the economy's aggregate supply schedule looks like SS_0 of Figure 7-3, and so we have drawn in a positively sloped SS_0 curve in the bottom frame of Figure 7-4.

Behavior of nominal and real wage rates. The interpretation of the Great Depression contained in Figure 7-4 raises an obvious question: Why did the aggregate supply curve fail to shift downward to bring the economy to its long-run equilibrium level of output along the vertical *QQ* line at a lower price level? A fixed aggregate supply curve, like that in the right-hand frame of Figure 7-3 or bottom frame of Figure 7-4, requires a rigid nominal wage rate. Data on the nominal wage rate are included in Table 7-1, column (9).

The year 1930 provides a particularly important example of nominal wage rigidity. Despite a decline of real GNP of 9 percent between 1929 and 1930, one of the steepest declines ever recorded, *the nominal wage rate did not decline at all.* A decline did begin in 1931 through 1933, but then in

1934 the nominal wage rate jumped by 12 percent despite an unemployment rate in that year of 22 percent! By 1937 the nominal wage rate was back to the 1929 level, despite an unemployment rate of 14 percent. Thus it is an exaggeration for the Keynesian model to treat the nominal wage rate as absolutely rigid. A decline did occur in 1931–33. But the nominal wage rate did not exhibit the continued decline after 1933 that would have been necessary to bring the economy back to an output ratio of 100 percent through the classical mechanism of self-correction.

Column (10) of Table 7-1 exhibits the real wage rate, which rose during the contraction phase from 1929 to 1933. But the increase in W/P was just 6 percent while hours of labor input was declining by 32 percent in the private non-farm economy and 41 percent in manufacturing. To be consistent with the Keynesian theory, in which a decline in labor input requires a movement from point E_0 to A in the left-hand frame of Figure 7-3, the labor demand schedule must be quite flat. Another possibility, that the economy does not remain on its labor demand schedule during a recession or depression, is explored in Chapter 8.

The rise in the nominal and the real wage rate after 1933, despite high unemployment, is attributed by some economists to government intervention. During 1934 and 1935 the National Industrial Recovery Act (NIRA) explicitly attempted to raise wages and prices, setting forth industry-specific codes that required law-abiding employers to raise wage rates. Although the NIRA was declared unconstitutional in 1935, it was succeeded in 1935 by the Wagner Act (National Labor Relations Act) that favored union membership and helped to raise union membership from 3.4 million in 1934 to 8.4 million in 1941. Nevertheless, many economists are skeptical that government policy can fully account for the failure of nominal wage rates to continue falling in the last half of the 1930s, in light of the continuing high level of the unemployment rate.

7-4 Imperfect Information and the "Fooling Model"

Weaknesses of the Classical and Keynesian Models

The preceding sections of this chapter contain a troubling element that has perplexed students and teachers for decades. For both firms and workers to be content with what they are doing, the economy must operate on *both* the labor demand and supply curves in the left-hand frame of Figure 7-3. Yet the Keynesian rigid wage assumption allows workers to move off their labor supply curve whenever real output differs from natural real GNP (Q^N). What justifies the Keynesian assumption of non-market-clearing in preference to the classical assumption of market-clearing?

In this section we begin our examination of several modern theories that have been developed to deal with the dilemma that the classical economists had no explanation of the business cycle, while the Keynesian theory relied on an arbitrary element, the rigid wage. The first of these is Milton Friedman's "fooling model," developed as part of his Presidential Address to the American Economic Association in 1967.[6]

---

[6]Milton Friedman, "The Role of Monetary Policy," *American Economic Review,* vol. 58 (March 1968), pp. 1–17.

Distinctive Features: Market-Clearing and Imperfect Information

Milton Friedman *(1912–) Friedman, 1976 Nobel Prize winner, is the most famous proponent of monetarism and the inventor of the permanent income hypothesis of consumption explained in Chapter 18.*

The first distinctive feature of Friedman's model is that firms and workers are never required to operate off the labor demand and supply curves. Such models are often called "classical," "equilibrium," or "market-clearing" models. The second distinctive feature is that business cycles can occur if workers *inaccurately perceive the price level,* hence the label "fooling model." This feature of the Friedman model is often called "imperfect information" and is a characteristic of many modern models of the market-clearing variety.

The fooling model is illustrated in Figure 7-5, which in the left frame copies the labor supply and demand curves of Figure 7-3, and in the right frame copies the aggregate supply curve and one of the aggregate demand curves (DD_0) from the same figure. Friedman's treatment of the labor demand curve is identical to the Keynesian model in Figure 7-3; that is, he assumes that the labor demand (N^d) curve depends on the actual real wage (W/P). Thus the *countercyclical* movement of the real wage occurs along the N^d line in Figure 7-5, just as in Figure 7-3. But Friedman adds one important

A BUSINESS CYCLE EXPANSION IN FRIEDMAN'S "FOOLING" MODEL

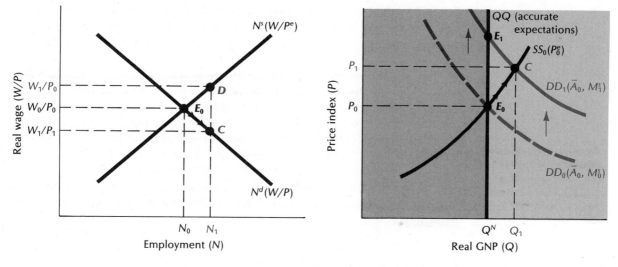

Figure 7-5 **Effects on the Price Index and Real Income of an Increase in the Nominal Money Supply from M_0^s to M_1^s While the Expected Price Level Is Fixed at P_0^e**

The position of the aggregate supply curve SS_0 is fixed by the assumed constancy of the price level expected by workers (P_0^e). A higher nominal money supply shifts the aggregate demand curve upward from DD_0 to DD_1, and the economy moves from point E_0 to C in both the left frame and the right frame. Because the actual price level has risen from P_0 to P_1, the firms are happy to hire additional labor input at point C in the left frame, but the workers think that their real wage has increased to point D and are happy to provide more labor input for as long as W/P^e remains high.

new element. In his interpretation, the labor supply curve depends on the "expected" real wage (W/P^e)—that is, the nominal wage rate (W) divided by the price level expected by workers (P^e).

Friedman's theory of the business cycle argues that an increase in aggregate demand raises the actual price level (P) and reduces the actual real wage (W/P), encouraging firms to hire more workers along their labor demand curve. For instance, in the right-hand frame of Figure 7-5 a rightward shift of the aggregate demand curve from DD_0 to DD_1 shifts the economy's short-run equilibrium from point E_0 to point C, raises real GNP from Q^N to Q_1, and raises the price level from P_0 to P_1. At point C in the left frame of Figure 7-5, N_1 workers are hired as the higher price level pushes the real wage down.

Yet only the firms know that the price level has increased; the *workers do not.* They still think the expected price level is P_0^e. If the firms raise the nominal wage rate from W_0 to W_1, workers will think that the expected real wage has increased from W_0/P_0^e to W_1/P_0^e and will happily work harder, moving up their labor supply curve to point D.

To explain business cycles, the Friedman model requires that the price level (P) differ from the expected price level (P^e). Thus in the right-hand frame of Figure 7-5, output can differ from Q^N along the SS_0 supply curve only if P differs from the expected price level P_0^e. What happens when the workers "catch on" to the fact that they have been fooled? Their expected price level will rise, and workers will demand a nominal wage increase sufficient to retain the original real wage level. As a result, the supply curve will shift up and to the left. This process will continue until workers have attained accurate expectations and output has returned to Q^N along the vertical QQ line at a point like E_1.

Because the level of output is always equal to natural real GNP (Q^N) when expectations are accurate, the vertical QQ line is labeled "Accurate Expectations" in the right-hand frame of Figure 7-5. Sooner or later any expectational errors will be corrected, so output cannot remain away from natural real GNP (Q^N) for long. Because of this feature, Friedman's fooling model is sometimes called a "natural rate" model, and in fact it was Friedman who is responsible for the terminology "natural real GNP" and "natural rate of unemployment." It is common to describe a model with a vertical long-run supply curve (like QQ in Figure 7-5) as obeying the **natural rate hypothesis.**

A model obeys the **natural rate hypothesis** when shifts in aggregate demand have no long-run effect on real GNP.

Criticisms of the Fooling Model

How does Friedman justify the claim of his fooling model that workers will hold incorrect expectations for any significant period of time? Friedman argues that *firms have more accurate information than is available to workers.* Such an "information advantage" for firms occurs because firms have a concentrated interest in a small number of prices of the products and monitor them continuously. Workers, on the other hand, are interested in a wide variety of prices of the things they buy and have insufficient time to keep careful track. Thus workers do not notice immediately when the price level rises.

But three questions can be raised about Friedman's model. First, workers and their families buy many goods, particularly gasoline, food, and drug items, on at least a weekly basis and would discover almost immediately if the prices of these items had risen. Second, if expectational errors really were the source of business cycles, workers could easily discover within a month or two that the aggregate price level had risen, since the media give prominent coverage to monthly changes in the Consumer Price Index. Third, if periods of high real GNP were *always* accompanied by an increase in the aggregate price level, workers would eventually suspect that a new interval of high production and easily available job opportunities would also be accompanied by an increase in the price level.

Each of these three criticisms raises serious doubts that workers would so easily be "fooled" as Friedman supposes. Suppose workers are not fooled; then an increase in demand that raises the general price level would bring instant demands by workers for nominal wage increases that exactly match the price increases. Yet equal-sized increases in W and P would leave the real wage (W/P) unchanged and would leave employment at its original level, N_0. There would be no business cycle in employment or output, so with reasonably intelligent workers the Friedman model fails as a theory of the business cycle.

7-5 The New Classical Macroeconomics and the Policy Ineffectiveness Proposition

The Assumption of Rational Expectations

Rational expectations need not be correct but make the best use of available information, avoiding errors that could have been foreseen by knowledge of history.

The **new classical model** is based on the three assumptions of market clearing, imperfect information, and rational expectations.

Despite its limitations, the Friedman model, with its twin assumptions of market-clearing and imperfect information, appealed to many economists. Preeminent among these was Robert E. Lucas, Jr., who took Friedman's model one step further by introducing an improved treatment of the way workers form their view of the expected price level (P^e). Instead of following Friedman's rather unsatisfactory assumption that workers only gradually adapted their expectations of the price level (P^e) to the actual value of the price level, allowing themselves to be fooled for weeks or even months, Lucas introduced the theory of **rational expectations.** Thus the **new classical model** contains three basic assumptions: market-clearing, imperfect information, and rational expectations.[7]

Expectations are rational *when people make the best forecasts they can with the available data.* It is important to recognize that these forecasts do not have to be correct, and so observing forecasting errors by individuals or professional economists does not constitute evidence against rational expectations. Instead, the theory of rational expectations argues that people do not consistently make the same forecasting errors.

[7]Robert Lucas did not invent the idea of rational expectations, but rather receives credit for applying it to macroeconomics. The original idea was applied to microeconomic issues and was set forth in John Muth, "Rational Expectations and the Theory of Price Movements," *Econometrica,* vol. 29 (July 1961), pp. 315–335.

Robert E. Lucas, Jr.
*(1937–   ) Lucas, the
leading developer of the
new classical
macroeconomics, merged
the concept of rational
expectations with the
assumptions of market
clearing and imperfect
information.*

For instance, the errors (or "fooling") of Milton Friedman's workers are not rational. If the observance of past history suggested that any increase in employment had always been accompanied by a reduction in the actual real wage below the expected real wage, then workers should anticipate that such *a reduction in the real wage would always accompany offers by employers of higher employment* and the workers should refuse such job offers. Workers would not provide more employment, since in Figure 7-5 employment cannot rise above N_0 along the workers' labor supply curve (N^s), unless the actual real wage rises above the original level W_0/P_0. More generally, individuals should not make errors in the same direction week after week, especially in circumstances similar to those that have occurred in previous history. The errors should be "random," that is, independent of previous forecasting errors.

The Friedman–Lucas Supply Function and the "Price Surprise"

The Friedman model implies a positively sloped aggregate supply curve, as in the right-hand frame of Figure 7-5. This supply curve is drawn again in Figure 7-6 and labeled $SS_0(P_0^e)$, with the term in parentheses indicating that the position of the SS curve is shifted whenever workers change their expectations of the price level. For instance, a higher expected price level (P_1^e) would shift the SS curve up from SS_0 to SS_1.

Note that we have drawn the supply curve in Figure 7-6 as a straight vertical line rather than as a curved line; this allows us to use a simple equation to represent the supply curve:

$$Q = Q^N + h(P - P^e). \tag{7.1}$$

Figure 7-6
The Short-Run Aggregate Supply Curve Drawn for Two Alternative Values of the Expected Price Level

The Friedman–Lucas Supply Curve is fixed in position by the price expectations of workers. Real GNP can rise above Q^N in the pink region only when the actual price level (P) rises above the expected price level (P^e). An increase in the expected price level from P_0^e to P_1^e shifts the curve up from SS_0 to SS_1.

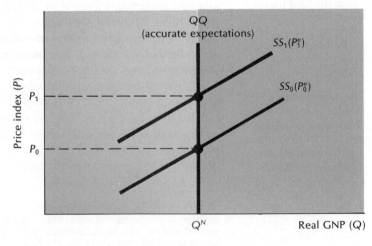

THE FRIEDMAN-LUCAS SUPPLY CURVE

This states that real GNP (Q) is equal to natural real GNP (Q^N), plus an amount that equals a coefficient h times the excess of the actual price level over the expected price level. This excess of P over P^e is sometimes called the "price surprise." For instance, if $P = 1.1$ and $P^e = 1.0$, while $Q^N = 4000$ and $h = 2000$, then the price surprise is 0.1 and actual real GNP will be:

$$Q = 4000 + 2000 (1.1 - 1.0) = 4200.$$

Although equation (7.1) or the equivalent SS curve in Figure 7-6 is now usually called the "Lucas supply function," such a function is also implied by Friedman's model. As a compromise, we describe it as the "Friedman–Lucas supply function." What Lucas contributed was to take Friedman's two assumptions of market-clearing and imperfect information, assumed in equation (7.1), and add the third assumption that expectations are formed rationally.

According to the Friedman–Lucas supply function, does a recession in which Q falls below Q^N require a price surprise? In which direction?

Why does a positive price surprise make firms produce more output, as assumed by the Friedman–Lucas supply function? Unlike the Friedman version of the model, which emphasizes the fooling of workers, the Lucas version emphasizes an information barrier shared by workers and firms alike. Firms sell in competitive markets and have no control over their own price, which rises and falls in response to demand. Lucas' firms are like small farmers producing wheat or corn, whose sales prices are determined at the Chicago Board of Trade. For firms to produce more, the price of their product must rise relative to marginal cost, which depends on the cost of raw materials and other goods purchased from suppliers. Firms know their own price, but information barriers prevent firms from knowing about prices charged in other markets. If there is a general increase in all prices, firms will observe first only their own price, while information barriers prevent them from observing prices charged by suppliers.

Slope of the supply function: Local versus aggregate price shocks. To overcome these barriers, firms use rational expectations to form the best possible estimate of the prices charged in other markets (P^e). If the price of their own product (P) rises relative to P^e, and thus relative to marginal cost, firms will anticipate higher profits and increase production. Hence Q rises above Q^N, as shown in equation (7.1). Thus the Lucas explanation of the business cycle hinges entirely on whether or not business firms believe that an increase in the price of their own product *will be experienced equally* by other firms. If firms guess that prices charged by their suppliers have risen as much as their own price, they will see no advantage to producing more now. If firms guess that prices charged by suppliers have *not* risen as much as their own price, they will produce more.

How do firms make this prediction? They apply rational expectations to their knowledge of past price behavior. If past movements in their own prices *have always been accompanied by similar movements in prices of suppliers,* then firms should expect that this will happen again. P^e will be assumed to rise in proportion to P, and output will not increase. But if the firm's price has often exhibited unique movements in response to "local conditions," for example, changes in weather altering the supply of wheat, then P may have risen without any accompanying increase in suppliers' prices. In this case firms may guess that P^e has not risen as much as P, and that this is a good time to produce.

In short, for products that in the past have experienced unique price movements in response to local conditions, firms may raise production substantially in response to a demand increase that raises the price of their own products. In contrast, for products that typically have experienced price movements that mimic those in the rest of the economy, firms will predict that their own price increase will be duplicated by increases in the costs of raw materials purchased from suppliers, and they will refuse to raise production.

A major contribution of Lucas' analysis is to conclude that the supply response (h in equation 7.1) will be high for firms that have previously experienced unique price movements, and low for firms that have experienced price movements mimicking those in the aggregate economy. Lucas also predicted that the supply response would be high in countries like the United States where the inflation rate has been relatively stable (making unique movements in individual prices more important). In contrast, the supply response would be small in countries like Brazil and Argentina where the inflation rate has ranged from zero to 1000 percent per year over the past few decades, and where movements in the aggregate price level *shared by all firms* completely swamp the influence of price movements for particular products. Lucas's key insight helps explain how countries like Brazil can have huge price movements with relatively small business cycles in real GNP.

7-6 Policy Ineffectiveness: A Proposition and Its Problems

The **policy ineffectiveness proposition** asserts that predictable changes in monetary policy cannot affect real output.

The concept of rational expectations, which states that individuals use all available information in forming their expectations, leads to a startling prediction by Lucas and his followers. In a modern version of monetary impotence, Lucas argues that *anticipated monetary policy cannot change real GNP in a regular or predictable way.* Usually called the **policy ineffectiveness proposition** (PIP), Lucas's argument for monetary impotence startled the economics profession when it was developed in the early 1970s.[8]

PIP can be understood in terms of equation (7.1), which states that the monetary authority (the Fed) can change output only if it can find some method of creating a price surprise. That is, the Fed must move P while not simultaneously moving P^e by the same amount. Yet if the public *knows* that an increase in the money supply raises the price level, and if the Fed's monetary stimulus is announced or can be *predicted* from the Fed's past behav-

---

[8]While Lucas receives the main credit for the basic ideas underlying the new classical macroeconomics, the formal case for PIP was made in Thomas J. Sargent and Neil Wallace, " 'Rational' Expectations, the Optimal Monetary Instrument, and the Optimal Money Supply Rule," *Journal of Political Economy,* vol. 83 (April 1975), pp. 241–254.

ior, then the public will boost the expected price level P^e along with the increase in the actual price level. Real GNP will not budge from natural real GNP (Q^N).

PIP can also be illustrated graphically. Figure 7-7 copies the SS_0 and SS_1 curves from Figure 7-6. Also included are two aggregate demand curves. DD_0 shows the level of aggregate demand before the Fed's monetary stimulus, and the initial position of the economy is at E_0. After the stimulus, which raises the money supply from M_0^s to M_1^s, the aggregate demand curve shifts up to DD_1. *If the Fed's monetary stimulus is announced or can be predicted from the Fed's past behavior,* then the public will understand the reason for the rising price level. The aggregate supply curve will shift up with the aggregate demand curve, and the economy will move from E_0 to E_1 without any deviation of Q away from Q^N.

Thus PIP suggests that the Fed cannot announce a monetary stimulus in advance if it wants to raise real GNP. But even worse, the Fed cannot create a monetary stimulus under conditions similar to those in which it has previously created a stimulus, *because people will anticipate the stimulus and adjust P^e accordingly.* PIP seems, then, to mark the demise of a regular **feedback rule** in which monetary policy would respond to higher unemployment by stimulating the economy, or would respond to higher inflation by restrictive actions. Seeing higher unemployment or higher inflation, individuals would anticipate the Fed's response by shifting their estimate of P^e, leaving the Fed's response without any effect on real GNP.

A **feedback rule** sets stabilization policy to respond in a regular way to a macroeconomic event, like an increase in unemployment or inflation.

Summary: The Policy Ineffectiveness Proposition states only that *fully anticipated changes in the money supply cannot affect real GNP.* It does not deny that a "money surprise" (an unanticipated change in the money supply) can alter the level of real GNP. But it implies that the Fed faces a considerable problem in creating such a money surprise, since the Fed cannot respond to economic events in the same way it has in the past.

Figure 7-7
Effect on the Price Level of an Increase in the Money Supply That Is Expected to Occur

In the new classical model, individuals have rational expectations. If they expect the money supply to increase or have prompt and accurate information on the money supply, their expectations of the price level will adjust in proportion to the expected change in the money supply. This is shown in the diagram by the upward movement of the Friedman–Lucas supply curve by exactly the same amount as the upward movement of the DD curve caused by the higher money supply.

THE NEW CLASSICAL BUSINESS CYCLE IS JUST LIKE THE OLD CLASSICAL BUSINESS CYCLE

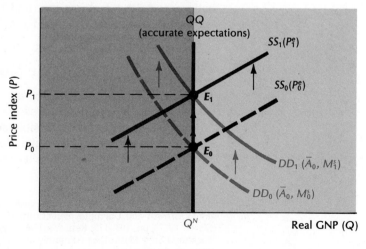

Weaknesses of PIP. Although PIP created a revolution that dominated macroeconomic discussion in the late 1970s, by the end of the decade several weaknesses of PIP had been pointed out. The problem was not the Lucas contribution of rational expectations. Rather, the weakness was in the twin assumptions inherited from Friedman, continuous market clearing and imperfect information, which made deviations of the current actual price from the expected price the *only* source of business-cycle movements in real GNP. The assumption of imperfect information implies that business cycles would be eliminated if we had accurate current information about the aggregate price level. All that is needed to eliminate the business cycle is for rational individuals to know that they could avoid departures from their own most efficient levels of activity if only they monitored published aggregate price information.

This "imperfect information" aspect of the new classical models has been widely criticized. Aggregate price information is easily available with short lags (announcements of monthly Consumer Price Index, CPI, changes are made on the nightly television news the day they are announced). With aggregate price information easily available, why should firms or workers take any action that might move them away from labor-market equilibrium, when all they have to do is wait a few days or weeks to learn the latest monthly change in the CPI? If business cycles really depended entirely on the absence of information on the monthly price level, then a private market would immediately develop in which entrepreneurs would gather their own weekly, daily, or hourly versions of the CPI and sell it to workers and firms.

The debate between the "new classical" economists and their "new Keynesian" critics in the late 1970s and early 1980s centered around complex statistical tests of PIP. Could the Fed influence real GNP or unemployment through a change in the money supply that was *anticipated* by the public? If so, PIP was invalid. The validity of PIP required that only Fed monetary changes that were *unanticipated* by the public could influence real GNP. After the statistical battles had been waged and the smoke had cleared, it was evident that the historical data did not support PIP. With monthly and even weekly data on the money supply available, people could make expectational errors about monetary changes lasting for only a few weeks, not nearly enough to explain business cycles lasting an average of four and one-half years in the postwar era, and twelve years for the period of high unemployment between 1929 and 1941.[9]

7-7 The Real Business Cycle Model

There appears to be increasing agreement that the Lucas "imperfect information" theory of the business cycle is unsatisfactory, since information lags are too short to be a plausible source of multiyear business cycles. New Keynesian economists favor abandoning new classical economics and the assumption of continuous market clearing. Instead, they concentrate on the

---

[9]The battle began with a paper by Robert Barro that claimed to support PIP, "Unanticipated Money Growth and Unemployment in the United States," *American Economic Review,* vol. 67 (March 1977), pp. 101–115. Return salvoes were fired by Frederic S. Mishkin, "Does Anticipated Monetary Policy Matter? An Economic Investigation," *Journal of Political Economy,* vol. 90 (Feb. 1982), pp. 22–51, and by Robert J. Gordon, "Price Inertia and Policy Ineffectiveness in the United States, 1890–1980," *Journal of Political Economy,* vol. 90 (Dec. 1982), pp. 1087–1117.

The **real business cy-
cle** approach explains
business cycles in out-
put and employment as
caused by technology
or supply shocks.

underlying sources of wage and price rigidity, as shown in the next chapter. Meanwhile, new classical macroeconomists have turned to an alternative theory of the business cycle that still assumes continuous market clearing. Their new theory is the **real business cycle** (RBC) approach to the analysis of economic fluctuations.

The RBC model assumes that the origins of the business cycle lie in "real" (or supply) shocks rather than "monetary" (or demand) shocks. In terms of our graphical analysis, the main source of shifts in output lies in swings in the aggregate supply curve, not the aggregate demand curve. This contrasts with the Lucas imperfect information approach, in which unanticipated monetary shocks led to cycles in real output and employment because information barriers prevented business firms from accurately anticipating movements in prices charged in markets other than their own. In terms of the Friedman–Lucas supply function (equation 7.1), the RBC approach is not based on price surprises, that is, deviations of P from P^e. Instead, the RBC approach states that fluctuations in Q are caused entirely by fluctuations in natural real GNP itself, Q^N.

What are these real or supply shocks that cause business cycles? They include new production techniques, new products, bad weather, new sources of raw materials, and price changes in raw materials. Recall that the Lucas model failed to consider that information barriers are too short-lived to explain the *length* and *persistence* of actual business cycles. In contrast, the RBC approach assumes that these supply shocks are highly persistent, meaning that a favorable shock lasts several years, dies away smoothly, and is replaced by an adverse shock that lasts several years. It is important to note that the RBC theory simply *assumes* and does not explain the persistence of business cycles that undermined the Lucas approach.

In the RBC model, the economy responds to these persistent supply shocks according to the new classical assumption of continuous equilibrium. Firms produce the amount they desire at prices and wages that respond flexibly to changing economic conditions, and hire the number of workers they want; workers obtain exactly the number of hours of work that they desire at the market-determined real wage.[10] Our aggregate supply curve diagram introduced in Chapter 6 illustrates these aspects of the RBC model.

A Graphical Analysis of the RBC Model

The top frame of Figure 7-8 exhibits the production function (*F*), which shows how much output can be produced by each additional worker. An adverse supply shock leads to a downward shift in the production function, for instance from the "normal" curve F_0 to the "bad shock" curve F_1, implying a decline in the productivity of each worker. In the lower frame the labor

---

[10]Two of the most influential papers in the development of the RBC approach are Finn E. Kydland and Edward C. Prescott, "Time to Build and Aggregate Fluctuations," *Econometrica,* vol. 50 (November 1982), pp. 1345–70, and Robert G. King and Charles I. Plosser, "Money, Credit, and Prices in a Real Business Cycle," *American Economic Review,* vol. 74 (June 1984), pp. 363–380. A sympathetic exposition is Bennett T. McCallum, "Real Business Cycle Models," National Bureau of Economic Research working paper 2480, forthcoming in Robert J. Barro, *Handbook of Modern Business Cycle Theory.* A critical exposition is contained in N. Gregory Mankiw, "Real Business Cycles: A New Keynesian Perspective," *Economic Perspectives,* 1989.

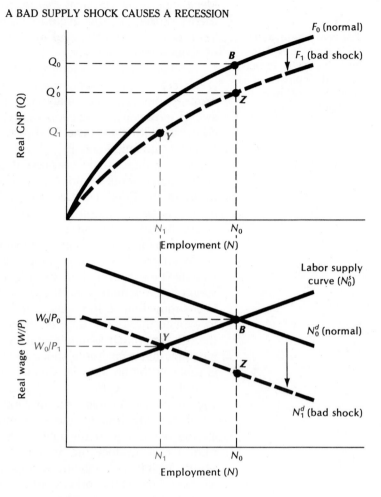

Figure 7-8

Effect of an Adverse Supply Shock on Output and Employment in the Real Business Cycle Model

F_0 in the top frame is the normal production function, identical to curve F_0 in Figure 6-7 and 6-8. N_0^d is the normal labor demand curve. An adverse movement in supply conditions, like bad weather for growing crops, shifts the production function down to F_1 and the labor demand curve down to N_1^d. In normal times the economy operates at point B in the upper and lower frames, and in bad times at point Y. The decline in employment depends on the slope of the labor supply curve; if the labor supply curve were a vertical line instead of a positively sloped line like N_0^s, the economy would move to Z instead of Y. Employment would remain fixed and output would fall only from Q_0 to Q_0'.

A BAD SUPPLY SHOCK CAUSES A RECESSION

demand curve, which shows the marginal product of labor, shifts down in response to the adverse supply shock from the line labeled N_0^d to the line N_1^d.

The effect of the adverse supply shock on both output and employment depends on the slope of the labor supply curve. As we learned in Section 6-6, if this slope is positive, as along the line labeled N_0^s, then a lower real wage induces workers to supply less labor (working longer hours or leaving the home to take a job or to work at two jobs). Since the economy is always in equilibrium in the RBC model, the demand for labor shifts as a result of the supply shock from point B to point Y. Employment falls from N_0 to N_1, while output falls from Q_0 to Q_1.

A different slope of the labor supply curve would lead to a different conclusion. Imagine that the labor supply curve, instead of N_0^s, is a vertical line rising above N_0 through points Z and B. Then the economy's equilibrium point would be shifted downward by the adverse supply shock from B to Z. The shock would cause no change in employment, and in the upper frame there would be a much smaller decline in output, from Q_0 to Q_0'. Thus the RBC model's ability to explain why employment declines in real-world recessions requires a positive slope of the labor supply schedule, as shown by the line N_0^s. According to this theory, employment falls in a recession because workers consider this a bad time to work. Rather than work at the lower real wage business firms pay in response to the adverse supply conditions, workers choose to enjoy leisure during recessions.

SELF-TEST   According to the RBC theory, why does output increase in a business expansion? What is the explanation of the theory for the increase in employment that takes place in high-employment years like 1973 and 1988–89?

Debating the Merits of the RBC Model

To validate the RBC approach, Edward Prescott of the University of Minnesota and others have developed a method called "calibration." A mathematical RBC model is developed on a computer, and important components like the slope of the labor supply curve are selected to be compatible with evidence from microeconomic studies of the U.S. economy. The supply shock process that drives the business cycle is not based on any data at all; rather, it is assumed to be of a magnitude and persistence that will allow the computer model to mimic actual U.S. business cycles. With so much resting on assumptions, and with the extent and duration of U.S. cycles based on an assumed supply shock, what can the calibration exercise demonstrate? Prescott and his colleagues judge their model to be successful if it can reproduce the cyclical properties of four main economic variables relative to output: consumption, investment, capital input, and labor input. In particular, the model should be able to duplicate such features of the U.S. economy as much greater cycles of investment than of consumption, and decreases in labor productivity in recessions.

Many economists, even some of the most prominent new classicists, question the relevance of the RBC approach.[11] First, they doubt that supply shocks are important enough to explain actual business cycles. Second, they note that RBC proponents have made no attempt to locate the specific shocks that cause the business cycles or to explain the behavior of such important macroeconomic variables as money and prices.

Nature of technology shocks. Unlike the Keynesian *IS-LM* model of Chapters 4 and 5, the RBC model does not incorporate a multiplier effect that can magnify the impact of shocks on the economy. Thus to explain big recessions the model needs big shocks. Skeptics doubt that any conceivable supply shock could explain why output fell by one third in the Great Depression of the 1930s. Only the oil price shocks of the 1970s, which we examine

---

[11]See Robert J. Barro, "Comments," in Stanley Fischer, ed., *NBER Macroeconomics Annual 1986*, M.I.T. Press, pp. 136–139.

in more detail in Chapter 10, qualify as a supply shock severe enough to explain the recessions that occurred in 1974–75 and 1980–82. Proponents of the RBC approach have failed to identify particular events in particular sectors that could be labeled supply shocks in earlier episodes like the Great Depression and postwar recessions before 1974. At an industry level, one would expect technology shocks to occur randomly. Highly distinctive technologies are used in different industries; for instance, an innovation that increases the speed of a Macintosh desktop computer has little impact on the productivity of coal miners. Favorable shocks in some industries would cancel out adverse shocks in other industries, which deepens the skepticism that (except for the oil shocks of the 1970s), the *average* effect of all the separate industry shocks could be large enough to explain actual booms and recessions.

Money and prices. The distinguishing feature of the RBC approach is the assumption that the dominant source of business cycle movements is supply shocks, with no role for demand shocks. But this leads to a troublesome implication: if business cycles occur when the aggregate supply curve shifts back and forth along a fixed aggregate demand curve, then prices should rise in recessions and fall in booms. The business cycle should behave like the market for wheat, with falling prices and rising output in years with good weather, and vice versa. But in actual business cycles prices rise more in booms than recessions.

Most RBC models simply omit money and any mechanism by which the aggregate price level is determined. A few others explain price movements as a reflection of passive movements in the money supply induced by the supply shocks. For instance, in a recession caused by a negative supply shock, prices fall rather than rise because the central bank sharply reduces the money supply. Any such passive decline in the money supply would have to be so strong that it *more than offsets* the price increases that naturally happen with a supply shock. Yet such reactions have not been observed in past episodes, most notably in the Great Depression when in 1929–33 the money supply fell much less than real output (see Table 7-1). No RBC proponent has yet tried to explain why prices fell in the Great Depression, why the inflation rate fell in most postwar recessions, and why the inflation rate rose in the recession of 1974–75. An adequate explanation requires an approach in which *both supply and demand shocks can cause business cycles;* we develop this more realistic model in the next three chapters.

Real wages and employment. The RBC model can explain fluctuations in employment over the business cycle only if the labor supply curve is positively sloped, as depicted in Figure 7-8. But with the exception of the supply shock period in the 1970s, real wages have not moved procyclically, as must occur in Figure 7-8 to induce a decline in employment during a recession. We have already learned that they do not move countercyclically either, as assumed in the original Keynesian model and the Friedman fooling model. The fact that real wages show no systematic fluctuations casts doubt on the RBC model, which induces workers to raise employment in booms and reduce employment in recessions through movements in real wages.

7-8 New Classical Macroeconomics: Limitations and Positive Contributions

The development of new classical macroeconomics has taken place in two phases, the Lucas approach based on information barriers, and the real business cycle (RBC) approach. Both phases attempt to explain how business cycles can occur in a model in which agents form expectations rationally and in which equilibrium is maintained continuously. In the new classical models firms and workers operate on their labor demand and supply curves. A common feature of the Lucas and RBC models is that *workers always have a choice about their hours of work; there is no such thing as a layoff notice telling a worker that his or her job has disappeared.*

We have seen that both the Lucas and RBC models have limitations. The Lucas model falters because information barriers in the real world are much too short-lived to explain why most business cycles last four years or longer. The RBC model is therefore the focus of current research on business cycles that maintain continuous equilibrium or market clearing. The main problems with the RBC model are discussed in the previous section. First, except for the oil shocks of the 1970s, no other technology shock has been strong enough to explain actual business cycles. Second, the RBC models ignore price behavior, thus missing the opportunity to use observed price fluctuations to help identify the source of business cycles, that is, whether they originate in supply or demand shocks. Finally, the RBC model wrongly implies procyclical fluctuations of real wages.

Positive Contributions of New Classical Macroeconomics

Since strong objections have been raised to both the Lucas and RBC versions of new classical theory, we naturally wonder why these models have had such a strong appeal to a broad range of economists. What explains this apparent paradox?

Rational expectations: Linking micro- and macroeconomics. The assumption of rational expectations appeals to economists, since it requires that people do not repeat their mistakes. Instead, people make the best use of all available information to guide their economic behavior. Such an approach is much more appealing than the alternative assumption that people make repeated mistakes in the same direction, period after period. The rational expectations hypothesis also has appeal because of its grounding in microeconomics. This means that the assumption of rational expectations in macroeconomics parallels the basic microeconomic assumptions of profit maximization and utility maximization.

The weakness of the new classical model lies not in the assumption of rational expectations, but rather in its assumption of continuous market clearing. As we shall learn in the next chapter, there are good reasons why the market for labor does not clear each period. Firms and workers find it advantageous to enter into contracts (written or unwritten) that reduce uncertainty about the future as well as reduce the costs of negotiating new wages every week. Such contracts are quite rational, and both firms and workers can have fully rational expectations when negotiating and signing such contracts. The rigidity that such contracts impart to nominal wage rates prevents markets from clearing and thus conflicts with the market-clearing assumption on which rests the new classical approach to business cycles.

The theory of efficient financial markets. Many of the ideas developed by the new classical economists have been applied successfully to markets where continuous market clearing is a much more reasonable assumption. This is particularly true of financial markets, including the stock market, bond market, foreign exchange market, and the markets for agricultural and crude commodities like sugar and gold. The theory of efficient markets incorporates the assumption of rational expectations. Expectations are assumed to incorporate all available information, implying that stock prices jump the instant new information is received, and that there are no opportunities to make extraordinary profits on the stock market without access to inside information.

Greater understanding of economic policy. The idea that individuals in the private part of the economy have rational expectations has improved our understanding of economic policy. Even if long-term wage and price contracts impede the flexibility of wages and prices, as discussed in the next chapter, those who negotiate contracts attempt to do so with full information on what policymakers are likely to do. For instance, wage negotiators who suspect that the government will allow rapid inflation after a supply shock are likely to demand full cost-of-living adjustments in their contracts. In contrast, past refusal of a government to allow rapid inflation following a supply shock, as in the case of the German Bundesbank in the 1970s, will increase wage negotiators' confidence that full cost-of-living protection is not necessary.

Recall that the policy ineffectiveness proposition (PIP) developed as part of the Lucas information-barrier approach implies that fully anticipated monetary policy changes have no effect at all on output. While PIP does not appear to be valid in U.S. history, a milder and more acceptable proposition is that fully anticipated policy changes have *smaller* effects than unanticipated changes. The expansionary policies pursued in the United States in the 1960s caused the output ratio to exceed 100 percent for a few years, but not permanently. In countries like Argentina and Brazil, in which inflationary policies have been conducted for several decades, there is relatively little response of output to changes in policy. Further, in extreme inflationary episodes ("hyperinflation"), radical changes in government policy seemed to halt inflation without a major decline in output.[12]

Pervasive effect on economic research. Even if the new classical theories of the business cycle are subject to substantial skepticism, new techniques of analysis introduced by these theories have had a major influence

---

[12]See Thomas J. Sargent, "The Ends of Four Big Inflations," Chapter 3 in his *Rational Expectations and Inflation* (Harper & Row, 1986).

on the way economists study such variables as consumption, investment, and the foreign exchange rate. The understanding of extreme episodes of inflation in places like Argentina and Brazil, as well as Israel, is just one contribution of techniques introduced by new classical economists. The distinction between anticipated policy changes and policy "surprises" has improved our understanding of policy changes. The new Keynesian models described in the next chapter emphasize institutional impediments to price flexibility, like long-term labor contracts, but the new classicists first pointed out that the form of the labor contracts may reflect what people anticipate about future economic policy.

Finally, the development of the RBC model has raised profound questions about the meaning of a business cycle. A simplistic view would be that "natural output" (Q^N) grows smoothly at the same rate forever. In the data developed for use in this book (and listed in Appendix A) we take the less extreme view that Q^N grows smoothly over each business cycle, and then in the next cycle grows smoothly again, but at a different rate. At the other extreme the RBC model eliminates the distinction between Q and Q^N and attempts to explain why there is a business cycle in Q^N. An intermediate view is that Q and Q^N are distinct but that Q^N itself may vary over the business cycle. Recent research claims that a substantial fraction of output fluctuations in quarterly data is associated with movements in long-run growth rather than purely transitory business cycles. This research aims to improve our understanding of the link between changes in long-run growth and cyclical swings and argues against a sharp dichotomy between policies to dampen cycles and those to stimulate growth. This research, while still in its formative stage, might not have raised these questions at all but for the stimulus provided by the controversy over the RBC version of new classical macroeconomics.[13]

SUMMARY

1. Classical economists believed that cycles in aggregate demand mainly affected the price level, not real output. The economy's self-correcting forces of price flexibility protected real output from fluctuations.

2. Keynes criticized the classical economists on two grounds. The first was that the aggregate demand curve might be vertical rather than negatively sloped, due to a failure of autonomous spending to respond to the interest rate (vertical *IS* curve) or to a liquidity trap (horizontal *LM* curve) or both. Pigou countered that falling prices raise wealth and spending, guaranteeing a negatively sloped aggregate demand curve.

3. Keynes also criticized the classical economists because he believed that wages were rigid, preventing prices from adjusting sufficiently to return real GNP to the level of natural real GNP.

4. Many economists disliked Keynes's arbitrary assumption of a rigid wage and attempted to build a theory of the business cycle based on continuous market clearing and imperfect information. The first of these theories was Milton Friedman's fooling model, in which workers are "fooled" into providing extra labor input because they do not have as prompt or complete information on the aggregate price level as do firms.

5. Robert Lucas developed the first version of the new classical model, which adds rational expectations to Friedman's assumptions of continuous market clearing and imperfect information. The central tool of the new classical model is the Friedman–

---

[13]See James H. Stock and Mark W. Watson, "Variable Trends in Economic Time Series," *Journal of Economic Perspectives,* vol. 2 (Summer 1988), pp. 147–174.

Lucas supply curve, which attributes business cycles in real output to expectational errors, also called "price surprises."

6. The central implication of the Lucas model is the policy ineffectiveness proposition, which states that monetary policy cannot affect output through either an *announced* policy change or through a change that reacts to past events in a consistent and predictable way.

7. The second new classical approach is called the real business cycle model. This explains business cycles in output and employment as the result of slowly changing (that is, persistent) shocks to supply conditions and technology.

8. Both versions of the new classical macroeco-

nomics have been criticized as theories of the business cycle, the Lucas version because actual information barriers are too short-lived to explain multi-year business cycles, and the real business cycle version because no one has yet identified specific technology shocks that are large enough to explain actual recessions and depressions.

9. Despite these criticisms, the new classical macroeconomics has been extremely influential, especially for studies of financial markets, consumption, investment, and foreign exchange rates. It has also led to a new view of policy, in which the institutional arrangements by which private firms and workers negotiate wages and prices depend on what they think policymakers are likely to do.

CONCEPTS

self-correcting forces
monetary impotence
rigid wages
deflation impotence
GNP gap
Pigou or real balance effect
Keynes effect
expectations effect
redistribution effect

persistent unemployment
market-clearing
non-market clearing
natural rate hypothesis
rational expectations
new classical model
policy ineffectiveness proposition
feedback rule
real business cycle

QUESTIONS AND PROBLEMS

Questions

1. According to the view of the classical economists, there should have been a movement down the *DD* curve during the 1930s. Explain why this type of movement would require a shifting *SS* curve. Did the *SS* curve shift during the Depression in the way expected by the classical economists?

2. What is meant by the term monetary impotence? According to Keynes, what two conditions could lead to monetary impotence? Were either of these two conditions present during the Great Depression?

3. Explain the role played by the interest rate in the Pigou effect.

4. Why does the existence of a potent Pigou effect guarantee a negatively sloped *DD* curve?

5. Does the Pigou effect alter the average propensity to consume in the economy?

6. The whole controversy regarding the location of the *IS* curve and the potency of the real balance effect becomes irrelevant if nominal wages are rigid downward. Why is this so? Use the *DD/SS* model to explain your answer.

7. According to the Friedman "fooling" model, how does the labor market clear when prices and output rise in the short run?

8. Explain how the Friedman "fooling" model predicts that an expansionary monetary policy can lead to increased output in the short run, while the new classical model suggests that such a policy would have no effect on real output.

9. In what ways are the Friedman "fooling" model and the Keynesian model similar? In what ways do they differ?

10. In what ways are the Friedman "fooling" model and the new classical model similar? In what ways do they differ?

11. If policymakers were trying to decrease output in a period of continuing inflation, would the existence of the Pigou effect have any impact? Can you explain, under these circumstances, how the redistribution effect and the expectations effect might affect the economy?

12. Given the existence of a Pigou or real balance effect, what do you predict will happen to the *IS* and *DD* curves if the economy experiences an unexpected increase in autonomous exports? (Assume that the economy begins in a long run equilibrium position where *DD* crosses the *QQ* line.)

13. What is meant by the term "price surprise"? What role does it play in determining the slope of the supply function in Lucas's "local" explanation of business cycles? Explain Lucas's explanation for why the supply function in Brazil is likely to be steeper than that in the United States.

14. How does the real business cycle (RBC) approach differ from the Lucas approach? How is it similar? Does it explain the persistence of business cycles?

15. What does real business cycle (RBC) theory predict will happen to prices, real wages, and employment in response to an adverse supply shock? Is this prediction matched by real world experience? What explanation(s) for the real world behavior of prices and real wages do real business cycle theorists offer?

Problems

1. Given the following Friedman–Lucas supply function:

   $Q = Q^N + h(P - P^e)$ where $Q^N = 5000$, $P^e = 1.5$ and $h = 2500$

   Calculate the level of real output (Q) for
   (a) $P = 0.75$
   (b) $P = 1.00$
   (c) $P = 1.25$
   (d) $P = 1.50$
   (e) $P = 1.75$
   (f) $P = 2.00$

2. Given the Friedman–Lucas supply function in problem 1, what would be the equilibrium level of income if people accurately expect that the price level is 1.00? 1.50? 2.00? Explain.

SELF-TEST ANSWERS

p. 187 The Pigou effect stabilizes the economy when demand is high; rising prices reduce the value of real balances and real wealth, which in turn reduces consumption. The expectations and redistribution effects destabilize the economy. The expectations effect causes people to spend sooner, since they expect future prices to be higher. This boosts demand when demand is already high. Similarly, the redistribution effect causes income to be redistributed from savers who spend little to borrowers who spend much, thus boosting demand when demand is already high.

p. 199 Yes, there must be a price surprise when Q falls below Q^N in a recession. When the price level is surprisingly low, firms conclude that the current period is a bad time to produce (since they receive an unrewardingly low price for their product.) Hence, they reduce production voluntarily.

p. 205 A business expansion is explained by RBC theory as the result of a favorable or beneficial supply shock which makes factors of production unusually productive. Employment increases as workers add more hours and accept more jobs in the belief that the higher real wage, paid out by firms as a result of high productivity, makes the period an attractive one in which to expend extra work effort.

"New Keynesian" Explanations of the Business Cycle: The Microeconomics of Wage and Price Stickiness

The price of commodities in the market is formed by means of a certain struggle which takes place between the buyers and the sellers.

—Henry Thornton, 1802

8-1 Essential Features of the New Keynesian Economics

Common Elements of the Original and New Keynesian Approaches

The adjective "new" distinguishes modern developments in Keynesian theory from the original Keynesian model that was developed during the Great Depression by Keynes and his followers and was reviewed in Section 7-2. The original Keynesian model combines a theory of shifts in aggregate demand based on the *IS-LM* model of Chapters 4 and 5 with a theory of aggregate supply based on the arbitrary assumption of a fixed nominal wage. Unlike the old and new classical models, with their assumptions of continuous equilibrium, or market clearing, the Keynesian approach does not insist that markets clear continuously. Hence the Keynesian model, either the original or new variety, is often dubbed a **non-market-clearing model**, conveying the failure of prices to adjust rapidly enough to "clear markets" within a relatively short interval after a demand or supply shock. If slow price adjustment makes the return of the economy to natural output a long, drawn-out process, the economy can remain in a state of disequilibrium for years.

In a **non-market-clearing model**, workers and firms are not continuously on their demand and supply schedules, but rather are pushed off these schedules by the gradual adjustment of prices.

The appeal of Keynesian economics stems from the evident unhappiness of workers and firms during recessions and depressions. Workers and firms *do not act as if they were making a voluntary choice to cut production and hours worked.* A simple thought experiment is enough. Ask yourself these questions about the real world: Can each worker during every day of a recession sell all the labor desired at the going wage and price? Would every worker in a recession refuse a job offer at the going wage and price? Then ask these related questions about business firms: Can each business firm sell all the output desired at today's prices? Would each business firm turn away customers at today's prices? The history of business cycles is punctuated by recessions and depressions lasting several years, during which workers and firms could not sell all the labor and output desired at the going wages and prices. Thus a theory of business cycles based on the failure of markets to clear, the new Keynesians believe, is more realistic than the new classical approach based on continuous market clearing.

Just as Keynes developed his non-market-clearing model by postulating a fixed nominal wage, which limited the amount by which the price level could decline in a period of low demand, the new Keynesian approach also bases its model on the assumption that prices adjust slowly. The implications of "sticky" or slowly adjusting prices for real output can be seen clearly when we review our basic definitions from Chapter 1. Recall that the GNP deflator (P) is defined as nominal GNP (Y) divided by real GNP (Q):

$$P \equiv Y/Q.$$

This definition can easily be reversed: real GNP (Q) is nominal GNP (Y) divided by the price level (P):

$$Q \equiv Y/P$$

This implies that:

$$q \equiv y - p$$

In words, the percentage change in real GNP equals the percentage change in nominal GNP minus the inflation rate.

Throughout the history of most industrial countries, fluctuations in nominal aggregate demand (y) have been accompanied by similar but smaller fluctuations of the aggregate price level (p). As a result, the new Keynesian model asserts that changes in *real* output (q) are determined *not* at the level that business firms desire, but as a "residual," the portion of the nominal GNP fluctuation (y) that is *not* absorbed by price movements (p). The "left-over" change in real demand, q, comes as news to firms, and their subsequent adjustments in employment come as news to workers.

In new classical models, business firms base their choice of the output level on news regarding their own price level obtained from auction markets like the Chicago Board of Trade. In contrast, Keynesian non-market-clearing models turn the role of prices and output upside down. New Keynesian business firms base their choice of the price level on news regarding their own sales obtained by watching the ebb and flow of customers coming through the front door.

The New Keynesian Model

The **new Keynesian economics** explains rigidity in prices and wages as consistent with the self-interest of firms and workers, all of which are assumed to have rational expectations.

What, then, is the difference between the original and **new Keynesian economics?** Both assume that prices adjust slowly. But unlike the original model, which assumed a fixed nominal wage, the new-Keynesian approach *attempts to explain the microeconomic foundations of slow adjustment of both wages and prices.* The new Keynesian approach borrows—some would say "steals"—the concept of rational expectations from new-classical economics. And it borrows from traditional microeconomics the core assumptions that firms maximize profits and workers maximize their own well being or utility. The achievement of new Keynesian economics is to show how choices made by firms and workers that maximize business profits and worker well-being at the microeconomic level have adverse social consequences at the macroeconomic level.

Two distinctions are essential to the new Keynesian model. The first is between wage setting in labor markets and price setting in product markets. Following the original Keynesian element of the "rigid wage," the first wave of new Keynesian theorizing attempted to explain why wages are sticky. Yet it is not enough for wages to be sticky. If profits were sufficiently flexible, prices could also be flexible, rising and falling in exact proportion to changes in nominal demand and leaving output fixed. This realization has shifted attention to the product market to uncover reasons why prices are insufficiently flexible to mimic fluctuations in nominal GNP.

The second distinction is between **nominal rigidity** and **real rigidity.** Markets will not clear if something prevents the full adjustment of nominal prices, that is, prevents movements in nominal prices (P) proportionate to movements in nominal demand (Y). The first group of new Keynesian theories explains wage or price stickiness as the result of factors that make prices costly to adjust. Included in this category are **menu costs** and overlapping **staggered contracts,** which limit the flexibility of both prices and wages. These factors are said to explain nominal rigidity because they deal with barriers to the adjustment of nominal prices.

New Keynesian theories also explain real rigidities, the stickiness of a wage relative to another wage, of a wage relative to a price, or of a price relative to another price. Theories that explain real rigidities in labor markets include the "implicit contract" and "efficiency wage" models, both of which we will examine later in the chapter. Critics note that theories of real rigidities do not explain nominal rigidity, since nothing prevents each individual agent from indexing nominal price to nominal aggregate demand, that is, automatically changing P by the same percentage change as Y, thus leaving real output (Q) unaffected. We will be particularly interested in the arguments given by new Keynesians as to the reasons for the absence of such full indexation, which in turn would suggest that theories of real rigidities *are* relevant to the explanation of sticky prices and wages.

It is important for us to study the new Keynesian ideas, not just to understand the reasons for price stickiness, but also to assess the new classical approach. Despite its unrealistic aspects, the new classical approach was popular and influential because it addressed the original Keynesian model's arbitrary and unexplained assumption of wage rigidity. To the extent that the new Keynesians have succeeded in developing a microeconomic theory of price stickiness, they will further reduce the appeal of the new-classical macroeconomics as a theory of business cycles.

A **nominal rigidity** is a factor that inhibits the flexibility of the nominal price level due to some factor, such as menu costs and staggered contracts, which make it costly for firms to change the nominal price or wage level.

A **real rigidity** is a factor that makes firms reluctant to change the real wage, the relative wage, or the relative price.

A **menu cost** is any expense associated with changing prices, including the costs of printing new menus or distributing new catalogs.

Staggered contracts are contracts setting the price of wage level which have differing expiration dates for different groups of firms or workers.

8-2 Why Small Nominal Rigidities Have Large Macroeconomic Effects

A basic insight of Keynesian theory, both old and new, is that decisions of individual business firms do not always serve the best interests of society. The original Keynesian model argued that stimulative fiscal policy might be needed to avoid an economic slump resulting from some combination of monetary impotence, deflation impotence, and fixed wages. The new Keynesian model does not place any special emphasis on fiscal policy as opposed to monetary policy. Instead, it shows how rational profit-maximizing decisions by business firms may have adverse consequences for society.

Price Setting by a Monopolistic Firm

An **auction market** is a centralized location where professional traders buy and sell a commodity or a financial security.

The new classical and new Keynesian approaches view business firm behavior from different perspectives. In the new classical model firms are assumed to be perfectly competitive "price takers" with no control over the price. This approach may describe farmers producing goods sold on an **auction market,** like wheat or corn sold on the Chicago Board of Trade. Such farmers choose how much to produce but have no control over price. However, the assumption of perfect competition does not apply to firms in most other sectors of the economy. "Monopolistic competition" describes a market in which the number of sellers is sufficiently small that each firm is a price setter rather than a price taker. For instance, manufacturing firms, airlines, and many other firms can choose exactly what price to set, but they have no control over the amount sold. An airline enters a price schedule into the reservations computer and then waits to see how many passengers show up on the plane.

The new Keynesian approach assumes that small menu costs will deter monopolistic firms from constantly changing their prices. Each price change would require firms to spend time and money holding meetings to decide on price changes, informing the sales staff of the new price schedule, and printing new menus or catalogs. New classical critics scoff at the "menu cost" explanation of price stickiness. Surely, they argue, menu costs are much too small to explain why society would endure 25 percent unemployment during the Great Depression![1] But new Keynesian theorists have shown that menu costs do not have to be large to explain price stickiness. To see why, look at the left-hand frame of Figure 8-1, where we review the elementary theory of price setting by a monopolist.[2] Our diagrams are particularly simple, since they assume that marginal cost is constant along the horizontal line labeled "initial MC_0." There are no fixed costs, so marginal cost and average cost are the same. The quantity produced (Q_0) is determined at the point where the marginal revenue line (MR_0) intersects the marginal cost curve. The price is determined at point E_0, where the chosen quantity Q_0 intersects the "initial demand" curve. The right-hand frame of Figure 8-1 shows exactly the same situation but identifies the areas indicating the business firm's profit and the consumer surplus enjoyed by the purchasers of the product.[3]

---

[1]Ironically, one of the most often-cited papers on the effects of menu costs on price-setting behavior was written by one of the developers of the new-classical approach. See Robert J. Barro, "A Theory of Monopolistic Price Adjustment," *Review of Economic Studies,* vol. 39 (1972), pp. 17–26.

[2]The presentation in this section is a simplified version of the first half of N. Gregory Mankiw, "Small Menu Costs and Large Business Cycles: A Macroeconomic Model of Monopoly," *Quarterly Journal of Economics,* vol. 100 (May 1985), pp. 529–537.

[3]**Review:** When the demand curve is a straight line, the marginal revenue curve is always drawn so that it lies halfway between the demand curve and the vertical axis. The demand curve shows how much each purchaser is willing to pay for the product. At the price P_0 any purchaser whose willingness to pay is greater than P_0 enjoys a consumer surplus, reflecting the fact that the price charged is less than the willingness to pay.

HOW A MONOPOLIST SETS PRICE TO MAXIMIZE PROFITS

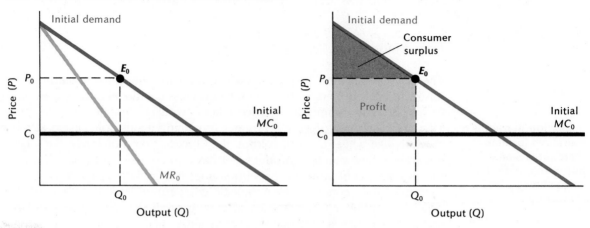

Figure 8-1   **The Price-Setting Decision of a Monopolist**
In the left frame the slanted red line is the initial demand curve and the pink MR_0 line is the marginal revenue curve. The horizontal black line is the initial marginal cost schedule MC_0. Output is chosen where MR equals MC. Price (P_0) is shown at point E_0, the intersection of the demand curve with the quantity produced. In the right frame the gray area shows the consumer surplus, the area below the demand curve and above the price level P_0. Profit is the pink rectangle, the area to the left of Q_0 between P_0 and C_0.

The Firm's Response to a Decline in Demand

To understand how recessions in real output may occur, let us now examine the effects of a decline in the demand for the product. This is shown in the left-hand frame of Figure 8-2 by the downward shift from the dashed red "initial demand" curve to the solid red "new demand" curve. To avoid a recession, the firm must produce the same amount as before, Q_0, which intersects the new demand curve at E_1. For unchanged output to be chosen by the profit-maximizing firm at point E_1, it is necessary that marginal cost decline by the amount shown between the "Initial MC_0" and "Required MC_1" lines. The lower black line is called "required" because this decline in MC is needed to avoid a recession.

Will the firm avoid cutting output by reducing price from P_0 to P_1? Perhaps not if there are menu costs, because the gain in profit by cutting price may not be sufficient to cover the menu costs. Recall from the right-hand frame of Figure 8-1 that the profit box is a rectangle lying above the MC line with its upper right corner at the equilibrium point E_0 or E_1. Comparing the two profit boxes, by lowering the price from P_0 to P_1 the firm gains the profit area marked B and loses the profit area marked A.

SMALL MENU COSTS CAN LEAD TO LARGE SOCIAL COSTS

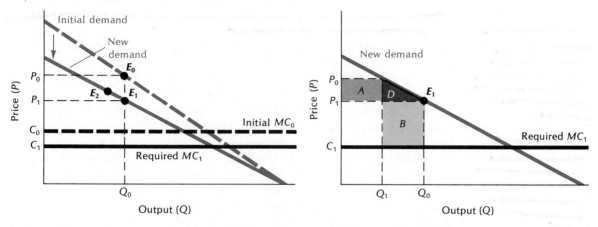

Figure 8-2 **The Price-Setting Choice of a Monopolist Facing a Decline in Demand**
In the left frame a decline in demand shifts the demand curve down from the
"initial demand" line to the "new demand" line. To maintain fixed output at Q_0, the
price must fall from P_0 to P_1 and marginal cost must fall to "required MC_1." In
deciding whether or not to reduce price to the profit-maximizing level P_1, the firm
weighs the gain in profit (area B minus area A in the right frame) against any menu
cost that may be involved in changing price. If the firm fails to cut price below P_0,
the level of output falls from Q_0 to Q_1, and society loses the area D plus B, which is
much larger than B minus A.

SELF-TEST   Why does area A measure the profit lost? Why does B measure the profit
gained? Why must the area B be greater than A?

Despite the gain in profit from cutting price, the firm may choose not to
cut price if the menu cost, which we can call *"z,"* is large enough. The firm
cuts price if the gain in profit B - A exceeds z but not if z exceeds B - A. As
drawn in Figure 8-2, the area B minus the area A is only 13 percent of the
total profit that would be earned at the lower price P_1. So a menu cost
greater than 13 percent of profit would deter the firm from cutting price.

But society loses much more if the firm decides not to cut price. Output
drops from Q_0 to Q_1, and society loses the consumer surplus area D and the
profit area B. In the diagram, the area D + B is 46 percent of the total profit
that would be earned at the lower price P_1. *Thus the firm's decision not to
cut price can cause society to lose more than triple the amount lost by the
firm.* And the firm will not cut price if the menu cost is greater than 13
percent. Thus it is possible for the menu cost to be a relatively small
amount, say 14 or 15 percent, and for society to lose an amount equal to 46
percent of the profit that would be earned at the lower price P_1.

The Macroeconomic Externality and the Effects of Sticky Marginal Cost

A **macroeconomic externality** is a cost incurred by society as a result of a decision by an individual economic agent (worker or business firm).

A **coordination failure** occurs when there is no private incentive for firms to act together to avoid actions that impose social costs on society.

Society's loss from the firm's profit-maximizing decision not to cut price is called a **macroeconomic externality.** The firm does not pay the costs its decision imposes on society, just as a firm causing air pollution or water pollution may not pay the costs imposed on the victims of dirty air and water. In the case of air and water pollution, society is better off if the government reduces the output of the polluting firm, for instance, by imposing a tax on smoke. Similarly, society would be better off if all firms cut price together. Their failure to do so, even though such price cuts are in society's best interest, is called a **coordination failure** because there is no guiding "invisible hand" to return to the firms some portion of the amount society as a whole would gain if they were to cut their price.

The analysis of Figure 8-2 assumes that the marginal cost declines instantly in proportion to the decline in demand. This is required to maintain output unchanged at the profit-maximizing price. Now let us look back at the left-hand frame of Figure 8-2 and consider the case in which marginal cost does not decline at all and remains at the line labeled "initial MC_0." Why might marginal cost be "sticky," failing to decline at all? There are many reasons, some of them discussed later in this chapter. Among these are contracts that fix the wage and contracts that fix the prices of materials purchased from suppliers. If the wage paid to labor and the price paid to all suppliers remained fixed, then the MC line would stay fixed as well. In this case the profit-maximizing price is at E_2, not E_1.[4]

Thus with sticky marginal cost the profit-maximizing price declines less than it would with flexible marginal cost, and output must fall. There are two implications. First, sticky marginal cost means that the menu cost needed to deter the firm from cutting price at all is less than before. But society's loss from maintaining the original price P_0 and not maintaining production at Q_0 is just the same as before.[5] Thus sticky costs strengthen the argument that menu costs create a macroeconomic externality and raise the ratio of society's loss to the menu cost.

More important, *sticky marginal cost implies that menu costs are not needed at all to explain how recessions occur.* Part of this is the idea in the original Keynesian model, already encountered in Figure 7-3, that a decline in price for a firm facing a fixed wage will raise the real wage and force the firm to reduce output and employment. New Keynesian theory extends this idea to purchases by firms from suppliers. Any factors that prevent supplying firms from cutting the price of materials, or even that delay such price reductions, will tend to make marginal costs sticky and imply that E_2 is the point that maximizes profit for the firm in Figure 8-2, not point E_1.

---

[4]To simplify Figure 8-2 the marginal revenue line is not shown. If you want to draw it in, find the point halfway along the horizontal axis between the vertical axis and the demand curve. Then draw a slanted line going up and to the left; it intercepts the lower "required MC_1" line directly above Q_0. Point E_2 lies directly above the place where this marginal revenue line intersects the higher "Initial MC_0" line.

[5]If price charged with sticky marginal cost, that is, the vertical intercept of point E_2, were to lie exactly halfway between P_0 and P_1, then in this example the firm's gain in profit by cutting price would be half as much as before, 6.5 instead of 13 percent, and any menu cost greater than 6.5 percent would suffice to deter to price cut. Social cost in comparing Q_0 and Q_1 is still 46 percent.

8-3 Long-Term Labor Contracts as a Source of the Business Cycle

Long-term labor contracts are agreements between firms and workers that set the level of nominal wage rates for a year or more.

Long-term labor contracts are an important source of sticky marginal cost faced by business firms. Just as the monopolistic firms described in the previous section impose social costs on society while maximizing profits, so too do firms and workers that enter into long-term labor contracts. Nevertheless, as the new Keynesian model emphasizes, there are good reasons why workers and firms desire such contracts. In this and the next two sections, we study the features of long-term labor contracts and the differences between labor contracts in the United States and those in other countries, particularly Japan. U.S. labor contracts introduce only real rigidities if they are fully indexed to nominal GNP (Y), but they introduce nominal rigidities if they are not fully indexed.

Characteristics of Labor Contracts

In the United States, with few exceptions, formal labor contracts are negotiated in the union sector, covering about 20 percent of the labor force. Industries that are heavily unionized include much of manufacturing (especially autos, electrical machinery, rubber, and steel), as well as substantial parts of the construction and transportation industries (especially airlines, railroads, and trucking). Industries that tend to be nonunion include fast food and other services, retailing, and parts of manufacturing (especially apparel and textiles).

The behavior of wage rates in the union sector of the economy is more important than this 20 percent figure would suggest, since the wage rates that are negotiated in the union sector "set a pattern" that is imitated (although not copied exactly) by nonunion workers. The leading role of unions in moderating the flexibility of nonunion wages is evidenced by the evolution of union and nonunion wages. Nonunion wages are only moderately more flexible than union wages over the business cycle, and they exhibit a substantial degree of stickiness. One reason that unions set a pattern for nonunion wages is that nonunionized firms (such as Delta Airlines) do not want their employees to quit and join a rival unionized firm (such as American Airlines) or to vote to become unionized, and so they tend to pay wage rates similar to those in unionized firms.

Wages negotiated under labor contracts are not completely rigid or fixed. Rather they change when a new contract is negotiated. Without labor contracts, the nominal wage rate would be free to change every day. With labor contracts, the nominal wage rate is set at the time of negotiation for the duration of the contract. Wage changes during the lifetime of the contract are allowed, but they are set in advance at the time of the negotiation.

Cost-of-living agreements provide for an automatic increase in the wage rate in response to an increase in the price level.

Scheduled wage changes and COLAs. These prenegotiated changes are of two types. First, there is usually a scheduled change that takes effect in each year of multiyear contracts. Second, there is sometimes a **cost-of-living agreement** (COLA) that sets in advance the change in the nominal wage that will be allowed for each percentage point of future inflation. For instance, a contract might specify that a worker would receive a 3.0 percent increase in each of the three years of a three-year contract, plus 100 percent of the inflation that occurred in each of the three years. Thus, if the actual inflation rate turned out to be 0.0 percent, the wage increase would be 3.0 percent. Alternatively, with an actual inflation rate of 10.0 percent, the wage increase would be 13.0 percent. A COLA contract giving workers a fixed increase plus 100 percent of the inflation rate is called "full COLA protection," whereas a fixed increase plus 50 percent of the inflation rate would be "half COLA protection."

COLAs are intended to help workers maintain their real wage. Without COLAs, the real wage rate is reduced by inflation. The following example shows that a sudden change of the inflation rate from zero to 10 percent will cause a sharp decline in the real wage when the worker has no COLA protection. With full COLA protection (a nominal wage change equal to 3.0 percent plus the inflation rate) the real wage change is unaffected by inflation. With half COLA protection, the nominal wage change in the example is equal to 3.0 percent plus 0.5 times the inflation rate.

	Nominal wage change with COLA protection			Real wage change with COLA protection		
	None	Half	Full	None	Half	Full
Inflation of zero	3.0	3.0	3.0	3.0	3.0	3.0
Inflation of 10 percent	3.0	8.0	13.0	−7.0	−2.0	3.0

In this example each of the figures for real wage change is equal to the corresponding figure for nominal wage change minus the assumed inflation rate.

SELF-TEST   Under what circumstances is the growth rate of the real wage rigid, showing no response at all to a change in the rate of inflation: with no COLA protection, half COLA protection, or full COLA protection?

Contract timing.   The two main characteristics of contract timing are the duration of the contract and the expiration date in relation to other contracts. Contract duration is the length of time over which the contract applies, for instance, three years. A system in which contracts do not all expire at the same time features "overlapping staggered contracts." In the United States the great majority (about 80 percent) of labor contracts are three years in length, whereas in Japan and in most European countries, one-year contracts are more common. And in the United States contracts are overlapping and staggered, in contrast to Japan, where the expiration date is simultaneous.

Figure 8-3 illustrates the difference between the Japanese and American contract systems. The left frame describes the Japanese system. Contracts all expire simultaneously and last for one year. Thus in the upper left corner we see that a wage "settlement" (that is, agreement) negotiated in 1988 covers wage changes for 1988. A wage settlement negotiated in 1989 covers wage changes for 1989, and so on.

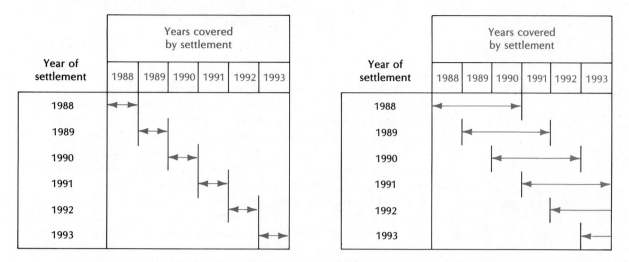

Figure 8-3   **Contrast of One-Year Labor Contracts with Simultaneous Expiration Dates with Three-Year Overlapping Staggered Labor Contracts**

In the left-hand frame the settlement for each year (like 1988) sets the wage rate just for that year (1988). In contrast in the right-hand frame there are three-year overlapping staggered contracts. The settlement in 1988 sets the wage for 1988, 1989, and 1990. Then in 1989 the settlement sets the wage for 1989, 1990, and 1991. The wage change in any one year like 1990 is therefore determined partly by 1990 settlements, partly by 1989 settlements made the previous year, and partly by 1988 settlements made two years before.

In contrast, in the United States contracts last for three years and have staggered expiration dates. Thus, in the right-hand frame the top line shows that contracts negotiated in 1988 set the wage changes that will occur in 1988, 1989, and 1990. The next line shows that contracts negotiated in 1989 set the wage changes that will occur in 1989, 1990, and 1991.

What is the significance of this difference between the United States and Japan? With one-year contracts that expire simultaneously, the Japanese can achieve a rapid adjustment of the nominal wage rate to changing macroeconomic conditions. The Japanese system makes it easier for the aggregate supply curve to shift soon after any shift in the aggregate demand curve, and to shift by the same amount, minimizing the extent and duration of cyclical unemployment caused by aggregate demand shifts. With staggered contracts, as in the United States, this rapid adjustment is impossible. Wages adjust slowly, and with a long lag, making marginal costs sticky for many business firms. Much of the economy's adjustment to shifts in aggregate demand takes the form of business cycles in output and unemployment.

CASE STUDY: Adjustment of U.S. Negotiated Wage
Settlements, 1980–90

The system of long-term overlapping staggered contracts makes the U.S. economy resemble a Keynesian fixed-wage economy in the way that it reacts to a decline in demand. For instance, the U.S. economy experienced a sharp decline in aggregate demand in 1981 and 1982. As shown in the bottom frame of Figure 8-4, the unemployment rate increased to a peak of 10.7 percent in the fourth quarter of 1982. However, wage changes negotiated in previous years prevented the rate of wage change from declining rapidly in response to this increase in the unemployment rate.

This role of overlapping staggered three-year contracts is illustrated in the top frame of Figure 8-4. Each line connects three points and shows the percentage rate of wage increase that was negotiated in the first year for that year and the next two. For instance, the "1980 settlements" line shows the percentage rate of wage increase negotiated in 1980 for 1980, 1981, and 1982. The 1980 line tilts down, indicating that workers were able to obtain higher wage increases in the first year of the contract than in the second and third years (this is called "front loading").

The role of overlapping staggered three-year contracts in slowing down the adjustment of wage changes is clearest for the year 1983. One third of the wage change for 1983 was determined by wage settlements negotiated in 1981, with a rate of change of 7.5 percent. One third of the wage change for 1983 was determined by 1982 wage settlements, with a rate of change of 7.0 percent. Only the 1983 settlements, with a much lower rate of 4.5 percent, reflect the influence of high unemployment during the 1981–82 recession in holding down wage changes. Even in 1984, the average change in wages was influenced by the 6.1 percent rate agreed in 1982 settlements to apply to 1984.

The American three-year overlapping staggered contract system made wages more rigid and thus made output and unemployment more variable than would have occurred with a Japanese-style one-year contract system with a simultaneous expiration date. One reason for this is obvious in Figure 8-4: if all U.S. contracts had been renegotiated in 1983, the rate of wage increase would have been slower than the actual rate, which was held up by the lagged effect of the 1981 and 1982 settlements.

But another reason is less obvious. Since workers in 1983 knew that the 1981 and 1982 contracts were still in effect, they knew that the wage costs of business firms were still rising, and that business firms would be likely to continue raising prices to cover their higher wage costs. This made them reluctant to accept a radical decline in the rate of wage increase in 1983 contract negotiations. In contrast, with a simultaneous contracting system like that in Japan, workers would not need to worry about the inflationary effects of preexisting contracts still in effect. If workers in 1983 *knew* that all contracts were expiring, they might have been willing to agree to *much lower* wage increases in 1983, perhaps even zero, instead of the 4.5 percent increase that actually occurred.

Figure 8-4

Percentage Rate of Wage Increase of Union Contract Settlements Plotted against the Actual Unemployment Rate, 1980–90

The top frame shows the rate of wage increase negotiated in the three-year settlements reached in each year shown. For instance, 1980 settlements called for wage increases of 9.5 percent in 1980, 8.8 percent in 1981, and 6.7 percent in 1982. Notice in the bottom frame that the actual unemployment rate soared during 1982, and in response 1983 settlements were much lower than 1982 settlements. Nevertheless, the *average* rate of wage increase in 1983 was held up by the increases for 1983 negotiated previously in 1982 and 1981 settlements. *Source:* For 1980–85, from Daniel B. Mitchell, "Shifting Norms in Wage Determination," *Brookings Papers on Economic Activity,* vol. 16 (1985, no. 2), Table 3. For 1986–88, from the Bureau of National Affairs data bank.

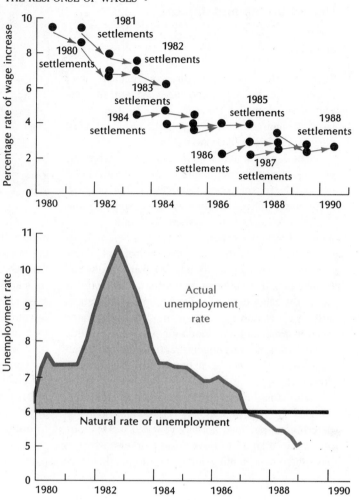

OVERLAPPING STAGGERED THREE–YEAR CONTRACTS SLOW DOWN THE RESPONSE OF WAGES

Scheduled Wage Adjustments in First, Second, and Third Years of Union Contracts

Percent

Year of settlement	Year in which wage adjustment is effective										
	1980	1981	1982	1983	1984	1985	1986	1987	1988	1989	1990
1980	9.5	8.8	6.7								
1981		9.6	8.0	7.5							
1982			7.0	7.0	6.1						
1983				4.5	4.8	4.5					
1984					4.0	4.0	4.0				
1985						3.7	4.0	3.9			
1986							2.4	3.0	3.0		
1987								2.4	2.8	2.8	
1988									3.5	2.5	2.8

Source: For 1980–85, Daniel B. Mitchell, "Shifting Norms in Wage Determination," *Brookings Papers on Economic Activity,* vol. 16 (1985, no. 2), Table 3. For 1986–88, figures are from the BNA Data Bank.

How Do Labor Markets Differ in the United States and Japan?

Japan

There are three unique features of Japanese labor markets, the lifetime employment system, the system of simultaneous one-year wage contracts, and large semiannual bonus payments based at least partly on the idea of profit-sharing.

The Japanese labor market is characterized by very low unemployment rates, averaging around 2 percent in recent years, relatively stable employment, and relatively flexible wages. Fostering these desirable features is the system of lifetime employment, in which workers and firms develop long-term attachments that last until retirement at the relatively early age of fifty-five. Workers rarely quit to take jobs at rival firms, and firms reciprocate by rarely resorting to layoffs. The lifetime employment system is not universal, but is mainly concentrated in large firms, and does not apply to women or employees of numerous subcontractors and other satellite firms that act as a buffer during economic downturns.

The most important aspect of lifetime employment is the role of seniority rather than ability in determining payment; all fifty-year-old workers are paid more than all forty-year-old workers, whereas pay differences among fifty-year old workers are minor. This payment system tends to foster a feeling of equality, in contrast to the class distinctions that are more evident in many American and European firms. Pay differences between top executives and blue-collar workers are much smaller in Japan (and some European countries like Sweden) than in the United States.

Greater equality in turn reduces the potential for conflict between workers and firms, thus lowering costs of negotiation and causing both sides to be less concerned about the possibility of strikes. With less fear of strikes, both sides are more willing to enter into one-year wage contracts, in contrast to the U.S. three-year contracts that are designed in part to reduce the frequency of strikes.

8-5   Why Long-Term Wage Contracts Are Advantageous for Workers and Firms

In this section we begin by learning why long-term wage agreements are *privately advantageous* to individual firms and workers, thus explaining how they can exist despite their tendency to aggravate business cycles. Then we learn that not only *wages* but also *prices* are subject to long-term contracts and other less formal agreements that limit their flexibility.

Private Advantages of Long-Term Labor Contracts

Long-term labor contracts impose heavy costs on the U.S. economy. By hindering the prompt adjustment of wage rates to shifts in aggregate demand, contracts indirectly create business cycles in output and unemployment. Yet

The United States

The unique American system of three-year overlapping staggered contracts reduces the flexibility of nominal wage rates and aggravates fluctuations in output and employment. This system can be traced to the 1948 contract between the United Auto Workers and General Motors, which established the first multiyear contract and the first COLA. It was the high cost of negotiation, as perceived by managers besieged in 1946–48 with annual strikes or threats of strikes, that led to the 1948 General Motors contract. The GM president had the idea of buying labor peace through a long-term contract, "bribing" the union with the first COLA protection. Since 1953 there have been eleven three-year contracts in the auto industry. And statistical data show that U.S. wages and prices have been less flexible since 1950 than in the decades before 1950.

In explaining why the United States developed three-year contracts but the Japanese did not, differences in the perceived importance of industrial conflict played a major role. The United States had unionized in a hurry after the 1935 Wagner Act provided legal protection to unions. The first large-scale industrial conflicts in the late 1930s were widely publicized. Partly because unionization took the form of large industrial unions in key industries, especially coal, steel, and automobiles, there was a widespread perception that strikes were costly.

In conclusion, economics provides some insight into labor market institutions by suggesting that contract forms may reflect a weighing of benefits and costs. For instance, three-year contracts achieve the benefit of reducing strikes at the cost of allowing a less frequent reaction by wage rates to macroeconomic events. But economics must be supplemented by sociology and history to provide a more complete understanding of why contract forms and duration differ across countries.[a]

[a]This analysis is excerpted from Robert J. Gordon, "Why U.S. Wage and Employment Differs from That in Britain and Japan," *Economic Journal,* vol. 92 (March 1982), pp. 13–44.

the firms and workers who enter into these contracts do not necessarily have to pay the costs imposed on society by their own preference for long-term agreements; for this reason, long-term contracts are said to impose a macroeconomic externality of the type introduced in Section 8-2.

Negotiation Costs and Strikes

What are the private advantages to workers and firms of entering into long-term labor contracts? First, firms and workers like to enter into agreements that last a long time because wage negotiations are costly and time consuming on both sides. Each negotiation requires research by both sides on wage rates being paid in comparable firms, the outlook for the firm's productivity and profits, and forecasts of future unemployment and inflation. A three-year contract means that these costly preparations and negotiations can be undertaken less frequently.

Second, when workers and firms have severe disagreements, workers may feel they have to strike. Firms dislike strikes intensely, since they disrupt production and shift business to competing firms. Workers dislike strikes for the obvious reason that they receive no wage income during the strike. Three-year contracts reduce the incidence of strikes by allowing firms and workers to go at least three years between strikes.

Absence of Full COLA Protection

Some contracts incorporate cost-of-living agreements (COLAs), as we learned above. Full COLA protection would allow wages to change automatically in response to changes in prices. Yet in the United States in 1989 only 40 percent of the negotiated settlements provided any COLA protection at all, and the average amount of COLA protection in those contracts was only about half (50 percent). Why do firms not offer workers full COLA protection? The main reason is that COLA protection is extremely risky for firms. If external forces (for example, higher oil prices charged by foreign nations) result in higher consumer prices, firms must boost their wage costs without any commensurate increase in the nominal demand for their product. U.S. steel and automobile producers encountered serious difficulties in the early 1980s, partly as a result of full COLA protection they had granted in the 1970s that raised their wage costs substantially faster than for foreign firms making the same products.

The aggregate demand-supply analysis of the new classical model in Figure 7-7 pointed out that business cycles in real output are avoided if the *SS* curve moves up and down simultaneously with the *DD* curve. So why can labor contracts not be set up to index wage rates to nominal aggregate demand—that is, the position of the *DD* curve? *Such demand (or nominal GNP) indexing has never been observed.* Why? An automobile manufacturing firm would resist a contract calling for an increase of 10 percent in wages in response to a 10 percent increase in aggregate demand, because the demand for automobiles might increase by a lesser amount or might even fall. But a union would not accept what the firm would prefer, indexation of the wage rate to automobile sales. The union would fear that auto sales might fall relative to aggregate demand as a whole, and they also might fear that auto companies would understate their sales figures in order to cut their wage payments. *It appears that neither firms nor workers are willing to take the risks involved in indexing wage rates to changes in nominal aggregate demand.* What we observe instead is that the amount people are paid per hour is negotiated for the life of the contract, three years in the United States, subject to only partial COLA protection. This means that labor contracts are a source of nominal rigidity and make marginal costs more sticky than otherwise.

8-6 Markup Pricing and Long-Term Price Agreements

Many of the private advantages of long-term agreements on wage rates in labor markets between *firms* and *workers* also are present in long-term agreements on prices in product markets between *firms and other firms*.

Auction Prices and Preset Prices

The distinctive fact about product markets is that the prices of *some products* are set in auction markets and change continuously, while the prices of *other products* are "preset." Among auction prices are those of wheat, corn, "pork bellies," stocks, bonds, and financial futures. Among preset prices are those of almost everything we buy, including items in retail stores marked with price tags, items in restaurants with preset prices on menus, and items in wholesale or mail-order warehouses with book-length price lists. Some items are sold both by auction and with long-term contracts, for instance crude oil.

Why aren't all products sold in auction markets? Some of the reasons for preset prices are similar to those for wages. Firms often enter into agreements to provide goods or services for a given price. For instance, aluminum companies enter into contracts to supply aircraft and wire companies, aircraft companies contract to supply airlines, coal firms contract to supply steel firms, steel firms contract to supply auto producers, and so on. These contracts are attractive to firms, because they reduce uncertainty. Buyers are assured of a certain supply, and suppliers are assured of a reliable buyer for at least part of their output. These advantages outweigh the fact that, by entering into contracts that limit price movements in advance, some future sales may be made at prices that are no longer appropriate under future demand or supply conditions.

Why retail prices are preset. Many other products, particularly at the wholesale and retail level, are sold with prices that are preset but not subject to a contract. The customer just comes into the store and sees a price tag on each product. What explains the absence of auction markets for retail goods? Auction markets occur at centralized locations far distant from the actual goods being transacted; there is no need to convey the actual merchandise (pork bellies) from buyer to seller inside the trading room. All that is being sold is a claim, usually registered on a computer. But I cannot buy my lunchtime hamburger on a hypothetical New York hamburger exchange. I need it in Evanston, Illinois, and I need it now!

The factors of heterogeneity (a wide variety of different goods), the need for direct physical contact between seller and buyer (hamburger maker and professor), and small transaction sizes all help explain why price-setting practices are common in sales by wholesale and retail outlets. Unlike the rigid nominal wage in the original Keynesian model, there is nothing arbitrary about preset prices. They simply substitute for preset auction markets by allowing transaction locations and times to be freely chosen (Burger King in Evanston at noon).[6] Interestingly, bargaining or "haggling" in retail outlets is more common in less developed countries than in the United States. Bargaining takes time, so it makes sense for bargaining to occur in countries where (because people are poor) the value of time is lower than in the United States.

---

[6]This section draws on Robert J. Gordon, "Output Fluctuations and Gradual Price Adjustment," *Journal of Economic Literature,* vol. 19 (June 1981), especially pp. 517–525.

Markup Pricing

With **markup pricing** the price is set at the level of the average cost of labor and materials inputs, times a certain fraction, called a markup, to cover capital cost and profits.

Some procedure must be devised to determine the prices that are preset in price contracts and in wholesale and retail outlets. The most common approach is **markup pricing.** The firm finds it most natural to set the price as the average cost of its "variable inputs" (materials and labor) times a "markup fraction" to cover its capital cost and profit.[7] Arthur M. Okun, one of the developers of the new Keynesian model, explains markup pricing by its efficiency and fairness. It is *efficient,* since it allows top management to save time by delegating to lower echelon employees many pricing decisions: "Just look up the cost and apply the usual mark-up." And it is *fair,* since it conveys a message from the firm to its customers that *the reason for price increases is increases in cost.* Thus price increases seem consistent with the "rules of fair play," rather than as an attempt by greedy management to take advantage of a situation of high demand.[8]

If the markup fraction were constant, prices would rise exactly in proportion to increases in cost. If wage costs were set by long-term labor contracts, and materials costs were constant, prices would be constant as well. Such a situation with constant costs and a constant markup fraction implies fixed prices and can be analyzed in what sometimes is called the "Fixprice" version of the non-market-clearing model, as in Section 8-10.

But even if wages are fixed by long-term labor contracts, the price level exhibits some response to changes in aggregate demand for two reasons. First, the prices of some raw materials are set in auction markets and respond promptly to changes in demand (or supply) conditions. Second, the markup for the economy as a whole is not constant. Firms find it easier to raise prices when demand is high, and they are forced to give discounts and rebates (that is, to cut the markup) when demand is low.[9]

8-7 "Real" Sources of Wage Stickiness

Thus far our discussion of the new Keynesian approach has emphasized nominal rigidities, particularly menu costs of changing nominal prices and long-term contracts for both wages and prices that are incompletely indexed. These contracts imply that a business firm's marginal cost does not respond instantly to a decline in demand. Consequently, the contracts reinforce the role of menu costs in dissuading firms from changing their prices

---

[7]If C^W is wage cost, C^M is the price of materials, and Z is the markup fraction, the price is set as:

$$P = (1 + Z)(C^W + C^M).$$

For example, if $Z = .2$, $C^W = 60$, and $C^M = 40$, then $P = 120$. If the markup fraction rises to .25, then P rises to 125. If C^W and C^M both double, and Z is at its original value of .2, then P doubles to from 120 to 240.

[8]See Arthur M. Okun, *Prices and Quantities: A Macroeconomic Analysis* (Washington, D.C.: Brookings Institution, 1981), esp. Chapter 4.

[9]Evidence supporting a variable markup is contained in numerous empirical research papers, including Robert J. Gordon, "The Impact of Aggregate Demand on Prices," *Brookings Papers on Economic Activity,* 1975, no. 3, pp. 613–662.

by the full amount needed to avoid changes in output and hence recessions. Now we turn to three theories that attempt to explain real rigidities, that is, the slow adjustment of wages relative to prices or other wages. The most prominent of these are the implicit contract theory and the efficiency wage theory.

The Implicit Contract Model

The implicit contract approach takes its name from the fact that agreements between workers and firms do not have to be written down formally in negotiated legal contracts. Instead, agreements may be more informal or "implicit." With his characteristic gift for coining phrases, the late Arthur Okun adapted Adam Smith's famous phrase "the invisible hand" and described implicit contracts as "the invisible handshake." Some commentators initially thought that the implicit contract theory amounted to a microeconomic explanation for Keynesian wage stickiness. The theory assumed that employees are more averse to risk, particularly instability of incomes over the business cycle, than their employers. After all, owners of firms had already shown that they were willing to take the financial risk of opening their own businesses; workers showed their distaste for risk by working for the owners. Firms maximize profits by providing stable incomes to their workers, who dislike variability, in effect providing a compensation package that consists partly of wage payments and partly of insurance services.

Economists soon recognized that this approach provides no satisfactory explanation of Keynesian unemployment. It justifies only a fixed-income contract (that is, tenure of the type enjoyed by many college professors) rather than the contracts actually observed in most firms, which feature relatively stable wages but highly variable employment. The only way the implicit contract theorists could explain variable employment was by adding the element of government-financed unemployment benefits, which in effect subsidize firms that discharge or lay off their employees during recessions. Since government unemployment benefits were introduced in the United States only in 1938, implicit contract theory cannot explain the economy's collapse in 1929–33. Further, workers are shown to care about stability in *real* income, not nominal income, and implicit contract theory cannot explain why workers do not insist on full indexation of wage contracts. This deficiency is common to all theories based entirely on real rigidities.

The Efficiency Wage Model

If any development in the microeconomics of labor markets could be called the "rage of the '80s," it is efficiency wage theory, based on the hypothesis that worker productivity depends on the level of the real wage. This theory falls into the category of those explaining real rigidities because it stresses the reasons why firms would not want to cut the wage that they pay *relative to the wage paid by other firms*. It does not explain why all firms do not index their wages to nominal demand and then achieve high worker productivity by paying a higher wage relative to other firms than the wage called for by the indexed contract.

Why does a firm believe that the productivity of its workers will increase if the firm pays a higher wage? Among the reasons are greater effort by workers, reduced "shirking" or "goofing off" on the job, lower turnover (which reduces training costs), the ability to attract higher-quality workers, and improved morale and loyalty. Virtually all the literature with implications for macroeconomics dates from the 1980s, although work on less-developed countries dating back at least three decades posited a linkage among wages, nutrition, and health.

The efficiency wage result is obtained in a simple model with identical, perfectly competitive firms. Each firm has a production function in which labor input is multiplied by an efficiency factor "e" that depends on the wage rate paid relative to that paid by other firms (W), as shown in the left frame of Figure 8-5. Raising W raises labor cost by making firms pay more to workers, but reduces labor cost per unit of output by making workers more efficient. As shown in the left frame, initially increases in W by 1 percent raise e by more than 1 percent, so labor cost declines as shown in the right frame. Firms continue raising W until it reaches the equilibrium value W^*, which occurs at the point where raising W by 1 percent raises efficiency by exactly 1 percent, thus leaving labor cost per unit of efficiency unchanged. Firms will refuse to raise W any further, since this would raise wage payments more than it would boost efficiency. The value W^* is called the "efficiency wage."

Because W^* is completely fixed by whatever technological and institutional factors that determine the "e" function, the firm's reaction to any

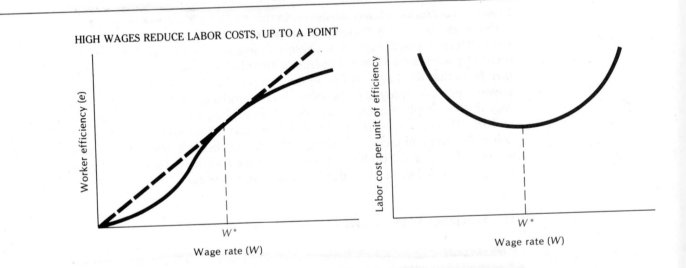

HIGH WAGES REDUCE LABOR COSTS, UP TO A POINT

Figure 8-5   **The Relationship Between the Relative Wage Rate and Worker Efficiency**
In the left frame worker efficiency increases faster than the relative wage up to point W^* and then more slowly thereafter. As a result, labor cost per unit of efficiency reaches a minimum at W^*, as shown in the right frame.

change in the demand for its product is to cut employment while maintaining the wage rate at W^*. Firms have no incentive to cut wages, since this would actually increase their wage bill per unit of output. The efficiency wage approach seems to explain numerous aspects of microeconomic labor market behavior, once we allow different groups of workers to have different levels of efficiency at any given relative wage rate. For example, the theory predicts the widely observed phenomenon that workers line up eagerly for high-paying jobs but firms hire only a few of them, maintaining the high wage in order to be able to pick and choose rather than reduce the wage rate in face of the abundant supply of workers. The theory also predicts that less productive workers, those whose labor cost per efficiency unit is high, will suffer higher unemployment rates than more productive groups. The model can explain why we do not observe "work sharing" in the form of fewer hours per week in periods of low demand; such reductions in hours would raise labor cost by cutting the wage income and hence the efficiency of the most productive workers.

SELF-TEST According to the efficiency wage theory, how is unemployment explained? Assuming that the unemployed are willing to work at a lower wage rate than existing workers, why does the firm not simply fire the existing workers and hire the unemployed in their place at a lower wage?

As a theoretical underpinning of the new Keynesian approach to wage and price rigidity, the efficiency wage model explains why firms resist cutting their wage rates in response to a decline in demand, and why they do not hire unemployed workers who may be willing to work for a lower wage. This approach is still subject to the same criticism as long-term wage contracts, that full wage indexation would allow firms simultaneously to maintain worker effort by paying the optimal relative wage W^* while maintaining a flexible nominal wage rate. However, for the reasons discussed in Section 8-5, firms and workers are unwilling to risk full wage indexation.

8-8 Coordination Failures and Indexation

Our discussion of the new Keynesian model has now covered a variety of factors that may inhibit the prompt adjustment of prices in response to a change in nominal GNP, thus automatically implying a response in real GNP. Leaving aside menu costs, the full adjustment of prices to demand shocks like that depicted in Figure 8-2 depends on the instantaneous response of marginal cost. Following a negative demand shock, output must fall if marginal cost declines less than marginal revenue. There are two reasons why firms may rationally expect marginal cost to move differently from marginal revenue. First, marginal revenue may move with aggregate nominal demand but marginal costs may not. This would occur if a firm believes that its costs depend on many specific factors other than the perceived level of aggregate nominal demand (for example, volatile supply conditions, price changes for imported materials, changes in cost created by exchange-rate movements). Second, with a fixed nominal aggregate demand, marginal cost would also remain fixed, while a local shift in demand (for example, a decline in beer drinking in response to drunk-driving laws) could reduce marginal revenue, providing another reason why marginal cost may move differently from marginal revenue.

The Input-Output Approach and the Absence of Full Indexation to Nominal Demand

8-9   To explain real price rigidity, the local-aggregate cost distinction must apply to a world with many different firms purchasing supplies from each other. The auto maker buys headlights from a firm that buys filament from a firm that buys copper from a firm that may mine copper using trucks purchased from the auto maker. The input-output model emphasizes the importance of multiple buyer-supplier relations; each firm is simultaneously a buyer and a seller. With only two firms, each supplying the other, firms could easily disentangle the local versus aggregate component of their costs. But with thousands of firms buying thousands of components, containing ingredients from many other firms, the typical firm has no idea of the identity of its full set of suppliers. Since the informational problem of trying to guess the effect of a demand shift on the average marginal cost of all these suppliers is probably impossible to solve, the sensible firm just "waits by the mailbox" for news of cost increases and then, as Okun suggested in his cost-based markup theory, passes them on as price increases.

The input-output approach provides a critical contribution not just to understanding real price rigidity, but also nominal rigidity. The standard accusation against the theories of real rigidity suggested above is that they are consistent with nominal flexibility achieved through indexation to nominal demand. Yet the input-output approach emphasizes the high fraction of a firm's costs that are attributable to suppliers of unknown identity, with some unknown fraction producing in foreign countries under differing aggregate demand conditions. This environment would give pause to any firm considering nominal-demand indexation of the product price, since the failure of all suppliers to adopt similar indexation could lead to bankruptcy.

There is nothing to guarantee any confidence that supplier firms will adopt any aggregate indexation formula, for no single supplier acting alone has any incentive to do so. The rewards are too small and the penalties of acting alone are too great, *for a firm's viability depends on the relation of price to cost, not price to nominal GNP.* No individual firm has an incentive to take the risk posed by nominal GNP indexation, which would take away from the firm the essential control required of the relation of price to cost.

Coordination Failures and Daylight Saving Time

The failure of marginal cost to decline instantly and fully in response to nominal demand reflects a coordination failure. Marginal cost would drop if all workers and firms cut wages and prices together by the same percentage as nominal demand. But each is afraid to act first, since they would lose out if other workers and firms failed to act also. Daylight saving time provides a simple example of government intervention in the face of a coordination failure. All firms may want to open and close later in the summer, but none does so because each store wants to keep the same hours as other stores. By simply decreeing a shift in the clock, the government solves the failure of individual stores to coordinate their actions.

The Business Cycle in the New Keynesian Model

We have now studied a number of explanations for wage and price rigidity provided by the new Keynesian model, based on rational expectations and profit-maximizing behavior. Now it is time to see how this theory explains business cycles in output and employment, and how it escapes some of the criticisms of the original Keynesian and new classical models. We shall start with a simple example in which *prices and wages are completely rigid.* This would occur if wage costs were fixed by long-term contracts and price mark-ups were constant, or if menu costs were sufficiently important to make prices completely rigid in the short run.

The Labor Market with a Fixed Price Markup

For decades economists have been bothered by two aspects of the diagrammatic analysis of the original Keynesian model, as set out in Figure 7-3. In the left-hand frame of that diagram, a decline in aggregate demand causes the economy to move from point E_0 to point A. Workers are pushed off their labor supply curve. This raises a first question: Why are workers willing to provide more or less labor input than is indicated by their labor supply curve? We have now suggested that this willingness is explained by the *private advantages* of long-term labor contracts.

The second troubling issue is the assumption that the economy always moves back and forth along its labor demand curve. Why are firms *on* their labor demand curve while workers are *off* their labor supply curve? This asymmetry is bothersome, since it does not seem to be justified by observed differences in the behavior of firms and workers. In addition the movements of the economy back and forth along the labor demand curve seem to imply *countercyclical movements of the real wage rate,* which do not seem to be a strong feature of real-world data.

The effective labor demand curve.   A resolution of these issues was suggested initially by Don Patinkin of the Hebrew University, Jerusalem. Patinkin's key insight was that our previous labor demand curve is inconsistent with the Keynesian income determination model. As originally developed in Chapters 6 and 7, our labor demand curve assumes that firms always hire *exactly the number of workers they want at today's real wage.* That previous labor demand curve is copied from Figure 7-3 in the left-hand frame of Figure 8-6 and labeled the "notional" labor demand curve. This "notional" curve may be thought of as the firm's "voluntary" labor demand, in the sense that it shows how many workers the firms would "voluntarily" hire at each real wage.

To see why the notional labor demand curve is incompatible with the model of Keynesian income determination in Chapter 3, consider a leftward shift in the aggregate demand curve from DD_0 to DD_1, shown in the right-hand frame of Figure 8-6. In Chapter 3, we assumed that the price level (P) was fixed, and we did not mention the wage rate. Here we can assume that the wage rate is held fixed in the short run at W_0 by labor contracts and that the price level is also held fixed at P_0 on the assumption that materials costs are fixed and that the price markup is fixed. Thus the real wage is fixed at W_0/P_0.

Shifts in demand move the "brick wall."   Starting at point E_0, the drop in aggregate demand means that firms will be unable to keep production fixed and will issue layoff notices to workers. If they reduce employment to

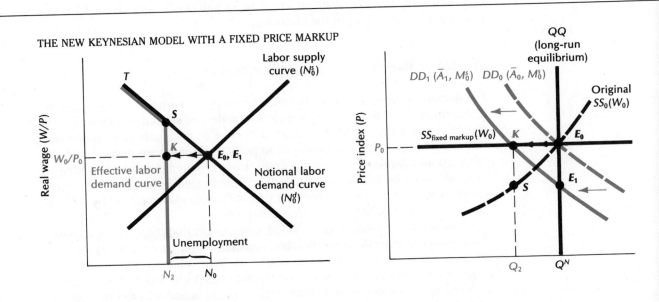

THE NEW KEYNESIAN MODEL WITH A FIXED PRICE MARKUP

Figure 8-6   **Effect on the Price Index, Real GNP, and Employment of a Decrease in Planned Autonomous Spending from $\bar{A}_0$ to $\bar{A}_1$.**

Here both the nominal wage rate and the price level are assumed to be fixed in the short run, due to long-term wage and price agreements. The reduction in autonomous spending shifts the aggregate demand curve leftward from DD_0 to DD_1 in the right frame, and the economy moves leftward from E_0 to point K. In the left-hand frame the "notional labor demand curve" is exactly the same as the "labor demand curve" from Figures 7-3 and 7-5. But now there is a second "effective" labor demand curve shown by the red line running through T, S, K, and N_2. Firms are forced to operate along the effective labor demand curve when they cannot sell all they would like to at the current real wage rate.

N_2, then they are operating at the new point K.[10] *Because the real wage is fixed at W_0/P_0, the firms have moved off the notional labor demand curve (N_0^d).* Instead they are operating along the red "effective" labor demand curve that consists of two line segments. The first coincides with the black notional curve between T and S (to the left of the employment level N_2) and the second drops vertically downward from S to K to N_2.

This vertical segment can be thought of as a "brick wall" that stands between firms and their desired sales level. At the real wage W_0/P_0, firms *want* to hire N_0 workers at point E_0. But they cannot sell all the output that the original N_0 workers can produce. The underlying source of the difficulty is not that the real wage is too high, for the real wage has remained fixed at W_0/P_0. Instead, the problem is the shift in the aggregate demand curve DD in the right frame, together with the assumed fixity of wages and prices in the short run.

Disequilibrium in the non-market-clearing model. Economists usually refer to the analysis presented in Figure 8-6 as the "non-market-clearing model." Sharing credit with Patinkin for the non-market-clearing model are Robert Clower of the University of South Carolina, Robert J. Barro of Harvard University, and Herschel I. Grossman of Brown University.[11] It can be contrasted to the original Keynesian model, in which workers are off their labor supply curve but firms are on their labor demand curve. As a reminder, the original Keynesian model has an aggregate supply curve like the dashed line in the right-hand frame of Figure 8-3 labeled $SS_0 (W_0)$. In contrast the non-market-clearing model discussed in this section implies a horizontal aggregate supply curve labeled "$SS_{\text{fixed markup}}$."

The "new Keynesian model" goes beyond this non-market-clearing model by postulating a *reason* for the short-run fixity of the nominal wage rate and the price level, that is, long-term wage and price agreements, markup price-setting, and other sources of nominal and real rigidity. These wage and price agreements are not carved in stone. After a few months or years they will be renegotiated. Point K in Figure 8-3 is not one of market-clearing equilibrium. There is an excess supply of labor, measured by the distance between K and E_0 in the left-hand frame of Figure 8-6. And firms are producing less than natural real GNP (Q^N), measured by the distance between K and E_0 in the right-hand frame. The unemployed workers are unhappy about their plight, as are the firms.

The process of adjustment toward long-run equilibrium. This widespread unhappiness will lead gradually to new wage and price contracts that reduce the wage rate below W_0 and the price level below P_0. Since the nominal wage rate is assumed fixed in drawing the horizontal line "$SS_{\text{fixed markup}}$"

---

[10]Output falls to Q_2 in the right-hand frame of Figure 8-6. The production function of Figure 6-7 determines the number of workers (N_2) needed to produce that level of output. The production function is omitted here to save space.

[11]The basic references are Don Patinkin, *Money, Interest, and Prices* (New York: Harper & Row, 1965), Chapter 13; Robert W. Clower, "The Keynesian Counterrevolution: A Theoretical Appraisal," in F. Hahn and F. Brechling, eds., *The Theory of Interest Rates* (London: Macmillan, 1965); and Robert J. Barro and Herschel I. Grossman, *Money, Employment, and Inflation* (Cambridge, England: Cambridge University Press, 1976).

in the right-hand frame, downward pressure on *both* wages and prices will allow that SS line to slide down the DD_1 schedule in the right-hand frame from K and E_1, where output is the same as originally at E_0. And this original level of output will allow firms to rehire the original employment level N_0 in the left-hand frame. Thus downward pressure on *both* wages and prices allows the "brick wall" of the effective demand curve for labor to shift rightward toward E_0.

Proponents of the new Keynesian model point out that there is no reason for the economy to *wait* for downward pressure on wages and prices to bring about a return to natural real GNP (Q^N). This way may take a long time, as in the Great Depression. Instead, the high unemployment may be reduced by a stimulus to aggregate demand that pushes the aggregate demand curve back from DD_1 to DD_0, allowing the economy to return to E_0 at the original nominal wage rate and price level.

Much more could be said about the non-market-clearing model. But here a summary of the main points is enough:

1. A recession can occur in which firms face an involuntary sales constraint, and workers face involuntary unemployment.

2. The recession can occur without any increase in the real wage from the original point E_0 in the left-hand frame of Figure 8-6. Instead, *both* the nominal wage rate and price level are too high in relation to the level of aggregate demand, and this prevents the economy from sliding southeast from K to E_1 along the aggregate demand curve DD_1 in the right-hand frame.

3. Because business firms are just as unhappy about recessions as are unemployed workers, it follows that the stickiness of prices is just as important a source of output fluctuations as the slow adjustment of the nominal wage rate.

4. The non-market-clearing model only examines the *consequences* of sticky wages and prices. The new Keynesian approach with its emphasis on the microeconomic sources of nominal and real rigidities, helps to explain *why* wages and prices do not adjust instantly to a change in aggregate demand.

SELF-TEST · Which theories of the business cycle require that the real wage moves countercyclically? Which require that the real wage moves procyclically? Which make no prediction about movements in the real wage?

Variable Price Markups and Auction Prices for Materials

Some economists have objected to the fixed-price version of the non-market-clearing model because in the real world prices are not completely fixed in the short run. There are two reasons why prices may change promptly when there is a shift in aggregate demand, *even if the nominal wage rate is fixed.* Each of these two reasons is compatible with the new Keynesian analysis of firm behavior in product markets.

First, some raw materials like wheat, corn, and pork bellies are traded on auction markets and are free to respond to changes in demand. Second, the markup of final goods prices over the average of labor and materials costs may vary in the short run. In periods of high output when competitors are producing all they can, a firm can charge a premium, thus raising its markup. And in recession, or when foreign competition is exacerbated by a strong dollar, it may be necessary to offer discounts or rebates to sell excess inventories of merchandise.

Both of these two reasons have the same implication, that the short-run aggregate supply curve is not horizontal like the "$SS_{\text{fixed markup}}$" line of Figure 8-6. Instead, the short-run aggregate supply curve may be positively sloped like the "$SS_{\text{variable markup}}$" in the right-hand frame of Figure 8-7, where a leftward shift in the aggregate demand curve takes the economy southwest from point E_0 to point L, rather than straight west to point K as before. At L prices are lower and output higher than at point K, because the price

THE NEW KEYNESIAN MODEL WITH A VARIABLE PRICE MARKUP

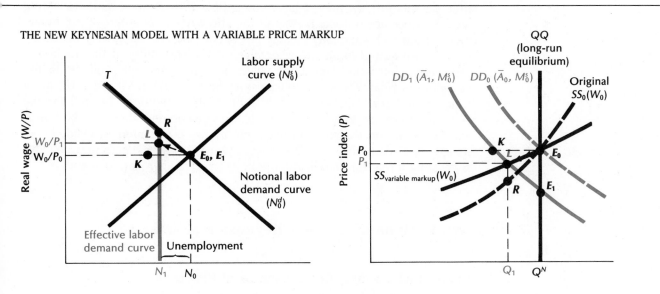

Figure 8-7   **Effect on the Price Index, Real GNP, and Employment of a Decrease in Planned Autonomous Spending from $\bar{A}_0$ to $\bar{A}_1$.**

Here the nominal wage rate is assumed to be fixed in the short run, due to long-term wage agreements. The markup of the price over the constant wage is allowed to depend positively on output, reflecting either a variable markup or the influence of cyclically sensitive raw materials prices set in auction markets. The reduction in autonomous spending shifts the aggregate demand curve leftward from DD_0 to DD_1 in the right frame, and the economy moves southwest from E_0 to point L. In the left-hand frame the "effective" labor demand curve shown by the red line runs through T, R, L, and N_1. Notice that the $SS_{\text{variable markup}}$ supply curve in this figure slopes positively, just like our original short-run supply curve in Chapter 6, but its slope is less steep. At a disequilibrium point like L there is pressure for change, and the SS curve will shift down when wage and price agreements are renegotiated.

markup shrinks as demand falls. Shown for contrast is the original SS_0 supply curve that assumes that firms are always on their notional labor demand curves. As long as the new $SS_{\text{variable markup}}$ line is less steep than SS_0, then firms are out of equilibrium and the non-market-clearing model works just the same way as in Figure 8-6.

The operation of the labor market with a variable markup is shown in the left-hand frame of Figure 8-7. The amount of employment (N_1) is limited by the amount of output that firms can sell (Q_1 in the right-hand frame). The price level has fallen from P_0 to P_1, enough to raise the real wage rate to W_0/P_1. The labor market operates at point L, which lies along the effective labor demand curve that goes through points T, R, L, and N_1. There is enough price flexibility to allow more employment and less unemployment than at K (the point reached in Figure 8-6 with a fixed price level). But there is not enough price flexibility to allow the firms to operate on their notional labor demand schedule at a point like R in both frames of Figure 8-7.

Implications of the variable markup. Thus a variable markup, or auction markets for raw materials, is compatible with the non-market-clearing model. Prices are not fixed, even in the short run. A countercyclical movement of the real wage may or may not occur, and *is not logically necessary as a by-product of business cycles.* Even if the variability of the markup is relatively small, and even if the share of auction market products in the economy is relatively small, business cycle movements of real GNP away from natural real GNP (Q^N) set in motion the conditions needed for the economy to return to Q^N. As contracts are renegotiated, there will be downward pressure on wages and prices that allows the economy to slide down its aggregate demand curve DD_1 toward point E_1. This process may be slow, suggesting a role for stabilization policy to revive aggregate demand.

8-10 Implications of the New Keynesian Model

Contrast with Supply Curve Analysis of Chapter 6

The analysis of the new Keynesian model brings us full circle to Chapter 6, where the aggregate demand and supply curves were introduced. The new Keynesian model in the right-hand frame of Figure 8-7 operates graphically in response to a demand shift exactly like Figure 6-10. There we saw that an *increase* in aggregate demand would increase *both* real output and the price level in the short run, but only the price level in the long run. Similarly, Figure 8-7 shows that a *decrease* in aggregate demand would decrease *both* real output and the price level in the short run, but only the price level in the long run.

The new Keynesian model introduces two improvements to our basic aggregate supply curve analysis of Chapter 6. In Chapter 6 we referred only to "pressure for change" to explain gradual shifts in the short-run aggregate supply curve along the road to long-run equilibrium, without providing any reason why the adjustment of the supply curve would not be instantaneous. The new Keynesian model provides the missing reasons for nominal and real rigidities that cause price adjustment to be gradual, not instantaneous.

The second improvement is *symmetry,* since the new Keynesian model allows *both* workers and firms to operate in disequilibrium, away from their notional labor demand and supply curves (as at point K in Figure 8-6 and point L in Figure 8-7).

Contrast with other theories.   The new Keynesian model seems to solve the main dilemma of the other business cycle theories examined in Chapter 7, that is, how to explain observed business cycles without the unrealistic elements of assuming away output fluctuations (as does classical economics), assuming complete wage rigidity (as does the original Keynesian model), assuming unrealistic fooling of workers (the Friedman model), failing to explain persistent unemployment in the presence of easily available information on prices and the money supply (the Lucas information barrier model); or failing to identify the source of supply shocks or explain price behavior at all (the real business cycle model).

Workers and firms in the new Keynesian model are rational, finding it *privately advantageous* to enter into long-term agreements that may have a *macroeconomic externality,* imposing employment and output losses on other workers and firms. The other approaches fail to provide an adequate theory of the business cycle, partly because they do not distinguish between the *private interest* (for instance, signing contracts) and the *collective interest* in avoiding business cycles.

Criticisms of the New Keynesian Approach

The new Keynesian model has been criticized for suggesting *too many* reasons why wages and prices are sticky. Some of these reasons, like staggered overlapping wage and price contracts, have been criticized on the grounds that business cycles were common before the rise of labor unions in the United States in the 1930s and 1940s. To explain business cycles in eras or industries where unions are not strong, we must rely on other new Keynesian explanations that do not require written contracts. Several of these, including the input-output approach and efficiency wages, do not depend on the existence of organized labor unions.

Testing of the new Keynesian approach is in its infancy. There is yet no agreement on which of the various sources of nominal and real rigidity have been most important. The degree of wage and price rigidity differs greatly across countries and in different historical eras. For instance, prices were more flexible before World War II in Japan and France than in the United Kingdom and United States. Prices are clearly more flexible in countries like Argentina and Brazil that experience high and variable inflation than in countries like the United States. Research that would explain why this is true has barely begun.

One reason that prices may be more flexible in some countries than in others can be linked to rational expectations. When firms and workers expect the government to pursue inflationary policies, they are more likely to insist on full cost-of-living protection and to invest time in trying to predict changes in government policy. They may also be unwilling to enter into long-term staggered contracts. In countries like West Germany, where the central bank has consistently pursued anti-inflationary policies since the early 1970s, there will be less demand for indexed contracts.

SUMMARY

1. The new Keynesian approach shares with the original Keynesian approach an explanation of business cycles based on the failure of prices to adjust sufficiently to maintain a continuous equilibrium in the labor market. The new Keynesian model differs by developing microeconomic explanations of wage and price rigidity based on rational expectations and profit-maximizing behavior.

2. Small menu costs can cause large social costs of recessions by giving profit-maximizing firms a reason not to adjust the price level to every change in demand. Sticky marginal costs imply that firms will reduce output in response to a reduction in demand, even in the absence of menu costs.

3. One source of sticky marginal costs is the role of long-term labor contracts in preventing the prompt adjustment of the nominal wage rate to changes in demand. The United States has three-year overlapping staggered labor contracts, in contrast to Japan, where labor contracts last for one year and expire simultaneously.

4. Long-term labor contracts are advantageous to both firms and workers by reducing negotiation costs and the frequency of strikes.

5. Prices of most products are preset rather than being determined in auction markets. Markup pricing is a standard method of setting these preset prices. Markups are not constant but do not change enough to allow preset prices to be fully flexible.

6. Two sources of real rigidity are implicit contracts and efficiency wages. In the efficiency wage model, firms are reluctant to cut wages for fear of reducing the efficiency of their employees and of causing their best employees to quit.

7. The input-output approach stresses that the large number of supplier-purchaser relations in the economy makes it hard for firms to guess how their marginal costs will adjust to a change in demand. It also helps explain why firms do not want to index their prices to aggregate variables like nominal GNP.

8. In the new Keynesian model business cycles push both firms and workers off of their notional demand and supply curves. Workers are prevented from obtaining the level of employment they desire by a "brick wall," the effective labor demand curve, that is moved back and forth by the level of aggregate demand.

9. The new Keynesian model is consistent with rational expectations. It emphasizes the fact that workers are not fooled and will respond to inflationary policies by demanding not just higher wage increases but also more contingency clauses (like COLAs) to protect them from such policies.

CONCEPTS

non-market-clearing model
new Keynesian economics
nominal rigidity
real rigidity
menu costs
staggered contracts

auction market
coordination failure
long-term labor contracts
macroeconomic externality
markup pricing

QUESTIONS AND PROBLEMS

Questions

1. What was the important assumption made with respect to wage rates in the original Keynesian model? How does the new Keynesian model differ in its approach to that assumption?

2. While the existence of long-term contracts is theoretically appealing, does the fact that only about 20 percent of the labor force have jobs in which labor contracts are formally negotiated make this addition to the theory unrealistic?

3. "Classical and new classical firms choose output, but new Keynesian firms choose price." Explain.

4. Explain why it is believed that greater pressure is placed on employment and output in response to shifts in aggregate demand under a situation of long-term, staggered labor contracts than would be the case under shorter-term, uniform expiration date contracts.

5. What is a macroeconomic externality? How do long-term agreements impose a macroeconomic externality on the economy? What other sources of macroeconomic externalities are identified in this chapter?

6. Explain the distinction between auction prices and pre-set prices. Which type of prices is more prevalent in the American economy? Why?

7. In what ways are the original Keynesian model and the new Keynesian model similar? In what ways do they differ?

8. According to both the original Keynesian model and the Friedman "fooling" model, workers move off the labor supply curve but firms move along the labor demand curve in response to a change in aggregate demand. Explain how the distinction between a notional demand curve and an effective demand curve helps resolve this asymmetrical behavior.

9. Explain the distinction between the "fixed markup" supply curve and the "variable markup" supply curve. Which supply curve is compatible with the non-market-clearing model?

10. On May 8, 1989, the *Wall Street Journal* reported that part-time and temporary contract worker employment in Japan is on the increase and now represents 12 percent of Japan's work force, a substantial increase in the number of people willing to forfeit the job security of traditional Japanese labor markets. "As temporary employees, their desire for a life style that doesn't center on their jobs fits neatly with Japanese businesses' need to reduce labor costs," states the reporter. If the trend continues, what implications does this phenomenon have for the future of business cycles in Japan? What do you think the reaction of traditional life-time employed workers to this trend is likely to be?

11. What is meant by the terms nominal and real rigidities? If nominal rigidities could be completely removed from the U.S. economy, would that solve the problem of output and employment fluctuations during business cycles?

12. Is it possible for there to be a business cycle without fluctuations in employment and output? Which, if any, school(s) of thought suggested that this would be the normal case?

Problems

1. Using Figures 8-1 and 8-2 as a guide, assume a price setting monopolist firm with no fixed costs and constant marginal cost (MC_0) of \$3.00 faces an original demand curve $P = 10 - .1Q$.
   (a) What is the equation of the firm's marginal revenue curve MR_0 (recall that for a linear demand curve, MR is twice as steep as demand)?
   (b) What quantity will the firm produce to maximize profits? What price will it set to insure that it sells all that it produces? (Hint: Recall that profit is maximized when $MC_0 = MR_0$.)
   (c) At the profit maximizing price, what is the firm's total revenue? Total cost? Profit?
   (d) What is the value of consumer surplus? (Hint: Recall that the area of a triangle equals one half the area formed by its two sides.)

2. Now assume that the firm described in question 1 faces a fall in demand such that the new demand curve is $P = 8 - .08Q$.
   (a) What is the equation for the firm's new marginal revenue curve (MR_1)?
   (b) If the firm is to maintain its original level of output (Q_0), what must happen to its marginal cost of production? What is the "require" marginal cost (MC_1)? (Hint: Set Q in MR_1 equal to Q_0.)
   (c) At what price on the new demand curve can the firm sell the original quantity of output?
   (d) If MC remains at \$3.00, and there are no *menu costs,* what output would the firm choose to produce to maximize profits? What price will it set? (Hint: Find the quantity and price associated with point E_2 in Figure 8-2.)
   (e) If the firm maintains the original price, what is the maximum quantity that it can sell, given the new lower level of demand? (Hint: Find Q_1 in Figure 8-2).
   (f) Calculate the profits lost and gained if the firm chooses to reduce the price from the original price to the new lower price associated with the original quantity. (Hint: Calculate the values for area A and area B Figure 8-2 as they apply to this problem.)

(g) What is the maximum value for *menu costs* under which we could expect this firm to maintain its original output (assuming that it could reduce its marginal costs to the required level)?

(h) If *menu costs* are greater than $22.00, and marginal costs cannot be reduced below $3.00 due to contractual input prices, would the firm seek to maximize profits by choosing the solution found in problem 2(d) above (that is, where $MC_0 = MR_1$)?

SELF-TEST ANSWERS

p. 217 If a price P_0 is charged, profit is the area between P_0, the new demand curve, and the "Required MC_1" line, that is, the sum of the rectangles A and F. If a price P_1 is charged, then profit is the area between P_1, the new demand curve, and the "Required MC_1" line, that is, the sum of the rectangles F and B. Since F is in common to both situations, shifting from a price of P_0 to a price of P_1 means losing the profit rectangle B and gaining the profit rectangle B. Why is B greater than A? Because E_1 is the position that maximizes profit with the new demand curve and the required MC_1 line. Thus total profits must be greater when producing at E_1 than at E_0 (given the reduction in demand), so the amount of profit gained by cutting the price from P_0 to P_1 must be positive.

p. 220 The growth rate in the real wage rate is completely unaffected by inflation when there is full COLA protection. Since this makes the growth rate in the nominal wage rate change fully in response to the change in the inflation rate, there is no change in the growth of the real wage rate, since this is defined as the growth rate of the nominal wage rate minus the inflation rate.

p. 231 The firm refuses to hire the unemployed, even at a wage lower than is being paid to current workers, because the firm does not believe that it would thereby lower its labor cost. It believes that the unemployed workers, if hired at a lower wage, will be less productive than the current workers and will be more likely to quit.

p. 236 Both the original Keynesian model and Friedman's fooling model require that the real wage fluctuate countercyclically (that is, the real wage goes down as employment increases), because firms are assumed always to operate on their downward sloping labor demand curve. The real business cycle (RBC) theory predicts that the real wage should fluctuate procyclically, since it explains cyclical increases in employment as a response by workers to the higher wage to be earned in a period of high productivity. Neither the Lucas imperfect information theory nor the new Keynesian theory imply anything about movements in the real wage.

PART IV
Inflation and Unemployment

CHAPTER NINE

Demand Inflation: Its Causes and Cures

Why is our money ever less valuable? Perhaps it is simply that we have inflation because we expect inflation, and we expect inflation because we've had it.

—*Robert M. Solow*[1]

9-1 Introduction

We are now ready to study the fundamental causes of inflation, and the determinants of the responsiveness of inflation to shifts in aggregate demand and supply. Does faster growth in the money supply cause faster inflation instantly, or only after some time has passed? Does the government, through its monetary and fiscal policy, bear the blame for the faster inflation experienced in the United States between 1965 and 1982? Can government management of aggregate demand avoid a revival of double-digit inflation in the 1990s?

The *SS-DD* model of Chapters 6 through 8 suggests that any event that can cause a *single rightward shift* in the economy's aggregate demand schedule (*DD* curve) can cause at the same time a *single upward jump* in the price index. But **inflation** is a continuous increase in the price index, not a single jump. Thus a sustained inflation requires a continuous increase in aggregate demand. To focus on the determinants of inflation, we now shift from the diagrams of Chapters 6 through 8, which measure the level of the price index on the vertical axis, to related diagrams that measure vertically the percentage rate of change of the price index—that is, the inflation rate itself. In Chapters 6 through 8, a continuous inflation results in a steady upward movement of the economy's equilibrium position so that the economy eventually moves off the upper edge of the page. Now, as we shift to the rate of inflation, the equilibrium position of an economy experiencing a steady inflation of, say, 6 percent remains fixed on the page.

In this chapter we will study the relationship between inflation and the level of real GNP, and we will see that in the absence of supply shocks, shifts in aggregate demand are the main cause of swings in real GNP and the rate of inflation. A level of real GNP above the natural level of real GNP cannot be sustained permanently without a continuous acceleration of inflation. We

Inflation is a sustained upward movement in the aggregate price level that is shared by most products.

[1]*Technology Review,* December/January 1979, p. 31.

will examine the unfortunate corollary to this fact, that a reduction of inflation cannot be achieved by aggregate demand policy without also involving a transition period of recession, with real GNP below natural real GNP.

Because inflation caused by supply shocks, such as the sharp increase in the price of oil in 1974 and 1979, raises different issues and requires different policy responses, we postpone until Chapter 10 a full treatment of supply-shock inflation. We also simplify our discussion by postponing until Chapter 11 an analysis of the relationship between real GNP and unemployment.

9-2 Real GNP and the Inflation Rate

A *continuous* increase in demand pulls the price level up *continuously*. This kind of inflationary process is sometimes called demand-pull inflation, describing the role of rising aggregate demand as the factor "pulling up" on the price level, and it is depicted in Figure 9-1. Here the top frame repeats the aggregate supply and demand schedules, with the minor changes that (for expositional simplicity) we have drawn both curves as straight lines, and we have introduced specific numbers on the vertical and horizontal axes. For instance, the natural level of real GNP is assumed to be 100 on the horizontal axis, and the economy is assumed to be at that level of output initially at point E_0, where the SS_0 and DD_0 curves cross. The initial values of the price index (P_0) and an index of the nominal wage rate (W_0) are both 1.0. The real wage rate (W_0/P_0) is initially at its equilibrium value of 1.0.

The short-run aggregate supply curve (SS) has a *positive slope,* meaning that a higher output level raises the price level. The SS curve in Figure 9-1 is based on the new Keynesian model developed in Chapter 8; it reflects the same economic reasoning as the "$SS_{\text{variable markup}}$" curve of Figure 8-7. Its positive slope reflects the impact of a higher output level in raising the markup of final goods prices over labor and materials costs, and in raising the prices of raw materials that are sold in auction markets. Figure 9-1 has been simplified by omitting the phrase "variable markup" and designating each positively sloped SS curve by a number. The *position* of the SS curve depends on the nominal wage rate, and the SS curve shifts up or down when new long-term wage contracts are negotiated.

Effects of an Increase in Aggregate Demand

If there should be a rightward shift in the aggregate demand curve from DD_0 to DD_1, because of an increase in the money supply or in government spending, the economy would move initially to point E_1, where the price level is $P_1 = 1.03$. Everywhere to the right of the vertical QQ line the price level exceeds the initial level P_0 on which workers based their current set of long-term wage agreements and contracts. As these contracts expire, there will be upward pressure on the nominal wage rate. Thus point E_1 and all other points to the right of the QQ line are not positions of long-run equilibrium.

What happens when people have the opportunity to renegotiate contracts? If their new contracts set $W_1 = 1.03$, the aggregate supply curve will

Figure 9-1
Relationship of the Short-Run Aggregate Supply Curve (*SS*) to the Short-Run Phillips Curve (*SP*)

In the top frame the economy starts in long-run equilibrium at point E_0. When aggregate demand shifts up from the DD_0 curve to the DD_1 curve, the price level moves to point E_1. The economy can stay to the right of the QQ line in the pink area only if aggregate demand shifts up continuously from DD_1 to DD_1' to even higher levels of aggregate demand. The nominal wage rate adjusts upward as wage contracts are renegotiated whenever the economy is in the area designated by the pink shading. Aggregate demand must keep ahead of the upward adjustment of the nominal wage rate, shown by the vertical path marked by red arrows. This continuous inflation of 3 percent per period is represented directly below in the lower frame at point E_1.

HOW A CONTINUOUS INCREASE IN AGGREGATE DEMAND CAUSES CONTINUOUS INFLATION

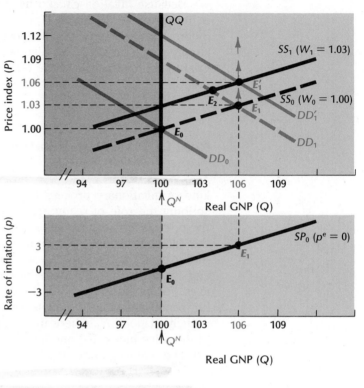

shift upward by the amount by which the nominal wage rate has increased. Thus the SS_1 curve drawn for the new nominal wage rate lies everywhere exactly 3 percent higher than the old SS_0 curve.

How Continuous Inflation Occurs

What happens to real GNP and the price level as the result of the upward shift from SS_0 to SS_1? There are two possibilities, both illustrated in the top frame of Figure 9-1.

A one-shot increase in aggregate demand. The first possibility is that aggregate demand stays at the level indicated by the DD_1 schedule. Then the upward shift of the supply curve to SS_1 would shift the economy from E_1 northwest to point E_2. What must happen to prevent the level of output from declining? The aggregate demand schedule DD must shift upward by exactly the same amount as the supply schedule SS. Thus if the nominal wage rate increases from 1.00 to 1.03, shifting supply up from SS_0 to SS_1, output can remain fixed *only if the demand curve shifts up* again, this time from DD_1 to DD'_1. Once again, however, the price level of 1.06 at point E_1 has raced ahead of the wage rate of 1.03, and there will again be upward pressure on the nominal wage rate as contracts are renegotiated.

A continuous increase in aggregate demand. To keep output from declining, aggregate demand must continuously increase; the economy will move straight upward along the path depicted by the red arrows in the top frame. The bottom frame shows the same process in a much simpler way. The horizontal axis is the same as in the top frame, but now the vertical axis measures not the price level but its rate of change, the inflation rate. Thus in the top frame when the price level is fixed in long-run equilibrium, as at point E_0, the percentage rate of change of prices (or inflation rate) in the bottom frame is zero, as at point E_0. Throughout the book we will write percentage rates of change as lowercase letters, p in the case of the inflation rate; thus the vertical axis measures off the zero rate of inflation occurring at point E_0 as $p = 0$.

The maintenance of a higher level of output requires a continuous increase in aggregate demand and in the price level, as depicted by the vertical path of the red arrows in the top frame. This same process of continuous inflation in the bottom frame is illustrated by *the single point E_1*, where each period the rate of change of the price level is 3 percent (just as in the top frame the price level rises by 3 percent between points E_1 and E'_1).

The *SP* curve. In the bottom frame of Figure 9-1 the upward-sloping line connecting points E_0 and E_1 is called the *SP* line. It shows that to maintain real GNP (Q) above natural real GNP (Q^N), aggregate demand must be raised *continuously* to create a *continuous* inflation (3 percent at point E_1). When real GNP is above Q^N, the price level has risen (because of variable markups and auction prices for raw materials) above the level that workers and firms anticipated when they entered into their current long-term labor contracts. As these contracts expire, there will be pressure to negotiate wage increases. But these wage increases just push the price level even higher, as in the movement in the top frame from point E_1 to E'_1 and even higher up.

Thus point E_1 in the lower frame, and indeed all points to the right of Q^N (indicated by the pink-shaded area), share the characteristic that the economy is not in a long-run equilibrium because the price level is constantly racing ahead of the nominal wage rate. The reason for the continuous upward pressure for higher wages is that contracts fail to *anticipate further inflation* and to *specify in advance the wage increases needed to keep up with inflation*. Such contracts are said to have an **expected rate of inflation** of zero. This is abbreviated $p^e = 0$ and is included as a label on the *SP* line, which is based on the assumption that people do not anticipate further inflation when they negotiate labor contracts.

The "*SP* curve" is an abbreviation for the **short-run Phillips curve** and is named after A. W. H. Phillips, who first discovered the statistical relation

The **expected rate of inflation** is the rate of inflation that is expected to occur in the future.

The schedule relating unemployment to the inflation rate achievable given a fixed expected rate of inflation is the **short-run Phillips curve**.

between real GNP and the inflation rate.[2] The SP curve slopes upward for the same reason that the SS curve slopes up in the new Keynesian model, that is, the possibility of variable price markups and the existence of auction markets for some raw materials. Its slope—that is, *how steep it is*—depends on how much business firms raise their markups in periods of high output, and what percentage of GNP is sold on auction markets. Its position is fixed by the rate of inflation that is expected at the time current wage contracts were negotiated (p^e), and p^e is zero in Figure 9-1. Because its position depends on expectations, the SP curve is sometimes called the **expectations-augmented Phillips curve.**

The **expectations-augmented Phillips curve** or *SP* curve shifts its position whenever there is a change in the expected rate of inflation.

SELF-TEST   From what you have learned so far, can you generalize about the accuracy of the expected rate of inflation in the bottom frame of Figure 9-1? In what area is actual inflation greater than expected inflation? In what area is actual inflation less than expected inflation? Where in the diagram does the expected rate of inflation turn out to be exactly right?

9-3 The Expected Price Level and the Expected Rate of Inflation

The remarkable thing about the inflation process illustrated in Figure 9-1 is that it presupposes that people never learn to *anticipate* inflation when they negotiate their long-term wage and price agreements and labor contracts. Each period the price level races ahead of the nominal wage rate along the path shown by the red arrows, but people fail to build this inflation into their price and wage agreements *ahead of time*.

The left frame of Figure 9-2 depicts exactly the same relationship between the price index and the nominal wage index as plotted in the top frame of Figure 9-1. Notice how the price level (P) follows the red line and each period stays ahead of the black line representing the nominal wage rate (W). For instance, at point E_1 (which corresponds to E_1 in Figure 9-1) the excess of the price level over the nominal wage rate is indicated by the first pink rectangle.[3]

---

[2]Phillips showed that over 100 years of British history the rate of change of wage rates was related to the level of unemployment. Because the change in wage rates in turn is related to inflation, and unemployment is related to real GNP, the research of Phillips popularized the idea depicted by the SP curve in Figure 9-1, that a high level of output is associated with a high inflation rate. See A. W. H. Phillips, "The Relation between Unemployment and the Rate of Change of Money Wage Rates in the United Kingdom, 1861–1957," *Economica* (November 1958), pp. 283–299. The curve should actually be called the "Fisher curve," since the relationship between the unemployment and inflation rates had been pointed out much earlier in Irving Fisher, "A Statistical Relation between Unemployment and Price Changes," *International Labour Review* (June 1926), pp. 785–792, reprinted in *Journal of Political Economy* (March/April 1973), pp. 596–602.

[3]The labels on the vertical axis of Figure 9-2 ignore the effect of compound interest. A steady 3 percent inflation would raise the price level to 1.030, 1.062, 1.094, 1.127, and so on.

ADJUSTING THE EXPECTED PRICE LEVEL IS NOT THE SAME AS ANTICIPATING
A CONTINUOUS INFLATION

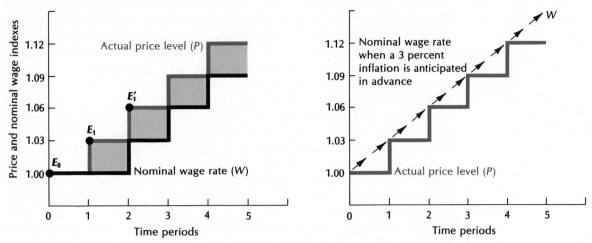

Figure 9-2 **The Adjustment of the Nominal Wage Rate (W) with Inaccurate and Accurate Expectations of Future Inflation (p^e)**

The left frame shows the relationship assumed in Figure 9-1 between the actual price level (P), depicted by the red line, and the nominal wage rate (W), depicted by the black line. Because W always is assumed to adjust upward one period later than P, the pink shaded rectangles indicate the excess of P over W at points E_1 and E_1' in the top frame of Figure 9-1. The problem is that a continuing inflation is not anticipated. A contrasting adjustment is illustrated in the right frame. Line W always keeps up with P, because W is always set at last period's value of P plus an extra 3 percent upward adjustment to reflect the expected inflation rate of 3 percent ($p^e = 3$).

Forming Expectations of Inflation

Contract negotiators are not likely to remain unaware of the potential for future inflation for very long. If the inflation rate remains at 3 percent for a while, they will begin to anticipate that it will continue next period. The nominal wage rate (W) will be adjusted upward from last period's level by the percentage inflation rate that is anticipated at the time of the contract negotiations (p^e). If initially the wage is $W_0 = 1.00$ and negotiators anticipate an inflation rate of 3 percent, then the nominal wage rate set for the subsequent period is not 1.00, but 1.03. The upward adjustment of the nominal wage rate when the expected inflation rate is 3 percent is illustrated by the black arrows in the right frame of Figure 9-2. There the price level (P) follows the same red path as in the left frame, but the nominal wage rate never falls behind. Instead, the contract is designed to set the nominal wage rate in advance, and the actual nominal wage rate keeps up with the price level in each period.

Changing inflation expectations shift the *SP* curve. Once negotiators expect inflation in advance, the short-run Phillips curve shifts, as illustrated in Figure 9-3. There the lower SP_0 short-run Phillips curve is copied directly from the bottom frame of Figure 9-1. Everywhere along the SP_0 curve no inflation is expected. At point E_0 the actual inflation rate is just what is expected—zero—and the economy is in a long-run equilibrium position with the price level completely fixed. At point E_1 as well no inflation is expected ($p^e = 0$), but the actual inflation rate turns out to be 3 percent.

When an expected 3 percent inflation occurs ($p = p^e = 3$), the long-run equilibrium position occurs at point E_3. The entire short-run Phillips curve has shifted upward by exactly 3 percent, the degree of adjustment of the expected inflation rate. The excess of Q over Q^N has led firms to raise their markups and workers have obtained larger wage increases in newly negotiated contracts. Now real GNP greater than Q^N (100) cannot be achieved along the new SP_1 schedule unless the actual inflation rate exceeds 3 percent, in which case the actual inflation rate would again exceed the expected inflation rate.

The economy is in long-run equilibrium only when there is no pressure for change. Point E_1 certainly does not qualify, because the actual inflation rate of 3 percent at point E_1 exceeds the zero inflation rate expected along the SP_0 curve when people made their long-term wage agreements. There is pressure for people to adjust their erroneous expectation ($p^e = 0$) to take account of the continuing inflation. At point E_3 the pressure for change ceases because expected inflation as been boosted enough ($p^e = 3$). Wage agreements allow *in advance* for a 3 percent inflation. This keeps the actual real wage rate, employment, and output all unaffected by inflation.

Thus point E_3 qualifies as a point of long-run equilibrium because expectations turn out to be correct, just as does E_0. There is no need for further revision of price markups or the expected inflation rate built into

---

Figure 9-3

Effect on the Short-Run Phillips Curve of an Increase in the Expected Inflation Rate (p^e) from Zero to 3 Percent

The lower SP_0 curve is copied directly from the bottom frame of Figure 9-1 and shows the relation between output and inflation when no inflation is expected ($p^e = 0$). But when people begin fully to expect the 3 percent inflation, the 3 percent actual inflation yields only the level of real GNP at E_3. The short-run Phillips curve has shifted upward by exactly 3 percent, the amount by which people have raised their expected inflation rate. The vertical *LP* line running through points E_0 and E_3 shows all the possible positions of long-run equilibrium where the actual and expected inflation rates are equal ($p = p^e$).

THE RELATION BETWEEN OUTPUT AND INFLATION DEPENDS ON THE RATE OF EXPECTED INFLATION (p^e)

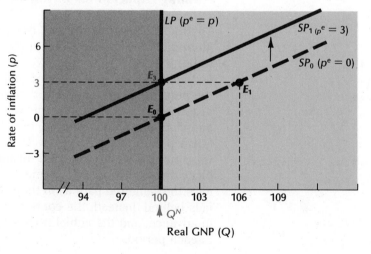

wage contracts. The only difference between points E_0 and E_3 is the inflation rate that is correctly expected, zero at E_0 versus 3 percent at E_3. Otherwise the two points share the correctness of expectations and the same real GNP level of 100, equal to natural real GNP (Q^N).

The *LP* "correct expectations" line. The vertical *LP* line connects E_0 and E_3 and shows all possible points where the expected inflation rate turns out to be correct. The *LP* stands for Long-run Phillips curve and can be thought of as the "correct expectations" line. Everywhere to the right of the *LP* line (indicated by the pink shading) inflation turns out to be higher than expected, and the expected inflation rate will be raised. Everywhere to the left (indicated by gray shading) inflation turns out to be lower than expected and the expected inflation rate will be reduced. The vertical *LP* line showing all possible positions of long-run equilibrium is analogous to the vertical *QQ* long-run supply schedule of Chapters 6 through 8. Its message is the same: real GNP (Q) cannot be pushed permanently away from its long-run natural level (Q^N).

The message of Figure 9-3 is simply that the combination of real GNP and inflation that the economy can achieve depends on the expected rate of inflation (p^e) built into current wage contracts. For any level of real GNP, the higher the expected inflation rate, the higher the actual inflation rate will be and thus the faster the nominal wage rate will increase. In this sense inflation is self-propelling—if people expect it, it will occur, even if output is at its long-run natural level. A cure for inflation will not succeed unless it cuts the expected inflation rate.

Are workers fooled? The two *SP* lines in Figure 9-3 are only two among many that might be drawn. To determine the *SP* line in effect today, we need to know the rate of inflation that was expected when labor contracts were negotiated. If many labor contracts are currently in effect, then the expected inflation rate (p^e) that determines the position of the *SP* curve is the *average* of the different inflation rates that were expected at the time of the many different contract settlements. For instance, the expected inflation rate might have been 4.0 percent at the time of a March 1988 settlement, 4.5 percent at the time of a March 1989 settlement, and so on.

How should we interpret the state of the economy in the pink area to the right of the *LP* line? Anywhere in that area the actual inflation rate (p) turns out to be faster than was expected (p^e) at the time contracts were negotiated. However, the new Keynesian approach (on which the positively sloped *SP* line is based) does not assume that workers are unable to observe the inflation that is occurring, or that they have some informational disadvantage compared to firms.

Instead, p^e represents the inflation that *both* workers and firms expected at the time of the last contract negotiation, say last year. Now, this year, there may be a shift in aggregate demand that pushes up the actual inflation rate above what *both* expected. If the wage contract does not expire for several months or years, both workers and firms may *accurately observe* the actual increase in the inflation rate but be unable to react to it until it is time for the contract to be renegotiated. For instance, in 1967 the U.S. inflation rate accelerated rapidly as the result of increased defense spending on the Vietnam War. However, wage contracts that had been negotiated in early 1965, and were still in effect were based on a much lower inflation rate.

Does full cost-of-living (COLA) protection prevent the economy from operating to the right of the *LP* line?

9-4 Nominal GNP Growth and Inflation

Once we have determined the value of p^e, the average inflation rate expected at the time contracts were negotiated, we know which *SP* curve applies to today's economy. This might be SP_0 or SP_1 in Figure 9-3 or another *SP* line (not drawn) that corresponds to some other value of p^e. But we still have a major question remaining if we are to understand the determination of real GNP and the inflation rate: *where will the economy's position be along the current SP curve?* For instance, along SP_0, will the economy be at point E_0, point E_1, or some other point?

To answer this question, we need to know the relationship between nominal GNP and both real GNP and the inflation rate. Recall from Chapter 8 that nominal GNP (Y) is defined as the price level (P) times real GNP (Q):

$$Y = PQ \tag{9.1}$$

Just as real GNP is determined in the *IS-LM* model of Chapters 4 and 5 by such factors as real government spending and the real money supply, so nominal GNP is determined by nominal government spending and the nominal money supply. In addition, nominal GNP is determined by any other *disturbance* to aggregate demand discussed in the preceding chapters, including changes in tax rates, autonomous taxes, the autonomous component of net exports, the shifts in business and consumer optimism.[4]

In this chapter we are interested in the *growth rate* of the price level, that is, the rate of inflation. We can convert (9.1) into a relationship that directly includes the rate of inflation if we recall a simple piece of arithmetic: the growth rate of any product of two numbers, such as P times Q in equation (9.1), is equal to the sum of the separate growth rates of the two numbers.[5] Writing the growth rates of variables in (9.1) as, respectively, y, p, and q, implies

$$y = p + q \tag{9.2}$$

---

[4]We can take our basic equation for the aggregate demand (*DD*) curve, developed in the appendix to Chapter 5, and repeat it here:

$$Q = k_1\overline{A} + k_2 M^s/P$$

This states that real GNP (Q) equals an autonomous spending multiplier times the value of planned *real* autonomous spending at a zero interest rate ($\overline{A}$), plus a monetary multiplier times the real money supply (M^s/P). When multiplied through by the price level (P), this becomes an expression that determines nominal GNP (Y) as equal to the autonomous spending multiplier times *nominal* autonomous spending at a zero interest rate ($P\overline{A}$), plus a monetary multiplier times the *nominal money supply*.

[5]The formal way to show this is to take the logarithm of the product of two terms, such as PQ:

$$\log Y = \log P + \log Q$$

Then the derivative of both sides is taken with respect to time:

$$\frac{d \log Y}{dt} = \frac{d \log P}{dt} + \frac{d \log Q}{dt}$$

This is the same as the first equality in equation (9.2), since y is defined as $(d \log Y)/dt$ and likewise for p and q.

Table 9-1 Alternative Divisions of 6 Percent Nominal GNP Growth between Inflation and Real GNP Growth

		Level of Variable			Growth Rate of Variable Between Periods 0 and 1		
	Period	Nominal GNP (y)	Real GNP (Q)	GNP Deflator (P)	Nominal GNP (y)	Real GNP (q)	GNP Deflator (p)
Alternative A:							
Inflation at 9 percent	0	100	100	1.00	6	−3	9
	1	106	97	1.09			
Alternative B:							
Inflation at 6 percent	0	100	100	1.00	6	0	6
	1	106	100	1.06			
Alternative C:							
Inflation at 3 percent	0	100	100	1.00	6	3	3
	1	106	103	1.03			

In words, this equation says that the growth rate of nominal GNP (y) equals the inflation rate (p) plus the growth rate of real GNP (q).

If the level of nominal GNP starts out at 100, as in period 0 in Table 9-1, then a growth rate of 6 percent will bring the level to 106 in period 1. As shown in Table 9-1, several different combinations of inflation and real GNP growth are compatible with a 6 percent growth rate for nominal GNP ($y = 6$).

Alternative B shows that if inflation is 6 percent, higher prices will absorb all of the 6 percent growth of nominal GNP so that nothing will remain for real GNP growth. Real GNP remains constant, then, at its initial level of 100.

Alternative C shows that if inflation is only 3 percent, than half of the 6 percent growth in nominal GNP will remain for real GNP to grow by 3 percent, from 100 initially to 103 in period 1.

Finally, alternative A shows that if inflation is 9 percent, then nominal GNP growth of 6 percent will not be sufficient to maintain real GNP constant at 100. Real GNP growth must be *minus* 3 percent, forcing the level of real GNP to fall from 100 in period 0 to 97 in period 1.

Example: When inflation is less than the growth rate of nominal GNP, real GNP must rise, just as in alternative C. When inflation is greater than the growth rate of nominal GNP, real GNP must fall, just as in alternative A.

	y	=	p	+	q
Years like Alternative C					
1977	11.0	=	6.5	+	4.5
1984	10.2	=	3.6	+	6.6
Years like Alternative A					
1974	8.0	=	8.6	+	(−0.6)
1982	3.7	=	6.3	+	(−2.6)

9-5 Effects of an Acceleration on Nominal GNP Growth

Now we are ready to see how changes in nominal GNP growth (y) affect real GNP (Q) and the inflation rate (p). We shall assume that initially the economy is in a long-run equilibrium in Figure 9-4 at point E_0. The actual and expected inflation rates are both zero ($p = p^e = 0$). Thus the SP curve that applies is SP_0, which assumes $p^e = 0$ and is copied from Figure 9-3.

If nominal GNP growth is also zero ($y = 0$), then the economy can stay at point E_0, since $y = p$. Why? In this situation, firms are all raising their prices at the same rate as the increase in nominal GNP, which leaves nothing for any increase in real GNP. As we can see by subtracting p from both sides of equation (9.2), when $y = p$, the growth rate of output (q) must be zero:

$$q = y - p, \quad \text{or in this case at point } E_0$$
$$0 = 0 - 0 \tag{9.3}$$

As long as $y = 0$, point E_0 is a long-run equilibrium, meeting the three conditions that (1) the economy is on the SP curve, (2) $y = p$ (so $q = 0$), and (3) that expectations are accurate ($p^e = p$).

Now let us assume that nominal GNP growth (y) accelerates permanently from 0 to 6 percent. What happens? The economy can no longer stay put at E_0 because it is no longer true that $y = p$. Instead, the 6 percent value of y exceeds the 0 percent initial value of p, and real GNP must grow. With no price increases at all, firms respond to rising expenditures by providing more goods and services. If real GNP (Q) grows, that makes the *growth rate*

Figure 9-4
The Adjustment Path of Inflation and Real GNP to an Acceleration of Nominal GNP Growth from Zero to 6 Percent When Expectations Fail to Adjust

The economy initially is at point E_0, with actual and expected inflation of 0 percent. A 6 percent acceleration in nominal GNP growth moves the economy in the first period to point F. If the expected rate of inflation ($p^e = 0$) fails to respond to faster actual inflation (an unrealistic assumption), the economy eventually arrives at point E_2.

THE IMPACT ON INFLATION AND REAL GNP OF FASTER NOMINAL GNP GROWTH

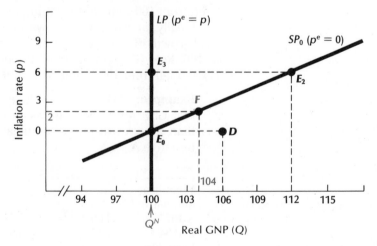

of real GNP (q) positive. Equation (9.3) teaches us the following key rule about the adjustment of real GNP and inflation:

Real GNP must grow, that is, the growth rate of real GNP is positive ($q > 0$), whenever nominal GNP growth exceeds the inflation rate ($y > p$).

Now it might seem that, as the result of an acceleration of y from 0 to 6, the economy must go to point D in Figure 9-4, where inflation (p) is zero but real GNP (Q) has grown from 100 to 106, so that the *growth rate* of real GNP is 6 percent ($q = 6$):

$$q = y - p, \quad \text{or, in this case at point } D,$$
$$6 = 6 - 0.$$

However, there is a problem with point D: *it does not lie on the SP curve* (SP_0), which shows the combinations of output and the inflation rate consistent with profit-maximizing behavior by businesses. We must find a point along the SP_0 curve that also satisfies equation (9.3). This is point F, which lies along SP_0 but also satisfies equation (9.3). At point F, the inflation rate is 2 percent ($p = 2$), while real GNP has grown from 100 to 104 ($q = 4$):

$$q = y - p, \quad \text{or in this case at point } F,$$
$$4 = 6 - 2.$$

Thus, starting from E_0, an acceleration in nominal GNP growth from zero to 6 percent will slide the economy up the SP_0 curve, since people initially expect an inflation rate of zero ($p^e = 0$). This extra 6 percent of nominal GNP growth is divided between inflation and output growth, according to equation (9.3). In this example, two percentage points of the total six percentage point acceleration in y are devoted to higher inflation at point F, and the remaining four percentage points are devoted to output growth, that is, raising real GNP from 100 to 104. Point F is a position of *short-run equilibrium*, since it (1) is on the SP curve and (2) satisfies equation (9.3).

The continuing adjustment. What happens next? The economy cannot stay at point F, because *F is not a position of long-run equilibrium.* It violates two of the three requirements stated earlier for long-run equilibrium—that $y = p$ and that expectations be accurate. First, if nominal GNP growth is 6 percent forever, and the inflation rate is only 2 percent at point F, then equation (9.3) tells us that real GNP growth must be positive and real GNP must increase, moving us right of point F in Figure 9-4. This means the economy cannot stay at point F. Second, *expectations have turned out to be incorrect.* Instead of the zero inflation expected along the SP_0 curve, inflation has turned out to be 2 percent.

Let us deal with the first of these issues and temporarily neglect the second. What happens if workers and firms negotiating contracts fail to react to the inaccuracy of their expectations. This means that the expected rate of inflation remains at zero ($p^e = 0$) and that we remain on the SP_0 curve. But we still have the first problem, that real GNP grows whenever nominal GNP exceeds the inflation rate, that $q > 0$ when $y > p$ as in equation (9.3). Since we have assumed that nominal GNP growth has accelerated permanently to 6 percent, this means that *real GNP must keep growing until inflation "uses up" all of nominal GNP growth,* that is, until $y = p = 6$. This occurs only at point E_2, where the inflation rate (plotted on the vertical axis) is equal to 6 percent, the same as the assumed permanent growth rate of nominal GNP.

But point E_2 is not satisfactory because of the second issue just mentioned, incorrect expectations. Granted E_2 is a position of short-run equilibrium, lying on the SP curve and satisfying equation (9.3). And real GNP has stopped growing, because $y = p$. However, the economy cannot stay at E_2 because this point has inflation racing along at 6 percent, while expectations of inflation (p^e) remain at zero. It is inevitable that labor contract negotiations will take the ongoing 6 percent inflation into account. As the rate of wage increase is raised to take account of the unfortunate reality of 6 percent inflation, the *SP* curve will shift upward. Thus, point E_2 is not a position of long-run equilibrium.

The *SP* curve will stop shifting upward only when the economy reaches a long-run equilibrium, satisfying the three requirements that (1) the economy is on the *SP* curve, (2) $y = p$ (so output stops growing, $q = 0$) and (3) expectations are accurate ($p^e = p$). While the first two conditions are met at point E_2, the third is satisfied only along the vertical *LP* "Correct Expectations" line. And where along the *LP* line do we satisfying the second condition, $y = p$? Given the assumed growth rate of nominal GNP ($y = 6$), this occurs only at point E_3, where $y = p = 6$.

9-6   Expectations and the Inflation Cycle

Forward-Looking, Backward-Looking, and Adaptive Expectations

How high can real GNP be pushed by the acceleration in nominal GNP growth, and for how long? Just as high as point F, or all the way out to point E_2? Everything depends on the speed at which p^e (the average rate of inflation expected when current contracts were negotiated) responds to higher inflation. This speed of adjustment depends on numerous factors.

Forward-looking expectations and the new classical macroeconomics.   First, are expectations forward-looking or backward-looking? **Forward-looking expectations** attempt to predict the future behavior of an economic variable, like the inflation rate, using an economic model that specifies the interrelation of that variable with other variables. Contract negotiators with forward-looking expectations might reason, for instance, that an acceleration of nominal GNP growth from zero to 6 percent implies 6 percent inflation in the long run, and immediately raise the expected rate of inflation to 6 percent. The growth rate of the nominal wage rate would speed up by 6 percent, and this would shift the *SP* curve directly upward by 6 percent, as in Figure 9-5.

The economy would move *immediately* from point E_0 to point E_3, without any period at all with real GNP (Q) greater than natural real GNP (Q^N). The new classical macroeconomic theory based on Lucas' idea of informa-

Forward-looking expectations attempt to predict the future behavior of an economic variable using an economic model that specifies the interrelationship of that variable with other variables.

Figure 9-5

The Adjustment Path of Inflation and Real GNP to an Acceleration of Nominal GNP Growth from Zero to 6 Percent with Forward-Looking Expectations

The economy is initially at point E_0, just as in Figure 9-4. However, now we assume that expectations are forward-looking. If nominal GNP growth increases *permanently* from zero to 6 percent, if all individuals in the economy expect this change to be permanent, and if there are no long-term contracts, then the SP curve will shift up from SP_0 to SP_2, and the economy will move straight up from point E_0 to point E_3. Unlike Figure 9-4, there is no expansion of real GNP.

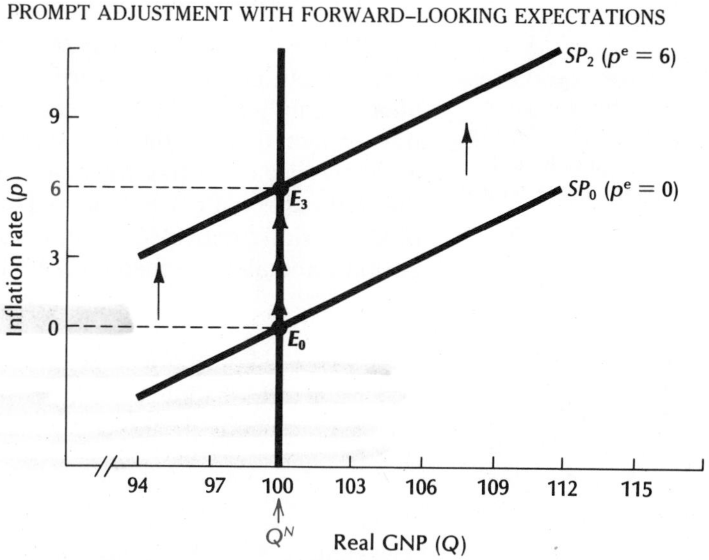

PROMPT ADJUSTMENT WITH FORWARD–LOOKING EXPECTATIONS

tion barriers (discussed in Section 7-5) has the implication, shown in Figure 9-5, that rational economic agents adjust their expectations immediately to avoid any business cycle in real GNP, as soon as they have accurate information on the behavior of nominal GNP.

The rationality of backward-looking expectations.   Another alternative, **backward-looking expectations,** does not attempt to calculate the implications of economic disturbances *in advance* but simply adjusts to what has *already* happened. For instance, the backward-looking approach bases expectations of inflation on the past behavior of inflation, without any attempt to guess the future path of nominal GNP growth or its implications. There are two important reasons why rational workers and firms may form their expectations by looking backward rather than forward.

Backward-looking expectations use only information on the past behavior of economic variables.

1. People may have no reason to believe that an acceleration in nominal GNP growth will be permanent. Nominal GNP growth has fluctuated before, making individuals reluctant to leap to the conclusion that the change is permanent. They may prefer just to wait and see what happens.

2. Even if the acceleration of nominal GNP growth were permanent, the existence of long-term wage and price contracts and agreements would prevent *actual* inflation from responding immediately. Since people know about these contracts and agreements, they know that changes in wages and prices will adjust *gradually* to the acceleration in nominal GNP. However, the exact speed of adjustment cannot be predicted in advance, since it depends on many factors, including the average length of wage and price contracts and agreements, and the importance of COLA protection in wage contracts. Further, *one* set of contract negoti-

ators may have no idea whether *other* negotiators expect future nominal GNP growth to be 6 percent, 0 percent, or some other number.

The most popular form of backward-looking expectations, which has been widely studied and verified, is called **adaptive expectations.**[6] The idea is simply that when people find that actual events do not turn out as they expected, they adjust their expectations to bring them closer to reality. A simple way of writing the adaptive expectations hypothesis for inflation is that the expected (or anticipated) rate of inflation (p^e) is set as an average of last period's expected inflation rate (p^e_{-1}) and the difference between last period's actual and expected inflation rates ($p_{-1} - p^e_{-1}$):

$$p^e = p^e_{-1} + j(p_{-1} - p^e_{-1}) \qquad (9.4)$$

Adaptive expectations base expectations for next period's values on an average of actual values during previous periods.

Here j represents the weight put on last period's difference between actual and expected inflation; j could be equal to zero, to 1.0, or to any fraction in between, depending on whether people expect last period's actual inflation rate (p_{-1}) to continue this period.

Alternative Speeds of Adjustment

Here are examples showing how the expected inflation rate is formed when j takes on different hypothetical values:

Value of j	Calculation of p^e	Example when $p^e_{-1} = 0$ and $p_{-1} = 2$
0	$p^e = p^e_{-1} + 0(p_{-1} - p^e_{-1}) = p^e_{-1}$	$p^e = 0$
0.25	$p^e = p^e_{-1} + 0.25(p_{-1} - p^e_{-1})$	$p^e = 0.5$
1	$p^e = p^e_{-1} + 1(p_{-1} - p^e_{-1}) = p_{-1}$	$p^e = 2$

In the first line of the table, j is zero. People do not adjust their expectations at all to the actual behavior of inflation, but instead they maintain their expectation (p^e) at its value in the previous period (p^e_{-1}). This behavior, which is not very realistic, is the same as in Figure 9-4, where the SP_0 curve remains in effect as a result of the failure by people to raise their expectation of inflation above $p^e = 0$.

In the second line of the table, j is at the intermediate value of 0.25. People compromise, basing part of their estimate of expected inflation on what actually happened last period (p_{-1}) and the remainder on what they previously expected. A value of j equal to 0.25 indicates that people believe that there is a one-quarter chance that the new rate of inflation will continue and a greater, three-quarter chance that inflation will return to what they previously expected.

The third line of the table shows the extreme case of $j = 1.0$, which means that the expected inflation rate is always set equal to what actually happened last period. In Figure 9-6, the acceleration of nominal GNP growth from zero to 6 percent, which raises actual inflation from zero to 2 percent as the economy moves from point E_0 to point F, would cause next period's

---

[6]The idea of adaptive expectations was first used in macroeconomics in a now-classic paper, Phillip Cagan, "The Monetary Dynamics of Hyperinflation," in Milton Friedman, ed., *Studies in the Quantity Theory of Money* (Chicago: University of Chicago Press, 1956), pp. 25–117.

Figure 9-6

Effect on Inflation and Real GNP of an Acceleration of Demand Growth from Zero to 6 Percent, with Different Speeds of Expectation Adjustment

When expectations do not adjust at all, the economy follows the black path northeast from E_0 to E_2, exactly as in Figure 9-4. When expectations adjust fully to last period's actual inflation ($j = 1.0$), the economy moves upward along the red path going northwest from point H.

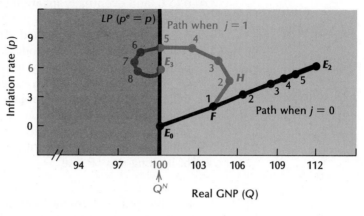

HIGHER NOMINAL GNP GROWTH RAISES INFLATION PERMANENTLY BUT RAISES REAL GNP ONLY TEMPORARILY

expected inflation rate to rise by the same amount, to 2 percent. An important, and simple, relation to remember is that when $j = 1$:

This period's expected inflation rate equals last period's actual inflation rate, or $p^e = p_{-1}$.

Adjustment Loops

The economy's response to higher demand growth depends on j, the coefficient of adjustment of expectations. In Figure 9-6 two responses are plotted, corresponding to two values of j: zero and 1.0. The black line moving straight northeast from point E_0 through point F to E_2 duplicates Figure 9-4. Since j is zero, expectations do not adjust at all and the economy remains on its original SP_0 curve.

The red line shows the opposite extreme of adjustment when $j = 1.0$. In each period the SP curve shifts upward by exactly the previous period's increase in actual inflation. Because actual inflation increases by two percentage points in going from E_0 to point F, in the next period the SP curve shifts upward by two percentage points and takes the economy northward from F to H. But then expectations adjust upward again, because at H inflation has risen above the 2 percent people expected. Eventually, after looping around the long-run equilibrium point E_3, the economy arrives there. (The appendix to Chapter 10 shows how to calculate the exact location of the economy in every time period along this path.)

The red path for $j = 1.0$ exhibits several basic characteristics of the inflation process.

1. An acceleration of demand growth as in Figures 9-4 and 9-6 raises the inflation rate and real GNP in the short run.

2. In the long run, if expectations adjust to the actual behavior of inflation, the inflation rate (p) rises by exactly the same amount as y, and any increase in Q along the way is only temporary. The economy eventually arrives at point E_3.

3. Following a permanent increase in nominal GNP growth (y), inflation (p) always experiences a temporary period when it "overshoots" the new growth rate of nominal GNP. For instance, in Figure 9-6 y increases from 0 to 6, and eventually inflation settles down to 6 percent at point E_3. But along the adjustment path the final equilibrium value of 6 percent inflation is temporarily exceeded. Along the red path, for instance, inflation reaches 8 percent in periods 4 and 5. Overshooting occurs along this path because the economy initially arrives at its long-run inflation rate ($p = 6$) in period 3 before expected inflation has caught up with actual inflation. The subsequent points that lie above 6 percent reflect the combined influence on inflation of (1) the upward adjustment of expectations and (2) the continued upward demand pressure that raises actual inflation above expected inflation whenever the economy is to the right of its long-run LP line.

SELF-TEST   Look at the red adjustment loop in Figure 9-6. Why is the line from point 1 to 2 steeper than from E_0 to point 1?

9-7   *CASE STUDY:*   The U.S. Inflation Cycle and Stagflation, 1964–71

For too long in the 1960s, economists preached that there was a tradeoff between inflation and unemployment. Along any SP curve, the enjoyment of higher real GNP requires tolerating more inflation. But no SP curve is likely to stay fixed for long if the inflation rate differs substantially from the expected rate of inflation. There is no positive relation between inflation and real GNP in the long run when expectations have adjusted to the actual inflation experience. The natural rate hypothesis states that in the long run real GNP is at a natural value (Q^N) independent of the inflation rate.

Some critics have claimed that "economics is bankrupt" because it could not explain **stagflation,** the simultaneous occurrence of inflation, recession, and high unemployment in the late 1960s and early 1970s. But stagflation is precisely what we have generated in Figure 9-6! *The red adjustment path displays segments in which the inflation rate is rising and real GNP is falling at the same time.* Along this path the economy suffers through several periods when inflation is higher than its long-run 6 percent value, while simultaneously real GNP is lower than its natural level, Q^N.

Stagflation is the simultaneous occurrence of inflation, recession, and high unemployment.

Inflation and Nominal GNP Growth

The real world never precisely duplicates any simple textbook model, but the U.S. rate of inflation and level of real output during the period 1964–71 provide a classic example of the effects of an acceleration in nominal GNP growth. If we compare the annual growth rate of nominal GNP (y) during the four-year interval 1960–63 in the first line of Table 9-2 with its growth rate during the three-year interval 1964–66, we observe an acceleration from 5.1 percent to 8.2 percent. And in the third line of Table 9-2, we see that the inflation rate accelerated steadily, from an average rate of 1.5 percent during 1960–63 to 4.5 percent during 1967–70.

Table 9-2   **Annual Growth Rates of Important Variables During Selected Intervals, 1960–70**

	(%) 1960–63	(%) 1964–66	(%) 1967–70
Growth rate of			
1. Nominal GNP (y)	5.1	8.2	6.9
2. Real GNP (q)	3.6	5.7	2.3
3. GNP deflator ($p = y - q$)	1.5	2.4[a]	4.5[a]
4. Output ratio (Q/Q^N) in last year of interval (%)	98.7	104.1	99.3

[a]Lines 2 and 3 do not add precisely to line 1, because of rounding errors. *Source:* Appendix A.

The table shows that the response of inflation to faster nominal GNP growth was not immediate, just as we observed in Figure 9.6. During the intermediate interval 1964–66, inflation only speeded up from 1.5 to 2.4 percent. This "left room" during 1964–66 for the growth of real GNP ($q = y - p$) to speed up from 3.6 to 5.7 percent, as shown on line 2.

Inflation and the Output Ratio

We want to draw a diagram showing how the experience of the United States in 1964–71 compares to our previous theory that analyzes inflation in response to a permanent acceleration in the growth rate of nominal GNP. To do this, in Figure 9-7 we plot inflation on the vertical axis, just as in Figures 9-4 and 9-6.

But we cannot duplicate those diagrams by plotting actual real GNP on the horizontal axis, since in our theory the *SP* curve shows the relation of actual and expected inflation (p and p^e) to the *deviation* of actual real GNP (Q) from natural real GNP (Q^N). The previous theoretical diagrams were able to plot actual real GNP on the horizontal axis only by assuming that natural real GNP (Q^N) is constant. In the real world, however, natural real GNP grows steadily, as a result of an increasing population and of improvements in worker productivity. To make Figure 9-7 consistent with the theory of the *SP* curve, we adjust for growth in Q^N by plotting on the horizontal axis, the **output ratio**—the *ratio* of actual to natural real GNP, Q/Q^N.

The **output ratio** (Q/Q^N) is a basic concept in macroeconomics, because it is closely connected with the two central targets of stabilization policy, inflation and unemployment.

1. In our theoretical diagrams (Figures 9-4 and 9-6) inflation accelerates when real GNP (Q) exceeds the natural level of real GNP (Q^N), assumed until now to be equal to a constant value of 100. Similarly, in the real world inflation accelerates when the output ratio (Q/Q^N) exceeds 100 percent. Thus a basic task of economic policy is to maintain a stable output ratio of 100 percent, in order to avoid an acceleration of inflation. The failure of policymakers to achieve this goal accounts for the inflation that developed between 1964 and 1971 and continued throughout the 1970s.

The **output ratio** (Q/Q^N) is the ratio of actual real GNP (Q) to natural real GNP (Q^N).

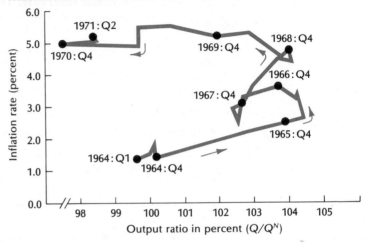

Figure 9-7

The Inflation Rate and the Output Ratio in the United States, 1964–71

Notice how faster demand growth initially raised the real GNP ratio, Q/Q^N. But then in 1967 and 1968 expectations adjusted upward and the economy moved almost straight up until a reduction of demand growth brought about the recession of 1970–71. *(Source: Appendix A.)*

2. As we shall discover in Chapter 11, the output ratio is closely related to the unemployment rate. When the output ratio is 100 percent, the unemployment rate is roughly 6 percent. When the output ratio *falls* significantly below 100 percent, as in the 1981–82 recession, unemployment *rises* substantially. Thus policymakers must walk a tightrope, maintaining the output ratio at 100 percent. A higher output ratio causes inflation to accelerate, while a lower output ratio pushes the unemployment rate above 6 percent.

The Acceleration of Inflation, 1964–71

The quarter-by-quarter evolution of the inflation rate (p) and the output ratio (Q/Q^N) during the period 1964–71 is traced in Figure 9-7. Here we see that the actual U.S. behavior of inflation and real GNP almost exactly mirrors the theoretical diagram, Figure 9-6. At first, in 1965 and 1966, the acceleration of nominal GNP growth occurred along a relatively fixed *SP* schedule, and a substantial increase in the Q/Q^N ratio was achieved at the cost of only a moderate acceleration in the inflation rate. After 1966, however, expectations of inflation appear to have begun a rapid adjustment upward, shifting up the *SP* schedule. As a result, inflation accelerated to about 5 percent without any further increase in the Q/Q^N ratio after early 1966.

But 1969 was not the end of the story. Expected inflation had not yet caught up with actual inflation, and the continuing adjustment of expectations shifted up the *SP* schedule even further. Inflation "overshot" its long-run equilibrium value and "used up" so much of nominal GNP growth that the output ratio Q/Q^N began to fall. The government added to the downward pressure on Q/Q^N by reducing nominal GNP growth substantially in 1970–71. By early 1971 the economy's real GNP level had fallen to only 99.3 percent of natural real GNP, lower than in early 1964, but now with an inflation rate of 5 percent instead of the initial 1.5 percent.

9-8 Recession as a Cure for Inflation

How To Achieve Disinflation

In the theoretical model summarized in Figure 9-6, an increase in nominal GNP growth causes an acceleration of inflation. Eventually, the inflation rate speeds up by as much as demand growth. In the same way in the United States between 1964 and 1971 a permanent acceleration in nominal GNP growth caused inflation gradually to accelerate from 1.5 percent per year in the early 1960s to about 5 percent per year in 1970–71.

Disinflation is a marked deceleration in the inflation rate.

Now we need to find out how to achieve **disinflation,** that is, a marked deceleration in the inflation rate. It seems obvious that the most straightforward way of eliminating inflation would be to set in reverse the process that created inflation. By causing demand growth (y) to slow down, the government could cause inflation to decelerate. Inflation would not respond immediately by the full amount of the slowdown in y, just as inflation did not instantly respond to faster demand growth in 1964–66. But eventually a policy of "slow y" would lead to low inflation.

The "Cold Turkey" Remedy for Inflation

The essential problem in stopping inflation is the slowness with which inflation adjusts to a deceleration in demand growth. If inflation responded instantly, the elimination of inflation would be a painless process. The fact that policymakers did not carry out a sustained policy of substantially cutting nominal GNP growth in the 1970s suggests that the costs of stopping inflation were perceived to be substantial. Finally a sharp decrease in nominal GNP growth was accomplished in 1981–82. The ensuing sharp slowdown in real GNP growth and accompanying increase in the unemployment rate support the suggestion that indeed stopping inflation is costly.

The response of inflation to a slowdown in nominal GNP growth is explored in Figure 9-8. This figure is a "twin" of Figure 9-4, except that here we begin with 10 percent inflation. On the horizontal axis we plot actual real GNP (Q) and assume that natural real GNP (Q^N) remains fixed at a value of 100. In the case of this diagram, expected inflation is assumed to be 10 percent along the SP_2 line.

The **cold turkey** approach to disinflation operates by implementing a sudden and permanent slowdown in nominal GNP growth.

In Figure 9-8 we assume that the government introduces a policy sometimes called **"cold turkey,"** suddenly reducing demand growth (y) from 10 to 4 percent. If the position of the SP_2 line remains fixed, with people expecting inflation of 10 percent because inflation last period was 10 percent, then the economy will move initially to point K. The government's policy cuts inflation from 10 percent at point E_4 to 8 percent at K, but at the cost of a recession as real GNP falls from 100 to 96.

Notice that the move from E_4 to point K in Figure 9-8 represents an exact reversal of the adjustment from E_0 to point F in Figure 9-4. In both cases, the initial reaction of the economy to the 6 percent change in nominal GNP is divided into two percentage points of adjustment of inflation and four percentage points of adjustment in real GNP. Thus in Figure 9-4 the six-

Figure 9-8
Initial Effect on Inflation and Real GNP of a Slowdown in Nominal GNP Growth from 10 Percent to 4 Percent

Initially the economy is in a long-run equilibrium at point E_4 with expected inflation (p^e) equal to the actual inflation rate (p) of 10 percent. When nominal GNP growth slows down suddenly and permanently from 10 percent to 4 percent, the economy initially moves to point K in the first period. Expectations are assumed to be adaptive, with $j = 1$, and so the expected rate of inflation in the first period is equal to 10 percent, that is, last period's *actual* inflation rate. Notice that the *drop* in real GNP and inflation between point E_4 and K in this figure is exactly equal to the *increase* in real GNP and inflation between point E_0 and F in Figure 9-4.

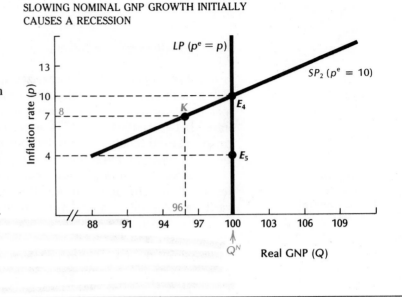

SLOWING NOMINAL GNP GROWTH INITIALLY CAUSES A RECESSION

percentage-point *acceleration* in y was accompanied initially by an increase of the inflation rate from zero to 2 percent, and an increase in real GNP from 100 to 104. Now in Figure 9-8 the six-percentage-point *deceleration* in y is accompanied initially by a decrease of the inflation rate from 10 to 8 percent, and a decline in real GNP from 100 to 96.

The Process of Adjustment to the New Long-Run Equilibrium

The process of adjustment finally comes to an end when inflation is equal to the new growth rate of nominal GNP ($p = y = 0$), and when the expected inflation rate has declined to its long-run equilibrium value of zero ($p^e = 0$). Recall that the vertical *LP* line shows all the different combinations of inflation and real GNP where expectations are correct. One such point on *LP* is E_5, where inflation is 4 percent and thus is compatible in the long run with nominal GNP growth of 4 percent. But to reach E_5, the *SP* line must go through that point, which requires that expected inflation fall to 4 percent, and, with adaptive expectations, this is unlikely to occur until people see that the inflation rate has actually declined to 4 percent.

Because individual households and firms are likely to take a "show me" attitude, refusing to believe that inflation will slow down until they see such a slowdown actually occur, the "cold turkey" cure for inflation is likely to be a long and drawn-out process. Even if we make the optimistic assumption that the weight (j) put on last period's inflation in forming expectations is 1.0 on an annual basis (that is, treating each "period" as lasting one year), the economy's arrival at point E_5 would take more than a decade, as illustrated in Figure 9-9.

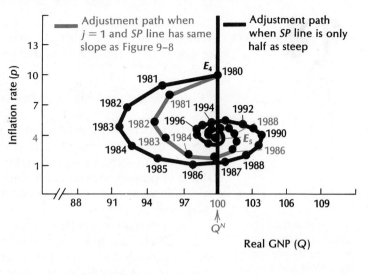

Figure 9-9

Adjustment Path of Inflation and Real GNP to a Policy That Cuts Demand Growth from 10 Percent in 1980 to 4 Percent in 1981 and Thereafter

The red line between 1980 and 1981 traces exactly the same path as between E_4 and K in Figure 9-8 and shows what happens in subsequent years. The black line as an alternative assumes that the SP line is only half as steep as in previous diagrams in this chapter. The flatter the SP line, the longer it takes for the economy to approach long-run equilibrium.

THE ECONOMY ADJUSTS TO A "COLD TURKEY" POLICY

The downward spiraling loop. In Figure 9-9 the economy starts at point E_4, the same point as in the previous diagram. Nominal GNP growth, actual inflation, and expected inflation are all 10 percent at point E_4 ($y = p = p^e$). The red loop running southwest from point E_4 shows what would happen if the rate of nominal GNP growth (y) were suddenly slowed down from 10 percent in 1980 and prior years to 4 percent in 1981 and all future years. The economy's initial reaction is to go to the point marked 1981, with inflation of 8 percent and real GNP that falls from 100 to 96 percent. *The point marked 1981 is exactly the same as point K in Figure 9-8.*

For 1982 and the following years, the economy follows the red path. This spiraling downward loop, which shows the effects of a permanent deceleration of y from 10 to 4, is the *mirror image* of the spiraling upward loop in Figure 9-6, which showed the effects of a permanent acceleration of y from 0 to 6. The economy "overshoots," with inflation falling temporarily below the 4 percent permanent growth rate of nominal GNP (y).

A fatter loop. The red path in Figure 9-9 is not the only possible outcome. We have seen before that the shape of the economy's adjustment loop depends on the speed of adjustment of expectations (j). However, the shape of the loop and the length of the adjustment period also depend on the slope of the SP (short-run Phillips) curve. The black line in Figure 9-9 shows an alternative outcome when the SP curve is only half as steep as we have assumed thus far in this chapter.[7] The flatter SP curve assumption results in a "fatter loop" in Figure 9-9, with a deeper recession, during which real GNP

---

[7]That is, the slope of the SP curve is assumed to be 1/2 in drawing the red line and 1/4 in drawing the black line. The slope of the diagrams earlier in the chapter is 1/2, because the SP line rises by one percentage point of inflation for every two percentage points of increase in real output.

falls to a minimum of 91.6 percent instead of a minimum of 94.7 percent along the red line, and a longer recession, with the economy returning to $Q = 100$ only in 1987, instead of 1985.

SELF-TEST

Why does the slope of the *SP* line affect the economy's adjustment path in response to a slowdown in nominal GNP growth?

"Cold Turkey" versus "Gradualism"

The two paths depicted in Figure 9-9 share in common the "cold turkey" approach to disinflation, that is, a sudden drop in nominal GNP growth from 6 percent in 1980 to zero forever afterward. The cost of disinflation is a slump in output, with real GNP declining by a greater amount if the *SP* curve is relatively flat, or if the speed of adjustment of expectations (j) is relatively low.

The **gradualism** approach to disinflation operates by implementing a slow and gradual reduction in nominal GNP growth.

An alternative method of achieving disinflation is called **gradualism.** This differs from the cold turkey approach by *gradually* (rather than suddenly) slowing down the rate of nominal GNP growth. Figure 9-10 illustrates the costs and benefits of gradualism as compared with cold turkey, plotted against the years (1980–99) over which the disinflation takes place. For contrast, Figure 9-10 also illustrates a "do nothing" or "live with inflation" policy, which in the top frame requires that nominal GNP growth remain permanently at 10 percent, in the middle frame implies that inflation remains permanently at 10 percent, and in the bottom frame allows real GNP to remain permanently at 100 percent of Q^N.

The top frame shows simply the growth rate of nominal GNP assumed in each policy. The thick solid line labeled "cold turkey" shows a sudden slowdown of nominal GNP growth from 10 percent in 1980 and before to 4 percent in 1981 and after. The dotted line labeled "gradualism" illustrates an alternative policy, which slows down nominal GNP growth by 1.0 percentage points per year (10 percent in 1980, 9 percent in 1981, 8 percent in 1982, down to 4 percent in 1986).

The evolution of inflation and real GNP. The bottom two frames of Figure 9-10 exhibit the evolution of the inflation rate and real GNP between 1980 and 1999. The thick solid line for the cold turkey approach *provides exactly the same information as the black line in Figure 9-9 that assumes a relatively flat SP curve.*

Compared to the cold turkey line, the dotted gradualism line shows the consequences of a gradual slowdown in nominal GNP growth. Not surprisingly, inflation decelerates more slowly, reaching 4 percent or below in 1987 instead of 1984. But there is a benefit, because real GNP never falls below 94.1 percent in the bottom frame of Figure 9-10 along the gradualism path, while it falls to 91.6 percent along the cold turkey path.

The "output cost" of disinflation and the "sacrifice ratio." Overall, however, cold turkey and gradualism lead to roughly the same *cumulative* output sacrifice, as compared to the living with inflation policy that keeps the inflation rate at 10 percent and real output at 100. With the cold turkey policy, over the six years 1981–86 the total amount by which real GNP falls below natural real GNP is 35.5 percent, an average of 5.9 percent per year for six years. Although the loss of output under the gradualism policy is not

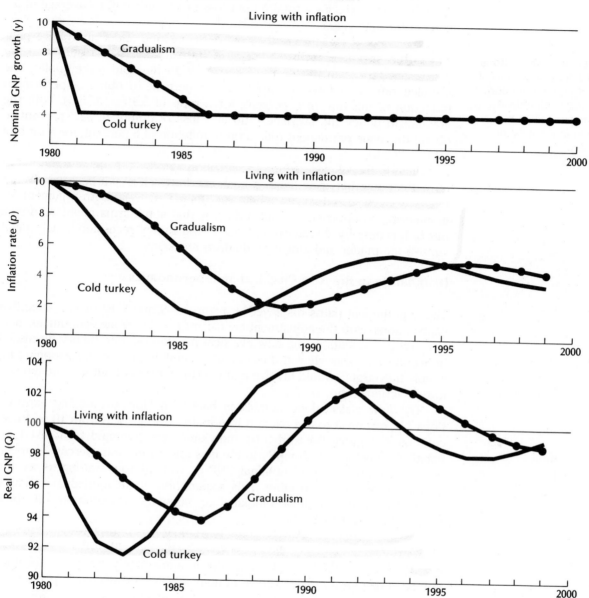

Figure 9-10 **The Effect on Real GNP and the Inflation Rate of Three Alternative Growth Paths of Nominal GNP**

In this figure the slope of the *SP* curve is assumed to be half as steep as in the theoretical diagrams earlier in this chapter, just as was assumed along the black loop in Figure 9-9. The paths labeled "cold turkey" correspond exactly to the black loop in Figure 9-9. For contrast, the effects on real GNP and the inflation rate are shown for two other paths of nominal GNP growth. The first is "living with inflation," which leaves both real GNP and inflation unchanged from the initial 1980 value. The second is the "gradualism" path, along which nominal GNP slows down by one percentage point per year between 1980 and 1986. By the year 2000 there is little difference between the "cold turkey" and "gradualism" paths, and the main difference is that the "cold turkey" path slows down inflation sooner at the cost of a sharper but shorter slump in real GNP.

as large in any single year, output remains below natural real GNP for nine years instead of six, for a total output loss of 32.2 percent, an average of 3.6 percent for nine years.

A convenient measure of the cost of disinflation under alternative policies is the **sacrifice ratio,** the ratio of the *cumulative* lost output to the permanent reduction in the inflation rate. With the cold turkey policy the sacrifice ratio is a loss of output of 35.5 percent to obtain a permanent reduction of inflation of 6 percent, for a ratio of 5.9 (= 35.5/6). With the gradualism policy the sacrifice ratio is a loss of output of 32.2 percent to obtain the same permanent reduction of inflation of 6 percent, for a ratio of 5.4 (= 32.2/6).

The **sacrifice ratio** is the cumulative loss of output incurred during a disinflation divided by the permanent reduction in the inflation rate.

Since both policies reduce the inflation rate by the same amount, the only difference between them is a choice between a sharper and shorter recession, contrasted with a milder and longer recession. An argument for gradualism, as opposed to cold turkey, is that some firms might be driven out of business by the sharp and short cold turkey recession which might survive the milder and longer gradualism recession.

Disinflation in the New Classical Macroeconomics

The hypothetical paths displayed in Figures 9-9 and 9-10 *assume* adaptive expectations, with the adjustment coefficient $j = 1.0$. Some economists, particularly proponents of the new classical macroeconomic theory discussed in Section 7-5, have viewed these paths as unduly pessimistic. Stopping inflation, they argue, would involve a much smaller loss of output, and a much lower sacrifice ratio.

The new classical economics is based on "forward-looking expectations." In response to a reduction in nominal GNP growth from 10 to 4 percent, as in Figures 9-9 and 9-10, individuals are assumed to adjust their inflation expectations promptly to the new lower rate (four percent) implied by the new lower rate of nominal GNP growth, without waiting to see the inflation rate *actually* decline. This assumption about individual behavior contrasts with the "backward-looking" or "show me" expectations on which Figures 9-9 and 9-10 are based.

If expectations adjusted as rapidly as they are assumed to by the new classical economists, disinflation could be achieved with little or no loss of output. The *SP* curve would shift down immediately by six percentage points, in response to a slowdown of nominal GNP growth by six percentage points. In a disinflation, the new classical economists would predict a straight vertical downward movement from E_4 to E_5 in Figure 9-8.

However, we reviewed in Section 9-6 several reasons why forward-looking expectations are not observed in the real world, particularly in economies like the United States where all individuals know that the response of inflation to a nominal GNP growth slowdown is *limited* by the existence of long-term wage and price agreements. As we shall see, the actual behavior of U.S. real GNP and the U.S. inflation rate in the early 1980s duplicated the "cold turkey" path in Figure 9-10 quite closely, providing impressive support for the hypothesis of backward-looking (specifically, adaptive) expectations upon which the theoretical diagrams of this chapter are based. After 1984 the correspondence was less close, simply because nominal GNP growth did not fall permanently but partly recovered.

A good test of our theory is to compare its predictions with actual data from the experience of the United States in the most recent recession. We have previously seen in Figure 9-7 that the acceleration of inflation that occurred between 1964 and 1971 describes a counterclockwise loop much like the theoretical adjustment paths in Figure 9-6. Did inflation in 1981–89 behave like the theoretical adjustment loop displayed in Figure 9-9?

To review, the main point of the previous section was that inflation (p) does not fully respond instantly to a slowdown in nominal GNP growth (y). Instead the slower nominal GNP growth (y) is initially divided between slower inflation (p) and slower real GNP growth (q). If real GNP growth (q) slows down below the growth in natural real GNP, then the output ratio (Q/Q^N) will decline. We will find the economy moving in a southwest direction on our diagram, experiencing slower inflation (p) and a lower output ratio (Q/Q^N) at the same time.

1981–82: A Classic Disinflation

During the recession of 1981–82, the output ratio fell for seven straight quarters, from 1981:Q1 to 1982:Q4. Figure 9-11 plots the inflation rate (p) and the output ratio (Q/Q^N) beginning in 1981:Q1. The economy follows the predicted path to the southwest, with a declining output ratio and declining inflation as well. The output ratio declined to 92 percent, the lowest

Figure 9-11
The Inflation Rate and the Output Ratio, 1981–89

Notice how slower growth in nominal GNP was divided between slower inflation and slower real GNP growth. Because real GNP (Q) fell while natural real GNP (Q^N) continued to rise, the output ratio fell from 98 percent in 1981:Q1 to about 91 percent in 1982:Q4. A revival in demand growth allowed the output ratio to increase between 1983 and mid-1984. Between 1984 and 1986 the output ratio stopped rising, while the inflation rate continued its decline. After 1986 the output ratio resumed its rise and the inflation rate accelerated.

DID THE ECONOMY FOLLOW THE TEXTBOOK ADJUSTMENT PATH?

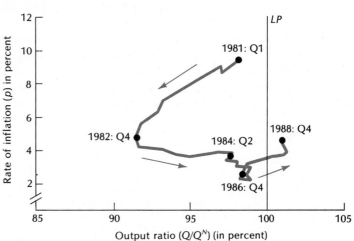

level of the postwar era, and there was a corresponding increase in the unemployment rate to 10.7 percent in 1982:Q4, the highest of the postwar era.

Data on the behavior of the main macroeconomic growth rates of nominal GNP (y), inflation (p), and real GNP (q) are displayed in Table 9-3. This shows in line 1 that in the four quarters ending in 1981:Q1, the last quarter before the recession began, the respective growth rates of y, p, and q were 11.2, 10.5, and 0.7 percent. But in the following seven quarters nominal GNP growth (y) dropped sharply to 4.1 percent, for a total deceleration of 7.1 percentage points. This is an even sharper slowdown than the 6 percent "cold turkey" nominal GNP slowdown depicted in our theoretical adjustment path in Figures 9-9 and 9-10.

Compared to the 7.1-point slowdown in nominal GNP growth, the table shows that inflation slowed by only 4.4 points, from an initial rate of 10.5 percent to an average of 6.1 percent during the seven quarters of the recession. Because inflation did not decline as promptly as nominal GNP growth, real output growth was -2.0 percent, so there was a slowdown in output growth of 2.7 percent (from $+0.7$ to -2.0 percent). Thus the level of real GNP (Q) was falling while natural real GNP (Q^N) was rising steadily, creating the decline in the output ratio (Q/Q^N) depicted in Figure 9-11.

How does the actual 1981–82 experience compare with the simple theoretical adjustment path in Figure 9-9? In the real-world recession inflation slowed down by 62 percent of the nominal GNP slowdown ($4.4/7.1 = 0.62$). In the theoretical diagram of Figure 9-9 nominal GNP growth experiences a six-point permanent slowdown, whereas the average slowdown of the inflation rate over the first two years (1981 and 1982) along the red line is 3.3 percent.[8] Thus the theoretical prediction is that over the first two years inflation absorbs 55 percent ($3.3/6 = 0.55$) of the slowdown in nominal GNP growth. This is remarkably close to the real-world experience.[9]

Disinflation During the 1982–89 Expansion

The theory developed in this chapter predicts that the inflation rate accelerates when the economy's output ratio (Q/Q^N) is above 100 percent and decelerates when the output ratio is below 100 percent. The theory has been validated during the business expansion that began in late 1982, both by the disinflation that occurred until late 1986 and by the inflation that began in 1987 as the economy arrived at an output ratio of 100 percent. The path of actual inflation and the output ratio during the expansion,

---

[8]As can be validated by working through the numerical example in the appendix to Chapter 10, inflation falls from 10 percent to 8 percent in the first year of the adjustment, and then in the second year to 5.3 percent. Thus the average inflation rate in the first two years is 6.7 percent for a slowdown of 10.0-6.7, or 3.3 percent.

[9]The text discussion should be qualified, because a portion of the decline in the inflation rate during 1981–82 was due to the partial reversal of the 1979–80 supply shocks. These are treated explicitly in the next chapter.

Table 9-3 **Inflation (p) and the Growth Rates of Nominal GNP (y) and Real GNP (q) in the 1981–82 Recession**

	Annual growth rates in percent		
	y	p	q
	(1)	(2)	(3)
1. Four-quarter growth rates before recession began	11.2	10.5	0.7
2. Average annual growth rate during recession	4.1	6.1	−2.0
3. Growth slowdown during recession (line 1 minus line 2)	7.1	4.4	2.7

shown in Figure 9-11, exhibits a downward loop similar to that predicted in the cold turkey loop of Figure 9-9.

Two crucial differences between the real world and the simplified theory of this chapter explain the zigzags in the economy's actual path in Figure 9-11. First, and most important, nominal GNP growth did not follow either a cold turkey or a gradualism path. Instead, nominal GNP growth exhibited ups and downs that can be connected to our study in Chapter 5 of fiscal deficits, crowding out, and the dollar. The second difference is that inflation dropped temporarily in 1986 from the path it would have otherwise followed in response to a sharp decline in oil prices. We postpone until the next chapter the analysis of "oil shocks" that may cause sharp upward or downward movements in the inflation rate.

Here our focus is on the rate of nominal GNP growth. We can see the sharply different growth rates that the economy experienced before the 1981–82 recession, during the recession itself, and during the three phases of the 1982–89 expansion:

	Nominal GNP growth
Prior to recession, 1977:Q1–1981:Q3	10.9
"Cold turkey" recession, 1981:Q3–1982:Q4	2.4
Expansion phases:	
Initial revival, 1982:Q4–1984:Q2	10.2
Midcourse correction, 1984:Q2–1986:Q4	5.5
Second wind, 1986:Q4–1989:Q2	7.4

These differences in nominal GNP growth help explain the differing directions taken by the economy after 1982 in Figure 9-11. Initially after the business-cycle trough was reached in 1982:Q4, the economy moved sharply to the right as a result of the sharp acceleration of nominal GNP that occurred during the "initial revival" phase. If the low cold turkey growth rate of nominal GNP had been maintained, instead the economy would have looped further downward, as in the theoretical loop of Figure 9-9. Between mid-1984 and late 1986, nominal GNP growth slowed sharply, and the economy resumed its path downward and to the right, as predicted by the theory. The disinflation reached its end in late 1986, partly because the economy had almost reached an output ratio of 100 percent and partly because that quarter marked the maximum beneficial impact of falling oil prices (which pushed inflation down more than predicted).

Why were the growth rates of nominal GNP so different during the three phases of the expansion? As we learned in Chapter 5, the federal government cut tax rates and boosted defense spending in 1981–84, leading to a large "natural employment deficit." This sharp shift toward fiscal stimulus helped bring the 1981–82 recession to an end and contributed to the rapid expansion during the "initial revival" phase. But then the international crowding-out effect began to sap the economy's strength. Net exports fell sharply as the appreciating dollar priced American goods out of foreign markets and made imports attractive in price. As we shall see in Chapter 17, the economy could easily have fallen into a recession as a result of the slump in net exports, but the Fed came to the rescue with extremely rapid growth in the money supply and a sharp decline in interest rates, allowing the output ratio to creep up slightly from mid-1984 to late 1986.

**The Expansion's "Second Wind" and the
Reacceleration of Inflation**

In early 1985 the dollar reached its peak and then began a rapid depreciation that, as we learned in Chapter 5, completely retraced the path of the appreciation and by 1987 brought the dollar back to its level of 1980. There was a substantial delay in the response of net exports, which continued to decline until 1986:Q3 but then began a sharp recovery in response to the more competitive prices of U.S. exports and the less competitive prices of U.S. imports. The turnaround in real net exports amounted to about 1.5 percent of GNP and stimulated a revival in nominal GNP growth that was sufficient to push the economy further to the right in Figure 9-11.

By mid-1989 inflation had accelerated more than two percentage points from the minimum rate reached in late 1986. Part of this resulted from the behavior of oil prices, but most resulted from the movement of the output ratio (Q/Q^N) above 100 percent. At that time, it was unclear how long the business expansion could continue, as the acceleration of inflation had alarmed the Fed and caused it to move toward a tighter monetary policy. Our theory predicts that an output ratio above 100 percent can be maintained only at the cost of an accelerating inflation, as occurred in the 1964–71 period that we studied in Figure 9-7.

More likely, the Fed's shift toward tight money will succeed in slowing down the economy enough to make actual real GNP grow more slowly than natural real GNP, thus reducing the output ratio back to or even below 100 percent. Accompanying this decline would be an increase in the unemployment rate and perhaps a further acceleration of inflation, that is, "stagflation." This possibility is illustrated by the adjustment loop between periods 2 and 5 in Figure 9-6, which illustrated the effects of accelerating inflation. By the time you read this book, you will know whether the model's predictions came true.

9-10 Conclusion: Is the Natural Rate Hypothesis Still Valid for the United States?

This chapter has developed a theory of inflation that combines the "natural rate hypothesis" invented by Milton Friedman with the emphasis of the new Keynesian economics on "gradual" or "sticky" price adjustment.[10] We have seen that in the long run the economy tends to return to an output ratio (Q/Q^N) of 100 percent at the long-run Phillips schedule (the vertical LP line) consistent with the full adjustment of wage and price contracts to the prevailing rate of inflation.

But in the short run the delays in adjusting prices, because of long-term wage and price contracts, and the other impediments described in Chapter 8 (menu costs, implicit contracts, efficiency wages, and others) can cause the economy to move substantially above or below the LP line. An output ratio above 100 percent tends to boost auction market prices and markups of prices over wages, and hence to cause inflation to accelerate. The time taken for all price and wage contracts to adjust prevents the rate of inflation from catching up promptly to an acceleration of nominal GNP growth; hence rapid real GNP growth causes the output ratio to rise above 100 percent (as in the late 1960s and in 1988–89). In a recession the reverse occurs. The inflation rate cannot slow down fast enough in a time of rapidly dropping nominal GNP growth, as in 1981–82, allowing the output ratio to fall well below 100 percent.

The theoretical model predicts periods of economic "bliss" when inflation slows down and the output ratio rises toward 100 percent, as in 1964–65 and 1986. It predicts periods of economic "misery" or "stagflation" when inflation accelerates and the output ratio falls, as occurred in 1970–71 and may occur after 1989. Other periods of stagflation can be caused by adverse supply shocks, as we learn in the next chapter. Finally, the theory implies that the job of stabilization policy is to maintain the output ratio at 100 percent.

The history of macroeconomics is filled with examples of theories that were abandoned after real-world episodes contradicted the theoretical predictions. In contrast, our textbook inflation model achieved a remarkable record of success in the 1980s as the disinflation and subsequent reacceleration of inflation proceeded along a path remarkably like the theoretical disinflation loops of Figure 9-9. The disinflation of 1981–86 cost about 25 percent of one year's GNP in lost output, roughly as the theoretical model predicted and contradicting the predictions made by some new classical economists in the early 1980s that such a disinflation could be achieved costlessly. And inflation began to reaccelerate within a few months of the economy's movement beyond the output ratio of 100 percent and below the natural unemployment rate of 6 percent.

Because the textbook inflation model works so well for the United States, the contrast between the experience of the United States and Europe in the 1980s is puzzling. Inflation stopped decelerating in Europe at an unemployment rate of 10 percent, much higher than Europe had enjoyed in the early 1970s. We treat the debate over high European unemployment, and

---

[10]The natural rate hypothesis was defined in the context of Milton Friedman's fooling model in Section 7-4.

its interpretation in terms of the textbook inflation model, at the end of the next chapter after we have learned how inflation behaves in the presence of supply shocks.

SUMMARY

1. The fundamental cause of inflation is excessive growth in nominal GNP. In long-run equilibrium, when actual inflation turns out to be exactly what people expected when they negotiated their labor contracts, the pace of that inflation depends only on the growth rate of nominal GNP.

2. Because a high rate of nominal GNP growth is sustainable only if it is fueled by a continuous increase in the nominal money supply, in the long run inflation is a monetary phenomenon. The Federal Reserve, by choosing growth rates for the money supply over a decade, determines roughly what the inflation rate will be over that decade.

3. In the short run actual inflation may be higher or lower than expected, and real GNP can differ from long-run equilibrium natural real GNP. An acceleration of nominal GNP growth in the short run goes partially into an acceleration of inflation, but also partly into an acceleration of growth in real GNP. But when expectations of inflation catch up to actual inflation, the economy will return to its level of natural real GNP.

4. The response of inflation to an acceleration in demand growth depends on the slope of the short-run Phillips curve (*SP*) and the speed with which expectations of inflation respond to changes in the actual inflation rate. The flatter is *SP*, and the slower is the adjustment of expectations, the longer it takes for inflation to respond to faster nominal GNP growth, and the longer is the temporary expansion of real GNP.

5. The 1964–70 period in the United States provides the classic example of the gradual response of inflation to a permanent acceleration in demand growth. After a temporary boom, real GNP by 1970 had fallen below natural real GNP.

6. A permanent end to inflation requires that nominal GNP growth drop to the growth rate of natural real GNP, assumed in the text to be zero. But this will cause a temporary recession in actual real GNP, the length and intensity of which will depend on the slope of the *SP* curve and the speed of adjustment of expectations.

7. The slow downward adjustment of inflation during 1981–86 is important evidence that a substantial time period is required for inflation to adjust downward and provides further support for the theory.

8. Inflation began to accelerate in 1987–89, as rapid nominal GNP growth caused the output ratio once again to exceed 100 percent. The model predicts that the boom will end in a period of stagflation.

CONCEPTS

inflation
expected rate of inflation
short-run Phillips curve
expectations-augmented Phillips curve
forward-looking expectations
backward-looking expectations
adaptive expectations

stagflation
output ratio
disinflation
cold-turkey approach
gradualism approach
sacrifice ratio

QUESTIONS AND PROBLEMS

Questions

1. In what ways are the *SS* curve and the *SP* curve similar? In what ways do they differ?

2. The main parameter of the *SP* curve is p^e. What is p^e? If $p^e = 0$, what is the relationship between the expected price level and the previous actual price level? What is the relationship between the expected price level and previous price levels if $p^e = 2$?

3. Why does the *SP* curve slope upward? What determines the rate at which the *SP* curve slopes?

4. If the equilibrium real wage rate remains constant, what happens to nominal wages when the inflation rate exceeds the expected inflation rate?

5. If the government chooses a more expansionary policy and workers and their negotiators realize that there will be an increase in inflation for the coming year, does the expected inflation rate, as defined in the model (p^e), change? Why or why not?

6. What are the three conditions for long-run equilibrium? Explain what happens if each of the conditions is violated.

7. Why can't the economy move from point E_0 to point D in Figure 9-4 when the level of real GNP increases?

8. Distinguish between forward-looking and backward-looking expectations. Which type of expectations would rational workers and firms be most likely to use? Explain why.

9. Assume that the economy is at Q^N and the level of Q^N does not change over time. If p^e remains constant and Q increases what will happen to the rate of inflation?

10. How would you answer question 9 if Q^N was increasing?

11. Explain the role played by the slope of the SP curve in determining the path taken by the economy when there is a deceleration of nominal GNP growth.

12. Compare the advantages and disadvantages of the cold turkey and the gradualism approaches to achieving disinflation.

Problems

1. Assume the following values for the initial period (t_0):

$P = 1.20$ $P^e = 1.20$ $W = 300$

(a) Assume that $p^e = 0$. What would be the expected price levels in periods 1 through 3?
(b) Assume that the expected inflation rate equals 4 percent ($p^e = 4$). What would be the expected price levels in periods 1 through 3?
(c) What is the actual real wage in t_0?
(d) What is the equilibrium real wage in t_0?
(e) If the equilibrium real wage remains constant and the labor market is always in equilibrium, what would be the nominal wage in periods 1 through 3 when $p^e = 0$? When $p^e = 4$?
(f) Assume that the actual inflation rate equals 5 percent ($p = 5$). What is the price level in time periods 1 through 3? What would be the actual real wage in time periods 1 through 3 if $p^e = 0$? If $p^e = 4$?
(g) What is the relationship of Q and Q^N in question (f)? Explain how you know what the relationship will be.

2. The following questions are based on the relationship between the nominal growth rate (y), the inflation rate (p), and the growth rate of real GNP (q). (See equations 9.1 and 9.2.)
(a) If the price level is equal to 1.00 and the level of real GNP (Q) equals 2000, what is the level of nominal GNP?
(b) If the level of real GNP increases by 4 percent and the price level remains the same, what is the new level of nominal GNP?
(c) If the level of real GNP is the same as in (a) and the price level increases by 4 percent, what is the level of nominal GNP?
(d) If $Q = 2000$ and $P = 1.00$ and both P and Q increase by 2 percent, what is the new level of nominal GNP?
(e) Explain why your answers to (b) through (d) are related as they are.
(f) Complete the following table:

	Period	Y	Q	P	y	q	p
Alternative A:							
Zero inflation	0	3900	3000	1.30	—	—	0
	1	4056	—	—			
Alternative B:							
2 percent inflation	0	3900	3000	1.30	—	—	2
	1	4056	—	—			
Alternative C:							
6 percent inflation	0	3900	3000	1.30	—	—	6
	1	4056	—	—			

3. Assume the *SP* schedule for the economy is the same as shown in Figure 9-4. Assume, as in Figure 9-4, that $y = 6$ and that Q^N remains fixed at 100. In time period 1, the economy is at point F in Figure 9-4 ($Q = 104$ and $p = 2$).

   (a) Assume that labor negotiators use an adaptive expectations approach to setting expectations and that $j = 1$. (See Equation 9.4.) What is the level of p^e in time period 2?
   (b) Draw a new *SP* curve based on your answer to (a).
   (c) What will be the new level of Q if policymakers want no further increase in the inflation rate (keep $p = 2$)? What is the rate of change in real GNP (q)? What will policymakers have to do to achieve this result?
   (d) Assume that, instead of following the policy in (c), policymakers want to keep $Q = 104$. What would be the value Q and for p? How would policymakers achieve this result?
   (e) Assume that, rather than following policies described in (b) or (c), policymakers again allowed nominal GNP to grow at 6 percent ($y = 6$). What is the new value of Q? What is the new inflation rate?

p. 248 Everywhere in the pink area actual inflation is greater than expected inflation (for instance, actual inflation of 3 percent at E_1 is greater than expected inflation of $p^e = 0$ along the SP_0 line). Everywhere in the gray area actual inflation is less than expected inflation. Only along the borderline between the pink and gray areas, that is, at $Q = 100$, is expected inflation correct.

p. 252 Does full COLA protection keep the economy from operating to the right of the *LP* line in Figure 9-3? The answer depends on whether such protection raises the wage rate instantly when prices rise. In real-world COLA contracts there is a substantial lag between the increase in prices and the resulting increase in wages. Thus, even with full COLA protection, it is possible for the wage rate to lag behind the price level, as depicted in the left frame of Figure 9-2.

p. 260 Why in Figure 9-6 is the line from point 1 to 2 steeper than from E_0 to point 1? The line is steeper because inflation is higher at point 2 than point 1, because the expected rate of inflation (p^e) has shifted up in response to the actual inflation that occurred at point 1. And, since nominal GNP growth (y) is the same at point 1 and point 2, but inflation (p) is higher, the growth of real GNP ($q = y - p$) must be less from 1 to 2 than from E_0 to point 1. Similarly, since inflation is even higher at point 3, real GNP growth must be even lower, and in fact negative, in going from point 2 to point 3.

p. 266 The dependence of the adjustment loop on the slope of the *SP* curve reflects the influence of the *SP* slope on the division of a change in nominal GNP between price change and real GNP change. Recall that the *SP* curve slopes upward to reflect price flexibility in auction markets and the tendency of firms to raise markups in expansions and reduce markups in recessions. If the tendency to reduce markups in recessions is small, then the *SP* curve to the left of Q^N is relatively flat, and most of the initial impact of a decline in nominal GNP growth will hit output rather than prices. Eventually the economy will adjust, but a flatter *SP* curve implies that the "cold turkey" curve for inflation will be long lasting and painful in terms of lost output.

CHAPTER
TEN

Supply Disturbances and Policy Responses

Since 1970 the Phillips curve has become an unidentified flying object.
—Arthur M. Okun[1]

Demand inflation is a sustained increase in prices that is preceded by a permanent acceleration of nominal GNP growth.

Chapter 9 showed that a permanent acceleration of nominal GNP growth would cause inflation to speed up gradually. Likewise, a permanent deceleration of nominal GNP growth would create a "disinflation"—that is, a gradual but permanent deceleration of inflation. After the period of adjustment is completed, the inflation rate in long-run equilibrium is the same as the rate of nominal GNP growth. Chapter 9 thus covered **demand inflation,** which is inflation caused by an acceleration or deceleration of the growth rate of nominal aggregate demand—that is, nominal GNP. Demand inflation can be caused by changes in any of the demand factors studied earlier in the book—consumer and business confidence, the money supply, government spending, tax rates, and net exports.

10-1 The Importance of Supply Disturbances

Supply inflation is an increase in prices that stems from an increase in business costs not directly related to a prior acceleration of nominal GNP growth.

In this chapter we study a second reason for changes in the inflation rate, that is, **supply inflation.** During the decade between 1971 and 1981, fluctuations in nominal GNP growth were a poor guide to the timing of fluctuations in the inflation rate; the U.S. inflation rate exhibited volatile accelerations and decelerations that were not preceded by changes in nominal GNP growth in the same direction. *In fact, the lowest nominal GNP growth of the decade was experienced in early 1975, when the inflation rate was the fastest.* Shifts in supply inflation also help us understand why inflation was so low in 1986 and why it accelerated in 1987–89.

Types of Supply Shocks

Supply inflation stems from sharp changes in business costs that are not related to prior changes in nominal GNP growth. The most important single cause of supply inflation in the 1970s and early 1980s in most industrialized

[1]"Postwar Macroeconomic Performance," in M. S. Feldstein, ed., *The American Economy in Transition* (Chicago: University of Chicago Press, 1980).

277

countries in the world was a sharp increase in the price of oil. A sharp decline in the price of oil in 1986 reversed some of the earlier harm done by supply inflation. Supply inflation can also result from an increase in the prices of other raw materials, particularly farm products, if they are sufficiently important.

In some countries (although not the United States), supply inflation has also been caused by sharp and spontaneous increases in wage rates related to labor-management strife rather than a previous acceleration of nominal GNP growth. An example of wage-led supply inflation occurred in France at the time of the 1968 general strike and in Italy in 1969, a time of conflict called the "hot autumn." We shall take a closer look at the unique aspects of European inflation at the end of this chapter.

A supply disturbance or supply shock is an event that changes the amount of output that firms are willing to produce at a given price level.

The events causing the sharp changes in business costs are called **supply disturbances** or **supply shocks.** Recall that an economic model analyzes the response of endogenous variables to exogenous disturbances. In this chapter the exogenous disturbance is a supply shock like an increase in the price of oil, and the endogenous variables that respond to the shock include inflation, unemployment, actual real GNP, and natural real GNP.

Sources: politics and the weather.   Exogenous supply shocks are those not caused by changes in other economic variables. Sometimes the causes of supply shocks are *political,* as in the case of the oil embargo imposed in the early 1970s by the Arab oil-producing nations belonging to the Organization of Petroleum Exporting Countries, better known as **OPEC.** OPEC caused two successive adverse "oil shocks," first in 1973–74 and again in 1979–80. A beneficial oil shock in 1986 resulted from the near-collapse of the OPEC cartel.

OPEC stands for the Organization of Petroleum Exporting Countries, the world's oil-producing cartel.

Sometimes the *weather* causes supply shocks, as in the case of a crop failure that causes a sharp increase in farm prices. Usually supply shocks caused by the weather are *temporary,* lasting only a year or two, after which conditions return to normal. The OPEC oil shocks, however, were *permanent,* causing an increase in the real price of oil that lasted from 1974 to 1986. We return to the distinction between temporary and permanent shocks in Section 10-5.

Supply shocks can be either *adverse* or *beneficial.* An adverse supply shock is one that makes inflation worse while causing real GNP to fall, as in the case of sharp increases in oil or farm prices in the early 1970s. A beneficial supply shock is one that reduces inflation while causing real GNP to rise, as in the case of the sharp decline in oil prices in 1986. Whether adverse or beneficial, supply shocks pose a difficult challenge for the makers of monetary and fiscal policy. Adverse supply shocks impose unpleasant choices on policymakers, who can avoid extra inflation only at the cost of higher unemployment, or vice versa. But even beneficial supply shocks may require policymakers to make choices.

Supply Shocks and the Macroeconomic Puzzles

Supply shocks help explain the first three puzzles introduced at the beginning of the book. The first two puzzles ask why the unemployment and inflation rates in the United States were so high and so variable in the 1970s and early 1980s.

PUZZLE 1: WHY HAS
UNEMPLOYMENT BEEN
SO HIGH AND SO VARI-
ABLE?

PUZZLE 2: WHY HAS
THE INFLATION RATE
BEEN SO HIGH AND SO
VARIABLE?

PUZZLE 3: WHY HAS
PRODUCTIVITY GROWN
SO SLOWLY?

In Chapter 9 the only factor shifting the *SP* curve was the expected rate of inflation (p^e); in this chapter we learn that the *SP* curve can also be shifted by supply shocks like a boost in oil prices or farm prices. By altering the position of the *SP* curve, supply shocks can make inflation, real GNP, and the unemployment rate more unstable.

In addition to their effect on inflation and unemployment, supply shocks also influence the rate of productivity growth. Supply shocks thus contribute a partial answer to the third puzzle, regarding the post-1973 slowdown in the rate of U.S. productivity growth. An adverse supply shock taking the form of higher oil prices necessarily reduces the economy's natural real GNP, resulting in a lower real income per person than if oil prices had not increased.

Direct and indirect effects.   The reduction in natural real GNP can be considered the *direct* effect of an adverse supply shock. It is unavoidable and cannot be escaped through the manipulation of monetary and fiscal policy tools. We turn to this direct effect first, in Sections 10-3 and 10-4, using the aggregate supply and demand model developed in Chapter 6. There we see that the effect of the supply shock on natural real GNP depends primarily on the nature of labor contract institutions in the economy.

The aggravation of inflation and unemployment can be considered the *indirect* effect of an adverse supply shock. Policymakers face a tradeoff in reacting to this indirect effect, since they may choose to have less inflation and more unemployment, or vice versa. The tradeoff is described by the short-run Phillips (*SP*) curve, developed in Chapter 9. We turn to the effect of supply shocks on the *SP* curve and the response of inflation and real output in Section 10-5.

10-2   CASE STUDY: Oil Prices and U.S. Inflation Since 1970

Now we take a brief look at the relationship between changes in oil prices and in the U.S. inflation rate since 1970. The top frame of Figure 10-1 displays nominal GNP growth (y) and the inflation rate (p). Since the growth rate of output is nominal GNP growth minus inflation ($q = y - p$), the shaded areas between the y and p lines show real GNP growth. Pink areas show periods when real GNP growth was positive and gray areas show intervals when real GNP growth was negative. Each of the three gray areas designates a recession (1974–75, 1980, and 1981–82).

The bottom frame of Figure 10-1 displays the nominal and real price of oil, measured in dollars per barrel. Here we can see clearly the two adverse supply shocks of the 1970s. The first "OPEC shock" occurred in 1973–74, when the nominal price of oil jumped from about $3.50 to about $13.00 per barrel after the Arab oil embargo that followed the 1973 Arab–Israeli Yom Kippur War. Again in 1979–80 the nominal price of oil jumped to almost $39.00 per barrel, as an aftermath of the 1979 Iranian revolution. In the 1980s the nominal price of oil leveled off, then fell gradually, and in early 1986 plummeted. By mid-1989 the *real* price of oil had fallen back to about $6.00 in 1972 dollars, below the real price in 1974 but still almost double the real price in 1972 and earlier years.

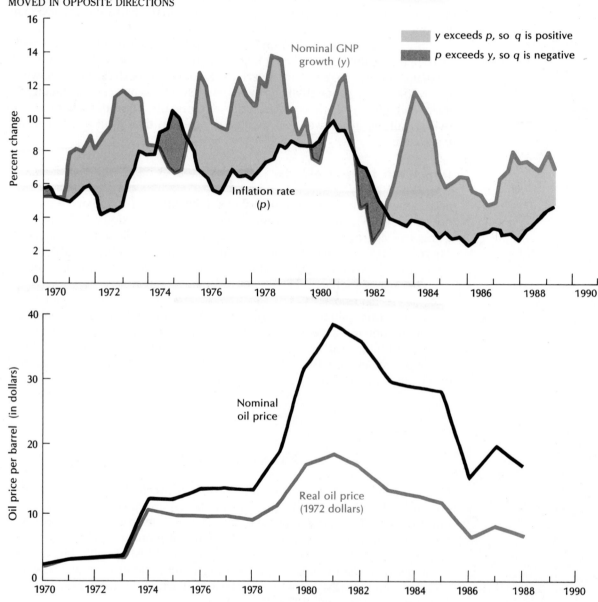

Figure 10-1 **Four-Quarter Growth Rates of the GNP Deflator and Nominal GNP and the
Level of Nominal and Real Oil Prices, 1970–89**

The top frame compares the inflation rate (p) with nominal GNP growth (y)
beginning in 1970:Q1. The pink areas show periods when real GNP growth q was
positive, and the gray areas show periods of negative real GNP growth. In the
bottom frame the nominal price of oil is compared with the real price of oil,
expressed with 1972 as a base year. Notice the upsurge of inflation in the top frame
at the times of the two oil shocks in the bottom frame.

A Mixture of Supply and Demand Inflation

Comparing the top and bottom frames, we can see the upsurge of inflation in 1973–74 and 1979–80, which occurred partly because of the influence of higher oil prices. Rapid nominal GNP growth also contributed to both the 1973–74 and 1979–80 accelerations of inflation. Just as demand and supply elements were mixed in the 1973–74 and 1979–80 periods when supply shocks were adverse, so were they mixed in the period after 1982 when supply shocks were beneficial. The main reason for the disinflation of the 1980s was the fact that nominal GNP growth slowed. But in addition the deceleration of the inflation rate resulted partly from the decline in oil prices and from the effects of the 1981–85 appreciation of the foreign exchange rate of the dollar, which caused the relative price of imports to fall.

10-3 Supply Shocks in the Static Aggregate Supply Model

This analysis of supply shocks begins by showing how the "direct effect" of an adverse supply shock reduces natural real GNP. A convenient tool for this analysis is the aggregate demand-supply model developed in Chapter 6. The aggregate demand and supply curves are used to illustrate the effects of supply shocks in two steps. First, Figure 10-2 shows how and why an adverse supply shock shifts the aggregate supply curve. Then Figure 10-3 sets forth the options open for the response of monetary policy. Should policymakers react to the higher price level caused by the supply shock with an increase in the money supply, a decrease, or neither?

OPEC Shifts the Aggregate Supply Curve

In Chapter 6 we derived the aggregate supply curve in a diagram just like Figure 10-2. We then used this diagram to show the effect of an adverse supply shock in the real business cycle model (Figure 7-8). The left two frames in Figure 10-2 are identical to Figure 7-8. In the lower left-hand frame the dashed "old labor demand curve" shows the amount of employment (N) at different levels of the real wage rate (W/P). In the upper left-hand frame the dashed "old production function" shows the amount of real GNP (Q) that can be produced at different levels of employment (N). Then in the lower right-hand frame the dashed SS_0 line shows the amount of output that will be produced at different price levels (P), *holding constant the nominal wage rate at W_0.*

What is the effect of an adverse supply shock in this diagram? We assume that the adverse supply shock takes the form of a sharp increase in the price of oil by the OPEC. Because firms reduce their energy use in response to the higher relative price of oil, the production function shifts down as shown in the upper left frame. The "new production function" (F_1) shows the smaller level of output that can be produced by additional workers, given the lower amount of energy used by firms after the supply shock.

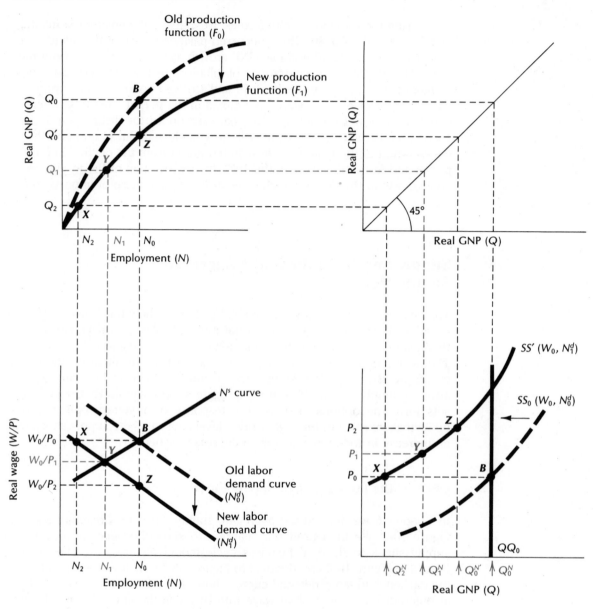

Figure 10-2 **Effect of a Supply Shock on the Labor Demand Curve, the Production Function, and the Aggregate Supply Curve**

In the left upper frame the supply shock shifts the production function downward, and in the left lower frame it shifts the labor demand curve downward. Of the three points X, Y, and Z, only point Y is a long-run equilibrium if the labor supply curve has the slope shown. Point Z is a long-run equilibrium position if the labor supply curve is vertical (not shown). The right frame shows how the aggregate supply curve shifts to the left. The position marked Q_1^N shows the new natural level of real GNP consistent with the new equilibrium real wage rate at point Y. If the labor supply curve were vertical, the natural level of real GNP would fall only to $Q_0^{N'}$.

The labor demand curve also shifts from N_0^d to N_1^d. This reflects the fact that the slope of the production function has become flatter, indicating a lower marginal product of labor at every level of employment. *Each extra worker is less productive since there is less energy to work with.* For instance, at the original level of employment (N_0), the marginal product of labor has shifted down from point B to point Z in the lower left frame. The "new labor demand curve" (N_1^d) goes through points X, Y, and Z.

Effect of real wage rigidity. At which point under these new conditions will the economy operate? This depends on the real wage. We assume that the nominal wage rate remains unchanged at W_0. Thus the real wage remains unchanged at W_0/P_0 *if the price level remains unchanged.* This corresponds to a marginal product along the "new labor demand curve" in the lower left frame at point X, and an employment level N_2. In the upper left frame, we see a point X demonstrating how much can be produced (Q_2) at the employment level N_2. Then in the lower right frame Q_2 is redrawn against the assumed price level (P_0) at point X. *This point X assumes that both the nominal wage (W_0) and real wage (W_0/P_0) are rigid.* Firms do not find it profitable to produce as much output (Q) or hire as much labor (N) as before the increase in oil prices.

Now consider an alternative outcome, with a *flexible* real wage rate that falls to W_0/P_1, where the labor supply curve (N^s) intersects the new labor demand curve N_1^d at point Y. Assuming the nominal wage rate remains rigid at W_0, the price level must rise to P_1 to provide an incentive to firms to hire more workers at point Y than point X. Employment in this case is N_1 and output is at Q_1. Notice in the right frame that point Y occurs where the assumed price level P_1 intersects the output level Q_1.

Effect of labor supply curve slope. But so far the employment level at X and Y has fallen below the original employment level N_0. What would happen if the labor supply curve were vertical, indicating that a constant number of people want to work? To maintain the original level of employment (N_0) the flexible real wage rate would have to fall to W_0/P_2. In each of the three frames the economy would operate at point Z. Despite the fixed level of employment, however, the level of output would fall from Q_0 to Q_0', as a result of the lower production function. This is shown in both the lower right and top left frames. Thus point Z assumes *both* real wage flexibility *and* a vertical labor supply curve.

OPEC and the Natural Level of Real GNP

The new short-run aggregate supply curve connects the alternative points X, Y, and Z. It is labeled SS' in the right frame of Figure 10-2, and it assumes that the nominal wage rate remains fixed at W_0, and that the labor demand curve has shifted down to N_1^d. Originally, before the OPEC supply shock, the natural level of real GNP, Q_0^N, occurred along the vertical QQ_0 line in the right frame. But now the action of OPEC in raising the relative price of oil has reduced the level of natural real GNP.

Three reasons why natural real GNP might fall. How far does natural real GNP fall as a result of the supply shock? We can use Figure 10-2 to identify three reasons why natural real GNP might fall:

Reason 1: Lower Production Function. The first reason that natural real GNP falls is *unavoidable*. This is the downward shift in the production function. Even if employment remains at the original level (N_0), output must fall from point B to point Z in the upper left-hand frame and in the lower right-hand frame. This first reason for the decline in natural real GNP is designated by the distance between $Q_0^{N'}$ and Q_0^N in the lower right-hand frame.

Reason 2: Voluntary Labor Supply Response. The original level of employment (N_0) may not be maintained. If workers react to a lower real wage by deciding that employment has become less attractive relative to leisure, there will be a voluntary decline in the supply of labor. The labor supply curve will then be positively sloped, like the line labeled "N^s curve" in the lower left-hand frame. If the real wage is flexible, then the economy will operate at point Y in the lower left-hand frame, where the labor supply curve (N^s) intersects the new labor demand curve (N_1^d). The economy will also operate at point Y in the other frames. This second reason for the decline in natural real GNP is designated by the distance between Q_1^N and $Q_0^{N'}$ in the lower right-hand frame.[2]

Reason 3: Real Wage Rigidity. To reach point Y, the real wage must be flexible. If instead the real wage is rigid at the original level (W_0/P_0), then the economy will operate at point X in the lower left-hand frame, where the rigid real wage rate (W_0/P_0) intersects the new labor demand curve (N_1^d). The economy will also operate at point X in the other frames. This third reason for the decline in natural real GNP is designated by the distance between Q_2^N and Q_1^N in the lower right-hand frame. Obviously Reason 2 (requiring real wage flexibility) and Reason 3 (requiring real wage rigidity) cannot both occur at the same time.

Labor supply curve slope and real wage rigidity. Which of the three reasons applied to the U.S. economy in the 1970s? The answer depends on whether the labor supply curve was vertical or positively sloped (that is, were we at point Y or Z?) and whether the real wage rate was rigid (that is, were we at point X instead of Y or Z?).

Let us deal with real wage rigidity first. In the United States the real wage actually fell at the time of both the 1973–74 and 1979–80 oil shocks, after an uninterrupted increase since the end of World War II. Between the middle of 1973 and early 1975, the real wage rate fell by about 3 percent. And between the middle of 1978 and early 1980, the real wage rate fell by about 2.5 percent.[3]

The basic reason for real wage flexibility in the United States was identified in the discussion of long-term labor contracts (Section 8-3). This is the

---

[2] Both reason 1 and reason 2 cause a decline in Q^N in the real business cycle model of Figure 7-8.

[3] Our real wage rate measure is the average hourly earnings index for the nonagricultural private economy (Bureau of Labor Statistics) divided by the GNP deflator.

fact that U.S. wage contracts do not offer workers the full protection of a cost-of-living adjustment (COLA). Thus when the price level increases sharply at the time of an oil shock, COLA protection is insufficient to boost wages in tandem with prices, and the real wage declines.

With real wage flexibility, the theoretical economy in Figure 10-2 goes to either point Y or point Z. Which description of labor supply behavior seems to apply best to the United States? The best *aggregate* measure of the slope of the labor supply curve is the behavior of the **labor force participation rate**—that is, the fraction of the working-age population who are either employed or unemployed. People not in the labor force are those staying at home, studying in school, or too discouraged to look for work. With a positively sloped labor supply curve, we would expect that the *decline* in the U.S. real wage rate that occurred in 1973–74 and 1979–80 would have *reduced* the labor force participation rate.

However, the first oil shock did not reduce the labor force participation rate. Instead, the rate increased slightly from 60.8 percent in 1973 to 61.2 percent in 1975. After the second oil shock, the rate stayed about the same, with rates of 63.7 in 1979, 63.8 percent in 1980, and 63.9 percent in 1981. Thus it would appear that the labor supply curve in the left frame of Figure 10-2 should be drawn as a vertical line at N_0 rather than as the positively sloped line N^s. *A vertical labor supply curve combined with real wage flexibility implies that the economy would operate after the supply shock at point Z in all three frames of Figure 10-2.*

> **The labor force participation rate** is the ratio of the labor force (total employed plus unemployed) to the working-age population.

SELF-TEST Does Figure 10-2 illustrate the direct or indirect effect of a supply shock? At point Z, what is the new level of the natural level of output? Can you express in words the reason or reasons why the natural level of output declines as a result of the supply shock at point Z?

10-4 Obstacles to Accommodation of Supply Shocks

The preceding section illustrates that even with some real wage flexibility and a vertical labor supply curve, people will be worse off after a supply shock. What are the options for the makers of monetary and fiscal policy following a supply shock? Should they raise or lower the rate of nominal GNP through changes in monetary or growth fiscal policy? The next two sections explore this policy dilemma. This section continues to use the static aggregate supply model, as in Figure 10-2. The next section then examines the same question with the dynamic inflation-output model based on the short-run Phillips (SP) curve.

The Fed's Alternatives

Figure 10-3 examines the Fed's alternatives. Based on the evidence in the preceding section that the labor supply curve is vertical and the real wage is flexible, we have concluded that natural real GNP would fall from Q_0^N to $Q_0^{N'}$ as the result of the adverse supply shock. The vertical QQ_0' line running through Z shows the economy's new long-run equilibrium. Only

Figure 10-3

Effect on Real GNP and the Price Level of a Higher Oil Price that Shifts the Short-Run Supply Curve from SS₀ to SS′

Initially the higher oil prices shift the economy from point B to point H if the nominal money supply is left unchanged at M_0^s. The natural level of real GNP is assumed to fall from Q_0^N to $Q_0^{N'}$. A monetary policy that leaves the nominal money supply unchanged at this level causes involuntary unemployment if point H happens to lie to the left of point z (with a steeper DD line, point H might lie to the right of point Z).

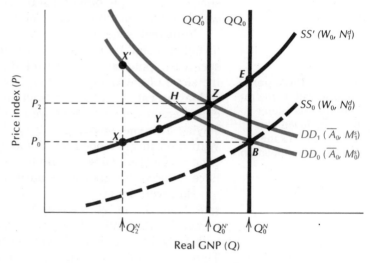

THE FED'S DILEMMA

along this new QQ_0' line is the real wage rate at its long-run equilibrium level (shown by point Z in the lower left frame of Figure 10-2). Anywhere to the left of the new QQ_0' line there will be downward pressure on the nominal wage rate when labor contracts are renegotiated, and anywhere to the right there will be upward pressure.

If the Fed maintains the *nominal* money supply at its initial level, M_0^s, and if autonomous planned spending also remains unchanged, then the aggregate demand curve remains fixed at DD_0, shown in Figure 10-3. As a result of the shock the economy moves initially from its starting place (point B) to point H, which is the intersection of the unchanged aggregate demand curve (DD_0) and the new aggregate supply curve (SS'). The higher price level at H causes a decline in the *real* money supply, a drop in real GNP, and layoffs of some workers. Notice that at point H the actual real wage is *higher* than the equilibrium real wage, because the price level is *lower* at point H than at point Z.

To eliminate unemployment, the Fed should raise the money supply by enough to make the DD curve intersect the new aggregate supply schedule at point Z. This is shown by the new DD curve labeled DD_1. *But it would be a mistake for the Fed to try to maintain the original level of output by shifting the DD curve up to point E.* This would require employment to rise above its initial level and would put upward pressure on the nominal wage rate, thus raising the SS curve again. An inflationary spiral could result. If the Fed raises the DD curve enough to prevent actual real GNP from falling below natural real GNP (along the new QQ line), it is said to have "accommodated" the supply shock. But is must be careful not to "overaccommodate," which may be difficult in the absence of adequate information on what has actually happened to the QQ line.

The perils of COLAs. The Fed can be stymied if all employees have cost-of-living adjustment clauses (COLA) in their labor contracts. Why do COLAs affect the Fed's ability to react to a supply shock? A COLA that gives full protection to a worker raises the nominal wage rate by the full amount of any increase in the price level.

> *Thus a COLA agreement that gives full protection rigidifies the real wage rate.*

In Figure 10-3 a full-protection COLA that rigidifies the real wage rate at W_0/P_0 makes the economy's natural real GNP decline from the original point B in Figures 10-2 and 10-3 to point X.

COLA implies an unpleasant choice for the Fed. Faced with real wage rigidity that reduces natural real GNP to Q_2^N in Figure 10-3, the choices of the Fed are unpleasant. Notice that the long-run equilibrium point X (which applies if the real wage rate is rigid) lies well below the aggregate demand curve (DD_0) drawn for the initial level of the nominal money supply (M_0^s). This means that to reduce the actual level of real GNP to the new natural level of real GNP (assuming full COLA protection and real wage rigidity), the Fed must reduce the nominal money supply by enough to shift the aggregate demand curve down so that it intersects with point X. This reduction in the nominal money supply would maintain the initial price level in Figure 10-3 (P_0) but would require a major loss of output.

What are the Fed's alternatives in the face of real wage rigidity (full COLA protection)? We have seen that a *reduction* in the real money supply would be necessary to bring the economy to point X in Figure 10-3, thus averting an increase in the price level above the initial level (P_0). If, however, the Fed *maintains* the initial level of the money supply, keeping the aggregate demand curves at DD_0, upward pressure on wage rates will shift the SS curve upward, moving the economy to point X', where the DD_0 curve intersects the new level of natural real GNP (Q_2^N, valid if the real wage rate is rigid).

Another Basic Obstacle: Nominal Wage Rigidity

With real wage rigidity (caused by full COLA protection), the Fed must accept a decline in real output, with no increase in the price level at point X if the money supply is reduced and a significant increase in the price level at point X' if the money supply remains the same. But even with real wage flexibility, the Fed has an unpleasant choice. For instance, the highest feasible level of output at point Z in Figure 10-3 requires that the price level increase from the initial P_0 to the new P_2.

Is there no way to attain the output level of point Z, yet avoid an increase in the price level? No, unless the nominal wage rate declines. Such a decline in the nominal wage rate, as shown in Figure 10-4, would make no difference for the *direct* effect of the supply shock. Natural real GNP would still shrink from the initial Q_0^N to the new $Q_0^{N'}$. But if the nominal wage rate were to decline enough, the short-run supply curve would shift *down* to the position SS'' in Figure 10-4. If this downward shift in SS were accompanied

Figure 10-4
Effect on the Price Level and Real GNP of an Adverse Supply Shock When the Nominal Wage Rate Is Flexible

The economy is initially at point B. The adverse supply shock reduces natural real GNP from Q_0^N to $Q_0^{N'}$. In contrast to Figure 10-3, here the nominal wage rate falls by enough to allow the new SS'' curve to intersect the new level of natural real GNP at point Z'', where the price level remains at the original level (P_0).

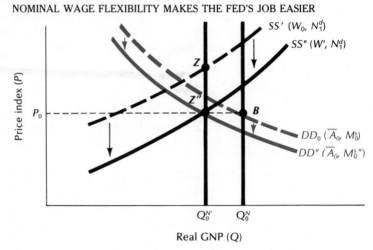

by a sufficient decline in the nominal money supply to push the aggregate demand curve down from DD_0 to DD'', the economy would go to point Z''. Here the price level remains at the initial P_0, while the level of output has declined only by the direct effect of the supply shock on natural real GNP (Q^N), with no *additional* reduction of output beyond that.

SELF-TEST   Does real wage rigidity or nominal wage rigidity prevent the Fed from maintaining the original price level (P_0) and the highest feasible level of output ($Q_0^{N'}$)?

10-5   The Response of Inflation and Real GNP to a Supply Shock

In Figure 10-1 we examined the relationship between oil price shocks and the U.S. inflation rate. There we saw that increases in the *level* of the real price of oil caused a change in the aggregate *rate of inflation*. Our analysis thus far has examined only the response of the aggregate *price level* to an oil shock. How does the rate of inflation react?

Effects of Supply Shocks on the Price Level and on the Rate of Inflation

Supply shocks may be temporary or permanent. We can distinguish between the effects of each type of shock on the *price level*, as compared to the effect of each type on the *rate of inflation*.

Temporary supply shock. One example of a temporary supply shock is a crop failure, caused by an untimely freeze or drought. The result is likely to be a temporary increase in the level of prices, followed by a return in the price index to its previous level. This occurred in the summer of 1988, when an unusually severe drought ruined much of the nation's wheat, corn, and soybean crop, causing an increase in prices in the fall and winter of 1988. But then normal weather returned in 1989 and the price index for these products dropped to its initial level. The following diagram assumes that initially the inflation rate is zero.

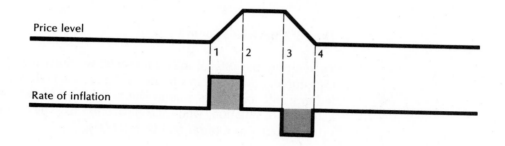

In the diagram, at time 1 the price level begins to rise, increasing the rate of inflation (which is, after all, just the rate of change of the price level). At time 2 the price index levels off, so that the rate of inflation returns to zero. At time 3 the price level begins to fall, so that the rate of inflation becomes negative, and finally both the price level and rate of inflation return at time 4 to their initial values. This type of supply shock is unlikely to cause any adjustment of the expected inflation rate, because most people will correctly view the initial inflation (indicated by the pink shaded area) as a temporary phenomenon.

Permanent supply shock. Examples of a permanent supply shock were the OPEC oil price increases of 1974 and 1979, which affected the economy for more than a decade until oil prices finally fell in 1986. Increasing energy prices pushed up the rate of inflation as firms adjusted to the higher price of oil, but then no further direct impact was felt on the price level. This type of "permanent" supply shock can be depicted as follow.

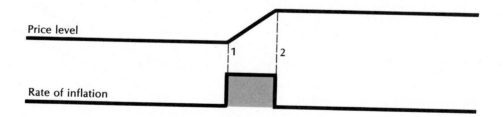

This diagram duplicates the previous one for the first two time periods, during which the price index rises to a new, higher level. The difference is that no subsequent drop in the price level occurs; the OPEC oil cartel did not allow the price of oil to return to its pre-1974 level until 1986, a long 12-

year interval, unlike the corn and soybean farmers who raised production promptly in 1989 after the 1988 drought had ended.

The analysis in Sections 10-3 and 10-4 focused on the effects of the *permanent* increase in the real price of oil on natural real GNP, actual real GNP and the aggregate *price level*. The upward movement of the aggregate price level shown in the in-text diagram between time "1" and time "2" was represented in the previous analysis by the upward shift in the *SS* curve in Figures 10-2 and 10-3. Now we are prepared to examine the effect of this permanent shock on the aggregate *rate of inflation,* shown by the pink area between time "1" and "2" in the in-text diagram.

The SP Curve Reappears

To see how the rate of inflation reacts, we must use the short-run Phillips (*SP*) curve, developed in Chapter 9. The SP_2 schedule in Figure 10-5 is copied from the same schedule in Figure 9-8. The vertical axis plots the aggregate rate of inflation, while the horizontal axis plots the output ratio—the ratio of actual to natural real GNP (Q/Q^N).

Allowing for a change in the output ratio. In Chapter 9 we assumed that natural real GNP (Q^N) was constant, implying that any movement in the output ratio (Q/Q^N) was identical to a movement in actual real GNP (Q). This assumption allowed us for simplicity to plot actual real GNP (Q) on the horizontal axis, instead of the output ratio (Q/Q^N). However, we know now from the analysis of Sections 10-2 and 10-3 that a supply shock will affect the level of natural real GNP (Q^N), and to allow for this change in Q^N we plot the output ratio (Q/Q^N) on the horizontal axis in this chapter.

Figure 10-5
The Effect on the Inflation Rate and the Output Ratio of an Adverse Supply Shock that Shifts the SP Curve Upward by 3 Percent

The economy is initially at point E_3, with an output ratio of 100 percent and both actual and expected inflation rates of 6 percent. The supply shock shifts the *SP* curve upward to SP_3. The movement of the economy depends on the policy response. With an accommodating policy the economy moves from E_3 to point N, with a neutral policy to point L, and with an extinguishing policy to point M.

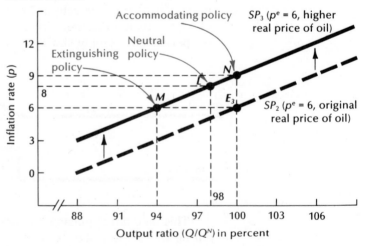

THE FED'S UNPLEASANT CHOICES AFTER AN ADVERSE SUPPLY SHOCK

Supply shocks and the SP schedule. Recall that each *SP* schedule has a positive slope, reflecting the impact of a higher output ratio in raising the prices of raw materials traded in auction markets, and in raising the markup of final goods prices above labor and materials costs. The vertical position of the *SP* curve depends on the rate of inflation that was expected (p^e) at the time that current wage contracts were negotiated. As long as the real price of oil remains constant, the only factor that could make the *SP* curve shift would be a change in the expected rate of inflation (p^e). But if a supply shock changes the real price of oil, then we have a second reason why the *SP* curve might shift up.

Point E_3 in Figure 10-5 depicts a situation of long-run equilibrium. Actual inflation is 6 percent, and initially the rate of nominal GNP growth is assumed to be 6 percent. Since the upward-sloping SP_2 schedule assumes that expected inflation (p^e) is 6 percent, the condition $p^e = p$, required for long-run equilibrium, is satisfied.

Now let us assume that OPEC suddenly doubles the price of oil over the course of a year, as occurred in 1979, and let us assume that its action is sufficient *to add three extra percentage points to the inflation rate at any given level of real GNP.* The three extra points of inflation are reflected in the upward shift of the *SP* schedule from SP_2 to SP_3 in Figure 10-5. Where will the economy move along the new SP_3 schedule?

Policy Responses to Supply Shocks

The response of the economy to the adverse permanent supply shock depicted in Figure 10-5 *depends on the response of nominal GNP growth.* The government can implement policy measures to alter nominal GNP growth. These policy actions determine where the economy moves along the new SP_3 schedule.

Neutral, accommodating, and extinguishing policy responses. There are three possible policy responses. The first is called a **neutral policy.** Such a policy would attempt to keep nominal GNP growth unchanged from the original rate (6 percent). This is shown by point *L* in Figure 10-5. Since real GNP growth by definition must be equal to nominal GNP growth minus the inflation rate ($q = y - p$), a *neutral policy makes the output ratio decline by the same amount as inflation increases.* Thus, at point *L*, the output ratio falls by 2 percent (from 100 to 98) and inflation rises by 2 percent (from 6 to 8 percent).[4] The sum of -2 and $+2$ is precisely zero, the assumed zero change in the growth rate of nominal GNP.

Does the government have any way to escape the simultaneous worsening of inflation and decline in the output ratio shown at point *L*? It can keep the output ratio fixed only if it is willing to accept more inflation. Or, it can keep inflation from accelerating above 6 percent only if it is willing to accept a greater decline in the output ratio.

> Following a supply shock a **neutral policy** maintains nominal GNP growth so as to allow a decline in the output ratio equal to the increase of the inflation rate.

---

[4]The text discussion of the graphical example in Figure 10-5 ignores the decline in Q^N discussed in the previous sections. The precise definition of a neutral policy is one involving no change in the excess of nominal GNP growth over the growth rate of natural real GNP from its initial value, assumed to be 6 percent ($y - q^N = 6$). This more precise definition is developed in the appendix to Chapter 10.

Following a supply shock an **accommo-dating policy** raises nominal GNP growth so as to maintain the original output ratio.

Following a supply shock an **extinguish-ing policy** reduces nominal GNP growth so as to maintain the original inflation rate.

An **accommodating policy** attempts to maintain the output ratio intact at point N. To do this, inflation must be allowed to rise by the full extent of the vertical shift in SP, so that inflation jumps from 6 to 9 percent per year. This acceleration of inflation requires an acceleration of nominal GNP growth.

An **extinguishing policy** attempts to eliminate entirely the extra inflation caused by the supply shock.[5] This requires cutting nominal GNP growth by enough to take the economy to point M, where the inflation rate is 6 percent, but the output ratio has fallen from 100 to 94 percent (instead of to 98 percent at point L). Why is the extra four-point decline in the output ratio necessary? To "extinguish" the extra two percentage points of inflation that occur at L compared to M, the output ratio must be cut by four percentage points, since the slope of the SP line is assumed to be 1/2 (two units in a vertical direction for each four units in the horizontal direction).

What Happens in Subsequent Periods

If the hypothetical supply shock occurs for just one period, then in Figure 10-5 the SP line shifts down to its original position (SP_2) after one period at position SP_3. The economy would then be free to return to the original output ratio and the original inflation rate. All that would remain of the effect of the supply shock would be its "direct" effect in reducing natural real GNP and raising the price level. The "indirect" effect on the output ratio (Q/Q^N) and on the rate of inflation would last for just one period.

But the SP curve returns to position SP_2 *only if the expected inflation rate remains at 6 percent.* The expected inflation rate must not respond to the one-period increase in the actual inflation rate that occurs at points L and N in Figure 10-5. Is this plausible? The response of the expected inflation rate depends on whether labor contracts incorporate cost-of-living agreements.

Why are COLAs crucial? Without COLAs, contract negotiators will recognize that it is possible for the economy to return to its original position (point E_3 in Figure 10-5) after the one-period effect of the supply shock. But with COLAs, the one-period increase of inflation (to point L or N) will be incorporated automatically into a faster growth of nominal wage rates *next period.* Contract negotiators in subsequent periods will see that COLAs have raised the rate of change of the nominal wage and will realize that this makes it impossible for the economy to return to point E_3. Their expected rate of inflation will shift up above the original 6 percent, and the SP curve will shift to a position above the original SP_2 in subsequent periods.

The policy dilemma. Thus once again we see that COLAs create a dilemma for the makers of monetary policy. In Figure 10-3, we saw that COLAs introduce real wage rigidity that reduces natural real GNP. Now we see that COLAs imply that a permanent supply shock will permanently raise the inflation rate *unless an extinguishing policy response to the initial impact of the supply shock prevents any increase at all of inflation and thus prevents any increase at all in the rate of change of nominal wage rates.*

---

[5]The phrase *extinguishing policy* was introduced in Edward M. Gramlich, "Macro Policy Responses to Price Shocks," *Brookings Papers on Economic Activity,* vol. 10, no. 1 (1979), pp. 125–178.

What should the Fed do when faced with this dilemma? It faces the classic trade-off between inflation and lost output. With even partial COLA protection for workers, a permanent adverse supply shock will permanently raise the inflation rate in the absence of an extinguishing policy. But this does not mean that the Fed should actually pursue such an extinguishing policy. The social costs of the loss in output may be severe, as Q/Q^N declines to point M in Figure 10-5, while the social costs of permanently higher inflation following a neutral or accommodating policy response may be relatively small. We turn in the next chapter to the social costs of lost output, unemployment, and inflation.

Effects of Favorable Supply Shocks

We have seen how the responses of inflation and real GNP to adverse supply shocks depend on the actions of policymakers. Exactly the same analysis can be used to predict the effects of a favorable supply shock, one that causes the SP curve to shift downward. Just as a crop failure or freeze in Florida can shift SP up, so bumper crops that lower relative farm prices could shift SP down. As an example of a much more important beneficial supply shock, in 1986 the SP curve shifted down as a result of a significant downward shift in the real price of oil (shown in the bottom frame of Figure 10-1). Another factor that can cause SP to shift downward is a freeze of wages and prices like that instituted by the Nixon administration from August 15, 1971 to April 1974. While the controls were not successful on a permanent basis, they did have the effect of temporarily holding down prices. A beneficial supply shock shifts SP downward.

The effect of a favorable supply shock can be interpreted with the help of Figure 10-6. The decline from SP_2 to SP_4 reflects the assumption that the favorable supply shock *reduces inflation by 3 percent at each level of real*

Figure 10-6

Effect on Inflation and Real GNP of a Favorable Supply Stock That Shifts the *SP* Line Down by Three Percentage Points

The economy is assumed to start at point E_3, with an initial output ratio = 100, expected inflation equal to nominal GNP growth (6 percent), and an initial inflation rate of 6 percent. If the *SP* line is shifted down by three percentage points by a favorable supply shock, the economy goes in the next period to point L' on the assumption that nominal GNP growth remains at 6 percent. If an accommodating demand growth reduction is chosen by policymakers, the economy goes to N', whereas an "extinguishing" policy that boosts demand growth enough to move the economy to M' can eliminate all of the price-reducing effects of the beneficial shock.

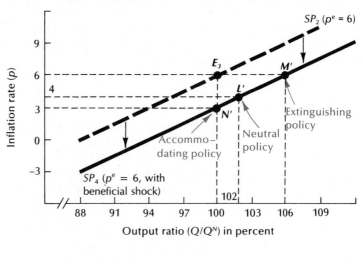

"GOOD SHOCKS" CAN REDUCE INFLATION WHILE RAISING REAL GNP

GNP. Our entire analysis of adverse supply shocks remains valid for this case of a "favorable supply shock," except that *everything happens in reverse*. If nominal GNP growth is held at the original 6 percent rate then the economy will move from E_3 to L'. If policymakers want to avoid this increase in the output ratio, nominal GNP growth can be reduced by three percentage points. This would shift the economy down to point N'. Policymakers can also "extinguish" the beneficial effects of the shock by boosting nominal GNP growth, as at M'. Events in subsequent periods depend on the duration of the favorable shock and the prevalence of COLA clauses, just as in the case of an adverse shock.[6]

SELF-TEST
> Imagine that the relative price of oil falls by half within a single year and exhibits no change thereafter. Under what circumstances will the inflation rate be reduced by this event in the year of the change? Thereafter?

10-6 Price Controls: Their Temporary Appeal and Their Permanent Damage

The Appeal of Price Controls

We learned in the last chapter that one cure for inflation is a recession that may last from several years to a decade. Because a recession is painful, it is not surprising that some economists and politicians periodically turn to price controls as a "way out." The Nixon administration turned to controls in frustration at the failure of the 1970 recession to achieve any significant slowing of inflation.

Controls are not a new idea. The Roman Emperor Diocletian imposed a comprehensive control program in A.D. 301. Offenders who violated the edict by charging prices or paying wages differing from those decreed by the emperor were sentenced to death! The program was abandoned as a failure after thirteen years. The United States had a comprehensive and compulsory system of wage and price controls during World War II, a more limited system during the Korean War, a period of voluntary wage-price guidelines in the Kennedy and Johnson administrations during 1962–66, and, finally, a full-fledged control program in the Nixon administration between August 1971 and April 1974.

In the example of Figure 10-6, price controls work just like a favorable supply shock in shifting down the *SP* schedule. But if expectations do not adjust downward, then the termination of price controls will cause a rebound in the price level. Thus the long-run success of controls depends on an adjustment of expectations that may not occur. Because there is a long historical record that price controls are abandoned sooner or later, expectations may fail to adjust because people *expect the controls to fail*. They hold this expectation because policymakers have rarely slowed down nominal GNP growth by as much as the controls shift down the *SP* curve.

[6]The analysis of supply shocks in this chapter was introduced in two papers. See Robert J. Gordon, "Alternative Responses of Policy to External Supply Shocks," *Brookings Papers on Economic Activity*, vol. 6, no. 1 (1975), pp. 183–206, and Edmund S. Phelps, "Commodity Supply Shocks and Full-Employment Monetary Policy," *Journal of Money, Credit, and Banking*, vol. 10 (May 1978), pp. 206–221.

The Case Against Price Controls

Controls cause shortages. If controls could reduce the growth rate of all wages and prices by the same percentage, without having any effect on the flexibility of relative prices or relative real wages, they would not be so harmful. But the relative prices of different products and the real wages of different groups of workers are continually changing as the private market-place uses the price system to allocate resources. Because government officials running the control program cannot possibly know how relative prices and real wages would be moving each day in the absence of controls, the controls prevent prices from moving sufficiently to equate supply and demand, thus leading to shortages when the price is held too low. The danger of shortages of products or labor skills is the chief argument against controls.

Effects of the 1971–74 price control program. We shall see in the case study in the next section that the controls program failed to reduce inflation permanently and destabilized the economy, aggravating the real GNP boom of 1972 and deepening the recession of 1974–75. But the harm done by the controls program goes further than this. By preventing relative price adjustments during the 1971–72 period, the controls program caused shortages of several products to develop.

Controls on the price of lumber in 1972 began to curtail the supply of lumber and caused sawmills to shut down operations. Shortages of molasses, fertilizer, and logs appeared because higher world prices pulled domestic supplies abroad while domestic producers were forbidden from raising prices within the United States. Reinforcing steel bars fell under the controls, but the steel scrap used in making the bars was excluded from the controls and shot up in price, squeezing the profits of the makers of steel bars, causing their production to shrink, and interfering with construction projects. Baling wire used by farmers to bundle crops also was in short supply because steel companies found that they were losing $100 on every ton of baling wire at the low controlled price.[7]

10-7   *CASE STUDY:*   Supply Shocks and the U.S. Economy
Since 1971

Inflation Triggers Recession, 1971–76   In mid-1976 the *New York Times* announced "A New Theory: Inflation Triggers Recession."[8] This idea is familiar to readers of the previous sections. Any upward shift in *SP*, whether caused by an upward revision in the expected rate of inflation, by the termination of price controls, or by a supply shock, can both raise the actual inflation rate and trigger a recession as long as nominal GNP growth (*y*) is held constant by monetary and fiscal policymakers.

---

[7]These examples are from C. Jackson Grayson, "Controls Are Not the Answer," *Challenge* (November/December 1974), pp. 9–12; and Walter Guzzardi, Jr., "What We Should Have Learned about Controls," *Fortune,* (March 1975), p. 105.

[8]*New York Times,* July 18, 1976, Section F 13.

Data relationships. Data for the period since 1971 are displayed in Table 10-1. To adjust for the growth rate of natural real GNP (q^N), the identity[9]

$$y \equiv p + q \tag{10.1}$$

is replaced by a new identity obtained by subtracting q^N from both sides of (10.1), implying the new identity:

$$y - q^N \equiv p + q - q^N \tag{10.2}$$

In words, equation (10.2) states that the *excess* of nominal GNP growth (y) above natural real GNP growth (q^N) is equal to the inflation rate (p) plus the *excess* of real GNP growth (q) above natural real GNP growth (q^N).

When the excess real GNP growth rate ($q - q^N$) is positive, the *level* of the output ratio (Q/Q^N) exhibits an increase. The real output of the economy is growing faster than the "natural" growth rate of real output that is consistent with a constant unemployment rate. In this situation the *unemployment rate is decreasing.* In contrast a negative excess real GNP growth rate ($q - q^N$) implies a decline in the output ratio (Q/Q^N) and *an increase in the unemployment rate.*

The first three columns of Table 10-1 provide data on the components of equation (10.2) for each year since 1971. In expansion years like 1972 and 1987, for instance, excess nominal GNP growth ($y - q^N$) exceeded the inflation rate (p), resulting in positive excess real GNP growth ($q - q^N$). In these and all other years when excess real GNP growth was positive, the level of the output ratio in column (4) increased from its value in the previous year. In contrast, recession years like 1974 and 1982 had excess nominal GNP growth rates below the inflation rate, resulting in *negative* excess real GNP growth ($q - q^N$) and a *decline* in the level of the output ratio from the previous year.

Data on supply shocks: food and energy inflation. The next two columns in Table 10-1 display the growth rates of two price indexes that show the effect of supply shocks. These are the real price deflators for food and energy shown in columns (5) and (6). An adverse supply shock occurs when the change in the real price deflator for food or energy is positive, and a beneficial supply shock occurs when these changes are negative. Adverse supply shocks occurred in years like 1974 and 1979, when there was "double-digit" growth of the real energy deflator in column (6). There was also growth in the real food deflator that almost reached double digits in 1973. A beneficial supply shock occurred in 1986, when the real energy deflator fell by 21 percent.

A convenient measure of the importance of supply shocks is provided by the *difference* between the growth rate of the "total" deflator for consumption expenditures, column (7) and of the "net" consumption deflator that *excludes* expenditures on food and energy, column (8). This difference between columns (7) and (8) is shown separately as the "food-energy effect" in column (9). Notice that substantial positive values of the food-en-

---

[9]In words, equation (10.1) states that nominal GNP growth (y) equals inflation (p) plus real GNP growth (q).

TABLE 10-1   **Nominal GNP Growth, Inflation, and Supply Shocks, 1971–88**

Four quarters ending in	Annual growth rates[b]			Level of output ratio (Q/Q^N)	Annual growth rates				
	$y - q^N$	p	$q - q^N$		Real[b] food deflator	Real[b] energy deflator	Total consumption deflator	Net consumption deflator	Food-energy effect
	(1)	(2)	(3)	(4)	(5)	(6)	(7)	(8)	(9)
1971:Q2	5.6	5.9	−0.2	98.4	0.3	−0.1	3.7	3.7	0.0
1972:Q4[a]	8.0	4.3	3.6	102.0	1.7	−0.4	3.5	3.1	0.4
1973:Q4	7.8	7.9	0.0	102.0	8.9	4.6	6.9	4.4	2.6
1974:Q4	3.9	9.5	−5.6	96.4	0.5	12.4	9.8	8.7	1.1
1975:Q4	7.2	8.0	−0.8	95.7	−0.2	4.5	6.5	6.1	0.4
1976:Q4	6.5	5.6	0.8	96.4	−4.4	0.2	4.9	6.2	−1.3
1977:Q4	8.3	6.6	1.8	98.2	−0.7	0.3	6.3	6.4	−0.1
1978:Q4	10.9	7.7	3.2	101.4	3.4	0.0	7.3	6.4	0.9
1979:Q4	6.3	8.5	−2.1	99.2	−0.8	20.4	9.3	7.4	1.9
1980:Q4	7.1	9.4	−2.4	96.9	−0.4	7.8	10.0	9.1	0.9
1981:Q4	6.6	8.3	−1.7	95.2	−2.6	3.8	7.6	7.9	−0.3
1982:Q4	0.8	5.0	−4.2	91.3	−1.4	−2.8	4.7	5.6	−0.9
1983:Q4	7.5	3.6	4.0	95.0	−1.3	−4.2	3.9	4.7	−0.8
1984:Q4	5.9	3.4	2.6	97.5	0.2	−3.0	3.6	3.9	−0.3
1985:Q4	4.1	2.9	1.2	98.7	−1.3	−2.6	3.7	4.2	−0.5
1986:Q4	2.3	2.7	−0.4	98.3	1.6	−21.4	2.4	4.1	−1.7
1987:Q4	5.7	3.1	2.6	100.9	−1.2	3.2	4.9	4.9	0.0
1988:Q4	4.6	4.2	0.4	101.4	0.9	−4.3	4.3	4.5	−0.2

[a]Growth rates shown are annual rates for the six quarters ending in 1972:Q4.
[b]Real food and energy deflators are the respective nominal deflators divided by the total consumption deflator.

ergy effect were registered in 1973–74 and 1978–80. These are the *adverse* supply shocks that afflicted the U.S. economy. *Beneficial* supply shocks in the form of negative food-energy effects occurred in 1976 and in each year between 1981 and 1986.

The following sections discuss the major features of the economy since 1971 and refer to the data in Table 10-1. To illustrate the relationship between the actual events and the theory, some of the data in Table 10-1 are also displayed for the 1971–76 period in Figure 10-7.

Prosperity and Price Controls, 1971–73

The main features of the early 1970s are evident in the first three columns of Table 10-1. Both excess nominal GNP growth and inflation accelerated in 1971–73, but in 1974 inflation accelerated further while excess nominal GNP growth $(y - q^N)$ declined sharply, resulting in an abrupt drop in the

Figure 10-7
The Output Ratio and the Inflation Rate, both Including and Excluding Food and Energy Prices, 1971–77

The black line traces the relation between the real GNP ratio (Q/Q^N) and inflation, excluding food and energy prices. Notice the southeast movement in 1971–72, when prices were controlled, and the northwest movement in 1974, when controls were terminated. The upper red line shows total inflation, including food and energy prices, and the pink area measures the impact on inflation of food and energy prices between early 1973 and early 1975. *(Source: National Income and Product Accounts, 1982 revision, Table 7.2.)*

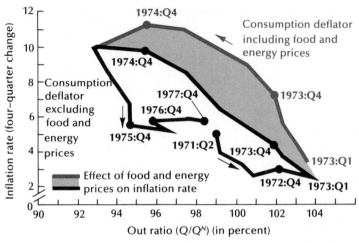

THE NEGATIVE RELATION BETWEEN INFLATION AND REAL GNP IN THE 1970s

output ratio (Q/Q^N). A basic source of accelerating inflation in 1973–74 is shown in columns (5) and (6) of Table 10-1, where it is evident that a dramatic increase in the real deflators for food and energy dominated this period.

Figure 10-7 has the same vertical and horizontal axes as the theoretical diagrams Figures 10-5 and 10-6. It allows us to examine some of the characteristics of the early 1970s for the inflation rate and the output ratio. The 1970s began with the comprehensive program of wage and price controls, introduced by the Nixon administration on August 15, 1971.

We can interpret the effect of the Nixon controls with the help of Figure 10-6, which shows a downward movement of the *SP* curve in response to a favorable supply shock. Recall that the economy's direction of movement after the imposition of controls depends on the actions of policymakers; the economy moves straight down with an accommodating policy (point N' in Figure 10-6), to the southeast with a neutral policy (point L'), and straight east with an extinguishing policy (point M').

The real-world economy depicted in Figure 10-7 at first moved southeast, from the point marked 1971:Q2 (the second quarter of 1971, the last "precontrol" quarter) until the middle of 1972 and then straight east until early 1973. The fact that the economy moved so far to the right in Figure 10-7 can be explained by the "extinguishing" nominal GNP growth policy followed during 1972 and 1973, with *such an acceleration of nominal GNP growth that inflation fell very little despite the controls.* In turn, rapid nominal GNP growth can be attributed to the rapid growth in the money supply that the Fed allowed in 1972–73.

The First Round of Supply Shocks, 1973–75

The end of controls in May 1974 contributed to high inflation in 1974–75 as firms tried to reestablish the no-controls level of prices.[10] Figure 10-7 separates the effect of price controls and their removal from the separate supply shock caused by the increase in the relative prices of food and energy. This is done by plotting two lines between early 1973 and early 1975. The continuous black loop shows the relation between the (Q/Q^N) ratio on the horizontal axis and the rate of inflation of consumer prices *excluding consumer expenditures on food and energy*. This rate is also shown in column (7) of Table 10-1. If the real prices of food and energy had remained constant, then the black line would show total inflation as well.

But 1973 and 1974 were years of dramatic jumps in the real prices of food and energy. As a result the total inflation rate, shown by the red line in Figure 10-7, considerably exceeded the inflation rate excluding food and energy products. The pink area shows the contribution of food and energy prices to overall inflation. This is the "food-energy effect," also shown in Table 10-1, column (9). We conclude that inflation would have accelerated in 1974 anyway as a result of the termination of controls, but that the food and oil supply shocks aggravated considerably this acceleration.

The year 1976 brought relief from supply shocks. There was no further increase in the relative price of energy during 1976, while the relative price of food actually dropped. And the temporary price-boosting effect of the termination of controls had ended. By late 1977 the economy had returned almost exactly to where it was in 1971:Q2, with about the same output ratio (Q/Q^N), and with about one percentage point additional inflation.

Supply Shocks Strike Again, 1978–81

The behavior of the U.S. economy after 1977 mirrored some of the main elements of the early 1970s. Once again supply shocks in 1978–81 caused inflation to accelerate and the output ratio to fall, as had occurred in 1973–74. Once again the supply shocks subsided after 1981, as had occurred after 1975. And the first and second supply shock episodes were roughly equal in size. We can see this in column (9) of Table 10-1, where the "food-energy effect" sums up to 4.1 percent in 1973–75 and to a similar 3.7 percent in 1978–80.

Differences between the first and second supply-shock episodes. But there were differences. *One important difference was the absence of price controls in the late 1970s.* Thus a major element that had contributed to the instability of inflation and the output ratio during 1971–75 was not repeated in 1978–81. A second difference was that there was a much more prolonged recession during and after the 1978–81 supply shock. This can

---

[10]For a quantitative assessment that distinguishes between the influence of the controls and the high output ratio, see Robert J. Gordon, "Can the Inflation of the 1970s Be Explained?" *Brookings Papers on Economic Activity,* vol. 8, no. 1 (1977), pp. 253–277. A more detailed treatment is Alan S. Blinder, *Economic Policy and the Great Stagflation* (New York: Academic Press, 1979).

be seen in the first three columns of Table 10-1. By maintaining a restrictive monetary policy, the Fed managed to keep excess nominal GNP growth $(y - q^N)$ below the inflation rate for four straight years, 1979–82. As a result, the output ratio (Q/Q^N) fell steadily from a peak of 101.4 percent in 1978:Q4 to a trough of 91.3 percent four years later, in 1982:Q4. In contrast, excess nominal GNP growth was held below the inflation rate for a shorter period in 1974–75.

A third difference between the first and second supply shocks was that the economy had only temporary relief in 1975–77 after the first supply-shock period. But the aftermath to the second supply-shock period lasted much longer, with a decline in the real price of energy that began modestly during 1982–85 but then became very sharp in 1986.

The Beneficial Oil Shock in 1986

The high price of oil in the early 1980s both reduced the demand for oil and stimulated the search for new supplies. Britain, Norway, Mexico, and many other producers outside of the Arab world raised their production of oil. For a while, during 1982–85, Saudi Arabia acted to prevent the drop in demand and increase in supply from causing the price of oil to collapse by cutting back on its production. But by early 1986 this cutback had gone too far, depriving the Saudi Arabian government of much revenue, and the Saudis raised production. At this point the price of oil fell almost by half, from $28 to about $15 per barrel.[11]

The sudden and sharp decline in the price of oil in early 1986 created a beneficial supply shock. As shown in the first three columns of Table 10-1, excess nominal GNP growth was relatively low during 1986. This slow growth in demand was largely a result of the decline in net exports caused by the previous 1980–85 appreciation of the dollar (we studied this episode previously in an earlier case study, Section 5-9). In this sense the beneficial supply shock was initially "accommodated," allowing all of its beneficial effect to take the form of a reduced inflation rate.

But then the economy caught its "second wind," as the falling dollar of 1985–87 stimulated net exports. As a result, excess nominal GNP growth more than doubled from 1986 to 1987–88. The output ratio exceeded 100 percent in 1988–89, and the inflation rate had accelerated by mid-1989 to the fastest rate observed since the early 1980s.[12] Inflation wound up higher in 1989 than it had been prior to the beneficial 1986 supply shock, largely because rapid excess nominal GNP growth had the effect of "extinguishing" the beneficial impact of the supply shock on the inflation rate.

---

[11]The collapse in the oil price was predicted several years in advance in Arlon R. Tussing, "An OPEC Obituary," *The Public Interest*, no. 70 (Winter 1983), pp. 3–21. This article also contains a short but fascinating history explaining why the price of oil was so low before 1973, and the process by which the OPEC cartel was formed.

[12]The acceleration of the inflation rate is particularly evident in the fixed-weight consumption deflator in Table 10-1, column (7). The implicit GNP deflator in column (2) accelerates less than the fixed-weight consumption deflator in column (7) or the fixed-weight GNP deflator plotted in Figure 9-11. This occurs largely as a result of a measurement error caused by the overweighting of electronic computer prices in the implicit deflator but not the fixed-weight deflator. See Martin N. Baily and Robert J. Gordon, "Measurement Issues, the Productivity Slowdown, and the Explosion of Computer Power," *Brookings Papers on Economic Activity*, vol. 19, no. 2, especially pp. 386–88.

10-8 Inflation and Output Fluctuations: Recapitulation of Causes and Cures

At the beginning of the book we introduced six puzzles of macroeconomic behavior. The first two puzzles were a high and variable rate of unemployment, and a high and variable rate of inflation. We learned early in the book that fluctuations in unemployment are a direct mirror image of fluctuations in the output ratio (Q/Q^N). In the past two chapters we have been engaged in an analysis of the interrelations between the inflation rate and the output ratio (Q/Q^N), and in so doing we have gained a considerable understanding of our first two macroeconomic puzzles. We have learned that an acceleration of inflation can be caused by excessive nominal GNP growth and by supply shocks. Supply and demand inflation are interrelated because the extent and duration of the acceleration of inflation following a supply shock depends on the response of nominal GNP growth, which is controlled in part by policymakers.

A Summary of Inflation and Output Responses

Figure 10-8 provides a highly simplified summary of our analysis in Chapters 9 and 10. Four cases are presented, corresponding to (a) demand shifts alone, (b) supply shifts alone, (c) demand and supply shifts in the same vertical direction, and (d) demand and supply shifts in the opposite vertical direction. In our discussion, we identify examples from U.S. history during 1963–86 that illustrate the four cases.

Case (a): Demand shifts alone. When we observe a marked increase in the output ratio with a modest or small increase in the rate of inflation, we can infer that there has been an acceleration of nominal aggregate demand growth with little if any shift in the *SP* curve. Expectations of inflation (p^e) remain roughly constant, and there are no supply shocks. The economy exhibited this type of response during 1963–66, when tax cuts and the beginning of Vietnam War spending, supported by monetary accommodation, boosted nominal GNP growth. A similar movement to the northeast occurred in 1987–89. An example of a shift in a southwestern direction, with a deceleration of nominal GNP growth, occurred in the first few quarters of the 1981–82 recession, when there was a sharp decline in Q/Q^N with little downward response of the inflation rate.

Case (b): Supply shifts alone. The United States experienced a straight northwestward movement in 1973–74, when food and energy supply shocks sharply boosted the inflation rate, with a relatively small change in the rate of nominal GNP growth. As a result the inflation rate and the output ratio (Q/Q^N) moved in opposite directions and by about the same amount. Between 1978:Q4 and 1980:Q4 a second supply shock had roughly the same impact. The only example of a southeastward movement occurred during the first few months of the Nixon price control period in late 1971, when the rate of inflation fell without much change in nominal GNP growth.

A SUMMARY OF INFLATION AND OUTPUT RESPONSES

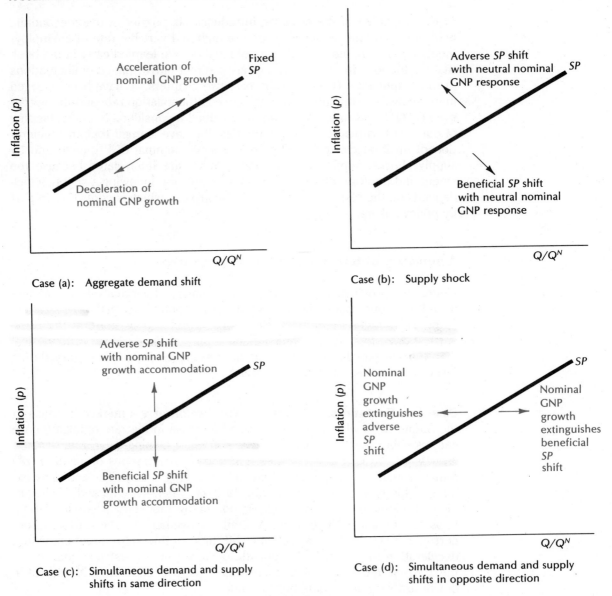

Case (a): Aggregate demand shift

Case (b): Supply shock

Case (c): Simultaneous demand and supply
shifts in same direction

Case (d): Simultaneous demand and supply
shifts in opposite direction

Figure 10-8 **Responses of the Inflation Rate (p) and the Output Ratio (Q/Q^N) to Shifts in Nominal GNP Growth and in the SP Curve**

In Case (a) an aggregate demand shift moves the economy to the southwest or northeast if there is no supply shift. In Case (b) a supply shift moves the economy to the northwest or southeast when nominal GNP growth is unchanged (a "neutral" policy response). Case (c) illustrates the northward or southward movement that occurs with an accommodative policy response to a supply shift. Case (d) illustrates the westward or eastward movement that accompanies a supply shift with an extinguishing supply response.

Case (c): Demand and supply shifts in the same vertical direction.
When we observe the economy move straight north on the diagram, with an acceleration of inflation but little change in the output ratio, we can infer that there is a simultaneous demand and supply shift. For instance, between 1967 and 1969 nominal GNP growth accelerated while the *SP* curve shifted upward in response to accelerating inflationary expectations (p^e). As a result inflation accelerated while the output ratio remained constant. The economy made a small southward movement in the first few quarters after the beneficial 1986 oil shock.

Case (d): Demand and supply shifts in the opposite vertical direction. The economy can move straight to the right when nominal GNP growth accelerates and cancels out the effect of a downward *SP* shift. This occurred in 1972, when the effect of the Nixon price controls program in holding down the inflation rate was offset by rapid nominal GNP growth. A leftward movement can occur when nominal GNP growth decelerates while the *SP* curve is shifting upward. This occurred during the 1969–70 recession, when nominal GNP growth slowed, while the *SP* curve was shifting upward as the expected inflation rate (p^e) continued its slow and delayed adjustment to the acceleration of actual inflation during 1966–69. This interpretation helps us understand why inflation in early 1971 was still as rapid as in 1969 despite an intervening decline in the output ratio.

SELF-TEST In Figure 10-8, which plots the inflation rate against the output ratio, it is possible for the economy to move in any direction. Can you explain why the economy would move in each possible direction: north? northeast? east? and so on for each other possible direction?

Cures for Inflation

Just as excessive nominal GNP growth and adverse supply shocks are the fundamental causes of inflation, the basic cure for inflation is to turn these causes on their head. The reverse of fast nominal GNP growth is obviously slow nominal GNP growth. A decision to reduce the inflation rate by restricting the growth rate of nominal GNP can be both effective and costly, as the nation learned in 1981–82. Inflation can be cut markedly, but only at the cost of a substantial and prolonged slump in the output ratio and a substantial increase in the number of jobless workers.

But government policy against inflation is not limited to creating a deceleration of nominal GNP growth. Whether there are adverse supply shocks or not, the government can attempt to create beneficial supply shocks. We learned in Section 10-6 that price controls act like beneficial supply shocks but have undesirable side effects and are unlikely to be effective for more than a short time. Instead, the government might create beneficial supply shocks by eliminating or weakening price-raising or cost-raising legislation, and by creative tax and subsidy policy.

Such cost-cutting government policies were recommended as a method of reducing the inflation rate *without* the massive loss of output and extra amount of unemployment that the economy actually experienced after 1981. Instead, government cost-cutting policies could have been used to shift the

SP curve downward, while restrictive aggregate demand policy could have been used to reduce the growth rate of nominal GNP and shift down the *DG* line at the same speed. By *coordinating* cost-cutting supply policies with aggregate demand policies, a disinflation could have been engineered without a substantial loss in output. On our basic diagram in Figure 10-8, the economy would have experienced a straight southward movement like that in case (c).[13]

Obviously, coordinated policies were not undertaken. Instead, a "cold turkey" policy of restricting nominal GNP growth pushed the economy to the southwest, not to the south. But we can speculate with the benefit of hindsight that a coordinated cost-cutting and demand restriction policy might have been successful. A key ingredient in the argument for a coordinated policy is the behavior of oil prices, as shown in Figure 10-1. Initially when OPEC raised the price of oil in 1973–74 and 1979–80, there was little adjustment of energy usage, but the movement toward conservation and efficiency gradually gained momentum as consumers invested in energy-saving devices and new automobiles. As a result, the real price of oil dipped substantially after the second OPEC oil shock. Thus substantial progress toward curing inflation would have occurred automatically after 1981 *through the partial unwinding of the 1979–80 oil shock.* Even without the cold turkey recession, the real price of oil would have declined under the pressure of greater efficiency and falling demand for energy relative to real GNP. This would have shifted the *SP* curve down, and nominal GNP growth could have slowed in tandem.

10-9 *CASE STUDY:* The Divergence of Unemployment Rates in the United States and Europe

The behavior of U.S. inflation and the output ratio seems to be well explained by the theory developed in Chapters 9 and 10. The disinflation experienced by the United States during 1982–86, and the reacceleration of inflation during 1987–89 both follow the predictions of our theory. As we shall see in the next chapter, the U.S. unemployment rate also behaves predictably, rising above 6 percent when the output ratio falls below 100 percent, and vice versa. The U.S. unemployment rate fell from a peak of 10.7 percent in late 1982 to slightly above 5 percent in early 1989.

But the behavior of European unemployment is another story. As shown in the top frame of Figure 10-9, unemployment in Europe has stayed close to 10 percent since 1984, falling only slightly in 1988–89, and has exhibited nothing like the decline in unemployment enjoyed by the United States. For five straight years, from 1984–88, 18 million Europeans were out of work. And, unlike the short duration of most U.S. unemployment, European unemployment is long-lasting and therefore much more serious. *In*

---

[13]Coordinated supply and demand policies to reduce the inflation rate are examined at length in Arthur M. Okun, *Prices and Quantities: A Macroeconomic Analysis* (Washington, D.C.: Brookings Institution, 1981), Chapter 8. Okun's position is similar to that taken in this section, except that this author does not share Okun's enthusiasm for tax-based incomes policies nor the extent of his concern that inflation should be reduced to a zero rate.

WHY DID UNEMPLOYMENT RISE IN EUROPE BUT FALL IN THE U.S.?

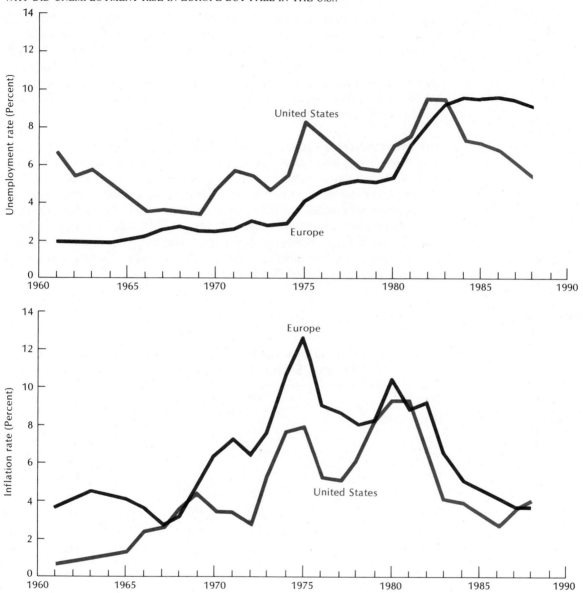

Figure 10-9 **Unemployment and Inflation Rates, United States and Europe, 1961–89**

The top frame exhibits the unemployment rates for the United States and Europe. In 1989 the U.S. unemployment rate was about the same as in the early 1960s, but the European unemployment rate was almost five times higher. The bottom frame shows that the inflation rate in Europe has behaved similarly to that in the United States since 1970 but has averaged about 2.5 percentage points higher. Finally in 1989 the European inflation rate fell below that in the United States for the first time since 1968.

many European countries more than half of the unemployed have been out of work for more than one year.

Table 10-2 displays historical unemployment data for individual European countries. Here two remarkable facts stand out. First, the average unemployment rate for the "Eleven European Countries" has increased steadily, from 1.9 percent in 1961, to 3.0 percent in 1972, to 5.0 percent in 1979, to 8.8 percent in 1989 (after reaching nearly 10 percent in 1986). Second, unemployment rates vary among the individual European countries, ranging in 1989 all the way from a minuscle 0.8 percent in Switzerland to 12.5 percent in the Netherlands.

The great American job machine.   Nothing stirs more envy in Europe than reference to the "great American job machine," the accomplishment of the U.S. economy in creating 16.7 million new jobs from 1980 to the end of 1988. Over the same period Europe, with a substantially larger working-age population, created only 3 million new jobs. Part of America's achievement, to be sure, occurred because its higher birth rate and more immigration increased the working-age population. But the reduction of the U. S. unemployment rate by half since the 1982 peak is also responsible for rapid job growth in the United States.

Table 10-2   **Unemployment Rates in North America, Japan, and Europe, Selected Years, 1961–89**

Country	1961	1972	1979	1986	1989
United States	6.7	5.5	5.8	7.0	5.3
Canada	7.1	6.2	7.4	9.6	7.8
Japan	1.4	1.4	2.1	2.8	2.3
Eleven European countries	1.9	3.0	5.0	9.8	8.7
France	1.2	2.7	5.9	10.4	10.0
Germany	0.8	0.8	3.2	8.0	7.5
Italy	5.1	6.3	7.6	10.3	11.0
United Kingdom	1.5	4.0	5.0	11.7	7.0
Austria	1.9	1.2	2.1	3.1	3.3
Belgium	2.1	2.7	8.2	11.3	9.5
Denmark	1.4	0.9	5.4	7.8	9.5
Netherlands	0.7	3.1	5.4	13.2	12.5
Norway	1.5	1.7	2.0	2.0	4.3
Sweden	1.4	2.7	2.1	2.2	1.5
Switzerland	0.0	0.0	0.3	0.7	0.8

Sources: All data are OECD "standardized unemployment rate" definitions and are from Robert J. Gordon, "Back to the Future: European Unemployment Today Viewed from America in 1939," *Brookings Papers on Economic Activity,* vol. 19, (1988, no. 1), Table 1, p. 275, except data for 1989 are OECD projections from *OECD Economic Outlook,* June 1989, Tables 41 and 42.

Chapter 10 / Supply Disturbances and Responses

European Inflation and the Natural Rate Hypothesis

If the United States and Europe had the same natural rate of unemployment, then we would expect that the high level of European unemployment would have caused inflation in Europe to slow down much more than in the United States. But this has not happened. Between 1980 and 1986, European inflation slowed down by about the same amount as in the United States. Only in 1987–89 did Europe's inflation behave differently, settling down at about 3.5 percent and avoiding the reacceleration displayed by the U.S. inflation rate. Yet according to the natural rate hypothesis, when there are no supply shocks, a steady rate of inflation like that experienced by Europe in 1987–89 occurs only when the economy is operating at its natural rate of unemployment.

Thus in 1987–89 the natural rate of unemployment in Europe must have been the same as the actual rate of unemployment, about 9 to 9.5 percent. Yet inflation was also steady in Europe in the early 1960s, when the actual unemployment rate was just 2 percent. Thus steady inflation in 1987–89 appears to imply that Europe is "stuck" at a high natural rate of unemployment of about 9 percent, fully 4.5 times higher than the 2 percent natural unemployment rate of the early 1960s. The mystery of high European unemployment can be summarized in this puzzle: *How could the natural rate of unemployment have quadrupled in Europe since the early 1960s, while in the United States it hardly changed at all?*[14]

10-10 New Theories to Explain High European Unemployment

The **structuralist hypothesis** holds that European unemployment is high because of specific impediments in the operation of the economy, including excessive real wages, high unemployment benefits, excessive government spending and regulation, high marginal tax rates, regional imbalances, and others.

The **hysteresis hypothesis** holds that the natural rate of unemployment follows automatically in the path of the actual unemployment rate; if the actual rate were lowered by stimulative policy, the natural rate would also decline automatically.

The puzzle of high unemployment in Europe has stimulated an outpouring of new theories of inflation and unemployment behavior. In this brief introduction we look at the two main competing explanations, the **structuralist** and **hysteresis** hypotheses.[15] The structuralist hypothesis holds that European unemployment is high because specific impediments in the operation of the economy, particularly the labor market, have raised the natural unemployment rate. Among these structural causes of the high natural rate are excessive real wages, high unemployment benefits, excessive government spending and regulation, high marginal tax rates, and regional imbalances. Because the natural unemployment rate is high as a result of particular

---

[14]The natural rate of unemployment for the United States is plotted at the beginning of the book in Figure 1-5. Historical data are provided in Appendix A.

[15]The most complete assessment of the structuralist hypothesis is Robert Z. Lawrence and Charles L. Schultze, eds. *Barriers to European Growth: A Transatlantic View* (Washington: Brookings, 1987). The most widely cited paper introducing the hysteresis interpretation is Olivier J. Blanchard and Lawrence H. Summers, "Hysteresis and the European Unemployment Problem," in S. Fischer, ed., *NBER Macroeconomics Annual 1986,* pp. 15–77. The two views are compared, with an application to the experience of the U. S. in the late 1930s, in Robert J. Gordon, "Back to the Future: European Unemployment Today Viewed from America in 1939," *Brookings Papers on Economic Activity,* vol. 19 (1988, no. 1), pp. 271–304.

causes, the actual unemployment rate cannot be reduced without either (1) an accelerating inflation or (2) changes in government policy that eliminate the structural impediments.

The hysteresis hypothesis holds that the natural rate of unemployment follows automatically in the path of the actual unemployment rate; if the actual rate were lowered by stimulative policy, the natural rate would automatically decline as well. The hysteresis view shares the prediction of the structuralist view that stimulative demand policy designed to reduce the actual unemployment rate will cause inflation to accelerate. But it is more optimistic than the structuralist view because it believes that the resulting acceleration of inflation will end after the economy settles down to a new and lower level of unemployment. In contrast, the structuralist view holds that inflation will accelerate forever if unemployment is allowed to decline from its current level.

The Structuralist and Hysteresis Views in Pictures

Both views agree that Europe is today operating at its natural unemployment rate. What they disagree about is the cause of the high natural rate and its implications for the future: will stimulative demand policy cause inflation to accelerate forever, or not? Figure 10-10 depicts the basic idea of both views, with the structuralist interpretation on the left and the hysteresis view on the right. Unemployment is plotted in the top frame and inflation in the lower frame, just as in Figure 10-9. In all frames three time periods are marked out. Time "t_0" marks a point in the past, the end of the period of decelerating inflation, "t_1" is the current period ("now"), and "t_2" is a hypothetical future period.

During the time prior to t_0, corresponding roughly to the interval 1980–85 in Europe, inflation was decelerating. In the absence of supply shocks, this implies that the actual unemployment rate was above the natural unemployment rate, as shown in both the left and right frames. During the time between t_0 and t_1 ("now"), inflation stopped decelerating and unemployment changed little. This implies that the natural unemployment rate must have risen and caught up with the actual unemployment rate, as shown in both frames.

The differences come to the right of t_1, which shows the consequences of a hypothetical decline in actual unemployment traced by the red dashed line. The structuralist view is based on the idea that specific impediments hold up the natural rate, and that it will not decline. As a result, the decline of the actual unemployment rate will cause inflation to accelerate for as long as unemployment stays below the natural rate. The more optimistic hysteresis view holds that the natural rate automatically follows the actual rate. Thus, the black dashed line in the upper right frame declines as the natural rate falls in response to the decline in the actual unemployment rate. Eventually the natural rate catches up to the actual rate, and as a result the inflation rate stops accelerating.

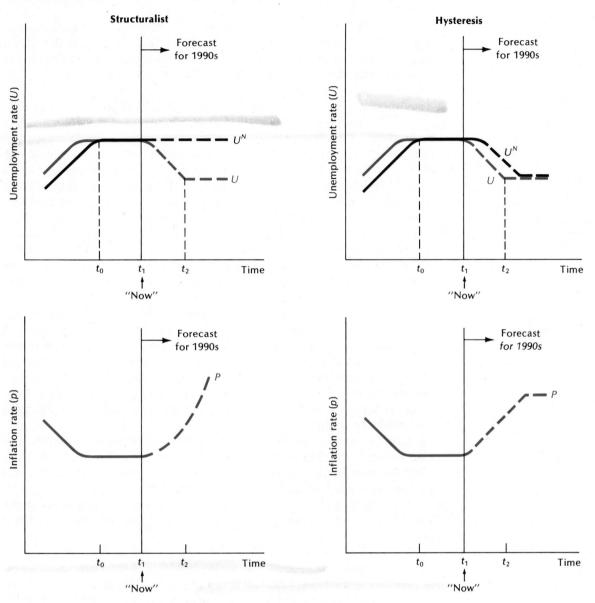

Figure 10-10 **Contrasting Interpretations of Structuralist and Hysteresis Hypotheses**
The left two frames describe the interpretation of the structuralist hypothesis; the right two frames the hysteresis hypothesis. Both agree that prior to time t_1 ("now") the natural rate of unemployment (U^N) increased enough to equal the actual rate of unemployment (U), thus explaining why inflation stopped declining. For the future the structuralist hypothesis predicts that U^N will remain high unless remedies for specific structural impediments are found. As a result, any decline in U will cause accelerating inflation, as shown by the dashed line in the lower left frame. The hysteresis hypothesis suggests that such a decline in U will cause U^N to follow along behind, thus stopping the acceleration of inflation at time t_2.

Assessing the Structuralist Hypothesis

The structuralist hypothesis advances specific reasons for the increase in Europe's natural unemployment rate between the 1960s and the 1980s. These fall into two groups, those that involve government regulation and the welfare state, and those that emphasize excessive real wages.

Eurosclerosis is an alleged European illness involving the effects of excessive government regulation and the encroachment of the welfare state in impeding the efficient operation of the labor market.

Eurosclerosis. Some writers describe Europe as suffering from a disease they call **"Eurosclerosis,"** the effects of excessive government regulation and the welfare state in impeding the efficient operation of the labor market. Europeans often describe themselves as trapped in webs of government regulation. Among the most frequently cited examples of restrictive legislation are layoff regulations, plant-closing laws, and shop-opening hours. Some critics doubt regulation is an important cause of the European problem, because regulations vary widely among individual countries and in some places seem little more burdensome than in the United States. Limitations on shop-opening hours, on the other hand, may be a legitimate complaint. By hindering the opening of convenience stores like 7-11, they prevent the growth of low-wage jobs of the types that have blossomed in the United States during the 1980s.

Much blame for high European unemployment has been ascribed to generous unemployment benefits which insulate the jobless for much longer against income loss. Yet careful studies have shown that European unemployment benefits have, if anything, become *less* generous during the period that unemployment has been rising. A similar skeptical verdict seems warranted for the claim that there is a worsening mismatch between the locations of vacant jobs and long-term jobless in Europe; quantitative measures find no evidence of this.

A more serious problem may be high European tax rates, which may hinder entrepreneurship and stifle the opening of small business firms, which have been a prime source of job growth in the United States. Yet these tax rates are not as high as the top-bracket U. S. rate of 70 to 90 percent in effect during the 1950s and 1960s, which did not prevent the United States from achieving growth in jobs and productivity during that period.

High real wages. Ever since the Great Depression, excessive real wages have been blamed for high unemployment. Indeed, in Chapter 7 we criticized the original Keynesian model for requiring real wages to move countercyclically, rising in recessions.[16] The European problem of high real wages developed in two stages. First, in 1968–70 workers pushed up real wages spontaneously in an attempt to create a permanent increase in their share of national income. Second, at the time of the 1974 oil shock, productivity growth slowed down in Europe as in the United States, but the growth of real wages did not slow down nearly as much as in the United States. In

---

[16]In figure 7-3 an increase in the real wage moves the economy from E_0 to A, creating unemployment.

terms of the theory presented earlier, Europe in the 1970s exhibited many of the symptoms of the "rigid real wage" designated by points X and X' in Figure 10-3.

However, after 1979 growth in European real wages slowed markedly, and labor's share of the national income declined back to its levels of the early 1970s. Thus most observers find that excessive real wages can no longer be blamed for high unemployment in Europe.

Assessing the Hysteresis Hypothesis

The term "hysteresis" means that which "comes after" or "is behind" and comes from the Greek word for "to be behind." In the right frame of Figure 10-10, the natural unemployment rate "follows behind" the actual unemployment rate.[17] We have already seen in Figure 7-4 how a self-correcting downward movement of the U. S. aggregate supply curve was notably missing in the late 1930s. Both Europe in the 1980s and the United States in the 1930s display behavior of unemployment and inflation that is consistent with the hysteresis hypothesis. When unemployment is high the natural rate "follows behind" and becomes high as well, thus eliminating any continuous downward pressure on the inflation rate.

Proponents disagree on the best theoretical explanation of the hysteresis phenomenon. Something happens to prevent the unemployed from bidding down wages. Some believe that long-term unemployment causes a decline in skills, so that the unemployed can no longer compete with those who have jobs. Others prefer the "insider-outsider" model, which makes no claim that "insider" job holders have better skills than the long-term unemployed "outsiders" but rather emphasizes the monopoly market power of the insiders to hold up wages. Why don't the firms fire the insiders? Costs of hiring and training outsiders, or the threat of strike actions by insiders, are two reasons. A final explanation of hysteresis is that the economy's capacity falls during a period of high unemployment, reducing the level of capacity to the level of actual output.

All the explanations of hysteresis imply that a stimulus to aggregate demand will raise the inflation rate. If the unemployed lack skills, firms will often raise wages to steal trained workers from other firms rather than retrain the unemployed. If the insiders have market power, they will insist on wage increases in response to more rapid demand growth. Further, insufficient capacity may lead to shortages of some goods, which in turn could cause inflation. But the three explanations also imply that the inflation will stop accelerating once unemployment settles at a new lower level, since by then the unemployed will have regained their skills, the outsiders will have become insiders, and new investment will have added the needed capital. This optimistic verdict for the future contrasts sharply with the structuralist approach.

---

[17]For an intellectual history, see Rod Cross and Andrew Allan, "On the History of Hysteresis," in Rod Cross, ed., *Unemployment, Hysteresis, and the Natural Rate Hypothesis* (Oxford and New York: Basil Blackwell, 1988), pp. 26–38.

Implications of the Debate for Macroeconomics

The debate is not yet settled. While the various structural factors seem to go in the wrong direction, or to be insufficiently powerful to explain why the natural unemployment rate in Europe is so high, the hysteresis approach also rests on a flimsy foundation. No one yet has adequately explained why hysteresis should have been prevalent in the United States in the 1930s and Europe in the 1980s, but not in the postwar United States. The argument that skills and capital depreciate during a period of high unemployment would seem to apply equally to Europe and the United States, leaving the sharp drop in U. S. unemployment during 1982–88 a mystery. And if the entire support for the hysteresis idea rests on the insider-outsider distinction, then one wonders what explains hysteresis in the United States in the 1930s, when labor unions were barely established and company-hired strikebreaking was common.

At the end of the 1980s, only one thing seemed sure. A stimulus to aggregate demand in Europe would benefit not only some of Europe's jobless individuals, but would also help to settle the debates of economists by demonstrating whether the behavior of inflation is more in keeping with the predictions of the structuralist or hysteresis advocates.

SUMMARY

1. The highly variable inflation experience of the United States in the 1970s and 1980s cannot be explained solely as the consequence of previous fluctuations in the growth rate of nominal GNP. Instead, supply shocks caused inflation to accelerate and decelerate independently of the influence of nominal GNP growth.

2. A supply shock has both a direct and an indirect effect. The direct effect of an adverse supply shock is to reduce natural real GNP and of a beneficial supply shock is to raise natural real GNP.

3. The amount by which natural real GNP declines in response to an adverse shock depends on the slope of the labor supply curve and the rigidity or flexibility of the real wage rate.

4. The indirect effect of the supply shock is the impact on the inflation rate and the ratio of actual to natural real GNP. Policymakers cannot avoid a worsening of inflation, a decline in the output ratio, or both. An "accommodating policy" keeps real GNP at its previous level but causes inflation to accelerate by the full impact of the supply shock; an "extinguishing policy" attempts to cancel out the acceleration of inflation but at the cost of a reduction in real GNP.

5. Accommodation would be an attractive policy if the upward shift in *SP* were expected to be temporary, and if expectations of inflation did not respond to the temporary jump in the inflation rate.

But accommodation may cause more than a temporary increase of inflation if wage contracts have cost-of-living adjustment clauses that incorporate the supply shock into wage growth.

6. Price controls can be treated as a favorable supply shock that shifts down the *SP* schedule, usually only temporarily. The response of inflation and real GNP depends on whether government policy accommodates the control by slowing down aggregate demand growth. In the early 1970s controls served only to destabilize the behavior of prices and real GNP with no long-run benefit, and in addition they interfered with the efficient operation of the economy.

7. The depth of the recession of 1973–75 can be explained by three supply shocks (the termination of price controls and increases in the relative prices of food and of energy), together with an extinguishing policy that slowed aggregate demand growth in response to the supply shocks.

8. In 1978–80 the economy was again beset by adverse supply shocks, involving once more an increase in the relative price of food and energy. Again the government responded with an extinguishing policy, which was more protracted and delayed than in 1974–75. The trough of the recession in 1975 occurred just five quarters after the first oil shock; in 1982 the trough occurred *fifteen* quarters after the second oil shock.

9. In 1986 oil prices fell sharply, creating a beneficial supply shock. An acceleration of nominal GNP growth in 1987–88 had the effect of "extinguishing" the downward pressure of this shock on the inflation rate.

10. After all the economic instability reviewed in the last two chapters, U.S. unemployment in 1988–89 was little different than in the early 1960s. In contrast, European unemployment had more than quadrupled since the early 1960s.

11. On explanation for high European unemployment is called structuralist and emphasizes the adverse effects of government regulations, the welfare state, and excessive real wages. Another explanation is called hysteresis, that the natural rate of unemployment automatically moves up and down in response to changes in the natural rate of unemployment.

CONCEPTS

demand inflation
supply inflation
supply disturbance or shock
OPEC
labor force participation rate
neutral policy

accommodating policy
extinguishing policy
structuralist hypothesis
hysteresis hypothesis
Eurosclerosis

QUESTIONS AND PROBLEMS

Questions

1. What empirical data suggest that the fluctuations in the inflation rate which took place during the 1970s were not examples of demand inflation (as described in Chapter 9)?

2. Supply shocks can be both non-economic in source (exogenous) or the result of changes in economic variables. Give examples of each type of shock.

3. Explain the distinction between the direct effect and the indirect effect of an adverse supply shock.

4. How does an adverse supply shock affect the production function? What is the effect of an adverse supply shock on the demand for labor function?

5. Based on labor participation data, what appears to be the shape of the aggregate labor supply curve? Given this type of labor supply curve, what change in the natural level of real GNP will result in response to an adverse supply shock?

6. If, in response to a supply shock, the Fed maintains the nominal money supply at its initial level, what will happen to the following economic variables: level of GNP, price level, unemployment rate, real wage? What is the relationship of the actual real wage and the equilibrium real wage in this situation?

7. Assume that the economy is at its natural level of real GNP. What would happen if the Fed, in response to an adverse supply shock, increased the money supply in an attempt to keep the level of real GNP unchanged?

8. Is labor better off if a COLA that gives "full protection" takes effect when an adverse supply shock hits the economy?

9. What differentiates an accommodating, extinguishing, and neutral policy response to an adverse supply shock? What happens to the rate of inflation and the real GNP ratio (Q/Q^N) in each of the three cases?

10. Under what conditions would a permanent supply shock cause a temporary increase in the inflation rate? If these conditions exist, are there any "permanent" effects of the supply shock on the economy?

11. Did the policymakers choose an accommodating, neutral, or extinguishing policy during the price controls of 1971–73? What was the result of the chosen policy?

12. What is the primary piece of evidence that suggests an increase in the European natural rate of unemployment between the 1960s and 1987–89? Summarize the alternative theories that purport to explain this phenomenon.

Problems

1. Assume that the price level in the initial period (period 0) in the economy was 1.00 and there had not been any inflation. Because of a widespread infestation in the Midwest, the supply of farm products decreases dramatically. As a result, the overall price index rises by 5 percentage points. Because the infestation was short-lived, the price index in the second period falls back to 1.00, its normal level.
   (a) What will be the price level for periods 1 through 3?
   (b) What will be the inflation rate for periods 1 through 3?
      Assume that the infestation causes permanent damage to the soil and farm prices remain at their new higher levels permanently.
   (c) What will be the price level for periods 1 through 3?
   (d) What will be the inflation rate for periods 1 through 3?
   (e) Explain why your answers to these two pairs of questions differ.
      Assume that in the initial period (period 0), there had been an existing four percent inflation rate.
   (f) What would have been the price level in period 1 if the infestation did not occur? If the infestation causes the overall price index to rise by an additional 5 percentage points, what is the price index in period 1? What is the actual level of inflation that takes place in period 1?

   (g) If in periods 2 and 3 the economy moves back to its preinfestation equilibrium, what would be the price levels in periods 2 and 3?

2. Assume that for every increase of 1 percentage point in the rate of inflation, firms are willing to increase output by 1 percentage point and that the level of output in the economy is currently at 200 (the natural level of output) and the rate of inflation is 4 percent.
   (a) Based on the above information, draw the SP curve.
   (b) What is the level of nominal GNP growth in the economy?
      An adverse supply shock rocks the economy such that the inflation rate associated with every level of output increases by 4 percentage points.
   (c) Draw the new SP curve.
   (d) The government chooses to follow a neutral policy in response to this shock. What will be the level of nominal GNP growth? What will be the new rate of inflation? What will be the new level of real GNP?
   (e) If the government chose to follow an accommodating policy, what would be the new inflation rate? The level of real GNP? The level of nominal GNP growth?
   (f) If the government chose to follow an extinguishing policy, what would be the new inflation rate? The level of real GNP? The level of nominal GNP growth?

SELF-TEST ANSWERS

p. 285 Figure 10-2 illustrates the direct effect of the supply shock in reducing the natural level of real GNP. The new level of natural real GNP at point Z is $Q_0^{N'}$.

p. 288 Both nominal wage rigidity and real wage rigidity prevent the Fed from attaining simultaneously the original level of prices and of natural output. Real wage rigidity causes output to fall well below the highest feasible level to Q_2^N and in addition the price level may rise to a point like X' in Figure 10-3 unless the Fed cuts the nominal money supply substantially. Even without real wage rigidity, the existence of nominal wage rigidity allows the highest feasible level of output ($Q_0^{N'}$) to be attained only if the price level rises substantially above P_0.

p. 294 The inflation rate will fall in the year of the decline in the relative price of oil, except in the case of an extinguishing policy which raises nominal GNP growth sufficiently to cancel out the oil price effect. And, if the inflation rate declines in the first year, it will also decline in subsequent years if the expected rate of inflation declines and/or if COLA agreements cause lower inflation in the first year to cause lower wage changes in subsequent years.

p. 303 North: An adverse supply shock accommodated by an increase in nominal GNP growth. Northeast: an acceleration of nominal GNP growth causing inflation during the period prior to the adjustment of expectations. East: a beneficial supply shock extinguished by an increase in nominal GNP growth. Southeast: a beneficial supply shock accompanied by an unchanged rate of nominal GNP growth. South: a beneficial supply shock accommodated by a reduction in nominal GNP growth. Southwest: a deceleration of nominal GNP growth causing disinflation prior to the adjustment of expectations. West: an adverse supply shock extinguished by a reduction in nominal GNP growth. Northwest: an adverse supply shock accompanied by an unchanged rate of nominal GNP growth.

The Elementary Algebra of Inflation, Real GNP, and Unemployment

Throughout Chapters 9 and 10 we have located the short-run equilibrium rate of inflation and level of real GNP along an *SP* line, as at point E_3 of Figure 10-5. Now we learn how to draw a second "*DG*" line that shows where the economy will operate along the *SP* schedule. We also learn how to calculate the inflation rate and level of real GNP without going to the trouble of making drawings of the *SP* and *DG* lines. We do this by solving together the equations that describe the *SP* and *DG* lines, just as we did in the appendix to Chapter 5, where we learned the equivalent in algebra to the *IS* and *LM* curves. We use *SP–DG* diagrams to show that either the algebraic or graphical method leads to the same answer.

The centerpiece of our model in this appendix is the deviation of the output ratio from 100 percent. One way to write this deviation is:

$$100(Q/Q^N) - 100$$

This deviation is zero, of course, when the output ratio (Q/Q^N) equals 1.0, which occurs when actual output (Q) equals natural output (Q^N).

Calculations in the model are more accurate and straightforward when we use logarithms. Since the logarithm of 1.0 is zero, the log of the output ratio is zero when the output ratio is unity. Thus a second way of expressing the deviation of the output ratio from 100 percent is the "log output ratio" expressed in percentage.

$$\hat{Q} = 100[\log(Q/Q^N)].$$

The following table shows that $\hat{Q}$ is very close in value to the deviation $100(Q/Q^N) - 100$:

Q/Q^N	$100(Q/Q^N) - 100$	$\hat{Q}$
0.90	−10	−10.5
1.00	0	0.0
1.05	5	4.9

In the rest of this appendix, a value of $\hat{Q}$ of zero corresponds to 100 on the horizontal axis of the diagrams in Chapters 9 and 10 that plot output or the output ratio against the inflation rate.

Equation for the *SP* Line

The *SP* line of Chapters 9 and 10 can be written as a relationship between the actual inflation rate (p), the expected inflation rate (p^e), and the log output ratio $(\hat{Q})$—that is, the log ratio of actual real GNP to natural real GNP (Q/Q^N).

General Linear Form

$$p = p^e + g\hat{Q} + x \qquad (1)$$

Numerical Example

$$p = p^e + 0.5\hat{Q}$$

Here the x designates the contribution of supply shocks to inflation, and initially in the numerical example we assume that the element of supply shocks is absent $(x = 0)$, so that we can concentrate on demand inflation. The numerical example also assumes that the slope of the *SP* line, designated g in the general linear form, is 0.5 in the numerical example as was assumed in all the figures of Chapters 9 and 10. Thus $g = 0.5$ indicates that the *SP* line slopes up by one percentage point in extra inflation for each two percentage points of extra real GNP relative to natural real GNP. We also note that when $\hat{Q} = 0$, the economy is on its vertical *LP* line where actual and expected inflation are equal $(p = p^e)$.

In order to understand what makes the *SP* line shift, we must copy here equation (9.3). This indicates that expectations of inflation (p^e) are formed adaptively as a weighted average of last period's actual inflation rate (p_{-1}) and last period's expected inflation rate (p^e_{-1}):

General Linear Form

$$p^e = jp_{-1} + (1 - j)p^e_{-1} \qquad (2)$$

Numerical Example

$$p^e = p_{-1}$$

The numerical example assumes that $j = 1$; that is, that expected inflation depends simply on what the inflation rate actually turned out to be last period, with the subscript "-1" indicating "last period."

When we substitute (2) into (1), we obtain a new expression for the SP line that depends on two current-period variables $(\hat{Q}$ and $x)$ and two variables from last period $(p_{-1}$ and $p^e_{-1})$:

General Linear Form

$$p = jp_{-1} + (1 - j)p^e_{-1} + g\hat{Q} + x \qquad (3)$$

Numerical Example

$$p = p_{-1} + 0.5\hat{Q}$$

Equation for the *DG* Line

But we need more information than that contained in (3) to find both current inflation (p) and the current log output ratio $(\hat{Q})$. In other words, we have two unknown variables and one equation to determine their equilibrium values. What is the missing equation? This is the "*DG* line" and is based on the definition that nominal GNP growth (y) equals the inflation rate (p) plus real GNP growth (q), all expressed as percentages:

$$y \equiv p + q \qquad (4)$$

In the theoretical diagrams of Chapter 9 the natural level of real GNP (Q^N) is constant. But now we want to be more general and allow Q^N to grow, as it does in the real world. We subtract the growth rate of natural real GNP (q^N) from each side of equation (4):

$$y - q^N \equiv p + q - q^N \qquad (5)$$

Let us give a new name, "excess nominal GNP growth" $(\hat{y})$, to the excess of nominal GNP growth over the growth rate of natural real GNP $(\hat{y} = y - q^N)$. We can also replace the excess of actual over natural real GNP growth $(q - q^N)$ with the change in the log

output ratio $(\hat{Q})$ from its value last period $(\hat{Q}_{-1})$[1]. When these replacements are combined, (5) becomes

$$\hat{y} \equiv p + \hat{Q} - \hat{Q}_{-1} \qquad (6)$$

Combining the *SP* and *DG* Equations

Now we are ready to combine our equations for the *SP* line (3) and *DG* line (6). When (6) is solved for the log output ratio $(\hat{Q})$, we obtain the following equation for the *DG* line:

$$\hat{Q} \equiv \hat{Q}_{-1} + \hat{y} - p \qquad (7)$$

This says that the *DG* relation between $\hat{Q}$ and p has a slope of -1, and that the relation shifts when there is any change in $\hat{Q}_{-1}$ or $\hat{y}$. Now (7) can be substituted into the *SP* equation (3) to obtain:

$$p = jp_{-1} + (1 - j)p^e_{-1} + g(\hat{Q}_{-1} + \hat{y} - p) + x \qquad (8)$$

This can be further simplified if we factor out p from the right-hand side of (8):[2]

General Linear Form

$$p = \frac{1}{1 + g}[jp_{-1} + (1 - j)p^e_{-1} + g(\hat{Q}_{-1} + \hat{y}) + x] \qquad (9)$$

Numerical Example

$$p = \frac{2}{3}[p_{-1} + 0.5(\hat{Q} + \hat{y})]$$

Now we are ready to use equation (9) to examine the consequences of any event that can alter the inflation rate and log output ratio in the short run and long run. The main subject of Chapter 9 was the

---

[1]This replacement relies on the definition of a growth rate from one period to another as the change in logs (here we omit the "100" that changes decimals to percents):

$$q = \log(Q) - \log(Q_{-1})$$
$$q^N = \log(Q^N) - \log(Q^N_{-1})$$

Subtracting the second line from the first, we have

$$q - q^N = \log(Q) - \log(Q^N) - [\log(Q_{-1}) - \log(Q^N_{-1})] = \hat{Q} - \hat{Q}_{-1}.$$

[2]To obtain (9) from (8), add gp to both sides of equation (8). Then divide both sides of the resulting equation by $1 + g$.

consequences of accelerations and decelerations in nominal GNP growth (y), so let us use equation (9) to reproduce the path of adjustment plotted in Figure 9-6 following an acceleration in y from zero to 6 percent per annum. Now, however, we shall perform the analysis for adjusted nominal GNP growth ($\hat{y}$), thus allowing it to remain valid for any value of q^N.

Example When $\hat{y}$ Rises from Zero to 6 Percent

We start out initially with zero inflation and with an output ratio of 100 percent, as at point E_0 in Figure 9-6. This means that the log output ratio ($\hat{Q}$) is zero. We also assume that there are no supply shocks ($x = 0$). Thus our initial situation begins with:

$$p_{-1} = p^e_{-1} = \hat{y} = \hat{Q}_{-1} = 0$$

Substituting into the numerical example version of (9) we can confirm that these values are consistent with an initial value of zero inflation:

$$p = \frac{2}{3} [0 + 0.5 (0 + 0)] = 0$$

Now there is an assumed sudden jump in $\hat{y}$ to 6 percent per year. What happens to inflation in the first period? Substituting $\hat{y} = 6$ into the numerical example, we have:

$$p = \frac{2}{3} [0 + 0.5(0 + 6)] = \frac{2}{3} (3) = 2$$

The new log output ratio can be found by using equation (7):

$$\hat{Q} = \hat{Q}_{-1} + \hat{y} - p = 0 + 6 - 2 = 4$$

Thus we have derived the combination of p and $\hat{Q}$ plotted at point F in Figure 9-6—that is, inflation of 2 percent and a log output ratio of 4.[3]

The adjustment continues in future periods, of course. We can compute the values of p and $\hat{Q}$ in the next few periods by substituting the correct numbers into the numerical example version of (9), using a

---

[3]In Figure 9-6 we assumed for simplicity that natural real GNP was not growing. Thus any change in Q/Q^N became simply a shift in Q itself, in this case a 4 percent increase from 100 to 104 in Figure 9-6.

pocket calculator. These values correspond exactly to the path labeled "$j = 1$" in Figure 9-6:

Period	p_{-1}	$\hat{Q}_{-1}$	$\hat{y}$	p	$\hat{Q}$
0	0.00	0.00	0	0.00	0.00
1	0.00	0.00	6	2.00	4.00
2	2.00	4.00	6	4.67	5.33
3	4.67	5.33	6	6.89	4.44
4	6.89	4.44	6	8.07	2.37

Exercise 1: Using the same numerical example, calculate what happens for the first four periods when the economy is in an initial long-run equilibrium at point E_4 in Figure 9-11 with $\hat{y} = p = p^e = 10$, and $\hat{Q} = 0$, and suddenly the adjusted growth rate of nominal GNP ($\hat{y}$) falls to a new permanent value of zero. How is your answer changed if the coefficient of adjustment of expectations is assumed to be $j = 0.25$ instead of $j = 1.0$?

(**Hint:** This requires that you substitute $j = 0.25$ and $g = 0.5$ into the "General Linear Form" version of equation (9) above.)

Learning to Shift the SP Curve and DG Line

In this section we learn how to draw graphs in which the SP curve and DG lines are accurately shifted, so that the economy's adjustment path can be traced out. In an example we will see how to trace out the path in Figure 9-6 marked "$j = 1$," showing how the economy reacts to a permanent six-percentage-point acceleration in nominal GNP growth.

Shifting the SP curve. The SP curves plotted in the left frame of Figure 10-11 are based on the numerical example of equation (1), repeated here for convenience:

$$p = p^e + 0.5 \, \hat{Q} \qquad (1)$$

The lower SP_0 line assumes that $p^e = 0$. Thus it shows that inflation (p) is zero when $\hat{Q} = 0$. When $\hat{Q}$ is 4, inflation is 2 percent. In our numerical example the inflation rate in period 1 is shown by point F on SP_0. If $j = 1$, so the expected rate of inflation always equals last period's actual rate of inflation ($p^e = p_{-1}$), then there is an easy rule for drawing the new SP line for the subsequent period:

Rule for Shifting SP When j = 1: If the economy is at point F in period 1, then the SP curve for period 2 can be drawn as intersecting the *LP* line at the same vertical coordinate as point *F*, shown by the point *F'*.

Thus in the example the *SP* curve for period 2 is SP_1, shown as having the same slope as SP_0 but intersecting *LP* at point *F'*. The vertical coordinate of the point where *SP* intersects *LP* tells us what expected rate of inflation (p^e) is being assumed along that *SP* curve. Along SP_1, for instance, p^e must be 2 percent, since the vertical coordinate of point *F'* is 2 percent.

Shifting the *DG* line. The *DG* lines plotted in the right frame of Figure 10-11 are based on equation (7), repeated here for convenience:

$$\hat{Q} = \hat{Q}_{-1} + \hat{y} - p \qquad (7)$$

Since p and $\hat{Q}$ are on the two axes, to plot a *DG* line we need to know the values of $\hat{y}$ and $\hat{Q}_{-1}$. The DG_1 line in the right frame of Figure 10-11 assumes that $\hat{y} = 6$ and $\hat{Q}_{-1} = 0$. This line has a slope of minus 45 degrees, sloping down one percentage point vertically for every percentage point in the horizontal direction.

When the economy is at point *F* in period 1 in our example, with an inflation rate of 2 percent and

an output ratio of $\hat{Q} = 4$, we must draw a new *DG* line for period 2. To develop a general rule for shifting *DG*, we draw a horizontal line *CQ*, which stands for "constant output." The *CQ* line is always horizontal, and its vertical coordinate is the assumed growth rate of $\hat{y}$, in this case 6 percent. It shows that if inflation were equal to $\hat{y}$, then by equation (7) the output ratio would be constant, $\hat{Q} = \hat{Q}_{-1}$, hence the name "constant output," or "*CQ*" line. Now we can write a general rule for shifting *DG*:

Rule for Shifting DG: Start from the economy's position in period 1, point *F* in this example. Then draw a horizontal *CQ* line at a vertical coordinate corresponding to the assumed value of $\hat{y}$, in this case 6 percent. Then the *DG* line for period 2 will be a line with a slope of minus 45 degrees intercepting the *CQ* line at the same horizontal coordinate as point *F*. This point of interception is labeled point *F"* in the right frame of Figure 10-11.

Thus in the example the *DG* line for period 2 is DG_2, shown as parallel to the DG_1 line but intersecting *CQ* at point *F"*. Note that the rule also applies to the DG_1 line. Since the economy in the previous period ("period 0") was at a log output ratio of 0, the DG_1 line

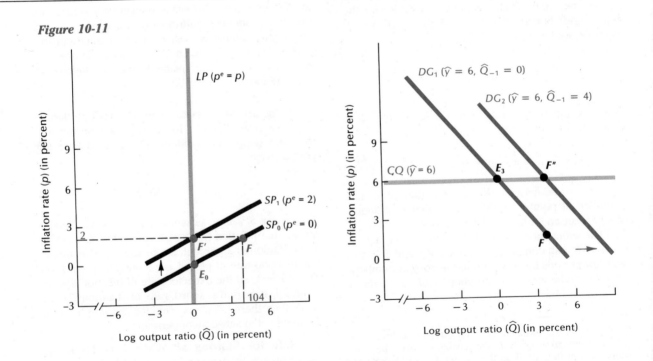

Figure 10-11

intercepts the CQ line at point E_3, which has a horizontal coordinate of 0.

Another equivalent way to remember the rule for shifting the DG line is simple. When $\hat{y}$ increases, the DG line shifts up *vertically* by the amount of the change in $\hat{y}$, for example, up by 6 percent between the lines DG_0 and DG_1. But when $\hat{Q}_{-1}$ increases, the DG line shifts to the right *horizontally* by the amount of the change in $\hat{Q}_{-1}$, for example, by 4 percent between the lines DG_1 and DG_2.

Tracing the economy's adjustment with shifts in SP and DG. Now we are prepared to draw a graph tracing the economy's adjustment to a permanent 6 percent acceleration in $\hat{y}$, from an initial value of zero to a new value of 6. In Figure 10-12 the economy starts at point E_0, on the SP_0 curve drawn for the initial assumed expected rate of inflation ($p^e = 0$), and on the DG_0 line drawn for $\hat{y} = 0$ and an output ratio last period $\hat{Q}_{-1}$ of 0.

The permanent acceleration of $\hat{y}$ fixes the CQ line at a vertical position of 6. We draw a new DG_1 line intersecting CQ directly above point E_0. The SP line does not shift in period 1, because expectations of inflation adjust with a one-period lag. Thus in period 1 the economy moves from E_0 to F, with an inflation rate (p) of 2.0 percent and an output ratio $\hat{Q}$ of 4.0 percent. Then in period 2 both SP and DG shift. We draw a new SP_1 line, as in Figure 10-9, as intersecting the LP line at the same vertical coordinate as point F. We draw a new DG_2 line, as in Figure 10-9,

as intersecting the CQ line at the same horizontal coordinate as point F. The two new lines, SP_1 and DG_2, intersect at point H, where the inflation rate (p) in 4.67 percent and the log output ratio is 5.33 percent. This is the same as the economy's position in period 2 calculated by the algebraic method in the preceding section.

The adjustment in period 3 is also shown in Figure 10-12. A new SP_2 line is drawn as intersecting the LP line at the same vertical coordinate as point H. A new DG_3 line is shown as intersecting the CQ line at the same horizontal coordinate as point H. The economy's new position in period 3 is at the intersection of the SP_2 curve and DG_3 line, labeled in Figure 10-10 as point I. Inflation has now risen to 6.89 percent and the log output ratio has fallen to 4.44 percent.

The general principles developed in this section can be used to show the economy's adjustment to either a shift in $\hat{y}$ or a supply shock. General characteristics of the adjustment process, shown in the example of Figure 10-12, are as follows:

> The SP line always shifts up in the subsequent period when the economy's position in the current period is to the right of LP, and it shifts down when the economy is to the left of LP. The DG line always shifts to the right in the subsequent period when the economy's current position is below the CQ line, that is, when inflation is less than $\hat{y}$. And the DG line shifts to the left in the subsequent period when the economy is

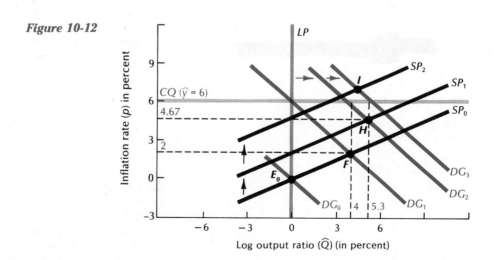

Figure 10-12

above the *CQ* line. Thus, in the example of Figure 10-12, the *DG* line drawn for period 4 would intersect the *CQ* line at the same horizontal coordinate as point *I* and thus would be to the left of the DG_3 line.

The Consequences of a Supply Shock

We have examined the effect on inflation of an acceleration of growth in nominal GNP. But another source of inflation may be a supply shock, such as an increase in the relative price of food or energy. Let us assume that we start in long-run equilibrium at point E_3 in Figure 10-5, with $\hat{y} = p = p^e = 6$, and $\hat{Q} = 0$. Initially the supply-shock variable x is equal to zero. But now let us assume there is a jump in the relative price of oil that boosts x to a value of 3 for two periods, followed by a return after that to $x = 0$.

The discussion of supply shocks emphasized that two crucial factors determine how the economy reacts to a supply shock. First, is $\hat{y}$ increased, decreased, or left the same by policymakers following the shock? Second, do expectations adjust to the temporary shock? Cost-of-living adjustment clauses in wage contracts are equivalent to an adjustment of expected inflation for the influence of the supply shock.

The simplest case to analyze is one in which there is no response of either demand growth ($\hat{y}$) or expected inflation (p^e). To trace the path of inflation and the real GNP ratio, we simply use the general formula (9) with $\hat{y}$ assumed to be permanently fixed at 6, and $j = 0$ (representing the failure of expectations to respond at all to actual inflation). The general form for this case becomes:

$$p = \frac{1}{1 + g} [p^e_{-1} + g(\hat{Q}_{-1} + \hat{y}) + x] \quad (10)$$
$$= \frac{2}{3} [p^e_{-1} + 0.5 (\hat{Q}_{-1} + \hat{y}) + x]$$

Now, starting in the initial situation, we substitute the required elements into this formula for each period in succession.

Period	p^e_{-1}	$\hat{Q}_{-1}$	$\hat{y}$	x	p	$\hat{Q}$
0	6	0.00	6	0	6.00	0.00
1	6	0.00	6	3	8.00	−2.00
2	6	−2.00	6	3	7.33	−3.33
3	6	−3.33	6	0	4.89	−2.22
4	6	−2.22	6	0	5.26	−1.48
5	6	−1.48	6	0	5.51	−0.99

This adjustment path shows what would happen to the economy with a two-period supply shock of $x = 3$, with a "neutral" aggregate demand policy that maintains steady excess nominal GNP growth, and with no response of expectations to the effects of the supply shock. In period 1 the inflation rate jumps from 6 to 8, exactly duplicating the movement from point E_3 to point L in Figure 10-5. In the next period inflation diminishes somewhat, since the position of the *DG* line depends on the current period's starting value of $\hat{Q}$, which has fallen from 0 to −2. Thus the intersection of *DG* and *SP* slides southwest down the stationary SP_3 line to $p = 7.33$ and $\hat{Q} = −3.33$. Then the supply shock ends, x returns to its original zero value, and the economy gradually climbs back up the SP_2 line to its long-run equilibrium position, $p = 6.0$ and $\hat{Q} = 0$.

Exercise 2: What rate of adjusted nominal growth should policymakers choose if they want to pursue an accommodating policy? An extinguishing policy? (**Hint:** An accommodating policy means that $\hat{Q}$ remains fixed at 0, which requires that $\hat{y} = p$. Substitute p for $\hat{y}$ in equation (10) and, in addition, note that $\hat{Q}_{-1} = 0$, thus obtaining $p = p^e_{-1} + x$. For an extinguishing policy, take (10) and set the left-hand side (p) equal to 6; then solve for the required $\hat{y}$.)

Exercise 3: For a neutral policy response, calculate the adjustment path of inflation and Q/Q^N in the first four periods when expectations respond fully to the extra inflation caused by the supply shock. That is, assume now that $j = 1$ instead of $j = 0$ as in the previous exercise. Next, maintaining the assumption that $j = 1$, calculate the same adjustment path when the policy response is accommodative. (See the hint for Exercise 2.) How would you describe the disadvantages of an accommodative policy when $j = 1$?

The Behavior of the Unemployment Rate

The unemployment rate (U) is very closely related to the log ratio ($\hat{Q}$), as we shall learn in Chapter 11. Corresponding to the natural level of real GNP (Q^N), defined as the level of real GNP at which expectations of inflation turn out to be accurate, there is a natural rate of unemployment (U^N). When real GNP is above Q^N, and inflation is accelerating, we also find that the actual unemployment rate (U) is below the natural rate of unemployment (U^N). This relationship can be written:[4]

General Linear Form

$$U = U^N - h\hat{Q} \qquad (11)$$

Numerical Example

$$U = U^N - 0.4\hat{Q}$$

How is this relationship to be used? First, we must determine the value of the natural rate of unemployment. In the United States in the early 1980s this appears to be approximately $U^N = 6.0$ percent. Then we take alternative values for $\hat{Q}$ and substitute these values into equation (11). Here are two examples:

Example 1: $\hat{Q} = -5$
Since $U^N = 6.0$, we use (11) to determine:

$$U = 6.0 - 0.4(-5) = 8.0,$$

that is, an unemployment rate of 8.0 percent.

Example 2: $\hat{Q} = 5$

$$U = 6.0 - 0.4(5) = 4.0,$$

or an unemployment rate of 4.0 percent. Thus we see that for every five percentage points by which $\hat{Q}$ exceeds 0, the unemployment rate lies two percentage points below U^N, the natural un-

employment rate of 6.0 percent. And for every five percentage points by which $\hat{Q}$ falls short of 0, the unemployment rate lies two percentages points above the natural unemployment rate of 6.0 percent.

There is also a simple short-cut way of calculating the *change* in the unemployment rate from last period (U_{-1}) to this period (U):[5]

General Linear Form

$$U = U_{-1} - h(q - q^N) \qquad (12)$$

Numerical Example

$$U = U_{-1} - 0.4(q - q^N)$$

Thus, starting with $U_{-1} = 6.0$, a value of $q - q^N$ of 1.0 will cause the unemployment rate to fall to $U = 5.6$.

Exercise 4: Go back through the previous exercises and calculate the unemployment rate for each period corresponding to Q/Q^N.

---

[4]**Caution:** In the appendix to Chapter 5 we used h to designate the income responsiveness of the demand for money, and in Chapter 7 for the slope of the Lucas—Friedman Supply curve.

---

[5]How can (12) be derived from (11)? Let us write down (11) and then subtract from it the value of (11) for last period:

$$U = U^N - h\hat{Q}$$
$$- U_{-1} = U^N_{-1} - h\hat{Q}_{-1}$$

If there is no change in U^N from one period to the next, then this difference is:

$$U - U_{-1} = - h(\hat{Q} - \hat{Q}_{-1})$$

But now we can substitute $q - q^N$ into this expression,

$$U - U_{-1} = - h(q - q^N)$$

To see why this substitution is valid, look back at footnote 1.

Unemployment and Inflation: Costs and Policy Options

Look at it this way: People who are unemployed or cannot sell what they grow, or see their business vanish into bankruptcy, suffer physical and mental damage much like victims of military campaigns. The psychic shellshock of hard times is perhaps more persistent than that of war. . . . There is no realistic hope that the men and women and children who have lost their jobs, homes, and peace of mind because of the current lingering recession will ever forget or will ever have the same sense of confidence that they had before the pink slip or the foreclosure notice or the auctioneer's gavel.

—Ben Stein[1]

Until now we have examined the behavior of only one measure of real activity in the economy: the ratio of actual to natural real GNP (Q/Q^N). But we are interested also in understanding the reason for fluctuations in unemployment. In this chapter we learn that the difference between the actual unemployment rate (U) and natural unemployment rate (U^N) is very closely related to the real GNP ratio Q/Q^N. We shall also learn why the natural unemployment rate U^N is so high in the United States, and what can be done to reduce it. Finally, we shall compare the costs of unemployment with the costs of inflation, in order to assess the choices policymakers face in situations when a reduction of unemployment requires faster inflation or vice versa.

11-1 The Dilemma of High Unemployment

PUZZLE 1: WHY HAS UNEMPLOYMENT BEEN SO HIGH AND SO VARIABLE?

In late 1982 the jobless rate soared to 10.7 percent, higher than in any year since the Great Depression. Why should society tolerate such high levels of unemployment, together with the waste that occurs when machines, factories, stores, and office buildings are underutilized? Should we conclude that

---

[1]Ben Stein, "Economic Purple Hearts," *New York Times*, January 12, 1983, Op Ed page.

there is some simple solution that economists understand but politicians refuse to accept? Or is the problem of high unemployment insoluble?

We were first introduced to the close relationship between real GNP and the unemployment rate in Figure 1-5. There we noticed that years when real GNP fell below natural real GNP were also years of high unemployment, when the actual unemployment rate exceeded the natural rate of unemployment. Our first task in this chapter is to quantify the relationship between real GNP and unemployment.

Because of the regular relation between real GNP and the unemployment rate, we already understand the main causes of *fluctuations* in unemployment. In Chapter 9 we concluded that the government has the power to raise real GNP (and thus reduce unemployment) by stimulating nominal GNP growth, but only for a temporary period. In Chapter 10 we learned that supply shocks can cause inflation to worsen and real GNP to decline at the same time, thus also causing higher unemployment.

What we have learned so far only helps us understand the causes of *changes* of actual unemployment above and below the natural rate of unemployment. So far we have said nothing that would explain why the natural rate of unemployment (U^N) is itself so high.

The first and most basic cause of high unemployment in the United States is that the natural rate of unemployment is not zero, but a much higher number, in the vicinity of 6.0 percent.

Frictional, Structural and Cyclical Unemployment

Frictional unemployment occurs in the normal process of job search by individuals who have voluntarily quit their jobs, are entering the labor force for the first time, or are reentering the labor force.

Structural unemployment occurs when there is a mismatch between the skill or location requirements of job vacancies and the present skills or location of unemployed individuals.

Cyclical unemployment is the difference between the actual and natural rates of unemployment.

Often unemployment is divided into three components, **"frictional," "structural,"** and **"cyclical."** We learn in the first part of this chapter why the natural rate of unemployment, the rate compatible with a steady rate of inflation, is not zero. The unemployment that the economy experiences when it is operating at the natural unemployment rate (with an output ratio Q/Q^N of 100 percent) consists of the frictional and structural components. We shall see that these components of unemployment are higher than necessary as a result of discrimination against blacks and women, barriers to mobility and the acquisition of job skills, and government regulations.

When the economy is operating at an unemployment rate above the natural rate, as in 1982 when the average unemployment rate for the year was 9.7 percent, the economy is said to be experiencing "cyclical" unemployment. This is the direct result of macroeconomic policies that cause nominal GNP growth to decelerate suddenly, combined with long-term wage and price contracts that prevent the inflation rate from shifting down rapidly enough in response to slower nominal GNP growth.

Although we use the phrase "natural rate of unemployment" throughout this book to refer to the unemployment rate compatible with steady inflation, the term "natural" is misleading. The natural unemployment rate is not carved in stone, immutable, or desirable. It can be changed either by the actions of private firms and households or by changes in government policy. A central theme of this chapter is to identify the sources of the high natural rate of unemployment and to determine how that rate might be reduced.

11-2   CASE STUDY: Unemployment and the Real GNP Ratio

Most of our task of understanding fluctuations in unemployment has already been completed. When the output ratio (Q/Q^N) rises, the unemployment rate declines, and vice versa. Although one cannot predict the unemployment rate perfectly by knowing the Q/Q^N ratio, nevertheless the unemployment rate is very closely related to Q/Q^N.

In Figure 11-1 notice the cluster of prosperous years, 1965–69, in the lower right corner, with values of Q/Q^N well above 100 percent and unusually low unemployment rates. The contrasting situation in the upper left

A HIGH REAL GNP RATIO GOES WITH LOW UNEMPLOYMENT, AND VICE VERSA

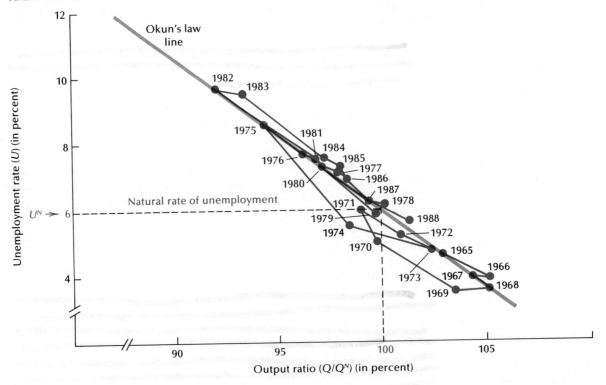

Figure 11-1 **The U.S. Ratio of Actual to Natural Real GNP (Q/Q^N) and the Unemployment Rate, 1965–88**
This diagram illustrates that unemployment (U) moves inversely with the real GNP ratio (Q/Q^N). In prosperous years, such as 1966–69, the observations are in the lower right corner, with a high real GNP ratio and low unemployment. The opposite extreme occurred in 1982, the observation plotted at the upper left corner. A recession occurred, the output ratio fell, and workers were laid off. The gray line expresses the relation between U and Q/Q^N, sometimes called Okun's law.

corner occurred in the recession years 1975 and 1982, when massive lay-offs caused record unemployment. The negative slope of the points connected by the red line in Figure 11-1 just reflects common sense. When sales slump, workers are laid off and the jobless rate rises. But when sales boom and Q/Q^N is high, some of the jobless are hired, and the unemployment rate goes down.

The close negative connection between the unemployment rate (U) and Q/Q^N was first pointed out in the early 1960s by the late Arthur M. Okun, formerly Chairman of the Council of Economic Advisers in the Johnson administration.[2] Because it has held up so well, the relationship is known as **Okun's law.** Not only does U tend to follow the major movements in Q/Q^N, but in addition the percentage-point change in the unemployment rate tends to be roughly 0.4 times the percentage change in the Q/Q^N ratio, in the opposite direction. For instance, the gray line is drawn so that an output ratio (Q/Q^N) of 100 percent corresponds to a natural unemployment rate of 6 percent, a situation in which the actual and expected rates of inflation are equal. A drop in the Q/Q^N ratio by five percentage points, from 100 to 95, would correspond to an increase in the unemployment rate of 0.4 as much, or 2 percentage points, as indicated by the gray line going through 8 percent unemployment on the vertical axis and 95 percent on the horizontal axis.[3]

Consider, for instance, the following examples in which a change in the real GNP ratio was accompanied by a change in the unemployment rate of a bit more than 40 percent as much in the opposite direction:

Years	Percentage change in Q/Q^N	Percentage change in U	Ratio of (2) to (1) (%)
1973–75	−7.9	3.6	−45.6
1979–82	−7.6	3.8	−50.0
1982–88	9.1	−4.2	−46.2

The Okun's law relationship shown as the negatively sloped gray line in Figure 11-1 can also be written as an equation:

General Linear Form

$$U = U^N - h[100(Q/Q^N) - 100]$$ (11.1)

Numerical Example

$$U = U^N - 0.4[100(Q/Q^N) - 100]$$

The general form states that the actual unemployment rate (U) equals the natural rate of unemployment (U^N) minus the slope coefficient (h) times the difference between the output ratio and 100 percent. (The "100" in

Okun's law states that there is a regular negative relationship between the output ratio (Q/Q^N) and the difference between the actual and natural rates of unemployment.

[2]Arthur M. Okun, "Potential GNP: Its Measurement and Significance," reprinted in Okun's *The Political Economy of Prosperity* (Washington, D.C.: Brookings Institution, 1970), pp. 132–145.

[3]The response is estimated to be 0.45 in Robert J. Gordon, "Unemployment and Potential Output in the 1980s," *Brookings Papers on Economic Activity,* vol. 15, no. 1 (1984), pp. 537–564. This figure is rounded off to 0.40 in the text. The original Okun article and much of the literature on Okun's law set the responsiveness of unemployment to Q/Q^N at 0.33, but this estimate seems to have been obsolete for many years, because the original articles on Okun's law ignored the substantial lag in the response of unemployment to Q/Q^N.

front of the Q/Q^N term is necessary to convert the output ratio into a percent.) You can use the numerical example in equation (11.1) to compute the unemployment rate for sample output ratios of 95 and 105, assuming that U^N equals 6 percent.

Another feature that stands out in Figure 11-1 is that the red line connecting the various annual observations tends to "loop around" the gray Okun's law line in a clockwise direction. This reflects the lag in the adjustment of unemployment to changes in Q/Q^N. In a year such as 1973 Q/Q^N expanded rapidly, but firms were slow to hire workers, delaying the decline in unemployment. In years such as 1970 and 1974, when Q/Q^N dropped sharply, firms were slow to fire workers, and there was a delay in the increase in the unemployment rate.[4]

11-3 How the Government Measures Unemployment

The Unemployment Survey

Many people wonder how the government determines facts such as "the teenage unemployment rate in December 1988 was 14.8 percent," because they themselves have never spoken to a government agent about their own experiences of employment, unemployment, and time in school. It would be too costly to contact everyone in the country every month; the government attempts to reach each household to collect information only once each decade when it takes the Decennial Census of Population. On the other hand it would not be enough to collect information just once every ten years, because policymakers would have no guidance for conducting current policy.

As a compromise, 1500 Census Bureau workers interview each month about 60,000 households, or about 1 in every 1400 households in the country. Each month one fourth of the households in the sample are replaced, so that no family is interviewed more than four months in a row. The laws of statistics imply that an average from a survey of a sample of households of this size comes very close to the true figure that would be revealed by a costly complete census.[5]

Questions asked in the survey. The interviewer first asks, for each separate household member, "What were you doing most of last week—working, keeping house, going to school, or something else?" Anyone who has done any work at all for pay during the past week, whether part-time, full-time, or temporary work, is counted as employed.

For those who say they did no work, the next question is "Did you have a job from which you were temporarily absent or on layoff last week?" If the

---

[4]See Robert J. Gordon, "The End-of-Expansion Phenomenon in Short-Run Productivity Behavior," *Brookings Papers on Economic Activity,* vol. 10, no. 2 (1979), pp. 447–461.

[5]The facts in this section are taken from *How the Government Measures Unemployment,* BLS Report no. 505 (Washington, D.C.: U.S. Bureau of Labor Statistics, 1977), updated with more recent newspaper reports.

person is awaiting recall from a layoff or has obtained a new job but is waiting for it to begin, he or she is counted as unemployed.

If the person neither works nor is absent from a job, the next question is "Have you been looking for work in the last four weeks?" If so, "What have you been doing in the last four weeks to find work?" A person who has not been ill and has searched for a job by applying to an employer, registering with an employment agency, checking with friends, or other specified job-search activities is counted as unemployed. The remaining people who are neither employed nor unemployed, mainly homemakers who do not seek paid work, students, disabled people, and retired people, are counted as not in the labor force.

Definitions based on the interview. Despite the intricacy of questions asked by the inteviewer, the concept is simple: "People with jobs are employed; people who do not have jobs and are looking for jobs are unemployed; people who meet neither labor market test are not in the labor force."[6] The **total labor force** is the total of the civilian employed, the armed forces, and the unemployed. Thus the entire population aged sixteen and over falls into one of four categories:

The **total labor force** is the sum of the civilian employed, the armed forces, and the unemployed.

1. Total labor force
   a. Civilian employed
   b. Armed forces
   c. Unemployed
2. Not in the labor force

The actual unemployment rate is defined as the ratio:

$$U = \frac{\text{number of unemployed}}{\text{civilian employed} + \text{unemployed}}$$

Example: In March 1989 the BLS reported an unemployment rate of 5.0 percent. This was calculated as the ratio:

$$U = \frac{\text{number of unemployed}}{\text{civilian employed} + \text{unemployed}} = \frac{6,128,000}{117,136,000 + 6,128,000}$$

$$\text{or } U = 5.0 \text{ percent}$$

And, as we learned in Section 10-3, the labor force participation rate is the ratio of the total labor force (civilian employed, armed forces, and the unemployed) to the population aged sixteen or over. In March 1989 this rate was 66.3 percent.

Flaws in the definition. The government's unemployment measure sounds relatively straightforward, but unfortunately it disguises almost as much as it reveals:

1. *The unemployment rate by itself is not a measure of the social distress caused by the loss of a job.* Each person who lacks a job and is looking for one is counted as "1.0 unemployed people," whether the person is the head of a household responsible for feeding numerous dependents

---

[6]*How the Government Measures Unemployment*, p. 6.

or a sixteen-year-old looking only for a ten-hour-per-week part-time job to provide pocket money. Only a minority of the unemployed can be described as workers who have lost one job and are looking for another.

2. *The government's unemployment concept misses some of the people hurt by a recession.* Some suffer a cut in hours, being forced by their employer to shift from full-time to part-time work. Still counted as employed, they never enter the unemployment statistics. An unemployment concept called "labor time lost" counts aggregate hours lost by the unemployed and those working part-time for economic reasons. This rate was 5.8 percent in March 1989, higher than the official unemployment rate of 5.0 percent.

3. *A person lacking a job must have performed particular specified actions to look for a job during the past four weeks.* What about people who have looked and looked and have given up, convinced that no job is available? They are not counted as unemployed at all. They simply "disappear" from the labor force, entering the category of not in the labor force. Those out of the labor force who would like to work but have given up on the job search are sometimes called "discouraged workers" or the "disguised unemployed." They numbered as many as 1.8 million in the 1981–82 recession.

Despite the inadequacies of the government unemployment concept, our graphs and tables emphasize the total official unemployment rate because it is most widely publicized and discussed by the public. To better understand the meaning of unemployment, however, we have to probe deeper.

11-4 Why Is the Natural Rate of Unemployment So High?

Distinguishing the Types of Unemployment

At the beginning of this chapter we were introduced to three concepts of unemployment—frictional, structural, and cyclical. How do each of these concepts relate to the natural rate of unemployment and to Okun's law?

Together the first two concepts, frictional and structural, make up the natural rate of unemployment. Frictional unemployment occurs in the normal process of job search by individuals who have voluntarily quit their jobs, are entering the labor force for the first time, or are reentering the labor force. Any economy can expect to have a moderate amount of frictional unemployment, and we shall see that there are good reasons for the United States to have more frictional unemployment than some other countries. Because frictional unemployment occurs in the normal process of "turnover" in the labor market, as people move between jobs and move in and out of the labor force, frictional unemployment is often called **turnover** unemployment.

Turnover unemployment is another name for frictional unemployment. It is one of the two components of the natural rate of unemployment.

Structural unemployment is the second component of the natural rate of unemployment. It occurs when there is a mismatch between the skill or location requirements of job vacancies and the present skills or location of unemployed individuals. Structural unemployment tends to last much longer than frictional unemployment, since longer is required for people to learn new skills or to move to new locations. Because structural unemployment involves a mismatch of skills, location, or both, it is often called **mismatch** unemployment.

Okun's law refers to the third type of unemployment, that is, cyclical unemployment. Okun's law has no explanation for the level of the natural rate of unemployment; it simply accepts whatever the natural rate of unemployment is. What Okun's law states is that the cyclical component of unemployment $(U - U^N)$ has a regular negative relationship to the output ration (Q/Q^N). Thus, rewriting equation (11.1), we have:

General Linear Form

$$U - U^N = -h[100(Q/Q^N) - 100] \qquad (11.2)$$

Numerical Example

$$U - U^N = -0.4[100(Q/Q^N) - 100]$$

For instance, using the numerical example, when the output ratio (Q/Q^N) is 95 percent, the cyclical component of unemployment is two percentage points. Thus if U^N is 6.0 percent, the actual unemployment rate is two percentage points higher, or 8.0 percent.

The government provides estimates of such actual concepts as the unemployment rate and the labor force, but not of the natural unemployment rate or of its two components, frictional and structural unemployment. The estimate that $U^N = 6.0$ rests on statistical research that attempts to estimate the slope of the *SP* curve of Chapters 9 and 10.[7] As for the breakdown of U^N between the frictional and structural components, the best we can do is guess that the two components of U^N are of roughly equal size. If so, then the following would be the breakdown of the U.S. unemployment rate in a year like 1987, when the actual unemployment rate was 6.2 percent:

Cyclical unemployment		0.2
Natural rate of unemployment		6.0
Frictional (turnover) unemployment	3.0	
Structural (mismatch) unemployment	3.0	
Total: Actual unemployment rate		6.2

There is one type of unemployment that does not appear in the figures, and this is **seasonal** unemployment that occurs as the result of seasonal fluctuations in employment opportunities. For instance, in areas with cold weather, construction workers are laid off for weeks or months at a time.

---

[7]For instance, see Robert J. Gordon, "Understanding Inflation in the 1980s," *Brookings Papers on Economic Activity,* vol. 16, no. 1 (1985), pp. 263–299, and "The Role of Wages in the Inflation Process," *American Economic Review Papers and Proceedings,* vol. 78 (May 1988), pp. 276–283.

The average annual unemployment rate of construction workers is high even if every construction worker is employed in the warm-weather months, since the average annual rate is an average of the rates for the cold-weather and warm-weather months. Thus if there were three cold months with unemployment rates for construction workers of 20 percent and nine warm months with unemployment rates of 0 percent, the average annual rate would be 5 percent. Seasonal unemployment may be considered a component of frictional unemployment and is thus part of the natural rate of unemployment.

We now turn to the reasons for frictional and structural unemployment. We begin with structural unemployment, since it constitutes a more serious social problem than frictional unemployment.

Vacancies and Unemployment in an Imaginary Economy

We can better understand the structural component of the natural unemployment rate (U^N) if we think of an imaginary society in which U^N is zero. All jobs are completely identical in their skill requirements, and all are located at exactly the same place. All workers are completely identical, with skill requirements perfectly suited for the identical jobs, and all workers live in the same location as the jobs. We can imagine a 10-mile-high combined factory-office-apartment skyscraper with very fast elevators at the corner of State and Madison Streets in Chicago.

In this imaginary economy it is impossible for vacancies and unemployment to exist simultaneously. Why? Imagine that initially some workers are unemployed, and that the government pursues expansive monetary and fiscal policies that stimulate aggregate demand. Additional jobs open up, but the unemployed workers are in exactly the right place and possess the right skills, so that they instantly zoom up or down the speedy elevators in the 10-mile-high skyscraper to the job's location. Each job vacancy disappears immediately, and unemployment declines.

Eventually all the unemployed will have found jobs. Any further job vacancies caused by an additional demand stimulus will not disappear because there are no available jobless people to fill them. Further aggregate demand stimulus will just expand the number of job vacancies.

Skill differences among jobs can cause structural unemployment. To be slightly more realistic, let us now assume that there are two types of jobs and workers in the 10-mile-high skyscraper, typists and computer programmers. As the economy expands, it gradually uses up its supply of trained computer programmers. Once all the computer programmers have jobs, all of the unemployment consists of jobless typists. If the government further stimulates aggregate demand, we assume that an equal number of job vacancies is created for programmers and typists. The typist vacancies disappear immediately as available typists are carried by elevator to fill the job openings. But there are no computer programmers left, and so the programmer job openings remain. *Vacancies and unemployment exist simulta-*

neously because firms refuse to hire typists to fill programmer vacancies. The costs of training are just too high.

In reality the actual economy is divided into numerous separate labor markets differing in location, working conditions, and skill requirements. If aggregate spending increases when the overall unemployment rate is 10 percent, then unemployed workers are available in almost every skill category and location, and firms do not have to raise wage rates to attract applicants. But in our economy at a 6 percent unemployment rate, any increase in aggregate spending generates job openings in some labor markets while many people remain unemployed in other markets. Some unemployed are able to fill developing job vacancies. But others are prevented from qualifying by the cost of moving to the locations of the job openings, by the cost of acquiring the required skills, and even by the "cost of information" involved in finding out what jobs are available.

Vacancies and upward pressure on wage rates.   In the imaginary economy with all jobs and workers alike and located at the same place, policymakers could use aggregate demand stimulus to push the unemployment rate to zero. There would be no job vacancies and no tendency for firms to boost wage rates to fill empty job slots. Thus it would be possible to experience zero unemployment without upward pressure on wages.

But in the real-world economy, with numerous separate labor markets, vacancies and unemployed workers can coexist. There may be many unfilled job openings for hotel workers in Boston while auto workers may be unemployed in Michigan. This type of unemployment is called "structural" or "mismatch" unemployment. Any attempt to use aggregate demand policy to push the total unemployment rate to zero will create numerous job vacancies for the types of skills that are in short supply and in the locations where labor is scarce. Firms will be desperate to fill the job vacancies and will boost wage rates, hoping to steal workers away from other firms. Higher wages will raise business costs and cause price increases. *Thus a situation with a low unemployment rate and lots of job vacancies maintained by rapid demand growth is one in which the inflation rate will continuously accelerate.*

Causes of and Cures for Mismatch Unemployment: Lack of Skills

All groups in the labor force, including adult men, adult women, and teenagers, are victims of mismatch between their own skills and locations, and the skill and location requirements of available jobs. Why does this worker-job mismatch occur? We begin with causes of skill mismatch and some suggested policy remedies, and then turn to the causes of and remedies for location mismatch.

Inflexibility of relative wages.   Elementary economics teaches that a surplus of a commodity develops when its price is too high. In the same way, many economists have argued that high unemployment of some groups, particularly teenagers, signals an excessive real wage for that group. In the

United States there is a uniform minimum wage for both adults and teenagers, but teenage unemployment is higher than adult unemployment, and some people have proposed a lower minimum wage for teenagers. Yet others argue that a lower minimum wage for teenagers would harm low-skill adult workers.

After several years in the late 1970s when the minimum wage increased rapidly, the minimum wage reached $3.35 in early 1981 and was not raised until 1989. Since the average wage rate of all workers increased after 1981, the *ratio* of the minimum wage rate to the average wage rate declined (from 46 percent in 1981 to 35 percent in 1989). However, this decline in the "effective" minimum wage did not seem to help groups with high unemployment such as teenagers and blacks. The unemployment rate of teenagers between 1980 and 1988 rose from 2.5 to 2.8 times the total unemployment rate, and the black unemployment rate rose from 2.0 to 2.2 times the total rate, despite the decline in the minimum wage rate relative to the average wage rate.

Lack of job training. Vacant jobs often have specific skill requirements. Sometimes firms are willing to train workers when the skills are specific to the particular job; for example, a secretary needs to know the filing system in a particular office. Although during a training period the firm may be paying workers more than their productivity, the firm can finance the training by paying workers less than their productivity after the training period is completed. But some training, for example, how to use a word processor or personal computer, is general in nature. Firms may be unwilling to train employees in general skills for fear that the employees will quit before the firm's training investment can be repaid. Yet schools may not be able to provide the training, either, lacking the equipment or properly trained instructors.

Solutions for low skills fall into three basic categories—better public education, subsidies for firms to train workers, and government-financed training programs. Better public education is essential, particularly for students from low-income families, since training subsidies and programs will not work if teenagers and young adults cannot read or perform arithmetic.

Employer training subsidies have been very successful in raising incomes of participants, both during and after the training period. The primary problem seems to have been persuading employers to participate. Firms that participated in such programs tended to be selective, choosing those who needed training least, and they have been reluctant to include young people.[8]

Among the most useful functions of government-financed training programs has been to provide basic skills not learned in the public schools. It has been possible on average to achieve a 1.5 year gain in reading ability and 1 year in math with just 90 hours of adult instruction. One program with

---

[8]The statements about subsidy and training programs are taken from an excellent and readable recent summary paper by Sar A. Levitan and Garth L. Magnum, "A Quarter Century of Employment and Training Policy: Where Do We Go from Here?" in William D. Nordhaus, ed., *Jobs for the Future: Strategies in a New Framework* (Washington, D.C.: Center for National Policy, 1984), pp. 39–49.

an excellent record is the Job Corps, which provides skill training in residential settings to young people from the most disadvantaged backgrounds.

Discrimination.   Some employers will not hire women, minorities, or teenagers. Much discrimination stems from long-standing customs and from social pressure. We observe that almost all secretaries, telephone operators, elementary school teachers, nurses, and typists are women, and that black workers are pushed into relatively unpleasant occupations. Despite the gains since the civil rights movement of the mid-1960s, less-educated blacks and women are still prevented in many cases from entering unions in blue-collar trades. Women also face discrimination from employers fearing that young female employees will quit work as the result of pregnancy. This in unfair to young women who plan to continue working while their children are young, and to those who plan to remain childless.

Several Western European nations have helped reduce discrimination against women by subsidizing maternity leaves and providing subsidized child care, allowing women with children to maintain more stable job records. A case could be made for similar subsidies in the United States to members of minority groups who were cheated in the past by segregated school systems, low expenditures on inner city schools, and outright job discrimination. Some barriers, particularly the limitation of many blue-collar craft unions to white males, may require legal rather than economic remedies.

Causes of and Cures for Mismatch Unemployment: Wrong Location

Often job vacancies and unemployment are very unequally distributed. Within the United States, the recovery and expansion of the economy after the 1982 recession was quite unequally distributed. By early 1989 six of the eight states with the lowest unemployment rates were the six New England states; the unemployment rate in Vermont had fallen to 2 percent but was still above 9 percent in Louisiana. Fast-food outlets in Boston were paying well above the minimum wage to teenagers, and the Berkshire Hilton in Pittsfield, Massachusetts, was so short-staffed that the manager had to double as a bellhop.[9] Such a regional imbalance of unemployment rates helps raise the natural rate of unemployment and put upward pressure on wage rates, as New England employers are forced to raise wages more than Louisiana employers reduce wages.

Why don't unemployed workers move from Louisiana to New England? Part of the reason is that they may lack needed skills. Another is that two-earner families have become more common, making it harder for families to move when one family member loses a job but the other does not. High housing prices (in the region where jobs are abundant) and the lack of ready cash to pay for moving expenses also help explain the persistence of un-

---

[9]"How Some U.S. Areas Cope with Anomaly: Surging Economies," *Wall Street Journal,* December 12, 1985, p. 1.

employment differences between regions. The same problems plague inner city residents who see nearby factories closing but cannot travel to distant suburban factories or offices where new jobs are opening up. Another reason for locational mismatch unemployment is simply that the unemployed do not know where the jobs are. Some European countries invest much more than the United States in centralized government employment services to provide informational and job counseling services. Finally, some unemployed people do not want to move away from relatives, friends, and familiar surroundings.

Several solutions, other than a better employment service, have been proposed to reduce the locational source of mismatch unemployment. One suggestion is subsidies to help unemployed workers pay the costs of relocating to areas with ample job openings. Another suggestion is "enterprise zones" to induce manufacturers to move their factories to depressed areas. While the United States has little experience with such programs, several European nations have attempted to "bribe" firms to locate in depressed areas. A successful example is a new electronics area called "Silicon Glen" between Glasgow and Edinburgh, Scotland, but similar programs in northern England and southern Italy have been largely unsuccessful.

11-5 Frictional (Turnover) Unemployment and Job Search

We have now examined the sources of structural (or mismatch) unemployment, one of the two components of the natural unemployment rate. A second component is frictional (or turnover) unemployment. What is the difference between structural and frictional unemployment? The barriers that stand between vacant jobs and *structurally* unemployed workers are serious and require substantial investments in training or moving to eliminate. But the barriers that stand between vacant jobs and *frictionally* unemployed workers are less serious, involving the costs of "job search" for a relatively short period in the local community for a suitable job.

One way of differentiating structural and frictional unemployment is the length of unemployment episodes ("spells"). In a year like 1987 when the economy was operating close to the natural rate of unemployment, half of all weeks of unemployment occurred in spells of at least three months duration.[10] Thus some of the unemployed find jobs quite rapidly, in a month or two, suggesting frictional unemployment. Many others take much longer, suggesting structural unemployment. Thus frictional and structural unemployment are not in conflict but both occur at the same time, to different people.

---

[10]This figure understates the importance of long-term unemployment, since some unemployment spells end by people dropping out of the labor force rather than finding jobs. Taking into account people who leave the labor force and then become unemployed a second time before finding a job, 40 percent of unemployment in 1974 was accounted for by unemployment spells lasting six months or more. See Kim B. Clark and Lawrence H. Summers, "Labor Market Dynamics and Unemployment: A Reconsideration," *Brookings Papers on Economic Activity,* vol. 10, no. 1 (1979), pp. 13–60.

Reasons for Frictional Unemployment

As we have seen, Census Bureau workers ask a number of questions in order to determine whether individual household members are unemployed. These questions allow the unemployed to be broken down into five groups:

1. persons laid off who can expect to return to the same job,
2. persons who have lost jobs to which they cannot expect to return,
3. persons who have quit their jobs,
4. reentrants who are returning to the labor force after a spell of neither working nor looking for work, and
5. new entrants who have never worked at a full-time job before but are now seeking employment.

Frictional unemployment consists primarily of individuals in categories 3 to 5, although reentrants and new entrants may spend a long time in futile search if their unemployment is structural.

The breakdown of the unemployed among these five categories is very sensitive to the business cycle. In recessions like that of 1981–82, the share of persons who have lost their jobs, either temporarily or permanently, rises substantially. In fact 90 percent of the increase in unemployment during the typical recession occurs in the form of job losses and layoffs. Thus we can regard cyclical unemployment as occurring in categories 1 and 2, although structural unemployment also occurs in category 2, "job loss."

Some reasons for unemployment are concentrated in particular demographic groups. For instance, job loss tends to be most concentrated among adult males. Since layoffs were so widespread in 1982, and were so concentrated among adult males, that year was the first in the entire postwar era when the overall unemployment rate of males exceeded that of females. Reentry unemployment is felt mainly by adult females and teenagers. New entry unemployment, of course, is mainly experienced by teenagers.

Table 11-1 shows how the types of unemployment are divided among the major demographic groups. The month illustrated is October 1987, when the economy was operating at its natural rate of unemployment. To simplify

Table 11-1 **Unemployment Rates by Reason, Sex, and Age in October 1987**

	Unemployment rate				Percentage of group unemployment			
	Males, 20 and over	*Females, 20 and over*	*Teenagers, 16–19 years*	*All groups*	*Males, 20 and over*	*Females, 20 and over*	*Teenagers, 16–19 years*	*All groups*
1. Job losers	3.1	1.9	2.6	2.8	67.1	36.1	15.0	45.0
2. Job leavers	0.7	0.8	2.5	0.8	14.6	15.8	14.6	15.0
3. Reentrants	0.7	2.1	4.7	1.6	15.4	40.3	27.4	27.4
4. New entrants	0.1	0.4	7.4	0.8	2.9	7.8	43.0	12.6
5. Total for group	4.6	5.2	17.2	6.0	100.0	100.0	100.0	100.0

Source: Employment and Earnings, November 1988, Table A–14.

the table the categories of temporary and permanent job loss are consolidated. A glance at the table reveals several important differences that help explain the higher unemployment of adult women and teenagers. The three groups are fairly close together on the percentage of the labor force out of work through job loss (line 1). Adult women and teenagers differ from adult males by their more frequent reentry unemployment. On line 4, over seven percentage points of the total 17 percent teenage unemployment rate appear to be due to the extra unemployment experienced by teenagers when they search for their first job ("new entrant").

Overall, perhaps the most striking contrast is between the large percentage of adult male unemployment caused by "lost job" (67.1 percent on line 1) as opposed to the small share of teenage unemployment caused by job loss (15.0 percent). Thus it would be fair to conclude in a year like 1987 that adult males experience mostly structural unemployment, while teenagers experience mostly frictional unemployment.

The economics of job refusal.   The basic reason for frictional unemployment is explained by the theory of "search" unemployment, which develops the idea that an unemployed person may sometimes do better to refuse a job offer than accept it! Why? Imagine a teenager who quits school and begins to look for his first job. He walks down the street and soon encounters a restaurant displaying a sign "Dishwasher Wanted." An inquiry provides the information that the dishwasher opening is available immediately and pays $4.25 per hour. Will the teenager accept the job without further search? Refusal may benefit the teenager if he is able to locate a job with higher pay or better working conditions.

Job search theory treats unemployment as a socially valuable, productive activity. Unemployed individuals "invest" in job search. The cost of their investment is the cost of the search itself plus the loss of wages that could be earned by accepting a job immediately. The payoff to their investment is the prospect of earning a higher wage for many months or years into the future. Because people do not always want the first available job and prefer to search, the only way for the government to bring down the natural rate of unemployment is either (1) to provide better employment agencies that provide information that shortens the period of job search, (2) to lessen entry into job search by reducing the reasons behind quitting, reentry, and initial entry, or (3) to change the economic incentives that unnecessarily prolong the search, particularly unemployment benefits and high taxes on the income of the employed, both of which cut the net earnings of taking a job immediately rather than remaining unemployed.

Effects of unemployment compensation.   Some economists blame the government for making frictional unemployment higher than necessary and advocate measures to reduce the duration in weeks of an average episode ("spell") of unemployment, as well as reducing the number of episodes per worker. In a series of articles, Martin S. Feldstein of Harvard University has focused on how the unemployment compensation system extends the duration of unemployment. A job with a before-tax wage of $200 per week may yield a worker only $146 in take-home pay. With no unemployment compensation or welfare benefits, the worker would have an incentive to search many hours per day and take a new job quickly. But the opportunity to receive an unemployment benefit of $120 per week cuts drastically the worker's incentive to search for a new job. The combination of taxes on income from work together with unemployment compensation imposes a tax rate of 87 percent—that is, the drop in take-home pay during unemployment ($146 − $120 = $26) is only 13 percent of the before-tax original wage. Many workers on layoff do not search at all but simply wait to be recalled to their old job.[11]

The incentive for temporary layoffs given by the unemployment compensation system occurs not only in recessions but also when the economy is operating at its natural rate of unemployment. The economy may be in equilibrium, with no tendency for inflation to accelerate or decelerate, yet a firm may find that its sales have dropped temporarily. The unemployment compensation system provides an incentive for the firm to adjust by laying off workers rather than by cutting hours per employee or simply by allowing inventories to grow.

SELF-TEST   Would the following events raise or lower the amount of frictional (turnover) unemployment? (1) A change in rules allowing the unemployed to earn unemployment benefits for one year instead of the present six months. (2) A reduction in the personal income tax rate. (3) A decrease in the fraction of the working-age population consisting of teenagers. (4) An increase in the price of pay telephone calls.

11-6 The Costs of Recessions and Stabilization Policy

Costs of Frictional and Structural Unemployment

So far we have examined the factors that make the natural rate of unemployment so high in the United States. A certain amount of frictional unemployment performs a valuable function by allowing individuals to explore without being forced to accept the first available job, which may pay little or have unattractive working conditions.

However, the rest of the unemployment that occurs when the economy is operating at the natural rate is structural. Far from refusing a wide variety of job offers, many unemployed people never have a job offer to consider. The costs of structural unemployment include, first, the private costs to the individual, including lost income and the erosion of job skills and confidence. Second, there are costs to society—not only the cost of unemployment and welfare benefits, but also the costs of additional crime committed by the unemployed, as well as the costs of higher rates of illness and even

---

[11]Martin S. Feldstein, "The Importance of Temporary Layoffs: An Empirical Analysis," *Brookings Papers on Economic Activity,* vol. 6, no. 3 (1975), pp. 725–744.

suicide among the unemployed. These private and social costs should properly be taken into account when weighing the budgetary costs of policies to reduce structural unemployment, including better public schools, training subsidies, and government-managed training programs.

Costs of Cyclical Unemployment

Recall that cyclical unemployment is the amount by which the actual unemployment rate exceeds the natural rate of unemployment. The costs of cyclical unemployment include the same types of private and social costs caused by structural unemployment. But in addition, the costs of recessions far exceed the private and social costs incurred by the individuals who actually become unemployed. Recall that Okun's law, plotted in Figure 11-1 and expressed in equations (11.1) and (11.2), states that the unemployment rate (U) is equal to the natural unemployment rate (U^N) plus 0.4 times the deviation of the output ratio (Q/Q^N) from 100 percent. Turning this relationship around, Okun's law implies that actual real GNP changes relative to natural real GNP by roughly 2.5 (that is, 1/0.4) times the change in the unemployment rate. Thus a recession that involves cyclical unemployment ($U - U^N$) of four percentage points lasting for a year involves the loss of 10 ($= 2.5 \times 4$) percent of one year's GNP, or about $500 billion at 1989 prices.

As we learned in Chapter 9, policymakers may create a recession as part of the process of "disinflation," the achievement of a permanent slowdown in the inflation rate. We learn in the next sections of this chapter why people dislike inflation, and why reducing the inflation rate is beneficial to society. But if disinflation is achieved by a recession, then these benefits of disinflation must be weighed against the costs of the recession required to achieve disinflation.

Why is the response of output as high as 2.5, making the output loss in a recession a larger percentage than the cyclical unemployment rate? First, some of the unemployed become discouraged and drop out of the labor force, so society loses their wages and the income taxes they paid while employed, even though they are not counted as among the unemployed. Second, overtime hours are cut substantially in a recession, reducing the take-home pay of many of those still employed. Third, business profits decline sharply as firms retain employees who are no longer needed (because firms want to retain the valuable skills of the employees and hope that the economy will soon revive). Fourth, all branches of government lose a substantial amount of tax revenue.

Balanced against these costs of recession, over and above the income loss of the unemployed themselves, is a minor gain in leisure time by those who are unemployed or work fewer overtime hours. Overall, it has been estimated that this leisure time factor requires only a minor downward adjustment to make the value of the GNP gap a reasonably accurate adjustment of the dollar cost of recessions.[12]

---

[12]See Robert J. Gordon, "The Welfare Cost of Higher Unemployment," *Brookings Papers on Economic Activity,* vol. 4, no. 1 (1973), pp. 133–195. See also Arthur M. Okun, *Prices and Quantities: A Macroeconomic Analysis* (Washington, D.C.: Brookings Institution, 1981), Chapter 7.

The Human Costs of Recessions

In assessing the costs of the disinflation policy of the early 1980s, we need to consider not only the hundreds of billions of dollars of lost output, but also the human costs of recessions. The basic difference between the costs of unemployment and inflation is that the unemployment of a household head hits the family like a hammer, whereas the costs of inflation are milder and spread more broadly across the entire population.

The human costs of unemployment are tragic. Researchers have found that with every 1 percent increase in the U.S. unemployment rate, 920 more people commit suicide, 650 commit homicide, 500 die from heart and kidney disease and cirrhosis of the liver, 4000 are admitted to state mental hospitals, and 3300 are sent to state prisons. In total, a 1 percent increase in unemployment is associated statistically with 37,000 more deaths, including 20,000 heart attacks. Unemployed workers are also more likely to experience dizziness, rapid heart beat, troubled sleep, back and neck pain, and high blood pressure.[13]

Common among the psychic costs of unemployment is a sense of being condemned to uselessness in a world that worships the useful. Just as serious are the long-term consequences. In 1981–82 as many as 25 million people may have been deprived of medical insurance as a consequence of unemployment, since such insurance is a job benefit typically paid by employers. Physical and mental health deteriorates, and this is exacerbated by alcoholism. The health of children also suffers, particularly when parents take out their frustration and rage on their children in the form of child abuse.

All these factors taken together strengthen the case for government stabilization policies that maintain the actual unemployment rate close to the natural rate, and for a vigorous pursuit of policies to reduce turnover and mismatch unemployment in order to push the natural unemployment rate well below 6 percent.

11-7 Costs of Inflation: Creeping Inflation Versus Hyperinflation

We have seen that unemployment imposes major costs on society. Yet high unemployment is often the result of deliberate government policies to create a recession in order to cut the inflation rate. Is the benefit of lower inflation worth the cost of higher unemployment? The rest of this chapter examines how inflation harms society, who is most hurt by inflation, and how government policies might reduce the costs of inflation.

At first glance, worry about inflation may appear misplaced. When inflation is zero, wages may increase at 1 percent a year. When inflation proceeds at 6 percent annually, wages may grow at 7 percent annually. Workers

---

[13]Barry Bluestone and Bennett Harrison, *The Deindustrialization of America* (New York: Basic Books, 1982), Chapter 3.

have little reason to be bothered about the inflation rate (p) if the growth in their wages (w) always stays the same distance ahead, as in this example:

	No inflation	6 percent annual inflation
Growth rate of nominal wages (w)	1	7
Growth rate of price deflator (p)	0	6
Growth rate of real wages ($w - p$)	1	1

However, we shall learn that inflation is felt primarily by owners of financial assets, not by workers whose only income is earned in the form of wages and who spend their entire wage income on consumption goods.[14] An unexpected "surprise" inflation hurts "ordinary people" by cutting the real value of individual savings accounts and hits particularly hard at the savings and at the pension funds of those who are retired or are about to retire.

Even when inflation is fully anticipated and is no surprise, everyone notices the shrinkage in the value of the cash in their pockets and people invest extra effort in managing their cash that would not be necessary in the absence of inflation. Furthermore, inflation creates real costs for society because the tax system does not state its rules in inflation-adjusted "real" dollars. More generally, the capricious redistribution of income caused by inflation creates uncertainty for everyone.

The distinction between "surprise" and "fully anticipated" inflation is central to understanding the costs of inflation and suggested methods of reducing those costs. We distinguish between nominal, expected real, and actual real interest rates, and show how both surprise and fully anticipated inflation affects savers and borrowers. Then we turn to the effects of surprise inflation and remedies that allow the nominal interest returns to savers to adjust more promptly to surprise inflation. Finally, we examine the effects of inflation that is fully anticipated and possible solutions, including reforms of the tax system and other institutions. We conclude the chapter by comparing the welfare costs of recessions with those of inflation.

11-8 Nominal and Real Interest Rates

The **nominal interest rate** is the market interest rate actually charged by financial institutions and earned by bondholders.

The **expected real interest rate** is the nominal interest rate minus the expected rate of inflation.

As Americans became accustomed to inflation in the 1960s and 1970s, they learned the difference between nominal and real interest rates, even if they had not been taught this economists' jargon.

*The **nominal interest rate** (i) is the rate actually quoted by banks and negotiated in financial markets. The **expected real interest rate** (r^e) is what people expect to pay on their borrowings or earn on their savings after deducting expected inflation ($r^e = i - p^e$). The expected real interest rate is what matters for investment and saving decisions. The ac-*

[14]The statement that workers do not lose refers to a normal inflation fueled by increasing aggregate demand. When the economy experiences a supply shock, as did the United States in 1974 and 1979–80 at the time of the oil price hikes, inflation experiences a temporary acceleration while real wages simultaneously decline. This is the "real wage flexibility" experienced in the United States, as discussed in Section 10-3.

tual **real interest rate** *is the nominal interest rate minus the actual rate
of inflation* $(r = i - p)$.

Effect of Fully Anticipated Inflation on Borrowers and Lenders

The nominal interest rate can be very different in two countries with different inflation rates, or in one country at different moments in history. But investment and saving decisions will be the same in the two situations as long as the expected real interest rate is the same. The following example illustrates a hypothetical situation in which a fully anticipated inflation would have no effect.

Sam and Pete with no inflation. Let us consider the example of Pete Puritan and Sam Spendthrift—two boys, both broke, who both want a new ten-speed bicycle. Both plan to earn $100 at part-time jobs over the next year, exactly the price of a new bicycle, but Sam impatiently buys his bike immediately with borrowed money, whereas Pete patiently waits until the end of the year. When there is no inflation, the price of the bicycle remains constant at $100:

	Pete Puritan	Sam Spendthrift
1. Sam purchases bicycle on January 1 with borrowed money	—	100
2. Earnings during year, put into savings account	100	100
3. Savings account on December 31, including 3 percent interest	103	103
4. Sam repays loan, including 3 percent interest	—	103
5. Pete buys bicycle	100	—
6. Balance at end of year (line 3 minus 4 and 5)	3	0

At the end of the year, each boy has his bicycle, but Pete has $3 left and Sam has nothing. Why? Pete has received a reward for his patience, the interest on his savings account. Sam has spent his interest earnings to pay the interest cost of his loan; he was not patient, and so he receives no reward for patience as does Pete.[15]

Fully anticipated inflation. Now we consider Pete and Sam's behavior in a second situation, in which inflation proceeds at a 6 percent annual rate instead of zero. If the expected real interest rate is to remain at 3 percent

---

[15]Notice the simplifying assumptions introduced to keep this example manageable. First, neither boy pays taxes on his wages. Second, we pretend that interest is earned on the $100 of wage earnings throughout the year, whereas, in fact, if work is distributed evenly in each month the average balance in the savings account is only $50. Third, the borrowing interest rate and savings account interest rate are both 3 percent, whereas in the real world borrowing rates are higher to compensate banks and other lenders for risk and for administrative costs. Fourth, we disregard the depreciation on Sam's bicycle, which is one year older than Pete's.

as in the first situation, the nominal interest rate on both savings accounts and bicycle loans must rise from 3 to 9 percent:

General Form | Numerical Example

$$r^e = i - p^e \qquad r^e = 9 - 6 = 3$$

With a 6 percent rate of inflation, the price of the bicycle rises from \$100 to \$106 by the end of the year, but the higher interest rate exactly compensates, and both boys wind up in exactly the same situation as before:

	Pete Puritan	Sam Spendthrift
1. Sam purchases bicycle on January 1 with borrowed money	—	100
2. Earnings during year, put into savings account	100	100
3. Savings account on December 31, including 9 percent interest	109	109
4. Sam repays loan, including 9 percent interest	—	109
5. Pete buys bicycle on December 31, which now costs \$106	106	—
6. Balance at end of year (line 3 minus 4 and 5)	3	0

As before, Pete receives a \$3 reward for his patience, while Sam is compensated not by money but by the nonmonetary benefit of an extra year's enjoyment of his bicycle. The extra \$6 that Sam earns on his savings account is exactly eaten up by the extra interest on his loan, whereas the extra \$6 that Pete earns on his savings account is exactly eaten up by the \$6 increase in the price of the bicycle.

Summary: This example was designed to illustrate an artificial situation in which inflation has no effect on economic well-being. Our current inflation would have no adverse consequences, and there would be no need for policymakers to try to reduce or stop inflation if these basic characteristics of the example were universally true in the United States:

1. Inflation is universally and accurately anticipated.

2. All savings are held in bonds, stocks, or savings accounts earning the nominal interest rate (i); no one holds money in accounts with an interest rate held below the market nominal interest rate. We will see that this condition is violated in the United States, where the interest rate on cash is maintained at zero and the interest rate paid on some types of checking and savings accounts is below the market nominal interest rate.

3. An inflation of p_0 percent raises the market nominal interest rate (i) for both saving and borrowing by exactly p_0 percent above the no-inflation interest rate.

4. Only real (not nominal) interest income is taxable, and only the real cost of borrowing is tax deductible.

5. Inflation raises the prices of all goods by the same percent (that is, any changes in the relative prices of goods are just the same as would have occurred in the absence of inflation).

11-9 Effects of Surprise Inflation

Redistributive Effects of an Inflationary Surprise

Now let us violate condition 1 in the preceding summary list, that inflation is accurately anticipated. In several postwar episodes, such as 1966–69, 1973–74, and 1978–80, the actual inflation rate accelerated well above the rate expected by most people.

Sam and Pete with unanticipated inflation. Let us assume that in the bicycle example both the savings and borrowing rate stay at 3 percent because banks expect a zero rate of inflation. Then, as a total surprise to everyone, the price of all goods jumps 6 percent on December 30, forcing Pete to pay $106 for his bicycle:

	Pete Puritan	Sam Spendthrift
1. Sam purchases bicycle on January 1 with borrowed money	—	100
2. Earnings during year, put into savings account	100	100
e. Savings account on December 31, including 3 percent interest	103	103
4. Sam repays loan, including 3 percent interest	—	103
5. Pete buys bicycle on December 31, which now costs $106	106	—
6. Balance at end of year (line 3 minus 4 and 5)	−3	0

Poor Pete's hopes have been dashed. He would never have bothered to save if he had known that his money would lose value during the year. Pete is the classic loser from inflation, the individual who has his savings eroded by an **unanticipated inflation,** but who does not (like Sam) have debts to match. Because most people start out in life with relatively few assets, and then gradually build up savings in preparation for retirement, those hurt most by an unanticipated inflation are those who have retired or who are about to retire.

When actual inflation (p = 6 percent in the example) turns out to be different than expected (p^e = 0 in the example), the actual real interest rate differs from that which was expected. In the example a 3 percent real interest rate was expected (r^e = 3), but after the fact (*ex post*) the actual real interest (r) turned out to be much less:

General Form	Numerical Example

$$r = i - p \qquad r = 3 - 6 = -3$$

Deflation hurts debtors. The basic case against unanticipated inflation, then, is that it redistributes income from creditors (savers) to debtors without their knowledge or consent. Conversely, an unanticipated deflation does just the opposite, redistributing income from debtors to creditors. Throughout history, farmers have been an important group of debtors who have been badly hurt by unanticipated deflation. The interest income of savers

Unanticipated inflation occurs when the actual inflation rate (p) differs from the expected (or anticipated) inflation rate (p^e).

hardly fell at all between 1929 and 1933, but farmers, badly hurt by a precipitous decline in farm prices, saw their nominal income fall by two-thirds, from $6.2 to $2.1 billion. Farmers were also badly hurt by the disinflation of the early 1980s.

Gainers from surprise inflation.   Clearly, Pete and all other savers lose from a surprise inflation. Who gains? Sam does not gain, because he has a debt and an asset to match when the price increase occurs. His bicycle has gained in value. But because all prices have increased together, his capital gain on the bicycle does him no good. If he wanted to sell his bike and buy schoolbooks, the higher price of schoolbooks would prevent him from buying any more schoolbooks than would have been possible in the absence of inflation. The real gainers from unanticipated inflation are those who are heavily in debt but who have no financial assets, only physical assets whose prices rise with inflation. Private individuals who have just purchased houses with small down payments are among the classic gainers from an unanticipated inflation.

Here is an example of Harold Homeowner, who purchases his $100,000 house on January 1 with a 10 percent down payment.[16] His financial statement appears as follows on January 1 and December 31, when an inflationary surprise increases the price of his house by 6 percent on December 30. His increase in net worth of $6000 is a "nominal **capital gain**," and the $5094 increase in his real net worth is called his "real capital gain."

*A **capital gain** is any increase in the value of a physical or financial asset.*

Besides homeowners, other classic gainers from surprise inflation are corporations, whose outstanding stocks and bonds are the counterpart of household assets. The government also gains from inflation because its outstanding liabilities are money (currency and bank reserves) and government bonds.

Harold Homeowner's Financial Statement, January 1 and December 31, when an Inflationary Surprise Increases the Price of His House by 6 Percent on December 30

	January 1	December 31
Assets		
House	$100,000	$106,000
Liabilities		
Mortgage debt	90,000	90,000
Net worth =		
assets −		
liabilities	10,000	16,000
Real net worth		
$= \dfrac{\text{net worth}}{\text{price index}}$	$\dfrac{10,000}{1.00} = \$10,000$	$\dfrac{16,000}{1.06} = \$15,094$

Redistribution among income classes.   Surprise inflation hurts savers and benefits borrowers. Does this mean that inflation redistributes wealth from rich to poor? No, it does not. Because poor people neither save nor borrow much (since they have little collateral to offer for loans), they are not much affected by surprise inflation, although poor people of working age

---

[16]The repayment of mortgage debt is ignored.

are major losers from recessions and high unemployment. Poor people near retirement who rely entirely on social security are protected by the indexation of social security benefits.

Instead, the major redistribution accomplished by inflation affects the rich and the middle class. Wealthy individuals hold the vast majority of nominal-fixed (that is, nonindexed) bonds, and they lose heavily from surprise inflation. Middle-income homeowners, like Harold Homeowner in the example earlier, are the major gainers from surprise inflation. So are middle-income farmers, who benefit from higher land prices on land that was financed by fixed interest mortgages. *Thus the major redistribution effect of surprise inflation is to transfer real wealth from the rich to the middle class, while a surprise deflation (or disinflation) transfers real wealth from the middle class to the rich.* America's middle-income farmers who had been big winners from the U.S. inflation of the 1970s, were among the much-publicized losers from the 1982–86 disinflation.

Surprise Inflation and the Effects of Uncertainty

Thus far we have discussed one major effect of surprise inflation, the redistribution of wealth from savers to borrowers. But there is another effect of surprise inflation that affects everyone, and this is uncertainty about the future price level. In the absence of indexed bonds, people are exposed to the effects of inflation on asset prices and returns in a way that does not occur with no inflation. There is a real fear that today's saving, intended to finance a child's college education or living expenses after retirement, will be inadequate.

In the inflation experienced in the United States in the 1970s and early 1980s, families who had previously bought their homes with low-interest mortgages, like Harold Homeowner, turned out to be very well protected against inflation. Even those who owned their homes free and clear were well protected, since the price of housing increased more than the average level. Similarly, the fear of inadequate living standards during retirement was alleviated by the indexation of social security benefits. But our hindsight knowledge of these facts does not lessen the insecurity felt by many people while the inflation was going on; nor does it lessen the genuine losses suffered by those who did not own homes and were not protected by social security or indexed wages. The fear of an uncertain future probably explains much of the dislike of inflation expressed in public opinion polls and the political pressure felt by policymakers in the late 1970s and in the early 1980s to shift to a policy of disinflation.

11-10 Costs of a Fully Anticipated Inflation

The redistributional effects of inflation disappear once the inflation ceases being a surprise and becomes fully anticipated. Because of the U.S. system of overlapping staggered wage contracts, it may take several years for all contracts to take account of the higher anticipated inflation rate. But because interest rates are free to adjust promptly, the nominal interest rate tends to rise as soon as people adjust their expectations of inflation. However, it takes people much longer to form their expectations of inflation, and it may take several months or quarters of continuing inflation to convince everyone that inflation will continue at a higher rate, and the nominal interest rate completes its upward adjustment.

What are the costs to society of allowing inflation to continue at a steady moderate rate like 5 or 10 percent, as long as everyone accurately anticipates that rate? The simple example of the effects of anticipated inflation on Pete Puritan and Sam Spendthrift enumerated five conditions that must be satisfied for inflation to have no effect. The first of these was accurate anticipations, which we will assume throughout this section. The other four conditions are (2) no one holds money earning any interest rate below the market interest rate, (3) inflation raises the nominal interest rate by 1 percent for each 1 percent of inflation, (4) only real interest income is taxable and the real cost of borrowing tax-deductible, and (5) inflation causes no changes in relative prices. Each of these conditions is violated in the real world, and the following discussion of the effects of anticipated inflation is organized into categories corresponding to the violation of these conditions—the effects of money holding, effects of nonadjustment of nominal interest rates, effects of the tax system, and effects of inflation on relative prices. This section examines the effects of inflation on money holding and the inconvenience that inflation creates to money holders, as well as the relationship between inflation and changes in relative prices. In the next section we examine the effects of regulations that prevent the adjustment of nominal interest rates and effects of the tax system.

Welfare Cost of Lower Real Money Balances

The market rate of interest is not paid on money for two main reasons. First, currency pays no interest. Second, banks earn no interest on the reserves (deposits) that they are required to keep at the Federal Reserve banks, so banks cannot afford to pay the market rate of interest on deposits. The fact that the market rate of interest is not paid on money has several consequences for society.

People demand money for its convenience services. The reason that fully anticipated inflation imposes welfare costs on society is that people do not desire money for itself, but rather for the **extra convenience services** that it provides. Inflation causes people to hold less money, so they suffer inconvenience. Money provides convenience to the consumer because purchases can be made instantly. If no money were held (that is, no currency and no checking accounts), then the consumer would have to suffer the inconvenience of going to the bank to make a savings deposit withdrawal, or—even less convenient—to sell a stock or bond before the purchase could be made.

The **extra convenience services** of money are the services provided by holding one extra dollar of money instead of bonds.

People hold currency even though it pays no interest. The reason they are willing to hold currency paying zero interest, instead of holding a savings certificate paying 7 percent interest, *must be* that the money provides them with at least 7 percent more convenience services than the certificate. How is this related to inflation? When the inflation rate increases, the nominal interest rate on all assets other than currency tends to increase. If the inflation rate rose by 5 percent then the nominal interest rate on certificates would tend to rise from 7 percent to 12 percent, that is, to a rate 5 percent higher than before. Thus people would cut back on their money holdings until the extra convenience services of money rose from 7 to 12 percent. They would hold less cash in their pockets, retain cash only for those expenditures where only cash is accepted (as for taxi rides and bus fares), and would hold less cash for nonessential purposes.

The "shoe-leather cost" of inflation.   The effect of higher inflation and higher interest rates in causing people to hold less cash is sometimes called the "shoe-leather cost" of inflation. Why? Higher interest rates cause people to hold less cash in their pockets at any given moment, so they must go more often to the bank to obtain cash by making withdrawals from savings accounts and other interest-paying assets. The inconvenience that people suffer while making these trips to the bank eventually wears out their shoes, hence the "shoe-leather cost."

Shoe-Leather Costs in Actual Inflations

Shoe-leather costs in the United States.   Financial deregulation has allowed the banking system to pay interest on most types of checking accounts. Thus it is only currency (and the nonpayment of interest on bank reserves at the Federal Reserve banks) that accounts for money's shoe-leather costs. Taking account of the payment of interest on bank checking accounts, it has been estimated that the value of convenience services lost from a 10 percent inflation in the United States is just 0.25 percent of GNP, or $13 billion at 1989 prices.[17] This loss is very small in comparison to the costs of the recession that would be needed to eliminate permanently a 10 percent fully anticipated inflation. And it could be reduced further if the Federal Reserve System paid interest on bank reserves.

Hyperinflation is an extremely rapid inflation, reaching 100 percent or more *per month.*

Shoe-leather costs during rapid inflation.   The inconvenience cost of inflation becomes much larger when inflation enters the triple-digit range, as in Israel in the early 1980s. For instance, at the 400 percent inflation rate that Israel experienced in early 1985, the inconvenience cost rises to 3.3 percent of GNP. The cost would be enormous in a **hyperinflation,** like that which occurred in Germany in 1922–23, at the end of which the inflation rate was 600 percent per month. In 1919 a farmer sold a piece of land for 80,000 marks as a nest egg for old age. All he got for the money a few years later was a woolen sweater. Elderly Germans can still recall the terrible days in 1923.

> People were bringing money to the bank in cardboard boxes and laundry baskets. As we no longer could count it, we put the money on scales and weighed it. I can still see my brothers coming home Saturdays with heaps of paper money. When the shops reopened after the weekend they got no more than a breakfast roll for it. Many got drunk on their pay because it was worthless on Monday.[18]

---

[17]See Stanley Fischer, "The Benefits of Price Stability," working paper, Massachusetts Institute of Technology, Cambridge, Mass., July 1984.

[18]Alice Segert, "When Inflation Buried Germany," *Chicago Tribune,* November 30, 1974.

The Bolivian inflation of 1985. The Latin American country of Bolivia experienced a hyperinflation that reached a rate of 50,000 percent per year by January 1985. Inflation had so eroded the value of money that the largest peso note—a 100,000 peso bill—was worth only $2.00 at the official exchange rate, bringing inconvenience into every aspect of life. When the dinner bill arrived at a restaurant, wads of money had to be pulled out to settle the bill, and credit cards were not accepted. Hotel bills were paid with suitcases of money, and when handing over two 100,000 peso notes for a pack of cigarettes costing 120,000 pesos, or $2.40, the buyer would receive a couple of inches of 1000 peso notes in change.

Many transactions took place on a barter basis, since using money had become so inconvenient and costly. Many commodities were hoarded as inflation hedges. One government official estimated that his employees worked only a third of the day in the office and spent the rest of their office time buying, selling, or trading among commodities held instead of money. A whole new profession of money changers developed, since the shrinking value of the peso made people want to convert pesos into dollars instantly. In every city, day and night, Bolivians were on the streets waving wads of pesos at passing cars. The holding of money fell dramatically, from the equivalent of $600 million in the early 1980s to $10 million in early 1985.[19]

Changes in Relative Prices

In the case of the Bolivian inflation, the cost to society involved more than just the payment of zero interest on currency (and a nominal interest rate far below the inflation rate on bank deposits). In addition relative prices of goods were altered. This often happens in open economies when policymakers attempt to manipulate the value of the foreign exchange rate or to prevent firms from buying certain types of imports. Sometimes certain prices are controlled, or are set by the government, and are slow to change. These changes in relative prices inevitably create shortages of some goods and surpluses of others and create extreme versions of the costs of price controls discussed in Chapter 10.

Even in more moderate inflations than the 1985 Bolivian episode, there tends to be a connection between inflation and changes in relative prices. The main reason was that analyzed in Chapter 10. Supply shocks begin as changes in relative prices, like a change in the real price of oil, and then turn into changes in the aggregate inflation rate when nominal wage rates are rigid and policymakers choose not to extinguish the effects of the supply shock by restrictive monetary policy. The absence of full COLA (wage indexation) protection for many workers (but its presence for some other workers and for social security benefits) also can cause changes in relative prices.

---

[19]Details on the Bolivian inflation were taken from "Amid Wild Inflation, Bolivians Concentrate on Swapping Currency," *Wall Street Journal,* August 13, 1985, p. 1, and other journalistic accounts.

11-11 Indexation and Other Reforms to Reduce the Costs of Inflation

There is a strong case for the institution of reforms that can cut substantially the costs imposed by inflation. These reforms fall into three categories: the elimination of government regulations that redistribute income from savers to borrowers, the creation of an indexed bond to give savers a secure place to save, and a restatement of tax laws to eliminate the effects of inflation on real tax burdens.

Decontrol of Financial Institutions

Much of the distortion caused by the inflation of the 1970s resulted from federal government-imposed interest rate ceilings on commercial banks and savings institutions (for more details, see the box in Chapter 16). The step-by-step deregulation introduced under the 1980 Depository Institutions Deregulation and Monetary Control Act (DIDMCA) has gradually solved this problem. By 1985 all regulations on the payment of interest on checking and savings accounts were lifted. Thus, inflation in the future will not have as great a redistributive effect as in the past, since all individuals, rich and poor alike, will be able to receive the market rate of interest on their savings.

Even if all checking and savings accounts paid a nominal interest rate that included a full inflation premium, savers would still suffer an erosion of purchasing power on their pocket cash. Inflation still causes people to work harder to keep their cash balances at a minimum.

Indexed Bonds

Even though lifting government interest-rate ceilings on savings and checking accounts will substantially cut the costs of inflation, many economists have recommended that the government go further and issue an indexed bond that would fully protect savers against any unexpected movements in the inflation rate.

An **indexed bond** pays a fixed real interest rate; its nominal interest rate is equal to this real interest rate plus the actual inflation rate.

An **indexed bond** protects savers from unexpected movements in the inflation rate by paying a fixed real interest rate (r_0) plus the actual inflation rate (p). Thus the saver's nominal interest rate would be:

General Form	Numerical Example
$i = r_0 + p$	(a) $3 = 3 + 0$
	(b) $13 = 3 + 10$

In numerical example (a), savers would receive a 3 percent return if the inflation rate were zero. If inflation suddenly accelerated to 10 percent, as in example (b), savers would find that the nominal return (i) rose to 13 percent, and they would be just as well off as without the inflation.

To fully protect savers from losing from surprise inflation, and to keep borrowers from gaining, indexed bonds would have to be universal. Private banks and savings institutions would also have to issue indexed bonds and indexed loans, including mortgages. Once indexed bonds were issued by the government, private financial institutions could afford to risk issuing their own, since they could invest funds in government indexed bonds to back their own indexed bonds. Saving for retirement would be freed from the risk of loss from surprise inflation, if insurance companies could start selling indexed retirement annuities.

Why has the government failed to offer an indexed bond? Governments have feared that the issuance of an indexed bond would be treated as a confession of failure, and this in turn might increase the rate of inflation that people expect when they negotiate their wage contracts. Further, indexed bonds cut the costs of surprise inflation to savers, which would deter political objections if the government were to create surprise inflation in the future. Both these factors suggest that indexed bonds might raise the future inflation rate.

Indexed Tax System

Another important reform made effective in 1985 is the partial indexation of the personal income tax system. This now raises the dollar amounts of tax credits, exemptions, standard deductions, and tax rate brackets each year by the amount of inflation that has been experienced. A 5 percent inflation thus caused the 1988 personal exemption of $1950 to rise to $2048 in the following year. Without an indexed tax system, inflation would raise individual incomes and push taxpayers into higher tax brackets.

But the government must do more than index credits, exemptions, deductions, and tax brackets in order to achieve a fully inflation-neutral tax system. It must end present rules that discriminate against savers and favor borrowers by taxing real rather than nominal interest and capital gains. Just as savers should be taxed only on real interest income and real capital gains, borrowers should be allowed to deduct from their taxable income only the real portion of the interest they pay on loans. These reforms would eliminate the present effect of inflation in the U.S. tax system of discouraging saving and encouraging borrowing and spending.

11-12 Conclusion to Part IV: The Inflation and Unemployment Dilemma

A monetary and fiscal policy that maintains actual unemployment at the natural unemployment rate will keep inflation from accelerating further if the economy is spared from supply shocks. However, such a policy will do nothing to curb the expectations of further inflation that are so crucial in the persistence of actual inflation from year to year. Instead, policymakers are faced with four options. They can try to cut the inflation rate by deliberately using restrictive monetary and fiscal policy to create a recession, causing a massive waste of workers and machines. They can try to use price and wage controls, but they stand little chance of succeeding without causing shortages of some products and of skilled workers. Third, they can attempt government-designed supply-side measures that help to reduce costs and prices. Finally, the government can issue an indexed bond to insulate savers from the effects of inflation, and it can redesign the tax system to make it "inflation neutral."

In the early 1980s the government relied too heavily on the first option, reducing the inflation rate substantially from that in the late 1970s, but at the same time raising the unemployment rate to the highest level experienced since the Great Depression. In deciding to cut the inflation rate by restrictive aggregate demand policy, the government may have created the likelihood of future instability, since the economic recovery may tend to "overshoot" the natural rate of unemployment (as shown in Figure 9-10) as appeared to be occurring in 1988–89. In Part V we discuss the types of activist stabilization policy necessary to prevent overshooting.

But even if the economy eventually settles into a long-run equilibrium with the actual rate of unemployment equal to the natural rate of unemployment, there is still much for the government to do. The natural unemployment rate is too high, and it can be lowered through policies that reduce structural unemployment. Inflation still occurs, so there is a need for an indexed bond and an inflation-neutral tax system to reduce the costs of inflation. Further, it may be possible to lower the inflation by remedies that reduce the burden of regulation, tariffs and quotas against imports, and taxes that are paid by consumers through higher prices.

Thus economists are not short on solutions for the inflation-unemployment dilemma; rather, the problem is political. Many of the reforms advocated in the previous paragraph raise the ire of special interest groups. Also, some of these policies require more expenditures (for example, training programs) or lower taxes (making the tax system inflation-neutral). Finally, it is hard for politicians to think about such problems in the presence of the large U.S. budget deficit.

SUMMARY

1. A primary concept in this chapter is the natural rate of unemployment, abbreviated U^N. The term implies not immutability or desirability but naturalness in the sense of equilibrium: the unemployment rate at which there is no pressure for the inflation rate to change.

2. The main reason for high unemployment in the United States is that the natural rate of unemployment is not zero but in the vicinity of 6.0 percent. Roughly half of the natural unemployment rate consists of frictional unemployment; the rest consists of structural unemployment.

3. The actual unemployment rate falls below the natural rate of unemployment when the real GNP ratio (Q/Q^N) rises above unity, and vice versa. Thus all the factors in Chapters 9 and 10 that cause the Q/Q^N ratio to fluctuate also cause the actual unemployment rate to change in the opposite direction. The difference between U and U^N is cyclical unemployment.

4. Structural unemployment is caused by a mismatch between the high skill requirements of available jobs and the low skills possessed by many of the unemployed. In an economy with flexible relative wages, the unskilled would be able to find jobs more easily but would receive lower wage rates. Any real cure for the problems of the unskilled—whether high unemployment, or low wages, or both—requires an increase in their skills and better matching of their locations with the locations of available job openings.

5. Policy proposals to cure mismatch unemployment include training subsidies and loans, better schooling, a lower minimum wage for teenagers, a reduction in discrimination, a better employment service, and moving subsidies or loans.

6. Frictional unemployment is another component of the high natural rate. The barrier that maintains frictional unemployment is the absence of perfect information, making necessary an investment in job search to locate job openings that offer higher wage rates or better working conditions.

7. Policy solutions to reduce frictional unemployment include an improved employment service to provide better information as well as changes in the present system of unemployment compensation, which provides a subsidy to workers who turn down job offers and continue to search or to remain at home awaiting recall to their old job.

8. The increase in the official unemployment rate during a recession understates the cost to society of the recession. Typically the gap between natural output (Q^N) and actual output (Q) grows by 2.5 percentage points for every 1 percentage point by which the actual unemployment rate rises above the natural unemployment rate.

9. Inflation is felt primarily by owners of financial assets. The financial effects of inflation are divided into two categories: the effects of a fully anticipated inflation, and the effects of unanticipated inflation.

10. An increase in the fully anticipated rate of inflation tends to reduce the average holdings of real money balances, as the cost of holding these balances—the nominal interest rate paid on alternative financial assets—increases along with the inflation rate. The extra effort made by corporations and households to maintain lower money balances is a real cost imposed on them by inflation.

11. The basic case against unanticipated inflation is that it redistributes income from creditors to debtors unfairly without their knowledge or consent. The gainers from unanticipated inflation are those who are heavily in debt and whose assets are primarily physical rather than financial.

12. The U.S. tax system has many rules that are stated in nominal rather than real terms. As a result, the tax system is far from inflation neutral. The present U.S. tax system causes all types of inflation, both anticipated and unanticipated, to redistribute income from savers to borrowers.

CONCEPTS

frictional unemployment
structural unemployment
cyclical unemployment
Okun's law
total labor force
turnover unemployment
mismatch unemployment

seasonal unemployment
nominal and real interest rates
anticipated and unanticipated inflation
capital gain
extra convenience services
hyperinflation
indexed bond

QUESTIONS AND PROBLEMS

Questions

1. Does the current technique of measuring unemployment tend to overestimate or underestimate the true social cost of unemployment? Explain your answer.

2. Which of the three types of unemployment are the subject of Okun's law?

3. "Policymakers may reduce temporarily the natural rate of unemployment by pursuing an expansionary monetary policy." Do you agree with this statement? Explain your answer.

4. How can vacancies and unemployed workers coexist? If policymakers pursue an expansionary policy to increase real GNP, what will happen to

the number of unemployed workers? What will happen to the number of vacancies as real output increases?

5. Explain how your answer to question 4 helps us to understand why wages tend to rise faster as real output increases (i.e., why the *SP* curve is upward sloping).

6. Explain why the length of unemployment episodes is one way of differentiating between structural and frictional unemployment.

7. In what way can unemployment be considered a socially valuable experience?

8. Explain the distinction among the following: the nominal interest rate; the expected real interest rate; and the actual real interest rate. Which of these interest rates is the most relevant to the saving/investment decision? Which of the rates has the most impact on determining the distribution of income?

9. What are the primary determinants of who wins and who loses in an unanticipated inflation? Using your answer as a starting point, explain why the major redistributional effect of unanticipated inflation is to transfer real wealth from the rich to the middle class.

10. Explain why people want to hold money up to the point where extra convenience services are equal to the nominal interest rate. How can this observation help us understand the net social loss to society of an inflation?

Problems

1. This question uses Okun's law to estimate values for unemployment rates and Q/Q^N. Refer to Equation 11-1. Assume $U^N = 5$ percent and h = 0.3.
   (a) If $Q^N = 100$, what is the unemployment rate when $Q = 96, 102, 106$?
   (b) Now assume that $Q^N = 120$. What must be the level of real GNP (Q) to have an unemployment rate of 8.0, 3.5, 5.75?

(c) If the current unemployment rate is 6.5 percent, by how much will output have to increase to lower unemployment to 5.9 percent?

2. Assume an individual is willing to save $1500 if the real rate of interest is 6 percent.
   (a) If that individual is expecting a rate of inflation of 3 percent, what does the nominal interest rate have to be in order to induce the individual to save?
   (b) If the nominal interest rate is at the rate found in (a), what is the nominal return (in dollars), from one year of saving?
   (c) If this individual's expectations are correct, what is the real return (in dollars) from that year of saving?
   (d) If the individual's expectations are not fulfilled and the actual inflation rate turns out to be 6 percent, what is the real return (in dollars)?

3. Bill borrows $200,000 for three years from Larry and agrees to pay Larry 8 percent interest, compounded annually. The entire amount of the loan plus interest will be paid at the end of the third year. The price level at the time of the loan is 1.00.
   (a) What is the amount that Larry will receive at the end of the third year? If the price level is 1.00 at the end of the third year, what is the real value of the payment received by Larry?
   (b) Assume that the inflation rate in the economy is 3 percent for each of the three years. What is the price level at the end of the third year? What is the real value of the payment received by Larry?
   (c) Again, assume that the inflation rate in the economy is 3 percent for each of the three years. However, in this case, Larry had indexed the loan in order to protect himself from inflation. What would be the nominal interest rate for each year of the loan? What is the nominal amount of the payment received by Larry at the end of the third year? What is the real value of the payment?

SELF-TEST ANSWERS

p. 337 (1) An extension of the time to earn unemployment benefits would reduce the cost of refusing a job and hence would extend the period of search and raise the frictional unemployment rate. (2) A reduction in the personal income tax rate would raise the cost of refusing a job, since it would increase the after-tax pay for any given pre-tax wage rate, and hence would reduce the period of search and the frictional unemployment rate. (3) Fewer teenagers would imply less turnover, since teenagers often engage in search unemployment when they look for after-school or summer employment, or work during years off from school. (4) A higher price of phone calls would raise the cost of search and hence would reduce the amount of search and reduce the frictional unemployment rate.

p. 349 Financial deregulation which allowed the payment of interest on checking accounts made the demand for money (that is, checking accounts plus currency) less responsive to an increase in the interest rate. Hence an increase in the nominal interest rate caused by higher inflation causes less shifting away from money than prior to deregulation, thus reducing the shoe-leather cost of fully anticipated inflation.

PART V

Macroeconomics in the Long Run: Growth, the Public Debt, and the Foreign Debt

CHAPTER TWELVE

Economic Growth and the Productivity Slowdown

In essence the question of growth is nothing new but a new disguise for an age-old issue, one which has always intrigued and preoccupied economics: the present versus the future.
—James Tobin[1]

One of the most perplexing economic problems in the United States since 1973 has been a slowdown in the growth rate of labor productivity. This, in turn, has led to a slowdown in the growth rate of natural real GNP. Although the productivity slowdown has also occurred in most other countries, the growth rate of productivity in the United States is lower than in any other industrialized nation. This was the third puzzle introduced at the start of the book.

The subject of economic growth has taken on new importance as the U.S. economy enters the 1990s. The productivity slowdown has persisted for almost two decades, and its very duration deepens the puzzle of its causes. Further, two new obstacles to economic growth emerged in the 1980s. First, the federal budget deficit has proven to be a longer lasting problem than some had predicted. The deficit adds to the ever-growing public debt and requires ever-growing interest payments to those who own the public debt, including foreigners. The budget deficit and growing public debt may hinder economic growth, because household saving diverted into financing the government budget deficit is unavailable to finance private investment spending, a source of economic growth.

The second obstacle to economic growth is the foreign trade deficit, which in a few years has converted the United States from a creditor nation to a debtor nation. Each year the United States owes more to foreigners and must pay a larger fraction of GNP to foreigners, thus reducing the growth in the standard of living of U.S. citizens.

Because economic growth has become such a critical macroeconomic problem, and because the government budget and foreign trade deficits may prevent future growth, we begin here a three-chapter discussion of these interrelated topics. In this chapter we examine the sources of economic growth and recent explanations for the slowdown in the growth rate of natural real GNP and productivity (output per hour). Then Chapter 13 reviews

---

[1]"Economic Growth as an Objective of Government Policy," *American Economic Review*, vol. 54 (May 1964), p. 1.

the debate over the measurement of and causes of the budget deficit, whether its effects are harmful, and the implications of the increasing public debt. We turn to international macroeconomics in Chapter 14, where we ask why the U.S. foreign trade deficit has been so intractable despite the substantial decline in the value of the U.S. dollar since 1985. What, if anything, can be done to prevent an ever-growing drain of interest payments to foreigners on the standard of living of American citizens?

12-1 Standards of Living as the Consequence of Economic Growth

The Poor United Kingdom

In economics, **economic growth** is the study of the causes and consequences of sustained growth in natural real GNP.

In 1870 average real GNP per person in the United Kingdom was about 18 percent higher than in the United States. But by 1988 average real GNP per person in the United States was 60 percent higher than that in the United Kingdom. How was this possible? Faster **economic growth,** meaning a higher average annual growth rate of real GNP per person, allowed the United States to overtake the United Kingdom in 1886 and to move ahead by a growing distance between 1886 and 1950. Although the United Kingdom kept pace with the United States after 1950, it was never able to close the gap. This was a race between the tortoise and the hare in which the tortoise never caught up.

The gap between the average real GNP per person in the two countries makes an enormous difference in their relative standards of living. Since the comparisons are made in a way that holds constant the prices of goods and services in the two countries, the average American can purchase all the goods and services bought by the average U.K. resident and still have 60 percent more left over for additional spending. And this difference is the result of a seemingly puny and insignificant difference in U.S. economic growth rate between 1870 and 1988—1.84 percent per year for the United States as compared to 1.29 percent for the United Kingdom.

> *Minor differences in economic growth rates sustained over a long period build up into substantial differences in relative living standards. As another example, in 1955 the United Kingdom enjoyed a living standard that was 12 percent higher than that of West Germany. But a West German economic growth advantage between 1955 and 1988 of 3.03 percent compared to 1.99 percent for the United Kingdom converted the 1955 situation into a totally different relationship in 1988, when the West German average per-person real GNP level was 26 percent higher than the British.*

Economic Growth: Something for Nothing?

It is easy to see why economic growth is such a fascinating topic. High rates of economic growth make it possible to have more of everything—higher defense spending and welfare benefits with plenty left over for more private consumption of goods and services. In contrast, a society with a low rate of economic growth suffers continual strife as difficult choices must be made about the allocation of a slow-growing pie. In this unfortunate society more defense spending may mean higher taxes or a cut in welfare benefits. In the 1960s the achievement of relative rapid U.S. economic growth gradually diminished concern and interest in the topic of growth. But in the 1970s and 1980s, U.S. performance faltered. Growth in real GNP per worker almost vanished, and no one has yet completely explained the slowdown. Concern with the topic of growth soared again.

We have two main concerns in this chapter. First, we want to identify the main determinants of the rate of economic growth. Second, we want to review the many explanations suggested for the slowdown of U.S. economic growth since 1973. We will also compare the recent growth experience of the United States with that of other countries.

12-2   CASE STUDY: The Growth Experience of Seven Countries Over the Last Century

Figure 12-1 shows the level of per-person GNP in seven leading industrial countries for selected years over the last century. The figures are expressed in 1988 U.S. dollars and are based on a careful study that bases the prices actually paid by inhabitants of other countries on the average paid in all industrialized countries.[2]

Table 12-1 summarizes some of the most important information contained in Figure 12-1, including the values in 1988 U.S. prices of per-person

[2]The source of the price comparisons is the major international study headed by Irving B. Kravis of the University of Pennsylvania. See Irving B. Kravis et al., *A System of International Comparisons of Gross Product and Purchasing Power* (Baltimore: Johns Hopkins Press, 1975). Details on the sources for Figure 12-1 are given in Appendix C.

Table 12-1   **Level and Growth Rate of Per Capita Real GNP in 1988 Dollars for Seven Countries, 1870–1988**

| | Level in thousands of 1982 dollars | | Average annual growth rate in percent | | | | |
	1870	1988	1870–1988	1870–1913	1913–55	1955–73	1973–88
United States	2303	20,091	1.84	2.01	1.64	2.07	1.61
Sweden	1207	16,675	2.22	2.03	2.23	3.21	1.57
Germany	1466	15,732	2.01	1.62	1.61	3.92	1.96
France	1717	15,198	1.85	1.46	1.26	4.26	1.70
Japan	712	14,784	2.70	1.48	1.33	7.82	3.87
United Kingdom	2728	12,519	1.29	1.00	1.05	2.40	1.49
Italy	1408	10,470	1.70	0.80	1.26	4.58	2.07

Source: See Appendix C.

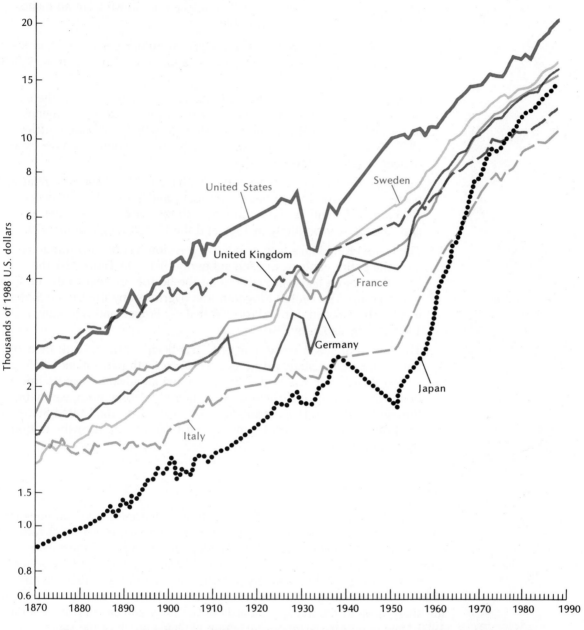

Figure 12-1 **Per-Person GNP in 1988 U.S. Dollars for Seven Countries, 1870–1988**

Notice that the United Kingdom (dashed gray line) had the highest per-person income level in 1870, but its slow growth now places it second from the bottom. Japan (dotted black line) was the growth champion, rising from last place as recently as 1966 to a level above both the United Kingdom and Italy in 1988, and close to a tie for second place. Notice that Germany and France, despite zigzags due to wars, have remained essentially tied for most of the period shown, and that both have raced past the once-mighty United Kingdom. (Wartime data are omitted for most countries; lines plotted connect final prewar and first postwar points.) (*Source:* See Appendix C.)

GNP in both 1870 and 1988 as well as the growth rates of per-person GNP during selected intervals. In the table countries are listed in order of 1988 per-person GNP. Several major conclusions can be drawn from an inspection of the figure and companion table:

1. All nations have enjoyed substantial growth in per-person GNP; in the United States there was an increase by a factor of almost 9, from $2303 in 1870 to $20,091 in 1988.

2. Figure 12-1 is plotted on a logarithmic scale. This means that the slope of each line indicates the economic growth rate; a steep line means fast growth and a flat line indicates slow growth. For most countries 1955–73 was the period of fastest growth, and all countries have experienced a growth slowdown since 1973.

3. Differing growth rates among countries have led to changes in relative positions. Japan's growth has been most rapid, particularly between 1955 and 1973, with an incredible growth rate of 7.8 percent per annum. Japan overtook Italy in 1966 and the United Kingdom in 1979.

4. The United Kingdom's loss of relative position has been continuous over the entire century. In each subperiod listed in Table 12-1 the United Kingdom had a growth rate at the bottom or next to the bottom of the group. The United Kingdom was overtaken by the United States in 1886, by Sweden during World War II, by France and Germany in 1960, and by Japan by 1979.

5. The United States is something of a "has-been" in the growth race, owing its high living standard to its superior growth performance before 1950. In particular, the United States gained an advantage in its freedom from wartime destruction as compared to some European nations. But since 1950 the U.S. advantage has eroded, with the United States at the bottom of the growth league during 1955–73, and near the bottom during 1973–88.

Types of Economic Change

If you look closely at Figure 12-1, you will note that the individual lines for each country display not only the process of economic growth that raises the standard of living decade after decade, but two types of shorter-term movements. The first of these is wartime destruction. Figure 12-1 excludes the years during and immediately after the two world wars, 1914–22 and 1940–50. Nevertheless, the effect of wartime destruction is clearly visible in the sharp drop in the living standards of Germany and Japan from 1940 to 1950. Making up for wartime destruction explains much of the rapid economic growth in these two countries in the 1950s and early 1960s.

The second type of short-term economic change visible in Figure 12-1 is the business cycle, on which we have focused throughout this book. The data for each country are annual, so the alternation of business recessions and expansions is visible, most notably during the depression years of the 1930s. The figure also highlights the unique nature of the Great Depression in the United States. Per-person real GNP declined much less in the other countries than in the United States. Whereas per-person real U.S. GNP declined 38 percent in 1929–33, the declines for the other nations ranged from 3 percent in Sweden to 13 percent in Germany.

12-3 The Production Function and the Sources of Economic Growth

The economic elements that directly produce real GNP are **factor inputs.**

The theory of economic growth has filled many academic journals with highly mathematical articles. Yet the basic ideas are very simple. The theory divides output growth into two categories: (1) growth of **factor inputs,** such as labor and capital, and (2) growth in output relative to growth in factor inputs. Thus the theory converts the question of how to achieve faster output growth into two subquestions: how to achieve faster growth in factor inputs, and how to achieve faster growth in output relative to inputs.

Throughout most of this book we have examined the causes and consequences of changes in the ratio of actual real GNP to natural real GNP, the ratio Q/Q^N. But now were are interested in changes in economic conditions over long periods during which the Q/Q^N ratio may be expected to be roughly constant. Thus our theory of economic growth refers to the growth of natural real GNP (Q^N).

The Production Function

The **production function,** a relationship usually written in algebra, shows how much output can be produced by a given quantity of factor inputs.

How much real GNP (Q) can be produced at any given time? This depends on the total available quantity of the two main factor inputs, capital (K) and labor (N), and also the behavior of output per average available factor input, which we call A (for the "autonomous" growth factor).[3]

The relationship between Q, A, K, and N is given by the **production function:**

General Form   Numerical Example

$$Q = A\,F(K, N) \qquad Q = A\,K^{0.25}\,N^{0.75} \qquad (12.1)$$

In words, the general form states that real GNP equals an autonomous growth factor (A), expressed as an index, multiplied by a function of an index of capital input (K) and labor input (N). In the numerical example, output depends on a geometric weighted average of K and N, with weights 0.25 and 0.75. The box on the facing page gives background information on the relationship between the general functional form and the numerical example.

Output per person and the capital-labor ratio. We have already learned in our our case study and in Figure 12-1 that the growth of the standard of living depends not on *total* real GNP, but on real GNP *per person,* which can be written as real GNP (Q) divided by the total amount of

---

[3]The use of the symbol A in this context and the decomposition of real GNP growth into growth in labor, capital, and the "residual" A date back to the seminal paper by Robert M. Solow, "Technical Change and the Aggregate Production Function," *Review of Economics and Statistics,* vol. 39 (August 1957), pp. 312–320. The symbol A stands for "autonomous growth factor" and should not be confused with A_p or $\overline{A}$, the symbols for autonomous planned spending in Chapters 3–6.

General Functional Forms and the Production Function

Until this point, we have used only "specific linear" forms for the behavioral equations. For instance, the demand for money in the appendix to Chapter 5 was written as:

$$\left(\frac{M}{P}\right)^d = hQ - fr$$

This equation can be stated in words as: The real demand for money $(M/P)^d$ is equal to a positive number (h) times real GNP (Q) minus another number (f) times the interest rate (r). The equation tells specifically how the real demand for money depends on real GNP and the interest rate.

The production function in this chapter can also be written in a specific form called the "Cobb–Douglas production function."[a]

General Form	Numerical Example
$Q = A K^b N^{1-b}$	$Q = A K^{0.25} N^{0.75}$

In words, this states that real GNP (Q) is equal to an autonomous growth factor (A), multiplied by a geometric weighted average of an index of capital (K) and of labor (N). The weights, b and $1 - b$, represent the elasticity (or percentage response) of real GNP to an increase in either factor.[b] For instance, in our numerical example if all variables are indexes initially at 1.0, a 4 percent increase in labor input will cause a 3 percent increase in real GNP. Initially:

$$1.0 = 1.0(1.0^{0.25} \, 1.0^{0.75})$$

After a 4 percent increase in labor input:

$$1.03 = 1.0(1.0^{0.25} \, 1.04^{0.75})$$

Thus the elasticity of real GNP with respect to a change in labor input is 0.75 ($= 3/4$).

Several other characteristics of the production function are evident. First, an equal percentage increase in both factors, capital and labor, raises real GNP by the same percentage. This characteristic, called **constant returns to scale,** occurs because the sum of the weights (b and $1 - b$) is unity. When both factor inputs increase by 4 percent, we have:

$$1.04 = 1.0(1.04^{0.25} \, 1.04^{0.75})$$
(after 4 percent increase
in both K and N)

A second characteristic is the direct one-for-one response of real GNP to the autonomous growth factor A. If A increases by 4 percentage points, while capital and labor input remain fixed at 1.0, real GNP increases by the same four percentage points:

$$1.04 = 1.04(1.0^{0.25} \, 1.0^{0.75})$$
(after 4 percent increase
in A)

The Cobb–Douglas production function is only one of many ways in which real GNP might be related to A, K, and N. Often in economics we want to make the simple statement that "Q is related to A, K, and N" but without restricting the particular form of the relationship. To accomplish this, we

---

labor input (N), that is, Q/N. Thus we are interested in isolating those factors that determine the increase in per-person real GNP, which can be written as follows when the production function is divided through by N:[4]

---

[4]How can (12.2) be derived from (12.1)? There are two intermediate steps. First, we multiply and divide K by N in equation (12.1):

$$Q = A \, F(NK/N, N) \qquad\qquad (12.1)'$$

If the function F displays constant returns to scale (see box), then there is a unit elasticity of Q with respect to an increase in N (which appears in the numerator of the first term inside the parentheses as well as in the second term), and this fact allows us to factor out the N term and rewrite (12.1') as follows:

$$Q = A \, N \, f(K/N, 1). \qquad\qquad (12.1'')$$

Notice here that we have given a new name (f) to the function. Equation (12.2) in the text is obtained by dividing through both sides of (12.1'') by N.

sometimes use a *general functional form*. An example of such a general form for the production function is:

$$Q = F(A, K, N)$$

In words, this states simply that real GNP (Q) depends on an autonomous growth factor (A), an index of capital input (K), and an index of labor input (N). The capital letter F and the parentheses mean *depends on,* and any alphabetical letter can be used.

Why is it interesting to know simply that one variable depends on others? By writing an alternative equation, one could state the *alternative hypothesis* that there is no role for an autonomous growth factor:

$$Q = F(K, N)$$

This states that real GNP depends *only on* capital and labor input.

Sometimes it is desirable to make a specific assumption about the form in which one variable enters, but not the others. This occurs in equation (12.1) in the text, which states that the elasticity of real GNP with respect to the autonomous growth factor is unity, but does not restrict the form of the relationship between real GNP and the other inputs, capital, and labor:

$$Q = A F(K, N)$$

Without further information one cannot look at these general functional forms and learn whether the assumed relationship is positive or negative. The positive relationship between real GNP and both capital and labor inputs can be written in either of two ways:

Method 1: $Q = A \underset{(+)(+)}{F(K, N)}$

Method 2: $Q = A F(K, N);\quad F_K > 0,\ F_N > 0.$

The terms to the right of the semicolon in method 2 can be put into these words: the response of real GNP to a change in capital input (F_K) and in labor input (F_N) is positive (> 0).

Exercise: Consider a general functional form for the demand for money:

$$\left(\frac{M}{P}\right)^d = L(Q, r).$$

State in words what this function states about the relationship between the real demand for money ($(M/P)^d$) and real GNP (Q) and the interest rate (r). Use both methods 1 and 2 to write down the facts that the real demand for money depends positively on real GNP and negatively on the interest rate.

[a]The function is named after an Amherst mathematics professor, Cobb, and a University of Chicago economics professor (later U.S. senator), Paul H. Douglas, and is described in a book by the latter, *The Theory of Wages* (New York: Macmillan, 1934), especially Chapter V.

[b]*Elasticity* is a term introduced in most elementary economics courses and refers to the percentage change in one variable in response to a 1 percent change in another variable.

$$
\begin{array}{cc}
\text{General Form} & \text{Numerical Example} \\
\dfrac{Q}{N} = A\, f\!\left(\dfrac{K}{N}\right) & \dfrac{Q}{N} = A \left(\dfrac{K}{N}\right)^{0.25}
\end{array}
\qquad (12.2)
$$

This important relationship states that there are just two sources of growth in the standard of living, that is, real GNP per person (Q/N). These are the autonomous growth factor (A) and the ratio of capital to labor input (K/N), which we simply call "capital per person." (In this chapter we simplify by treating "persons" and "employment" as synonyms, ignoring changes in the ratio of employment to the population.

Equation (12.2) is the per-person version of the production function. It is illustrated in Figure 12-2. This production function is drawn by assuming that the autonomous growth factor is fixed at A_0. Like the production functions presented in Chapters 6 and 10 that plotted output against labor input,

Figure 12-2
A Production Function Relating Per-Person Output to Per-Person Capital Input

The production function shows how much output per person can be produced by different amounts of capital per person. One possible position for the economy is point B, but other positions are possible as well. We cannot tell from this diagram how large the economy's per-person capital stock will be.

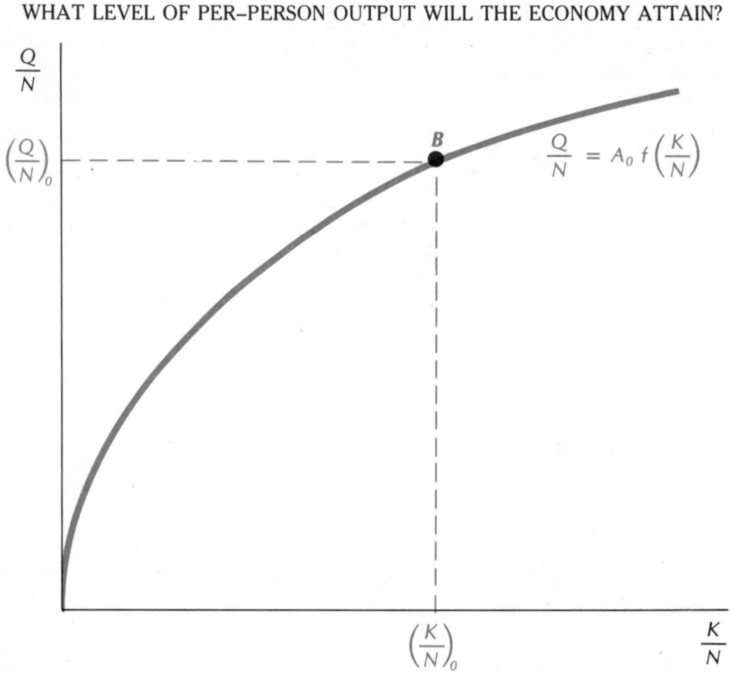

this one exhibits diminishing returns. Thus any addition to the per-person stock of capital (K/N) yields less and less of an increase in per-person output (Q/N). In the diagram, point B represents one possible level of production, with capital input per person $(K/N)_0$ producing output per person $(Q/N)_0$.

SELF-TEST   What happens to the ratio of output to capital (Q/K) as more capital per person is accumulated?

The production function in Figure 12-2 is just a start toward an adequate theory of economic growth. So far our analysis tells us simply that the main sources of growth in the standard of living are an autonomous factor (A) and growth in capital per person (K/N). But this does not explain the differences among countries or periods evident in Figure 12-1 because it does not tell us why these two sources of growth differ among countries or among historical eras. We do not yet know why the autonomous growth factor in Figure 12-2 is A_0 rather than some other amount, nor do we know what determines the level of K/N.

Our study of what determines the autonomous growth factor is deferred until Sections 12-5 and 12-6. Here, we focus on the determinants of growth of capital per person (K/N). We begin by reviewing the basic relationship between saving and investment, which we first encountered in Chapter 2.

Saving and the Growth in Capital Per Person

How is growth in K/N related to total national saving? This relationship is important, since it represents the link between the government's fiscal policy and the long-run growth of output per person. The concept of saving (S) that matters for economic growth is not the household saving of Chapter 3, but rather total national saving, *including the saving of households, corporations, and the government.* When the government runs a budget deficit, this is a negative component of *national saving,* offsetting part of the positive national saving of households and corporations.

If we then define S to include not just the private saving of households and corporations but also the government budget surplus or "government saving" (a budget deficit is treated as negative government saving) and assume that net exports are zero, total *national* saving (S) equals private investment (I):[5]

$$S = I \qquad (12.3)$$

Our task is to determine how the growth in capital is related to investment, and hence to total national saving (S). The first step is to divide total private investment (I) into two parts, "net investment" (I^n) that creates growth in capital and the remaining portion called "replacement investment" (D) that replaces old capital that wears out or becomes obsolete:

$$I = I^n + D \qquad (12.4)$$

Net investment is simply the change in the capital stock from one period to the next, where we use the Δ symbol, introduced in Chapter 3, to designate "change in":

$$I^n = \Delta K \qquad (12.5)$$

The other part of total investment, replacement investment, is assumed to be a fixed fraction (the "depreciation rate" d) of the capital stock (K):

$$D = dK. \qquad (12.6)$$

Our aim is to find a relation between national saving (S) and the growth in capital (ΔK). We take (12.4) and replace each element in turn, replacing I by S from (12.3), I^n by ΔK from (12.5), and D by dK from (12.6):

$$S = \Delta K + dK \qquad (12.7)$$

We can introduce the rate of change of capital ($\Delta K/K$) into (12.7) by dividing and multiplying the first term by K, and then simplifying:

$$S = \frac{K\Delta K}{K} + dK = \left(\frac{\Delta K}{K} + d\right)K \qquad (12.8)$$

In words, this states that national saving equals gross investment, which in turn equals the growth rate of capital plus the depreciation rate times the

---

[5]Rewriting equation (2.9), which shows the relation of private saving (S) to government saving ($T - G$), private investment (I), and net exports (X), we have:

$$S + (T - G) \equiv I + X$$

When S is redefined to include both private saving and government saving, we have:

$$S = I + X$$

This is the same as equation (12.3) in the text, with X set equal to zero.

capital stock. Now we have found the necessary connection between national saving and the growth rate of capital ($\Delta K/K$). This equation (12.8) can be combined with the per-person version of the production function (12.2) to illustrate the simple theory of economic growth.

12-4 Solow's Theory of Economic Growth

Can an increase in national saving (S) create a permanent increase in the growth rate of output? The answer is "no." This was the most surprising result of a new theory of economic growth originally developed in the 1950s by MIT's Robert M. Solow,[6] research for which he was awarded the Nobel Prize in 1987. We have already developed the major building blocks of Solow's theory. These are the per-person production function of equation (12.2) and Figure 12-2, and the relationship between saving and the growth in capital in equation (12.8).

Saving and Investment in the Steady State

A **steady state** is a situation in which output and capital input grow at the same rates, implying a fixed ratio of output to capital input.

The centerpiece of Solow's analysis is the idea of a **steady state.** In the simplest case, when there is no growth in A, then the steady state occurs when the economy stands still at a point like B in Figure 12-2. This occurs when the growth of Q and K are both equal to growth in N, implying that the ratios plotted in the figure, Q/N and K/N, are constant. Using lowercase letters to designate growth rates, we have:

$q = \Delta Q/Q$ = growth rate of real output or GNP,

$k = \Delta K/K$ = growth rate of capital input, and

$n = \Delta N/N$ = growth rate of labor input.

Thus the condition for a steady state in which capital per person (K/N) is constant can be written simply as:

$$k = n \qquad (12.9)$$

In common-sense terms, (12.9) states the condition necessary for the economy to stand still at a point like B in Figure 12-2: the amount of capital per person (K/N) must be constant. But if labor input and the population are growing at a rate n, then capital (K) must be growing exactly as fast as N to keep K/N constant. This requires that the growth of K (designated by k) equal the growth of N (designated by n).

Looking back at equation (12.8), we already have a relation between saving and the growth in capital ($\Delta K/K$). Let's rewrite (12.8), using the steady-state condition in (12.9) to replace $\Delta K/K$ (or k) by n. Starting with (12.8),

$$S = \left(\frac{\Delta K}{K} + d\right)K, \quad \text{we obtain} \qquad (12.8)$$

$$S = (n + d)K, \quad \text{which implies}$$

$$s\frac{Q}{K} = n + d \qquad (12.10)$$

---

[6]Robert M. Solow, "A Contribution to the Theory of Economic Growth," *Quarterly Journal of Economics,* vol. 70 (February 1956), pp. 65–94.

To obtain the final line of (12.10), we redefine total national saving (S) as the ratio of national saving to output (s = S/Q) times output (Q), and then divide both sides of the equation by K. In words, the first line of (12.10) states that a steady state requires total saving (S) to equal the level of "steady state investment," which is the amount of investment that will make the capital stock grow at the rate of population growth (nK) while allowing for depreciation of capital (dK). The final line of (12.10) states that saving per unit of capital must equal the sum of the population growth rate and the depreciation rate, which in turns is the amount of steady-state investment per unit of capital.

SELF-TEST   There are four components of equation (12.10), s, Q/K, n, and d. Which, if any, of these components changes its value as we move along the production function in Figure 12-2?

Solow's Insight

Robert M. Solow (1924–   ). *Solow, 1987 Nobel Prize winner, invented both the modern theory of economic growth and the standard method for empirically distinguishing the roles of capital and of technological change in the growth process.*

The algebra of equation (12.10) had been worked out in the 1940s by Sir Roy Harrod, an English economist, and Evsey Domar, who later taught at MIT. In their "Harrod-Domar" model of economic growth all of the elements of (12.10) are constant. But then, why does the left side of (12.10) equal the right side? This equality seems an unlikely coincidence, since the elements of (12.10) depend on totally unrelated factors. The ratio of national saving to output (s) on the left-hand side of the equation is determined by the saving decisions of households and the government, while the ratio of output to capital (Q/K) is determined by technological factors. And the rate of population growth (n) and depreciation rate (d) on the right-hand side of (12.10) are determined by totally different considerations—birth rates, death rates, immigration, and the rate at which old capital wears out or becomes obsolete. In Solow's words, describing a simple version of (12.10) in which d is omitted:

> Discomfort arose because . . . all three of the key ingredients—the saving rate, the rate of growth of the labor force, and the capital-output ratio— were given constants, facts of nature. The saving rate was a fact about preferences; the growth rate of labor supply was a demographic-sociological fact; the capital-output ratio was a technological fact. . . . The possibility of steady growth would be a miraculous stroke of luck. Most economies, most of the time, would have no equilibrium growth path. The history of capitalist economies should be an alternation of long periods of worsening unemployment and long periods of worsening labor shortage.[7]

In Solow's words again, "I began tinkering with the theory of economic growth, trying to improve on the Harrod-Domar model . . . I thought first about replacing the constant capital-output (and labor-output) ratio by a richer and more realistic representation of the technology." What Solow did, in short, was to marry the per-person production function of equation (12.2)

---

[7]Robert M. Solow, "Growth Theory and After," *American Economic Review*, vol. 78 (June 1988), p. 307.

with the saving-investment relation in (12.10). The implications of this marriage can be seen either in algebra or on a graph.

The Solow model in equations. To introduce the production function into (12.10), we simply multiply both sides of the equation by K and divide both sides by N:

$$s\left(\frac{Q}{N}\right) = (n + d)\frac{K}{N} \tag{12.11}$$

On the left-hand side we have total national saving per person, and on the right-hand side we have the amount of steady-state investment per person, that is, the amount of investment needed to equip each new population member with the same capital per person as the existing population, and to replace worn-out or obsolete capital. Because of diminishing returns in the production function, the ratio of Q to K is not a constant, but becomes ever lower as more capital is accumulated. If the left-hand and right-hand sides of (12.11) are not initially equal, capital per person will automatically grow or shrink until they are equal and a steady state is reached.

How much will per-person capital grow or shrink? The change in per-person capital is $\Delta(K/N)$. This, in turn, is the amount of per-person saving that remains after allowing for depreciation and equipping each new member of the population with the existing per-person level of capital:[8]

General Form   Numerical Example

$$\Delta\left(\frac{K}{N}\right) = s\left(\frac{Q}{N}\right) - (n + d)\left(\frac{K}{N}\right) \qquad .03 = 0.15\left(\frac{2}{3}\right) - (.01 + .06)(1) \tag{12.12}$$

Thus whenever the left-hand side of (12.11) exceeds the right-hand side, (12.12) states that saving is in excess of that needed for new workers and for depreciation, thus allowing per-person capital to grow, that is, $\Delta(K/N)$ is positive. Only when per-person capital stops growing, which requires that (12.11) be satisfied, does the economy reach a steady state.

One aspect of this theory may seem puzzling. We learned in Chapter 3 that an increase in the saving rate (s) depresses the economy by reducing consumption spending. How can we be so sure here that an increase in the saving rate will stimulate the growth of per-person capital? The answer is that *the Solow model is intended for long-run analysis* (decades, not months or years) *and assumes continuous full employment and flexible prices.* Thus when the saving rate rises in this model, consumption and the price level both decline. The interest rate falls by enough to stimulate sufficient investment to guarantee that saving and investment will remain equal.

---

[8]To obtain (12.12), take (12.8), solve for ΔK, divide both sides by K, and restate S as sQ.

$$\frac{\Delta K}{K} = s\left(\frac{Q}{K}\right) - d$$

This is the growth rate of capital (k). The change in per-person capital $(k - n)$ is simply the right-hand side of this expression minus n:

$$k - n = s\left(\frac{Q}{K}\right) - (d + n)$$

This states that the growth rate of capital is equal to the amount of saving per unit of capital that remains after providing for depreciation. To obtain (12.12) in the text, multiply both sides of the equation by K/N, noting that $(k - n)(K/N) = \Delta(K/N)$.

The numerical example assumes that $s = 0.15$, $Q/N = 2/3$, $n = 0.01$, $d = 0.06$, and $K/N =$ unity. Under these conditions, the economy is not in a steady state, and per-person capital grows at 0.03 percent per year. But each year that this occurs, K/N grows faster than Q/N, so more and more of saving is used up in equipping new workers and for depreciation, and each year the growth of K/N slows down. Eventually the per-person capital stock stops growing. In the example, this occurs after K/N has risen about 60 percent and Q/N has risen about 15 percent.[9] The Harrod-Domar coincidence does not apply, since any initial imbalance between saving and steady-state investment automatically generates a change in Q/K until saving equals steady-state investment. In this example, the Q/K ratio falls from an initial 2/3 to 0.466.

The Solow model in pictures. The same relationships are illustrated in Figure 12-3. Here the upper curved line is the per-person production function, copied from Figure 12-2. The economy's initial position at B, also cop-

---

[9]To solve this problem, we also assume that the specific production function relating Q/N to K/N is the numerical example of (12.2), which is consistent with the numerical example in (12.12) if $A = 2/3$. With these parameters, $\Delta(K/N)$ reaches zero when K/N rises from 1.0 to 1.609. The production function implies that this would produce an increase in output from 2/3 to 0.75, for saving of 0.1125 and investment of (0.07) times 1.609, or 0.1126. 1.609 is the value of K/N that solves:

$$0.15(2/3(K/N)^{0.25}) = 0.07(K/N)$$

Figure 12-3
Adjustment of Per-Person Capital When Saving Exceeds Steady-State Investment

Initially the economy produces at B. Per-person saving is at C, while the steady-state investment requirement is at D. Excess saving allows per-person capital to grow from $(K/N)_0$ to $(K/N)^*$. When the economy reaches point E, per-person saving equals steady-state investment, and K/N stops growing. The new level of per-person output, $(Q/N)^*$, is shown at point G.

THE ECONOMY HEADS FOR ITS STEADY STATE

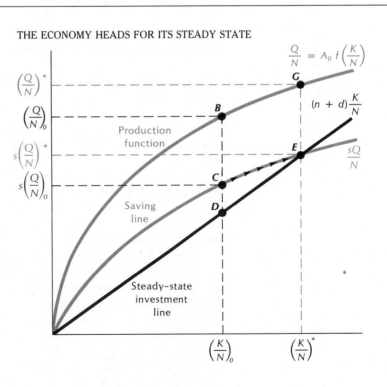

ied from Figure 12-2, is not a steady state. Why? Because at this level of output equation (12.11) is not satisfied. We see this from the two new lines in the diagram, which correspond to the two sides of (12.11).

The lower red "saving line" represents the left-hand side of (12.11)—the saving rate (s) times per-person output (Q/N). It has the same shape as the per-person production function but lies below it because s is a fraction below unity. When per-person output is at B, per-person saving is directly below at point C. The upward sloping straight black line, called the "steady state investment line," represents the right-hand side of (12.11), which multiplies the horizontal axis by the fraction ($n + d$). Starting at an initial per-person capital stock $(K/N)_0$, the amount of investment needed to equip new workers with capital, and to replace old capital, is shown at D.

The difference between the red and black lines, the distance CD, represents *additional saving available to fuel growth in per-person capital.* Thus the economy moves to the right up the red saving line whenever the red saving line is above the black steady-state investment line, as at C. Starting with output B and saving C, the per-person capital stock continues to rise until it reaches $(K/N)^*$ and the economy reaches E. This level of capital generates output level $(Q/N)^*$, shown at point G. At E and G the condition for a steady state is realized. The left-hand side of (12.11) represented by the red saving line equals the right-hand side, represented by the straight black steady-state investment line. There is no excess saving left to fuel growth in per-person capital, and the per-person capital stock becomes fixed at $(K/N)^*$. Similar reasoning applies if the economy starts out with a per-person capital stock to the right of E; then saving is insufficient to replace worn-out capital and equip each new worker with as much capital as existing workers, and the per-person capital stock shrinks.

Implications of the Solow Growth Model

The most important implication of the Solow model startled economists. In contrast to the long-standing view that the key to raising the economy's growth rate was to increase the saving rate, Solow's analysis implied that *the economy's steady state growth rate depends only on the growth rate of the population (n) and is completely unaffected by changes in the saving rate.*

To understand this implication, let us begin with an economy that has an initial steady state, as at point E in Figure 12-4. Here we have copied the production function, the steady-state investment line, and the "old saving line" directly from Figure 12-3. Initially the economy's saving-investment equality occurs at point E, and its level of per-person real GNP, the amount $(Q/N)^*$, is shown at point G. Now we introduce a sudden increase in the saving rate from s_0 to s_1, which shifts the red saving line up and causes the economy to move from E to E' along the saving line, and from G to G' along the per-person production function. After the economy arrives at the new steady state, Q/N is fixed, and output grows at the same rate as N, just as was true prior to the increase in the saving rate, at point E.

Thus the saving rate matters, but not as people had previously believed. An increase in the saving rate raises the standard of living, from $(Q/N)^*$ to $(Q/N)'$ in Figure 12-4. To achieve this increase in Q/N, the growth rate of Q

Figure 12-4
Effect of an Increase in the Saving Rate

Initially the economy produces at point G, with per-person saving and capital stock shown at E. If the saving rate increases from s_0 to s_1, there is excess saving above the level of steady-state per-person investment, shown along the black steady-state investment line. The economy's capital-labor ratio grows from $(K/N)^*$ to $(K/N)'$, the level of production from point G to G', and the intersection of saving and steady-state investment from E to E'.

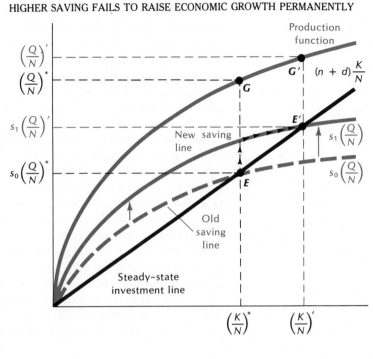

HIGHER SAVING FAILS TO RAISE ECONOMIC GROWTH PERMANENTLY

is temporarily raised above the growth rate of N. But the higher saving rate does not create a permanently higher growth rate of output, which depends only on population growth. In the steady state Q/N is fixed, so that Q and N must grow at the same rate. Intuitively, the extra saving finances only a higher *level* of the capital stock per person (K/N), not continuing *growth* in the capital stock per person. The extra saving is "eaten up" by the extra replacement investment implied by the higher capital stock, and the extra net investment required to equip each worker with the higher level of capital stock per person.

SELF-TEST   What is the effect of a reduction in the rate of population growth (n)? Is there a change in the growth rate of output?

12-5   Technology in Theory and Practice

At first glance the Solow growth model seems to contain a major flaw. As presented thus far, the model implies that the permanent growth rate of output should be the same as the growth rate of the population, and that the standard of living (Q/N) should be fixed. How, then, does the theory explain the sharp increase in the standard of living for each of the major industrialized nations, as plotted in Figure 12-1?

Two Types of Technological Change

Solow used two methods to make the model consistent with history. Both methods introduce an added element into the story: growth in technology in all its forms, including better schooling, improved organization, and all the fruits of innovation and research. The two methods for introducing technological change into the Solow growth model are to assume (1) that technology makes each worker more efficient, and (2) that technology shifts the production function relating per-person output to per-person capital.

"Labor-augmenting" technological change. This approach leaves our previous discussion of the Solow growth model, including the diagrams, completely intact. We simply need to adopt a broad definition of growth in "effective labor input." Instead of just counting the number of bodies at work, we count the "effective labor supply," taking account of improved education and the storehouse of technology that makes today's workers more efficient than workers a century ago. We now interpret N as effective labor input, and n as the growth rate of effective labor input. In the steady state output can grow at 3 percent ($q = 3$) if effective labor input grows at 3 percent ($n = 3$), leaving the ratio of output to effective labor input (Q/N) fixed. Now K/N remains fixed if the capital stock grows at 3 percent. Effective labor input growth of 3 percent exceeds population growth of, say, 1 percent, allowing the standard of living (Q per person) to grow at 2 percent.[10]

"Neutral" technological change. One problem with the first approach is that it assumes that technology only makes workers more efficient, with no impact on capital input. A more realistic assumption is that technology makes *both* labor and capital input more efficient. This "neutral" type of technological change simply means that the autonomous growth factor in equations (12.1) and (12.2) grows over time. Here we copy (12.2) for convenience:

General Form   Numerical Example

$$\frac{Q}{N} = A\, f\!\left(\frac{K}{N}\right) \qquad \frac{Q}{N} = A \left(\frac{K}{N}\right)^{0.25} \tag{12.2}$$

If education, innovations, and research raise the value of A every year, then per-person GNP can increase steadily. The growth rate of per-person GNP ($q - n$) is:

General Form   Numerical Example

$$q - n = a + b(k - n) \qquad q - n = a + 0.25(k - n) \tag{12.13}$$

Here a is the growth rate of the autonomous growth factor, and b is the elasticity of output with respect to capital input, assumed to be 0.25 in the

---

[10]Labor-augmenting technical change can be introduced into our original production function from equation (12.1) by defining effective labor input as a technological factor (T) times the population:

$$Q = F(Q, TN).$$

When T enters in this form, it is sometimes called "Harrod-neutral" technical change.

numerical example of (12.2). An economy might, for instance, have values of $a = 1.5$ and $k - n = 2$, which would be consistent with a steady-state in which

$$q - n = a + b(k - n) = 1.5 + 0.25(2) = 2.0.$$

In this example, there is a steady state, because per-person output and capital are growing at the same rate, allowing Q/K to remain fixed. After introducing neutral technological change into the diagrams of the Solow growth model, the production function shifts upward steadily, thus shifting the saving line up and to the right along a fixed steady-state investment line. Q/N and K/N rise in the steady state, but at the same rate.

SELF-TEST   Calculate the percentage growth rate of real GNP per person ($q - n$) from the numerical example of equation (12.13), assuming that b always equals 0.25, for the following combinations of the rates a, k, and n:

a	k	n	$q - n$
0	0	4	_____
0	4	4	_____
4	0	0	_____
4	4	4	_____

Shifts in the Production Function

Soon after Solow developed his theory of growth, he applied the theory to the measurement of the autonomous growth factor (a) in (12.13). His idea was to turn (12.13) around, so that a could be calculated from the other components:

$$a = (q - n) - b(k - n). \tag{12.14}$$

Since data were available on the growth rates of output (q) and of both capital and labor input (k and n), the only trick in determining the value of a was to identify the elasticity b. Here Solow's idea was to apply the theory of profit maximization in a competitive firm. Solow pointed out that such firms would also set the return on capital equal to the marginal product of capital, which implies that the elasticity b can be measured by the share of capital income in total GNP.[11]

Solow's finding was controversial. Fully seven eights of the growth in output per hour of work ($q - n$) over the period he studied (1909–57) was attributed to "technical change in the broadest sense," including education, research, innovations, and other improvements, while only the remaining eighth was attributed to growth in the capital stock per hour of work

---

[11] Let r be the rate of return to capital. Then competitive firms will set r equal to the marginal product of capital (MPK). The share of capital in GNP is rK/Q, which competitive firms will set equal to $(MPK)(K/Q)$, which is equal to the elasticity of output with respect to capital, $(dQ/dK)(K/Q) = (dQ/Q)(dK/K)$.

$(k - n)$. But an equation like (12.14) addresses economic growth and the sources of its slowdowns (like that which has occurred worldwide since 1973) only superficially. Knowing that some mysterious a factor was important in the growth process does not tell us, for instance, what caused a to grow more slowly after 1973. Some skeptics believe that a should not be given a name like "technological change," which implies we know precisely what determines a. They suggest that we call a instead the **residual** or, more frankly, "the measure of our ignorance." Government agencies like the U.S. Bureau of Labor Statistics, which now routinely calculate a, describe a as the growth in **multifactor productivity** or **total factor productivity.**

The **residual** is the amount that remains after subtracting from the rate of real GNP growth all of the identifiable sources of economic growth.

The growth in **multifactor productivity** or **total factor productivity** is the growth rate of output per hour of work, minus the contribution to output of the growth in the quantity of other factors of production per hour of work, notably capital but sometimes including energy, raw materials, or other factors of production.

The Many Sources of Growth in the Residual

What causes per-person output to increase, other than raising the capital stock per worker? There are many such causes, some of which involve factors unrelated to "technological change." Evaluating these factors forms the main agenda of studies of the "sources of economic growth," an example of which we study in the next section.

Education.   College graduates are paid more than high-school graduates, largely because their extra knowledge and skills make them more productive. Thus it follows that a better-educated society is a more productive one. But it is hard to tell exactly how much more. The return to extra education fluctuates over time, having fallen in the 1970s and risen in the 1980s. Further, the higher earnings of college graduates may also reflect the fact that many college graduates have a higher level of native ability than those who do not attend college.

Age-sex composition.   Just as college graduates are paid more than high-school graduates, adult men on average are paid more than adult women, and both are paid more than teenage workers. Does this mean that society becomes less efficient when the share of women and teenagers in the work force goes up? Clearly this is a controversial issue, especially for women who may be paid less because of present or past discrimination, not because they are less productive. It stands to reason, however, that experienced adult workers are more productive than inexperienced teens.

Movement off the farm.   A traditional source of economic growth in the early stages of industrialization is the movement of workers from the farm to the city. Since the average farm worker produces less than the average city worker, such movement helps make society as a whole more efficient. Eventually this source of growth diminishes, simply because there are fewer farm workers left. Further, the gap between farm and city productivity narrows; in the United States farm output per hour was only 25 percent of the economy-wide average in 1948, but had risen to 75 percent in 1987, largely as a result of a great increase in farm machinery and fertilizer per farm worker.

Crime and the environment.   Both crime and pollution of air and water can slow the growth of multifactor productivity. Crime may lead business firms to hire workers like security guards, who do not produce goods and services. Air and water pollution may directly reduce productivity; for instance, air pollution may lead to illness that affects the job performance of workers. Further, the government's efforts to stem pollution lead to regulations that require business firms to hire workers who do not directly produce measured output. For instance, electric utilities have been required to install "scrubbers," which require extra maintenance personnel who do not contribute directly to the production of electricity. Since our GNP statistics do not treat the resulting improvement in air quality as an increase in output, measured productivity falls. If society only undertakes those antipollution measures whose costs are balanced by the benefits of cleaner air and water, then the reduction in measured productivity caused by antipollution devices could be considered a measurement error rather than a true source of lower productivity.

Research and innovation. This is what people have in mind when they refer to "technological change." Some types of technical change, like the transistor and new types of chemicals, occur in research laboratories. Many other types occur on the production line as workers improve production methods (process innovations) or the design and quality of products (product innovation).

Improvements in labor quality. The benefits gained from research and innovation are sometimes hard to distinguish from the benefits of education and skills learned through on-the-job experience. All of these factors form the broadly defined level of "knowledge" or "technology." Society rarely experiences a decline in such knowledge. Even after World War II, when the destruction of German and Japanese cities caused a temporary decline in per-person output, knowledge and skills were not forgotten. Once these nations rebuilt their buildings and machines, their economies recovered rapidly.

12-6   *CASE STUDY:*   Sources of U.S. Growth and the Post-1973 Productivity Growth Slowdown

Why has productivity in the United States grown faster at some times than at others? And why have some nations, like Japan, grown faster than others, like the United Kingdom? For the past three decades Edward F. Denison of the Brookings Institution has been engaged in painstaking research to identify the sources of the growth in real GNP of the major industrialized countries.

Denison's method is based on Solow's equation (12.13), in which growth in output per unit of labor $(q - n)$ is divided between an autonomous growth factor or "residual" (a) and the contribution of growth in capital per unit of labor $(k - n)$. Denison has carefully adjusted measures of labor input (n) to take into account factors like education that change the quality of labor input. Thus Denison explains the growth in total output (q), not just in $(q - n)$:

General Form   Numerical Example

$$q = a + bk + (1 - b)n \qquad q = a + 0.25k + 0.75n \qquad (12.15)$$

We obtain this equation from (12.13) simply by adding n to each side. Denison's method involves estimating the magnitude of the main elements q, b, k, and n. Like Solow, Denison then determines the final element a as a "residual," whatever is left over. However Denison then tries to identify the fraction of a attributable to such factors as the movement of labor off the farm, and the effects of crime and pollution.

SELF-TEST

Denison's equation (12.15) has five elements, q, a, k, n, and b. Assuming that b always equals 0.25, any of the four remaining elements can be calculated if the other three are known. Fill in the blanks:

q	a	k	n
4	___	4	1
___	4	4	1
4	3	4	___
3	0	___	1

Sources of Growth in the United States

The Denison method. Table 12-2 illustrates the main components of Denison's method for the United States in three time periods, 1929–48, 1948–73, and 1973–82. The first line lists the percentage growth rates of real national income, which differs from real GNP growth (q) only by excluding depreciation and indirect business taxes.[12] Next, Denison must calculate the weights (b and $1 - b$) to be applied to the growth in capital and labor input. His b weights, like Solow's, are based on the share of labor and capital in total national income; thus b is set equal to the fraction of national income consisting of income of all types of capital (corporate profits, interest, rent) while $1 - b$ is set equal to the fraction consisting of compensation of employees.[13] In calculating the growth rate of capital (k), Denison makes straightforward use of government data and arrives at the results shown on line B.1 in Table 12-2. For instance, the figure 0.11 percent on line B.1 for 1929–48 represents the weight b (about 0.2) times the growth rate of capital (k) during that period.

The next section of the table on line B.2 and the following lines shows the contribution to economic growth of labor input growth divided into several categories. First, Denison calculates the growth in employment. Then he makes adjustments for increases or decreases in the quality of labor and for hours worked per employee. The major quality adjustment is for increased education: based on comparisons of the earnings of college graduates and high school graduates, Denison assumes one college-graduate employee represents more labor input than one high-school-graduate employee. Further adjustments are made on line B.2.d to measure the effect on production of the shift in the labor force toward a larger share of women and teenagers and a smaller share of adult men.[14] Each component

---

[12] **Review:** Figure 2-6.
[13] Income of the self-employed is allocated partly to labor and partly to capital.
[14] This shift is shown in Table 11-1.

Table 12-2 **Sources of Growth of Real National Income in the United States, Selected Periods, 1929–82 (Contributions to Growth Rates in Percentage Points)**

	1929–48	1948–73	Difference: (2)–(1)	1973–82	Difference: (4) – (2)
	(1)	(2)	(3)	(4)	(5)
A. Real national income	2.57	3.89	1.32	2.61	−1.28
B. Total factor input	1.56	2.23	0.67	2.53	0.30
1. Capital	0.11	0.77	0.66	0.67	−0.10
2. Labor	1.45	1.46	0.01	1.86	0.40
a. Employment	1.05	1.28	0.23	1.90	0.62
b. Hours of work	−0.21	−0.24	−0.03	−0.33	−0.09
c. Education	0.38	0.40	0.02	0.44	0.04
d. Age-sex composition	0.00	−0.15	−0.15	−0.24	−0.09
e. Unallocated	0.23	0.17	−0.06	0.09	−0.08
C. Output per unit of input	1.01	1.66	0.65	0.08	−1.58
1. Movement from farms and small business	0.29	0.30	0.01	0.07	−0.23
2. Economies of scale	0.22	0.32	0.10	0.21	−0.11
3. Legal and human environment	0.00	−0.04	−0.04	−0.17	−0.13
4. Miscellaneous	0.01	−0.01	−0.02	0.02	0.03
5. Residual: "advances in knowledge"	0.49	1.09	0.60	−0.05	−1.04

Source: Edward F. Denison, *Trends in American Economic Growth, 1929–1982* (Washington, D.C.: Brookings Institution, 1985), Table 8-2.

of the "labor" category in section B.2 of the table is shown after multiplication by the $1 - b$ weight (approximately 0.8).

The bottom part of Table 12-2 shows additional estimates that link part of the autonomous growth factor (a) to specific causes. For instance, line C.1 lists the addition to economic growth caused by the movement of workers from farms where their productivity was relatively low to urban jobs where their productivity was higher. Line C.2 shows an estimate of the effects of "economies of scale," the benefits of growing market size that allow greater specialization of firms, longer production runs, and larger transactions. An interesting category is line C.3, the "Legal and human environment," representing Denison's estimate of the negative impact on productivity of increased pollution, environmental legislation, and the rising crime rate.

After a final estimate of various miscellaneous factors, Denison arrives at his residual, an estimate of the contribution to growth of advances in knowledge. This is calculated by subtracting from output growth in line A the total contribution of factor input growth in line B and the other growth sources listed in lines C.1 through C.4. The residual simply stands for all those sources of growth that Denison cannot account for.

The acceleration of economic growth during 1948–73. We now want to examine Denison's specific numerical answers to two questions. First, why did the rate of economic growth speed up between the first period list in column (1), 1929–48, and the next period listed in column (2), 1948–73? To find the answer, we look at column (3), which subtracts column (1) from column (2). There we see on line A that real national income growth accelerated by 1.32 points. About half of this can be attributed to advances in knowledge on line C.5. There was also a speedup in the growth of capital input (line B.1), which is not surprising since during the first period, 1929–48, the Great Depression had depressed the demand for new capital goods and during World War II investment was postponed in order to concentrate resources on war production.

Explaining the growth slowdown after 1973. The second question is why growth slowed after 1973. To answer this, we move farther rightward in Table 12-2 to column (4), which shows the sources of growth in the most recent period, 1973–82. Column (5) compares 1973–82 to the previous period, 1948–73. There we see that economic growth slowed down by a substantial 1.28 percentage points per year, about the same as the 1.32 point speedup between the first two periods. Denison attributes almost all of the slowdown to the "residual" category. A modest acceleration in the growth of employment is more than offset by a decline in the growth of output per unit of input (line C). While a slower rate of movement from farm to city (C.1), and the impact of environmental legislation and crime (C.3) explain part of the puzzle, most of its left unexplained in line C.5.

Thus, despite all of the work that goes into preparing the estimates of the sources of growth, Denison's method does not seem to provide a complete explanation of the slowdown after 1973. This can be seen more clearly if we summarize the analysis in Table 12-2 as follows:

	Slowdown, 1973–82 from 1948–73
A. Real national income	−1.28
B. Total factor input	0.30
C. Output per unit of input,	−1.58
of which "residual" equals	−1.04
Residual as percent of slowdown	83

12-7 Competing Hypotheses to Explain the Productivity Slowdown

The case study in the preceding section identified several sources of economic growth that help explain why productivity growth in the United States was relatively rapid before 1973, and much slower after 1973. Nevertheless, most of the productivity slowdown remains unexplained in the Denison study. Economists are still debating the causes of the productivity growth slowdown. Some analysts attribute the entire slowdown to one or two major factors. Others believe that many different factors have each made a small contribution. In their view, to use the analogy devised by Lester Thurow of MIT, the productivity slowdown has been like "death from a thousand cuts." In this section we examine some of these competing explanations.

Dimensions of the Productivity Slowdown

Has U.S. productivity performance improved since 1982, the end of Denison's study period? Is the slowdown equally serious for growth in output per hour $(q - n)$ and multifactor productivity growth (a)? The more recent data are displayed in Table 12-3. In the top half of the table the red line displays $q - n$ for four time periods. There was an overall slowdown of 1.61 percentage points between 1948–73 and 1973–87, but a slight improvement from 0.48 to 1.11 points from 1973–79 to 1979–87. Thus the productivity growth slowdown continues to be a serious problem, but is not quite as severe as it was in the 1970s.

The next two lines display a sharp contrast in performance between the manufacturing and nonmanufacturing sectors. Manufacturing $q - n$ revived so strongly after 1979 that the post-1973 productivity growth slowdown almost disappeared. Not shown in the table is the main source of the manufacturing revival. Rather than being spread evenly, *almost two thirds of the manufacturing productivity recovery occurred in the computer industry.*[15]

---

[15]This fact is documented, and many other aspects of the industrial aspects of the productivity slowdown are discussed, in Martin N. Baily and Robert J. Gordon, "Measurement Issues, the Productivity Slowdown, and the Explosion of Computer Power," *Brookings Papers on Economic Activity,* vol. 19, no. 2 (1988), pp. 347–420.

Table 12-3 **Average Annual Aggregate Productivity Growth, 1948–87, Selected Periods (Percent per Year)**

Measure	1948–73	1973–79	1979–87	1973–87	Change, 1948–73 to 1973–87
Output per hour $(q - n)$					
Business	2.94	0.62	1.32	1.02	−1.92
Nonfarm business	2.45	0.48	1.11	0.84	−1.61
Manufacturing	2.82	1.38	3.39	2.52	−0.30
Nonmanufacturing	2.32	0.16	0.33	0.25	−2.07
Multifactor productivity (a)					
Business	2.00	0.10	0.61	0.39	−1.61
Nonfarm business	1.68	−0.08	0.45	0.22	−1.46
Manufacturing	2.03	0.52	2.56	1.68	−0.35
Nonmanufacturing	1.55	−0.29	−0.28	−0.30	−1.85

Source: U.S. National Income and Product Accounts and U.S. Bureau of Labor Statistics.

The nonmanufacturing part of the economy, about three times larger than manufacturing, reveals virtually no post-1979 revival, and near-total stagnation of productivity since 1973.

The bottom half of Table 12-3 displays the growth rate of multifactor productivity (a) for the same time periods and sectors of the economy. As in equation (12.14), a is obtained from $q - n$ by subtracting the contribution of growth in capital per worker hour. Hence all the numbers for a in the bottom half of Table 12-3 are smaller than those for $q - n$ in the top half. Otherwise, adjusting for growth in capital input leaves all the basic features of the productivity slowdown intact, suggesting that slower growth in capital input contributes only slightly to the overall productivity growth problem. We still have a slight revival after 1979, concentrated in computer manufacturing. The story in nonmanufacturing is even more dismal with *negative* growth in multifactor productivity.

The U.S. productivity slowdown has become very serious simply because it has lasted so long, especially the slowdown outside of the manufacturing sector. What explanations have economists devised for this puzzle? Here we review some of the leading explanations briefly, starting with those that center on slower growth in inputs other than quantity of labor hours; these include the quantity and quality of capital, the quantity of raw materials, and the quality of labor. Then we turn to hypotheses that try to explain the slowdown in the growth of a—that is, the Denison–Solow "residual" that remains after the quantity and quality of inputs have been taken into account.

Slower Growth in Measured and Unmeasured Inputs

Measured capital per labor hour. The growth of measured capital per labor hour slowed in the United States after 1973, both because the growth of the capital stock slowed down, and because the growth of labor hours increased in response to a massive movement by women from home activity into labor force participation. One leading hypothesis to explain slower growth in the capital stock is associated with Martin Feldstein of Harvard University. In collaboration with several coauthors, Feldstein has focused on the fact that the rules of the U.S. tax system are set in nominal rather than real terms. When the rate of inflation accelerates, saving by corporations and individual households is overtaxed, and saving is discouraged. In addition, the saving that actually occurs is diverted from productive purposes, like fixed investment in factories and equipment, to less productive purposes, like residential housing and speculation in gold and farm land. Feldstein is correct that the 1970s was a good decade to borrow money and a poor decade to lend money.[16] But some critics point out that the overall saving rate of households did not change much during the decade and in fact declined in the 1980s when inflation and tax rates both decreased. And, as we have seen in Table 12-3, slower growth in capital input explains only a small part of the slowdown in $q - n$.

---

[16]Martin Feldstein, "The Effect of Inflation on the Prices of Land and Gold," *Journal of Public Economics,* vol. 14, no. 3 (December 1980), pp. 309–317.

There is another explanation of the slowdown in the growth of capital per labor hour, which concentrates on the fact that the growth rate of labor hours speeded up after 1973 in the United States but not in other countries. The real wage rate in the United States declined substantially in response to the supply shocks of 1973–74 and 1979–80. Yet in Europe real wage rates grew substantially faster than productivity in the 1970s, finally moderating only in the 1980s. As a result labor was relatively cheap in the United States after 1973 and relatively expensive in Europe. The German economist Herbert Giersch has pointed to this difference in real wage behavior to explain why European countries enjoyed faster productivity growth and higher unemployment than in the United States. For more on high unemployment in Europe, see pages 304–314.

Raw materials and energy.   Michael Bruno, Governor of the Central Bank of Israel, and Jeffrey Sachs of Harvard believe that the worldwide character of the productivity slowdown after 1973 suggests the likelihood of a common cause. Bruno and Sachs stress the direct effect of the higher relative prices of energy and raw materials, together with the restrictive macroeconomic policies that were introduced in response to those increases in relative prices. They calculate that more than half of the slowdown in manufacturing productivity can be ascribed to the direct effect. This involves the impact of higher energy prices on reducing the usage of energy, which in turn reduces the productivity of both capital and labor. An additional indirect effect occurred in nonmanufacturing, where the combined impact of lower real income and contractionary macroeconomic policy reduced demand and cut the utilization of plants, machines, and "overhead" labor. Then there is a dynamic effect of slower growth, which Denison attempts to capture in his "economies of scale" factor, but which Bruno and Sachs consider to have been even more important.[17] A problem with the Bruno–Sachs analysis is that the increase in oil prices and raw materials prices has been reversed in the 1980s, yet productivity growth has not yet begun to revive, particularly in nonmanufacturing.

Decline in labor quality.   The role of labor quality in the productivity slowdown is still debated. The percentage of teenagers and adult women in the labor force rose after 1973, yet their average wages still lag behind those of adult men. Consequently, analysts who measure the relative productivity of groups of workers by their relative wages conclude that the quality of the workforce declined as its "age-sex composition" shifted. Looking back at line 2d of Table 12-2, we see that Denison assigns a small contribution to the age-sex shift. However, other economists believe that low relative wages of women reflect, at least in part, the effects of discrimination. Economists also note the decline in scores on SAT and other standardized tests that occurred in the 1970s and 1980s, and the more general problem that the U.S. school system is not training enough graduates with the skills needed to cope with the demands of modern technology. Altogether, the labor quality issue might explain 0.2 to 0.3 of the total productivity slowdown of 1.61 points (show on the upper red line in Table 12-3).

---

[17]Michael Bruno and Jeffrey Sachs, *Economics of Worldwide Stagnation* (Cambridge: Harvard University Press, 1985).

Running Out of Resources and Ideas

Because the productivity slowdown has been so pervasive and longlasting, some economists believe that the fundamental cause goes beyond slower growth in factor inputs. William Nordhaus has helped popularize the "depletion" hypothesis, which is a much more pessimistic approach than those reviewed earlier in the section. Whereas the other hypotheses imply that the productivity slowdown will be temporary, the Nordhaus depletion hypothesis suggests that there is no solution to the problem.

Part of the hypothesis is that a substantial portion of the rapid growth in productivity in the industrialized nations before 1973 was temporary, a "catch-up" phenomenon after World War II, and was bound to come to an end. Another aspect is the depletion of natural resources, in particular the decline in the rate of finding new productive oil wells in the United States. This has reduced productivity growth, since there are more people engaged in searching for less and less available oil. A final aspect of the depletion hypothesis is a decline in the rate of invention and innovation. Yet, in an assessment based on a large amount of detailed investigation at the industry-by-industry level, Zvi Griliches of Harvard University has concluded that, while research and development (R&D) is an important contributor to economic growth, the share of R&D in the economy has not changed enough since 1973 to explain any significant part of the observed slowdown in productivity growth.[18] Overall, while some elements of the Nordhaus approach may be on the right track, it has attracted as much criticism as endorsement from other economists.[19]

Problems of Particular Industries

One aspect of the productivity slowdown that seems to point in the directional of "death by a thousand cuts," that is, a multipart explanation, is the diversity of the experience of major industries. In the United States, for instance, three major industries have experienced a productivity growth slowdown that is about triple the average of other industries. One extreme case, the mining industry, illustrates the workings of the Nordhaus depletion hypothesis. Here most of the slowdown appears to have been caused by a reduced rate of finding new and productive oil wells. This part of the slowdown has a direct connection to the post-1973 rise in energy prices, which prompted oil firms to drill in less productive areas that previously had been neglected. Environmental and health legislation has also had a negative impact on productivity in coal mining.[20]

The construction industry is also an extreme case, with a *negative* growth rate of productivity since 1965. Productivity in the construction in-

---

[18]Zvi Griliches, "Productivity Puzzles and R&D: Another Nonexplanation," *Journal of Economic Perspectives,* vol. 2 (Fall 1988), pp. 9–21.

[19]The Nordhaus approach is set out in William D. Nordhaus, "Economic Policy in the Face of Declining Productivity Growth," *European Economic Review,* vol. 18 (May/June 1982), pp. 131–158. For some critical comments see the remarks of the discussants in the same volume.

[20]Our GNP accounts do not include any benefits from a better environment or better health resulting from such legislation. To the extent that the productivity slowdown can be traced to such legislation, then the slowdown is illusory on the condition that the legislation yields benefits to society (unmeasured in the GNP accounts) that are equal to its costs.

dustry has fallen back to the levels of the early 1950s. However, faulty data may be a source of error here. One possibility is that the growth in the price deflator for construction has been overstated, so that real GNP in the construction industry is understated. If so, a correction of this statistical problem would raise the growth rate of total GNP but would have an even greater effect in raising the growth rate of the capital stock, which includes the output of the construction industry. Thus any such hypothetical improvement of measurement techniques would not solve the puzzle of slower growth in multifactor productivity (a).

Public utilities compose the third extreme industry, with most of the problem concentrated in electricity generation. Several hypotheses come together here. Government regulation has required costly investment in antipollution equipment. Higher energy prices, together with slower growth in output due to restrictive macroeconomic policies, have reduced the use of existing electric generation equipment. The lack of advances since the 1960s in equipment design may also have slowed productivity growth. In fact, we may have gone backward. Billions of dollars have been wasted on the construction of nuclear power plants that have never been put into service. The complexity of the diagnosis of the productivity problem in this industry suggests that we should be skeptical of simple hypotheses that attribute all of the problem to one cause and promise a solution with a single proposed policy change.[21]

12-8 Preview: The Role of Policy

Throughout this chapter we have tried to solve "Puzzle 3," the mysterious slowdown in the growth rate of labor productivity in the United States since 1973. One of the most important objectives of economic policy is to obtain an increase in the standard of living of the average citizen. In the long run the growth rate of the standard of living, that is, income per person, depends on the growth rate of productivity, that is, output per hour of work ($q - n$). As the post-1973 slowdown in productivity growth continues, with a recovery in manufacturing but not in nonmanufacturing, concern about its causes has deepened.

We have seen that slower growth in capital input explains only a small part of the slowdown in growth of output per hour: comparing 1973–87 with 1948–73, multifactor productivity growth (a) slowed by 1.46 percentage points, almost as much as the 1.61 point slowdown in output per hour of work. Thus we have searched for causes elsewhere, and have found higher relative prices of oil and other raw materials, expenditures to control crime and pollution, a shift in the work force toward less experienced workers, a decline in quality of education, and the special problems of the mining, construction, and public utility industries.

How can government policy promote a more rapid growth in the nation's standard of living? One approach is to adopt policies to improve education and the skill of the workforce; some of these were discussed in our section on mismatch unemployment in Chapter 11. But the major focus of

---

[21]For more on the problems of individual industries, see the Baily-Gordon article cited in footnote 15.

policy discussions is on the role of the twin deficits, the federal government budget deficit and the foreign trade deficit. The federal budget deficit influences growth because it directly reduces national saving. The foreign trade deficit matters because a buildup of debt to foreigners will reduce the future output available for improvements in living standards by requiring future Americans to pay an increasing fraction of their income as interest to foreigners.

Greater private investment requires an increase in national saving, which can be achieved by any combination of more government saving and more private saving. Raising government saving, that is, reducing the budget deficit, has proven difficult because the administration and Congress have yet to agree on a set of spending cuts or tax increases. Tax reforms to stimulate business and personal saving are another approach but are politically difficult, simply because rich people save proportionately more of their incomes than poor people. Thus any measure to reduce the taxation of income from capital and raise consumption or income taxes would tend to benefit the rich and hurt the poor and much of the middle class.

Does the Saving Rate Matter for Growth?

A major lesson of this chapter has come from our study of the Solow model of economic growth. Solow showed, as in Figure 12-4, that an increase in the national saving rate (achieved by cutting the budget deficit or raising the private saving rate) *will not permanently raise the rate of economic growth.* Growth increases temporarily, but eventually all of the extra saving is needed for "steady state investment," that is, for equipping new members of the workforce with the existing per-person capital stock, and for replacing worn-out and obsolete capital. Does Solow's model imply that we do not need to worry about the federal budget deficit, or the low U.S. saving rate?

Table 12-4 **The Relationship between the Personal Saving Rate and Per-Capita Income Growth**

	Personal saving as percentage of personal disposable income, average of 1973 and 1987	*Growth in per-capita GNP, 1955–88*
Saving rate above 10 percent		
Italy	26.4	3.43
Japan	18.6	6.02
France	15.8	3.10
West Germany	13.0	3.03
Saving rate below 10 percent		
United Kingdom	7.9	1.99
United States	6.5	1.86
Sweden	0.6	2.46

Sources: Saving rate from *OECD Economic Outlook,* December 1988, Table R12. Growth rates from this chapter, Table 12-1.

Solow himself has cautioned us against taking his model too literally. He is impressed by findings of Edward N. Wolff of New York University, who has found that, over the history of the major industrialized countries since 1880, there is a very strong positive relationship between the growth rate of per-person capital $(k - n)$ and the rate of technological change (a). This stands in contrast to Solow's equation (12.14), which treats a and $k - n$ as unrelated. Wolff's point is consistent with Table 12-4. Per-capita growth rates are not perfectly correlated with household saving rates; nevertheless the four countries with the highest saving rates also grew the fastest, and those with the lowest saving rates also grew the slowest.

We conclude this chapter by leaving open the possibility that growth in productivity and per-capita income may be more closely related to the saving rate than is implied by the Solow growth model. In Solow's words,

> It appears that the [countries] that invested fastest were best able to take advantage of the available knowledge. . . . the way remains open for a reasonable person to believe that the stimulation of investment will favor faster intermediate-run growth.[22]

---

[22]Robert M. Solow, "Growth Theory and After," p. 315.

SUMMARY

1. Divergences between the economic growth rates of individual nations sustained over long periods of time can create substantial differences in living standards. Although Britain had the highest level of real GNP per capita in 1870 among the seven nations displayed in Figure 12-1, by 1988 Britain was second from the bottom as a consequence of its slow rate of economic growth during the intervening century.

2. The production function explains real GNP as depending on the quantity of factor inputs (capital and labor) and on an autonomous growth factor that reflects the influence of research, innovation, and other factors. An increase in the growth rate of real GNP per person requires either an increase in the growth rate of capital per person or an increase in the growth rate of the autonomous growth factor.

3. National saving is the sum of government saving (which in turn is the government surplus or minus the deficit) plus private saving. National saving equals private investment, which in turn equals the change in the capital stock plus the investment expenditures required to replace capital goods that wear out or become obsolete.

4. The Solow theory of economic growth defines an equilibrium called the "steady state" in which output, capital, and labor input are all growing at the same rate. If per-person saving exceeds steady-state investment per person, the capital-labor ratio will grow until per-person steady-state investment is high enough to halt the growth in the capital-labor ratio. At this point, the economy reaches a new steady state with a constant capital-labor ratio.

5. In the Solow model, in the long run the economy's growth rate of output depends only on its rate of population growth, or, more broadly, on the growth rate of "effective" labor input (which takes account of improvements in education, skills, and technology). An increase in the saving rate does not change the economy's steady-state growth rate of output.

6. The rate of population growth in the Solow model can be interpreted as any source of economic growth other than growth in per-person capital input. These include education, reallocation of labor between farm and city, research, and innovation.

7. The growth rate of labor productivity slowed markedly after 1973. A greater slowdown occurred in nonmanufacturing than in manufacturing. Little of the slowdown is explained by slower capital accumulation.

8. Other causes of the productivity slowdown include the effect of crime and environmental regulation, higher energy prices, lower quality of labor, and special factors in three industries, mining, construction, and electric utilities.

9. While Solow's growth model states that the saving rate does not affect the growth rate of output, the strong relationship between saving rates and growth rates in different countries over long periods of time suggests that saving and growth are related in a way not explained by the Solow growth model.

CONCEPTS

economic growth
factor inputs
production function
steady state

residual
multifactor productivity
total factor productivity

QUESTIONS AND PROBLEMS

Questions

1. In terms of the theories of growth presented in this chapter, is it important to distinguish between growth of output and growth of per person output? Why or why not?

2. "The United States is something of a *has-been* in the growth race." Explain. What explanations for this phenomenon does the author suggest are most appropriate? Which does he reject?

3. If the production function is characterized by constant returns to scale, what happens to real GNP when labor and capital inputs both double? What happens when labor and capital inputs double and the autonomous growth factor (A) also doubles in size?

4. Assuming that the autonomous growth factor (A) remains unchanged, explain why the gains in output associated with an increase in the capital-labor ratio inevitably fall following increases in the level of investment.

5. What is the most important implication of the Solow growth model? Does it imply that an increase in the rate of private saving is useless as a means to increase the standard of living in the long run?

6. Why do Denison and other researchers use the observed shares of capital and labor income as estimates of the weights on capital and labor in the production function (b and $1 - b$)?

7. Explain why, in spite of the suggested steady state outcome of Solow's model, that the national saving rate is treated in this chapter as playing such an important role in determining the rate of economic growth.

8. What is the major distinction between the growth model developed by Solow and that applied by Denison?

9. Lester Thurow argues that the productivity slowdown experienced by the Unitied States since 1973 has been like "death from a thousand cuts." Explain.

10. In what way could the oil crisis of the 1970s and the resulting higher price of energy have affected the growth rate of real GNP per person? What is the problem with such an explanation?

Problems

1. Assuming that U.S. output is characterized by a Cobb–Douglas production function with constant returns to scale and that the share of capital income to total GNP is 0.25, consider the following five cases:

Case I:	growth rate of labor (n) =	1%
	growth rate of capital (k) =	4%
	growth rate of autonomous growth factor (a) =	2%
Case II:	growth rate of labor (n) =	2%
	growth rate of capital (k) =	3%
	growth rate of autonomous growth factor (a) =	0.75%
Case III:	growth rate of labor (n) =	1%
	growth rate of capital (k) =	5%
	growth rate of autonomous growth factor (a) =	2.4%
Case IV:	growth rate of labor (n) =	3%
	growth rate of capital (k) =	3%
	growth rate of autonomous growth factor (a) =	0%

Case V: growth rate of labor (n) = 0%
growth rate of capital (k) = 0%
growth rate of autonomous
growth factor (a) = 3%

(a) In each case, what is the elasticity of output to capital input? Explain.

(b) In each case, what is the rate of growth of output?

(c) In each case, what is the growth of per-person output?

(d) Assuming that the autonomous growth factor is a "neutral" type of technological change, which cases(s) would be consistent with steady state growth?

2. Recalculate your answers to 1 a-d if the elasticity of output to labor input were 0.6.

3. If income in the economy over the past 25 years has been growing at a rate of 3.1 percent while labor input has been growing at 1.5 percent and capital input has been growing at 2.5 percent, what part of the total growth is accounted for by autonomous growth factors (technological change, education, and so on)? (Assume the economy is characterized by the following production function: $Q = AK^{0.25}N^{0.75}$.)

4. Consider an economy characterized by the following production function: $Q = AK^{1/3}N^{2/3}$, with a capital stock of, say, $3000 billion and current net investment of $120 billion.

(a) If the growth rate of autonomous factors is zero and the growth rate of labor is 1 percent, what is the current growth rate of per person output? Is this a steady state situation?

(b) If the government wanted to increase the growth rate of per-person output by an extra percentage point through tax and subsidy policies that affected capital growth alone, by what percentage would it have to raise investment?

(c) In the unlikely event that the government successfully stimulated the required investment, at what rate of growth in per-person output would the economy arrive in the steady state according to the implications of the simple Solow growth model? What assumptions about the nature of capital investment does this outcome imply? Does the text accept this assumption? Why or why not?

p. 362 Q/K declines as K/N increases. The answer is evident in the numerical example of equation (12.2), where Q/N rises with an elasticity of 0.25 to an increase in K/N, implying that Q increases much less rapidly than K, so that Q/K declines. This can also be seen by drawing a straight line from the origin (lower-left corner) of Figure 12-2 to point B. The slope of this line is the Q/K ratio. As we move to the right along the production function, the slope of this line from the origin to points on the production function will decrease.

p. 367 Only Q/K varies as we move along the production function in Figure 12-2, which plots Q/N against K/N. The other parameters s, n, and d are all held constant and are not introduced into the graphical analysis until Figure 12-3.

p. 371 A decline in the growth rate of population (n) causes the growth rate of output (q) to decline by exactly the same amount, after the economy reaches a new steady state. But the lower rate of population growth raises the standard of living (Q/N). Be sure that you can explain why: start from point E in Figure 12-4, assume that the old saving line remains valid, and rotate the steady-state investment line downward to the right, as required by the decline in the growth rate of population (n).

p. 373 The following are the growth rates of real GNP per person ($q - n$) corresponding to the four blanks: $-1.0, 0.0, 4.0, 4.0$.

p. 376 The following are the growth rates to be inserted in the four blanks: $a = 2.25$; $q = 5.75$; $n = 0.0$; $k = 9.0$.

Fiscal Policy and the Government Debt

In contrast to the original notion of activist fiscal stabilization policy, the budget decisions are now regarded as important because of their long-term effects on resource allocation.
—*Martin S. Feldstein, 1988*

13–1 Introduction: Fiscal Policy and the Debate Over the U.S. Budget Deficit

The *IS-LM* model of Chapters 4 and 5 portrayed fiscal and monetary policy as alternative tools available to control the level of output, or GNP. It showed that a given level of output, for instance natural real GNP (Q^N), could be achieved with a variety of different combinations of monetary and fiscal policy. With tight fiscal and easy monetary policy, Q^N would be compatible with a low interest rate. With easy fiscal and tight monetary policy, the same value of Q^N would be compatible with a higher interest rate. In this sense, monetary and fiscal policy represent two tools or "instruments" for controlling two "targets," that is, the level of output and the interest rate.

If the *IS* and *LM* curves have their normal slopes, and are neither vertical nor horizontal, the *IS-LM* model treats either monetary or fiscal policy as equally well suited to the task of controlling GNP. Yet economists have gradually come to agree that monetary policy is better suited than fiscal policy for controlling GNP because the Federal Reserve can make decisions promptly on policy changes necessary to control the money supply. In contrast, fiscal policy decisions (at least in the United States) tend to be made slowly and only after a difficult process of compromise between Congress and the administration. If monetary policy succeeds in stabilizing real GNP at the desired level of output, that is, natural real GNP, then fiscal policy by default becomes responsible for the level of real interest rates. This is an implication of our previous analysis of the mix of monetary and fiscal policy (Figure 5-6 on p. 132).

Real interest rates link the present and the future. They help determine how much of today's output will be invested rather than consumed, and thus available to produce more goods and services in the future. If monetary policy is given the task of controlling GNP in the short run, then fiscal policy becomes a major determinant of real interest rates and indirectly of the economy's rate of long-term economic growth. A successful economy does not consume all of its current production; it saves some fraction of that income in order to increase the nation's stock of productive wealth—not only structures and equipment, but also knowledge and education. Investment in new machines is the main channel by which advances in technology are incorporated into the productive process. Thus a country with low saving and investment may stagnate technologically while other countries steadily introduce more modern and efficient methods of production.

National Saving Evaporated in the 1980s

As we learned in the last chapter, there are two major components to national saving, private saving (S) and government saving. Government saving is the same thing as the government budget surplus ($T - G$). A government budget deficit reduces national saving. National saving is available to be lent to business firms for domestic private investment (I), or to be invested abroad as net foreign investment, which is the same as net exports (X). These relations are true by definition and are summarized by equation (2.9), which is repeated here as (13.1):

$$S + (T - G) \equiv I + X \qquad (13.1)$$

Figure 13.1 illustrates the components of the left side of (13.1) for three periods, with each component defined as a percentage of net national product.[1] The first is a historical base period, 1951–80, chosen to show how much the 1980s differed from the earlier postwar decades. The second and third are 1984–86 and 1987–88, chosen to show that national saving continued to evaporate in 1987–88 even as the economy recovered from its long slump and finally reached its natural level of output (Q^N). In the historical base period, 1951–80, the government deficit was only 1.2 percent; national saving of 8.0 percent was only slightly smaller than private saving of 9.2 percent.

But in the 1980s national saving fell by more than half. In 1984–86 the culprit was mainly the government deficit of 5.0 percent, which made national saving of 3.1 percent much smaller than private saving of 8.1 percent. In 1987–88 the government deficit decreased somewhat, but national saving shriveled further to 2.4 percent as private saving dropped from 8.1 to 6.3 percent.

National saving, the left-hand side of equation (13.1), is available to finance domestic private investment and foreign investment. This is shown in Figure 13-2, where in 1951–80 national saving of 8.0 percent financed domestic private investment of 7.6 percent, with 0.4 percent left over for foreign investment. But in the 1980s, when national saving fell far short of domestic private investment, the United States had to borrow rather than lend. The equality illustrated in the second two periods in Figure 13-2 can also be shown in equation (13.2), which solves (13.1) for the amount of domestic private investment:

$$I \equiv S + (T - G) - X, \quad \text{or} \qquad (13.2)$$

private domestic investment $\equiv$ national saving + foreign borrowing

---

[1]Figures 13-1 and 13-2 are adapted from Thomas E. Mann and Charles L. Schultze, "Getting Rid of the Budget Deficit: Why We Should and How We Can," *Brookings Review* (Winter 1988/89), pp. 3–17.

Figure 13-1
Private Saving, National Saving, and the Government Deficit, as Shares of Net National Product, Selected Intervals, 1951–88.

The left bar shows that during the three-decade period 1951–80, the government deficit was relatively small, so that private and national saving were almost the same. The center and right bars show that national saving fell by more than half in 1984–88, entirely because of the government deficit during 1984–86, but also because of a decline in private saving in 1987–88.

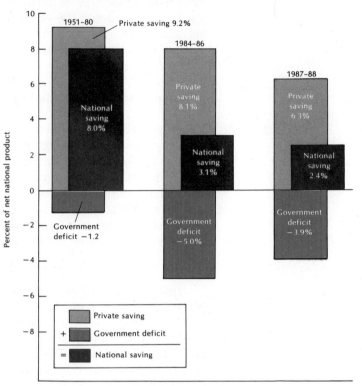

HOW THE TWIN DEFICITS ARE RELATED

Figure 13-2
National Saving, Domestic Private Investment, and Foreign Lending or Borrowing, Selected Intervals, 1951–88

Domestic private investment declined very little in the 1980s, as compared to the three-decade period 1951–80. As a result, the sharp drop in national saving was balanced by a shift from a small amount of foreign lending in 1951–80 to a large amount of foreign borrowing in 1984–88.

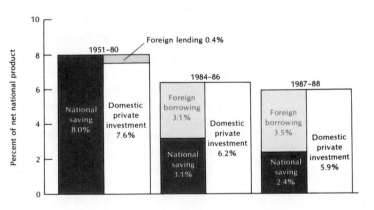

As shown in Figure 13-2, by 1987–88 foreign borrowing had reached 3.5 percent of GNP, almost equalling the government deficit of 3.9 percent.

SELF-TEST   When X is positive, does this indicate foreign lending or foreign borrowing? When X is negative? Be sure that you can explain whether positive net exports coincide with foreign borrowing or lending, and why.

The Debate Over the Government Budget Deficit

As the 1980s drew to a close, little progress had been made in reducing the government deficit. Economists debated not only the solutions to the problem, but also the extent of it. Some said, in essence, "Since it's difficult to eliminate the deficit, why bother?" Another group claimed that the deficit was improperly measured and did not really exist. Others viewed the large deficits as a disaster.

In this chapter we focus on the causes of the budget deficit and its consequences. Were tax cuts or spending increases primarily responsible for the deficit? What are the effects on society of a year-by-year buildup of the government debt? What is the burden of the government debt? Is there a limit to the rate at which the government debt can increase? Can we ignore the deficit problem if the ratio of the government debt to GNP does not increase? Throughout the chapter, we focus on the long-run effects of fiscal policy on the government debt and the rate of economic growth. The difficulty of achieving quick changes in fiscal policy, and the likelihood that temporary changes in fiscal policy will have little effect on private spending decisions, cause us to make monetary policy the main tool of stabilization policy, responsible for stabilizing output at the natural level of real GNP. We will return in Chapter 17 to the limitations of both monetary and fiscal policy, and the reasons many economists have concluded that monetary is superior to fiscal policy for the task of short-term stabilization. In Chapter 15 we will consider the more general question of whether *any* attempt to stabilize real GNP in the short run is possible or desirable.

13-2 Long-Run Effects of Fiscal Policy on Economic Growth and Welfare

In the previous chapter we concluded that an increase in the national saving rate is likely to stimulate economic growth, at least in the intermediate run of, say, the next decade or so. In this case, then, society must decide whether or not to save more, which requires the sacrifice of consumption *now* to obtain extra consumption *in the future.* This choice depends on society's **rate of time preference**, the extra amount people would be willing to pay to have consumption goods now instead of in the future. For instance, if people are willing to pay $1.10 to obtain a good today that they could have for $1.00 one year from now (by borrowing at a 10 percent real interest rate), then they are said to have a rate of time preference of 10 percent.

The **rate of time preference** is the extra amount a consumer would be willing to pay to be able to obtain a given quantity of consumption goods now rather than a year from now.

Raise saving or do nothing? Figure 13-3 illustrates two of the choices open to society, paths A and B. Path A reflects a "do-nothing" policy that maintains the growth rate of per-person consumption after time t_0 at the same rate as before. Path B reflects a policy that deliberately at time t_0 raises the incentive to save and invest while reducing the incentive to consume. Consumption along path B initially drops below path A by an amount shown by the gray shading. But then the higher rate of investment makes the capital stock grow faster, and consumption begins to grow faster along path B than path A, eventually catching up at time t_1 and moving ahead thereafter. The question for growth policy is: which path is better, A or B?

Figure 13-3
Two Alternative Paths of Consumption Per Person

Before time t_0 both paths involve exactly the same consumption per person. Along path A consumption per person continues to grow at the same steady rate after time t_0. But along path B a policy decision is made to consume less in order to save and invest more. At first, between t_0 and t_1, consumption along path B drops below path A by an amount shown by the gray shading. Then, after t_1 (and forever thereafter), consumption along path B exceeds that along path A as shown by the pink shading.

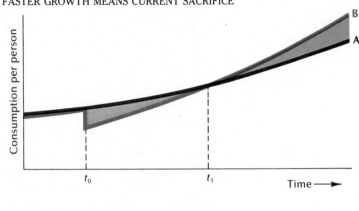

FASTER GROWTH MEANS CURRENT SACRIFICE

If the rate of return on extra capital investment is greater than society's rate of time preference, then $1 shifted from present consumption to investment will yield enough future consumption to be worthwhile. For instance, if the rate of return is 10 percent, $1 less of consumption today will yield $1.10 next year. If the rate of time preference is less than 10 percent, say 5 percent, then people are equally happy with $1.05 next year and $1 this year, so that clearly they would prefer $1.10 next year to $1 this year. In this situation, with a rate of return higher than the rate of time preference (sometimes called the rate at which individuals "discount" future consumption), society should save more and consume less, as along path B. This principle can be stated:

> *The U.S. saves too little if the rate at which individuals discount future consumption is less than the national rate of return on private investment.*[2]

In recent years the real rate of return on private investment in the corporate sector has been about 12 percent, and the rate of time preference of individuals is less than that. How much less? We know that the *real* interest rate on corporate bonds has been roughly 4 percent for the last twenty years, and that many individuals have been willing to save despite the low real interest rates available to them. Thus it is accurate to say that the United States now saves too little, because a dollar diverted from present consumption to present saving could earn a real return of about 12 percent, more than the real return after taxes now earned by most savers. People would want to save more if they were offered a real return of 12 percent than they save now at a real return of 4 percent or less.

---

[2]Martin S. Feldstein, "National Saving in the United States," in Shapiro and White (eds.), *Capital for Productivity and Jobs* (New York: The American Assembly, Columbia University), 1977.

Economic Growth and the Natural Employment Surplus

Two methods for stimulating national saving, and hence the growth of the capital stock and future consumption, are for policymakers (1) to create incentives that raise private saving (S), or (2) to run a larger government surplus (or smaller deficit). These two methods involve raising one (S) or the other ($T - G$) components of national saving in equation (13.1). The outcome for economic growth of a policy shift toward a larger government surplus depends on how this shift is carried out. First, the fiscal shift toward a "tighter" policy must be accompanied by enough of a boost in the money supply to maintain the output ratio (Q/Q^N). In terms of Section 5-5, this would be a shift in the "monetary-fiscal policy mix" that would lower the real interest rate, which in turn would induce firms to borrow the extra funds made available by the larger government surplus. In other words, an increase in S won't stimulate I unless monetary policy keeps the economy at a stable output ratio. More saving without more investment could cause a recession, as we learned in Chapter 3.

A second feature of the fiscal shift is that its stimulus to investment will be greater if it reduces private consumption rather than private saving. Thus preferable methods would be an increase in taxes on consumption goods or a reduction in transfer payments, rather than an increase in income taxes that would further reduce the after-tax return to private saving. Each of the methods that would provide the greatest stimulus to investment would tend to hurt poor people more than rich people, and hence is politically controversial.

Incentives to Private Saving

In addition to measures taken to raise the government surplus, equation (13.1) points to incentives for private saving as the second main way to stimulate private investment. Total private saving consists of business saving (both depreciation and retained earnings) and private household saving. Numerous economists have called attention to reforms that could stimulate the supply of both forms of private saving.

Private business saving. Two types of reforms have been suggested to stimulate business saving. The first would simply eliminate the corporate income tax. If corporations were to pay out as higher dividends their extra profits obtained by the elimination of the corporate income tax, then the government could tax back part of the funds through the personal income tax (which is levied on dividends). But extra profits that were retained by corporations would automatically become part of private saving (S) and would be available for private investment. While many economists endorse an elimination of the corporate income tax, Congress has not moved in this direction because it would create substantial revenue losses, and a revenue offset in the form of higher taxes on consumption or wage income would generate strong opposition by consumers and workers.[3]

A more popular reform would be to eliminate the effects of inflation on the corporate income tax. An "indexed tax system" would allow corporations to take larger depreciation deductions based on the current replacement costs of assets rather than their lower historical cost, thus raising business saving and reducing government tax collections. Other reforms in an indexed tax system would stimulate household saving and reduce borrowing to finance consumption, including the taxation of real interest returns (that is, the actual interest rate earned minus the inflation rate) and real capital gains (the actual percent capital gain per year minus the annual rate of inflation over the time the asset was held).

Private household saving. One of the most interesting differences between the United States and other large industrialized countries is the small fraction of disposable income saved by U.S. households, as shown in Table 12-4 in the last chapter. There are many disincentives to private saving common to the United States and other countries, but there are differences as well. Perhaps the most important disincentive in the United States is the tax system, which imposes the full personal income tax rate on the nominal rate of return on saving rather than on the real rate of return. Since the full nominal interest rate on borrowed funds is deductible (after 1989 for home mortgage loans but not other consumer loans) the system discourages saving and encourages borrowing. Other countries avoid this disincentive to saving by partially or completely exempting interest income from taxation; for instance, in the past Japan has offered a substantial government subsidy for household saving.[4]

13-3 The Future Burden of the Government Debt

We have already seen in equation (13.1) that a government budget deficit reduces national saving, the amount available to finance domestic private investment and foreign investment. Domestic private investment can be maintained at a level greater than national saving only by borrowing from foreigners. Whenever the government spends one dollar more than it receives in tax revenues, it must finance its deficit by issuing one more dollar of government debt. We ask in this section whether this extra government debt is harmful. How do we assess the "burden" placed by extra dollars of government debt on the well-being of future generations?

---

[3]A comprehensive discussion of the corporation income tax is in Joseph A Pechman, *Federal Tax Policy* (Washington, D.C., Brookings Institution, 1987), Chapter 5.

[4]See Fumio Hayashi, "Is Japan's Savings Rate High?" *Federal Reserve Bank of Minneapolis Quarterly Review,* Spring 1989, pp. 3–9; for a different perspective, see Lawrence J. Christiano, "Understanding Japan's Saving Rate: The Reconstruction Hypothesis," same source, pp. 10–25.

The idea is very simple: whether or not there is a burden depends on whether the extra dollars of government debt pay for government expenditures on investment goods or consumption goods. There is no burden if the government deficit finances productive government investment projects, like schools and highways. Such investment raises the well-being of society in the future by enough to pay the interest on the extra government debt issued to pay for them. In this case the government acts just like a private corporation, say AT&T, which pays for much of its new plant and equipment by selling bonds to the public. But there is a burden if the extra dollars of government debt pay for consumption goods that yield no future benefits. Such expenditures would include, for instance, ammunition fired at target practice by soldiers, fuel for the B-2 bomber, or groceries purchased by recipients of social security benefits.

The Burden of the AT&T Debt

What is the difference between the "burden of the AT&T debt" and the "burden of the government debt"? No one has ever accused AT&T of creating a burden on future generations by issuing bonds, and for good reason. Like any other corporation, AT&T is in business to make a profit for its stockholders. It attempts to estimate the future rate of return on each planned investment project—that is, the annual future profit likely to be contributed by each project divided by its cost. When each project is ranked in order of its rate of return, AT&T is ready to make its investment decisions. Projects with rates of return greater than the interest rate that AT&T must pay to sell bonds (AT&T's borrowing rate, say r_0) are approved. Projects with a rate of return below the borrowing rate (r_0) are rejected.

The contribution to revenue and expenses of the marginal AT&T project is summarized on the first line of Table 13-1. Net of all operating expenses (labor, materials, fuel, and so forth), the marginal project generates a rate of return (r_0) just equal to the borrowing rate (r_0), and thus contributes zero to net profit.[5] There is no burden on present or future generations. Individuals make voluntary purchases of AT&T bonds without compulsion. Workers and firms voluntarily build AT&T telephone exchanges and new installation equipment because they are paid with the money that AT&T raises from the bond purchasers. Thus in the present generation everyone acts voluntarily in his or her own best interests and there is no burden on anyone.

In future generations the bondholders receive the interest payments that induced them to purchase the bonds in the first place. Where does AT&T obtain the money to pay the interest payments? By definition the marginal investment project creates exactly enough revenue (over and above operating costs) to pay the interest costs. Thus in future generations everyone

---

[5]This discussion neglects explicit consideration of corporation and personal income taxes. The AT&T rate of return on line 1 can be calculated after payment of corporate income taxes. Although personal income taxes must be paid on interest payments to individuals by both AT&T and the government, this factor makes no essential difference in the discussion.

Table 13-1 **Comparison of Consequences of AT&T Debt with That of Public Debt**

	(1) Rate of Return	(2) Interest Payment	(3) Net of Interest Return
1. AT&T marginal investment project	r_0	r_0	0
2. Government marginal investment project	r_0	r_0	0
3. Government deficit-financed consumption expenditure	0	r_0	$-r_0$

is acting voluntarily. The investment projects create extra revenue for AT&T that pays the interest to keep the bondholders happy.

Investment Versus Consumption

If AT&T bonds do not create a burden for present or future generations, what is meant by the burden of the public debt allegedly created when the government issues bonds? The discussion depends on the way the government spends the proceeds of the bond floated to finance its deficit. If the government spends the proceeds on an investment project that yields a return to society sufficient to pay the interest costs on the bonds, then there is no future burden. In this case the government is acting exactly as does AT&T. But if the government spends the proceeds on consumption, then there is no future benefit to pay for the future interest payments, leaving future generations with a net burden.

Government investment projects, such as the construction of government hospitals, schools, and public universities, generate a future rate of return. The return does not take the form of a monetary profit, since the government is not in business to make a profit; rather the return consists of the benefits to future society created by the project. Assuming that a hospital is utilized to cure sick patients, society is better off having the hospital than letting patients go uncured. The hospital's rate of return is the annual stream of benefits to society (net of the hospital's operating costs) divided by the cost of the hospital. Some recent economic research suggests that government investment spending, particularly on projects like the Interstate Highway System, is highly productive in yielding future benefits to society. This research suggests that, in fact, a reduction in government investment spending in the 1970s contributed significantly to the productivity growth slowdown discussed in the last chapter.[6]

---

[6]See David Aschauer, "Is Government Spending Productive?" *Journal of Monetary Economics* (March 1989).

If the government chooses to invest only in projects yielding future benefits to society that on an annual basis equal or exceed the government's borrowing rate, then the bonds floated to finance government investment projects are exactly analogous to AT&T bonds. As illustrated on line 2 of Table 13-1, the marginal government investment project generates a rate of return in the form of future benefits to society that just suffice to pay the interest on the government bonds. If the interest rate on government bonds—like that on AT&T bonds—is r_0, and the social rate of return of the government investment project is the same rate r_0, there are no future burdens on society. The AT&T bond and the government bond are identical.[7]

The main difference between AT&T bonds and government bonds is that people pay voluntarily to receive telephone service, automatically generating revenue to pay the interest on AT&T bonds without compulsory taxation, whereas the government must use taxes to pay the interest on its bonds. No burden on future taxpayers exists if they are the same individuals who benefit from the government investment project. For a local road or rapid transit project financed by local property taxes, the beneficiaries and the taxpayers are assumed to be the same people. For federal projects this assumption may be invalid. Benefits may be concentrated on certain constituencies (the often-publicized flow of federal dollars to the sunbelt), whereas taxes are widely dispersed across all households. In this case government deficit spending to finance investment projects creates not an aggregate burden but rather a redistribution from some members of future generations to others.

True Burdens of the Debt

The true burden on future generations is created by government deficit spending that pays for goods that yield no future benefits—for example, ammunition used for target practice. As illustrated on line 3 of Table 13-1, absolutely nothing is generated in the future as a rate of return; all benefits accrue in the present. The government must pay interest to keep bondholders happy, just as AT&T must pay interest, yet in current government deficit-financed consumption, there is no future benefit or income to pay the interest. Future taxpayers are forced to hand over extra payments to the government to cover the interest cost on the debt, and the taxpayers receive no benefit in return.

Debt owed to foreigners. As we learned in Chapter 5, the United States ran large budget deficits in the 1980s, and the high real interest rates caused by these deficits attracted a large flow of capital from foreigners desiring to buy U.S. securities. As a result, much of the additional federal government debt created during the 1980s is held by foreign investors, and the interest payments on this debt will flow abroad for as long as they hold this debt.

---

[7]Problems involved in the choice of the interest rate ("the social discount rate") that should be used in evaluating government investment projects have been elegantly analyzed by A. C. Harberger in "Our Measuring the Social Opportunity Cost of Public Funds," in his *Project Evaluation* (Chicago: Markham, 1972), Chapter 4, pp. 94–122.

The obligation to make these interest payments to foreigners will require higher taxes for U.S. citizens and create a burden of the debt that is not balanced by any future benefit.

The analysis of debt held by foreigners is similar to that for debt held by domestic residents, since the extent of the burden depends on whether the debt was originally created to finance consumption or investment projects. If the federal government creates debt to build a beneficial long-lasting project, then the return on the project is available to cover the interest payments to foreigners. If the debt is created to pay for current consumption, as was for the most part true for the United States in the 1980s, there is no future return to balance the extra taxes needed to pay the interest to foreigners.

The only way the United States can avoid this future interest burden is to end inflows of capital from foreign investors. This would result from a low real interest rate in the United States that would be unattractive to foreign investors. This low real interest rate could be achieved by shifting to an easy-money and tight-fiscal policy mix and would be accompanied by a further depreciation in the dollar and a shift from a trade deficit to a trade surplus.

We can view such a change in policy in terms of equation (13.1), which is repeated here:

$$S + (T - G) \equiv I + X$$

Assume that we begin with a government deficit ($T - G$ negative) and foreign borrowing (X negative). A policy shift to a tight-fiscal and easy-monetary policy mix would, if large enough, eliminate the government deficit (moving $T - G$ from a negative amount to zero) and raise national saving (the sum of $S + T - G$), while reducing the need to rely on foreign borrowing (moving X from a negative amount to zero). Domestic private investment (I) would remain fixed as a result of this policy shift if national saving ($S + T - G$) is raised by exactly the same amount that foreign borrowing is reduced.

13-4 The Government Budget Constraint and the Financing of Government Expenditures

The **government budget constraint** relates government spending to the three sources available to finance that spending: tax revenue, creation of bonds, and creation of money.

A household must withdraw its savings or borrow if its expenditures exceed its income; the same is true of the government. The options open to the government for financing its expenditures are summarized in the **government budget constraint.** This divides government spending into two parts, spending on goods and services (G) and interest payments (iB), where i is the nominal interest rate on government bonds and B is the dollar amount of government bonds outstanding. Government revenue sources are tax revenue net of transfer payments (T), the issuance of additional bonds (ΔB), and the issuance of additional government monetary liabilities (ΔH). In keeping with our subsequent discussion of financial markets in Chapter 16, government monetary liabilities, which consist of currency held by the government and of bank reserves, are called "high-powered money" and abbreviated H. Both B and H are part of the government debt; the only difference is that bonds pay interest and high-powered money does not.[8]

The Government Budget Constraint Equation

The government budget constraint can be expressed in a simple formula:

$$\underbrace{G - T}_{\text{basic deficit}} + \frac{iB}{P} = \frac{\Delta B}{P} + \frac{\Delta H}{P} \qquad (13.3)$$

Here $G - T$ is called the "basic deficit," that is, the deficit that the government would run excluding its interest payments on outstanding bonds. In fiscal year 1988 (that is, the year ending September 30, 1988), the total U.S. government deficit including interest payments was $155.1 billion. Since interest payments were $151.7 billion, the "basic deficit" was just $3.4 billion. The budget deficit that must be financed, however, is the full $155.1 billion, as shown by the left-hand side of equation (13.3). Because the symbols G and T are expressed in real terms, we must divide the other terms in (13.3) by the price level (P) to express them in real terms as well.

Bond Creation versus Money Creation

The right-hand side of equation (13.3) shows the two methods available to finance the total government budget deficit. These are the issuance of additional government bonds, represented by ΔB (recall from Chapter 3 that "Δ" means "change in"), and the issuance of additional high-powered money, represented by ΔH. When the government raises H the total nominal money supply (M) tends to increase, which, as we learned in Chapters 4–6, is a major determinant of aggregate demand.[9]

Since an increase in H raises aggregate demand more than an increase in B (because a higher H raises the money supply and eliminates the crowding-out effect), the government may want to finance its budget deficit through issuing more H when the economy is weak and by issuing more B when the economy is strong. Specifically, when actual output is below natural output (Q^N), financing government deficits through creation of extra H helps achieve the goals of stabilization policy by pushing the economy

---

[8]In the United States H is issued by the Federal Reserve, which holds B as assets to cover its monetary liabilities, H. Thus the proper concept of B for discussions of the government budget constraint is the total value of government bonds held outside the government, that is, excluding bonds held by the Fed and other government agencies. At the end of the fiscal year 1989, for instance, the total government debt was $2869 billion, but "only" $2194 billion of that was held outside the government by private owners of bonds and high-powered money.

[9]Recall that the position of the demand curve, first derived in Chapter 6, depends on the amount of autonomous spending planned at a zero interest rate, and on the nominal money supply. As we learn in Chapter 17, the money supply (M) is a multiple of high-powered money (H) if the demand for currency and for bank reserves are stable fractions of the amount of bank deposits.

closer to Q^N without increasing inflation. But when demand in the economy is strong, and Q is above Q^N, then it is undesirable for the government to finance its budget deficit by raising H, since this will boost Q even further above Q^N.

There is a difference between issuing B and H that relates to our discussion of the burden of the government debt in the previous section. When the government runs a budget deficit and finances it by issuing bonds, the bonds create an obligation for citizens to pay extra taxes in the future to cover the interest on the bonds. As we have seen, the future interest payments create a burden of the government debt, unless the budget deficits result from productive investment spending. But financing the budget deficit by creating high-powered money entails no such future burden, because no interest is paid on either currency or bank reserves, the two components of H. Why does the government not simply escape the entire burden of the government debt by financing it entirely through creation of more H? This would tend to create too much demand in the economy and cause an accelerating inflation; instead of an easy-fiscal tight-money policy mix, we would have an easy-fiscal *and* easy-monetary mix, leading to too much aggregate demand and an acceleration of inflation.

Effects of Inflation

Inflation may seem to aggravate the government's problem of financing its basic deficit, since inflation raises the nominal interest rate (i) that appears on the left-hand side of (13.3). However, inflation also eases the government's problem. This is not evident in equation (13.3), where the inflation rate (p) does not appear. However, we can slightly rearrange (13.3) by multiplying the first term on the right-hand side by B/B and the second term by H/H. This converts (13.3) into:

$$G - T + \frac{iB}{P} = \frac{\Delta B B}{BP} + \frac{\Delta H H}{HP} \tag{13.4}$$

The reason for this step may seem unclear, since the inflation rate (p) still does not appear in (13.4). But ($\Delta B B/BP$) is the percentage change in bonds ($\Delta B/B$) times the amount of real bonds outstanding (B/P) and ($\Delta H H/HP$) is the percentage change in high-powered money ($\Delta H/H$) times the amount of real high-powered money (H/P) outstanding. Clearly, if B/P and H/P are to remain stable, then the percentage growth rate of B, represented by a lowercase b, and the growth rate of H, designated by a lowercase h will have to equal the inflation rate (p):

$$\Delta B/B = b = \Delta H/H = h = p \tag{13.5}$$

These are conditions for a steady state in which B/P and H/P are stable.[10] Substituting from equation (13.5) into (13.4) and moving the amount of government interest payments over to the right-hand side, we have a final state-

---

[10]Recall from the last chapter that a steady state in the basic Solow growth model is a situation in which the growth rates of Q, K, and N are the same, so that the Q/N and K/N ratios are constant.

ment of the government's budget constraint that applies to a steady state with stable B/P and H/P:

$$G - T = \frac{pH}{P} - \frac{(i - p)B}{P} \qquad (13.6)$$

basic deficit   seignorage   real interest
or   on bonds
inflation tax

The term pH/P represents the inflation rate times real high-powered money, the revenue that the government receives when it creates just enough H to maintain fixed the real amount H/P. This revenue that the government gets from inflation is called **seignorage;** from the point of view of private households and firms who must add to their nominal quantity of H enough to keep real H/P constant, this same revenue is called the **inflation tax.**

Inflation does not eliminate the government's obligation to pay interest on its outstanding bonds held by private households and firms. But the government budget constraint illustrates that the government only has to worry about paying the *real* interest expense of servicing the bonds. While it pays bond holders the nominal interest rate (i), bond holders have to give part of i back to the government to purchase sufficient additional bonds to keep their real bond holdings (B/P) constant.

To see how this works in an example, imagine that we start with $100 of bonds, a 5 percent inflation rate per year, an 8 percent nominal interest rate, and a 3 percent real interest rate. The government must pay $8 in interest. But, to keep the real quantity of bonds (B/P) constant, the government sells $5 in new bonds to the public, raising the value of outstanding bonds to $105. The government's net interest expense is just $3 (the real interest rate of 3 percent times the original $100 of bonds). Why? Because the government *pays* $8 in interest but *receives* $5 as a payment by the public for the new bonds.[11]

Thus the government benefits from inflation in two ways. First, it obtains an extra source of revenue, called seignorage or the inflation tax. The government can then lower ordinary taxes, or increase spending more than it could otherwise. Second, the government may gain if inflation raises the nominal interest rate by less than inflation itself. Sharp increases of inflation, particularly during the oil shock periods of the 1970s, are often accompanied by an increase in the nominal interest rate of less than one-for-one, thus reducing the real interest rate (see Figure 1-10). And, as shown in equation (13.6), it is the real interest rate that matters for government finance.

SELF-TEST   Assume that after centuries of a zero budget deficit and a zero debt, the nation of Abstinia runs a one-year deficit equal to 1 percent of GNP, which it finances by creating H/P equal to 1 percent of GNP. If inflation over the next decade occurs at 5 percent per year, what must be true of the basic deficit and the level of H for Abstinia to end the decade with the same level of H/P equal to 1 percent of GNP?

Seignorage is the revenue the government receives from inflation and is equal to the inflation rate times real high-powered money.

The **inflation tax** is the revenue the government receives from inflation and is the same as seignorage, but viewed from the perspective of households.

[11]To simplify the presentation, both equation (13.6) and the numerical example in this paragraph neglect the taxation of interest earnings, which further reduces the government's net real interest expense.

13-5 Is the Size of the Government Deficit Exaggerated?

Robert Eisner of Northwestern University has argued that inflation is just one of several reasons why conventional measures of the government budget deficit exaggerate the size of the deficit. In collaboration with Paul Pieper of the University of Illinois, Eisner has created provocative new measures of the federal budget deficit that make the deficit disappear entirely in some years and make it much smaller in others. While the official measures show that by 1988 the federal budget deficit had fallen from a peak of 5 percent of GNP in 1983 to about 3 percent, Eisner claims that a proper measure of the total government deficit, including all branches of government, was actually in surplus in 1988!

To review Eisner's methods, we need to separate two different issues. It is one thing to argue, as does Eisner, that the official measures exaggerate the size of the deficit. But it is quite another to argue that the deficit is not a problem. It would be quite possible for a properly measured deficit of zero to indicate a problem with the government budget *if the desirable condition of the properly measured government budget is a large surplus.* As we shall see, some economists argue that the federal government should run a surplus to offset the tendency of private American households to save too little. Others argue that the government as a whole should run a surplus to save up for the next century, when many workers born in the "baby boom" years of 1947–65 will retire and require greatly increased government expenditures for social security benefits.

The Eisner-Pieper Adjustments

Eisner and Pieper make three major adjustments that we summarize here.[12] Each of these tends to make the government budget deficit smaller than in the official measure, as shown in Figure 13-4. Here in the top frame we see that the "adjusted deficit" that incorporates the Eisner–Pieper corrections is always smaller (or the surplus is larger) than in the "official deficit" measure. The corrections were a very small share of GNP in the late 1950s, but have gradually grown and by 1988 reached 3.2 percent of GNP, or $155 billion. The bottom frame of Figure 13-4 is an expanded view of the 1978–88 decade and breaks down the Eisner–Pieper adjustments into three effects, the "inflation effect," "state-local effect," and "government investment effect."

Inflation effect.   We learned in the last section that the government earns revenue from inflation because it can issue more high-powered money and bonds without raising the real quantity outstanding. This source of revenue is omitted in the official deficit measures, so Eisner and Pieper adjust for

---

[12]The most accessible introduction for the general reader is Robert Eisner, *How Real Is the Federal Deficit?* (New York: The Free Press, 1986). In this brief summary we omit one of the major Eisner-Pieper adjustments, that for changing interest rates, both because of its complexity and because the adjustment tends to zigzag, reducing the official deficit measure in years of rising interest rates and raising that measure in years of falling interest rates.

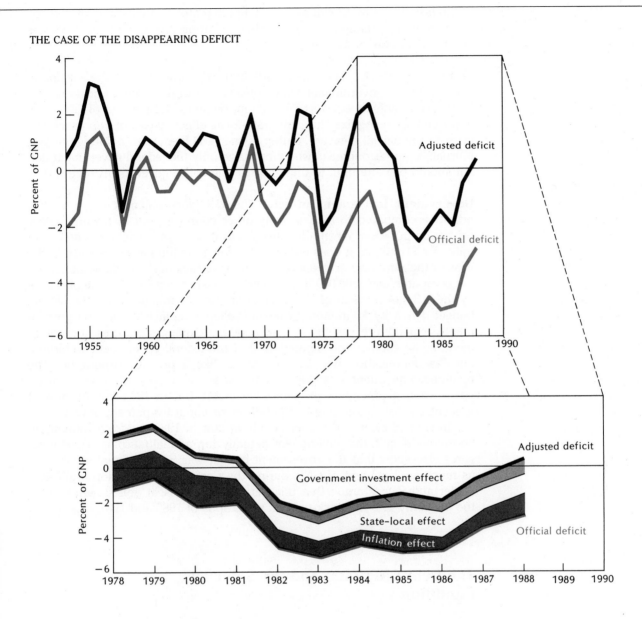

Figure 13-4 **Official Federal Budget Deficit and Eisner–Pieper Adjusted Deficit, as Percent of GNP, 1953–88**

The top frame shows two concepts of the federal budget deficit. The red line is the official concept, and the black line is the Eisner–Pieper adjusted concept. The bottom frame magnifies the top frame for the final decade and exhibits the three components of the Eisner–Pieper adjustments. *(Source:* Robert Eisner and Paul Pieper, "Deficits, Monetary Policy and Real Economic Activity," in Kenneth Arrow and Michael Boskin, eds., *The Economics of Public Debt* (Macmillan, 1988), pp. 3–38. Data kindly provided by the authors.)

this omission by multiplying the outstanding stock of government debt by the percentage change in prices. Their inflation adjustment for 1988 was about $60 billion, or 1.2 percent of GNP.

State-local effect. The second adjustment simply adds in the surplus of state and local governments, which offsets part of the federal budget deficit. In 1988 this adjustment was $56 billion, or about 1.2 percent of GNP. It is important to recognize that the state-local effect does not represent any error in the official measure. Rather, Eisner and Pieper are pointing out that journalists and economists who emphasize only the federal government deficit should pay attention to the deficit of the entire government sector.

Government investment effect. The U.S. government budget is very primitive compared to that of many other countries, not to mention every private corporation. When a private corporation buys a machine, say a computer for $1 million, it does not treat the full $1 million as an expense in the year of the purchase. It deducts from its revenues only the depreciation on the computer, say $200,000 if the computer lasts five years. Yet the purchase by the U.S. government of a new computer for $1 million raises the federal budget deficit by $1 million. Eisner and Pieper replace the federal government's expenditures on investment goods, including structures and equipment, by an estimate of the amount that the federal government would deduct as depreciation if it kept its books like a private corporation. The resulting adjustment is small in many years, and even negative in some years when depreciation exceeds investment. But in 1988 the adjustment was substantial, amounting to $39 billion, or about 0.8 percent of GNP.

In short, Eisner and Pieper conclude that in 1988, far from running an enormous deficit, the government actually ran a small surplus. Their measures also show that the government budget was in substantial surplus, by as much as 2 percent of GNP, during the Carter Administration (1977–81). Eisner and Pieper argue that this period of tight fiscal policy helped push the economy into the back-to-back recessions of 1980 and 1981–82.

13-6 The Debt-GNP Ratio and the Solvency Condition

Another approach to the measurement of deficits is to abstain from talking about deficits altogether. What matters, according to this approach, is the ratio of the outstanding nominal federal debt ($D = B + H$) to nominal GNP (PQ). The federal deficit can be substantial, yet the $D/(PQ)$ ratio can nevertheless decline instead of rise.

This paradox seems less mysterious when we recognize that the nominal government budget deficit is equal to the change in the debt ΔD. How large can the deficit be and keep the debt-GNP ratio, $D/(PQ)$, constant? It will remain constant as long as the change in the debt-to-GNP is zero.

We can see this by noting that the growth rate of the debt-to-GNP ratio (D/PQ) is the difference between the growth rate in debt (d) and the growth rate in nominal GNP ($p + q$):

$$d - (p + q)$$

For stability in the debt-to-GNP ratio, we need the growth rate of debt (d) equal to the growth rate of nominal GNP ($p + q$):

$$d = p + q \qquad (13.7)$$

When we multiply both sides of (13.7) by the size of the debt (D), we obtain the allowable deficit (that is, addition to debt) that is consistent with keeping the debt-to-GNP ratio constant:

<table>
<tr><td>General Form</td><td>Numerical Example</td><td></td></tr>
</table>

$$dD = (p + q)D \qquad (0.07)(\$2000 \text{ billion}) = \$140 \text{ billion} \qquad (13.8)$$

This simple expression (13.8) leads to a surprising conclusion: *the debt-GNP ratio remains constant if the deficit equals the outstanding debt times the growth rate of nominal GNP.* In the numerical example, outstanding federal government debt in 1988 was about $2000 billion, times a growth rate of nominal GNP in 1988 of about 7 percent, equals an "allowable deficit" of $140 billion. Since the official measure of the deficit was close to this amount, the debt-GNP ratio stabilized in 1988.

Thus a focus on the ratio of debt to GNP leads to the same conclusion as that of Eisner and Pieper, that the deficit problem was much less serious than implied by the official deficit measure. By 1988 the U.S. federal budget deficit was small enough so that the public debt was no longer growing in relation to the size of the economy, that is, the debt-GNP ratio had stabilized. But what is the optimum debt-GNP ratio? Should the ratio be stable? Is there any reason why the debt-GNP ratio should not rise?

The Solvency Condition

Surely there is a limit to the size of the government debt, expressed as a ratio to GNP. The government must pay interest on the debt held by the public in the form of bonds. Does not the obligation to pay interest set a limit on the size of the government debt? Some observers have pointed out that it is possible for the government to pay the interest on its outstanding debt by issuing more bonds. A typical bondholder holding $100,000 in bonds, let us call her Claudia R. Asset, would expect to earn $5000 in interest each year when the overall economywide interest rate is 5 percent. Surely the government could simply issue $5000 in extra bonds to meet its interest obligations, without needing to levy taxes on future generations to pay this interest bill.

The government can meet its interest bill by issuing more bonds *only if the economy's real growth rate of output and income equals or exceeds its real interest rate.* Let us assume, unrealistically, that the real growth rate is 5 percent and the real interest rate is 5 percent. Then each year the government could issue 5 percent additional debt, raising Claudia's holdings from $100,000 to $105,000, without raising the ratio of outstanding debt to GNP (which also has grown 5 percent by assumption). Claudia would receive the $5000 payment that she expects, but the government would not have to levy additional taxes.

Clearly, if the real growth rate of output is less than the real interest rate, this method of financing the government debt is not available. If the real interest rate is 5 percent, Claudia expects to receive her $5,000, but with a real growth rate below 5 percent any issuance of $5,000 of extra debt *will raise the ratio of debt to GNP.* Next year, another $5,000 of interest will be due. To finance this interest obligation by printing more debt, the government will further raise the ratio of debt to GNP. Eventually, the ratio of debt to GNP will grow and grow, reaching infinity.

Thus the government faces the solvency condition whenever the real interest rate exceeds the economy's real growth rate. This seems likely to be a relevant condition in the early 1990s, when the real long-term government bond rate is likely to be about 4 percent and the economy's real growth rate of natural real GNP (q^N) about 2.5 percent. Under such conditions, the government cannot run a deficit in the long run. In fact, the government must run a sufficient surplus to pay the part of its interest bill that cannot be met by printing more bonds, and this surplus must equal the current government debt times the excess of the real interest rate over the economy's real growth rate of output. Without meeting this condition, the government debt will grow without limit as a ratio to total GNP.

13-7 *CASE STUDY:* Historical Behavior of the Debt-GNP Ratio Since 1789

Figure 13-5 exhibits the ratio of the U.S. federal government debt held by the private sector (excluding government bonds held by the Federal Reserve and other government agencies) since 1789. The most consistent feature of the historical record is the tendency of the debt ratio to jump during wars and to shrink during succeeding years until the next war breaks out. The Revolutionary War, Civil War, World War I, and World War II all created major jumps in the debt ratio, while in most other periods the debt ratio fell. Less visible, but also important, is the effect of economic recessions and depressions in raising the public debt through the effect of automatic stabilization (which reduces government revenue automatically as Q/Q^N falls, requiring an increase in the public debt to finance ongoing government expenditures). The most important example of this was the decade of the Great Depression, when the debt ratio rose from 15 percent in 1929 to 43 percent in 1939.

The bottom frame of Figure 13-5 magnifies the period since 1955 in order to exhibit the debt ratio under peacetime conditions. Until 1974 the debt ratio fell. From 1974 to 1976 the ratio rose, but then leveled off at about 23 percent until 1981. From 1981 to 1987 the ratio rose by more than 50 percent, indicating that the federal budget deficits were sizeable enough to make the government debt grow much faster than nominal GNP.

However, in 1988 the ratio stabilized at 38 percent, both because the deficit fell somewhat as a percent of GNP and because the "allowable" size of the deficit had risen. As shown on the right-hand side of equation (13.8), the allowable deficit (that is, allowable if the debt-GNP ratio is to remain constant) is the nominal debt times the growth rate of nominal GNP. In the late 1980s the nominal debt was increasing, as was the growth rate of nominal GNP. As the 1990s began, the slight downturn in the debt-GNP ratio seemed only temporary, as a period of slow economic growth appeared likely to raise the debt further as a share of GNP.

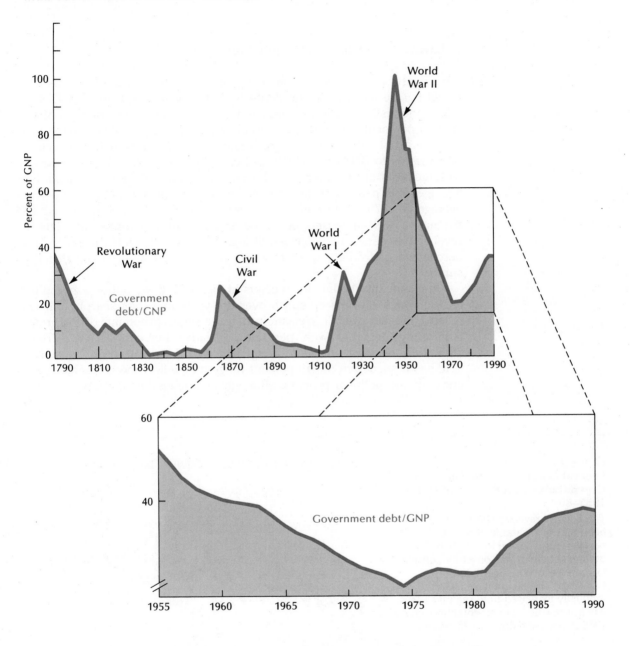

Figure 13-5 **The Ratio of U.S. Government Debt to GNP, 1789–1990**

The ratio of debt to GNP has ranged widely throughout American history, rising during wartime and falling between wars. During peacetime periods the debt/GNP ratio increased only during the Great Depression decade of the 1930s and during the "deficit decade" of the 1980s. (*Source:* See Appendix C.)

13-8   Sources of the Deficits and the Debate Over the Size of Government

Behavior of Revenue and Expenditure Ratios

What contributed to the radical change in fiscal policy in the 1980s, as illustrated by the increase in the debt-GNP ratio evident in Figure 13-5? Some U.S. economists point to the massive three-year phased introduction of substantial personal and business tax cuts enacted in 1981, while others claim that the problem is excessive government spending. Figure 13-6, which exhibits ratios to GNP of federal receipts and expenditures, seems consistent with the latter claim, at least on the surface. In 1983–85 federal expenditures averaged 24.5 percent of GNP, an increase of 3.3 points from the 21.2 percent average of 1970–79. In contrast, federal receipts in 1983–85 averaged 19.4 percent of GNP—*precisely the same* as the 1970–79 average. By 1989 the revenue percentage had changed little at 19.0 percent, while the expenditure percentage had fallen to 22 percent. This is what allowed the deficit to shrink.

PUZZLE 5: WHY HAS THE GOVERNMENT BUDGET DEFICIT PERSISTED IN THE 1980S?

In examining the line for receipts in Figure 13-6, we notice a zigzag pattern in which receipts creep up over the years and then sharply fall. This reflects "bracket creep" (an elasticity of tax revenues to nominal GNP of greater than unity) together with periodic legislative tax cuts (1964, 1970–71, 1975, 1982–84) that offset the creep. The fact that the ratio of receipts to GNP has remained in the 19 percent range may reflect the "revealed preference" of the political process, although politicians have hardly been idle,

---

Figure 13-6
Federal Government Revenues and Expenditures as a Percent of GNP, 1955–89

The Federal revenue share in GNP has been amazingly stable at about 19 percent. An increase in the share caused by bracket creep was offset by periodic tax rate reductions legislated by Congress. The expenditure share gradually increased until the mid-1980s, when it reached 24 percent, although by 1989 it was back down to 22 percent.

EXPENDITURES CREPT UP BUT REVENUES DIDN'T KEEP PACE

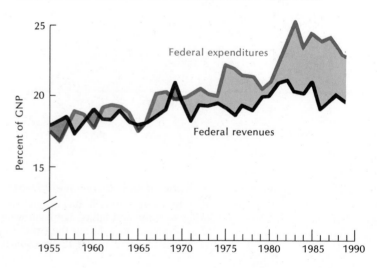

since they increased the share of payroll taxes from 2.1 to 7.1 percent of GNP from 1960 to 1989 while reducing the percentage for all other taxes from 16.4 to 11.9 percent.

The same political process allowed an upward creep in the ratio of expenditures to GNP until 1985. The expenditure percentage was 18.1 in 1955–59, 20.1 in 1960–69, 21.2 in 1970–79, and 22.7 in 1980–89. The left hand giveth and the right hand taketh away at different rates (or, "the right hand doesn't know what the left hand is doing").

Categories of Spending

What has caused the upward drift in the percentage of expenditures in GNP? As illustrated in Figure 13-7, virtually all of the increased share of government spending in GNP can be attributed to transfer payments, mainly social security and medicare, which went from 2.3 percent of GNP in 1960 to 8.9 percent in 1989. Second, other nondefense programs were cut substantially in the Reagan period, from 9.3 percent in 1980 to 7.3 percent in 1989. Third, the share of defense spending fell from 9.7 percent in 1960 to 5.3 percent in 1980 and increased only slightly to 5.8 percent in 1989.

A central cause of U.S. fiscal problems is an unintended increase in the well-being of social security recipients in the 1970s that neither Congress nor the administration has the courage either to finance or to reverse. During the 1970s, social security benefits per retiree rose 50 percent after adjustment for inflation, while average real earnings per employee did not increase at all, amounting to a substantial redistribution of income from workers to the elderly. This occurred because generous indexation clauses

Figure 13-7

Components of Federal Government Expenditures as Percent of Natural GNP, 1955–88

The diagram has five "slices" corresponding to the shares in GNP of the five major types of federal government spending. The sum of the five slices is the share of total federal government spending in natural GNP; this differs from the red line in Figure 13-6, which computes the share of federal government spending in actual GNP. The increase in the share of federal government spending in GNP is mainly accounted for by transfer payments throughout the period and by net interest payments in the 1980s. The share of national defense declined until 1979 and then rose. Grants and subsidies rose until 1978 and then declined.

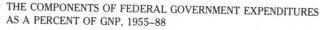

THE COMPONENTS OF FEDERAL GOVERNMENT EXPENDITURES AS A PERCENT OF GNP, 1955–88

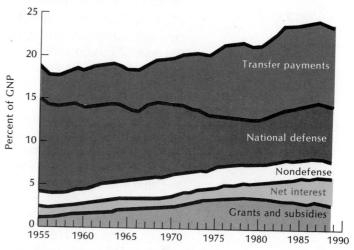

more than compensated retirees for inflation (which itself was exaggerated by measurement errors in the Consumer Price Index), while most workers outside of the unionized sector had little or no formal indexation protection. An important by-product was a marked reduction of the percentage of the elderly who have incomes below the official poverty line, from 35.2 percent of the over-65 population in 1959 to just 12.4 percent in 1984.

The Gramm-Rudman-Hollings Act: A Fiscal Revolution?

In 1985 Congress passed and the president signed the Gramm-Rudman-Hollings (GRH) Act. As amended in 1987, it mandates a steady decline in the federal government budget deficit to zero by 1993. The GRH Act, often called "Gramm-Rudman," is controversial and potentially revolutionary because it requires that if Congress cannot agree on sufficient expenditure cuts to achieve the required deficit reduction in a particular year, then spending will be cut *automatically* by the amount needed to meet the target. The automatic cuts would be administered by the comptroller general rather than Congress or the administration.

The GRH Act was passed because of a growing frustration by Congress at its own inability to control the increase in the expenditure share illustrated in Figure 13-6. Although the goal of reducing the deficit and moving toward an easy-money and tight-fiscal policy mix is desirable, the GRH Act contains a number of undesirable features.

1. No account is taken of the state of the economy. We have learned that automatic stabilization occurs when the output ratio (Q/Q^N) rises or falls, since the federal budget deficit automatically increases as the economy weakens. The GRH Act could require expenditure cuts during a recession, which potentially could make the recession even worse. The federal budget would shift from an automatic stabilizer to an automatic destabilizer. This would repeat the folly of Herbert Hoover, who raised tax rates in 1932 near the bottom of the Great Depression.

2. There is no magic in the GRH target of a zero deficit. The federal government ran deficits during most of the postwar period, but nevertheless the debt/GNP ratio fell until 1974. It is possible for the debt/GNP ratio to remain stable, as we have seen, even when the government is running a deficit, as long as that deficit is sufficiently small to keep the growth of the total government debt equal to the growth rate of nominal GNP.

3. The GRH Act exempts "entitlements" (mainly social security and medicare) and part of the defense budget from the automatic budget cuts. Thus, the burden of the automatic cuts would fall disproportionately on nondefense spending for purposes other than entitlements. Some critics feel that these exemptions are unfair, particularly since budget reductions during the Reagan administration were concentrated on nondefense nonentitlement spending.

During the period 1987–89, Congress and the administration managed to meet the GRH targets without actually reducing the deficit substantially. This apparent contradiction is resolved when we note the various tricks that

Congress and the administration developed to make the *forecast* of the next year's budget deficit appear to be much smaller than the *actual* deficit turned out to be. These tricks included forecasting unrealistically high economic growth and low interest rates. Congress also developed methods of pushing some expenditures (like Chapter 16's thrift institution bail-out) "off the budget," creating a new way of issuing government debt that was not counted as part of the budget deficit by traditional accounting rules.

One of the authors of GRH, Senator Warren Rudman of New Hampshire, once called his law "a bad idea whose time has come." But as the 1990s began without substantial progress in reducing the actual deficit, many observers echoed the sentiments of Lee Hamilton, a prominent Ohio congressman, who summed up the situation: "We have developed considerable skill and sophistication in meeting deficit-reduction targets—without reducing the deficit."[13]

13-9 New Views of Fiscal Policy: Supply-Side Economics

With the enactment of President Reagan's budget and tax packages in August 1981, the stage was set for the most dramatic shift in fiscal policy of the postwar era. We have already studied in Chapter 5 the effects of this program on the natural employment deficit (NED), interest rates, the value of the dollar, and net exports. And we have seen that the result was an increase in the ratio of debt to GNP by over half between 1981 and 1989.

Supply-Side Argument for Reagan Tax Cuts

The Reagan program differed from previous episodes of fiscal policy stimulus, for its primary motive was *not* a belief that the economy was so weak, nor that unemployment was so high, nor that monetary policy was so impotent that a fiscal stimulus was required. Instead, the Reagan administration believed that tax rates were simply too high and that the government sector was too large. According to the doctrine called **supply-side economics,** embraced by the Reagan administration, high tax rates stifled individual initiative and saving.

Supply-side economics predicts that a reduction in marginal income tax rates will create an increase in the supply of output, that is, in natural real GNP.

The supply-side theory makes one uncontroversial statement, and two controversial claims:

1. Income taxes reduce the after-tax reward to work and saving.

2. An increase in the after-tax reward to work and saving would create a *significant increase in the amount of work and saving.*

3. The resulting increase in work and saving would be so significant that after the tax cuts the federal government would collect more revenue than before the tax cuts.

---

[13]Howard Gleckman, "The Bottom Line: Gramm–Rudman Isn't Working," *Business Week,* April 10, 1989, p. 36.

Response of work effort and saving. The first statement is uncontroversial, because everyone admits that taxes reduce the after-tax reward to work and saving. In the second statement, the supply-siders argue that reductions in personal income taxes, such as those implemented by the Reagan tax package in 1981, will lead people to work longer hours, will encourage more people to take second "moonlighting" jobs, and will allow people to save more. Many economists were skeptical of these claims, however, and their skepticism seems to have been justified. At the time of the original 1981 debate about supply-side economics, Charles Schultze (chairman of the Council of Economic Advisers during 1977–81 under President Carter) quipped that "There's nothing wrong with supply-side economics that division by ten couldn't cure."

As it turned out, even Schultze's skeptical assessment may have been too optimistic. When we compare the economy four years before to the economy after the Reagan tax cuts, we find that the amount of work effort, as measured by the labor-force participation rate, grew more slowly after 1981 than before, and the personal saving rate fell after rising during 1977–81. The only bit of support for supply-side doctrines is that hours per employee fell more slowly after 1981 than before.

	Labor force participation rate	Hours per employee	Personal saving rate
1977	62.6	36.0	6.6
1981	64.2	35.2	7.5
1985	64.8	34.9	4.4
1988	65.9	34.7	4.1

Response of productivity growth. Some supply-side advocates also predicted a rebound in productivity growth. Everyone agreed in 1981 that the U.S. productivity growth record had been dismal since 1973, with a slowdown in productivity growth that no one fully understood. The post-1973 productivity slowdown, that we studied in Chapter 12, is the third puzzle introduced at the beginning of this book.

PUZZLE 3: WHY HAS PRODUCTIVITY GROWN SO SLOWLY?

As we learned in Chapters 10 and 12, one reason for the productivity growth slowdown after 1973 was the succession of oil shocks that occurred in 1974 and 1979–80. Since the real price of oil fell after 1981 (Figure 10-1), we should expect that productivity growth would have been more rapid after 1981 than before even without the supply-side tax cuts. As it happened, there was a modest recovery of productivity growth after 1981 but not enough to attribute a beneficial effect to the tax cuts after taking account of the falling real price of oil. Further, much of the post-1981 productivity revival is attributable to electronic computers, which surely would have existed even without the tax cuts.

	1948:Q4–1973:Q4	1973:Q4–1981:Q3	1981:Q3–1988:Q4
Private nonfarm output per hour (annual growth rate in percent)	2.3	0.6	1.4

The Laffer curve. The third supply-side claim, that tax cuts raise government revenue, is even more controversial than the second. This claim was widely touted in 1981 during the debate about the Reagan tax cuts, because critics had claimed that such large tax cuts would create unprecedented government budget deficits. Supply-side proponents argued that the tax cuts would "pay for themselves."

Their argument was illustrated by the famous Laffer curve, which Arthur Laffer of Pepperdine College in California had drawn on a napkin in a Washington restaurant in an inspired moment in 1974. The Laffer curve, reproduced in Figure 13-8, starts from the obvious point that the government will raise no tax revenue at all if tax rates are zero, as at point *A,* and if tax rates are 100 percent, as at point *E.*[14] In between, as the tax rate rises from zero to 100 percent, tax revenues will first rise and then fall. If the government introduces a tax cut (like the 1981 Reagan package) starting from point *B,* the economy would move leftward along the Laffer curve and government revenue would fall. But a tax cut starting from point *D* would cause a leftward movement that would raise government revenue.

Was the economy at point *B* or point *D* in 1981? Clearly, one can draw a Laffer curve with its peak at any tax rate—20, 50, or 80 percent. The peak at 70 percent in Figure 13-8 is completely arbitrary. During the debate, Arthur Laffer and two co-authors presented evidence based on the 1964 tax cut episode showing how both real GNP and tax revenues subsequently expanded.[15]

---

[14]Even this is not clear. Some people seem to enjoy their work so much that they might continue to work even at a tax rate of 100 percent!

[15]The Laffer paper and several critiques of supply-side economics are contained in Laurence H. Meyer, *Supply-Side Effects of Economic Policy* (St. Louis: Center for the Study of American Business, formal publication no. 39, May 1981).

Figure 13-8
The Laffer Curve

The curve shows that total government tax revenue depends on the tax rate. With either a zero or 100 percent tax rate, the government collects no revenue. Maximum revenue occurs at point *C.* If tax rates are cut starting from point *B,* government revenue declines, but if tax rates are cut starting from point *D,* government revenue increases.

WILL A TAX CUT REDUCE GOVERNMENT REVENUES
OR RAISE THEM?

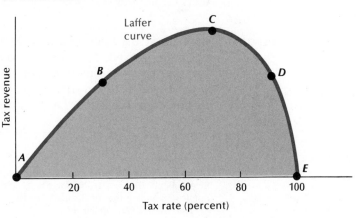

However, the Reagan administration ignored the difference between the expansionary monetary policy that accompanied the 1964 tax cut and the restrictive policy that accompanied the initial 1981 and 1982 stages of the Reagan tax cuts. In 1964–65 both the *IS* and *LM* curves moved to the right. But in 1981 and 1982 the *IS* curve moved to the right while the *LM* curve moved to the left by a greater distance, thus creating a recession. The administration assumed that the causes of output and inflation could be separated, with fiscal policy used to stimulate output and monetary policy used to cut inflation. This approach conflicts with our analysis of inflation in Chapter 9, which shows that what matters is the growth rate of nominal GNP. In 1981–82 the growth rate of nominal GNP plummeted, reducing both the output ratio and the inflation rate.

Supply-Siders a Decade After

Most economists have written off supply-side economics after observing the absence of a positive response of natural real GNP to the Reagan tax cuts that followed the 1981 legislation. However, hard-core advocates of supply-side economics continue to "keep the faith." How do they explain the economy's behavior in the 1980s?

True supply-siders argue that the policies pursued by the Reagan administration after 1981 undermined the effect of the 1981 tax cuts. First, in 1982 some of the 1981 incentives to business investment were reversed. Second, supply-siders blame the Reagan administration for failing to control spending. As shown in Figure 13-6, government spending as a percentage of GNP remained higher in 1982–88 than in any postwar year prior to 1982. While the Reagan administration in 1981 promised to pay for a large buildup in defense spending with cuts in nondefense spending, political pressures kept these nondefense spending cuts from occurring at the rate originally intended by the administration. Third, supply-siders blame the absence of higher labor-force participation, hours, saving, and productivity on the tight monetary policy pursued by the Federal Reserve in 1981–82. This third argument, however, lost its credibility as the economy recovered in 1983–88 from the "Fed's recession" without exhibiting the promised supply-side effects on natural real GNP.[16]

SELF-TEST   Looking at the Laffer curve in Figure 13-8 and assuming that government spending is fixed, does a reduction in tax rates starting from point *B* raise or lower the government budget deficit? Starting from point *D?* Which point, *B* or *D*, was believed in 1981 to describe the position of the U.S. economy by the following: Arthur Laffer? President Reagan? Critics of supply-side economics?

---

[16]The supply-side defense is taken from Paul Craig Roberts, "Can Reagan Resurrect His Supply-Side Policy?" *Business Week,* August 16, 1985, p. 18. Scholarly assessments of supply-side economics, including that of Reagan's advisor Martin Feldstein, appear in the *American Economic Review,* (May 1986), pp. 26–42.

13-10   New Views of Fiscal Policy:
The Barro–Ricardo Equivalence Theorem

**Robert J. Barro
(1944–   )**

Barro's fame stems from his theory of fiscal policy, the Keynesian non-market-clearing model (Section 8-9), and his tests of the policy ineffectiveness proposition (Section 7-6).

We have seen in the previous section that the supply-siders depart from the traditional Keynesian analysis of fiscal policy by predicting a large effect on supply (Q^N), not just on demand. Another attack on the traditional Keynesian analysis of fiscal policy was launched in 1974 by Robert J. Barro of Harvard University.[17] Because Barro's approach echoed a theme originally proposed by the classical economist David Ricardo in the early nineteenth century, his point has become known as the "Barro–Ricardo equivalence theorem."

Barro's point denies the efficacy of discretionary fiscal policy taking the form of tax changes because tax cuts are balanced by an increase in saving rather than an increase in consumption. Why? Barro points out that any tax cut is financed by deficit spending, which will require future tax payments to meet the interest on the public debt. People who see their taxes cut will say to themselves, "This just means lower taxes today and higher taxes in the future when the government needs to pay the interest on the debt; I'll just save today in order to build up a savings account that will be needed to meet those future taxes."

Bequests Imply Concern About Children

While economists had recognized that taxpayers might perceive their future obligation to meet government interest payments, most had not taken seriously the possibility that people would view higher future taxes as *completely equivalent* to lower current taxes (hence the name "equivalence theorem"). Economists had previously pointed out that much of the future interest burden of the higher public debt would occur after today's taxpayers are dead. Barro's unique contribution was to argue that people leave bequests to their children, implying that they care about their children and hence, indirectly, about the tax burden that they face. His striking deduction was that *today's taxpayers, reacting to a tax cut today, would raise their saving so as to increase their bequests to their children in order to pay for future taxes levied by the government.*

Another way to understand Barro's argument is that today's holdings of government bonds do not represent net wealth. When the government prints an additional one-dollar bond to pay for a tax cut, bondholders feel richer by one dollar, but taxpayers feel poorer by the same dollar since they recognize that one dollar's worth of future taxes will have to be levied to pay the interest on the bonds.

---

[17]Robert J. Barro, "Are Government Bonds Net Wealth?" *Journal of Political Economy,* vol. 82, (November/December 1984), pp. 1095–1117.

Criticism of the Equivalence Proposition

Barro's ingenious argument let loose a torrent of criticism. The link between bequests and concern for children was doubted. Decision horizons of private individuals are often quite short. Some parents do not care about their descendants. Perhaps more important, the absence of "perfect" rental markets for consumer housing and household possessions means that almost everyone is likely to die with a significant positive net worth in the form of housing and furnishings, which will be left as a bequest to some heir even if the deceased does not care about the exact standard of living that the heir achieves.

A separate criticism pointed out that most individuals pay a substantially higher interest rate to borrow than does the government (for example, 18 percent on credit cards compared to a long-term government bond rate in mid-1989 of 9 percent). This means that people apply a much higher "discount rate" to future government tax levies than the interest rate the government has to pay on its bonds. This point applies with special force when it is recognized that the typical adult consumer has an expected life span of about thirty-five years. If the government cuts taxes by raising the public debt, most of the burden of servicing or repaying the debt will be borne within that thirty-five year lifetime. Only a very small portion of the debt burden will be passed on to future generations, making moot the debate about the motives for bequests.

Evidence from the 1981 Tax Cuts

Most of the skepticism about the Barro-Ricardo equivalence theorem emerged immediately after the 1974 publication of Barro's article and was based on general principles. However, saving behavior after 1981 provided additional reason for doubt. In August 1981 Congress and the president enacted a substantial reduction in tax rates that was to take place over the three following years (1982–84). If consumers had behaved in the forward-looking way postulated by the Barro proposition, consumption would have remained unaffected while saving would have jumped to "pay for" the future tax burden created by the extra federal debt. However, the personal saving rate *fell* after 1981, from 7.5 percent in 1981 to an average of 5.9 percent in 1982–85. To set aside sufficient saving to pay for the future tax burden of the extra debt, households should have raised their saving rate from 7.5 percent in 1981 to roughly 11 percent in 1985, but *actual behavior went in the opposite direction.*

SUMMARY

1. National saving is the sum of private household and business saving, plus government saving (positive with a government budget surplus and negative with a budget deficit). U.S. national saving declined substantially in the 1980s, as the government ran a persistent budget deficit while private saving fell as well, and the decline in national saving was balanced by foreign borrowing rather than a decline in private domestic investment.

2. The two methods for stimulating national saving are for policymakers to create incentives that raise private saving or to run a larger government surplus (or smaller deficit).

3. Deficits that raise the future level of the public debt create a burden on future generations, if the deficits finance government consumption expenditures which yield no future benefits to balance the burden of taxes required to pay the interest on the debt.

4. The government budget constraint shows that the government's budget deficit must be financed either by issuing high-powered money or by issuing bonds. Financing with high-powered money leads to inflation while bond finance requires that the real interest rate be paid by the government on the outstanding bonds.

5. Critics argue that the U.S. federal government budget deficit is mismeasured because it does not take account of inflation, of state and local government surplusses, and of government investment.

6. The government faces a solvency condition, which states that it cannot run a deficit in the long run if the real interest rate exceeds the economy's real growth rate of output (natural real GNP).

7. The U.S. ratio of the public debt to GNP fell throughout the postwar period until 1974, and then rose through 1988, when it stabilized. The deficit in the 1980s was due to a higher ratio of government spending to GNP, not a lower ratio of tax revenue to GNP. In turn, most of the higher spending was due to an increase in transfer payments.

8. The Laffer curve predicts that, if tax rates are initially high enough, a cut in tax rates raises government tax revenue. Supply side economists predicted in the early 1980s that tax rate cuts would not only raise government tax revenues but also stimulate saving and work effort. The predicted effects did not occur.

9. The Barro–Ricardo equivalence theorem states that deficit-financed tax cuts will stimulate saving rather than consumption, as individuals try to build up their savings accounts to pay the future taxes required to service the higher government debt.

CONCEPTS

rate of time preference
government budget constraint
seignorage

inflation tax
supply-side economics

QUESTIONS AND PROBLEMS

Questions

1. Economic policymakers are concerned with both economic growth and economic stabilization. Explain the distinciton between them. Are different policies used for the two purposes? Give some examples.

2. Explain why the national saving rate plays such an important role in determining the rate of economic growth.

3. If the level of real GNP is held fixed by monetary policy at some given amount, which of the following will provide the greatest stimulus to saving?
   (a) increase in the personal income tax rates paid by the rich
   (b) increase in the personal income tax rates paid by the poor
   (c) introduction of a federal retail sales tax

4. In the years prior to 1983, many American economists argued that the high rate of foreign lending by the U.S. was good both for our domestic economy and for the nations which were the recipients of our net foreign investment. Does this argument work in reverse? What is the major problem associated with the U.S. becoming a net foreign borrower rather than a net foreign lender?

5. In 1989, the full effect of the tax reforms passed into law in 1986 took effect. A major provision of that law made interest payments on mortgages fully deductible from pre-tax income, but removed similar provisions that applied to interst paid on consumer loans and credit card companies. What impacts with respect to the saving rate do you predict this would have in the U.S. economy? What other impacts are predictable?

6. "In the steady state, the government benefits from inflation." Explain.

7. "Unnecessary fears of the rising government deficit have restricted desirable government spending." Explain.

8. The supply side argument for tax cuts is based on two controversial claims. What are they? Has the empirical record supported or refuted these claims?

9. What are the two ways of financing a government deficit? Explain the conditions under which the financing of the deficit would be inflationary.

10. How does the real interest rate affect the government's ability to finance long-term debt?

11. We rarely hear concern about the "burden" of privately held debt, and yet many people share a concern about the public debt. Why is this so? Is the concern reasonable?

12. Under what circumstances would it be appropriate to increase the level of national saving?

Problems

1. Assume that in 1990 real GNP equals 500 million, the government debt is 200 million and the real interest rate is 2.5%. Also assume that the growth rate of real GNP is 2.5%.
   (a) What is the value of the ratio, government debt to GNP?
   (b) What is the amount of interest paid on the debt in 1990? What percentage of GNP is that interest?

(c) What is the level of real GNP in 1989? If the government issues new debt to cover the interest charges on the debt, what will be the new level of the government debt? How much interest will be paid in 1991?

(d) Compare the percentage of GNP going for interest payments in 1991 to that for 1990. Compare the government debt to GNP ratio for the two years. Explain the results.

(e) Assume that the real interest rate was actually 5 percent and not 2.5 percent. How does this change in rates affect your answers to (c) and (d)?

2. Given the following data, use equation 13.2 to calculate (a) the level of national saving, (b) the level of private domestic investment, and (c) foreign lending or borrowing.

Government revenue	600
Government expenditures on goods and services	750
Disposable income	1000
Depreciation	200
Consumption	800
Corporate retained earnings	35
Exports	200
Imports	250

3. Assume that the current rate of inflation is 4 percent and that nominal GNP is $5000 billion and is growing at 2 percent. If the current deficit is $100 billion and the debt ratio is 20 percent and the government wants to maintain it at that level, by how much should it increase or decrease the deficit next year?

SELF-TEST ANSWERS

p. 390 A positive X corresponds to foreign lending, and a negative X to foreign borrowing. A positive X indicates positive net exports, that is, exports greater than imports. After paying for imports, an excess of foreign currencies is available to purchase assets in foreign countries. The opposite is true when X is negative, and when imports exceed exports. After foreigners have paid for their purchases of U.S. exports, they have sufficient excess earnings from sales of imports to the United States that they have dollars available to lend to the United States; hence negative net exports imply U.S. foreign borrowing.

p. 401 If inflation occurs at 5 percent per year for a decade, then the price level grows at 5 percent per year. To keep H/P constant, H must grow at 5 percent per year. Seignorage, the pH/P term in

equation (13.6) is equal to 5 percent ($p = 0.05$) times 1 percent of GNP ($H/P = 0.01$ times GNP), or 0.05 of 1 percent of GNP. Thus the government must run a basic deficit of 0.05 of 1 percent of GNP in order to end the decade with a fixed level of H/P.

p. 414 A reduction in tax rates moves the economy to the left in Figure 13-8, the Laffer curve diagram. Thus, starting from point B, tax revenues fall as we move to the left, raising the government deficit if government expenditures are fixed. Starting from point D, tax revenues rise and the government deficit declines. Arthur Laffer and President Reagan believed that the 1981 economy was at point D, and critics of the supply-side economists believed that the 1981 economy was at point B.

International Adjustment and
Foreign Debt

*Business fortunes are made on the ability to forecast such changes in the values of national
currencies, while political futures become frayed as a result of these changes.*
—Robert Z. Aliber[1]

14-1 Pervasive Effects of International Factors on
the Domestic Economy

Throughout this book we have emphasized international aspects of macroeconomics. We began in Chapter 1 by learning that the foreign trade deficit
is one of the six central macroeconomic concepts, and its volatility in the
1970s and 1980s is one of our six macroeconomic puzzles. We also noted
international aspects in the development of our simple *IS-LM* model of income determination. Autonomous shifts in net exports are one source of
shifts in the *IS* curve and can potentially create instability in aggregate demand, while the dependence of imports on income reduces the multiplier
and helps to stabilize aggregate demand.

Effects of the international economy on the domestic economy were a
central theme of Chapter 5. There we learned that a shift in the mix of
monetary and fiscal policy can affect the real interest rate and the foreign
exchange rate. For instance, the early 1980s in the United States were a
period of tight monetary policy and a shift of fiscal policy toward ease, as a
result of 1981 tax rate reductions and a buildup in defense spending. This
policy mix raised the U.S. real interest rate, attracted inflows of foreign capital, and caused an appreciation of the dollar by 50 percent between 1980
and early 1985. American consumers benefited, in contrast to American
firms and workers making U.S. exports and products in competition with
foreign imports. In short, the shift in the monetary-fiscal policy mix caused
international crowding out.

The U.S. economy can be influenced not just by the international repercussions of American monetary and fiscal policy, but also by foreign policies
and events. For instance, the appreciation of the dollar in the early 1980s
was caused not only by the shift toward ease of U.S. fiscal policy, but also
by the shift toward tightness of fiscal policy in several foreign nations, including Japan, Germany, and the United Kingdom. Supply shocks, studied in

---

[1]*The International Money Game* (New York: Basic Books, 1973), p. 4.

Chapter 10, provide another example of the effects of foreign events on the domestic economy. The adverse oil shocks of 1974 and 1979 aggravated U.S. inflation and unemployment, while the beneficial oil price reduction of 1986 reduced inflation and unemployment.

International Monetary Economics and Exchange Rate Regimes

This chapter supplements our previous treatment of international or "open-economy" macroeconomics. Goods, services, and capital flow among nations; problems arise when inflows do not balance outflows. How is such an imbalance to be corrected? In this chapter we present two primary ways of adjusting to an imbalance between international receipts and expenditures. The most straightforward is to maintain a flexible exchange rate, which corrects an imbalance in the flow of goods and services by changing the prices paid by foreigners for a nation's exports and by that nation's citizens for its imports from abroad.

The alternative method requires that a nation hold the exchange rate fixed and correct an imbalance in the flow of goods and services through some other means. For instance, a solution to a trade deficit, with exports too small to pay for imports, might be contractionary monetary and fiscal policy to reduce a nation's inflation rate and make the prices of its export goods more attractive. In the meantime, while awaiting a response of the domestic inflation rate, the nation must pay for its excessive imports by spending its stock of **international reserves.** Problems arise when the stock of international reserves runs low, just as a family faces difficulties when it runs out of money.

International reserves are internationally acceptable assets that each nation maintains to pay for any deficit in its balance of payments.

Thus a central debate in international monetary economics is over the alternative exchange rate "regimes" of flexible versus fixed exchange rates, and the related question as to whether some intermediate system is possible. The world has shifted from the fixed exchange rate system that was in effect between the end of World War II and early 1973 to a system in which exchange rates are flexible and change every day. However, the flexible exchange rate system has not insulated domestic economies from foreign events as much as its proponents had originally predicted, and the exchange rate of the dollar has turned out to be highly volatile. A prominent issue in the late 1980s is the feeling that exchange rates are *too* flexible, and that an intermediate system of "managed floating" or "target zones" might be desirable to limit exchange rate flexibility.

The Trade Deficit and the Foreign Debt

The foreign trade deficit resembles the government budget deficit in many respects. Just as a government budget deficit implies the buildup of government debt issued to pay for the deficit, so a foreign trade deficit implies a buildup of foreign debt as funds are borrowed from foreigners to allow imports to exceed exports. When the government debt rises, as in the United States in the 1980s, then the burden of interest payments implies that achieving a zero total deficit requires that the "basic budget" be in surplus. Similarly, after a buildup in foreign debt, the burden of interest payments to foreigners implies that the zero total deficit needed to end the increase in foreign debt must be accompanied by a foreign trade *surplus*. Just as the total government budget can be in deficit to a limited degree without implying an increase in the ratio of government debt to GNP, so the total foreign deficit can be in deficit to the same degree without implying an increase in the ratio of foreign debt to GNP.

From a position of zero foreign debt at the end of 1984, when international assets balanced international liabilities, the U.S. foreign debt ballooned to more than $500 billion by the end of 1988. In this chapter we examine the effects of an international payments imbalance on a nation's international asset and debt position. We learn how the balance-of-payments accounts measure a nation's international transactions. Then we turn to the determination of the foreign exchange rate, the debate about alternative exchange rate systems, and the struggle to explain the failure of a sharp decline in the dollar from 1985 to 1988 to return the U.S. trade position from deficit to surplus.

14-2 Flows of Goods, Services, Capital, and Money

Not only does the U.S. Department of Commerce keep track of the total flows of goods and services in the U.S. domestic economy in its national income and product accounts (reviewed in Chapter 2), but it also is the official recordkeeper for U.S. international transactions. Table 14-1 summarizes international inflows and outflows during 1988, including goods and services sold by Americans to foreigners and purchased from foreigners, income earned on foreign assets, gifts and transfers, loans and borrowing, and the flows of international reserves that "pay" for any imbalance. The data in Table 14-1 are sometimes called the balance-of-payments (BP) statistics, even though they include not only the net balance between inflows and outflows, but also the individual components of the flows.

The Balance of Payments

The **current account** is the portion of the balance of payments that includes exports and imports of goods and services, as well as transfers and gifts.

The **capital account** is the portion of the balance of payments that includes direct investment and trade in both long-term and short-term securities.

Table 14-1 is divided into three sections. The top (white) section is the **current account,** including flows of goods, services, and transfer payments. The middle (gray) section is the **capital account,** including borrowing and lending by banks and purchases of U.S. private assets by foreigners and foreign assets by U.S. individuals and by the U.S. government. The bottom (pink) section of Table 14-1 shows how the balance-of-payments (BP) surplus or deficit is financed. The table is arranged so that the sum of all the items in the right-hand, balance column is zero. If the total of the items in the current account and capital account sections is negative, as in 1988, then the United States is running a BP deficit (see line 7) and there must be an exactly equivalent negative financing item to offset the deficit (see line 10).

Every figure in Table 14-1 is preceded by a plus or minus. Plus items are credits, any transactions that provide the United States with an additional supply of foreign money. Examples of current account credits are exports of wheat, travel by foreigners on American-owned airlines and ships, and income earned by American holdings of assets abroad (for example, the Ford Motor Company, H. J. Heinz, and many other firms own factories in foreign

Table 14-1   U.S. International Transactions, 1988 ($ Billions)

Line number	Items	Credits (+)	Debits (−)	Net credit (+) or debit (−)	Balance
	CURRENT ACCOUNT				
1.	Exports and imports of goods and services				
	a. Goods	+319.9	−446.4	−126.5	
	b. Current services	+139.7	−137.5	+ 2.2	
	c. Income on foreign assets	+ 48.2	− 45.6	+ 2.6	
	d. *Balance on goods and services*	+507.8	−629.5		−121.7
2.	Net transfers				
	a. Government grants			− 10.1	
	b. Government pensions and private remittances			− 3.5	
	c. *Net unilateral transfers*				− 13.6
3.	Balance on current account				−135.3
	CAPITAL ACCOUNT				
4.	Increase in U.S. assets abroad (−)				− 88.4
5.	Increase in foreign assets in U.S. (+)				+188.2
6.	Balance on capital account				+ 99.8
7.	Official reserve transactions balance				− 35.5
	METHOD OF FINANCING				
8.	Increase in U.S. official reserve assets (−)				− 3.6
9.	Increase in foreign official assets in the United States (+)				+ 39.1
10.	Total financing of surplus				+ 35.5

Note: Line 5 includes the statistical discrepancy.
Source: Adapted from *Survey of Current Business,* March 1989, Tables A, D, J, K, pp. 26–33.

countries). Examples of capital account credits are investments by Arab sheikhs in the U.S. stock market and construction of a Japanese-owned Honda assembly plant in Ohio. In each of these cases, households or firms in the United States are paid in foreign money—British pounds sterling, Japanese yen, and many others—and a demand for dollars is created as the American recipients take the foreign money they have received to their banks and turn it in for the U.S. dollars they want.

Minus items are debits, the opposite of credits, and are any transactions that provide foreigners with an additional supply of dollars. Examples of current account debits are imports of Scotch whiskey and French wine, travel by Americans on foreign-owned airlines and ships, and dividends paid to Arab sheikhs who own stock in U.S. companies. Capital account debits occur when General Motors builds a factory abroad or when an American deposits funds in a Swiss bank account.

What was the situation of the United States in 1988? Total debits slightly exceeded total credits, so that the United States ran a balance-of-payments (BP) deficit. After we examine the main sources of the deficit, we will learn in the bottom pink part of Table 14-1 how the United States managed to finance its excess supply of dollars.

The Current Account

The first line of Table 14-1 states that U.S. exports of goods (a credit that supplies the United States with foreign money) were $ 319.9 billion. Imports of goods of $446.4 billion far exceeded exports of goods, by $126.5 billion. The main reasons for this trade deficit are reviewed later in this chapter. The deficit in the trade of goods was partly offset by a surplus of $2.6 billion of income from foreign assets.

Net exports is the excess of exports over imports, and a negative total for net exports means that imports exceed exports.

The sum of the first three lines (1.a, 1.b, and 1.c) is called the balance on goods and services (line 1.d), sometimes called **net exports** of goods and services. This balance is a component of GNP and directly contributes to production and employment.[2] A deterioration in this balance causes just as serious a decline in production and employment as would have been caused by a drop by the same amount in private investment or government spending. The negative balance in line 1.d reflects in part the crowding out effect of easy fiscal policy as discussed in Chapter 5. Transfers are flows of money without any corresponding return flow of goods and services, and hence make no contribution to GNP. Most of this (line 2.a) is in the form of government grants, or foreign aid. The remainder consists of a variety of items (line 2.b), including government pensions to employees who have retired abroad and private remittances, including gifts from Americans to their children and other relatives living overseas.

The total balance in the white portion of Table 14-1 is called the balance on current account, and it summarizes all the current transactions. In 1988 the U.S. current account balance was a huge minus number, about—$135.3 billion. Any surplus or deficit on current account must be exactly balanced by capital transactions in the gray block of the table or by financing items in the pink area.

The Capital Account

Foreign lending by the United States is a debit item because we supply dollars to foreigners as we buy assets in other nations, whereas investment by foreigners in the United States is a credit item. These are shown separately on lines 4 and 5. These changes in assets include "long-term" purchases of hotels, factories, and bonds, and "short-term" changes in bank deposits and loans.

Line 6 shows that the United States in 1988 ran a large surplus on capital movements. But the enormous capital account surplus on line 6 was enough to offset the current account deficit on line 3, leading the United States to run an overall deficit on line 7.

The **official reserves transactions balance** is the balance-of-payments surplus or deficit that includes all trade in goods and securities.

Significance of the Official Reserve Transactions Deficit

Line 7 is the fundamental U.S. balance-of-payments measure. The name **official reserve transactions** (ORT) **balance** refers to the fact that only

---

[2]Net exports were introduced as a component of GNP in Section 2-5 and analyzed extensively in Sections 5-6 and 5-7.

movements of international reserves by governments and official agencies are excluded from the components of the ORT balance on lines 1 through 6. Thus any changes in international reserves serve as a means of financing the ORT surplus or deficit, as illustrated for 1988 in lines 8 and 9.

The United States holds its international reserves in two main forms, (1) gold and (2) its reserve position at the International Monetary Fund (analogous to reserves that banks hold at the Federal Reserve). One way for the United States to cover a deficit is to draw down its holdings of gold. In 1988, however, U.S. reserve assets increased, and this increased the amount to be financed.

The second method to finance a deficit is an increase in holdings of dollars by foreign central banks in their official international reserves. This method of financing the deficit appears as a "plus" item on line 9.

The U.S. ORT Deficit and the End of the Fixed Exchange Rate Era

In the era of the fixed exchange rate, discussions of the "balance-of-payments problem" focused on the ORT surplus or deficit (Table 14-1, line 7). Foreign nations noticed particularly the advantage that the United States had, because it could finance its ORT deficit in two ways. First, it could run down its official reserve assets; this would be a positive (financing) item on line 8. Second, it could finance its deficit in a way that no other nation could, with the exception of the United Kingdom. Because other nations held dollars as reserves, any additional demand by foreign central banks for U.S. dollars to hold as reserves could be satisfied by the United States "exporting dollars." Each dollar added to the reserves of foreign central banks could finance the U.S. balance-of-payments deficit as readily as an extra dollar of exports. Such additions would be a positive (financing) item on line 9.

During the final years of the fixed exchange rate system (1968–73), the United States was able to run virtually any ORT deficit that it desired. It could buy more imports than the exports it sold, without any capital account surplus, because foreign governments had no way of "getting rid" of the dollars they accumulated as income for their sales of products to the United States. This occurred because after 1968 the United States refused to allow governments to purchase any part of the U.S. gold stock by cashing in their dollars. As a result, nations with BP surpluses against the United States had only two choices: they could cause their exchange rates to increase, or appreciate, in order to make their sales to the United States more expensive and thus less attractive, or they could expand their economies in order to cause more inflation and also make their exports to the United States more expensive.

In 1971 and 1972 Germany and Japan were so inundated with unwanted U.S. dollars that they allowed their respective exchange rates to appreciate. By early 1973 the system of fixed exchange rates had collapsed, and a system of flexible exchange rates was introduced. The new system helps to explain why the U.S. ORT surplus was such a small item in relation to the huge flows of exports, imports, and capital listed in the upper sections of Table 14-1.

Distinction Between ORT Deficits and Current Account Deficits

The remarkable aspect of the U.S. balance of payments in 1988 was the imbalance between the huge current account deficit and the equally huge capital account surplus. Clearly, if the only negative aspect of the balance of payments were an ORT deficit, then the observed U.S. ORT deficit seemed relatively small, less than 1 percent of GNP. However, the role of capital inflows in balancing the large U.S. current account deficit (due mainly to negative net exports) has serious implications for the future.

The problem is evident in Table 14-2, which displays data on the net investment position of the United States. For the United States to have a positive net investment position, over the whole of American history, it must have sent more capital abroad than foreigners have sent to the United States. For decades before 1985 this was the case, and in 1982 the United States reached a peak positive net investment position of $147 billion. However, the large current account deficits after 1982, largely balanced in each year by capital account surpluses, meant that foreigners were sending cap-

Table 14-2 **Net Investment of the United States, 1978–88**

	Billions of dollars; end of period								
	1980	*1981*	*1982*	*1983*	*1984*	*1985*	*1986*	*1987*	*1988*
U.S. assets abroad	607.1	719.8	824.9	873.9	896.0	950.3	1071.4	1167.8	1259.8
Official reserve assets	26.7	30.1	34.0	33.7	34.9	43.2	48.5	45.8	49.4
Other government assets	63.8	68.7	74.5	79.5	84.8	87.6	89.5	88.4	84.8
Private assets	516.6	621.0	716.4	760.7	776.3	819.5	933.4	1033.6	1125.6
Foreign assets in U.S.	500.8	578.7	688.0	784.5	892.6	1061.0	1340.6	1536.0	1746.7
Foreign official assets	176.0	180.4	189.1	194.5	199.3	202.6	241.7	283.1	322.1
Other foreign assets	324.8	398.3	498.9	590.0	693.3	858.4	1098.9	1252.9	1424.6
Net investment position	106.3	141.1	136.9	89.4	3.4	−110.7	−269.2	−368.2	−486.9

Source: Survey of Current Business, June 1989.

ital to the United States at a much faster rate than American investors were sending capital abroad. As a result, foreign assets in the United States grew much faster than U.S. assets abroad, as shown by Table 14-2, and by 1985 the United States had reached a "net debtor" position, that is, a negative net investment position. The net debtor position grew each year, reaching −$533 billion in 1988.

The Net Debtor Position for the United States and Growth in the Standard of Living

U.S. assets abroad generate income for American residents in the form of interest and dividend payments. However, foreign assets held in the United States generate interest and dividend income that the United States must send abroad. The emergence of the United States as a net debtor country suggests that in the 1990s Americans will have to make net payments of investment income to foreigners. These payments are a deduction from domestic output and income. Also, to generate sufficient export sales to pay for these extra payments of investment income, the dollar will have to depreciate more than otherwise, and this reduces the real income of Americans (whose unchanged wages must pay higher prices for Japanese cars, Italian cheese, and Scotch whiskey).

In short, the United States will have a problem in maintaining growth in its standard of living in the 1990s that is entirely separate from the productivity growth slowdown examined in Chapter 12. As an example, assume that the U.S. net foreign debt is $600 billion, roughly the level reached by the end of 1989. At a 10 percent interest rate, the United States would have to pay $60 billion per year, or about 1.2 percent of GNP, in interest to foreigners. Thus fully 1.2 percentage points of output growth would have to be set aside to service the growing foreign debt. Since growth of income per capita in the long run is limited by growth in output per hour, which has been running at about 1.2 percent per year, the foreign trade deficit *in effect fully wipes out U.S. economic growth for one full year,* making it unavailable to support a higher standard of living. If the foreign debt was to grow by another $600 billion over the next decade, the need to service this debt would wipe out yet another year's economic growth. In short, the United States is losing the fruits of one year's economic growth every eight to ten years by the need to service its foreign debt.

14-3 The Market for Foreign Exchange

When an American tourist steps into a taxi at the London airport, the driver will expect to be paid in British currency, not American dollars. To obtain the needed British currency, the tourist must first stop at the airport bank and buy British pounds in exchange for U.S. dollars. Banks that have too much or too little of given types of foreign money can trade for what they need on the foreign exchange market. Unlike the New York Stock Exchange or the Chicago Board of Trade, where the trading takes place in a single location, the foreign exchange market consists of hundreds of dealers who sit at desks in banks, mainly in New York and London, and conduct trades by phone. In London, 256 banks are authorized to deal in foreign currencies.

The results of the trading in foreign exchange are illustrated for four foreign nations in Figure 14-1. Each section of the figure illustrates the ex-

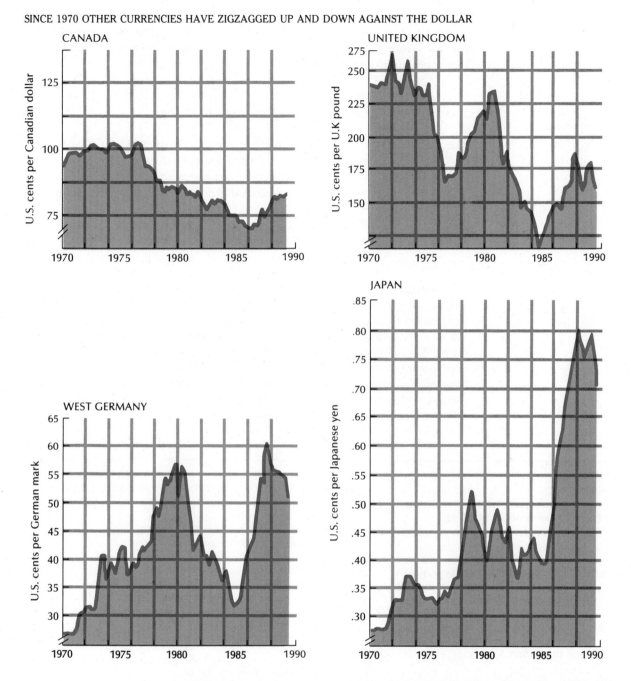

SINCE 1970 OTHER CURRENCIES HAVE ZIGZAGGED UP AND DOWN AGAINST THE DOLLAR

CANADA

UNITED KINGDOM

JAPAN

WEST GERMANY

Figure 14-1 **Foreign Exchange Rates of Four Major Industrial Nations, Quarterly, 1970–89**
Each foreign exchange rate is expressed as U.S. cents per unit of foreign currency.
Note that each rate displays quarter-to-quarter fluctuations together with a trend
that lasts several years or more. The Canadian dollar fluctuated within a narrow
range until 1976, then dropped about 30 percent, and after 1986 recovered only
about one third of its post-1976 loss. The British pound displays more erratic
behavior, ranging between 115 and 260 cents. It also has failed to recover its
depreciation of the early 1980s. Both the German mark and Japanese yen have
appreciated since the early 1970s, with a marked interruption during the period of
the dollar's strength in 1980–85. But the time pattern is different. The yen did not
decline as much as the mark in the 1980–85 period, and so in 1989 it was much
higher than its 1980 value, whereas the mark was roughly the same as in 1980.

change rate, expressed in terms of U.S. cents per unit of foreign currency. The data expressed are quarterly, so they conceal additional day-to-day and month-to-month movements. As is obvious from each section of the figure, major changes occurred during the years plotted.

The Demand for and Supply of Foreign Exchange

The factors that determine the foreign exchange rate and influence its fluctuations can be summarized on a demand-supply diagram like that used in elementary economics to analyze many problems of price determination. In Figure 14-2 the vertical axis measures the dollar price of the British pound, the same concept as is plotted in the upper right frame of Figure 14-1 for the actual 1970–89 behavior of the pound. The horizontal axis shows the number of pounds that would be demanded or supplied at different prices.

Why People Hold Dollars and Pounds

Currencies such as the U.S. dollar and the British pound are held by foreigners who find dollars or pounds more convenient or safer than their own currencies. For instance, sellers of goods or services may be willing to accept payment in dollars or pounds, but not in the Finnish markka or the Malaysian ringgit. Thus a change in the preference by holders of money for a currency such as the British pound will shift the demand curve for pounds and influence the pound's exchange rate.

Figure 14-2
Determination of the Price in Dollars of the British Pound Sterling
The demand curve D_0 slopes downward and to the right, reflecting the increased demand for pounds induced by depreciation (a lowering in the pound's price). The supply curve S_0 is assumed to slope upward, although this does not always occur (see text). The equilibrium price of the pound in the diagram is assumed to be $1.50, at the crossing point of the D_0 and S_0 curves.

THE EXCHANGE RATE OF THE POUND DEPENDS ON THE LAW OF SUPPLY AND DEMAND

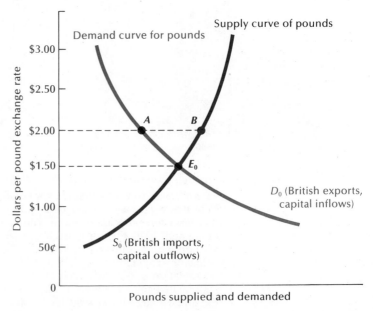

All currencies, whether or not they are demanded as a means of money holding, have a demand that is created by a country's exports and a supply generated by a country's imports. Figure 14-2 and Table 14-1 are related. The British balance-of-payments statement contains entries for the same items as the American BP statement in Table 14-1. British credits for exports create a demand for the pound. So, too, do credits generated by foreigners who invest in British factories, who repay previous loans, who send to Britain dividends and interest payments on British overseas investments, and who are attracted by high British interest rates to put money into British savings accounts and government securities. Thus the demand curve for pounds D_0 in Figure 14-2 is labeled with two of the credit items that create the demand (British exports, capital inflows). In the same way, the supply curve of pounds S_0 depends on the magnitude of the debit items—mainly British imports and capital outflows.

Slopes of Demand and Supply Curves

What explains the slopes of the demand and supply curves as drawn in Figure 14-2? Imagine that a British automobile costs £6000. If the exchange rate is $2 per pound sterling, as at point A, an American would have to pay $12,000 for the automobile. A decline in the exchange rate from $2 to $1.50, however, would cut the dollar price from $12,000 to $9000 as long as the British domestic price remains fixed at £6000. If the demand for British automobiles in the United States is price elastic, so that a decline in price raises the quantity purchased, the demand for British pounds will rise as the exchange rate falls and the number of British automobiles purchased goes up. The demand curve D_0 will be vertical only if the price elasticity of American demand for British imports is zero—that is, completely insensitive to changes in price.

The supply curve of pounds, S_0, depends on the price elasticity of British demand for imports from the United States. First, imagine that the price elasticity is zero. Will the supply curve be vertical? The answer, surprisingly, is no. Imagine that a U.S. automobile sells for $12,000 and that the British always buy one auto regardless of its price. Then at an exchange rate of $2 per pound sterling, the British will spend £6000 on the auto. But at the lower exchange rate of $1.50, the same automobile will cost £8000. Thus with a completely inelastic demand for imports, the British supply curve of pounds will have a negative slope, opposite that depicted in Figure 14-2. The supply curve will be vertical if the price elasticity of demand for imports is -1.0, so that expenditures in pounds are independent of the exchange rate.[3] Only

---

[3]The price elasticity of demand, a concept used in most elementary economics courses, is defined as

$$\text{elasticity} = \frac{\text{percentage change in quantity}}{\text{percentage change in price}}$$

When the elasticity is -1.0, the percentage change in quantity is equal to and opposite in sign from the change in price, so that revenue (= price × quantity) does not change. For the American automobile, a drop in the exchange rate from $2 to $1.50 would raise the price of the car from £6000 to £8000, an increase in price of 33 percent, and would cause a reduction in quantity purchased from 1.0 to 0.67 autos. Total British expenditure originally was £6000 (1.0 autos times £6000 price) and in the new situation is still £6000 (0.67 automobiles times £8000 price).

if the price elasticity is greater than unity (in absolute value) will the supply curve slope positively, as drawn in Figure 14-2.

SELF-TEST   For each of the following events, state whether there is a shift in the supply or demand curve for pounds in Figure 14-2, and whether the curve shifts to the left or right: (1) an increase in the desire of British households to buy videotapes of old Hollywood movies; (2) the discovery of oil in the North Sea that results in exports of British oil to the United States; (3) American Airlines discontinues a flight from Dallas to London that attracts mainly British passengers; (4) Americans start producing imitation Scotch whiskey, which displaces imports of the real thing.

Determination of the Foreign Exchange Rate

The foreign exchange rate is determined where the demand curve D_0 crosses the supply curve S_0 in Figure 14-2. As the curves are drawn, the equilibrium exchange rate is $1.50 per pound at point E_0, exactly the rate reached in June 1989. At a higher exchange rate, say $2, the supply of pounds exceeds demand by the distance AB. British imports and capital outflows exceed the demand for pounds created by British exports and capital inflows. In order to induce foreigners to accept their currency, the British will have to accept a lower exchange rate, $1.50.

If the British government wants to maintain the higher exchange rate of $2, it can do so only by intervention in the exchange market. It must buy up the excess supply of pounds from the foreigners who have received payments in pounds sterling from British purchasers of imports. How does the government pay for these pounds obtained from foreigners? This is the purpose of international reserves (holdings of gold and U.S. dollars). If the government does not intervene, or if it runs out of international reserves so that it cannot intervene, the foreigners holding excess pounds will sell them on the foreign exchange market, driving the price down to $1.50.

14-4   ### CASE STUDY: Determinants of Exchange Rates in the Long Run

The Theory of Purchasing-Power-Parity

The **purchasing-power-parity** (PPP) theory holds that the prices of identical goods should be the same in all countries, differing only by the cost of transport and any import duties.

The most important determinant of exchange rates is the fact that in open economies the prices of traded goods *should be the same everywhere*, after adjustment for customs duties and the cost of transportation. This is called the **purchasing-power-parity (PPP) theory** of the exchange rate. It can be written as follows:

General Form

$$\text{domestic price } (P) = \frac{\text{foreign price } (P^f)}{\text{foreign exchange rate } (e')} \quad \text{or} \quad P = \frac{P^f}{e'} \quad (14.1)$$

As an example of a situation when PPP is satisfied, consider a bushel of wheat selling for \$3 on the world market and for £2 in Britain, with an exchange rate (e') of \$1.50 per pound sterling:

Numerical Example

$$P = \frac{P^f}{e'} = \frac{\$3}{\$1.50/£} = £2$$

If PPP were not satisfied, the situation would be unsustainable. For instance, if the British price of wheat were only £1.50, then foreigners would be able to obtain wheat in Britain cheaper than the \$3 world price. They would pay

price of British wheat to foreigners $= Pe'$

$$= (£1.50)\left(\frac{\$1.50}{£}\right) = \$2.25$$

Foreigners would rush to Britain to buy up all the cheap British wheat, and the higher demand would push up the British price into equality with the \$3 world price.

The PPP Theory of Exchange Rates

As written in (14.1), the PPP approach is a theory for determining the domestic price, given foreign prices and the exchange rate. But the same equation can be turned around to state the PPP theory of exchange rates:

$$e' = \frac{P^f}{P} \tag{14.2}$$

This states that if the world price level (P^f) increases faster than the domestic price level (P), there is an increase in P^f/P and the exchange rate appreciates. In the wheat example, if a worldwide inflation were to raise the price of wheat from \$3 to \$4, but there were no inflation in Britain to alter the fixed £2 price of British wheat, the British exchange rate would increase from \$1.50 per pound sterling to \$2 per pound:

$$e' = \frac{P^f}{P} = \frac{\$4}{£2} = \$2/£$$

Exactly the opposite would occur if British prices were to rise faster than foreign prices. If British inflation were to double the price of British wheat from 2 to 4 pounds sterling, whereas foreign prices remained fixed at \$3, the British exchange rate would depreciate from \$1.50 per pound to \$0.75 per pound:

$$e' = \frac{P^f}{P} = \frac{\$3}{£4} = \$0.75/£$$

PPP in Action: 1973–89

Another way of writing equation (14.2) is to express the exchange rate and the two prices in terms of rates of growth.[4]

$$\Delta e'/e' = p^f - p \tag{14.3}$$

_____

[4]The growth rate of a ratio such as P^f/P is equal to the growth rate of the numerator (p^f) minus the growth rate of the denominator (p).

In words, this states that the rate of change of the foreign exchange rate ($\Delta e'/e'$) equals the difference between the foreign inflation rate (p^f) and the domestic inflation rate (p). For Canada and the United States this relationship goes in the right direction for the interval between 1973 and 1989.

	Annual rate of change of Canadian–U.S. exchange rate	Annual rate of change of U.S. GNP deflator	Annual rate of change of Canadian GNP deflator
Theory:	$\Delta e'/e'$	$= p^f$	$- p$
Actual for Canada:	-1.3	$\cong 5.9$	-6.7

The relation does not hold exactly in each year, partly because the balance of trade is not in long-run equilibrium each year.

The PPP theory contains an essential kernel of truth: that nations that allow their domestic inflation rate (p) to exceed the world rate will experience a depreciation of their exchange rate, and vice versa. But there are numerous exceptions to the relationship, because the demand for and supply of foreign currency depend on factors other than the simple ratio of domestic and foreign aggregate price indexes. Consider the same relationship (14.3) for Japan and the United States over two recent intervals.

	Annual rate of change of Japan–U.S. exchange rate	Annual rate of change of U.S. GNP deflator	Annual rate of change of Japanese GNP deflator
Actual for Japan:			
1973–79	$+3.7$	$\neq 7.5$	-7.7
1979–89	$+5.5$	$\neq 4.7$	-2.1

How can we explain the appreciation of the Japanese exchange rate (dollars per yen) between 1973 and 1979, knowing that Japanese inflation was slightly faster than U.S. inflation, and the greater appreciation of the year in 1979–89 than the difference of inflation rates? At least three crucial factors can cause the behavior of the exchange rate to differ from the simple difference between foreign and domestic inflation rates.

Technology and Natural Resources

Imagine that the Japanese and U.S. inflation rates were absolutely identical over some time period, as was almost true for 1973–79. Then, according to PPP, there should have been no change in the Japanese exchange rate versus the dollar over the same period. But imagine also that over this period the Japanese produced several new products that U.S. firms and households imported in great numbers, such as color television sets and videotape recorders, without any similar addition of new products sold by U.S. exporters. As a result there would be an increased U.S. demand for the yen to pay for the color television sets and videotape recorders and no change in the supply of yen. The price of the yen would have to increase (appreciate) to keep the foreign exchange market in equilibrium.

Discoveries of natural resources have the same effect on the exchange rate as applications of new technology. With identical inflation rates in Britain and the United States, the British exchange rate would be bound to appreciate as a result of the discovery of oil in the North Sea. British oil imports would fall, cutting the supply of pounds, and Britain might eventually be able to export some of its oil, raising the demand for pounds. Indeed, the British pound did appreciate for this reason between 1977 and 1980, even though inflation in the United Kingdom occurred at a faster rate than in the United States.

Capital Movements

The exchange rate depends not just on the products exported and imported by a country, but also on the demand for its money by foreigners. Customers from all over the world send funds to Switzerland for deposit in anonymous numbered bank accounts. Partly as a result, Switzerland enjoyed a substantial appreciation of its exchange rate over the 1973–79 interval, by much more than the difference between U.S. and Swiss inflation.

	Annual rate of change of Swiss–U.S. exchange rate	Annual rate of change of U.S. GNP deflator	Annual rate of change of Swiss GNP deflator
Actual for Switzerland:			
1973–79	+11.3	≠ 7.5	− 3.6
1979–89	+ 0.4	≠ 4.7	− 3.6

A nation with an attractive currency, such as Switzerland, can enjoy a low rate of domestic inflation because the higher prices of imports charged by foreigners are offset by exchange-rate appreciation, which makes a growing number of dollars available per Swiss franc. But problems are created for exporters, such as producers of Swiss watches.

Government Policy

Even if there are no changes in technology, no discoveries of natural resources, and no capital movements, the PPP relationship of equation (14.3) still may not hold. Governments can interfere in several ways. First, a trade surplus generated by low domestic inflation may not cause an appreciation if the government gives the surplus away by supporting a large defense establishment overseas or by making large grants of foreign aid to other nations. Such government actions partly explain why the United States ran an overall balance-of-payments deficit in the early 1960s despite a large trade surplus and a low domestic inflation rate. Second, a government facing a trade surplus may decide to stimulate the domestic demand for imports by cutting customs duties. Third, a government may try to prevent the exchange rate from appreciating by barring or taxing capital inflows, a tactic used by Germany in the early 1970s. In contrast, the United States in the 1960s tried partially to offset a balance-of-payments deficit, caused mainly by Vietnam War spending, by taxing capital outflows. Finally, a government may cause its currency to appreciate by running a tight-money and easy-fiscal policy, as did the United States in 1980–85.

Purchasing-Power-Parity and the Real Exchange Rate

The **real exchange rate** is equal to the average nominal foreign exchange rate between a country and its trading partners, with an adjustment for the difference in inflation rates between that country and its trading partners.

Chapter 5 introduced the concept of the **real exchange rate** and explained that movements in the real exchange rate are closely related to movements in the net exports of the United States. The real exchange rate is calculated by taking the average of the nominal exchange rates of all U.S. trading partners, weighted by their share in U.S. foreign trade, and adjusting for differences between the average inflation rate of these trading partners and the U.S. inflation rate. Because of their effects on real net exports, and hence on real GNP, movements in the real exchange rate are a *major source of instability in aggregate demand.*

If the PPP theory of exchange rates were valid at all times, the real exchange rate would not move. Why? Using the same symbols as in equation (14.3), the *change* in the real exchange rate ($\Delta e/e$) is defined as the change in the nominal exchange rate ($\Delta e'/e'$) plus the difference between domestic (p) and foreign (p^f) inflation. Thus the real exchange rate would remain unchanged, for instance, if the dollar appreciated at a rate of 2 percent per year ($\Delta e'/e' = 2$), U.S. inflation was 4 percent per year ($p = 4$), and foreign inflation was 6 percent per year ($p^f = 6$):

$$\Delta e/e = \Delta e'/e' + p - p^f \tag{14.4}$$
$$0 = 2 + 4 - 6$$

This is precisely what the PPP theory of exchange rates predicts, since it claims that $\Delta e'/e' = p^f - p$, or $2 = 6 - 4$ in this example.

We learned in Chapter 5 that major changes in the real exchange rate of the U.S. dollar occurred in the 1970s and 1980s, that these changes were caused by changes in the mix of U.S. monetary and fiscal policy, and that these changes in turn caused the huge U.S. trade deficit (negative net exports) evident in Table 14-1. Figure 14-3 repeats (from Figure 5-9) the time path of the U.S. real exchange rate. These movements in the real exchange rate cannot occur, according to the PPP theory; thus the movements in Figure 14-3 constitute strong evidence that the PPP theory may not hold over periods as long as five years.[5]

SELF-TEST

We have now learned that movements in the real exchange rate reflect the failure of PPP to hold at every moment of time. Looking back at the data displayed in the section "PPP in Action: 1973–89" on pp. 431–432, did the real exchange rate of the dollar appreciate or depreciate (1) against the Canadian dollar over 1973–89? (2) against the Japanese yen over 1973–79? (3) against the Japanese yen over 1979–89? (4) against the Swiss franc over 1973–79? (5) against the Swiss franc over 1979–89?

---

[5]It is now widely recognized that the PPP theory of exchange rates cannot explain major movements in exchange rates since 1973. See Jacob Frenkel, "The Collapse of Purchasing Power Parities during the 1970s," *European Economic Review,* vol. 16 (May 1981), pp. 145–166.

Figure 14-3
The Real Exchange Rate of the Dollar, 1960–89 (1980 = 100)

The real exchange rate of the dollar declined dramatically in the early 1970s, after the collapse of the fixed exchange rate period. There was another period of weakness for the dollar in 1977–79, followed by a large and sustained appreciation through early 1985. The depreciation of the dollar in 1985–88 wiped out almost all of the 1980–85 appreciation.

MOVEMENTS IN THE REAL EXCHANGE RATE DEMONSTRATE THE FAILURE OF PPP

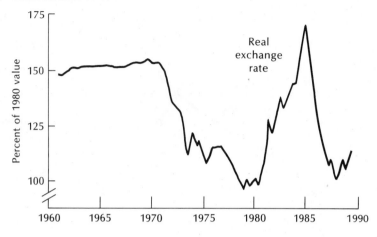

14-5 Determinants of Exchange Rates in the Short Run

Inelastic Short-Run Supply and Demand

Why do governments intervene to limit the fluctuations of their exchange rates rather than allow the exchange rate to adjust freely according to PPP? The problem is that without government intervention drastic up-and-down movements in exchange rates may be necessary to equate demand and supply in the short run, and these fluctuations in turn can cause undesirable movements in domestic prices and output. The most important cause of large fluctuations in exchange rates is the low elasticity of demand for imports and exports, particularly in the short run.

The slow adjustment of demand and supply. A nation may face two sets of demand and supply curves for foreign exchange. In the short run the supply and demand elasticities may be close to zero, but in the long run the elasticities may be substantial. The transition from the short run to the long run is illustrated in Figure 14-4. The demand and supply curves indicated by the solid lines, D_1 and S_1', are valid in the long run. At an initial exchange rate of $1.50, Britain is running a trade deficit shown by the distance between the D_1 and S_1' curves, the distance E_0F. After enough time has passed, the British trade deficit can be eliminated at point E_1 if the exchange rate is allowed to decline to $1.25.

But what happens in the short run, before British producers have time to increase their production of exports and import substitutes? The relevant schedules reflecting inelastic short-run demand and supply are the dashed red d_1 and dashed black s_1 curves. A decline in the exchange rate to $1.25 will widen the trade deficit to the distance HG, the distance between d_1 and

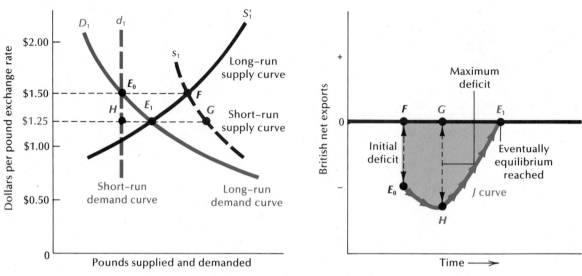

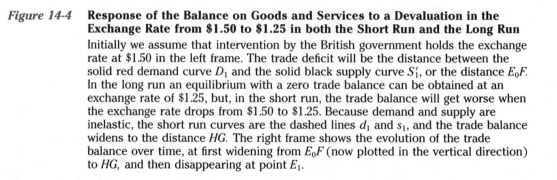

Figure 14-4   **Response of the Balance on Goods and Services to a Devaluation in the
Exchange Rate from $1.50 to $1.25 in both the Short Run and the Long Run**

Initially we assume that intervention by the British government holds the exchange
rate at $1.50 in the left frame. The trade deficit will be the distance between the
solid red demand curve D_1 and the solid black supply curve S_1', or the distance E_0F.
In the long run an equilibrium with a zero trade balance can be obtained at an
exchange rate of $1.25, but, in the short run, the trade balance will get worse when
the exchange rate drops from $1.50 to $1.25. Because demand and supply are
inelastic, the short run curves are the dashed lines d_1 and s_1, and the trade balance
widens to the distance HG. The right frame shows the evolution of the trade
balance over time, at first widening from E_0F (now plotted in the vertical direction)
to HG, and then disappearing at point E_1.

s_1. No reduction in the exchange rate, no matter how drastic, can bring the
trade deficit into balance in the short run. The British government will be
forced to intervene to keep the exchange rate from falling below $1.25 by
buying up the excess pounds that foreigners have obtained from the import
purchases of British firms. Only by patient waiting will the needed improvement in the trade balance occur. If the exchange rate is held at $1.25 by the
government, the demand and supply curves will slowly change shape. The
s_1 curve will pivot clockwise until it becomes the S_1' curve. The d_1 curve will
pivot counterclockwise until it becomes the D_1 curve. And the trade balance
will gradually shrink from the large amount HG to zero at point E_1.

The *J* curve and U.S. net exports in 1985–88.   The right frame of Figure
14-4 illustrates the evolution of the trade balance (net exports) as time
passes. Now the trade balance is plotted in a vertical rather than a horizontal direction. The initial trade balance is the distance E_0F. After the ex-

change rate depreciates to \$1.25, at first the trade balance widens to the distance *HG*, and then it narrows to eventually reach zero at E_1. The red line running between E_0, *H*, and E_1 has the shape of the capital letter *J*, tipped over on its side. Thus the situation of a trade balance that deteriorates in the short run following a depreciation in the exchange rate is called the *J-curve phenomenon*.[6]

The **J-curve phenomenon** is the short-run decline in net exports following an exchange rate depreciation, followed by an improvement in net exports.

The experience of the United States in 1985–88 provides a good example of the operation of the *J* curve. The dollar reached its peak in the first quarter of 1985, and by the fourth quarter of 1987 had depreciated by about 50 percent. The U.S. trade balance did not finally begin to improve until early 1988. Why? In the short run the demand for imports proved to be highly inelastic. Consumers continued to purchase Japanese automobiles and compact disc players, despite price increases that raised the U.S. import bill, expressed in dollars. Further, the prices of Japanese goods were not raised in the same proportion as the incredible doubling of the yen exchange rate between 1985:Q1 and 1987:Q4. Many Japanese producers willingly suffered reduced profit margins in order to avoid doubling the prices of goods sold to U.S. consumers. This also helps explain why U.S. imports did not decline promptly in response to the depreciation of the dollar against the yen and most European currencies.

14-6 Why Was the U.S. Trade Deficit So High After the Dollar's Fall?

In 1980 the U.S. trade accounts, including investment income, were roughly balanced, with neither a trade surplus nor deficit. After 1980 the dollar appreciated through 1985 and then depreciated, returning almost to its 1980 value by early 1988. If the rise and fall of the dollar were the only determinant of the trade balance, then we would have expected the trade balance to swing into deficit in response to the higher dollar during 1980–85, and then to return to a zero deficit in response to the falling dollar. The *J*-curve effect causes some delay, but surely one might expect that most of the movement of the trade balance from a large deficit to zero would have been completed by early 1989.

However, the improvement in the trade balance was surprisingly small. From a peak of about 3.4 percent of GNP in 1987, the U.S. current account deficit (defined in Table 14-1) fell only to about 2.3 percent of GNP in 1989. Why was the improvement in the trade balance so slow?

The Actual and Equilibrium Real Exchange Rate

One possibility is that trading conditions for the United States deteriorated between 1980 and 1989. Journalists often lament the lack of international

---

[6]Evidence on the *J* curve is presented in Rudiger Dornbusch and Paul Krugman, "Flexible Exchange Rates in the Short Run," *Brookings Papers on Economic Activity*, vol. 7, no. 3 (1976), especially on pp. 558–566. The authors conclude that "there is a significant price responsiveness, but adjustment lags are important and run to years, not quarters" (p. 566). See also Jeffrey D. Sachs, "The Current Account and Macroeconomic Adjustment in the 1970s," *Brookings Papers on Economic Activity*, vol. 12, no. 1 (1981), pp. 201–268.

trade "competitiveness" of the United States. In terms of economics, we can describe the problem as a decline in the equilibrium real exchange rate of the dollar. We have seen in our discussion of PPP that a country benefitting from oil discoveries or the development of new technology can enjoy an increase in its real exchange rate and a higher standard of living as its imports become cheaper. The problem is that foreign nations are discovering oil, developing new technology, and building new factories faster than the United States is. Hence these other countries enjoy an increase in their real exchange rate, which must mean a decline in the equilibrium real exchange rate for the United States.

The equilibrium real exchange rate is the exchange rate that would be consistent with a balanced current account after all lags of adjustment are completed.

We can define the **equilibrium real exchange rate** simply as the value of the exchange rate that would be consistent with balance in the current account, after all *J*-curve delays in adjustment are completed. If the current account exhibits a large deficit at the actual value of the exchange rate, then the equilibrium exchange rate must lie below the actual exchange rate. This interpretation is illustrated in Figure 14-5. Rather than plotting actual data, here we give a stylized view of what happened. The actual exchange rate appreciated from *A* to *B* (1980 to 1985) and then depreciated from *B* to *C* (1985 to 1990). However, since the current account was not balanced by 1990, and there had been plenty of time for *J*-curve lags to occur (since most of the dollar's decline had already occurred by late 1987), the equilibrium value of the dollar must lie below the actual value, shown at point *D* for 1990. Achieving balanced trade in "the future" as at point *E* would require a substantial further decline in the dollar.

Figure 14-5
The Relationship Between the Actual and Equilibrium Real Exchange Rate in the 1980s and 1990s

The red line going from *A* to *B* to *C* is a schematic representation of the behavior of the actual real exchange rate. The black line from *A* to *D* is a hypothetical series for the equilibrium real exchange rate, which must have been below the actual rate in 1990 in light of the negative trade balance. Even if the equilibrium rate were to remain constant in the future, the actual exchange rate would have to decline to achieve balanced trade.

WHY THE DOLLAR'S FALL DID NOT FIX THE TRADE DEFICIT

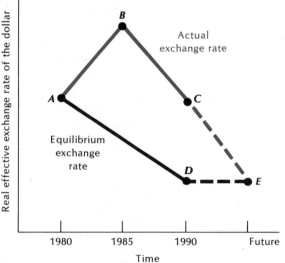

What caused the U.S. equilibrium exchange rate to decline after 1980? There are a number of factors, all of which either raise the U.S. demand for imports, raise the supply of imports, reduce the foreign demand for U.S. exports, or, finally, reduce the supply of exports.

Asian "newly industrialized countries" (NICs).   The NICs are countries like South Korea, Taiwan, Hong Kong, and Singapore, whose exports have expanded rapidly in the last two decades and which account for a growing part of U.S. imports. The NIC phenomenon pushes the U.S. equilibrium exchange rate downward as the NICs build factories capable of producing goods that Americans want to buy. However, the flexible exchange rate system does not work to raise the purchases by the NICs of U.S. exports, for two reasons. First, several of these countries, particularly Hong Kong, "peg" their currency to the U.S. dollar, so the needed depreciation of the dollar against their currency does not occur. Second, others protect their domestic manufacturers by making it difficult for U.S. firms to sell exports to them, either levying tariffs, limiting imports by quotas, or simply discriminating against imports.

Inelastic supply of U.S. import-competing goods.   Because the United States does not make particular goods, like VCRs, changes in the exchange rate have little effect on the trade deficit. If foreign firms raise the prices of VCRs imported by the United States, demand will decrease, but there will be no shift of purchases to U.S. producers. Eventually, if the dollar depreciates enough, foreign firms will find it desirable to open plants in the United States to produce those goods that U.S. businesses do not produce. This has already occurred in the automobile industry, where the Japanese have built factories capable of building 2 million cars bearing Japanese nameplates like Nissan and Toyota. As yet Korean or Taiwanese firms have not opened factories in the United States because wage rates in those countries are still well below U.S. levels.

Slow growth abroad.   One factor aggravating the trade deficit, at least until 1989, was the rapid growth of the U.S. economy relative to several foreign economies, particularly those in Europe. This raised the U.S. demand for imports faster than the increase in the demand by foreigners for U.S. exports. This factor will become less important if the U.S. goes through a recession or period of slow growth in the early 1990s as the Fed tries to prevent a reacceleration of U.S. inflation.

Farm products.   There is growing evidence that U.S. farmers, who have traditionally been a major source of U.S. exports, have been undermined by subsidies to foreign farmers, tariffs, quotas, and increasing farm production abroad. The "Green Revolution" in several of the less developed countries is a bad omen for the revival of the U.S. farm economy.

Latin America.   The U.S. traditionally was the dominant supplier of exports to Latin America. Yet in the late 1970s and early 1980s, several major Latin American nations financed imports from the United States by accumulating massive amounts of debt, and since then have drastically reduced imports as a condition for debt restructuring and repayment. For this reason, the U.S. trade surplus in 1980 was unsustainable, and the equilibrium exchange rate may have actually been lower than the actual exchange rate in that year.

14-7 The Debate Over Exchange Rate Systems

The Case for Fixed Exchange Rates

After the economic debacle of the Great Depression, and the economic havoc caused by World War II, leaders of the Western world were determined to create an economic system for the postwar period that would not be vulnerable to the risk of another depression. One component of the new economic era was a fixed exchange rate system, agreed upon in a famous conference at Bretton Woods, New Hampshire, in 1944. The **Bretton Woods system** remained in effect until the early 1970s when it broke down and was replaced by the present flexible exchange rate system. An understanding of the original arguments for fixed exchange rates, and the factors that led to the breakdown of the Bretton Woods system, is essential background for the current debate about the possibility of devising a new system.

The **Bretton Woods system** maintained fixed exchange rates over the period from the end of World War II to 1971.

The first argument in favor of fixed exchange rates is really an argument against flexible rates. Under a flexible system, exchange rates can exhibit highly volatile movements, due partly to the low short-run elasticity of demand and supply illustrated in Figure 14-4. These movements away from any reasonable estimate of an "equilibrium rate" that is compatible with balanced trade can persist for many years, as is demonstrated by the evidence on the U.S. real exchange rate in Figure 14-3. A persistent deviation of an asset price away from its equilibrium value is sometimes called a "speculative bubble" or "speculative run." Examples of such bubbles can be found throughout history, including the Dutch tulip bubble of 1635, the South Sea and Mississippi bubbles of 1720, the Florida land boom of the 1920s, and, some think, the stock market boom of 1928–29 and subsequent crash. Recent technical literature supports the view of the original proponents of the Bretton Woods system, adding a modern analysis based on rational expectations. Several economists have shown that, even with rational market participants, the market for foreign exchange can be subjected to "whims and fads" that are not supported by fundamental factors.[7]

The other argument for fixed exchange rates is based on the improved efficiency of world trade when importers and exporters can predict relative

---

[7]Among the many scholarly articles developing this view are Olivier Blanchard, "Speculative Bubbles, Crashes and Rational Expectations," *Economics Letters,* vol. 3 (1979), pp. 386–389; Maurice Obstfeld, "Rational and Self-Fulfilling Balance-of-Payments Crises," *American Economic Review,* vol. 76 (March 1986), pp. 72–81; and Robert Flood and Peter Garber, "Gold Monetarization and Gold Discipline," *Journal of Political Economy,* vol. 92 (February 1984), pp. 90–107.

prices accurately in advance rather than contending with the volatile movements of a flexible exchange rate system. Charles Kindleberger of the Massachusetts Institute of Technology argues, in fact, that the case for fixed exchange rates is analogous to the case for a single currency within the fifty states of the United States:

> The main case against flexible exchange rates is that they break up the world market. . . . Imagine trying to conduct interstate trade in the USA if there were fifty different state monies, no one of which was dominant. This is akin to barter, the inefficiency of which is explained time and again by textbooks.[8]

The breakdown of the Bretton Woods system. We learned in Section 14-4 that there are many reasons why exchange rates may need to change. First is the basic point of the purchasing-power parity theory, that the exchange rate between two nations cannot remain fixed if inflation rates in the two nations diverge substantially over time. In the 1960s the United States experienced an acceleration of inflation, as noted in Chapter 9, caused partly by Vietnam War spending by the government and partly by an accommodating monetary policy response. The accelerating U.S. inflation gradually caused a decline in its ever-more-expensive exports and an increase in its ever-cheaper imports. As a result, it became impossible to maintain fixed exchange rates between the dollar and other currencies.

For a few years, between 1968 and 1971, the United States tried to ignore this problem under a policy called "benign neglect." The United States had an unfair advantage under the Bretton Woods system because other countries like Germany held dollars as international reserves. Whenever the United States ran a trade deficit with Germany it could "pay for" its deficit by printing more dollars. However, the reverse was not true. The United States held no deutsche marks as reserves, so Germany did not have the option of running a deficit and paying for this deficit by printing deutsche marks. Essentially the system allowed the United States to run growing deficits without paying for them.[9] Foreign countries accumulated ever-increasing stocks of dollar reserves that they had received from the United States as payment for U.S. imports, but they were prevented by the United States from cashing these in for gold. In some countries the accumulation of dollars, by raising the assets of the central bank, directly caused an acceleration in the growth of the money supply and of the inflation rate.

By 1971 it had become clear that countries like Germany and Japan could no longer tolerate the buildup of dollar reserves that was forced on them by the Bretton Woods system. As a result, in two stages (the late 1971 Smithsonian Agreement and the final transition in early 1973) the industrial world converted to a flexible exchange rate system.

---

[8]Charles Kindleberger, *International Money* (London: Allen and Unwin, 1981), p. 174.

[9]Foreign governments generally held their dollar reserves in the form of interest-bearing short-term U.S. government securities, and so the United States was obliged to pay them interest.

The Case For and Against International Policy Coordination

Since the flexible exchange rate era began in 1973, most major industrial nations have pursued their own chosen monetary and fiscal policies without much regard for the resulting effects on the foreign exchange rate.[a] The most important example of this was the movement of the United States toward fiscal deficits in the 1980s, while most other large nations were moving toward fiscal surpluses. For this reason the dollar appreciated strongly between 1980 and 1985 (as shown in Figures 14-1 and 14-4). However, in 1985 there was a growing consensus among the finance ministers of the major nations that the appreciation of the dollar and the U.S. trade deficit had gone far enough.

Starting with the "Plaza Accord" of September 1985 (negotiated at the Plaza Hotel in New York City), the finance ministers of the five most important industrial nations (Group of Five, or "G-5") agreed to "intervene" in foreign currency markets in an attempt to achieve desired changes in foreign exchange rates, particularly of the dollar.[b] The Plaza Accord took place at a time when the dollar was widely agreed to be overvalued, and so involved an agreement to achieve a depreciation of the dollar.

Intervention may be desired either to change or stabilize a particular exchange rate. As we have seen, in 1985 policymakers agreed that the dollar had appreciated too much and intervened to try to create a depreciation. Then, between 1985 and 1987, the dollar depreciated back to its 1980 value. In 1988–89 policymakers appeared to endorse the new lower level of the dollar and maintain it. This required intervention from time to time in 1988–89 to keep the dollar from appreciating as higher U.S. interest rates increased the demand for dollars.

Intervention and the Case for Policy Coordination

Clearly, the effects of intervention will depend on whether policymakers coordinate their actions. Should the United States wish to create an appreciation of the dollar against the mark, for instance, it must create an excess demand of dollars relative to marks by reducing the U.S. money supply. This will not work if Germany simultaneously tries to create an excess demand for marks to prevent the mark from depreciating as the dollar appreciates. The result will be a stalemate and the appreciation of the dollar against the mark desired by the U.S. policymakers will fail to occur due to the lack of cooperation by the German policymakers.

If policies in each of two countries can affect the other, then the case for policy coordination would seem to be obvious. Policy coordination is viewed as more important in the modern world, since economic disturbances are communicated more rapidly from country to country. In the absence of policy coordination, policy decisions made in one country are more likely than previously to destabilize other economies. This can create problems if the goals pursued by different nations are inconsistent. If both the United States and Germany desire to create an appreciation in their currency by reducing their money supplies, neither will succeed, and both will suffer from higher unemployment than either intended.

Both the United States and Germany were subject to the criticism in the 1980s that they did not coordinate their policies sufficiently with each other and with other nations. The United States was criticized for its government budget deficit and resulting trade deficit, while Germany was criticized for tight monetary policies which slowed the growth of real GNP in Europe. Advocates of coordination argued that the United States should negotiate to reduce its deficit and that Germany should loosen its monetary policy.

The Case Against Policy Coordination

Some criticisms of policy coordination are very general. Governments might be tempted to avoid

politically painful decisions and then blame foreign governments for whatever mismanagement resulted. More specifically, governments cannot achieve effective coordination and still reflect the desires of their political constituents, if those constituents have truly incompatible objectives. German voters, for instance, are widely believed to place more weight on the avoidance of inflation than French or British voters. Another argument is that economic knowledge is insufficient to achieve effective policy results in a single country (this is part of the monetarist case against activism reviewed in the next chapter), and knowledge is even more limited when many countries are involved. Policy coordination, then, might be as likely to destabilize the world economy as to stabilize it.

A consistent opponent of international policy coordination is Martin Feldstein of Harvard, former chairman of the Council of Economic Advisers in the Reagan Administration.[c] Feldstein believes that coordination will not work for the United States as a result of the large U.S. trade deficit. To eliminate that deficit, it would be necessary for the dollar to decline further toward the equilibrium value of the dollar (as shown in Figure 14-5). But this is incompatible with the repeated desire of European and Japanese government officials to achieve a stable value of the dollar. It is also incompatible with the objectives of advocates of target zones, whose views are discussed in the text of Section 14-7.

Feldstein argues that attempts at coordinated policies to stabilize the dollar will be both harmful and ineffective. If market participants expect stability in exchange rates, they may create unwanted movements in domestic interest rates. For instance, if they observe a depreciation of the dollar and believe that this is not desired by policymakers, then they may anticipate a reduction in the money supply and cause interest rates to jump at a time when this is inconsistent with the domestic policy targets of policymakers. Feldstein also believes that domestic political forces, particularly the controversy between the U.S. administration and Congress regarding the best method to reduce budget deficits, are deeply rooted and will not be eliminated by international agreements to stabilize policy. Further, with the constitutional separation of powers and independent Federal Reserve system, no official of an American administration can promise to carry out specific actions called for by international agreements.

What should we conclude about international economic coordination? The events of the 1980s suggest that, while stability in exchange rates is desirable to foster efficient planning by businessmen and consumers, it is possible for actual exchange rates to move so far away from equilibrium exchange rates (as in Figure 14-5) that movements of actual exchange rates become desirable. As we shall see in the next chapter, the task of stabilizing the domestic economy is difficult on its own, and can be made only more difficult by the additional element of international agreements that may require domestic policymakers to take actions having destabilizing effects on the domestic economy.

---

[a]An exception to the pursuit of independent national policies is the European Monetary System (EMS), discussed in Section 14-7.
[b]The Group of Five (G-5) nations are France, Germany, Japan, the United Kingdom, and the United States. At the annual Summit Conferences, seven nations are represented, including the G-5 plus Canada and Italy.
[c]Martin S. Feldstein, "Distinguished Lecture on Economics in Government: Thinking About International Economic Coordination," *Journal of Economic Perspectives,* vol. 2 (Spring 1988), pp. 3–13.

The Case for Flexible Exchange Rates and Recent Experience

The traditional case for flexible exchange rates is similar to the case for free competition rather than monopoly in markets for goods.[10] Adherence to fixed exchange rates inevitably leads to a divergence between the fixed rate and the equilibrium exchange rate determined by the forces of supply and demand. In order to maintain the fixed rate during such disequilibrium, governments resort to devices that interfere with the free flow of goods and capital. These include tariffs, quotas, exchange controls, and taxes on capital inflows and outflows.

Further, fixed exchange rates are not really fixed. As pointed out in the discussion of purchasing power parity in Section 14-4, numerous factors change the equilibrium exchange rate, including differential inflation rates between nations, inventions, oil discoveries, and other factors that influence the demand or supply for a nation's currency. These factors can cause the equilibrium exchange rate to diverge from the fixed rate by enough for a nation to begin losing its international reserves (gold or dollars). For a time, the nation attempts to maintain the fixed rate and stem the loss in reserves by contractionary monetary or fiscal policy and by quotas on imports and restrictions on capital outflows. But inevitably these attempts are futile, and an exchange "crisis" occurs when investors rush to sell a currency because they believe that the government is about to change from one fixed exchange rate to another in a "devaluation." For instance, in October 1967, the United Kingdom, after several years of crisis measures, devalued its currency from $2.80 per pound to $2.40. The reality of devaluation under a fixed exchange rate system lies behind Milton Friedman's claim, made prior to the demise of the Bretton Woods system, that exchange rates would be no more volatile under a flexible system than a fixed system.

Another of the original arguments for flexible rates was that it would allow nations to conduct independent monetary policies. Under the Bretton Woods system Germany and Japan, in 1968–71, were forced to expand their money supplies faster than they desired because of the influx of international reserves. They would have been willing to avoid such an expansion of their money supplies under a flexible exchange rate system.

The reality, 1973–89. Part of the case for flexible exchange rates has been validated by the fact that since 1973 some nations have been able to pursue more independent monetary policies. For instance West Germany and Switzerland shifted to a tight monetary policy, while monetary policy was still relatively expansionary in the United States, the United Kingdom, and other nations. As a result, West Germany and Switzerland experienced significantly less inflation at the time of the first oil shock, during the period 1973–75. Also, in the late 1970s West Germany and Japan resisted the United States' plea for expansionary monetary policy. The United States was left to conduct expansion by itself, which resulted in a decline in the exchange rate of the dollar during the period of the Carter administration, 1977–80.

However, there has been a major surprise in the operation of the flexible exchange rate system. Exchange rates of major nations, as shown in Figure

---

[10]The classic statement is Milton Friedman, "The Case for Flexible Exchange Rates," in his *Essays in Positive Economics* (Chicago: University of Chicago Press, 1953).

14-1, have been much more volatile than had been anticipated. The enormous movements up and down have lasted for several years and have carried actual exchange rates far away from equilibrium exchange rates. The appreciation of the dollar in 1980–85 and subsequent depreciation in 1985–88 is the best example of this. Many U.S. manufacturing firms and farmers were needlessly put out of business by the strong dollar, whereas with a more stable exchange rate they might have remained in business.

We learned in Chapter 5 that a major reason for the rise of the dollar in 1980–85 was the mix of monetary and fiscal policy in the United States, with tight money accompanied by an easy fiscal policy. In contrast, fiscal policy was tightened in other major industrial nations. Thus the absence of *international policy coordination* was at the heart of the instability of exchange rates in the 1980s.

The Debate about Managed Floating and Target Zones

The volatility of exchange rates, particularly of the dollar, has led to growing support for a partial return to fixed exchange rates. This has already been accomplished within Europe, where the European Monetary System (EMS) has been operating with relative success to maintain exchange rates among European nations, within a relatively narrow band, since the late 1970s. But this success has been achieved only by a coordinated set of monetary and fiscal policies, in which other European nations have mimicked the contractionary policies of West Germany (the largest European nation), with the consequence of unemployment rates near or above 10 percent. Nations that have attempted to pursue an expansionary policy on their own, particularly France in 1981–82, have been forced to adjust their exchange rates and to retreat from any unilateral expansion, and the United Kingdom, unwilling to tie its monetary policy to that of West Germany, has refused to join the EMS.

Managed floating is a system intermediate between fixed and flexible exchange rates, in which the exchange rate is allowed to respond to movements in the long-run equilibrium exchange rate but not deviations from that equilibrium rate.

Managed floating is a compromise system in which exchange rates are allowed to change in response to changes in the "fundamentals," that is, in the equilibrium exchange rates. But volatile short-term movements are controlled by central bank intervention (buying and selling of a nation's currency in the foreign exchange market). The **target zones** proposal specifies a particular band (for example, plus or minus 10 percent) within which an exchange rate is allowed to fluctuate, with the requirement that intervention occur whenever the exchange rate moves outside the band or "zone."[11] The two systems are similar, but the target zones proposal is somewhat more formal, whereas the idea of managed floating is less specific about how much the exchange rate would be allowed to move.

The **target zones** proposal specifies intervention by central banks whenever exchange rates move outside a specified band or zone.

The debate over managed floating and target zones revolves around the issue that caused both the breakdown of the Bretton Woods system and the excessive volatility of the dollar in 1980–89. This is the traditional absence of international policy coordination—that is, an agreement by all countries to move toward tighter or looser monetary and fiscal policies at the same

---

[11]See John Williamson, "Target Zones and the Management of the Dollar," *Brookings Papers on Economic Activity,* vol. 17, no. 1, (1986), pp. 165–174. This issue also contains critiques and discussion of the Williamson proposal.

time. Supporters argue that the very act of signing an agreement for target zones would force a government to shift its policies in the direction of the policies pursued by other nations. Movement of a currency close to the edge of its zone might be perceived by domestic policymakers as requiring prompt action to bring monetary and fiscal policies more into line.

Skeptics of the target zones proposal believe that it would be subject to many of the same problems as the Bretton Woods system. Speculators would be tempted to "attack" a currency when it reached the edge of the zone, forcing a nation to devalue by changing the boundaries of the zones. Skeptics also doubt that nations actually would coordinate their policies sufficiently to maintain the system; the clash between easy fiscal policy in the United States and tight fiscal policy in nations like the United Kingdom and West Germany persisted in the 1980s despite the obvious dislocations caused to domestic producers and consumers. The debate over target zones is similar to the debate (reviewed in the next chapter) between the monetarists and activists, in that most arguments reveal differing degrees of optimism or pessimism about the willingness of politicians to pursue worthy economic objectives.

SELF-TEST   Classify each of the following statements into one of these groups: (A) part of original case for flexible exchange rates; (B) part of case against fixed exchange rates; (C) now recognized to be true of both flexible and fixed exchange rate systems. The statements are (1) exchange rates will be no more volatile; (2) international policy coordination is necessary; (3) allows nations to pursue independent monetary policies; (4) leads to destabilizing speculation.

SUMMARY

1. The international transactions of any nation are divided into three categories—*current* transactions involving the export or import of goods and services, together with unilateral transfer payments; *capital* transactions involving long-term and short-term borrowing and lending; and *financing items* required to offset any deficit or surplus on the current and capital accounts taken together.

2. If governments allowed the exchange rate of their currency to fluctuate from day to day to eliminate any imbalance on current and capital accounts, no financing items would be necessary. But if a government intervenes to maintain a fixed exchange rate, then there is likely to be a surplus or shortage of foreign exchange, which in turn causes an increase or decrease in the government's stock of international reserves (or, when the reserves run low, borrowing from abroad).

3. In the absence of government intervention, the foreign exchange rate tends to appreciate when there is an increased demand for a currency due to

higher exports or capital inflows. The rate tends to depreciate when there is an increased supply of a currency due to higher imports or capital outflows.

4. In the long run, the main determinants of the exchange rate between the currencies of two nations are their relative inflation rates, their comparative rates of innovation and technological change, their comparative rates of discovery of natural resources, and the balance of flows of capital and government transfer payments between them.

5. In the short run, the exchange rate can fluctuate widely around the long-run equilibrium exchange rate, because the price elasticities of imports and exports may be smaller in the short run than in the long run, and because neither the government nor private speculators have enough knowledge to stabilize the exchange rate at its long-run equilibrium level.

6. The Bretton Woods system of fixed exchange rates broke down as a result of the accelerating U.S. inflation during the Vietnam War period, which made it impossible to maintain fixed exchange rates between the dollar and other currencies.

7. The case for flexible exchange rates rests on the impossibility of maintaining fixed exchange rates in a world with divergent policies in different nations. Since 1973, flexible exchange rates have allowed some nations to maintain tighter monetary policies than other nations.

8. Since 1973, exchange rates have been more volatile than had been predicted previously by proponents of flexible rates. This has led to new proposals for "managed floating" or "target zones" that would limit variations in exchange rates.

9. The high volatility of exchange rates has also led to increased pleas for international policy coordination, but such coordination has been difficult to attain because of the divergent domestic policy priorities of the major industrial nations.

CONCEPTS

international reserves
current account versus capital account
net exports
official reserve transactions deficit
purchasing-power-parity theory of the exchange rate
real exchange rate

J-curve phenomenon
equilibrium real exchange rate
Bretton Woods system
managed floating
target zones

QUESTIONS

1. There are two main ways of adjusting to an imbalance between international receipts and expenditures. What are these ways? How do they work?

2. Explain the difference between a credit and a debit in the balance of payments.

3. In which categories of Table 14-1 would you include the following international transactions of the United States?
   (a) Purchase of a $100,000 Caterpillar tractor from the Peoria, Illinois factory by an Italian road-building contractor.
   (b) Short-term loan to the Italian contractor by the First National Bank of Chicago to finance the tractor.
   (c) Purchase of a $600 round-trip ticket to Paris on Air France by a student at Indiana University.
   (d) A $100 gift sent by a recent Italian immigrant in the United States to her mother in Torino.
   (e) Purchase of an Old General Motors factory in California by the Toyota company of Japan for $60 million.
   (f) A $100 million increase in the holdings of short-term U.S. government bonds by the Bank of England (the central bank of the United Kingdom).

4. Why was the negative value of net exports in the United States so large in the early part of the

1980s? Why didn't net exports recover in the late 1980s, given the changes in the foreign exchange rate that occurred?

5. In the 1980s there has been a dramatic change toward a surplus in the capital account in the U.S. balance of payments. What are the causes and implications of this change?

6. What determines the supply and demand for U.S. dollars in the foreign exchange markets? Why is the foreign demand for U.S. dollars the same as the foreign supply of foreign exchange?

7. Explain why the failure of real exchange rates in the United States during the 1970s and 1980s to behave as predicted by the purchasing price parity theory lends support to the activist's case.

8. Summarize the major advantages and disadvantages of fixed exchange rates.

9. While economists expected exchange rates to fluctuate under a system of flexible exchange rates, the movements in exchange rates under that system have been much more volatile than had been anticipated. Why did this volatility result?

10. What is the distinction between a *managed floating* system of exchange rates and the *target zone* system? What are some of the issues in the debate over these two systems?

p. 425 (1) line 1b, current services, debit; (2) line 1c, income on foreign assets, credit; (3) line 2b, private remittance, credit; (4) line 1b, current services, credit; (5) line 1a, exports and imports of goods and services, credit.

p. 430 (1) shifts the supply curve for pounds to the right; (2) shifts the demand curve for pounds to the right; (3) shifts the supply curve for pounds to the left (assuming the majority of passengers shift from American to British Airways); (4) shifts the demand curve for pounds to the left.

p. 434 In each answer, the real exchange rate stays fixed if the nominal exchange rate of the foreign currency increased (that is, the dollar depreciated) by the same amount as the difference between the U.S. inflation rate and the foreign inflation rate. (1) Canadian dollar, 1973–89, real exchange rate of the U.S. dollar was roughly constant; (2 and 3) Japanese yen, 1973–79 and 1979–89, the yen appreciated more than the difference between U.S. and Japanese inflation, so the real exchange rate of the dollar depreciated; (4) Swiss franc, 1973–79, the Swiss franc appreciated more than the difference between U.S. and Swiss inflation, so the real exchange rate of the dollar depreciated; (5) Swiss franc, 1979–89, the Swiss franc appreciated less than the difference between U.S. and Swiss inflation, so the real exchange rate of the dollar appreciated.

p. 446 Statement 1 is in group A, 2 in C, 3 in A, 4 in B.

PART VI

Taming Business Cycles: Macro Policy and the Sources of Instability

The Debate Over Activist Stabilization Policy

Economic forecasting is the occupation that makes astrology respectable.[1]

15-1 Link to Previous Chapters: The Central Role of Demand Disturbances

Unrealistic Precision of Policy Control in Previous Chapters

Demand disturbances include changes in business and consumer optimism, changes in net exports, and changes in government spending or tax rates (for example, in wartime) not related to stabilization policy.

Policy activism uses the instruments of monetary and fiscal policy actively to offset changes in private spending.

Until now it has been assumed that aggregate demand can be controlled exactly. But in the real world, life is more difficult for policymakers. Exogenous demand shocks or **demand disturbances** can shift the level of nominal GNP, but policymakers cannot neutralize these disturbances instantly because nominal GNP reacts to policy changes with a lag and by an uncertain amount. As a result, many economists argue against **policy activism,** that is, the use of monetary and fiscal policy to offset exogenous demand disturbances.

In Part II (Chapters 3–5) we identified the determinants of aggregate demand. Among the key disturbances that originate in the private sector are changes in business and consumer optimism or in net exports. Demand disturbances can also originate in the government, since government expenditures or tax rates sometimes change for reasons other than stabilization policy. For instance, a war may escalate defense spending and thereby create a demand disturbance that the government may try to offset by changes in tax rates or in monetary policy.

Part III (Chapters 6–8) combined these sources of demand disturbances, summarized by the *DD* curve, with alternative theories of aggregate supply. There the old and new classical models of aggregate supply, in which demand disturbances mainly alter the price level, were contrasted with the original and new Keynesian models, in which demand disturbances mainly cause changes in output and in the unemployment rate.

Part IV (Chapters 9 and 10) provided a dynamic analysis of aggregate demand and supply, based on the new Keynesian model in which long-term wage and price contracts impede the adjustment of the inflation rate, so that

---

[1]David Dremas, "The Madness of Crowds," *Forbes,* September 27, 1982, p. 201.

demand disturbances affect the output ratio and unemployment rate in the short run. Eventually, as contracts are renegotiated, this model shows that permanent changes in nominal GNP growth affect only the inflation rate in the long run.

The economy as supertanker. Throughout Parts II, III, and IV, we assumed, unrealistically, that the growth of aggregate demand (or nominal GNP) could be controlled precisely. The assumption was that, faced with a demand disturbance, policymakers are capable of calculating the change in the money supply, in government spending, or in tax rates that would *exactly* offset the demand disturbance. Unfortunately, policymakers cannot steer the economy back and forth as easily as a driver steers an automobile. Changing aggregate demand is much more like steering a giant supertanker. Even if the captain gives the signal for a hard turn, it takes a mile or so to see a change in the supertanker's direction, and 10 miles before the supertanker makes the turn. In the same way, the real-world economy has a momentum of its own, and policy shifts cannot control aggregate demand instantly or precisely.

Our discussion of longer run issues of economic growth and the behavior of the government and foreign debt in Part V mainly concerned issues that determine the long-term growth rate of natural real GNP (Q^N) and of the standard of living. Now we return to the need to tame business cycles and keep actual real GNP as close as possible to natural real GNP. This is the job of stabilization policy, both monetary and fiscal. In this chapter before treating the detailed implementation of monetary and fiscal policy, we ask whether the government should even try to carry out an "activist" control of aggregate demand.

The modern school of thought called **monetarism** denies that the benefits of activist government control of aggregate demand are worth the cost.[2] In fact, it is a basic tenet of the monetarist position that government interference does more harm than good and actually may stabilize the economy. The group of economists labeled "monetarist" were given this name to reflect the emphasis they placed on steady growth in the money supply as the basic tenet of stabilization policy.

Monetarism is a school of thought that opposes activist government policy intervention aimed at stabilizing aggregate demand.

The Monetarist–Activist Debate and Alternative Theories of the Business Cycle

How is monetarism related to the alternative models of the business cycle that we developed in Chapters 7 and 8? Most proponents of policy activism are adherents to the new Keynesian model based on long-term wage and price agreements. In fact, their endorsement of activism is directly related to the inflexibility of the price level. The new Keynesian model implies that demand disturbances will cause undesirable movements in actual real GNP away from natural real GNP (Q^N). The issues separating the monetarists from the activists involve the sources of demand disturbances and the effect of policy on *aggregate demand,* and do not involve the particular model of *aggregate supply* used to explain the business cycle.

[2]The term *monetarism* was introduced in Karl Brunner, "The Role of Money and Monetary Policy," *Federal Reserve Bank of St. Louis Review,* no. 50 (1968), pp. 9–24.

This chapter begins by discussing the relationship between monetary policy, fiscal policy, and other types of policy. This allows us to identify the unique role of monetary policy as a tool that activists believe can dampen the swings of real GNP during business cycles. We distinguish the opposing roles for monetary policy, "rules" versus "discretion," favored respectively by monetarists and activists. Then we examine the historical record to evaluate the claims made by the monetarists and their activist opponents. This record also allows us to evaluate the new classical macroeconomists' criticisms of policy activism.

15-2 Stabilization Targets and Instruments in the Activists' Paradise

What are the monetarists and new classical economists attacking? This section sets forth the traditional analysis of stabilization policy favored by the activist proponents and explains why the activists feel that multiple policy instruments are needed, and how they perceive the roles of monetary and fiscal policy. We then focus on the concerns of monetarists by identifying a number of idealized assumptions that would be necessary for policy activism to work promptly and precisely, an ideal called (for ease of reference) the "activists' paradise."

The Need for Multiple Instruments

When the driver of a car has a destination to reach on a map, he or she is trying to hit two targets: a particular latitude (north-south position) and a specific longitude (east-west position). To reach these two targets, the driver needs two basic instruments in the car, an engine to move the car forward or back and a steering wheel to move it left or right. Activist stabilization policy attempts to "hit" several targets. Just as for an automobile, hitting two targets requires at least two instruments of stabilization policy. For instance, Chapter 5 showed that the money-supply instrument could not simultaneously achieve both a target level of real GNP and a target interest rate. Both monetary and fiscal policy must be manipulated to achieve an intersection of the *IS* and *LM* curves at a given combination of the interest rate and real GNP.

Monetary, fiscal, and structural employment policies. Monetary and fiscal policy acting together are the two main instruments that control nominal GNP growth and the interest rate. In the long run the unemployment-rate target is beyond the control of monetary and fiscal policy. A permanent reduction in unemployment requires a permanent drop in the natural rate of unemployment, which requires in turn a separate instrument. That instrument is the mixture of structural employment policy tools discussed in Chapter 11—reform of unemployment compensation, training subsidies to firms, and so on.

But we are not finished yet. Fiscal policy really consists of two types of **policy instruments:** government spending and tax rates. A given government deficit can be achieved with high spending and high tax rates or low

Policy instruments for monetary policy are the money supply and interest rate; for fiscal policy they are government spending and tax rates.

spending and low tax rates. Thus within fiscal policy the mixture between spending and tax rates determines yet another target of policy, the division of total real output between public and private spending.

So far we are up to four instruments and four targets:

Instruments	Targets
Structural employment policy	Unemployment rate
Monetary policy	Inflation rate
Government spending	Interest rate
Tax rates	Division of real GNP between public and private spending

Figure 15-1 gives a more complete illustration of the principles of economic policy. The goal of economic policy is economic welfare, represented by the

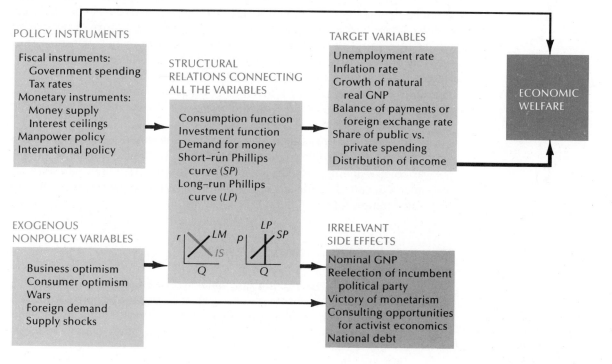

Figure 15-1 **A Flowchart Showing the Relation between Policy Instruments, Policy Targets, and Economic Welfare**
Both policy instruments and exogenous nonpolicy variables are ingredients fed into the structural relations that connect the exogenous (policy and nonpolicy) variables with the endogenous (target and nontarget) variables. Total economic welfare at the upper right depends on the achieved values of the target variables, and thus it depends in turn on the decisions of policymakers on the settings of the policy instruments.

box in the upper right corner of Figure 15-1. Economic welfare can be thought of as simply happiness, the things that individual members of society want—stable prices, full employment, and a high standard of living.

Targets, Instruments, and Structural Relations

Target variables are the economic aggregates whose values society cares most about, society's goals.

Looking left from the economic welfare box in Figure 15-1 we find a box that lists the main policy **target variables** that influence social welfare. Some are more important than others. The distribution of income is quite different from the other targets; any policy shift that raises the income of one group at the expense of others (rich versus poor; creditors versus debtors) is bound to be controversial and lead to political conflict.[3]

In the upper left corner of Figure 15-1 is a list of some of the policy instruments that the government can use to try to achieve the targets. The upper left instrument box is linked with the upper right target box through the large central box containing the structural relations that link the variables. The *IS* and *LM* curves of Chapter 4 and *SP* and *LP* curves of Chapter 9 summarize the main relations that link money, taxes, and government spending to unemployment and inflation. But those curves can be shifted as well by several exogenous factors not under the direct control of policymakers, as by a burst of business or consumer optimism or higher export sales (shifting the *IS* curve upward) or a supply shock (shifting the *SP* line upward). Wars have also been listed in the exogenous box rather than the instrument box, because the level of government spending in wartime is almost always set in accord with the goals of military strategy rather than economic stabilization.

Exogenous and instrument variables are ingredients in the structural economic relations in the middle box and yield particular values of the target variables—unemployment, inflation, and the others. Other variables are also affected, called irrelevant in the lower right rectangle because they are not major determinants of economic welfare.

Monetarism and the Activists' Paradise

A **constant-growth-rate rule (CGRR)** advocates a fixed percentage growth rate for the money supply, in contrast to the variable growth rate recommended by policy activists.

Monetarists oppose activist countercyclical swings in the money supply and think that the economy will be better off with a **constant-growth-rate rule** (CGRR) for the money supply.[4] They believe that activist stabilization policy may do more harm than good. "Activist economists," they claim, "require a

---

[3]An introduction to these and other targets is Arthur M. Okun, "Conflicting National Goals," in Eli Ginzberg (ed.), *Jobs for Americans* (Englewoods Cliffs, N.J.: Prentice-Hall, 1976).

[4]When he received his Nobel Prize in December 1976, Milton Friedman remarked that it was no thanks to him that the Central Bank of Sweden, which donated the money for his prize, still exists. "My monetary studies have led me to the conclusion that central banks could profitably be replaced by computers geared to provide a steady rate of growth in the quantity of money. Fortunately for me personally, and for a select group of fellow economists, that conclusion has had no practical impact . . . else there would have been no Central Bank of Sweden to have established the award I am honored to receive. Should I draw the moral that sometimes to fail is to succeed?" (Quote from the mimeographed text of the remarks, provided by the author.)

utopian set of assumptions about the economy if they expect an activist stabilization policy to do more good than harm."

The utopian "activists' paradise" is a hypothetical world in which activist policy achieves almost perfect control over total aggregate demand. It has these main characteristics:[5]

1. Ability by policymakers to forecast perfectly future changes in the private demand for and supply of goods and services.

2. Ability by policymakers to forecast perfectly the future effect of current changes in monetary and fiscal policy.

3. Possession by policymakers of policy instruments that powerfully affect aggregate demand.

4. Absence of any costs of changing policy instruments.

5. No political constraints on using the policy instruments for the desired purposes.

The activists' paradise is an extreme set of positions that no economist actually believes. Its purpose is to highlight the unrealistically optimistic set of assumptions that an activist proponent would have to embrace in order to be *sure* that activist policy intervention would be successful in dampening the swings of real GNP during business cycles. *The core of the activists' paradise is a deep faith in the power of macroeconomics as a science. The activists' paradise requires policymakers to be able to forecast perfectly not just future changes in demand, but also the future effect of current changes in policy.*

The other characteristics of the activists' paradise can be summarized as requiring policy to have powerful effects but no side effects. Activist proponents must therefore be a special blend of pessimist and optimist, remaining pessimistic about the ability of the private economy to remain close to its natural level (of Q^N or U^N) while being firmly optimistic about the power of macroeconomic forecasting and policy. Not least among the certitudes required of activist policymakers is the ability to identify the economy's natural rate of operation (Q^N or U^N), so that a particular situation can be described as "too high" or "too low" and the required offsetting policy response can be identified.

In contrast to the activists' paradise is the "monetarist platform" developed in the next section. This does not consist of a simple rebuttal of the assumptions of the activists' paradise. Instead, it contains statements of two types—expressing not only *pessimism* about the likely success of stabilization policy, but also doubt about the *need* for stabilization policy because of an *optimistic* faith in the ability of the private economy to remain stable on its own without policy intervention. Thus, one easy way to think about the monetarist-versus-activist debate is to note the differing locus of optimism and pessimism. Policy activists are pessimistic about the self-correcting powers of the private economy and optimistic about the efficacy of sta-

---

[5]The term *activists' paradise* and its major characteristics originate in Arthur M. Okun, "Fiscal-Monetary Activism: Some Analytical Issues," *Brookings Papers on Economic Activity,* vol. 3, no. 1 (1972), pp. 123–163. The rest of this chapter relies heavily on the late Arthur Okun's analysis of the arguments for and against activism. The author's tribute to the unique talents of Okun appears in *Brookings Papers on Economic Activity,* vol. 11, no. 1 (1980), pp. 1–5.

bilization policy. In contrast, the monetarists are optimistic about the underlying stability of the private economy but pessimistic about the efficacy of stabilization policy.[6]

15-3 A Monetarist Platform

The continuing disagreements between monetarists and activists can be traced to several assumptions of the monetarist platform with which activists disagree.[7]

Plank 1: *Without the interference of demand shocks introduced by erratic government policy, private spending would be stable.* The stability of private spending stems from the **permanent income hypothesis** of consumption explored in Chapter 18. Consumption, the largest component of private spending, changes only gradually as households adjust their estimate of their long-run or permanent income. Another stabilizing factor is the flatness of the *IS* curve due to the broad range of assets whose demand depends on the interest rate.

The **permanent income hypothesis** holds that consumption spending depends on the long-run average (permanent) income that people expect to receive, rather than on current income.

Plank 2: *Not only is private spending relatively stable, so is the demand for money.* As a result, the velocity of money grows at a steady and predictable rate, implying that adherence to a strict rule (CGRR) for the growth rate of the money supply would imply stable growth of nominal GNP.[8] And stable growth for nominal GNP would undeniably imply a stable inflation rate in the long run.

Plank 3: *Even if private planned spending and the demand for money are not completely stable, an activist monetary and fiscal policy is likely*

---

[6]Traditionally, macro textbooks have interpreted the monetarist debate as about the strength of policy multipliers. An extended statement that attempts to reorient the monetarist debate is Franco Modigliani, "The Monetarist Controversy, or, Should We Forsake Stabilization Policy?" *American Economic Review,* vol. 67 (March 1977), pp. 1–19. An earlier paper is Milton Friedman, "Why Economists Disagree," in *Dollars and Deficits* (Englewood Cliffs, N.J.: Prentice-Hall, 1968), pp. 1–16. Friedman on pp. 6–9 shares the same orientation as this chapter, although on pp. 10–16 he places considerably more weight than we do here on the influence of money on inflation. Our orientation reflects Friedman's own influence. There remain very few economists who disagree with him that in the long run inflation is a monetary phenomenon.

[7]The monetarist platform is not copied directly from any monetarist publication but is my own invention suggested by the continuing policy debate. It is, however, similar to the overall interpretation of Modigliani in "The Monetarist Controversy," cited on footnote 6. An extended debate between Modigliani and Milton Friedman that casts additional light on our interpretation is contained in "The Monetarist Controversy," Federal Reserve Bank of San Francisco, *Economic Review Supplement* (Spring 1977). Another interpretation of the debate, which shares our interpretation of activism is James Tobin, "How Dead Is Keynes?" *Economic Inquiry,* vol. 15 (October 1977), pp. 459–468.

Early drafts of this section benefited from the suggestions of Milton Friedman, Allan Meltzer, and Franco Modigliani. Almost all their suggestions have been adopted together with, in some cases, their own suggested wording in an effort to make this chapter an accurate and unbiased reflection of the monetarist-activist debate.

[8]**Review:** Velocity (V) is defined as nominal GNP (Y) divided by the money supply (M^s), $V = Y/M^s$. This implies that the growth rate of velocity (v) is equal to the growth rate of nominal GNP (y) minus the growth rate of the money supply (m^s), $v = y - m^s$. Thus if v is stable and predictable, then a fixed growth rate for m^s implies a stable and predictable growth rate of $y = v + m^s$.

The Monetarist Platform and the Activist Response

The Monetarist Platform	The Activist Response
Plank 1: Without the interference of demand shocks introduced by erratic government policy, private spending would be stable.	**Plank 1:** Shifts in business and consumer attitudes and expectations represent a substantial source of economic instability that should be countered by offsetting policy actions.
Plank 2: Not only is private spending relatively stable, but so is the demand for money. As a result, the velocity of money grows at a steady and predictable rate.	**Plank 2:** Since 1982 the growth of velocity has been extremely erratic, implying that a constant-growth-rate rule for the money supply would have destabilized the growth rate of nominal GNP.
Plank 3: Even if private planned spending and the demand for money are completely stable, an activist monetary and fiscal policy to counteract private demand swings is likely to do more harm than good.	**Plank 3:** Economic knowledge is now sufficiently advanced to allow countercyclical policy actions to stabilize the economy in the face of destabilizing swings in the private demand for commodities and for money.
Plank 4: Even if prices are not completely flexible, so that the economy can wander away from U^N in the short run, there can be no dispute regarding the increased flexibility of prices, the longer the period of time allowed for adjustment.	**Plank 4:** The period of time required for flexible prices to bring the economy automatically back to U^N is intolerably long, and there is no reason for government policymakers to tolerate the persistence of high unemployment and low levels of output that occur in the meantime.

to do more harm than good. All policy changes affect the economy with a long and uncertain lag, so that the effect of policy may be felt after it is needed and in some cases may occur so late that it pushes the economy in the wrong direction. The forecasting abilities of economists are too limited to short-circuit this lag in the effect of policy.

Plank 4: *Even if prices are not completely flexible, so that the economy can wander away from the natural level of real GNP (and natural rate of unemployment) in the short run, there can be no dispute regarding the increased flexibility of the price level, the longer the period of time allowed for adjustment.* Furthermore, it is unwise to base policy changes on short-run considerations because the long run is a succession of short runs. It is best to set a constant-growth-rate rule (CGRR) for the money supply compatible with steady inflation (or even zero inflation) in the long run and avoid the temptation to tinker with the economy in the short run. In economic jargon, monetarists have a relatively low rate of "time preference"; they put little emphasis on short-run events and pay primary attention to the consequences of present actions in the future.

Perspective on the Monetarist Platform

The monetarist platform evokes a comparison with the original classical macroeconomics, described in Chapter 7. Plank 4, with its belief in the long-run self-correcting powers of price stability, echoes the original classical theory of business cycles, in which price flexibility offsets any influence of aggregate demand instability on real GNP. How then do monetarists interpret the unemployment that has occurred in the 1970s and the 1980s?

Attitude of monetarists toward unemployment. Milton Friedman and other monetarists have argued that the unemployment data, properly interpreted, show unemployment to be a much less serious problem than the raw numbers suggest and show that a substantial portion of unemployment is voluntary.[9] Nevertheless, monetarists generally deny either disregard for unemployment or excessive concern for inflation.

In some periods of recession and high unemployment, such as 1975 and 1982 in the United States, the monetarist distaste for activist policy would appear to condemn the economy to a longer recession than the alternative activist approach of monetary or fiscal stimulation. Yet monetarists deny that their recommendation reflects a choice between more or less unemployment now, but only between *a lesser reduction in unemployment now and a greater increase in unemployment later.* Why? They distrust the political process, which is said to block the achievement of sensible economic policy. The economy is bound to overshoot any target, they argue, and politicians are unlikely to have the courage to apply the brakes to the economy soon enough to allow a "soft landing" at the target unemployment rate. Instead, the economy will be allowed to expand too far and too rapidly, inflation will accelerate, and the Federal Reserve will be forced to cause another recession and bout of unemployment to fight the renewed acceleration of inflation.

In the end the debate over policy recommendations by economists does not originate in irreconcilable analytical differences that call into question the scientific claims of economics. The dispute over plank 3 involves the greater willingness of activists to trust the government to follow the advice of economists, as contrasted to the fundamental distrust of the political process exhibited by monetarists. Planks 1 and 2, on the instability of private spending and the demand for money, remain in dispute because, in principle, monetarists can argue that any observed instability just reflects the side effects of manipulation of the money supply or other activist policy intervention. Finally, the disagreement over plank 4, on the importance of the short run as opposed to the long run, reflects not only differing value judgments, but also the much smaller degree of optimism held by monetarists regarding the likely payoff of short-run policy shifts.

---

[9] A classic monetarist attempt to reinterpret the meaning of an increase in unemployment is Milton Friedman, "Unemployment Figures," *Newsweek,* October 20, 1969, reprinted in his *An Economist's Protest,* 2d ed. (Glen Ridge, N.J.: Thomas Horton, 1975), pp. 105–107. An extended answer to Friedman's article is Robert J. Gordon, "The Welfare Cost of Higher Unemployment," *Brookings Papers on Economic Activity,* vol. 4, no. 1 (1973), pp. 133–195.

Classify each of the following statements by the group of economists that would advocate it, monetarists or activists. (1) Policymakers are able to forecast the effects on real GNP of monetary policy; (2) an attempt to raise the money supply during a recession will do more harm than good; (3) the demand for money is stable; (4) reliance on flexible prices to eliminate high unemployment may require an excessive time delay.

15-4 Sources of Instability in Private Planned Spending

This section investigates the first plank in the monetarist platform, the claim that private spending is stable. We shall see that instability has often prevented stabilization policy from achieving its basic aim, to keep the actual unemployment rate equal to the natural rate of unemployment (U^N). To achieve this aim, real GNP should be kept equal to the economy's natural real GNP level—the amount that the economy can produce each year when its unemployment rate is kept equal to U^N.

How successfully has actual real GNP (Q) been kept equal to natural real GNP (Q^N)? The postwar record illustrated in Figure 15-2 is decidedly mixed. Although economic policy has prevented mass unemployment, and a repeat of the Great Depression, nevertheless Q has diverged repeatedly from Q^N, sometimes for many years in the same direction. Between 1958 and 1963 Q was continuously below Q^N, reaching shortfalls of 4 percent in the recessions of 1958 and 1961. On the other hand, between 1965 and 1969 the reverse was true. For five straight years Q overshot and remained 3 percent or more too high. The worst year of all was 1982, when Q dropped almost 10 percent below Q^N.

Government Spending

Three expenditure components that contributed to unstable actual output growth are illustrated in Figure 15-2. Monetarists correctly note that much of the postwar instability has resulted from uneven changes in real government expenditures on goods and services (G). The most notable episode of erratic growth occurred during the Korean War, when G increased by 82 percent in the interval 1950–53. The Vietnam War buildup caused another period of rapid growth, 23 percent between 1965 and 1968. On the other hand, G hardly grew at all between 1968 and 1982.

Activists protest any attempt by the monetarists to discredit stabilization policy by pointing to erratic growth in G in Figure 15-2. "Erratic G growth is just one of many reasons why we need activist stabilization policy," reply the activists. "Wartime bursts in defense spending result from political decisions, not economic ones, and it is the job of stabilization policy to recommend offsetting actions that will keep the wartime expenditures from causing total real GNP to overshoot Q^N. Tax increases and tight monetary policy are appropriate activist actions to be taken in wartime situations."

BOTH GOVERNMENT AND PRIVATE SPENDING CONTRIBUTED TO ECONOMIC
INSTABILITY IN THE POSTWAR ERA

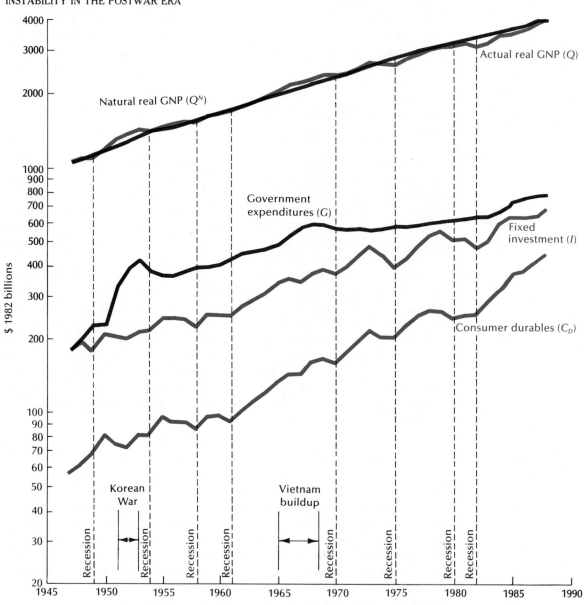

Figure 15-2 **Actual and Natural Real GNP and the Real Values of Government Spending,
Fixed Investment, and Consumer Durable Expenditures, 1946–88**

Fluctuations in government spending (*G*) were about as important as shifts in fixed
investment (*I*) and consumer durable expenditures (*C_D*) in contributing to
economic instability. The scale is logarithmic, so the steeper increases and
decreases in the *G, I,* and *C_D* lines than in the actual real GNP line indicate that the
three spending components were more unstable than total real spending. *(Sources:
Actual and natural real GNP, see Appendix A of this book; spending components (G,
I, C_D), U.S. Department of Commerce.)*

Private Spending

Activists then point to the behavior of the other two series plotted in Figure 15-2 fixed investment (I) and consumer purchases of durable goods (C_D), as evidence against plank 1 of the monetarist platform. Real private spending does not tend to grow steadily each year at 3 or 4 percent, but tends to exhibit periods of a few years of boom followed by several years of slump.

Business people who make investment decisions are not entirely to blame for the instability of private spending. There is very little difference in Figure 15-2 between the behavior of the fixed investment series (I) and that plotted directly below, consumer expenditures on durable goods. It is true, as monetarists may argue, that at least some of the fluctuations in I and C_D result from disturbances introduced by the government. For instance, controls on consumer credit held down C_D during the Korean War, and their elimination partly caused the 1955 spending boom.

Heart of the activist case. The instability of fixed investment and consumer durable spending lies at the heart of the activist case in favor of stabilization policy intervention. Short, sharp fluctuations in private planned spending would not be terribly serious if they lasted only six or nine months. But the behavior of I and C_D in Figure 15-2 indicates that periods of boom or bust tend to persist. Both I and C_D were weak between 1958 and 1961, both were strong through most of the 1960s, and both fluctuated widely in the 1970s and 1980s.

15-5 Money Demand Instability and Alternative Policy Targets

Plank 2 of the monetarist platform states that because private spending and the demand for money are stable, the velocity of money grows at a steady and predictable rate. This suggests that adherence to a strict rule (CGRR) for the growth rate of the money supply would create stable growth of nominal GNP. Activists dispute both points and deny, on the basis of the historical evidence in Figure 15-2, that private spending is stable; they also deny that the demand for money is stable. In this section we look first at the implications for monetary policy of unstable private spending and an unstable demand for money in our theoretical *IS-LM* model. Then we examine the historical behavior of velocity and, in particular, its erratic movements in the early 1980s.

Policy Targets in the *IS-LM* Model

We learned in Section 15-1 that the activist approach to stabilization policy involves the use of policy instruments to influence target or goal variables like the unemployment and inflation rates. In contrast, the monetarist approach based on a CGRR *makes the growth rate of the money supply the single target variable of monetary policy.* Figure 15-3 allows us to examine the consequences of "money supply targeting" in contrast with other approaches.

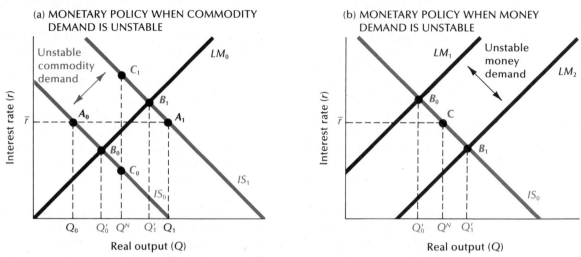

Figure 15-3   **Effects on Real Output of Alternative Policies That Stabilize the Interest Rate
or the Real Money Supply When Either Commodity Demand or Money
Demand Is Unstable**

In the left frame the demand for commodities is unstable, fluctuating between IS_0
and IS_1. A policy that maintains a fixed real money supply and a fixed LM_0 curve
leads to smaller fluctuations of output than an alternative policy that stabilizes the
interest rate at $\bar{r}$ *by shifting LM.* The contrary is true in the right frame, where the
demand for money is unstable. In this case a policy of stabilizing the interest rate
at $\bar{r}$ will keep real output more stable than an alternative policy that stabilizes the
real money supply. When the real money supply is held fixed, shifts in the *LM* curve
from LM_1 to LM_2 are caused by unstable money demand, causing output to fluctuate
between Q'_0 and Q'_1.

As in Chapters 4 and 5, Figure 15-3 illustrates the workings of the *IS-LM*
model on a diagram that plots the interest rate on the vertical axis and the
level of real output on the horizontal axis. As in Chapters 4 and 5, we assume that the expected inflation rate is zero, so that the nominal and real
interest rates are the same; both are labeled simply as the "interest rate" on
the vertical axis. The assumed fixity of the price level is an acceptable simplification if long-term wage and price contracts in the real world limit the
flexibility of the price level in the short run, so that the shifts in the *IS* or
LM curves of Figure 15-3 mainly influence the level of real output in the first
few months or quarters after the shift.

The *IS* curve shows all the combinations of the interest rate and real
output that maintain equilibrium in the commodity market, while the *LM*
curve shows the combinations that maintain equilibrium in the money market. The position of the *IS* curve can be shifted by changes in business and
consumer optimism, by changes in net exports, and by changes in govern-

ment spending and tax rates. When *commodity demand is unstable* because of swings in optimism, net exports, or government policy, the *IS* curve shifts back and forth as shown in the left-hand frame of Figure 15-3. The position of the *LM* curve can be shifted by a change in the real money supply; the LM_0 curve in the left-hand frame assumes that the real money supply is fixed.[10]

Implications of unstable commodity demand. William Poole of Brown University first popularized the use of the *IS-LM* model to compare targeting of the money supply with the alternative of targeting the interest rate.[11] Unstable commodity demand, shown by the shifting *IS* curve in the left-hand frame of Figure 15-3, calls into question the monetarist emphasis on achieving a constant growth rate of the money supply. When the real money supply is held constant and the *LM* curve remains fixed at LM_0, the economy moves back and forth between positions B_0 and B_1 in the left-hand frame, and real output moves over the limited range between Q_0' and Q_1'.

Monetarists correctly argue that fixing the *LM* curve by targeting the money supply is superior to a policy of maintaining stable interest rates. When commodity demand is high (as along IS_1), a stable-interest-rate policy means that the real money supply must be allowed to rise to prevent the interest rate from increasing. The Federal Reserve must increase the money supply to "accommodate" the additional demand for money that occurs when commodity demand is high. The stable-interest-rate policy causes the economy to fluctuate between points A_0 and A_1, and it allows real output to vary over the range between Q_0 and Q_1.

Instead of targeting interest rates or following the monetarist prescription of targeting the money supply, an alternative approach for the Fed would be to target real GNP itself. The policy of stabilizing real output directly is illustrated in the left-hand frame of Figure 15-3 by the points C_0 and C_1. Any fluctuations in commodity demand would have to be offset by fluctuations in the supply of money in the *opposite* direction. If the *LM* curve can be promptly moved in the opposite direction when an unstable demand causes a shift in the *IS* curve, then the economy could remain at natural real GNP (Q^N). And, as we learned in Chapters 9 and 10, maintenance of the economy at Q^N is consistent with steady inflation in the absence of supply shocks.

The analysis with unstable money demand. The right-hand frame of Figure 15-3 assumes that commodity demand is fixed, so that the *IS* curve remains fixed at IS_0. But, in opposition to plank 2 of the monetarist platform, the demand for money is assumed to be unstable. Although we continue to assume that the real money supply is fixed, *an unstable demand for money causes the LM curve to move about unpredictably between LM_1 and LM_2 despite the fixity of the money supply.* The constant-money-supply policy recommended by the monetarists leads to fluctuations in the economy between

---

[10]A fixed real money supply *(M/P)* and a fixed *LM* curve can be achieved either with a constant nominal money supply *(M)* and a fixed price level *(P)* or with the money supply growing at the same rate as the price level *(m = p)*.

[11]William Poole, "Optimal Choice of Monetary Policy Instruments in a Simple Stochastic Macro Model," *Quarterly Journal of Economics,* vol. 84 (May 1970), pp. 197–216. A little-known earlier reference is M.L. Burstein, *Economic Theory* (New York: Wiley, 1966), Chapter 13.

points B_0 and B_1, with output varying between Q_0' and Q_1'. A superior policy is to change the money supply in order to maintain a constant interest rate. When the demand for money grows, the interest rate is prevented from rising by the provision of a larger money supply, and vice versa. This constant-interest-rate policy keeps the economy pinned to point C, with a fixed interest rate $\bar{r}$ and a fixed output level Q^N. In this diagram, an interest rate target and a natural real GNP (Q^N) target amount to the same thing.

The Case for a GNP Target

In the left-hand frame of Figure 15-3, an unstable demand for commodities makes a real GNP target superior to a money-supply target, which in turn is superior to an interest-rate target. In the right-hand frame, with an unstable demand for money, a real GNP and interest rate target are the same, and both are superior to a money-supply target. Since activists disagree with both planks 1 and 2 of the monetarist platform, they predict instability in both commodity and money demand, which makes a real GNP target superior to an interest rate target.

In a world with no supply shocks of the types we studied in Chapter 10 (such as sharp changes in the price of oil), there would be no difference between real GNP targeting that attempted to maintain actual real GNP at the level of natural real GNP (Q^N) and nominal GNP targeting that fixed the growth rate of nominal GNP. If the economy were initially operating at Q^N, with excess nominal GNP growth ($y - q^N$) equal to the rate of inflation, a policy of maintaining $Q = Q^N$ would be the same as maintaining nominal GNP growth equal to the present inflation rate plus the growth rate of natural real GNP ($y = p + q^N$).

Supply shocks, however, make nominal GNP targeting different from real GNP targeting. A policy that fixes the growth rate of nominal GNP would, in the aftermath of an adverse supply shock, allow real GNP to fall below natural real GNP, as at point L in Figure 10-5. In contrast, a policy of maintaining $Q = Q^N$ would require an accommodating monetary policy and an acceleration of nominal GNP growth in response to an adverse supply shock. Because of the likelihood that accommodation of an adverse supply shock would lead to a permanent acceleration of inflation, many activists recommend that the Fed target nominal GNP growth rather than the level or growth rate of real GNP.

Velocity Falls Off the Rails in the 1980s

We have already observed evidence in Figure 15-2 regarding the historical fluctuations in the demand for particular types of commodities; investment goods, consumer durables, and government spending. Figure 15-4 exhibits the historical record on the velocity of money (the $M1$ concept) in the period since 1970. For plank 2 of the monetarist platform to be valid, velocity growth should be stable so that a fixed growth rate of the money supply implies a fixed growth rate of nominal GNP. Why? Velocity (V) is defined as

Figure 15-4

The Velocity of the Money Supply (*M1*), 1970–88

Velocity is defined as nominal GNP divided by the money supply. Between 1970 and 1980 velocity grew at 3.4 percent per year. Therefore, monetarists recommended that a constant-growth-rate rule for the money supply be set at 3.4 percentage points below the desired growth rate of nominal GNP. However, velocity departed radically from its 1970–80 trend after 1980, and actually declined through 1987 at an erratic rate.

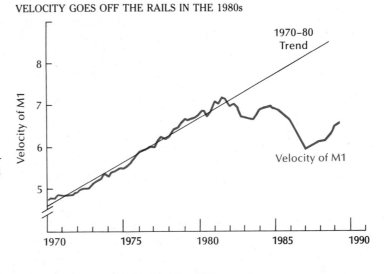

VELOCITY GOES OFF THE RAILS IN THE 1980s

nominal GNP (*Y*) divided by the money supply (*M^s*), so that stable growth in *V* and *M* would imply stable growth in *Y*. With such stability, money supply targeting and nominal GNP targeting would amount to the same thing.

However, after growing steadily at an average annual rate of 3.4 percent between 1970 and 1980, velocity "fell off the rails" in the 1980s. Not only did velocity stop growing, but it fell rapidly in 1982–83 and again in 1985–86. If the Federal Reserve had maintained a CGRR for the money supply in 1982–83 and 1985–86 instead of allowing double-digit growth in the money supply (as it did), then nominal GNP growth would have been so weak in those years that real GNP would have been much lower and unemployment much higher than the actual figures.

A key issue for GNP targeting: Persistence of shocks. We shall return to the velocity shifts of the 1980s when we study the demand for money in more detail in Chapter 16. For now, we are interested in the implications of unstable money demand for the controversy between the monetarists and activists. The preference for GNP targeting (either real or nominal) by activists raises a key question: Are the unstable swings in commodity and money demand long-lasting or short-lived? If the swings last for only a quarter, then there is not enough time for them to be offset by changes in the money supply. But if the swings last for several quarters or several years, there is ample time for shifts in the money supply to stabilize real GNP. The feasibility of a monetary policy that targets GNP thus hinges on the duration of swings in the demand for commodities and the demand for money. Monetarists doubt that the Fed can change the money supply rapidly enough to stabilize rather than destabilize real GNP, whereas activists optimistically believe that such stabilizing actions are possible.

SELF-TEST Using the *IS-LM* model analysis of Figure 15-3, which neglects both lags and inflation, rank three types of policies (stable money supply, stable interest rate, countercyclical money supply) by their ability to maintain stable real GNP under two sets of circumstances: (1) unstable commodity demand and (2) unstable demand for money. In each case, rank first the policy that is most likely to maintain stable output, then the next best policy, and then the third best.

15-6   CASE STUDY: The Performance of U.S. Forecasters Since 1970

The **lag of monetary policy** is the time delay between policy changes by the Fed and the resulting response of private spending.

There are ample reasons for monetarists to question the feasibility of GNP targeting. Monetarists fault the activists for making overly optimistic assumptions about the ability of forecasters to foresee future demand and supply disturbances. The ability to look into the future is required by the **lag of monetary policy.** An increase in the money supply in December 1989 may not have its main influence on spending until the fall of 1990. Thus *policymakers must be able to look ahead to determine whether private demand in the fall of 1990 is likely to be too high or too low.*

In this section we learn that U.S. forecasters have experienced some dramatic failures since 1970, as illustrated in Figure 15-5. The diagram compares the actual growth rate of nominal GNP (y), real GNP (q), and the GNP price deflator (p) with the change predicted one year in advance of the illustrated date by five well-known forecasting organizations. Most of these forecasters sell their forecasts to business firms and have every incentive to take account of all relevant factors that might affect the economy in the coming year.

As an example, in the upper left corner of the diagram we see that in the year ending in the second quarter of 1971 (1971:Q2) nominal GNP ac-

Figure 15-5   **Actual and Predicted Values of the Unemployment Rate (U) and of the Growth Rates of Nominal GNP (y), Real GNP (q), and the GNP Deflator (p), 1971–88**

For each of the four variables plotted, the pink areas show the periods when the actual value was higher than the predicted value, and the gray shading shows the periods when the actual value was lower than the predicted value. The most important forecasting errors were an underprediction of inflation throughout 1973 and 1974, and of nominal and real GNP in 1982. Note that between 1973 and 1976 most of the errors in forecasting inflation caused errors in forecasting real output in the opposite direction. *(Source: Errors are from Stephen S. McNees, "Which Forecast Should You Use?"* New England Economic Review *(July/August 1985), Table 1, p. 37, updated with supplementary data supplied by McNees, who calculated the median error from the four-quarter-ahead forecasts of these five forecasters: (1) Data Resources, Inc., (2) Chase Econometric Associates, Inc., (3) the MAPCAST group at the General Electric Company, (4) the Wharton Econometric Forecasting Associates, Inc., and (5) the median forecast from a survey conducted by the American Statistical Association and the National Bureau of Economic Research.)*

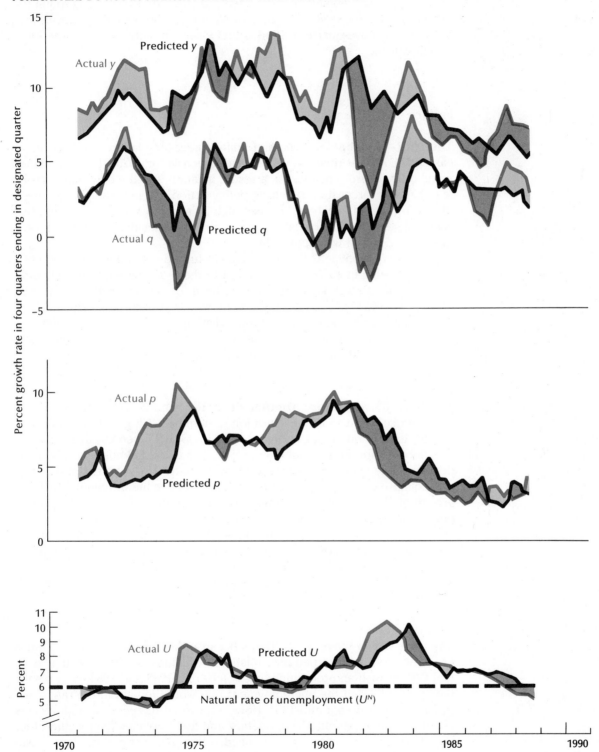

tually increased 8.5 percent (the red actual y line), whereas the median forecast made one year earlier in 1970:Q2 had been for an increase of 6.9 percent (this is the value for predicted y plotted for 1971:Q2). Through the middle of 1972 forecasts of nominal GNP growth (y) were fairly accurate, but then for a five-quarter period actual y substantially exceeded the forecasted values.

Failure of Forecasting

The 1974–75 debacle.   The first major forecasting failure occurred in early 1974. At that time the year-ahead forecasts for 1975:Q1 overpredicted y and q by record amounts. As a result, inflation was the only major problem that was forecast as requiring policy action. Unemployment was predicted to rise only slightly. Because high inflation was predicted, the forecasts suggested to policymakers that restraint rather than stimulation of aggregate demand was appropriate.

Yet what happened? Real GNP growth turned out to be -3.8 percent in the year ending in 1975:Q1, as opposed to the $+2.2$ percent forecast, and unemployment soared during that year from 5.0 percent in 1974:Q1 to 8.9 percent in 1975:Q2. Although there is no way to prevent a supply shock from raising both unemployment and inflation simultaneously, activist economists think in retrospect that some policy stimulus should have been applied in the last half of 1974 and early 1975.

The 1981–82 recession: Another debacle.   The 1981–82 recession was characterized by a sharp deceleration in nominal GNP growth from a four-quarter growth rate of 13.4 percent in 1981:Q3 to 2.6 percent in 1982:Q3. The deceleration in nominal GNP growth was caused almost entirely by a decline in the velocity of $M1$, as we saw in Figure 15-4. Forecasters missed this collapse of velocity almost entirely. Of the decline in nominal GNP growth of 10.8 percentage points, forecasters predicted only 2.1 percentage points four quarters in advance. This error was split between real GNP growth and inflation. This record implies that the Federal Reserve Board received no early warning signals from forecasters in 1981 that a deep recession lay ahead. Interest rates were allowed to stay too high for too long in 1981 and early 1982 because forecasters took such an unrealistically optimistic view of the economy.

The post-1982 recovery.   Perhaps because they had been overly optimistic, forecasters then turned pessimistic, forecasting too little nominal and real GNP growth and too much inflation during 1983 and 1984. As a result, they predicted that the unemployment rate would remain in the range of 9 to 10 percent through mid-1984. However, even if the pessimistic forecasts resulted in more stimulative monetary and fiscal policies than would otherwise have occurred, the economy needed this policy stimulus, since U was so far above U^N during the first part of the post-1982 recovery. Later, in 1988, forecasters again underestimated the strength of the economy.

Reasons for Forecasting Errors

Why did forecasting errors occur? No matter how sophisticated their forecasting models, economists must still make guesses on two key ingredients of any forecast.

1. First, they must guess the settings of the various policy instruments. Often forecasters make several forecasts: first an initial control forecast that assumes that policy remains unchanged, then additional forecasts that vary these policy assumptions in specified ways.

2. Second, they must guess the values of the nonpolicy exogenous variables. Among these, as depicted in Figure 15-1, are export demand, supply shocks, and any special aspects of business and consumer optimism that might invalidate the consumption function and investment function of the forecasting model.

There also must be a structural model that ties together the structural exogenous variables, the policy instruments, and target variables. In the first part of this book we developed a simple version of such a model. Modern forecasting uses **econometric models** that estimate the values of the parameters by statistical study on computers of past episodes.

An **econometric model** is a set of equations having statistically estimated parameters that can be solved to provide forecasts under alternative assumptions about policy instruments and nonpolicy exogenous variables.

Why forecasts were so far off. In addition to the two guesses listed above, econometric models must estimate numerical values for a large number of parameters: the response of money demand to changes in the interest rate and income (the *LM* curve); the response of consumption spending to changes in disposable income and wealth and the response of investment to changes in output and various financial variables (the *IS* curve); the response of inflation to real GNP given expected inflation (the *SP* curve); and other relationships.

Actual mistakes made by forecasters in Figure 15-5 reflect each of these elements:

1. Forecasters have failed to guess accurately the future behavior of the main instrument of monetary policy, the growth rate of the money supply.

2. Nonpolicy exogenous variables contributed the most to forecasting errors. These included the supply shocks of 1974 that caused an unforeseen acceleration of inflation and deceleration of real GNP.

3. The econometric models were flawed. An important weakness of the models is that, inevitably, their parameter estimates are based on a long historical period over which conditions may have changed.

Implications for activism. The forecasting errors in 1974–75 and 1982–83 raise serious doubts about the activist position. As long as there are lags in the effect of monetary policy, then forecasting is necessary to determine what the condition of the economy will be in future months when the economy reacts to monetary policy. Errors in forecasting imply that in some historical episodes, policymakers were not able to predict instability in the growth rates of nominal or real GNP. In response, activists note that forecasters can usually predict the multi-year deviations of actual unemployment (U) from the natural unemployment rate (U^N) with accuracy, as shown in the bottom frame in Figure 15-5.

15-7 Other Flaws in the Activist Case: Uncertainty, Lags, and the Time Horizon

Chapters 3–5 developed a set of multiplier formulas indicating the size of the change in real GNP that would result from a change in a policy instrument, such as tax rates, government spending, or the money supply. But the *IS-LM* models summarized in those chapters were very simple. This section shows that we do not know nearly as much about the values of the multipliers as the *IS-LM* model assumes.

Also, in the early chapters of this book we simplified the exposition of income determination by ignoring the time lag between changes in policy instruments and the resulting effect on the target variables. An essential part of the monetarist case against activism is that the lags in the effects of policy changes are likely to be both long and variable.[12]

Multiplier Uncertainty

Dynamic multipliers are the amount by which output is raised during each of several time periods after a $1 increase in autonomous spending.

Figure 15-6 illustrates several sets of **dynamic multipliers** calculated from various econometric models. The horizontal axis is successive quarters after the policy change. For each model the graph shows the cumulative total change in real GNP (Q) caused by a sustained $1 billion increase in real government spending. Because government spending is part of GNP, the multiplier would be exactly 1.0 if there were no stimulus at all to consumption or investment spending in the initial quarter of the increased government spending. For instance, the MPS model yields a multiplier that starts out only a bit above 1.0. Then the MPS multiplier rises to a peak of about 2.4 after seven quarters, reflecting the stimulus of higher income to both consumption and investment. Later, however, the multiplier begins to fall.

What should policymakers do if they predict that the economy needs $15 billion of stimulus to aggregate demand four quarters from now because unemployment is forecast to be higher than desired at that time? The models leave policymakers highly uncertain about the size of the policy stimulus needed. Multipliers for other policy instruments not shown in Figure 15-6 also indicate considerable divergence between the econometric models. Though **multiplier uncertainty** does not make activist policy intervention impossible, it does require that policymakers be conservative in setting their instruments, taking a smaller action than that dictated by the average multiplier.[13]

Multiplier uncertainty concerns the lack of firm knowledge regarding the change in output caused by a change in a policy instrument.

Long Lags

The "humped" multiplier pattern, as yielded by the MPS model in Figure 15-6, raises another problem. The effects of a stimulative policy may linger

---

[12]The most extensive discussion of the monetarist position is Milton Friedman, "The Lag in Effect of Monetary Policy," *Journal of Political Economy,* vol. 69 (October 1961), reprinted in *The Optimum Quantity of Money and Other Essays* (Chicago: Aldine, 1969), pp. 237–260.

[13]See William Brainard, "Uncertainty and the Effectiveness of Policy," *American Economic Review,* vol. 57 (May 1967), pp. 411–425. Brainard's formula suggests that the expected gap between actual and target GNP should be closed by only a fraction of the gap, but that fraction depends on correlations that we are most unlikely to know. An earlier analysis is Milton Friedman, "The Effects of a Full-Employment Policy on Economic Stability: A Formal Analysis," *Essays in Positive Economics* (Chicago: University of Chicago Press, 1953), pp. 117–132.

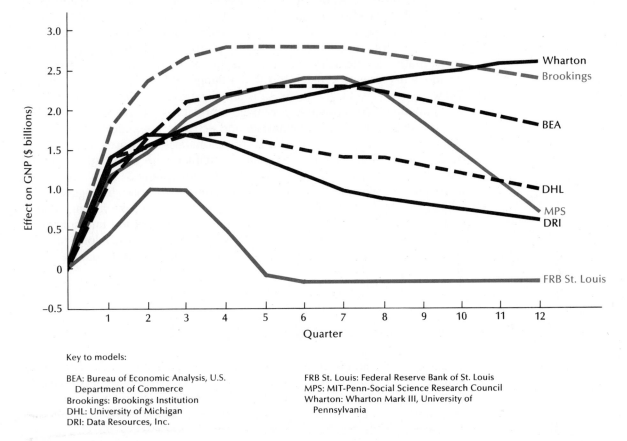

Key to models:

BEA: Bureau of Economic Analysis, U.S.
    Department of Commerce
Brookings: Brookings Institution
DHL: University of Michigan
DRI: Data Resources, Inc.

FRB St. Louis: Federal Reserve Bank of St. Louis
MPS: MIT-Penn-Social Science Research Council
Wharton: Wharton Mark III, University of
    Pennsylvania

Figure 15-6   **Change in Real GNP Induced by a Permanent $1 Billion Increase in Real Government Nondefense Spending: Estimates of Seven Econometric Models**

Each line corresponds to the estimate of a different econometric model. For instance, the line labeled Brookings indicates that, according to the Brookings model, a $1 billion increase in real government nondefense spending causes an increase in real GNP by $1.8 billion in the first quarter, $2.4 billion in the second quarter, and so on. A peak is reached at $2.8 billion in quarters 4–7, after which the impact declines. *(Source: Gary Fromm and Lawrence R. Klein, "A Comparison of Eleven Econometric Models of the United States,"* American Economic Review, *vol. 63 (May 1973), Table 5, p. 391.)*

long after they are wanted or needed. An anticipated shortfall of aggregate demand next quarter may be followed by an anticipated excess in subsequent quarters. A policy stimulus now may boost demand by only a small amount next quarter, when the stimulus is needed. But it may boost demand by a great deal five to eight quarters from now, *when the stimulus is not desirable and in fact restraint is required.*

Activism, Politics, and the Time Horizon

So far, the proponents of activism concede that the artificial assumptions of the activists' paradise are unrealistic. But they argue that forecasting uncertainty, multiplier uncertainty, lags, and costs and imprecision in the setting of policy instruments call for caution in setting stabilization policy, not its outright abandonment. They believe the monetarist emphasis on a fixed rule for monetary growth creates too much danger that the economy will drift away from policy targets over substantial periods of time, as in 1981–82 when nominal GNP growth experienced a precipitous decline.

The debate between monetarists and activists continues over the relationship between planks 3 and 4 of the monetarist platform. The inherent obstacles to an effective activist policy combined with the political realities that often cause irrational government behavior (plank 3) lead monetarists to prefer to leave the private economy alone. Even though sluggish price adjustment may imply that the private economy may take a long time to correct deviations of actual unemployment from the natural unemployment rate, monetarists are willing to wait. They prefer to emphasize long-run consequences and to deemphasize short-run flaws in the performance of the economy (plank 4).

15-8 The New Classical Attack on Policy Activism

In Chapter 7 we first introduced new classical macroeconomics, abbreviated here as NCM.[14] One of the foundations of new classical macroeconomics is the concept of rational expectations, the hypothesis that people make the best forecasts they can with the available data. Therefore, the new classical macroeconomists *place much more emphasis than either activists or monetarists on the public's expectations regarding future policy.* This leads to a sharp distinction between **rigid policy rules, feedback policy rules,** and **discretionary policy.** Adherence by policymakers to either a rigid rule or a feedback rule allows the public to form expectations about the future outcome of macroeconomic variables. The only difference is that a rigid rule, for instance a CGRR for the money supply, allows no change at all in a policy instrument. In contrast, a feedback rule raises the growth rate of the money supply by a specified amount in response to an increase in unemployment, or reduces the growth rate of the money supply in response to an increase in the inflation rate. Even if policymakers do not respond to changes in unemployment or inflation by a specific and preannounced formula, they *systematically* raise monetary growth when the unemployment

A **rigid rule** for policy sets a key policy instrument at a fixed value, as in a constant-growth-rate rule for the money supply.

A **feedback rule** sets stabilization policy to respond in a regular way to a macroeconomic event, like an increase in unemployment or inflation.

Discretionary policy treats each macroeconomic episode as a unique event, without any attempt to respond in the same way from one episode to another.

[14]In Chapter 7 we learned that there are two types of NCM models, that developed by Lucas ("Mark I") and the "Mark II" real business cycle models developed by Edward Prescott. Since the "Mark II" version of NCM holds that the *entire* cause of business-cycle fluctuations consists of supply shocks, and because it does not include money or prices in its models, it has no role in stabilization policy at all. Actual and natural output are always the same. Hence the discussion in the text refers only to the "Mark I" Lucas information-barrier version of the NCM.

rate rises as we learned in Chapter 7. The most dramatic NCM claim is that a feedback policy rule for the money supply is ineffective and that *activism is futile.*

The NCM approach leaves no room for a feedback policy rule to be effective. Incorrect expectations cannot cause Q to deviate from Q^N *if the policymaker announces the feedback rule in advance.* If the public *knows* that an increase in the money supply raises the price level, then any increase in the money supply called for by a feedback rule will be anticipated by the public, and a feedback rule for monetary policy must be ineffective.

Disinflation, Credibility, and Time Inconsistency

The NCM also implies *painless disinflation.* If the Federal Reserve Board announces a new path of monetary growth consistent with zero inflation instead of 10 percent inflation the public instantly adjusts its expectations, according to the NCM, and the *actual* inflation rate instantly slows down to zero without the need for a recession in real GNP. However, the public must *believe* that the Fed will actually carry out the new disinflationary monetary policy. For this reason, in their writings the new classical economists place a strong emphasis on **policy credibility.** If the policy lacks credibility, then the public does not believe that the Fed will maintain the new lower growth rate path and will refuse to adjust its expectations of inflation. Without such an adjustment of expectations, then any *actual* slowdown in monetary growth created by the Fed (which the public does not believe will continue) will lead to a recession in Q below Q^N.

Policy credibility is the belief by the public that the policymakers will actually carry out an announced policy.

Related to the need for credibility is the problem of **time inconsistency** in macroeconomic policy.[15] Once a policy of disinflation has become "credible" and the public has lowered its expectations of inflation, policymakers have the temptation to deviate from the preannounced policy. For instance, if policymakers deviate by raising the rate of monetary growth, and create an inflationary surprise, Q will rise above Q^N. If the policymaker can engineer such an increase in Q (and the accompanying reduction in the unemployment rate) immediately before an election, the incumbent is more likely to be reelected. If people recognize the problem of time inconsistency, that is, the temptation of policymakers to deviate from presently announced policies, then it will be much harder for *any* preannounced policy to remain credible.

Time inconsistency describes the temptations of policymakers to deviate from a credible policy once it is announced.

The time inconsistency problem, identified by proponents of NCM, contributes useful insights into the policy debate. First, disinflation is harder to achieve because the public will recognize that the Fed has a temptation to deviate from a disinflationary plan; the public will not find such a plan credible, thus worsening the recession that will result from the plan. Second, it helps explain why both monetarists and NCM advocates prefer rigid rules to

---

[15]The concept of time inconsistency was introduced in Finn Kydland and Edward Prescott, "Rules Rather Than Discretion: The Inconsistency of Optimal Plans," *Journal of Political Economy,* vol. 85 (June 1977), pp. 473–491.

feedback rules or discretion, since a rigid rule would tie the hands of the monetary policymaker and prevent any deviation from the rule brought about by the temptation of time inconsistency.

SELF-TEST   Are the following statements true or false? (1) For any given deceleration of nominal GNP, the recession will be shorter and less severe if the central bank possesses policy credibility with the public. (2) For any given deceleration of nominal GNP, the recession will be shorter and less severe if the public believes that the central bank's policy is subject to time inconsistency. (3) Policy credibility increases the merits of a "cold turkey" disinflation as compared to a policy of "living with inflation." (4) The possibility of time inconsistency strengthens the case of the activists against a constant-growth-rate rule of the money supply.

Supply Shocks and Disinflation in the NCM

The Friedman–Lucas NCM approach developed in Section 7-5 requires markets to clear continuously, and it relies entirely on incorrect expectations to explain departures of Q from Q^N. Yet in the real world, Q has departed from Q^N for years (a decade in the 1930s)—much longer than the month or two needed for individuals to obtain accurate information on the current price level.

Does the disinflation of the 1980s support or contradict NCM? Recall that NCM predicted that a credible disinflationary policy would stop inflation with much less recessionary pain than the activist economists believed. It is clear from the large increase in unemployment (the bottom frame of Figure 15-5) that the 1981–86 disinflation was not painless. But NCM advocates can find some solace in the prediction errors of Figure 15-5, for the unexpected drop in real GNP growth shown in the top frame is entirely attributable to *an unexpected decline in nominal GNP growth*. Thus, the public did not anticipate the decline in nominal GNP growth engineered by the Federal Reserve to stop inflation, which indicates that the Fed's disinflation policy *was not credible*.

Summary: Activism Versus the New Classical Macroeconomics

The NCM proponents stress the inability of monetary feedback rules to affect real GNP, and urge instead the same rigid CGRR approach to monetary policy advocated by the monetarists. NCM proponents support a CGRR for the credibility that it would bring to monetary policy. If people expect the Federal Reserve to maintain a CGRR for the money supply, their expectations of the inflation rate will be stable. This will minimize expectational errors in prices and thereby the need for unnecessary movements of Q about Q^N.

Activists counter the NCM approach for the same reasons that they criticize the first two planks in the monetarist platform; activists interpret the historical evidence as demonstrating the instability of the demand for commodities and money. A CGRR, they feel, would condemn the economy to needless business cycles caused by long-lasting persistent shifts in the *IS* and *LM* curves. Further, activists believe that monetary policy actions have powerful effects, whether or not they are correctly anticipated by the public—as shown by the sharp recession of 1982 following the high interest rates of 1981.

Because the new Keynesian model stresses long-term wage and price contracts, monetary policymakers do not need to worry about establishing credibility, since sticky wages and prices make output and employment respond to actual movements in money and not "surprise" movements in money. Activists contend, therefore, that what matters for the economy is not what the Fed policymakers *say,* but what they *do.* Both NCM proponents and activists would agree, however, that policy credibility may be more important in nations without long-term contracts, and especially important when policymakers are trying to stop a hyperinflation (as in the examples of Bolivia and Israel in Chapter 11).

Shifts in the pendulum of ideas. Despite all the intellectual energy that had been invested in analyses of the NCM approach, it seemed to be losing rather than gaining adherents in the late 1980s. As usual, ideas followed the tide of economic events. The fatal flaw of the NCM approach seemed to be its inability to explain the persistence of output fluctuations within the context of the Friedman–Lucas market-clearing approach. Expectational errors seemed an implausibly weak reed on which to rest a theory of business cycles.

The tide was also shifting away from the monetarists, who had warned about an impending upsurge in inflation implied by double-digit monetary growth in 1982–83 and again in 1985–86. As the months went on, and inflation slowed down rather than speeded up, monetarists were forced to retreat from their predictions. Their approach had been undermined by instability in money demand, which broke the tight link between money supply and nominal GNP growth. Also, inflation remained low in 1985–86 because of beneficial supply shocks and the lingering role of high unemployment in 1982–83. The low rate of inflation in 1985–86 and subsequent acceleration in 1987–88 (when money growth slowed) seemed more consistent with the new Keynesian analysis based on long-term contracts and supply shocks, as developed in Chapters 8–10, than with the monetarist approach with its stress on an inexorable link between monetary growth and inflation.

SUMMARY

1. In earlier chapters we assumed that the growth of aggregate demand could be controlled precisely by the monetary and fiscal policymakers. We now recognize that in the real-world economy, policy shifts cannot control aggregate demand instantly or precisely.

2. There are several targets of stabilization pol-

icy, which necessitates the use of several policy instruments. The conditions required for activist policy intervention to be effective are quite stringent, including accurate forecasting, possession of powerful tools, absence of costs of changing policy instruments, and absence of political constraints on their use.

3. The monetarist-activist debate centers on

the location in the economy of the principal source of economic instability. Monetarists believe that the private economy is basically stable and that fixed policy rules are necessary to protect the economy from ill-conceived and poorly timed government actions that in the past have caused economic instability. In contrast, the activist group considers private spending and the demand for money to be the primary sources of instability and hence supports an activist government counter-cyclical policy to achieve economic stability.

4. Although they recognize the problems introduced by forecasting uncertainty, multiplier uncertainty, lags, and costs and imprecision in the setting of policy instruments, the proponents of activism nevertheless favor caution in setting stabilization

policy rather than its outright abandonment. Some monetarists admit that sluggish price adjustment may prolong the adjustment of the economy to insufficient or excess demand, but they are more interested in long-run consequences than short-run transition periods.

5. The new classical macroeconomics attacks the claim by activists that monetary policy has strong effects on real output. Advocates of NCM claim that a regular feedback rule would be ineffective and stress the need for policy credibility, preferably by establishing and sticking to the same constant-growth-rate rule for the money supply favored by monetarists. Activists counter that the new classical model cannot explain the persistence of output fluctuations away from the natural level of output.

CONCEPTS

demand disturbances
policy activism
monetarism
new classical macroeconomics
policy instruments
target variables
constant-growth-rate rule (CGRR)
permanent income hypothesis
lag of monetary policy

econometric model
dynamic multiplier
multiplier uncertainty
rigid rule
feedback rule
discretionary policy
policy credibility
time inconsistency

QUESTIONS

1. Why do most adherents of the new Keynesian model based on long-term wage and price agreements endorse an activist approach to stabilization policy? How would the monetarist argue against this position?

2. To the new classical macroeconomists, the monetarist-activist debate referred to in question 1 is irrelevant. Why?

3. The case for activist intervention in the economy would work best in a world which could be dubbed on "activist paradise." What are some of the characteristics of this world?

4. One way of describing the monetarist–activist debate is to compare the beliefs of each side re-

garding the self-correcting powers of the economy and the efficacy of stabilization policy. What does each side believe about these issues?

5. Why do the monetarists believe that the *IS* curve is relatively flat? How does the issue of the flatness of the *IS* curve fit into the monetarist platform?

6. Under the constant growth rate rule, the single target for the policymaker becomes the growth rate of the money supply. Does this statement suggest that monetarists are not concerned with the level of real output and employment?

7. Under what circumstances would interest rate targeting and GNP targeting lead to the same re-

sult? Under what circumstances would different results occur?

8. What problems do long and variable lags present to the policymaker? If lags are long and fixed (rather than long and variable), do any problems remain?

9. Distinguish between a rigid rule and a feedback rule. Give an example of each. Explain why the new classical macroeconomists argue that any use of feedback rules must be ineffective.

10. Both monetarists and new classical macroeconomists agree regarding the use of a constant growth rate rule (CGRR) approach to monetary policy. However, the two groups reach this conclusion for different reasons. Explain how the rationales for the CGRR differ for the two groups.

SELF-TEST ANSWERS

p. 459 (1) activist; (2) monetarist; (3) monetarist; (4) activist.

p. 466 Unstable commodity demand: countercyclical monetary policy (best), then stable money supply, then stable interest rates. Unstable money demand: countercyclical monetary policy and stable interest rates (tied), then stable money supply.

p. 474 (1) true; (2) false; (3) true; (4) false.

Financial Markets and the Demand for Money

Money is what the state says it is. The state claims the right not only to enforce the dictionary, but also to write the dictionary.

—*John Maynard Keynes, 1925*

16-1 Money in a World of Many Financial Assets and Liabilities

Monetary and fiscal policy are the two main tools of stabilization policy, the set of actions taken by the government to achieve stable economic growth and dampen business cycles. In the 1950s and 1960s Keynesian economists favored fiscal policy, particularly temporary changes in income tax rates, as the primary tool of stabilization policy. The monetarists disagreed, emphasizing monetary policy and recommending a constant-growth-rate rule (CGRR) for the money supply, as set down in plank 2 of the monetarist platform in Chapter 15.

Gradually in the last two decades monetary policy has emerged as the major tool of stabilization policy, at least in the United States. Policymakers have gradually realized that fiscal policy is severely flawed as a means of controlling the economy over the short run (a year or two). The flaws of fiscal policy arise because fiscal policy changes require debate in Congress, which can last a long and unpredictable amount of time, and because temporary income tax changes have small and unpredictable effects. Further, in the 1980s fiscal policy became caught up in an ideological and political battle over the size of the government, leading to a government deficit that, as we learned in Chapters 5 and 13, is without precedent in peacetime for its persistence year after year.[1] This political battle further discredited fiscal policy as a stabilization tool.

The emergence of monetary policy in the policy spotlight did not, however, give the monetarists the victory that they expected. As we learned in the last chapter, rigid control of the money supply does not lead to rigid

---

[1] Nations with differing political institutions than in the United States may still be able to use fiscal policy as a tool of stabilization policy. For instance, in the United Kingdom the Chancellor of the Exchequer (equivalent of the U.S. Secretary of the Treasury) gives an annual budget speech in mid-March in which he announces changes in tax rates that go into effect the very day he speaks.

control of nominal GNP when the demand for money is unstable. With an unstable demand for money, the Federal Reserve will achieve tighter control over nominal GNP with an interest-rate target than with a money-supply target. And, indeed, it was the Federal Reserve's emphasis after 1982 on controlling interest rates that helps explain the success of monetary policy in achieving the long economic expansion of the 1980s.

The stability of the demand for money is central to the conduct of monetary policy. Thus in this chapter we study the demand for money. We begin by asking: What is money and why is it held? We shall see that the process of **financial deregulation** has allowed more and more assets to serve as money. This creates a serious problem in defining what the money supply actually is in the United States—and in stabilizing its demand. It also means that we cannot limit our discussion to money alone.

Since money is just one of many assets in **financial markets,** our objective is to study the demand for money in the context of the financial market as a whole. Thus we define the specific role of money by examining the flow of funds through financial markets.

We then turn to the major theories of the demand for money. These theories explain why the demand for money is related to income, the interest rate, and other variables, and why the demand for money appears to be stable at some times and unstable at other times. Then we conclude the chapter by learning how the deregulation of financial markets contributed to the volatility of interest rates in the 1980s.

Financial deregulation occurred in the United States in the late 1970s and early 1980s, allowing financial institutions to offer many new types of assets offering both interest payments and check-writing privileges.

Financial markets are organized exchanges where securities and financial instruments are bought and sold.

PUZZLE 4: WHY WERE INTEREST RATES IN THE 1980s HIGHER THAN EVER BEFORE?

16-2   Money and Financial Markets

Some economic units, like Sam Spendthrift in Chapter 11, spend more than they earn and need to borrow funds. Others, like Pete Puritan, earn more than they spend and need a place to keep their savings. Financial markets and **financial intermediaries** perform the essential function of channeling funds from those with surplus funds (savers) to those in need of funds (borrowers).

Financial intermediaries make loans to borrowers and obtain funds from savers, usually by accepting deposits.

Reasons for Saving and Borrowing

Because businesses cannot operate without borrowed funds, efficient financial markets that allow the exchange of funds between savers and borrowers are essential. A newly opened Burger King needs funds for its building and equipment before it can earn a single dollar selling hamburgers. A new airline must borrow to purchase a plane before it can fly a single passenger. Even long-established businesses like the Boeing Aircraft Company may need to borrow if a surge of orders creates a temporary need for cash to buy materials and components. And farmers frequently borrow money in the spring to purchase seed and fertilizer, repaying the loans when the crops are sold in the fall.

Whereas the business sector is a net borrower, the household sector is a net saver. Individuals save for many reasons, to provide funds for their retirement or their children's education, or simply for a "rainy day." Many people save and borrow at the same time, setting funds aside for long-term needs like retirement while borrowing funds to purchase their car, their house, and other goods and services. The total saving of the household sector, however, greatly exceeds its borrowing.

What about the other two major economic units, the government and the foreign sector? The "twin deficits" that we have emphasized throughout this book represent the unprecedented succession of federal budget deficits and foreign trade deficits that occurred in the 1980s. We have gotten used to thinking of the government sector and foreign sector as perennial net borrowers; historically, however, each sector has alternated between saving and borrowing.

Because borrowers have profitable uses for borrowed funds, they are willing to pay interest on them. And savers are happy to save when the interest they receive exceeds the benefit they would receive by spending the funds immediately. Thus fluctuations in the interest rate help create an equilibrium between the funds available from savers and those demanded by borrowers. And the Fed, through its control of monetary policy, can influence interest rates by its control over the creation of currency and bank reserves.

Financial Institutions and Financial Markets

Funds are channeled from savers to borrowers either directly or indirectly. The direct channel is through financial markets, exchanges where securities or financial instruments are bought and sold. Financial markets provide direct finance, because borrowers issue securities directly to savers. The securities, for example, General Motors stock or commercial paper, are a liability or debt of the issuer (General Motors) and an asset of the security holder.

The indirect channel operates through financial intermediaries. These are institutions, such as Citicorp Savings, that issue liabilities in their own name. The intermediaries balance their liabilities, say, a savings account held by Pete Puritan, with assets, say, a loan to Sam Spendthrift.

What determines whether savers channel their funds through financial markets and intermediaries? The simple answer is that savers are only willing to purchase securities through the direct channel, via financial markets, from borrowers large enough to have established a reputation for paying back borrowed money. Most large business firms and units of government issue securities directly through financial markets. But most individuals cannot do so because they have not established a reputation, and it is too costly for individual savers to research the credit-worthiness of every other individual in the country (or the world). Pete Puritan is happy to entrust his savings to Citicorp Savings, but he is not willing to accept an I.O.U. scribbled out by Sam Spendthrift.

Financial intermediaries function by *spreading risk* and by *collecting information efficiently*. Thus Citicorp makes loans to many borrowers, only a small fraction of which will fail to repay their loans. Citicorp sets aside a contingency fund to cover the losses from borrowers who do not repay and adds the cost of this fund to the rates charged to borrowers. Citicorp is large enough to hire specialists to assess credit risks, that is, to assess the likelihood that prospective borrowers will repay their loans. Further, groups of financial intermediaries can band together and support credit information agencies to collect this information even more efficiently. Thus it is less risky for Citicorp to lend to Sam than for Pete to use all of his savings to buy Sam's I.O.U.

Figure 16-1 illustrates the role of financial markets and institutions. The gray box on the left represents savers, and the gray box on the right represents borrowers. The upper pink box represents the financial intermediaries, and the lower pink box, the financial markets. The red lines connecting the boxes indicate the flows of funds from savers to borrowers. Notice that financial intermediaries not only provide funds directly to borrowers (a loan to Sam) but also purchase financial-market instruments. Banks and other intermediaries hold billions of securities, mostly issued by the government, in addition to loans granted directly to borrowers.

Figure 16-1
The Role of Financial Intermediaries and Financial Markets

Shown on the left are the savers, any economic unit with surplus funds. These funds can be held as currency, deposited in a financial intermediary, or used to purchase a money-market instrument or capital-market instrument in the financial markets. Financial intermediaries both purchase financial-market instruments and lend directly to borrowers. So borrowers have two sources of funds, loans from intermediaries and funds that come from issuing financial-market instruments.

HOW FUNDS FLOW FROM SAVERS TO BORROWERS

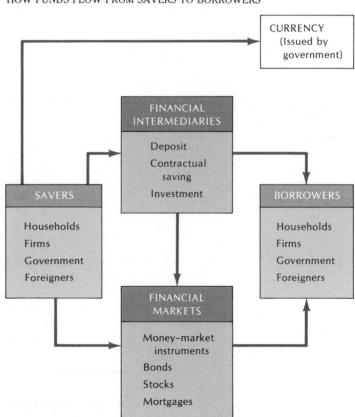

Where Money Fits In

Money includes currency and certain types of checkable deposits, that is, deposits of funds at financial intermediaries on which checks can be written. Currency is issued by the government and held directly by savers. It is shown in the upper right-hand corner of Figure 16-1 as a separate category, since it is neither issued by financial intermediaries nor traded on financial markets. It is a liability of the government, which can finance its deficit either by printing currency (like $20 bills) or by printing and selling government bonds. Both are considered borrowing by the government; the main difference is that the government pays interest on bonds but not on currency.

Money also consists of certain types of checkable deposits issued by financial intermediaries, mainly banks and savings institutions. Financial intermediaries include deposit institutions, contractual saving institutions, and investment institutions. We will learn later that one definition of the money supply ($M1$) includes only certain deposits issued by deposit institutions, while other definitions, for instance $M2$, also include money-market mutual funds, which are liabilities of investment institutions.

In short, "money" consists of currency and other items, but those other items do not correspond neatly to the distinction between financial institutions and financial markets illustrated in Figure 16-1. There are numerous definitions of "the money supply" in the United States, and some, but not all, liabilities of financial institutions are included in one or another definition of money.

Categories of Financial Institutions and Instruments

Table 16-1 displays the size and variety of U.S. financial intermediaries and instruments. Shown in the top half are three main categories of intermediaries; these correspond to the three categories indicated in the top pink box in Figure 16-1. Shown in the bottom half are financial market instruments corresponding to the bottom pink box in Figure 16-1. In general, financial deregulation and innovation have greatly increased the variety of financial market instruments and reduced the importance of banks in comparison with other types of financial intermediaries. As we shall see, this complicates the control of the economy through monetary policy.

Depository institutions. Commercial banks comprise by far the largest category of depository financial intermediary. Commercial banks issue deposits, both checkable and savings, hold government securities, and grant a wide variety of loans, including home mortgages, installment loans, and credit cards. Savings and loan institutions (S&Ls), notorious for their many failures in the 1980s, traditionally have been required by regulation to concentrate on mortgage loans. Prior to financial deregulation in the 1980s, S&Ls could issue only saving deposits but now also issue checkable deposits. However, although S&Ls now engage in the same activities as commercial banks, they are often less secure. Their large holdings of long-term fixed-rate mortgages were granted many years ago at interest rates that cannot in some cases cover the costs of obtaining funds today. Mutual savings

Table 16-1 The Main Financial Intermediaries and Instruments

Type of financial intermediary	Value of assets, end of 1988, $ billions
Depository institutions	
Commercial banks	2409
Savings and loan associations	1350
Mutual savings banks	263
Credit unions	194
Contractual savings institutions	
Insurance companies	1566
Private pension funds	1123
State and local government retirement funds	609
Investment intermediaries	
Finance companies	488
Mutual funds (bonds and stocks)	475
Money market mutual funds	338

Financial Market Instruments	Amount outstanding, end of 1988 $ billions
Money market instruments	
Large-denomination negotiable certificates of deposit	593
Commercial paper	452
Federal funds and repurchase agreements	387
Eurodollars	102
Bankers acceptances	61
U.S. Treasury bills	414
Capital market instruments	
Corporate bonds	1234
U.S. government securities	1390
U.S. government agency securities	348
State and local government bonds	589
Corporate stocks (market value)	3594
Commercial and consumer loans	1473
Mortgages	3180

Sources: *Flow of Funds Accounts* (March 1989), *Federal Reserve Bulletin* (May 1989), and *Economic Report of the President* (January 1989).

Thrift institutions include two types of financial intermediaries, savings and loan institutions and mutual savings banks. They used to obtain most of their funds from savings deposits and made most of their loans in the form of mortgages, but in recent years have been allowed to become more like commercial banks.

banks are similar to S&Ls, except for their corporate structure, while credit union loans and deposits are usually limited to a specific group, such as employees of a particular firm. Together, S&Ls, mutual savings banks, and credit unions are called **thrift institutions.**

Contractual savings institutions. A primary form of saving for many households consists of contributions to retirement plans. Usually these contributions are deducted from the paycheck in a fixed amount previously determined as part of a written or unwritten "contract" between employer and employee. Thus retirement contributions and other forms of saving are called "contractual savings." Contractual savings institutions are the financial intermediaries, including insurance companies (particularly life insurance companies), private pension funds, and state and local government retirement funds, that receive contributions from households and pay out benefits upon retirement. These institutions tend to hold long-term assets like corporate bonds, corporate stock, and mortgages. The existence of contractual savings is important in our subsequent discussion of stabilization policy, which is less likely to influence decisions by households on how much to consume or to save when saving is mainly in contractual form.

Investment intermediaries. These intermediaries differ from banks in the types of assets they hold, the types of liabilities they owe, or both. Finance companies, like banks, make consumer loans but raise funds not from depositors but from the financial markets, especially through issuance of commercial paper. Mutual funds, like banks, raise funds from consumers but then invest these funds in stocks and corporate bonds. Closest to banks are money-market mutual funds, whose shareholders, like bank depositors, can write checks. However, these intermediaries mainly hold short-term financial-market instruments, whereas banks mainly hold commercial and consumer loans. Because their assets have very short maturities, money-market mutual funds can raise their rates faster than banks can in a period of rising short-term interest rates like 1988–89.

Financial Market Instruments

As shown in Figure 16-1, savers can purchase financial market instruments not only directly, but also indirectly through financial intermediaries like banks and money-market mutual funds. Thus not all financial market instruments provide a direct one-step channel of finance from savers to borrowers. Financial market instruments fall into two categories, **money-market instruments** and **capital-market instruments.** Money-market instruments have short maturities, usually less than one year, small fluctuations in price, and minimal risk. Capital-market instruments have longer maturities, larger fluctuations in price, and greater risk.

Money-market instruments are assets sold on financial markets that have short maturities, usually less than one year, small fluctuations in price, and minimal risk.

Capital-market instruments are assets sold on financial markets that have relatively long maturities, can experience large fluctuations in price, and expose investors to the risk of capital loss.

Money market instruments. Negotiable large-denomination certificates of deposit make up the most important category of money-market instruments. They are issued by banks but are called "negotiable" because, once issued, they can be traded like shares of stock and are held by many types of savers and financial institutions. Commercial paper can also be issued by banks but also by other types of private borrowers, particularly large corporations. Bankers' acceptances are promises by firms to repay funds at a future date and are guaranteed by a bank, while repurchase agreements are equivalent to loans by corporations to banks. Federal funds are temporary loans between banks of the reserves at the Federal Reserve System, while Eurodollars are dollars deposited in foreign banks that U.S. banks can borrow. Finally, treasury bills are a means of short-term borrowing by the U.S. government, equivalent to commercial paper for private corporations, and are the most actively traded and safest of all money-market instruments.

A given type of business firm, say a bank or large corporation, may be involved both in saving and borrowing. Seasonal and other fluctuations in the stream of receipts and expenditures may create temporary surpluses or shortages of funds. Consequently, one division of a corporation may be investing surplus funds while another is borrowing. For instance, a large corporation may borrow through the use of a money-market instrument like commercial paper in one week and then lend surplus funds the next week through a repurchase agreement with a bank.

Capital market instruments.   The last and best-known category are the long-term capital-market instruments, including stocks and bonds. Bonds are issued by large corporations and by the government. They generally offer a fixed nominal interest payment and fluctuate in price in the opposite direction of interest rate movements (see box, pages 492–93). Stocks are claims on the profits of private corporations. They are riskier than bonds because bondholder interest is paid first and stockholders have a claim only on what is left over. Furthermore, dividend payments to stockholders are not fixed (as for bonds) but can vary, and corporations are even free to omit dividends entirely. Many corporations pay no dividends, and investors hold these stocks in hope that the stock price will appreciate. Capital market instruments also include mortgages and bank loans to business firms and consumers. While some mortgages are traded in the financial markets, others are not and are held until maturity by the depository institution that granted them. Commercial and consumer bank loans are also rarely traded.

SELF-TEST   Without looking at Table 16-1, answer the following. Which is the largest single type of financial intermediary? For each of the following, state whether it is classified as a financial intermediary, money-market instrument, or capital-market instrument: federal funds, money-market mutual funds, state government bonds, state government retirement funds, corporate bonds, and commercial paper.

16-3   Why People Use Money

We have seen that households and businesses hold their funds in numerous ways. Corresponding to this plethora of financial instruments are several alternative definitions of money, which incorporate either a narrow or broad range of financial instruments. To make sense of these definitions, we begin by examining the traditional functions of money. Different financial market instruments fulfill one or more of these functions.

A Medium of Exchange

The most important function that differentiates money from other assets is its role as a **medium of exchange.** Money is one of the most important inventions in human history because it has allowed society to rise above the cumbersome method of exchange known as the barter system. With barter, one good or service is exchanged directly for another. If, as a professor, I want a leaky faucet fixed, I must find a plumber who wants to learn about economics. It might take weeks or months to find such a plumber, since the matching of services requires a "double coincidence of wants."

A **medium of exchange** is used for buying and selling goods and services and is a universal alternative to the barter system.

A barter society remains primitive because people have to spend so much time arranging exchanges that they have little remaining time to produce efficiently. As a result, to avoid arranging exchanges they must become self-sufficient (I would have to fix my own leaking faucet), thus failing to take advantage of the essential role of specialization in the development of an advanced economic system. Money eliminates the need for barter and the double coincidence of wants.

Which types of assets serve as a medium of exchange? Thirty years ago, almost all exchanges in the United States involved coins, currency, or checking accounts that paid no interest. Gradually other methods of exchange have developed, including interest-bearing checking accounts, savings accounts and money-market mutual funds against which checks can be written, and, of course, credit cards.[2] The requirements for an asset to qualify as a medium of exchange include ready acceptability, protection from counterfeiting, and divisibility (ability to use for small transactions).

A Store of Value

People do not always spend their income the instant they receive it. Some receipts may be spent a day or two later, but others may be saved for a substantial period of time. People need some way of storing the purchasing power of their receipts until a later time. Any asset that performs this function is called a **store of value.** There are many financial instruments that serve as a store of value but not as a medium of exchange, including passbook savings accounts that do not provide check-writing services, as well as bonds and stocks.

When people store their receipts, they want their purchasing power to remain intact. For this reason they prefer, as a store of value, an asset paying an interest rate that is free to increase when there is inflation. We learned in Chapter 11 that the safest protection against inflation would be an "indexed bond," currently offered in some high-inflation countries but not in the United States. Coins and currency are not desirable stores of value, since they pay no interest and lose *real* value during inflation. For this reason, inflation makes those who still keep money in cookie jars and under mattresses seem downright irrational.

A Unit of Account

Money is also used for accounting purposes. How much your employer will pay you in wages, how much you owe the bank, how much a firm has earned, and how much a bond is worth are all recorded in some **unit of account.** This unit is called "dollars" in the United States, "pounds" in the

A **store of value** is a method of storing purchasing power when receipts and expenditures are not perfectly synchronized.

A **unit of account** is a way of recording receipts, expenditures, assets, and liabilities.

---

[2]Credit cards are not included in any of the definitions of money discussed in the next section. This is because a purchase by credit card does not represent a payment for an item from the point of view of the purchaser. Payment is made only when a check is written to settle the credit card bill; before that the credit card transaction represents a loan from the credit card company to the purchaser. The great advantage of credit cards is that they allow households to take out loans (within prescribed limits) in small amounts at the place of purchase. Banks pay merchants promptly but extend credit to the holders of credit cards.

United Kingdom, "marks" in Germany, and so on. The dollars that are entered on accounting records do not physically exist, in the sense that there is not a coin or piece of currency corresponding to each one. Some dollars that serve as bookkeeping entries can also serve as a medium of exchange without any piece of paper actually changing hands, as in wire transfers between bank accounts.

16-4 Definitions of Money and Financial Deregulation

Should the official U.S. definition of the money supply include just those items that are a medium of exchange, or should the definition also include items that cannot be used directly for exchange but serve as a store of value? The Federal Reserve has not made a decision on this issue, and instead compiles several measures of the money supply. The two most important of these are *M*1, which corresponds roughly to the medium-of-exchange function of money, and *M*2, which adds to *M*1 some but not all assets that can be used solely as a store of value. As we shall see, however, the rapid pace of financial deregulation has blurred the distinction between *M*1 and *M*2, and the two definitions do not correspond precisely to the distinction between the medium-of-exchange and store-of-value functions of money.

*M*1 is the U.S. definition of the money supply that includes currency, demand deposits, and traveler's checks.

*M*2 is the U.S. definition of the money supply that includes *M*1, savings deposits, savings certificates, repurchase orders, Eurodollar deposits, as well as money-market deposit accounts and money-market mutual funds.

The M1 Definition of Money

Originally, *M*1 included only those assets that could be used for exchange: currency, and checking accounts ("demand deposits"). Between the 1930s and the late 1970s, the distinction between checking accounts and savings accounts was legally enforced by Federal Reserve regulations: only checking accounts could be used for payments by check, but checking accounts paid no interest; savings accounts could not be used for transactions, but they paid interest.

Beginning in the late 1970s, however, the regulations were relaxed in three ways. First, the Federal Reserve allowed banks to pay interest on checking accounts. Second, it allowed banks to issue checkbooks for savings accounts. Third, institutions other than banks and thrift institutions were allowed to offer money-market mutual funds, on which checks could be written and which paid interest. Sometimes they paid better interest than banks paid on checking or savings accounts. By the mid-1980s the distinction between checking accounts, savings accounts, and money-market mutual funds had largely vanished. Each could be used for checks, and each paid interest at close to the short-term market interest rate. The only remaining differences were restrictions imposed by the banks and financial institutions on service charges and the minimum allowable size of a check.

Table 16-2 shows the various components of the Fed's *M*1 and *M*2 definitions of the money supply. Three main categories are shown for *M*1.

1. **Currency** includes coins and paper currency, consisting of notes ranging in denomination from $1.00 to $100.00.

Table 16-2   **Components of the *M*1 and *M*2 Measures of the Money Supply, December 1988 ($ Billions)**

	Component of M1	Component of M2
Currency	$ 211.7	
Transactions accounts		
Demand deposits	288.1	
Other checking deposits	280.5	
Traveler's checks	7.5	
Equals *M*1		787.8
Savings deposits		431.6
Small-denomination time deposits and certificates		1027.2
Overnight RPs and Eurodollars		78.0[a]
Money-market deposit accounts		502.0
Money-market mutual funds		240.8
Equals *M*2		3067.4

[a]Calculated as a residual from remaining items.
Source: Federal Reserve Bulletin, March 1989, p. A13.

2. **Transactions accounts** include demand deposits (non-interest earning checking accounts) at commercial banks and other deposits on which checks can be written. Demand deposits were traditionally the major component of *M*1, besides currency, but have been joined by numerous types of "other checkable deposits." These include negotiable orders of withdrawal (NOW) accounts and "Super NOW" accounts at thrift institutions, automatic transfer system (ATS) accounts at commercial banks that allow automatic transfers from savings accounts to cover overdrafts, and similar accounts at credit unions.

3. **Traveler's checks** outstanding have been purchased from a bank or other financial institution but have not yet been used for purchases.

The *M*2 Definition of Money

Also shown in Table 16-2 is the *M*2 definition of money. This includes a hodgepodge of different financial instruments, some of which were defined in the previous section. They all are stores of value, but only some can be used as a medium of exchange. The major components are these:

1. ***M*1.** Everything included in *M*1 is also included in *M*2.

2. **Savings deposits** include passbook savings accounts, as well as statement savings accounts that allow deposits and withdrawals to be made by mail.

3. **Savings certificates** are included in $M2$ if they are less than $100,000 in denomination. These have maturity dates ranging from six months to several years and have either fixed or floating interest rates.

4. **Overnight repurchase agreements** ("RPs") allow business firms to escape the regulations that allow only households to hold interest-bearing NOW accounts.

5. **Overnight Eurodollars.** Some of these are used as a medium of exchange and some as a store of value.

6. **Money-market deposit accounts** allow the writing of a limited number of checks per month and have a rate of interest comparable to money-market mutual funds (category 7 below).

7. **Money-market mutual funds** allow writing of unlimited numbers of checks over a certain minimum value.

Which financial-market instruments are excluded from the $M2$ definition of the money supply? Comparing Tables 16-1 and 16-2 we can see that $M2$ mainly consists of liabilities of depository institutions and investment intermediaries (money-market mutual funds but not stock or bond mutual funds). Of the money-market instruments, none are included in $M2$ other than RPs and Eurodollars. And no capital-market instruments are included in $M2$. Thus, even though $M2$ is comprehensive, it does not include every financial-market instrument, leading to potential instability in the demand for $M2$ if assets included in $M2$ become more or less attractive relative to assets not in $M2$. And instability in the demand for $M1$ is even more likely to occur, due to the similarity between assets included in $M1$ (like super NOW accounts) and those included in $M2$ but not $M1$ (like money-market deposit accounts).

Money-Supply Definitions and the Instability of Money Demand

As we saw in Tables 16-1 and 16-2, there are many different types of financial instruments, some but not all of which are included in the Federal Reserve's official definitions of the $M1$ and $M2$ money supply. This complex financial system creates severe difficulties for monetarists, the group of economists endorsing a constant-growth-rate rule (CGRR) for *"the* money supply." To implement the CGRR, they have to decide which money-supply measure should have its growth rate held constant.

The notion of a stable money-demand function linking "money" to "income" is a central theme of the theories of the demand for money that we shall survey in the rest of this chapter. However, most of these theories are relevant for a simple world in which only money can be used for exchange but *pays no interest.* Since people can be assumed to vary their holdings of money as their income changes (and thus their need to exchange money for goods changes), the simple-world theories assume a regular relationship between money and income that is subject only to the effect of changes in interest rates.

Effect of financial deregulation on the money-demand schedule. This was the idea on which we based the stable *LM* curve of Chapter 4, starting from the downward sloping money-demand schedule of Figure 4-5. This money-demand schedule is repeated in the left-hand frame of Figure 16-2, where the interest rate is drawn on the vertical axis and the level of real money balances, and is defined by the *M*1 definition (*M*1/*P*) on the horizontal axis. Here *P* stands as always for the aggregate price level.

The interest rate (*r*) on the vertical axis *is the average interest rate on assets not in M1, like passbook savings accounts*. Since *M*1 pays no interest in the left-hand frame, an increase in interest rates on alternatives to money will cause people to shift out of money into alternatives. This accounts for the negative slope of the money-demand schedule.

The downward-sloping money-demand schedule is drawn for a fixed assumed level of income (Q_0); it intersects the assumed level of the real supply of *M*1 ($M1/P)_0$ at an interest rate of 5 percent. As long as the level of income remains fixed at Q_0, the simple theory predicts that the demand for money schedule will remain fixed, as shown in the left-hand frame.

Now let us examine the implications of financial deregulation, which allows banks to issue new types of interest-bearing checking accounts like the NOWs (included in *M*1). At a 5 percent interest rate on alternatives to money like passbook savings accounts, people will be much more willing to

FINANCIAL DEREGULATION CAUSES MONEY DEMAND INSTABILITY

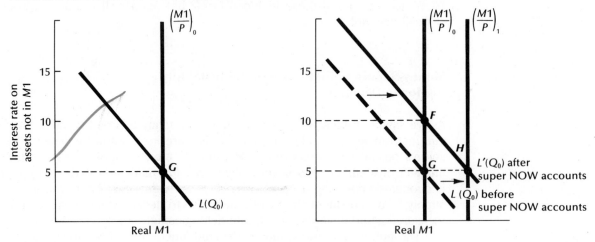

Figure 16-2 **Effect on the Demand for Money Schedule of the Invention of Interest-Bearing Checking (Super NOW) Accounts**

In the left-hand frame is copied our original money demand schedule that was used in Figures 4-5 and 4-6 to derive the *LM* curve. In the right-hand frame the money-demand schedule shifts rightward as a result of the invention of Super NOW accounts. If the Federal Reserve leaves the money supply fixed, the result is an increase in the interest rate from point *G* to point *F*. If the Fed wants the interest rate to be stable, it must raise the money supply from point *G* to point *H*.

hold $M1$. The interest paid on $M1$ now has the effect of shifting the $M1$ demand schedule as people cash in their passbook savings accounts to obtain NOW accounts. The higher demand for this new component of $M1$ causes a rightward shift in the $M1$ demand schedule from the old $L(Q_0)$ to the new $L'(Q_0)$.

Consequences of financial deregulation for the monetarist CGRR. Now we can see the dilemma that financial deregulation causes for monetarist advocates of a CGRR. If the Federal Reserve holds the supply of $M1$ rigidly fixed at $(M1/P)_0$, then the invention of NOW accounts will cause the interest rate to rise from 5 percent at point G to 10 percent at point F. The higher interest rate will reduce interest-sensitive spending like investment, and, by causing an appreciation of the dollar, will also reduce net exports. *In this situation monetarist adherence to a CGRR has destabilized both interest rates and output.* For this reason, many economists think that the Fed's attempt to move at least partially from interest-rate targeting to money-supply targeting during 1979–82, at a time when financial deregulation was occurring, helps explain part of puzzle 4, regarding high and volatile interest rates.

PUZZLE 4: WHY WERE INTEREST RATES IN THE 1980s HIGHER THAN EVER BEFORE?

Faced with the effects of financial deregulation, the Fed has another alternative. Instead of maintaining a CGRR for $M1$, the Fed could raise the supply of $M1$ to $(M1/P)_1$ and allow the economy to go to point H, where the original interest rate of 5 percent is consistent with the original level of real GNP, Q_0. This analysis explains why the Fed allowed very rapid growth of the $M1$ money supply in 1983 and 1985–86 in response to the increase in the demand for $M1$ caused by financial deregulation.

The course of financial deregulation in the late 1970s and early 1980s did not always raise $M1$. Some of the newly invented accounts, particularly money-market mutual funds and money-market deposit accounts, are included in $M2$ but not $M1$. When these were invented, many people reduced their holdings of non-interest-bearing checking accounts, part of $M1$, and thus caused a *leftward shift* in the money-demand schedule.

Thus financial deregulation has caused both leftward and rightward shifts in the demand for $M1$. As a result, the *velocity* of $M1$, defined as nominal GNP divided by $M1$ ($PQ/M1$), has been extremely unstable in the 1980s (see Figure 15-4).

Would it be preferable to use $M2$ for a monetarist CGRR? The same problem plagues $M2$, although perhaps to a lesser degree, since the invention of accounts that allow both check-writing and the payment of interest has caused many people to keep funds in money-market accounts (part of $M2$) that previously were kept in short-term securities like treasury bills that are not part of $M2$. Thus the money-demand schedule for $M2$ has also been influenced by financial deregulation. We examine data on the velocity of $M1$ and $M2$ in Section 16-8.

SELF-TEST   For each of the following, state whether the event shifts to the right or left the demand curves for $M1$ and for $M2$: (1) the introduction of money-market mutual funds; (2) the introduction of automatic transfer system (ATS) accounts at commercial banks that allow automatic transfers from savings accounts to cover overdrafts; (3) the introduction of money-market deposit accounts.

Side Effect of Financial Deregulation: The Thrift Institution Debacle

Dimensions of the Thrift Crisis

Thrift institutions ("thrifts") include savings and loan associations (S&Ls) and savings banks. At the end of 1988 there were about 3000 S&Ls and about 400 savings banks in the United States, holding about $1600 billion in deposits, substantially less than the $2400 billion held by the commercial banks (see Table 16-1). Over the decade of the 1980s more than 15 percent of the thrift institutions failed, and by 1987 fully one third of the nation's remaining thrifts were insolvent or in very weak financial condition.

Unlike the Great Depression, when many households lost their life savings as the result of bank failures, depositors at the thrifts in the 1980s did not lose the value of their deposits. How did the failed and insolvent thrifts repay their depositors? This was the job of the Federal Savings and Loan Insurance Corporation (FSLIC), which provided insurance to depositors and paid off depositors when thrifts failed. However, the scale of the failures and insolvencies in the 1980s was so great that the FSLIC ran out of funds. This required Congress and the administration to step in and appropriate the necessary funds to reimburse depositors. The administration predicted in 1989 that the total cost to the American taxpayer of resolving the thrift institution debacle would amount to $109 billion over the decade 1989–99.[a]

How Did It Happen?

Historically, thrifts were the only sources of long-term capital for home building. They played a major role in enabling people to become homeowners and spurred the postwar suburbanization of the United States. From 1933 until the early 1980s, thrifts were sheltered from competition, both in their ability to attract deposits from savers and in their ability to dominate the market for mortgage loans. From 1933 to 1980, the interest rate that thrifts could pay on savings deposits was fixed by the Fed, but beginning in the late 1970s financial deregulation provided attractive alternatives to savers. When market interest rates increased, people withdrew their savings from thrifts and shifted to newly developed alternatives, particularly money-market mutual funds.

The thrifts now faced a no-win situation. Congress responded to their plight by repealing the interest rate ceilings, allowing the thrifts to pay higher interest rates to depositors. But the thrifts were still "stuck" with low-yielding assets in the form of fixed-rate mortgages paying the same low interest rate over the life of the mortgage, often as long as 30 years. Since they had to pay higher rates to depositors than the low fixed rates on some of the old mortgages, many thrifts began to lose money. In 1982 the thrift industry lost $8.8 billion and 252 thrifts failed.

A Risky Business

Financial institutions take two types of risk, "credit risk" and "interest-rate risk." Banks try to keep the maturity of their assets and liabilities the same, so they face little interest-rate risk, since the interest rates on their assets and liabilities go up and down together. Instead, banks mainly take credit risk, that is, the risk of loss when people do not pay back the money they have borrowed in bank loans. Thrift institutions, in contrast, take little credit risk, since their loans are backed by the value of the home on which the mortgage is issued (although in some regions of the country the thrifts were hurt by falling home prices, which made the value of the home fall below the amount to be repaid on the mortgage). Primarily, thrift institutions take interest-rate risk because the maturity of their deposits is so much shorter than that of their mortgage loan assets.

As they were squeezed by the rising interest rates they had to pay on mortgages, some thrifts turned in the early 1980s to short-term nonmortgage loans. The thrifts tried to make "easy money" without building up the necessary expertise to assess the credit risk of the new short-term loans. Many of these loans defaulted, accounting for the

insolvency of many of the thrifts. Another approach was for the thrifts to shift to adjustable-rate mortgages (ARMs), with interest rates that went up and down in line with the interest rates on deposits and could eliminate interest-rate risk for the thrifts eventually (after all the old fixed-rate mortgages were paid off). Unfortunately, ARMs are no panacea either. They increase credit risk, since households may default if higher interest rates boost their monthly payments beyond their ability to pay.

The Role of Government

What caused the thrift debacle? Many blame financial deregulation. This is only half true; financial deregulation would not have made life so difficult for the thrifts if it had not been combined with volatility of interest rates (which we study in Chapter 17). The old system of regulation of interest rates paid to thrift depositors had to break down eventually, just as any system of price controls is defeated by changes in the equilibrium price established by supply and demand.

The problem, however, involved more than mere financial deregulation. It was aggravated by blunder and delay by federal regulators. Inadequate supervision allowed many thrifts to violate capital requirements (that is, the required minimum net worth in relation to deposits). Instead of the needed "early intervention" with problem thrifts, government regulators practiced a policy of nonintervention in the early 1980s. Insolvent thrifts were allowed to remain open too long; with nothing to

lose, they gambled heavily on risky short-term loans. Rather than deal with real customers, they bought both loans and deposits from brokers, growing rapidly in the process. When many of the loans defaulted, they would up even deeper in the hole than when the problem began in 1981–82. An extreme example imposed an unbelievable cost on the taxpayer:

> This anecdote is tantamount to a news report that a drunken motorist has wiped out the entire city of Pittsburgh. A company [American Diversified Savings, a California S&L] with $11 million in assets lost $800 milion. With perhaps $0.5 million in equity, it destroyed $800 million of insured deposits, a kill ratio of 1600 to 1.[b]

Having delayed too long while these losses ballooned, the government then compounded the problem by bribing potential buyers with tax benefits and other subsidies to take over insolvent thrifts. It has been estimated that the eventual cost to the government of these buyouts will be two to three times greater than simply to have allowed the failed banks to disappear.

What is the ultimate solution, now that the American taxpayer is stuck with a bill of $110 billion, and probably more? Some government officials believe that deregulation caused the problem, and that the solution is reregulation. But many others believe that any such return to the old system would expose thrifts to just the kind of interest-rate risk that brought them down. Instead of going back, other observers believe that the time has come to eliminate the distinction between thrifts and commercial banks, and to merge the regulatory structure applying to each. Under this proposal, healthy thrifts would become banks, the weaker ones would be liquidated.[c]

[a]Two excellent recent sources of detailed information are R. Dan Brumbaugh, Jr., Andrew S. Carron, and Robert E. Litan, "Cleaning Up the Depository Institutions Mess," *Brookings Papers on Economic Activity,* 1989, no. 1, and David O. Beim, "Beyond the Savings-and-Loan Crisis," *The Public Interest,* Spring 1989, pp. 88–99.
[b]Jonathan Gray, *Financial Deregulation and the Savings and Loan Crisis,* as quoted by Beim, p. 97.
[c]This is the conclusion reached by both sources cited in footnote a.

16-5 The Quantity Theory of Money

Now we turn to the traditional theories of the demand for money that apply to a simple world in which only money can be used as a medium of exchange, and in which money does not pay interest. Our interest in learning about the demand for money particularly concerns the role of the interest rate. For, as was explained in Chapters 4 and 5, the potency of monetary and fiscal policy depends in part on the *interest responsiveness of the demand for money*.

The dominant analysis of macroeconomics before Keynes's *General Theory* was based almost entirely on the assumption of a stable demand for money. Not only was the demand for money assumed to be stable, but little or no attention was given to the dependence of the demand for money on the interest rate.

The **quantity theory of money** begins with the famous quantity equation, which is called a tautology because it is true by definition:

$$MV \equiv PQ \tag{16.1}$$

> The **quantity theory of money** in its strong version assumes that real output is fixed, so that price changes are proportional to changes in the money supply.

Here M as before is the money supply, P is the price level, Q is real GNP, and V is the velocity of money. Equation (16.1) is a definition for the simple reason that velocity (V) is defined as (PQ/M). The right side of the equation corresponds to the transfer of goods and services between economic units, and the left side to the matching monetary payment for those goods and services.[3]

Implications of Constant Desired Money Holdings

As it stands, the quantity equation is not a theory, but we can convert it into a theory by postulating that people choose to hold a constant fraction ($1/V^*$) of their nominal income (PQ) in the form of money (M):

$$M = \frac{PQ}{V^*} \tag{16.2}$$

As written, equation (16.2) appears merely to be a transformation of (16.1) that divides both sides of the earlier equation by V. *The definition becomes a theory* when we assume that the fraction of income that people desire to hold in the form of money ($1/V^*$) is a constant. Starting with an initial money supply of M_0, any increase in the money supply will raise nominal GNP (PQ). Why? If the initial supply of money was the desired fraction ($1/V^*$) of income, any additional money will be considered excess by households and firms and will be spent.

---

[3]In this discussion we limit our attention to the income version of the quantity theory and ignore for lack of space the transactions version, which replaces Q in equation (16.1) by the total transactions in the economy, including not only current goods and services, but also transactions in capital assets and intermediate goods. In that version velocity (V) is interpreted as the current value of annual transactions divided by the money supply, or the total turnover of money per year. A more complete discussion of the quantity theory, and a summary of the limitations of the transactions version, are contained in Milton Friedman, "A Theoretical Framework for Monetary Analysis," *Journal of Political Economy,* vol. 78 (March/April 1970), pp. 193–238, reprinted in Robert J. Gordon (ed.), *Milton Friedman's Monetary Framework* (Chicago: University of Chicago Press, 1974), pp. 1–62. See also Milton Friedman, "Money: Quantity Theory," in *International Encyclopedia of the Social Sciences* (New York: Macmillan, 1968).

In its original pre-Keynesian version, prices were generally assumed to be relatively or completely flexible, so that almost all the adjustment of nominal income (PQ) would take the form of price changes and almost none the form of quantity changes. We can distinguish two versions of the quantity theory. The weak version states that, because the desired fraction of income held in the form of money ($1/V^*$) is constant, a change in the money supply causes a proportional change in nominal GNP in the same direction. The strong version adds the assumption that all or almost all the adjustment of nominal GNP takes the form of changing prices and none or almost none the form of changing output.

Determinants of Desired Money Holdings

The earlier quantity theorists did not believe that the fraction $1/V^*$ was fixed forever. They discussed a wide variety of factors that could alter $1/V^*$. For instance, some writers emphasized that the amount of money needed for conducting transactions would change as the technology of transactions changed. Although the dependence of the demand for money on the interest rate was implicit in the pre-Keynesian quantity theory, the meaning of this assumption was neither fully appreciated nor incorporated into formal analysis.[4]

16-6 The Keynesian Transaction and Speculative Motives

Keynes in the *General Theory* divided the demand for money into two compartments. The first portion of money was held to satisfy the "transactions motive," which is the same as the medium of exchange function of money introduced earlier in this chapter. Individuals with high incomes need more money for transactions than people with low incomes, so the total demand for money for transactions purposes depended on total nominal GNP (PQ) and was written $L_1(PQ)$.

The second portion of money was held to satisfy the "speculative motive" based on the assumed role of money as a store of value. Speculators continually try to make themselves richer by switching their asset holdings back and forth between money and bonds. Imagine a bond that promises to pay the holder $1 per year forever. An individual would be willing to pay a price of $1/r$ dollars for that bond. For instance, when the interest rate is 5 percent or 0.05, the price of the bond will be $20.[5]

---

[4]Alfred Marshall and A. C. Pigou of Cambridge University were two pre-Keynesian economists who recognized that individuals kept a fraction of their total assets in the form of money, and that the attractiveness of money for asset-holding would depend on its return compared to that of other assets.

[5]The simple inverse relationship between the bond price and the interest rate is strictly valid only for a perpetuity, a bond that pays interest forever but that never pays off its principal. For bonds with finite maturities, say thirty years or less, the relationship between bond prices and the interest rate is still inverse but not perfectly proportioned. The inverse relation between the interest rate and the price of bonds was introduced in the box on page 89.

If the normal interest rate is 5 percent or 0.05, then the normal bond price is $20. What would happen to the willingness of speculators to hold bonds if the actual interest rate were to drop to 0.04 and the bond price were to rise to $25? Some investors might feel that a $25 bond price was *too far above normal* and that bond prices were likely to fall in the future. To avoid the risk of capital loss, the speculators might sell their bonds and hold money instead.

Thus when the interest rate is low and bond prices high, the speculative demand for money is high. Conversely, when the interest rate is high and bond prices low, the demand for money is low.

The Interest Rate and the Speculative Motive

The behavior of speculators as outlined here was the only explanation put forth by Keynes of the sensitivity of the demand for money to the interest rate. The portion of money demand held to satisfy the speculative motive was called $L_2(r)$. Thus the total demand for money (M) was the total of the transaction demand $L_1(PQ)$ and the speculative demand $L_2(r)$:[6]

$$M = L_1(PQ) + L_2(r) \qquad (16.3)$$

Keynes's equation has been criticized on several grounds. Critics question the idea that speculative money holding occurs only because some investors believe that the interest rate is below normal and bond prices are above normal. This idea cannot explain why the demand for money remains high over an extended period of low interest rates, such as the 1930s. As time goes by, speculators should begin to revise downward their idea of the normal interest rate. Thus the deviation between the actual and normal interest rate should gradually disappear and speculative money holding should disappear as well.

16-7 Modern Theories of the Demand for Money

Since the publication of his *General Theory* over fifty years ago, Keynes's speculative motive for money holding has drifted out of favor as an explanation of the demand for $M1$. Why should speculators necessarily hold $M1$ during those periods when they are trying to avoid a capital loss? Other assets, particularly savings deposits and other components of $M2$, are not only free from the risk of capital loss but pay interest as well. Surely the reason speculators prefer $M1$ to savings accounts or certificates is its acceptance as a medium of exchange.

Interest Responsiveness of the Transaction Demand for Money

The abandonment of the speculative motive does not mean that the demand for money is independent of the interest rate, nor that the *LM* curve is vertical. In the early 1950s William J. Baumol of Princeton and New York Uni-

---

[6]This is exactly the equation Keynes used; *General Theory,* p. 199

versity and James Tobin of Yale demonstrated that the transactions demand for money depends on the interest rate. Therefore, the *LM* curve can have a positive slope even when there is no speculative demand.[7] The funds people hold for transactions, to "bridge the interval between the receipt of income and its disbursement," can be placed either in *M*1 (currency and demand deposits, which are assumed by Baumol and Tobin to pay no interest) or in time deposits. The higher the interest rate, the more individuals will tend to shift their transactions balances into interest-bearing time deposits and other components of *M*2 that do not serve as a medium of exchange.

Baumol analyzes the money-holding decision of a hypothetical individual who receives income at specified intervals but spends it gradually at a steady rate between paydays. An example is illustrated in the left frame of Figure 16-3, where the person is assumed to be paid $900 per month (*Q*) on the first of each month. How will the person decide whether to convert all

---

[7]William J. Baumol, "The Transactions Demand for Cash: An Inventory Theoretic Approach," *Quarterly Journal of Economics* (November 1952). James Tobin, "The Interest-Elasticity of the Transactions Demand for Cash," *Review of Economics and Statistics* (August 1956), pp. 241–247

THE HOLDING OF CASH DEPENDS INVERSELY ON THE ATTRACTIVENESS
OF HOLDING SAVINGS DEPOSITS

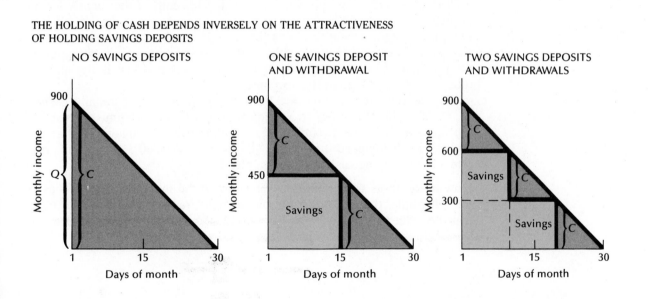

Figure 16-3 **Alternative Allocations of an Individual's Monthly Paycheck Between Cash and Savings Deposits**
In the left frame the individual holds the entire paycheck in the form of cash, indicated by the gray triangle, which shrinks as the paycheck is spent on consumption purchases. In the middle frame only half as much cash is held, because the individual finds it advantageous to hold half the paycheck in a savings deposit for half the month. In the right frame even less cash is held, because initially two thirds of the paycheck is deposited into a savings account.

of the paycheck into currency and demand deposits ($M1$), which bear no interest, or to deposit part of the paycheck in a time deposit that pays a monthly interest rate r?[8]

Costs and benefits of holding money. The individual compares the costs and benefits of holding $M1$ instead of the time deposit. The main cost of $M1$ is the interest rate on savings (r) lost when $M1$ is held instead of time deposits. The main benefit of holding $M1$ is the avoidance of what Baumol calls the "broker's fee" of b dollars charged every time (T) cash is obtained either by cashing the original paycheck or by obtaining cash at the savings bank. The broker's fee in real life includes the time and transportation expense required to make an extra trip to the savings bank to obtain cash from a savings deposit.

The number of times the broker's fee is incurred equals the size of the paycheck (Q) divided by the average amount of cash (C) obtained on each trip. For instance, the left frame of Figure 16-3 involves no savings account; the paycheck of \$900 (Q) is cashed at the beginning of the month ($C = 900$), and the broker's fee is incurred only one time ($T = Q/C = 1.0$).

In the middle frame half the paycheck is cashed on the first of the month ($C = 450$), and the other half is deposited in a time deposit. Interest is lost by holding cash in an amount equal to the interest rate times the value of the average amount held in cash, which is half the value of the cash withdrawal ($rC/2$). Why? In the first half of the month the individual starts with \$450 in cash and winds up with zero on the fifteenth of the month, for an average holding of \$225. Then the person converts the time deposit into cash, incurring a second broker's fee. The \$450 of cash dwindles again to zero on the last day of the month, so that the average cash holding during the last half of the month is again \$225. Total interest lost is the interest rate times $C/2$, or \$225 in this example.[9]

In the right frame only one third of the paycheck is initially cashed ($C = 300$), while the other two thirds are deposited in the time deposit. On the tenth and on the twentieth again withdrawals are made, so that the broker's fee is incurred three times ($T = Q/C = 900/300 = 3$). The interest rate lost by holding cash is once again $rC/2$.

How many trips to the bank? How should the individual behave—as in the left frame, the middle frame, or the right frame, or should even more trips be made to the bank? The answer is that the combined cost of broker's fees (bT) and interest lost ($rC/2$) should be minimized:

$$\text{cost} = bT + \frac{rC}{2}, \text{ or}$$

$$= b\frac{Q}{C} + \frac{rC}{2} \tag{16.4}$$

---

[8]Throughout this section we assume that no interest is paid on demand deposits, in contrast to the real world where interest is paid on some components of $M1$ and $M2$ that can be used for transactions. Our analysis remains valid as long as a higher interest rate on nonmoney assets raises the average interest rate paid on $M1$ less than proportionately, thus reducing the demand for $M1$.

[9]What is the area of the gray triangle in the left frame? The formula for the area of a triangle is one half times the height times the length, or $1/2(900)(1)$, where the length is expressed in months. This equals 450. In the middle are two gray triangles, each with an area $1/2(450)(1/2)$, or $1/2(450)(1)$ for both triangles. This equals 225. On the right are three triangles, each with an area $1/2(300)(1/3)$, or $1/2(300)(1)$ for the three triangles. This equals 150

It can be shown that the average value of the cash withdrawal (C) that minimizes cost is.[10]

$$C = \sqrt{\frac{2bQ}{r}} \tag{16.5}$$

This equation says that the average cash withdrawal equals the square root of the following: two times the broker's fee times income divided by the interest rate. A higher broker's fee (b) raises cash holdings by discouraging extra trips to the savings bank. But a higher interest rate (r) does just the opposite, reducing cash holdings as individuals shift more funds into time deposits to earn the higher interest rate.

Summary: The Baumol and Tobin contributions are of major importance. They show that the interest sensitivity of the demand for money is based not on a flawed theory of speculation but on a transactions motive that is shared by almost everyone. The theoretical underpinnings of the positively sloped *LM* curve are solid, implying that changes either in private spending desires or in fiscal policy will change both real output and the interest rate, at least in the short run.[11]

The Portfolio Approach

At about the same time as the Baumol–Tobin contributions, several articles rehabilitated the demand for money as a store of value from the criticisms aimed at the Keynesian analysis of the speculative motive.[12] In particular James Tobin, in another classic article, showed that most people prefer to hold a balanced portfolio with several types of assets.

Tobin's contribution. Some assets, particularly those in $M1$ and $M2$, maintain the nominal value of their principal and are thus "safe" or "riskless."[13] Other assets, particularly stocks and long-term bonds, have a market value (principal) that varies in price every day and are called risky assets. If investors do not like risk in the form of variations in asset prices, they will

---

[10]Here elementary calculus is required. Cost is minimized by changing C to make the derivative of cost with respect to C equal to zero:

$$\frac{\partial(\text{cost})}{\partial C} = \frac{-bQ}{C^2} + \frac{r}{2} = 0$$

When this is solved for C, we obtain the square-root expression shown as equation (16.5).

[11]The Baumol theory has the extra advantage of being specific, since the result in equation (16.5) provides a square-root hypothesis of money holding that can be tested against the data. Both the output elasticity and interest-rate elasticity of real money demand should be one-half. Why? Let us rewrite (16.5) in exponential form:

$$C = (2bQ)^{1/2}(r)^{-1/2}$$

Thus a one-percentage-point change in Q raises C by 1/2 percent. For a more advanced treatment that allows the theoretical elasticities to differ from 1/2, see Edi Karni, "The Transactions Demand for Cash: Incorporation of the Value of Time into the Inventory Approach," *Journal of Political Economy,* vol. 81, no. 5 (September/October 1973), pp. 1216–1225.

[12]The most important of these articles was James Tobin, "Liquidity Preference as Behavior Towards Risk," *Review of Economic Studies,* vol. 25, no. 67 (1958).

[13]"Riskless" is placed in quotes because $M1$ is not free of risk when prices are flexible, since inflation causes a capital loss on holdings of $M1$. This is one of the costs of inflation emphasized in Chapter 11

be unwilling to hold risky assets unless they are "bribed" by a higher average interest return. Otherwise, why should they be willing to needlessly expose themselves to risk?

Faced with various safe and risky assets, with the former paying less interest than the latter, most investors compromise, diversifying their portfolios of assets. To choose only risky assets would yield a high average interest return but would expose investors to too much risk. To choose entirely safe assets would eliminate risk completely but would yield a low average return. A mixed, diversified portfolio is usually the best approach, and each person can choose a slightly different balance between risk and return.

Although the portfolio approach is very appealing as an explanation for diversifying individual portfolios, it does not explain why anyone is willing to hold currency or non-interest-bearing checking accounts. Investors can achieve the goal of safety by holding interest-bearing components of $M1$ or $M2$. The major contribution of the portfolio approach is to explain why most households desire a mixture of safe interest-bearing components of $M1$ and $M2$ and risky stocks and bonds, rather than a portfolio consisting wholly of either one or the other.

Friedman's version. At roughly the same time that Tobin was writing, Milton Friedman developed a similar approach to the demand for money.[14] Friedman's was a generalization of the older quantity theory, in which he treated money as one among several assets including bonds, equities (stocks), and goods. Friedman emphasized that in principle any category of spending on GNP could be a substitute for money and may be stimulated by an expansion of the real money supply. Because he viewed a wider range of assets as being substitutes for money than did Tobin, Friedman tended to view monetary policy as having more potent effects on spending. This did not lead Friedman to support activist policies, but rather the monetarist approach based on a constant-growth-rate rule for the money supply.

The portfolio approach pioneered by both Tobin and Friedman makes the demand for money a function of both income and wealth, not just income. The possible response of the demand for money to wealth has an implication for the efficacy of fiscal policy. A stimulative fiscal policy financed by deficit spending raises real wealth if people treat government bonds as part of their wealth (see Chapter 13). This in turn will raise the demand for money and shift the LM curve to the left, cutting back on the fiscal policy multipliers that we calculated in Chapters 4 and 5, where the wealth effect on the demand for money was ignored.[15]

SELF-TEST   According to the Tobin and Friedman versions of the portfolio theory, would an increase in the supply of $M1$ tend to raise or lower prices in the bond market? In the stock market?

---

[14]Friedman's approach is explained in more detail in his "The Quantity Theory of Money—a Restatement," in Friedman (ed.), *Studies in the Quantity Theory of Money* (Chicago: University of Chicago Press, 1956), pp. 3–21

[15]A formal analysis of the wealth effect in the demand-for-money function is the subject of Alan S. Blinder and Robert M. Solow, "Analytical Foundations of Fiscal Policy," in *The Economics of Public Finance* (Washington, D.C.: Brookings Institution, 1974), pp. 45–57. See also Benjamin M. Friedman, "Crowding Out or Crowding In? Economic Consequences of Financing Government Deficits," *Brookings Papers on Economic Activity,* vol. 9, no. 3 (1978), pp. 593–641

CASE STUDY: Money Demand Puzzles

The quantity theory of money in equation (16.2) was based on the idea that people want to hold a constant fraction ($1/V$) of their income in the form of money. The more modern theories predict that the fraction $1/V$ will decline when there is an increase in the interest rate—the major cost of holding money. This is confirmed during the postwar years when interest rates rose (a graph illustrating the postwar increase in interest rates is presented in Figures 1-10 and 17-4). In the top frame of Figure 16-4, the downward-sloping line labeled $1/V1$ plots the ratio of the money-supply concept $M1$ to nominal GNP (PQ) and confirms the downward drift of money holdings relative to income, at least through 1981.[16]

The downward drift in $1/V1$ was not uniform each year. In years of rising interest rates, the decline in $1/V1$ was faster than normal, as in 1965–66. This occurs because, as we recall, the demand for money depends *negatively* on the level of the interest rate. Similarly, in recession years of falling interest rates, the decline in $1/V1$ was interrupted. Indeed, in a much-cited paper, Stephen M. Goldfeld explained almost all of the movements in $1/V1$ during the 1952–73 period as depending on movements in real GNP, the interest rate paid on time deposits, the market interest rate on commercial paper, and last quarter's value of the real demand for $M1$.[17]

Goldfeld's equation explains the pre-1973 decline of $1/V1$ as a result of two main factors. First, the interest rates on time deposits and on commercial paper increased fairly steadily, and they have a negative effect on the demand for money. Second, a 1.0 percent increase in real GNP raises money demand by only about 0.5 percent in the long run, causing $M1/P$ to grow more slowly than Q. This obviously causes $1/V1$ ($= M1/PQ$) to decline.

The Case of the Missing Money

The bottom frame of Figure 16-4 is an enlargement of the top frame for the years 1974–88. Whereas the top frame illustrates the behavior of annual data, the bottom frame shows the behavior of quarterly data over a shorter interval. The black line labeled "1959–73 trend" shows what would have happened to the real demand for $M1$ if $1/V1$ had continued to decline at the same rate between 1974 and 1988 as it did between 1959 and 1973. The red line showing the actual quarterly values of $1/V1$ is below the black trend line throughout the period between 1975 and 1983. The actual value then rose far above the trend line during 1985–89.

This shortfall of the demand for money in the late 1970s corresponds to a discovery that Goldfeld and others made—Goldfeld's equation lost its ability to track the demand for money successfully after 1973.[18] Overall,

---

[16]Since $V1$ is defined as $PQ/M1$, it follows that $1/V1 = M1/PQ$.

[17]Stephen M. Goldfeld, "The Demand for Money Revisited," *Brookings Papers on Economic Activity,* vol. 4, no. 3 (1973), pp. 577–638.

[18]Two of the many references are Stephen M. Goldfeld, "The Case of the Missing Money," *Brookings Papers on Economic Activity,* vol. 7, no. 3 (1976), pp. 683–730, and Richard D. Porter, Thomas D. Simpson, and Eileen Mauskopf, "Financial Innovation and the Monetary Aggregates," *Brookings Papers on Economic Activity,* vol. 10, no. 1 (1979), pp. 213–237

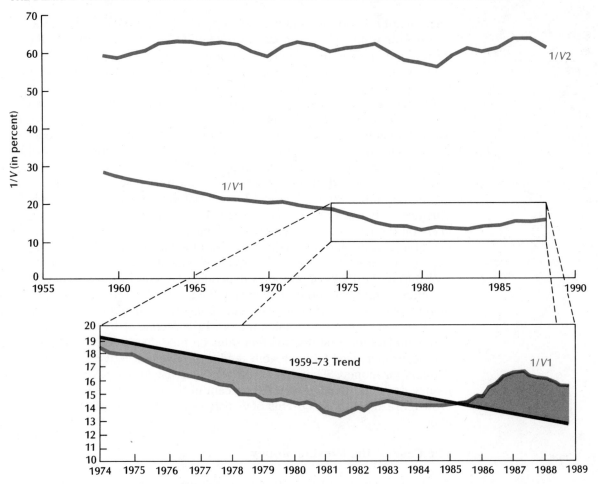

Figure 16-4   **Ratios of Money to Nominal GNP (1/V) for both M1 and M2, 1959–88**

Notice in the top frame that the demand for M2, as shown by 1/V2, exhibited no trend from 1960 to 1988. But it exhibited quite marked fluctuations around its average value of 62 percent. The demand for M1, as shown by 1/V1, experienced an irregular decline throughout the postwar period until 1981. In contrast to the top frame, which shows annual values, the bottom frame shows quarterly values for 1/V1 from 1974 to 1988. If 1/V1 had continued to decline smoothly at the rate experienced between 1959 and 1973, it would have followed the black "1959–73 trend" line. Instead, there was a substantial decline in 1/V1 below the trend line between 1975 and 1978, then a rise back far above the trend line in 1982–87.

households and businesses were holding much less money than predicted by Goldfeld's equation, given the prevailing values of income and interest rates. The shortfall amounted to about $55 billion in early 1979.[19]

---

[19]Prediction errors are those reported by Porter, Simpson, and Mauskopf, "Financial Innovation and the Monetary Aggregates," Table 1, p. 214

The Missing Money Reappears

After 1981 the money-demand puzzle shifted. Instead of too little money, there was suddenly *too much money*. We have already studied the effect of this instability in the demand for money on the monetarist case for a constant-growth-rate rule (CGRR) for $M1$. In fact, Figure 16-4, which shows the behavior of $1/V1$, is just the inverse of Figure 15-4, which shows the velocity of $M1$ ($V1$) over the shorter period 1970–88. Just as $V1$ starts falling after 1981 in Figure 15-4, so in Figure 16-4 $1/V1$ starts rising after 1981.

Notice that the reversal of trend of $1/V1$ does not apply to $1/V2$, plotted in the top part of Figure 16-4. Because $1/V2$ was at about the same level in 1988 that it was in 1960, the demand for $M2$ grew at almost the same rate as nominal GNP over this long period (recall that $1/V2$ is defined as $M2$ divided by nominal GNP, or $M2/PQ$). Despite this "trendless" behavior, $1/V2$ was still insufficiently stable to permit the control of $M2$ to achieve a stable growth rate of nominal GNP. Even if the supply of $M2$ had been maintained at a rigid growth rate of 10 percent in every year from 1977 to 1988, the growth rate of nominal GNP implied by the observed behavior of $1/V2$ would not have been stable. It would have ranged between 5.5 and 13 percent on an annual basis, and by more on a quarterly basis.

Solutions to the Case of the Missing and Reappearing Money

The reasons for the shortfall of the demand for $M1$ between 1974 and 1980 and its resurgence after 1981 have been much discussed.[20] Among the most important factors are:

1. **Early stages of financial deregulation.** The early stages of deregulation allowed the development of money-market mutual funds, which pay interest and allow checks to be written. These accounts grew from only $8 billion in September 1978 to over $200 billion in 1982. Also developed at this time were repurchase agreements, which allow business firms to earn interest on funds in checking accounts. Because both money-market mutual funds and repurchase agreements are included in $M2$ but not $M1$, their attractiveness drained funds out of the checking accounts that are included in $M1$.

2. **Later stages of financial deregulation.** As we have seen, $M1$ includes NOW, Super NOW, and ATS accounts that were introduced in the early 1980s. No longer was $M2$ the only repository of assets that paid interest and allowed checks to be written. With this newly attractive set of assets included in $M1$, the demand for $M1$ soared—particularly in 1982–83 and again in 1985–86. Because the main effect of deregulation at this later stage was to shift funds from assets included only in $M2$ to assets included in both $M1$ and $M2$, the demand for $M2$ showed more stability than the demand for $M1$.

---

[20]This section draws on my study, Robert J. Gordon, "The Short-Run Demand for Money: A Reconsideration," *Journal of Money, Credit, and Banking*, vol. 16 (November 1984), pp. 403–434

3. **Effect of supply shocks.** Although most theories of the demand for money are stated in real terms, people manage portfolios of *actual* (nominal) dollars. When there is a supply shock, such as the increase in oil prices in 1974 and 1979–80, the price level rises suddenly but people do not necessarily change their holdings of money right away, since (as the Baumol-Tobin theory emphasizes) financial transactions are costly. As a result, the level of real balances ($M1/P$) that investigators like Goldfeld are trying to explain may drop suddenly.

4. **Federal Reserve's change of target variables.** As we shall see in the next chapter, the Fed targeted interest rates before 1979. To stabilize interest rates whenever there was a change in commodity demand, the Fed was forced to move the real money supply ($M1/P$) in the same direction as output (Q). This led to the positive response of $M1/P$ to Q that the Baumol-Tobin theory predicts and that Goldfeld found for the 1952–73 period. Gradually in the 1970s and particularly during 1979–82, the Fed began to deemphasize interest rate targets and focus on a money-supply target. With the Fed now controlling the money supply, the response of $M1/P$ to Q was under the Fed's control. A rigid CGRR for $M1$ (and gradual adjustment of P in the absence of supply shocks) would imply no response of $M1/P$ to Q, and Goldfeld's pre-1973 coefficient would not accurately describe the behavior of real balances.

16-9 Financial Deregulation and the *IS-LM* Model

This chapter began by introducing the wide variety of financial instruments and showed how changes in financial regulations introduced new substitutes for money, thus contributing to instability in the demand for money. In addition, with the deregulation of financial markets, an active countercyclical monetary policy is likely to increase the volatility of interest rates. This section explains how the elimination of previous regulations and other related changes in financial markets have helped contribute to the volatility of interest rates.

Until 1985 **Regulation Q** fixed interest rates on some types of bank deposits.

Effects of Regulation Q. Until 1985, the Fed's **Regulation Q** fixed ceilings on the interest rate that could be paid on commercial bank demand deposits and time deposits, and similar regulations controlled interest rates at thrift institutions. During a period when the market interest rate on short-term federal funds or Treasury bills increased, either because of a rightward shift in the *IS* curve or an increase in the demand for money function, a substantial gap could open up between the interest rates on short-term securities and the interest rates on deposits that were *held down by Regulation Q.*

Any such gap between the interest rate on Treasury bills and on passbook savings accounts caused a massive withdrawal of funds from commercial banks and thrift institutions (TIs) and any such substantial downward shift in the demand for savings deposits had a disproportionate deflationary effect on the housing market, because (TIs) were required by law to hold almost all their assets in the form of mortgages. The supply of mortgage finance declined for purchasers of both new and used homes. The shift toward bonds and Treasury bills and away from TIs was called **disintermediation.** An outflow of funds from the TIs, a drop in mortgage finance, and a decline in housing expenditure occurred in every postwar episode of high interest rates before 1983.

Financial Deregulation and the *IS* Curve

Financial deregulation since 1978 has included the introduction of new interest-sensitive certificates at the TIs, the removal of deposit-rate ceilings, and the development of mortgage-backed securities have largely eliminated rationing of finance for new and existing homes. A fourth innovation has been the **adjustable-rate mortgage** (ARM). Previously all mortgages carried nominal interest rates fixed for the life of the mortgage. Some of the previous potency of tight monetary policy on the housing market resulted from the postponement of home purchases by buyers who preferred to wait for lower interest rates. Now home purchasers can opt for an ARM and purchase their house now, knowing that they will benefit from lower interest rates in the future when financial-market conditions permit.[21]

Thus before the 1980s home buyers often postponed plans to purchase homes either because they were denied credit by TIs suffering from disintermediation, or because they chose to wait for lower interest rates. Now credit rationing plays a smaller role and fluctuations in interest rates play a greater role in balancing supply and demand.

Recall that the *IS* curve displays all the combinations of real output (Q) and the interest rate (r) that are consistent with equilibrium in the commodity market. The slope of the *IS* curve indicates how much an increase in the interest rate reduces interest-sensitive spending, and thus reduces real output. Changes in financial markets have made the *IS* curve steeper, shown in the left frame of Figure 16-5, because a given increase in the interest rate on financial assets will cause a smaller reduction in expenditures than previously.

Why the *LM* Curve Became Steeper

Chapter 4 showed that the *LM* curve normally slopes up because the demand for $M1$ responds to the interest rate paid on bonds and other nonmonetary assets, which is the interest rate (r) plotted along the vertical axis of Figure 16-5. Our previous analysis, and the curve in Figure 16-5 labeled "old LM curve," assumed that the interest rate paid on $M1$ (r_m) was zero.

Disintermediation was the process of fund withdrawal from thrift institutions when market interest rates went above the interest rates on savings accounts that were fixed by Regulation Q.

An **adjustable-rate mortgage** has an interest rate that can change frequently in response to changes in financial-market conditions, in contrast to a fixed-interest mortgage.

---

[21]There indeed were outflows from TIs in 1988–89, but this was not the old type of disintermediation caused by a temporary shift in monetary policy. Instead, it reflected doubt by depositors in the solvency of the thrift industry in general and of individual TIs in particular.

FINANCIAL DEREGULATION TILTS THE *IS* AND *LM* CURVES

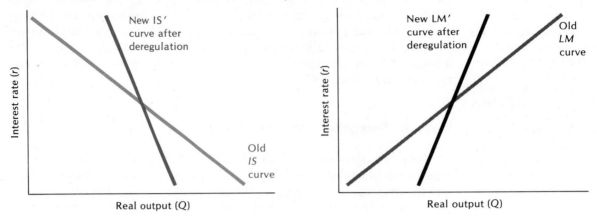

Figure 16-5   **Effect of Financial Deregulation in the Commodity and Money Markets**
In the left-hand frame deregulation causes the *IS* curve to become the steeper line *IS'* as the result of the discontinuation of regulation Q, of the introduction of new types of deposits at banks and TIs with flexible interest rates, of the development of mortgage-backed securities, and of the introduction of adjustable-rate mortgages. In the right-hand frame the *LM* curve becomes the steeper line *LM'* because a given increase in the interest rate in financial markets does not cause as much of a reduction of the demand for *M1* as previously, since banks and TIs are now able to raise the rates they pay for deposits.

Thus an increase in r raised $r - r_m$ by the same amount and created an incentive for individuals to reduce their holdings of $M1$.

This analysis still is valid for holdings of currency, which continue to pay no interest. But financial reforms have allowed banks to offer their customers interest-bearing checking NOW and Super NOW accounts. The interest rate on these accounts is variable and rises in response to increases in the interest rate paid on nonmonetary assets (r). Thus r_m, which is an average of the zero interest rate on currency and the positive interest rate paid on NOW and Super NOW accounts, responds partially to changes in r. So the difference $r - r_m$ rises by less than the amount of any increase in r, providing less of an incentive than previously for individuals to reduce their checking account balances. The result has been to make the *LM* curve steeper in the right frame of Figure 16-5.

Effects on Interest Rates

Now we can put our analysis into action and learn why the main effect of deregulation is likely to be more volatility of interest rates. In Figure 16-6 both frames show the *LM* curve shifting to the left by the same horizontal distance, as the result of a decision by the Fed to tighten monetary policy.

The difference between the frames is that the left-hand frame shows the economy before deregulation, with the flat "old *IS* curve" and "old *LM* curve" copied from Figure 16-5. The right-hand frame shows the economy after deregulation, with the new curves *IS'* and *LM'*, also copied from Figure 16-5. The economy moves from point *A* to *B* in the left frame and from point *A* to *B'* in the right frame, with a much greater increase in the interest rate under the new deregulated environment.

This analysis helps explain the fourth puzzle involving interest rates. And it shows that deregulation can have adverse side effects that may partially offset the benefits of greater efficiency and fairness when the price system (that is, interest rate movements) plays the main role in balancing the supply and demand for funds in financial markets.

Two qualifications are required of the analysis in this section. First, adjustable-rate mortgages (ARMs) help insulate the housing market from the effects of tight money by eliminating one reason home purchasers used to postpone home buying. But the increase in ARMs on *existing mortgages* in a period of tight money can put a financial squeeze on other consumers and

WHY DEREGULATION MAKES INTEREST RATES MORE VOLATILE

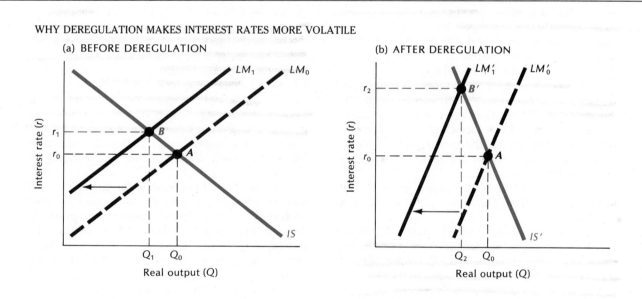

Figure 16-6   **The Effect of a Lower Money Supply on Interest Rates and Output**
Both frames show the effects of the same leftward horizontal shift in the *LM* curve as the result of a decision by the Fed to tighten monetary policy. In both frames the *IS* curve remains fixed. The difference is that the left frame uses the flat *IS* and *LM* curves from the period before deregulation of financial markets, copied from Figure 16-5. The right frame uses the new steeper *IS'* and *LM'* curves, also copied from Figure 16-5. As a result of the steeper curves, a given leftward shift in the *LM* curve creates a much bigger increase in the interest rate in the right frame than in the left frame.

cause them to postpone purchasing other items like autos and appliances. This leads us to expect that a period of tight money now will hit housing less, and other consumer spending more, than formerly.

The second qualification was introduced in Chapter 5. With an open economy and flexible exchange rates, tight money can restrict spending through the additional channel of an appreciating exchange rate, which then reduces net exports. Our conclusion in Chapter 5 that the *IS* curve is flatter with flexible exchange rates contrasts with our conclusion in this section that the *IS* curve becomes steeper as a result of financial deregulation. We return to this issue in the next chapter, where we find that on balance these changes may have steepened the *IS* curve in the short run but made it flatter in the long run. And there is no doubt that the *LM* curve has been made steeper as a result of financial deregulation without any offsetting impact from flexible exchange rates.

SUMMARY

1. The demand for money is a basic economic relation that determines how the money supply and total expenditures are related. Instability in the demand for money can make it difficult for the Federal Reserve to achieve precise control of spending through control of the money supply.

2. Surplus funds from savers are channeled to borrowers by way of financial intermediaries and financial markets. The main types of financial intermediaries are deposit, contractual saving, and investment intermediaries. The main types of financial market instruments are money-market and capital-market instruments.

3. The three functions of money are its use as a medium of exchange, as a store of value, and as a unit of account.

4. The United States has two major definitions of the money supply. *M*1 includes currency, demand deposits, and traveler's checks. *M*2 is comprised of both *M*1 and other assets, including savings deposits and certificates, repurchase orders, Eurodollar deposits, money-market deposit accounts, and money-market mutual funds.

5. Before the late 1970s, interest was not paid on checking accounts. But between 1978 and 1985 several types of new accounts were introduced that allowed interest to be paid and checks to be written on the same account. This era of financial deregulation contributed to the instability of the demand for money, as individuals switched back and forth between different types of accounts.

6. Several theories have been developed to explain the relation between the demand for money, income, wealth, and the interest rate. The demand for money for transaction purposes depends on the interest rate, because people will take the trouble to make extra trips to the bank and keep more of their income in savings accounts (and other interest-earning assets) when the interest rate is high.

7. The portfolio approach emphasizes the household decision to allocate its wealth among money, savings accounts, bonds, and other assets. Any event that raises wealth, such as a stimulative fiscal policy, will tend to raise the demand for money.

8. In 1974–79 the demand for money *declined* mysteriously compared to the predictions of most economists. As a result, the actual rate of growth in demand deposits and currency (*M*1) allowed by the Federal Reserve was adequate to finance a much faster growth rate of nominal GNP than had been expected.

9. In 1982–87 the demand for money *increased* mysteriously compared to the predictions of most economists, largely as the result of financial deregulation. As a result, the growth rate of nominal GNP dropped relative to that of *M*1. The nation suffered a serious recession in 1982, and the Fed was forced to allow double-digit *M*1 growth to maintain the recovery of output.

10. Deregulation of financial markets has made both the *IS* and *LM* curves steeper, so that a given change in the supply of money now has a greater effect on interest rates.

financial markets
financial deregulation
financial intermediaries
thrift institutions
money-market instruments
capital-market instruments
medium of exchange
store of value
unit of account

quantity theory of money
transaction motive
speculative motive
portfolio approach
$M1$ versus $M2$
Regulation Q
disintermediation
adjustable-rate mortgage

QUESTIONS AND PROBLEMS

Questions

1. Explain why stability of the demand for money is so important to the monetarist case. What happens to the monetarist argument if money demand is unstable?

2. What are the two most important functions for money? Give examples of assets which perform both functions. Give examples of assets which perform one of the functions but not the other.

3. How does the financial deregulation which has taken place in the 1980s affect the demand for money schedule introduced in Chapter 4? How does it affect the *LM* curve?

4. Explain why there is a long-run downward trend in the velocity of money. How does this phenomenon affect the quantity theory of money?

5. According to the Keynesian theory of money, if people believe that the interest rate is unusually low, will their demand for money be relatively high or low? Explain your answer.

6. What are the three major criticisms of the Keynesian theory of money? Which of the criticisms is most crucial?

7. Explain the significance of the Baumol–Tobin analysis of the transactions demand for money.

8. In what ways are the portfolio approaches developed by Tobin and Friedman similar? In what ways do they differ?

9. How does the inflation rate affect the velocity of money?

10. Describe the puzzling behavior of money demand after 1973. How have economists explained this phenomenon?

11. What is meant by the term financial markets? Given the existence of financial markets, why do we have financial intermediaries?

12. What is meant by the term disintermediation? What impact did deregulation of financial markets have on the process?

Problems

1. Assume the following equations summarize the structure of the economy before and after deregulation. (Note: the structure of the economy before deregulation is the same as that in question 2 at the end of Chapter 5).

   Economy *before* deregulation:
   $C = a + .75Q_d$ $G = 400$
   $a = 50 - 10r$ $M_s/P = 300$
   $T = 200 + .2Q$ $h = .4$
   $I_p = 300 - 30r$ $f = 50$
   $X = 400 - .2Q - 5e$ where the exchange rate
     $e = dr = 10r$

   Economy *after* deregulation:
   $C = a + .75Q_d$ $G = 400$
   $a = 50 - 5r$ $M_s/P = 300$
   $T = 200 + .2Q$ $h = .3$
   $I_p = 200 - 5r$ $f = 15$
   $X = 400 - .2Q - 5e$ where the exchange rate
     $e = dr = 10r$

   Using the information above,

   a) What is the equation of the *IS* curve before deregulation? What is the equation of the *IS* curve after deregulation?

   b) What is the equation of the *LM* curve before deregulation? What is the equation of the *LM* curve after deregulation?

c) What are the equilibrium levels of income (Q) and interest (r) before and after deregulation?

d) How do your answers to (a), (b), and (c) above differ before and after deregulation.

e) If the money supply decreases to 250, what is the new level of income and interest rate in the situations before and after deregulation? Do these results verify the explanation given in Figure 16-6? How does this problem differ, if at all?

SELF-TEST ANSWERS

p. 485 Commercial banks are the largest single type of financial intermediary. Federal funds are money-market instruments, money-market mutual funds are financial intermediaries, state government bonds are capital market instruments, state government retirement funds are financial intermediaries, corporate bonds are capital market instruments, and commercial paper is a money-market instrument.

p. 491 (1) This new type of account, which allows interest to be earned and checks to be written, is part of $M2$, and so its invention shifts the demand for $M2$ to the right and the demand for $M1$ to the left; (2) This new provision, included in $M1$, allowed savings automatically to be transferred to cover checking overdrafts, and its invention shifted the demand for $M1$ to the right and the demand for $M2$ to the left; (3) same as (1). The case study in Section 16-8 explains how the demand for $M2$ shifted to the right in the early stages of financial deregulation in 1978–82 and the demand for $M1$ shifted to the right in the later stages in 1982–83.

p. 500 Starting from an initial equilibrium, an increase in the supply of $M1$ creates an excess supply of $M1$. According to Tobin and Friedman, $M1$ is a substitute for both bonds and stocks, and so some of the $M1$ that is in excess of the initial demand will be used to purchase bonds and stocks. (Strictly speaking, the Tobin version makes stocks and bonds a substitute only for the interest-bearing part of $M1$, not non-interest-bearing currency and checking deposits).

CHAPTER SEVENTEEN

The Conduct of Stabilization Policy

There is a strong presumption . . . discretionary actions will in general be subject to longer lags than the automatic reactions and hence be destabilizing even more frequently.

—Milton Friedman, 1953

17-1   The Link Between Stabilization Policy and Long-Run Growth

The traditional theory of income determination, developed in Chapters 4–6, places monetary and fiscal policy on an equal footing. The level of output and interest rates can be influenced either by monetary policy, through its control over the money supply, or by fiscal policy, through its control over government spending and tax rates. Policymakers can achieve many combinations of output levels and interest rates by varying the "mix" of monetary and fiscal policy.

For instance, the mix of relatively easy fiscal policy and tight monetary policy in the United States in the 1980s resulted in high real interest rates. In a closed economy such a policy mix would "crowd out" investment and slow the rate of long-run economic growth. In an open economy like the United States this direct connection between the stabilization policy mix and the rate of long-run growth is broken, because an open economy can maintain the level of domestic investment by borrowing from foreigners. In the standard analysis of the policy mix, the levels of interest rates and output are determined simultaneously, and the stance of both monetary and fiscal policy matters for both the determination of output and of the interest rate. Hence both policies matter for stabilization and growth.

Lags and the Choice of Policies

The "comparative static" analysis of Chapters 4–6 neglected the dynamic elements that influence the role of monetary and fiscal policy. Beginning in Chapter 15, we recognized that stabilization policy acts with a time lag. Because their policies have a delayed impact on spending, the makers of monetary and fiscal policy must try to forecast where the economy will be six or twelve months into the future. But these forecasts are imperfect, so policymakers have a strong incentive to use for stabilization purposes the type of policy that operates with the shortest lags.

In the United States in the 1980s a political stalemate led to fiscal deficits of unprecedented persistence for a peacetime period. Fiscal policy ceased to operate with any regard whatsoever for the needs of stabilizing output growth and taming the business cycle. By default, then, stabilization policy came to consist entirely of monetary policy. Fiscal policy was thrust into the background role of determining the overall level of real interest rates, making fiscal policy the central variable in relation to the rate of long-run economic growth and the buildup of foreign debt.

Correspondingly, this chapter on the conduct of stabilization policy is primarily devoted to monetary policy. But fiscal policy is not neglected entirely. In other eras fiscal policy was used for stabilization purposes. We will review the past performance of fiscal as well as monetary policy, in order to understand those problems that may affect their usefulness in the future. In other countries, where the political process does not inhibit the use of short-run fiscal policy changes as part of stabilization policy, it is still interesting to debate the relative merits of monetary and fiscal policy. The political environment in the United States could change in the future, and bring fiscal policy back into consideration for stabilization purposes.

Limitations of Activist Monetary Policy

We learned in the last two chapters that precise control over the money supply does not guarantee precise control of aggregate demand. Changes in consumption, investment spending, net exports, government spending, and tax rates can shift the *IS* curve when the money supply is constant. In addition, changes in the amount of money demanded at a given level of real GNP and the interest rate can shift the *LM* curve even though the money supply is fixed.

Thus stable growth in nominal GNP appears to require an activist countercyclical monetary policy (Section 15-5). But an activist monetary policy may do more harm than good, as claimed in plank 3 of Chapter 15's monetarist platform, because of time lags in the effects of a change in the money supply on aggregate demand. And, as we learned in Chapter 16, the 1980s saw the deregulation of financial markets and the development of new financial instruments. These changes eliminated disintermediation, a process that tended to give monetary policy prompt control over housing construction through quantity rationing. Because effects of monetary policy rest more now on price effects of higher interest rates, and less on credit rationing, the lags of monetary policy may be even longer than they were a decade ago. Flexible exchange rates enhance the potency of monetary policy, but lags in the response of net exports to changes in the exchange rate also seem to be very long. Thus, just as it has been thrust by default into the spotlight as the economy's only tool to fight business cycles, monetary policy may be more prone than ever to long time lags. As the monetarists argue, countercyclical monetary policy may do more harm than good.

Until now we have assumed that the money supply can be set at any desired value. We begin this chapter by examining the methods by which the Federal Reserve controls the money supply. We then turn to evidence on lags in both monetary and fiscal policy and to case studies that illustrate the pitfalls encountered in past attempts to conduct an effective stabilization policy.

17-2 High-Powered Money and Determinants of the Money Supply

The *IS-LM* model shows how real output and the interest rate are jointly determined by the positions of the *IS* and *LM* curves. The position of the *LM* curve depends mainly on changes in the real money supply, that is, the nominal money supply divided by the price level (M^s/P). While the Federal Reserve does not directly control the price level, it does have the ability to control the nominal money supply. In this section we review the standard theory of how banks create money, and we learn that the Fed's actions have a multiplier effect on the total supply of money. We learn later that the elementary model of the money supply is too simple, and that the Fed cannot control the money supply as precisely as the simple theory implies.

Money Creation on a Desert Island

The role of the Fed in the money supply process is best understood by starting with a simple banking system where there is no Fed. We begin with the First Desert Island Bank, which is started by a banker who receives a deposit of 100 gold coins. Initially the bank holds the gold as an asset and has deposits of 100. However, the banker is missing an opportunity to make a profit: 100 gold coins sit in the vault, and only 20 are ever withdrawn by the initial depositor. The banker decides to keep "reserves" equal to just 20 percent of total deposits and to grant loans equal to the remaining 80 percent of total deposits.

It is possible to show the creation of money step-by-step. For instance, the banker sets aside 20 gold coins as reserves and makes a loan of 80, which is redeposited in the bank by the borrower, say, a used raft dealer. This brings total deposits to 180, consisting of the initial deposit of 100 and the new deposit of 80. Because the used raft dealer has redeposited the 80 gold coins received as a loan, the banker still has the original 100 gold coins, yet only 36 (20 percent of 180) are needed as reserves.

Required Conditions for Money Creation

When the process is completed, the banker's total reserves (100 gold coins) are equal to the total required to be held, 20 percent of total deposits. This allows the banker to continue granting loans until total deposits reach 500. At that point, the banker's actual reserves (100) equal required reserves (100 = 0.2 times 500). Thus the original deposit of 100 gold coins leads to the creation of 500 units of money, all in the form of bank deposits. The First Desert Island Bank has succeeded in creating $5 of money for every $1 of cash that it initially received.

How has this magic occurred? Five conditions are necessary for the banker to turn 100 gold coins into a money supply of 500.

1. **Equivalence of coins and deposits.** Paper receipts claiming ownership of bank deposits must be accepted as a means of payment on a one-for-one basis—that is, a deposit representing a claim to one gold coin is accepted by sellers as equivalent to payment of one gold coin. People must be able to withdraw a portion of their deposit in the form of cash (gold coins in the example).

2. **Redeposit of proceeds from loans.** Any consumer or business firm receiving a cash payment from the proceeds of a loan must redeposit the cash into his or her own account at the same bank. We assumed in the example that the used raft dealer redeposited the 80 gold coins received as the proceeds of the first loan.

3. **Redeposit of checks written on bank accounts.** When sellers receive any payment in the form of a check written on a bank account, they must redeposit the check in their own bank account in the same bank.

4. **Holding of cash reserves.** The bank must hold some fraction of its reserves in the form of cash (20 percent in gold coins in this example).

5. **Willing borrowers.** Someone must be willing to borrow from the bank at an interest rate that at least covers the bank's cost of operation. If the First Desert Island Bank could find no lending opportunities, then it could not grant any loans and the money creation process could not occur.

The Money-Creation Multiplier

High-powered money is the sum of currency held by the nonbank public and bank reserves.

If all five conditions are met, then the entire process of money creation can be summed up in a simple equation. We let the symbol H denote **high-powered money**—that is, the quantity of the type of money that is held by banks as reserves. In the example, H consists of the 100 gold coins, which are "high-powered" because they generate the multiplier expansion of money by the First Desert Island Bank. The symbol D represents the total of bank deposits. The symbol e represents the fraction of deposits that banks decide to hold as reserves. The *demand* for high-powered money to be held as reserves (eD) is then equal to the *supply* of high-powered money (H):

General Form   Numerical Example

$$eD = H \qquad 0.2(500) = 100 \qquad (17.1)$$

The same equation can be rearranged (dividing both sides by (e) to determine the size of the stock deposits (D) relative to the quantity of high-powered money (H) and the bank reserve-holding ratio (e):

General Form   Numerical Example

$$D = \frac{H}{e} \qquad 500 = \frac{100}{0.2} \qquad (17.2)$$

Comparison with income-determination multiplier. The money-creation multiplier is $1/e$, or $1/0.2 = 5.0$ in the numerical example. This is the second usage of the word *multiplier* in this book. In Chapters 3–6 we examined the factors determining the income-determination multiplier. In its simplest version, that multiplier in Chapter 3 was written as follows:

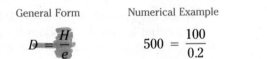

$$\text{Income-determination multiplier} = \frac{\text{autonomous planned spending } (A_p)}{\text{marginal propensity to save } (s)}$$

An increase in autonomous planned spending (A_p) is multiplied in Chapter 3 because spending creates income, a fraction of which *leaks out* into saving and taxes and the remainder of which goes into additional spending. The multiplier process ends only when the total of extra induced leakages equals the original increase in A_p.

The intuitive reasoning behind the money-creation multiplier is the same. An increase in high-powered money *(H)* is multiplied (17.2) because the initial deposit of *H* becomes reserves of the bank, a fraction of which *leaks out* into required reserves and the remainder of which is lent out and comes back as additional deposits of the stores and business firms that receive the loan proceeds. The money-creation multiplier process terminates only when the total of extra induced leakages into required reserves has used up the original increase in *H*.

Comparison with real-world conditions. Now it is time to recognize that some of the five conditions describing money creation on the desert island may not exist in the real world.

Condition (2) required that any seller receiving a cash payment from the proceeds of a loan redeposit the cash into the bank. If the cash does not come back to the bank, the multiplier process of money creation cannot occur at that bank. If the cash is redeposited at another bank, then the second bank will find itself with excess reserves, allowing the multiplier process to proceed.

Conditions (2) and (3) can be revised to apply to any group of banks, say, all the banks within the United States. As long as sellers receiving loan proceeds in the form of either cash or checks redeposit the funds in a U.S. bank, the money-creation multiplier in equation (17.2) remains valid for the U.S. banking system as a whole.

Cash holding. The money-creation multiplier is changed, however, if everyone wants to hold not only demand (checking) deposits at banks but some pocket cash as well. Imagine that everyone wants to hold a fixed fraction *(c)* of his or her deposits, say 5 percent, in the form of cash.[1] Then this source of cash holding adds an extra amount *(cD)* to the total demand for high-powered money. In a revised desert-island example, the demand for gold coins, the only form of high-powered money, might be 20 percent of deposits for bank reserves *(eD = 0.2D)*, plus 5 percent of deposits for pocket cash *(cD = 0.05D)*.

The total demand for high-powered money *(eD + cD)* can be equated to the total supply *(H)*:

General Form		Numerical Example	
Demand	*Supply*	*Demand*	*Supply*

$$eD + cD \quad = H \qquad\qquad 0.2D + 0.05D = 100$$
$$\text{or } (e + c)D = H \qquad\qquad \text{or} \qquad 0.25D = 100 \qquad (17.3)$$

Dividing both sides by *(e + c)*, we can solve for deposits:

$$D = \frac{H}{e + c} \qquad\qquad D = \frac{100}{0.25} = 400 \qquad (17.4)$$

---

[1]The cash fraction *c* has nothing whatsoever to do with the marginal propensity to consume *(c)* of Chapter 3. Also, the reserve holding ratio *(e)* has nothing to do with the foreign exchange rate *(e)* of Chapter 5. At this stage we have run through the alphabet and are requiring some letters to perform double duty. See the guide to symbols provided in the inside front and back covers.

In words, the total of deposits is equal to the supply of high-powered money *(H)* divided by the fraction of deposits that leaks into reserves *(e)* plus the fraction that leaks into pocket cash *(c)*.

Although specialized courses in monetary economics develop complicated formulas that relate the U.S. money supply to high-powered money and numerous other factors, for our purposes equation (17.4) is an entirely adequate explanation.[2] We can modify (17.4) slightly by recognizing that the total money supply *(M)* includes not only deposits *(D)* but also cash (including currency and coins) held in an amount equal to the cash-holding ratio times deposits *(cD)*:

$$M = D + cD = (1 + c)D \qquad (17.5)$$

Substituting for *D* in (17.5) from (17.4), we obtain:

$$M = (1 + c)D = \frac{(1 + c)H}{e + c} \qquad (17.6)$$

Money Creation in Pictures

Just as we used a simple diagram to illustrate the workings of the income-determination multiplier, we can use the same type of diagram to show the determinants of the money supply. The basic money supply formula, equation (17.6), is derived from equation (17.3), where the demand for high-powered money is set equal to the supply of high-powered money. The supply of high-powered money *(H_0)* is plotted as a horizontal line in the top frame of Figure 17-1. The demand for high-powered money from equation (17.3) is *(e + c)D*. Then, equation (17.5) shows how the money supply is related to deposits, allowing us to write:

$$\text{Demand for high-powered money} = \frac{(e + c)}{1 + c}M \qquad (17.7)$$

The upward-sloping straight line in the top frame of Figure 17-1 is the demand for high-powered money. The supply of money *(M_0)* is determined where the supply of and demand for high-powered money intersect, at point *A*.

The diagram allows us to visualize the two major ways in which the supply of money can change. First, as in the middle frame of Figure 17-1, the supply of high-powered money can be increased from H_0 to H_1, raising the money supply from M_0 to M_1. Second, as in the bottom frame of Figure 17-1, the demand for high-powered money may fall *for a given quantity of M*. This could occur if banks reduce *e* by holding less reserves per dollar of deposits, or if the public reduces *c,* the cash-holding ratio, by holding a smaller amount of currency per dollar of deposits. As shown in the bottom frame, a reduction in the reserve ratio from e_0 to e_1 will raise the money supply from M_0 to M_2.

---

[2]Students interested in a more detailed treatment of the money-supply process should consult Frederick S. Mishkin, *The Economics of Money, Banking, and Financial Markets,* Second Edition (Glenview: Scott, Foresman, 1989), Chapters 12–14.

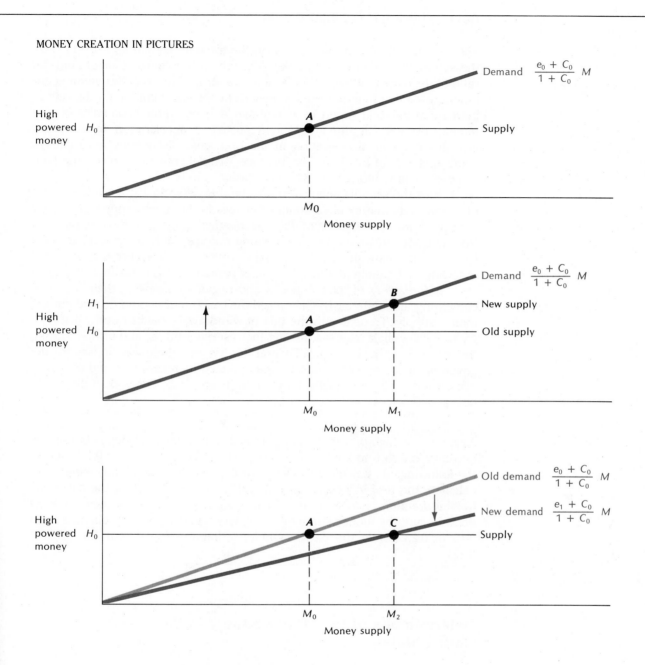

Figure 17-1 **Effects on the Money Supply of Changes in the Supply of and Demand for High-Powered Money**

In the top frame the supply of high-powered money is plotted as a black horizontal line, and the demand (given by equation 17.7) as an upward-sloping red straight line. The middle frame shows the effect of an increase in the supply of high-powered money from H_0 to H_1, shifting the new equilibrium from A to B and raising the money supply from M_0 to M_1. The bottom frame shows the effect of a reduction in the bank reserve-holding ratio from e_0 to e_1, shifting the new equilibrium from A to C and raising the money supply from M_0 to M_2.

Gold Discoveries and Bank Panics

The supply of money depends only on the three terms that appear in (17.6): the supply of high-powered money *(H)*, the cash-holding ratio *(c)*, and the ratio of deposits that the banks hold in the form of reserves *(e)*. In an economy in which all high-powered money *(H)* consists of gold, then the rate of increase in the total supply of money may depend on the economics of gold mining. Because in the long run a sustained acceleration in monetary growth causes an acceleration in inflation, gold discoveries have caused some episodes of inflation. For instance, price increases followed the gold discoveries in California in 1848 and Alaska in 1898.

Before the establishment of the Federal Reserve in 1913, the U.S. economy was at the mercy of capricious changes in the money supply stemming not only from the influence of gold discoveries on the growth of *H*, but also from episodes in which the cash-holding ratio *(c)* and the reserve ratio *(e)* fluctuated dramatically. During banking panics, which occurred about once a decade and culminated in the serious panic of 1907, depositors began to fear for the safety of their deposits and began withdrawing their deposits, converting them into cash. This raised the cash-holding ratio *(c)* and cut the money supply. To deal with the tide of withdrawals, banks in turn began to try to bolster their reserves, raising the reserve ratio *(e)* and further cutting the money supply.[3] In the pre-Federal Reserve era, there was no way for the government to raise *H* to offset panic-induced increases in *c* and *e*. Panics caused a drop in the money supply and in aggregate demand, cutting both output and prices.

SELF-TEST   Assume that high-powered money is 500, the fraction of deposits held as currency is 0.25, and the fraction of deposits held as reserves is 0.15. Answer the following: (1) Calculate the value of deposits and the money supply; (2) calculate the new value of deposits and the money supply if the currency-holding fraction changes from 0.25 to 0.35; (3) calculate the new value of deposits and the money supply if the reserve-holding fraction changes from 0.15 to 0.25 (while the currency-holding fraction remains at the original 0.25).

17-3   Determinants of the Money Supply in the United States

The Federal Reserve System was established in late 1913 upon the recommendation of a commission set up to study the causes of the 1907 banking panic and to recommend solutions to prevent future panics.[4] Banks now

---

[3]Notice in equation (17.6) that any increase in *e* reduces the quantity of money *(M)*. Although *c* appears in both the numerator and the denominator, an increase in *c* reduces the money supply as long as the reserve-holding ratio *(e)* is less than 1.0.

[4]A spirited narration on the establishment of the Federal Reserve System is in John Kenneth Galbraith, *Money* (Boston: Houghton Mifflin, 1975), Chapter 10. See also Milton Friedman and Anna J. Schwartz, *A Monetary History of the United States, 1867–1960* (Princeton, N.J.: Princeton University Press, 1963), pp. 168–172 and 189–196.

were to hold most of their reserves in the form of deposits at the Federal Reserve banks. High-powered money now consisted of two major portions: (1) cash as before and (2) bank deposits at the Federal Reserve banks.

The exact details of monetary control by the Fed have changed in minor ways since 1913, but the basic structure has remained intact and is illustrated in Table 17-1. The table is a simplified representation of the elements of the money-supply process, with numerical examples for December 1988. The right half of the table shows the balance sheet of the nation's commercial banks. Bank liabilities consist of deposits owed to the depositors, with a total amount of $1609 billion in December 1988.

Bank assets are of two types. First, banks hold reserves to back up their deposits, just as the Desert Island Bank kept gold coins on hand to meet withdrawals by depositors. U.S. bank reserves include vault cash and deposits at the Fed, both of which the banks accept as equivalent, because they can use their deposits at the Fed to obtain more vault cash if they need to

Table 17–1

All figures are for December 1988 in $ billions

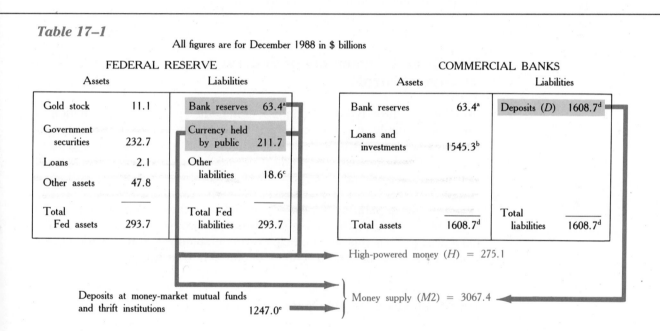

Source notes: M2 and currency held by the public are from *Federal Reserve Bulletin* (March 1989), Table 1.21. Federal Reserve assets from same source, Table 1.18. Other items are calculated as indicated in the lettered notes below, where table numbers all refer to the same source.

[a]Bank reserves from Table 1.25 include commercial bank reserves at the Fed plus currency and coin held by commercial banks as vault cash.

[b]Loans and investments are calculated as deposits minus bank reserves. Since total liabilities include several other major items not shown here, particularly borrowings and deposits that are not included in M2, this method understates loans and investments.

[c]Calculated as total Fed liabilities from Table 1.18, minus the currency component of M2, minus bank reserves calculated as in note a.

[d]Calculated as commercial bank transaction deposits and savings deposits from Table 1.25, plus small-denomination time deposits from Table 1.21.

[e]Calculated as M2 minus commercial bank deposits from note d minus currency held by the public.

accommodate an unusually large withdrawal. The other portion of bank assets consists of loans to households and business firms and investments in various types of federal, state, and local government bonds.

The Fed's balance sheet. The new element in Table 17-1 is the balance sheet of the Federal Reserve. The Fed's balance sheet has some similarity to that of the commercial banks because a portion of the Fed's liabilities consists of deposits (the bank reserves that the Fed "owes" to the banks). The asset side includes both loans and investments, a small $2.1 billion in loans to commercial banks and a much larger $232.7 billion of investments in government bonds.

But there are differences. The Fed can issue currency, whereas commercial banks are prohibited by law from doing so. The Fed's major liability item consists of currency held by the public.[5] Second, a portion of the Fed's assets consists of gold, which the commercial banks are prohibited from holding. Third, unlike the banks, which are required to keep a specified fraction of their deposits on hand in the form of reserves, the Fed does not have to maintain any fixed relation among its assets.

17-4 The Three Instruments of Federal Reserve Control

Decisions by three types of economic units enter into the determination of the money supply in equation (17.6). The job of the Federal Reserve is to calculate the total *M* that it desires, based on its current target for aggregate demand. The Fed must also predict the public's desired cashholding ratio *(c)*, over which the Fed has no control. Then the Fed can adjust the two remaining variables in equation (17.6), *H* and *e*, to make its desired *M* consistent with the public's chosen *c*. The Fed uses three main instruments to accomplish this task, the first two of which control *H* and the last of which influences *e*. Thus this section helps us understand which real-world events would cause the changes in *H* and *e* depicted in Figure 17-1.

First Tool: Open-Market Operations

Open-market operations are purchases and sales of government bonds made by the Federal Reserve in order to change high-powered money.

The first tool is by far the most important. The Fed can change *H* from day to day by purchasing and selling government bonds. In Table 17-1 the Fed's liabilities are the major component of *H,* and government bonds are the major asset of the Fed. By purchasing bonds, the Fed raises its assets and liabilities at the same time, thus increasing *H*. By selling bonds, the Fed reduces its assets and liabilities, lowering *H*. Any change in *H* caused by Fed **open-market operations** causes an even larger change in *M* through the money-creation multiplier.

---

[5]Take a dollar bill and examine it—above George Washington's picture are the words "Federal Reserve Note" and to the left is a circle indicating the regional Federal Reserve bank that issued the note.

Federal Reserve policy is decided on the third Tuesday of each month at a meeting of the Federal Open-Market Committee (FOMC) held in a large and imposing room in Washington and attended by the seven governors of the Federal Reserve Board and the presidents of the twelve regional Federal Reserve banks.[6] Each meeting results in a directive sent to the Fed's open-market manager in New York, a position held in 1989 by Peter Sternlight.

H is created out of thin air. Let us say that Mr. Sternlight's directive from the FOMC calls for continued moderate growth in the money supply, and that he has decided that the time has come for a $100 million increase in high-powered money (H). All Mr. Sternlight has to do is pick up the phone and place an order with a New York government bond dealer, say Salomon Brothers, for $100 million in U.S. government bonds. The act that creates H "out of thin air" occurs when the Fed writes a $100 million check on itself to pay for the bonds. Salomon Brothers deposits the check in its account at a commercial bank, say Chase Manhattan. Just as the Desert Island Bank decided to hold a fixed fraction of its new deposits in the form of gold-coin reserves, so Chase Manhattan holds a portion of its new deposit, say $10 million, in its reserve account at the Fed.

The Chase Manhattan does not let Salomon Brothers' remaining $90 million deposit sit idly as excess reserves. Why? Because reserves earn no interest. To earn interest, the Chase lends out the $90 million immediately, say to Sears Roebuck. And the process continues, creating bank deposits again and again at each stage.

Thus Mr. Sternlight has "created money," not just the original $100 million, but a sizeable multiple of $100 million. Yet at no stage has he made anyone wealthier, nor has he given anyone a gift. Salomon Brothers has $100 million more in its bank account, but owns $100 million less in government bonds. Sears has $90 million more in its bank account, but now owes $90 million to the Chase.

Effect on interest rates. Sternlight's action influences not only the total supply of money but also the interest rate. When he buys the original $100 million in bonds, his action tends to raise bond prices and reduce the interest rate on bonds.

> **Review:** An important lesson in Figure 15-3 is that the Federal Reserve System cannot simultaneously control both the interest rate and the money supply. Mr. Sternlight's bond purchase that raises the money supply shifts the LM curve to the right, moving the economy's equilibrium position southeast down the IS curve and thus reducing the interest rate. Similarly, the Fed cannot sell a bond and reduce the money supply without raising the interest rate. The Fed can reduce the money supply without increasing the interest rate only if fiscal policy moves the IS curve to the left at the same time.

Sometimes the Fed must engage in open-market operations even when it has no desire to raise or lower the money supply. For instance, during the

---

[6]All twelve regional presidents attend, but only five may vote. The New York Fed president always has a vote and the other four votes are rotated.

Christmas shopping season, the public needs more cash for transactions and raises its desired cash-holding ratio *(c)*. Without action by the Federal Reserve this increase in the denominator of the money-supply equation (17.6) would reduce the money supply. Banks would use the reserves to provide cash to the public and would have fewer reserves left over to support deposits, so that the money supply would shrink by a multiple of the public's cash withdrawals. The Fed can avoid this shortage by conducting a "defensive" open-market purchase of bonds, providing banks with the extra reserves they need to handle the public's cash withdrawals.

SELF-TEST   Be sure you can answer this question without looking back at the preceding text: If the Fed wants to reduce the money supply, does it conduct an open-market purchase of bonds or sale of bonds? What does it do if it wants to raise the money supply?

Second Tool: Rediscount Rate

The **rediscount rate** is the interest rate the Federal Reserve charges banks when they borrow funds.

Banks decide how much to borrow from the Federal Reserve System by comparing the interest rate charged by the Fed, the **rediscount rate**, with the interest rate the banks can receive by investing the funds received from the Fed. Federal Reserve loans tend to be high when the interest rate on short-term investments, such as the interest rate on Federal funds, is substantially above the Fed's rediscount rate. And Fed loans tend to be low when the Federal funds rate is low relative to the rediscount rate.

Because $100 million in Fed loans provides banks with $100 million in bank reserves, as does a $100 million open-market purchase, the Fed can control high-powered money *(H)* either by varying the rediscount rate or by conducting open-market operations. Monetary control can be achieved with either instrument and does not require both. The only justification for continuing the practice of lending by the Fed is the possible need for help by individual banks suffering from an unexpected rush of withdrawals, but these cases are rare and could be handled individually. Many economists have criticized the Fed for continuing its lending, because in periods of high interest rates the Fed tends to keep its rediscount rate low enough to induce substantial borrowing by banks. This in turn reduces the precision of the Fed's day-to-day control over *H*.

Third Tool: Reserve Requirements

Required reserves are the reserves that banks must hold according to Federal Reserve regulations.

Reserve requirements are the rules that stipulate the minimum fraction of deposits that banks must maintain as required reserves.

Unlike the desert island, where the banker chose voluntarily to keep 20 percent of the bank's deposits on hand in the form of gold-coin reserves, in the United States, commercial banks that are members of the Fed must keep a specified fraction of their deposits as **required reserves.** Bank reserves can be held in the form of reserve accounts at the Fed or as vault cash (currency and coin). **Reserve requirements** vary with different types of deposits.

As is evident in equation (17.6) and the bottom frame of Figure 17-1, the Fed can raise the money supply by reducing bank reserve requirements *(e)*, or vice versa. Thus a reduction in *e* accomplishes the same increase in the money supply as an open-market purchase of the appropriate amount. Why does the Fed need to retain its control over reserve requirements? The only real justification is that a high level of reserve requirements can come in handy in wartime when the government needs to run a large budget deficit. In World War II, for instance, the government would have been required to pay very high interest rates to induce the public voluntarily to finance its entire deficit. To avoid this tactic, the government sold a large quantity of bonds to the Fed, causing H to double between 1940 and 1945.[7] To minimize the inflationary pressure created by the large wartime increase in H, the Fed maintained bank reserve requirements at a level much higher than at present.

17-5 Limitations of Countercyclical Monetary Activism: Lags and Volatility in Interest Rates

Countercyclical movements in the real money supply can achieve a more stable path of real output than a CGRR at the cost of greater fluctuations in the interest rate. (**Review:** Figure 15-3.) The two main objections to countercyclical activism are (1) that lags prevent the monetary changes from influencing the economy until it is too late and (2) that the extra fluctuations in the interest rate caused by activism are undesirable. Monetarists have generally emphasized only the first objection.[8]

The Five Types of Lags

Several types of lags intervene that prevent either monetary or fiscal policy from immediately offsetting an unexpected shift in the demand for commodities or money. There are five main types of lags, some of which are common to both monetary and fiscal policy and the rest of which are more important for one or the other:

1. The data lag
2. The recognition lag
3. The legislative lag
4. The transmission lag
5. The effectiveness lag

To explain the meaning of each lag and to estimate its length, let us take the example of the "pause" in the 1981–82 recession that occurred between

---

[7]Imagine that the government writes a $100 check during the war to pay a soldier's wages. The Fed actually writes the check and debits the government's account at the Fed (part of the Fed's liabilities). To restore the previous balance in its account at the Fed, the government sells the Fed a $100 bond, for which the Fed "pays" by adding $100 to the government's balance.

[8]See Milton Friedman, "The Lag in Effect of Monetary Policy," *Journal of Political Economy,* vol. 69 (October 1961), reprinted in his *The Optimum Quantity of Money and Other Essays* (Chicago: Aldine, 1969), pp. 237–260.

January and May 1982. During the pause, the economy appeared to be recovering, giving no hint of the further decline in real GNP that occurred in the second half of 1982.[9]

1. **The data lag.**   Policymakers do not know what is going on in the economy the moment it happens. Although a few industries have sales reports with a lag of only a few days, the first sign of the 1982 pause did not appear until mid-March, when the news of an increase in real manufacturing and trade sales became known. It was not until mid-July that the quarterly GNP figures revealed that the growth rate of real GNP had risen from an annual rate of -6.1 percent in 1982:Q1 to $+1.2$ percent in 1982:Q2.

2. **The recognition lag.**   No policymaker pays much attention to reversals in the data that occur for only one month. The usual rule of thumb is to wait and see if the reversal continues for three successive months. If the 1982 pause had been more prolonged, three months of data would not have been available until July, and a second reading on quarterly GNP growth would not have been available until mid-October.

3. **The legislative lag.**   Although most changes in fiscal policy must be legislated by Congress, an important advantage of monetary policy is the short legislative lag. Once a majority of the Federal Open-Market Committee (FOMC) decides that an acceleration in monetary growth is needed, only a short wait is necessary until the next meeting of the FOMC, which occurs once every month.

4. **The transmission lag.**   This lag is the time interval between the policy decision and the subsequent change in policy instruments—the money supply, government spending, or tax rates. Again, it is a more serious obstacle for fiscal policy. Once the FOMC has given its order for the open-market manager to make open-market purchases, the expansion in the money supply begins almost immediately, although the full multiple money-creation process may require one or two months.

5. **The effectiveness lag.**   Almost all the controversy about the lags of monetary policy concerns the length of time required for an acceleration or deceleration in the money supply to influence real output. Milton Friedman is on record, from his extensive historical studies of U.S. monetary behavior between 1867 and 1960, as arguing that the effectiveness lag is both "long" and "variable."

A Short but Variable Lag

Many estimates of the lag of monetary policy are available. Let us first develop an informal estimate of the average lag between the month of maximum monetary tightness and the subsequent onset of recession in the six post-Korean War recessions, recognizing that each recession was influenced by factors other than monetary policy.

---

[9]The Department of Commerce "index of four coincident indicators" reached a peak of 108.4 (1982 = 100) in July 1981. It fell to 102.1 in January 1982, then revived slightly to 103.0 in Febuary, and fell to a final trough of 97.0 in December 1982.

Business cycle peak of	Month/year of peak in:		
	$M1/P$	Coincident indicators (CI)	Average lag (months)
1957	4/56	2/57	10
1960	7/59	1/60	6
1969	2/69	10/69	8
1973	1/73	11/73	10
1980	8/79	1/80	5
1981	11/80	7/81	8
Average	—	—	7.8

Here the date of cyclical peaks are indicated for the real money supply *(M1/P)*—the same variable plotted in Figures 17-3 through 17-6. Our measure of real economic activity is taken to be the government's index of coincident indicators (CI).[10] In each business cycle the peak in $M1/P$ has occurred before that in CI. The lag between the peaks in $M1/P$ and CI ranges from five to ten months. Thus the label "short and variable" would appear to describe the monetary effectiveness lag better than Friedman's "long and variable."

To summarize this section on lags, let us add up the total delay between an unexpected economic pause and the arrival of stimulus from a reaction to that event by the Fed:

Time of lag	Estimated length (months)
1. Data	2.0
2. Recognition	2.0
3. Legislative	0.5
4. Transmission	1.0
5. Effectiveness	7.8
Total	13.3

Thus the Fed could not counteract the economic slump that began in August 1981 until September 1982, although the variability of the effectiveness lag might have shortened or lengthened the total lag by two or three months. By the time the Fed's stimulus arrived, the economy might not need additional stimulus (although in this case a stimulus was badly needed in September 1982). Or, looking at the problem another way, the Fed would have had to forecast the 1981–82 slump as early as July 1980.

The New Uncertainty About Monetary Policy Lags

This evidence on the length of monetary policy lags may seem ancient history. But, as of mid-1989, the economy had not experienced a recession caused by tight money since 1982. Two major changes that occurred in the

---

[10]This is an average of these four series: (1) employees on nonagricultural payrolls, (2) real personal income less transfer payments, (3) index of industrial production, and (4) real manufacturing and trade sales. We use the CI series in preference to real GNP, since the latter is not available on a monthly basis.

1980s reduced the relevance of the episodes in 1979–82 and before. First, as we learned in Section 16-9, financial deregulation ensured that in the future, any episode of tight money would have to work through high interest rates pricing people out of purchases, without the quick impact of credit rationing in housing markets that had been important in earlier episodes. Back in the era of disintermediation, since victims of credit rationing could not escape its impact, monetary policy lags were relatively short. Today, those whose purchasing decisions are affected by high interest rates have the choice of extra borrowing or drawing down their savings in order to purchase houses, automobiles, and other goods.

The second change has been the impact of flexible exchange rates. While high interest rates in the early 1980s eventually led to a major appreciation of the dollar and a financial squeeze on American farmers and manufacturers, the response of net exports was a long slow process. Even slower was the recovery of the U.S. trade deficit after the 1985–87 decline in the dollar (see Figure 14-3). While some part of an economic slowdown caused by a future episode of tight monetary policy would occur through the channel of influence that runs from interest rates to the exchange rate to net exports, economists are now extremely uncertain of the size of the effect or the time lag involved. This uncertainty, and the likelihood that future lags may be longer and more variable than those in the past, strengthens Milton Friedman's longstanding argument against countercyclical monetary policy.

17-6 Limitations of Nominal GNP and Money Supply Targeting: Volatility in Interest Rates

Interest-Rate Volatility

In 1979 the Fed changed its "operating procedures" to place more emphasis on controlling $M1$ and less on controlling the interest rate. The result was a marked increase in the volatility of short-term interest rates, particularly in the period between early 1980 and early 1982. What are the costs of such volatility? As we first saw in Figure 15-3, an economy with a shifting IS curve will have a more volatile interest rate when the Federal Reserve chooses a money-supply target than when it chooses an interest rate target. A GNP target produces even more volatility in the interest rate, as long as IS shifts predominate. When money demand shifts predominate, however, the interest rate is more volatile with a money-supply target than with either an interest rate or GNP target. This volatility in the interest rate is illustrated in Figure 17-2.

Effects on financial markets.   One commentator described the effects of the 1980–82 experience on financial markets as "virtual bedlam." Market participants became obsessed with weekly fluctuations in $M1$ data, since they knew that the announcement of any increase in the money supply above the Fed's $M1^*$ target (as from point A to B in Figure 17-2) would require the Fed, in the following week, to move the economy from B to C in order to reachieve the target $M1^*$.

Figure 17-2

Two Demand Schedules for Nominal M1.

The higher demand schedule reflects any factor that might increase the demand for M1, including the invention of Super NOW accounts, an increase in the interest rate on Super NOW accounts, or a reduction in minimum deposits or service charges on such accounts. If the Fed wants to keep the money supply at M1*, it cannot prevent the interest rate from rising above r* to r'. If it wants to keep the interest rate at r*, it cannot prevent the money supply from rising above M1* to M1'.

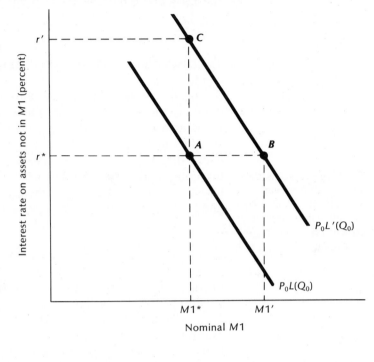

WHY THE FED CAN'T CONTROL BOTH THE INTEREST RATE AND THE MONEY SUPPLY AT THE SAME TIME

Fluctuations in the federal funds rate not only became larger, but also spread faster to other short-term rates and to long-term interest rates—particularly long-term government bonds. The long-term interest rate volatility translated into greater price volatility of long-term bonds and exposed traders to greater risk. Many were unwilling to take this risk, which reduced their participation in the market and made the market "thinner" and still more volatile. Others raised the markup of their selling price over their buying price, thus increasing costs for those attempting to raise funds on the bond market. Some observers suggested that the free-market mechanism for raising capital through the bond market by corporations, as well as state and local governments, was thus impaired by the volatility of interest rates during the 1980–82 period.

Effects of financial deregulation on interest-rate volatility. The Fed's new emphasis on money-supply targeting was not the only contributor to more volatile interest rates in the early 1980s. As we learned in Section 16-9, the overall effect of financial deregulation and the spread of adjustable-rate mortgages has been to steepen the *IS* and *LM* curves. Figure 16-6 showed the implication of the steeper *IS* and *LM* curves. Now any given decline in the money supply achieved by the Fed is likely to cause a greater increase in the level of interest rates than before. The steepness of the *IS* and *LM* curves helps explain why interest rates in the 1980s remained relatively volatile even after 1982, when the Fed abandoned its short-lived attempt to maintain a stable rate of monetary growth. For instance, the Treasury bill rate fell from over 10 percent in mid-1984 to about 5 percent in late 1986, and then rose again to 9 percent in early 1989.

17-7 Techniques of Monetary Targeting

During the early 1980s discussions of monetary policy focused on techniques of monetary targeting, which the Federal Reserve adopted in October 1979 and maintained until September 1982. Although there was considerable volatility in $M1$ growth during 1979–82, participants in financial markets *believed* that $M1$ was being used as a target. Whenever $M1$ neared or reached the upper end of its **target zone,** speculators would bid up short-term interest rates in the belief that the Fed would be forced to bring $M1$ back in line (as occurs in a movement between point B and point C in Figure 17-2).

The **target zone** is the level of a target variable like $M1$ implied by the allowable range of growth rates under current policy.

Target Zones and Monetary Cones

Recognizing that instability in the demand for commodities and for money would make it impossible to hit a precise $M1$ target every week, the Fed in 1975 established a range of allowable values for $M1$ called a "target zone." The range of a target zone is illustrated in Figure 17-3, which plots $M1$ in billions of dollars against time over the period between late 1984 and the end of 1986. We focus on the 1984–86 period in this example, because the failure of $M1$ to remain in the target zone during these years led the Fed to abandon the target zone approach for $M1$ soon afterward in early 1987. At the end of 1984, the Fed announced that its target growth rate for $M1$ was the range between 4 and 7 percent, over the period between 1984:Q4 and 1985:Q4.

In Figure 17-3 a cone-shaped wedge is shown with its left-hand corner at the actual value of $M1$ in November 1984, and its lower edge terminating at a value for November 1985 equal to 1.04 times the November 1984 value. The upper edge is defined in the same way, using a factor of 1.07 (that is, 7 percent higher). Under normal circumstances, the 1985 cone would have remained in effect for a year, and would have been followed by a new cone for 1986.

The money-supply explosion of 1985. In early 1985 $M1$ began to surge far above the original 1985 cone. To avoid the necessity of pursuing restrictive policies that would have brought $M1$ back within the original 1985 cone, the Fed simply declared the original cone obsolete and established a new higher cone. The same $M1$ surge happened again in the last half of 1985, taking $M1$ well beyond the limit allowed even by the revised 1985 cone. In the end, $M1$ growth between November 1984 and November 1985 was 11.9 percent, as compared to the original target range of 4 to 7 percent.

Why did the Fed fail to keep $M1$ within the cones when the monetarists insist that the most essential job of policymakers is to maintain a CGRR for

Figure 17-3
Actual Values and Target Zones for the Money Supply (*M*1), November 1984 to December 1986

The red line shows the actual values of the money supply from November 1984 to December 1986. The lines enclosing the "original 1985 cone" show the upper and lower bound for an *M*1 growth rate ranging between 4 and 7 percent. As *M*1 outran the original 1985 cone, a new revised cone was established, calling for a target range of *M*1 growth between 3 and 8 percent, beginning in May 1985. The third cone is the 3 to 8 percent range for 1986, starting from November 1985.

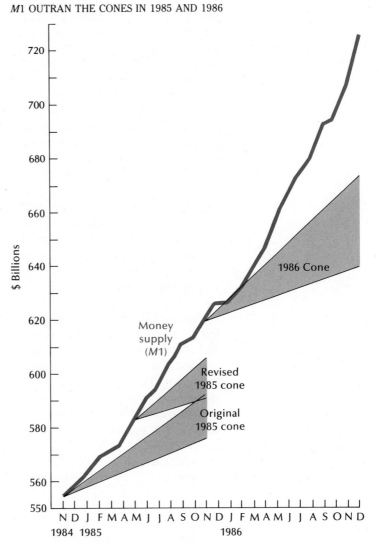

*M*1 OUTRAN THE CONES IN 1985 AND 1986

the money supply? Part of the reason was instability in money demand; falling interest rates made NOW and Super NOW accounts (included in *M*1) relatively more attractive compared to assets not included in *M*1 (see Chapter 16). Another factor was weakness in the economy, with the unemployment rate still above 7 percent and a huge trade deficit that was eroding the viability of the U.S. manufacturing and farm sectors (as we learned in Chapter 5). To have restrained *M*1 within the original 1985 cone, the Fed would have had to push up interest rates (as between points *B* and *C* in Figure 17-2), causing lower investment, a further appreciation of the dollar, and further weakness of net exports.

Cones for other money-supply definitions. Another reason for the Fed's reluctance to restrain $M1$ growth, which would have required higher interest rates, was that the money supply definition $M2$ (see Table 16-2) remained within its cone. The Fed defines target growth rate zones for $M2$ and two broader definitions, $M3$ (which includes large-denomination certificates of deposit and certain other assets) and total debt (the total outstanding debt of the nonfinancial sector, including all levels of government, households, and nonfinancial businesses).

During some intervals in the 1980s, the growth rates of $M2$, $M3$, or debt were more stable than the growth rate of $M1$, since financial deregulation caused much shifting about *among* assets within $M2$, but only some of which are in $M1$. Reflecting this, beginning in early 1987 the Fed stopped publishing any target zones at all for $M1$. However, the Fed was unwilling to choose one or more of the broader aggregates as a single target variable, due to the difficulty of achieving Fed control of $M2$, $M3$, or debt. There is much slippage between Fed open-market operations that directly change the quantity of high-powered money ($275 billion in December 1988), and the resulting change in the myriad of checking, savings, and deposit accounts, savings certificates, and money-market mutual funds that make up $M2$ ($3067 billion in December 1988).

Defects of the cone approach. The Federal Reserve's practice of targeting $M1$ growth cones suffered from another widely recognized defect. In Figure 17-3, we note that each successive cone begins at a higher level than the last. This "drift" of each successive cone to a higher starting point implies that the cumulative growth rate of the $M1$ money supply was much higher than the Fed originally intended when it began its new operational procedures in October 1979. This is evident in the following table which stops at the end of 1986, when the Fed abandoned zones for $M1$:[11]

Four quarters ending	4th quarter to 4th quarter growth rates of $M1$		
	Fed's target range	Midpoint of range	Actual outcome
1980:Q4	4.0–6.5	5.3	7.2
1981:Q4	3.5–6.0	4.8	5.1
1982:Q4	2.5–5.5	4.0	8.3
1983:Q4	4.0–8.0	6.0	9.7
1984:Q4	4.0–8.0	6.0	5.1
1985:Q4	4.0–7.0	5.5	11.3
1986:Q4	3.0–8.0	5.5	14.5
Mean annual growth rate		5.3	8.7

Over the interval from 1979:Q4 to 1986:Q4, the actual growth rate of $M1$ was 8.7 percent per year—quite a bit faster than the 6.3 percent growth rate achieved during the inflationary 1970s. This contrasts with the 5.3 percent mean growth rate that the Fed had intended to achieve through its announced target ranges for the growth rate of $M1$. This discrepancy, com-

---

[11]For 1980 and 1981, target ranges are for $M1B$ rather than $M1A$ and incorporate Fed's official adjustments for the introduction of NOW and ATS accounts. Actual outcomes are from official data for $M1B$, now $M1$, available in March 1989.

pounded through the 1979–86 period, implies that in 1986:Q4 $M1$ was $150 billion, or 27 percent, higher than the Fed had intended as a *result of the drift of the target zones.*

This table also highlights an important irony of the 1980s. Despite the fact that actual realized $M1$ growth proceeded at a faster rate than the Fed intended, and faster than in the inflationary 1970s, a significant disinflation occurred. The rigid link between growth in $M1$ and inflation, so stressed by monetarists, had been broken by the money demand (velocity) debacle, which in turn was caused by financial deregulation. In fact, research has shown that inflation responds to shifts in nominal GNP growth and to supply shocks, just as in our analysis of Chapters 9 and 10. There is no separate effect of $M1$ growth on inflation once the effect of nominal GNP growth has been taken into account.[12]

Monetary targeting in the late 1980s.   Though it abandoned target zones for $M1$ in early 1987, the Fed continued to publish zones for $M2$, $M3$, and total debt. But the Fed learned its lesson from the 1984–86 debacle. First, it made the target zones so wide as to be meaningless. And, when one of the broader monetary aggregates drifted outside of its wide cone, the Fed ignored this fact, just as it refused to tighten monetary policy during the $M1$ explosion of 1985–86. For instance, $M2$ drifted below its cone of 5.5 to 8.5 percent in 1987, growing only 4.0 percent between 1986:Q4 and 1987:Q4. Nevertheless the Fed did not allow interest rates to decline, as would have been necessary to push $M2$ growth up to the lower limit of the target zone. By 1989, a full decade after it began the 1979–82 experiment with monetary targeting, the Fed had returned almost completely to management of monetary policy through interest rates.

Despite the Fed's movement away from monetary targeting, some economists suggested that a monetarist CGRR policy should still be carried out using the money supply definition $M2$. They pointed out that the velocity of $M2$, shown at the top of Figure 16-4 on page 502, had not been nearly as unstable as the velocity of $M1$. Others doubted that the Fed should target $M2$ growth and cited a changing relation of total credit to $M1$ and increased international flows of money. Even Milton Friedman, the most famous monetarist, concedes that there is no tight linkage between $M2$ and nominal GNP growth over short periods, and that "$M2$ only indicates the economy's long-run behavior."[13]

SELF-TEST   Figure 17-3 shows that the Fed allowed a rapid increase in $M1$ above its stated targets. What would have happened to interest rates and to the foreign exchange rate of the dollar during this period if the Fed had restrained $M1$ growth to fall within its original target zone? Explain in terms of movements in the IS and LM curves. Similarly, what would have happened if the Fed had raised $M2$ growth in 1987 to remain within its stated target zone?

---

[12]See Robert J. Gordon, "Understanding Inflation in the 1980s," *Brookings Papers on Economic Activity,* vol. 16 (no. 1, 1985), pp. 263–299.

[13]Lindley H. Clark and Alfred L. Malabe, Jr., "Monetary Figures Are Putting Economists in a Dither," *Wall Street Journal,* June 28, 1989, p. A2.

CASE STUDY: Monetary Policy in Selected Postwar Episodes, 1957–79

This case study allows us to illustrate many of the issues set out in Chapters 15–17. We focus in this section on monetary policy in selected cyclical episodes before 1979, and in the next case study on the period after 1979. In each major cyclical episode, we ask whether the Fed's monetary policy stabilized or destabilized the economy. Would a monetarist rule calling for a constant growth rate of money have performed better than the monetary policy actually pursued?

Monetary Policy in Pictures

Our analysis uses the data displayed in Figure 17-4, which plots the key indicators of monetary policy over the period 1955–89. The top frame shows the four-quarter percentage growth rates of nominal GNP and $M1$. The difference between the growth rates of nominal GNP and of $M1$ is the growth rate of the velocity of $M1$ (this velocity concept was called "$V1$" in our case study on the demand for money, illustrated in Figure 16-4). Periods of positive growth in $V1$, the norm before 1979, are indicated by pink shading and negative growth in $V1$ by gray shading.

The middle frame of Figure 17-4 compares the output ratio (Q/Q^N) with the real money supply, $M1/P$. Our criterion for evaluating policy is that *stabilization of the economy would have been achieved by maintaining the Q/Q^N ratio as close as possible to 100 percent.* The bottom frame of Figure 17-4 displays the behavior of two *nominal* interest rates over this period, the short-term federal funds rate and the interest rate on long-term government bonds.

Looking over the full history displayed in Figure 17-4, several facts stand out. All three frames show major changes after 1979, justifying our choice to cover the pre-1979 and post-1979 periods in separate case studies. In the top frame the pink area shows that $V1$ growth was almost always positive before 1979, and that the growth rates of nominal GNP and $M1$ tended to fluctuate together, although the fluctuations of nominal GNP were greater, particularly in the 1950s. After 1979 the alternation of gray and pink areas illustrates the instability of $V1$ growth, already evident in our discussion of the demand for money and of financial deregulation in the previous chapter.

The overall message of the middle frame is that real $M1$ and the output ratio (Q/Q^N) fluctuated together until the post-1983 period, when real $M1$ exploded. This provides evidence that the Fed's control of $M1$ aggravated business cycles, both before 1979, when the Fed's main instrument was the targeting of interest rates, and in the 1979–82 interval, when the main instrument was the targeting of $M1$ (although in practice $M1$ growth fluctuated significantly during 1979–82, as is evident in the top frame).

Three themes stand out in the bottom frame. First, the overall level of interest rates has increased each decade. Second, short-term rates have always been more volatile than long-term rates, except after 1982 when they tended to move together. Third, short-term rates were especially volatile during the 1979–82 period, and long-term rates were unusually volatile throughout the 1980s.

MONETARY POLICY AT A GLANCE, 1955–89

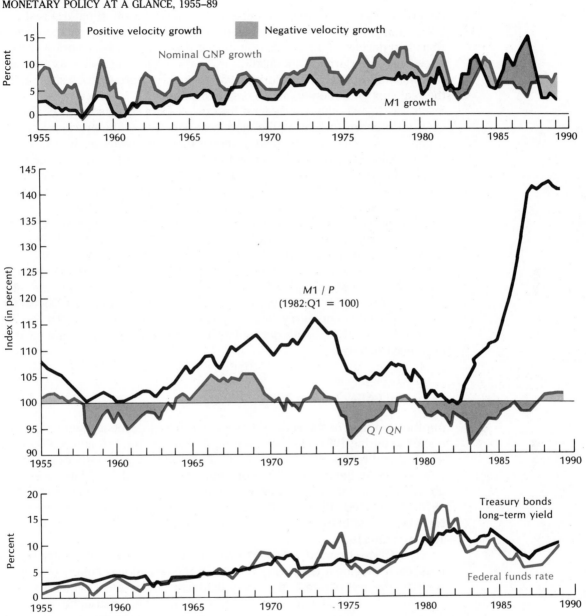

Figure 17-4
The Behavior of Nominal and Real *M*1, Nominal GNP, the Output Ratio, and Two Interest Rates, 1955–89

The top frame shows that nominal GNP growth was higher and more volatile than *M*1 growth before 1979, and that velocity growth (the pink area) was almost always positive. After 1979 velocity growth zigzags sharply back and forth, reflecting instability in money demand. The middle frame shows the procyclical movements of real *M*1 and the output ratio (Q/Q^N) in many key cyclical episodes, and the explosion of real *M*1 after 1983 reflects the decline in velocity growth evident in the top frame. The bottom frame shows that the short-term federal funds interest rate has always been more volatile than the long-term Treasury bond yield, and that both were more volatile after 1979 than before.

Monetary Policy During 1956–61

Policymakers in 1956 were not familiar with the concept of natural real GNP, a magnitude we have calculated with full knowledge of all accelerations and decelerations of inflation during the entire postwar period. They knew only that during 1956 inflation was proceeding and monetary restriction was appropriate. Thus during 1956 nominal $M1$ growth was slow, and the real supply of money ($M1/P$) declined steadily.

It was in 1957 that the Federal Reserve made a serious mistake. The Q/Q^N ratio began to drop as the monetary tightness of the previous year began to take effect. But instead of moderating the downward pressure, the Fed intensified it. Nominal $M1$ growth was actually allowed to become negative in late 1957, and the decline in real $M1/P$ continued even though a precipitous decline in the Q/Q^N ratio was under way. *Thus the Fed appears to have acted procyclically in 1957, aggravating the 1957–58 recession.*

This perverse behavior was repeated in 1959–60. Throughout 1960 the real money supply fell below its mid-1959 level, aggravating the 1960–61 recession and helping John F. Kennedy squeeze by Richard M. Nixon in the very close presidential election of 1960. It is hard to dispute the monetarist argument that a steady growth rate of $M1$ would have resulted in more stable behavior of Q/Q^N than the policies actually followed during 1956–61. On the other hand, a countercyclical nominal GNP targeting policy that achieved fastest $M1$ growth during late 1957 and during 1960 would have been even better.

Monetary Policy During 1964–71

Another example of the Federal Reserve's *procyclical* money-supply policy occurred during 1964–71. Twice during this period the Fed allowed both nominal and real money to accelerate *while Q/Q^N substantially exceeded 100 percent.* In the middle frame of Figure 17-4 the red Q/Q^N line rose above 100 percent in early 1964 and remained at a very high level until 1970. Yet the Fed allowed both real and nominal money to accelerate in two stages, first between mid-1965 and early 1966 and then between early 1967 and late 1968.

The 1964–71 period was punctuated by two periods of monetary tightness, each causing a temporary decline in the real money supply ($M1/P$). Why did the first period of monetary tightness during late 1966 fail to reduce Q/Q^N back to 100 percent, whereas the 1969 period of tightness succeeded? Two fundamental differences between the episodes stand out. First, the 1966 reduction in $M1/P$ was shorter-lived than in 1969–70. Second, the stance of fiscal policy was completely different in the two episodes. In 1966–67 real government expenditures were rising very rapidly, whereas in 1968–71 they were falling. In terms of our previous theoretical analysis, in 1966–67 the *IS* curve was moving rightward up the *LM* curve, causing the crowding out of investment.[14] During 1969–70, however, both the *IS* and *LM* curves were moving to the left.[15]

---

[14]A case study of this period was presented in Section 4-11.

[15]The swift leftward movement of the economy in 1969–70 is shown in the *SP* diagram, Figure 9-7.

Monetary Policy During 1971–79

Nominal $M1$ growth was more stable in the 1970s than in the previous two episodes; *nevertheless the output ratio* (Q/Q^N) *and inflation were both more unstable.* And almost without exception, monetary policy worsened the instability of the economy. First, in 1972 the temporary effect of price controls in holding down inflation allowed the Q/Q^N ratio to rise rapidly above 100 percent, as shown in the middle frame of Figure 17-4. Yet monetary policy did nothing to resist the overexpansion of real GNP, instead "pouring on the gas" and raising $M1$ growth in late 1972 to the highest four-quarter rate experienced in the postwar years up to that time.

Extinguishing the supply shocks. In 1974 the Q/Q^N ratio dropped precipitously as oil and food supply shocks, together with the termination of price controls, caused inflation to race ahead of nominal GNP growth. But monetary policy exacerbated the recession by allowing $M1$ growth to slow down steadily at the same time. The Fed could have chosen partially to accommodate the supply shock by allowing $M1$ growth to speed up, or to remain neutral by holding $M1$ growth constant. Instead, the Fed's choice of a partially "extinguishing" policy reaction made interest rates higher and the recession deeper than otherwise.

The best countercyclical monetary policy to encourage a rapid recovery from the 1975 recession would have been rapid $M1$ growth in 1975–76 when Q/Q^N was low and unemployment was high, followed by a gradual tapering off of $M1$ growth as the Q/Q^N ratio approached 100 percent. *Instead the Fed's policy was just the opposite,* with $M1$ growth that steadily accelerated as the economy recovered. A Fed policy of slow monetary growth in 1978 would have stabilized the economy compared to what actually happened.

Thus, despite the improvements in economic knowledge that took place over the postwar period, there was no improvement in the Fed's performance. Instead of stabilizing nominal GNP growth by conducting a countercyclical monetary policy, the Fed carried out a procyclical monetary policy that made swings in nominal GNP growth (and hence in real output and unemployment) greater than necessary.

17-9   *CASE STUDY:*   Monetary Policy in the 1980s:
The Velocity Recession and the Longest
Peacetime Expansion

This section reviews three main issues in the evaluation of monetary policy in the 1980s. First is the adoption by the Federal Reserve of new operating procedures in October 1979, which were abandoned in 1982. Second is the effect of unstable money demand in changing the economy's response to monetary policy. Third is the role of the Fed in prolonging the expansion after 1982, which continued through 1989.

Adoption of New Operating Procedures

On October 6, 1979, the Federal Reserve adopted new operating procedures. Why were the new procedures thought to be necessary, and why were they abandoned only three years after they were adopted?

Reasons for the change. We learned in the previous case study that during 1956–79 the Fed allowed the money supply to fluctuate procyclically, despite the fact that interest rates also fluctuated procyclically. This is consistent with the interpretation within the *IS-LM* model that the Fed attempted to stabilize interest rates, creating procyclical fluctuations in the money supply. However, the Fed was unwilling to stabilize interest rates completely, which would have caused even greater procyclical fluctuations of the money supply, or to stabilize the money supply, which would have created greater fluctuations in the interest rate (at least in the short run—in the longer run stable money growth would have prevented the acceleration of inflation that accounted for much of the post-1965 increase in interest rates).

Gradually, in the late 1970s, the Fed began to realize that its old procedures had allowed too much procyclical movement in the growth rate of money without stabilizing the interest rate. In an unusual Saturday meeting on October 6, 1979, the Federal Reserve Board shifted from short-term monetary control based on maintaining the federal funds rate within a "zone of tolerance" to direct control of **nonborrowed reserves.**

It was expected that this change in procedures would achieve something close to a constant-growth-rate rule (CGRR) for the money supply, as the monetarists had long advocated. Control over nonborrowed reserves, however, does not guarantee control over $M1$. Let us review the money-supply equation (17.6):

$$M = \frac{(1 + c)H}{e + c} \tag{17.6}$$

Here M is the money supply, H is high-powered money, e is the bank required reserve ratio, and c is the cash-holding ratio. We can see several factors that could make M deviate from nonborrowed reserves, the Fed's policy instrument after 1979.

> **Nonborrowed reserves** are total bank reserves minus bank borrowings from the Fed.

1. *H differs from nonborrowed reserves. H* also consists of bank borrowing from the Fed, and currency. An increase in bank borrowing or an unpredicted increase in the demand for currency could raise H even if the Fed held nonborrowed reserves rigidly fixed.

2. *The bank reserve holding ratio (e) can change.* This was especially true under the Fed's complex system (discontinued in the mid-1980s) of setting different reserve requirements for different types of assets. As the public shifted from one asset to another, e would change, often unpredictably.

3. *The cash-holding ratio (c) can change.* While cash-holding behavior is fairly predictable, unexpected movements can alter the ratio of M to H.

Behavior of Key Monetary Variables

Figure 17-4 shows that $M1$ growth was quite volatile in the first three years of the Fed's experiment (1980–82), ranging from 4.0 percent in 1980:Q2 to 9.9 percent in 1981:Q2. But it is hard to tell from the diagram whether monetary growth was more unstable than in previous postwar periods. To make this comparison we can calculate the mean and standard deviation of the four-quarter growth rate of $M1$ from each of five periods.[16]

	Mean of $M1$ growth	Standard deviation of $M1$ growth
1956–61	1.6	1.48
1964–71	4.9	1.53
1971–79	6.5	1.41
1979–82	6.9	1.55
1983–88	8.9	4.02

This table suggests that the Fed's new operating procedures failed to achieve their stated goals. Monetary growth was slightly more volatile in 1979–82 than in previous periods. Thus the October 1979 procedures do not seem to have smoothed out the growth path of money. For this reason, Milton Friedman and other monetarists reject the suggestion (made by many journalists) that the Fed during 1979–82 was conducting a "monetarist policy." Between 1979 and late 1981, the usual procyclical behavior of the Fed is evident, just as in previous postwar episodes. This is shown by the behavior of the real quantity of $M1$, labeled $M1/P$ in the middle frame of Figure 17-4, which fell right along with Q/Q^N until early 1982.

Reasons for the Fed's failure.   The Fed made everyone unhappy during 1979–82. In Chapter 11 we examined the plight of the unemployed, the victims of the high interest rates that were a by-product of the Fed's policy. Monetarists were dismayed at the volatility of money growth. They pointed out that the Fed allowed overly volatile monetary growth because it had not managed to escape from its old operating procedures. It continued to pay considerable attention to smoothing weekly and monthly fluctuations in interest rates, and it was prepared to allow the growth rate of money to deviate from its stated CGRR target if it felt that it was important to resist a particular movement in interest rates.[17]

---

[16]To calculate a standard deviation, use the following formula, where x_i are the individual observations, $\bar{x}$ is the mean, and n is the number of observations:

$$\sqrt{\frac{\sum_i (x_i - \bar{x})^2}{n}}$$

[17]An excellent exposition of the technical reasons for the Fed's failure is contained in William Poole, "Federal Reserve Operating Procedures: A Survey and Evaluation of the Historical Record since October 1979," *Journal of Money, Credit, and Banking,* vol. 14 (November 1982, Part 2), pp. 575–596.

In October 1982 the Federal Reserve discontinued any attempt to maintain $M1$ within its stated target zones. There was explosive growth in $M1$ in the year beginning in October 1982 and double-digit growth again in 1985 and 1986. The wave of innovations set loose by financial deregulation, reviewed in the last chapter, had made $M1$ much more attractive than previously, and the velocity of $M1$ had become more volatile than previously. Finally, in early 1987 the Fed completed its transition away from the monetarist CGRR recommendation when it discontinued issuing target zones for $M1$ in its official semiannual policy statements. For the broader monetary aggregates, $M2$ and $M3$, the target zones were so broad, for example, 4.0 to 8.0 percent in 1988, that $M2$ and $M3$ could remain within the zones despite substantial volatility in monetary growth rates.

Monetary Policy in the Longest Peacetime Expansion

The last U.S. recession reached its trough in November 1982, and the economy began to expand after that point. As of July 1989, the expansion had lasted 80 months, or almost seven years. At that point the 1982–89 expansion had exactly matched the 80-month 1938–45 expansion that included World War II. The 106-month 1961–69 expansion, which included the years of the Vietnam War buildup, remained the grand champion. A long period of expansion is favorable, regardless of the speed of the expansion, since long expansions imply infrequent recessions. People dislike variance in economic activity; that is why, for example, they require a premium to hold securities with volatile returns. Thus people prefer a slow and continuous economic expansion to an alternation of soaring expansions followed by ruinous recessions that yields the same rate of long-run growth.

The three phases of the expansion. Which elements of macroeconomic analysis explain the longevity of the 1982–89 expansion? Clearly, we need to consider both demand and supply aspects. It also helps to distinguish three phases of the expansion, the "initial revival" six-quarter phase through 1984:Q2, the "midcourse pause" 10-quarter phase through 1986:Q4, and the "second wind" phase after 1986:Q4. The respective annual growth rates of real GNP during the three phases were as follows:

Initial revival, 1982:Q4–1984:Q2   6.8
Midcourse pause, 1984:Q2–1986:Q4   2.6
Second wind, 1986:Q4–1989:Q2   4.0

Three elements dominate the behavior of demand in the current expansion—monetary policy and the twin deficits, that is, the federal budget deficit and the foreign trade deficit. The expansion began soon after the Fed abandoned the 1979–82 operating procedures. The sharp drop in interest rates in the autumn of 1982 stimulated an economic revival that proceeded at a rapid pace until mid-1984. The drop in short-term interest rates and the sharp revival in nominal GNP growth and in the output ratio (Q/Q^N) are all visible in Figure 17-4. The initial revival was fueled not just by lower interest rates, but also by consumer spending stimulated in part by the Reagan tax cuts, which were phased in mainly during 1982 and 1983. In terms of our textbook analysis, Chapter 5's fiscal budget line (*BB*) moved sharply downward, and the *IS* curve moved sharply to the right in 1983. The relaxation of Fed policy also moved the *LM* curve to the right.

After mid-1984 the expansion slowed, as the economy entered the "midcourse pause." During this period the negative impact of the rapidly growing foreign trade deficit sapped the economy's strength. The foreign trade deficit was interpreted in Chapter 5 as the counterpart of the fiscal deficit. Recall that fiscal deficits caused a high level of real interest rates, which in turn caused an appreciation of the dollar, making imports cheap and pricing U.S. exports out of many markets. During this middle phase of the expansion, the economy might have slipped into a recession were it not for skillful management by the Fed. Short-term interest rates were allowed to fall by half, from about 10 percent to about 5 percent, between mid-1984 and late 1986, and *M*1 was allowed to grow at double-digit rates in both 1985 and 1986. In short, the Fed pushed hard on the *LM* curve as the foreign trade deficit kept worsening.

Finally the long-predicted turn in the trade balance occurred, and the economy entered its "second wind" phase. During the two years after 1986:Q4, real exports soared at an annual rate of 15 percent. Working through the usual multiplier effects (see Chapter 3), the export boom stimulated a marked acceleration in real GNP growth and a decline in the civilian unemployment rate from the 1985–86 plateau of 7.0 percent to 5.0 percent in early 1989. The Fed no longer had to push hard to keep the expansion going, and it allowed short-term interest rates to rise substantially and M1 growth to fall to a growth rate of precisely *zero* percent in the year ending in June 1989.

Role of the dollar and oil prices.   In one sense, the unusual longevity of the expansion could be attributed to the ups and downs of the dollar. If the dollar had remained stable throughout, the 1984–86 expansion would have been substantially more rapid, and the economy's strength might have petered out in 1987–88. But this ignores the crucial role of the Fed. Just as the Fed kept the economy going in 1984–86, it could have achieved the same effect in 1987–88 under this "stable dollar" scenario.

This analysis primarily credits the Fed with perpetuating the expansion by aggressively applying a monetary stimulus during 1984–86 when other elements of demand were weak. And it goes further by stating that the Fed would have and could have kept the expansion going in 1987–88 even if the export boom had not come to the rescue. But all this raises a deeper question: why did the Fed push expansion in 1984–86 after bringing earlier expansions to a halt in 1969–70, 1973–74, and 1979–81? The answer must lie in the importance the Fed attaches to the inflation rate, and the very different behavior of the inflation rate during 1984–88 from that in any previous expansion since the early 1960s.

We learned in Chapters 9 and 10 that two factors explain the marked deceleration of inflation over the 1980–86 period. First and most important was the effect of weak demand over this entire period from 1980 to 1986. A continuous series of small but uniformly beneficial supply shocks during 1981–87 further aided the process of disinflation. These took the form of a gradual decline in the real price of oil and food, followed by a sharp decline in nominal and real oil prices in 1986. Lower oil prices worked together with the Fed's aggressive monetary stimulus to keep the expansion going. In terms of Figure 9-11, which plots the inflation rate against the output ratio, the combined effect of oil prices and the Fed's actions pushed the economy to the southeast in 1986–87, reminiscent of the 1971–72 period when monetary stimulus was combined with the beneficial (but temporary) effects of price controls.

It was the deceleration of inflation that gave the Fed the latitude to pursue monetary stimulus as aggressively as it did without having to worry about an acceleration of inflation. Once unemployment fell below 6 percent, in 1988 and 1989, inflation began to accelerate and the Fed returned to its traditional policy of raising interest rates to keep the economy from "overheating." As of mid-1989 it was unclear whether the Fed's policy would cause a recession that would bring the 1982–89 expansion to an end, or would simply cause slow real GNP growth without the period of negative growth that marks a recession. Slow real GNP growth without a recession would represent the miracle of a "soft landing" that the Fed had never previously achieved in the periods of tight money that occurred in 1956–57, 1959–60, 1969–70, 1974–75, and 1981–82 reviewed in this and the previous case study.

17-10 Limitations of Fiscal Policy: Lags, Effectiveness, and Inefficiency

As we have noted before, the long debate about cures for the U.S. federal budget deficit in the 1980s prevented the use of fiscal policy for short-run stabilization purposes. For this reason, we have already completed our main treatment of fiscal policy in Chapter 13, in connection with the effects of the deficit and the buildup of the public debt on the prospects for long-run growth. For the same reason, most of this chapter has been devoted to monetary policy and some of the new problems that have emerged in conducting it.

This section concentrates on the stabilization aspects of fiscal policy. While fiscal policy appears to be suspended, at least temporarily, as a stabilization tool in the United States, there are three good reasons to review the limitations of fiscal policy for stabilization purposes. First, to understand history we need to know if it was desirable to use fiscal policy for stabilization purposes in the years prior to the budget stalemate of the 1980s and, accordingly, if it would be desirable to use fiscal policy in the future after the stalemate is resolved. Second, we noted in this chapter and the last that structural changes in the economy, especially financial deregulation and flexible exchange rates, may make the lags of monetary policy longer than before, possibly tilting the balance toward fiscal policy. Third, fiscal policy for stabilization purposes is of continued interest in other nations that have not experienced a budget debate similar to that in the United States.

In the *IS-LM* model of Chapters 4 and 5, the conduct of fiscal policy is a simple matter. If real output is too low, then the government can increase spending or cut taxes. Since the *IS-LM* model has no time dimension, there is no apparent difference between monetary and fiscal policy in the ability to stimulate output (unless the *IS* or *LM* curve has an extreme horizontal or vertical slope). But in reality there are important limitations on the use of fiscal policy for stabilization purposes. The first is the existence of lags, which is also a problem in the use of monetary policy. The main difference is that the legislative lag of fiscal policy is longer, although the effectiveness lag may be shorter. The other problems are more specific to fiscal policy. There are good reasons to suspect that temporary changes in tax rates may have little impact on spending. Finally, changes in expenditures may be inefficient if the objectives of stabilization policy cause sudden fluctuations in government purchases.

Lags in the Operation of Fiscal Policy

Of the five types of lags listed in Section 17-5, the data and recognition lags are common to monetary and fiscal policy. We concluded that these lags introduce a delay of about four months between a change in economic conditions and the earliest feasible response of the policy authorities.

The third source of delay, the legislative lag, is much more important for fiscal than for monetary policy because both Congress and the president are involved. For example, President Kennedy's economic advisers convinced him to press for a permanent income tax reduction in mid-1962, but Congress did not pass the necessary legislation until March 1964. Another long lag occurred between mid-1966, when the buildup of Vietnam spending made clear the need for additional tax revenues, and mid-1968, when Congress finally enacted the income tax surcharge. Not all lags are uniformly long, however. Congress took only two months to pass a tax "rebate" (a temporary rate cut) proposed by President Ford in January 1975.

The fourth source of delay, the transmission lag, varies in length for different types of fiscal policy. A change in income tax rates can alter paychecks within weeks, as soon as new withholding tax tables are printed and mailed to employers. But an increase in government spending (for example, public works expenditures) is subject to a long transmission lag because of the time required to create designs, draw up plans, submit bids, sign contracts, and begin work.

The final delay, the effectiveness lag, varies among alternative types of fiscal policy. Further, econometric models differ in their estimates of the multipliers associated with individual types of policy change. For instance, in the first quarter following a $1 billion increase in government spending, estimates of the resulting increase in nominal GNP range between $0.7 and $1.8 billion. After three quarters have elapsed, the estimates range between $1.2 and $2.7 billion.[18] Thus policymakers who want to raise spending by, say, $25 billion have no firm guidance on the exact size of the fiscal stimulus that is required.

The evidence examined in Section 17-5 suggests that the effectiveness lag of monetary policy is only around two quarters, and is thus fully comparable with that of fiscal policy. This lag of monetary policy might, however, have become longer in the 1980s. Should we conclude that countercyclical monetary policy is superior to fiscal policy because its legislative lag is shorter and more predictable? Such a verdict appears premature, since the side effects of monetary and fiscal stimulus are different and must be considered in light of other policy objectives, such as those of promoting investment and economic growth and of minimizing inflation.

---

[18]Source: See Figure 15-6.

Possible Ineffectiveness of Tax Rate Changes

Changes in personal income tax rates in 1964, 1968, and 1975 designed for stabilization purposes were largely absorbed by offsetting changes in saving, as you will see in the next chapter. Thus ineffectiveness is a fundamental limitation of changes in tax rates as a tool of discretionary fiscal policy. Very large shifts in the natural employment deficit (NED) may be necessary to achieve significant changes in total spending and unemployment. To achieve a given unemployment target through tax policy alone, the NED may have to be shifted from its desired level by four or five times more than if the same unemployment target were reached through changes in government spending.

Several tax instruments are available besides the personal income tax. Any tax or subsidy on spending, such as a sales or excise tax or an investment credit, is ideally suited for stabilization if legislative lags are sufficiently short. Imagine that a U.S. national sales tax of 5 percent were levied on all products and that in a recession the sales tax were eliminated for six months. The temporary nature of the tax cut would aid in stimulating economic recovery because it would induce households to make their purchases of durable and semidurable goods (automobiles, clothing) earlier than would otherwise have occurred.

The major disadvantages of temporary changes in sales taxes are practical. First, the effect will be perverse during congressional debate of the measure; households will delay spending during a recession if they think that proposed tax cuts will make goods cheaper in the future after congressional action. Second, there is no national sales tax in the United States that can be used for countercyclical stabilization. The federal government could subsidize state and local governments to reduce their own sales taxes during recessions, but this proposal has the disadvantage of inequity, since some states (albeit a minority) do not have a state sales tax and thus would be unable to take advantage of the federal subsidy.

Possible Inefficiency of Expenditure Changes

Changes in government expenditures are presumed to be more effective than changes in tax rates because 100 percent of the extra spending initially becomes extra GNP. The main disadvantages of spending changes as compared to tax changes are (1) delays in timing and (2) the possibility that the social value of the extra output produced may be relatively low. The timing problem is most acute. It may not be administratively possible to spend extra billions productively within a short period. Even after the legislative lag is surmounted, there are usually long delays while projects are planned and funds allocated.

Just as questions of equity cloud any discussion of tax-rate changes, changes in spending on public projects raise the same questions of fairness. Spending on what? Cleaning up Boston Harbor? A new expressway in Houston? Another disadvantage of spending changes is that they are not easily reversible. Frequent changes in government spending plans can lead to a lack of confidence in the promises of government officials and considerable difficulties in hiring employees, who may fear subsequent dismissal when economic conditions change.

To conclude, lags, ineffectiveness, and inefficiency are potential defects of most types of fiscal policy that might be used for stabilization purposes. The best prospects for fiscal policy as a stabilization tool seem to occur in other countries. In Britain, where the government can announce and implement tax changes on the same day, there is no legislative lag, and the excise taxes controlled by the federal government have short effectiveness lags. In Japan the central government does not have to worry as much as the United States about balancing the conflicting demands of different regions and has demonstrated its ability to increase and slow down the pace of public works projects to balance excessive or insufficient demand in the private economy. In the United States, such a public works speedup was carried out successfully by the Eisenhower administration in the 1957–58 recession, but apparently not since that time.

17-11 Conclusion: The Case For and Against a Nominal GNP Target

Fiscal stabilization policy does not appear likely to play an important role in the United States in the early 1990s. This leaves monetary policy carrying the full burden of stabilization policy. How can the Fed avoid the unfortunate record evident in our case studies in this chapter? From the mid-1950s to the early 1980s the Fed's monetary policy destablized the economy more often than not, prolonging tight money too long into each recession and prolonging easy money too long into each boom.

The Case for Nominal GNP Targeting

In the aftermath of financial deregulation and the volatile swings of velocity in the 1980s, numerous economists began to advocate nominal GNP as a target for monetary policy instead of the two traditional targets, the interest rate and the money supply. This approach, they argue, has many advantages. Like the money supply, nominal GNP as a target provides a *"nominal anchor"* for the economy, since in the long run the inflation rate is tied to the rate of nominal GNP growth.

More precisely, as we learned in Chapter 9, inflation *by definition* is equal to:

$$p \equiv (y - q^N) - (q - q^N)$$

The first term in parentheses is "excess nominal GNP growth"—that is, the excess of nominal GNP growth (y) over natural real GNP growth (q^N). The second term is the difference between actual and natural real GNP growth ($q - q^N$), which in turn is equal to the change in the output ratio (Q/Q^N). In the long run the second term must be zero, meaning that in the long run inflation is equal to excess nominal GNP growth. By setting a target of nominal GNP growth, then, the Fed determines the long-run rate of inflation.

Nominal GNP growth is a superior target to money supply growth if the demand for money is unstable, as evidenced by the 1982–83 episode of volatile movements in velocity. One proposal to implement nominal GNP targeting calls for the Fed to specify a desired long-run path for nominal GNP.[19] Whenever the best available forecast calls for nominal GNP to exceed this desired long-run target path, the Fed would raise interest rates, and vice versa.[20]

The Forecasting Pitfall

In some past episodes, particularly 1982, a recession occurred when a decline in nominal GNP growth was not forecast in advance, and in such cases nominal GNP targeting might not allow the Fed to react any faster than it has in the past.[21] Some critics do not approve of the use of forecasts at all, believing that financial markets would speculate on the outcome of the Fed's internal forecasting exercises. This objection is not very persuasive, however, because speculation is inherent in financial market behavior. During 1979–82, financial markets speculated that the Fed would push interest rates up when they learned of unexpectedly high growth in $M1$; in the late 1980s financial markets speculated that the Fed would push interest rates up whenever monthly announcements of inflation were high or of unemployment were low.

Some use of forecasts in the implementation of nominal GNP targeting seems inevitable. To use no forecasts at all, and to react entirely to past movements in nominal GNP, would tie the hands of the Fed unnecessarily. And, despite the flaws of past forecasts, the use of a nominal GNP target based on, say, a four-quarter-ahead forecast would have stabilized the economy in some episodes. The Fed would have been forced to tighten the economy in some periods when the economy was overheated (1965–66, 1972–73, and 1978–79) and to loosen monetary policy when the economy tumbled into recession (1974–75, 1981–82).

---

[19]See Robert J. Gordon, "The Conduct of Monetary Policy," in Albert Ando, Hidekazu Eguchi, Roger Farmer, and Yoshio Suzuki, *Monetary Policy in Our Times* (Cambridge, Mass.: MIT Press, 1985), pp. 45–81. Appraisals of nominal GNP targeting include Charles R. Bean, "Targeting Nominal Income: an Appraisal," *Economic Journal,* vol. 93, pp. 806–819, and John B. Taylor, "What Would Nominal GNP Targeting Do to the Business Cycle?" *Carnegie-Rochester Conference Series on Public Policy,* vol. 22 (New York: North-Holland, 1985), pp. 61–84.

[20]A comprehensive survey of monetary policy in the 1980s, covering a wide range of countries and a large body of literature, is Charles Goodhart, "The Conduct of Monetary Policy," *Economic Journal,* vol. 99 (June 1989), pp. 293–346. Goodhart emphasizes in a worldwide context, as does this chapter in a U.S. context, the movement away from monetarism resulting from unstable changes in velocity.

[21]If we look back at Figure 15-5, we observe numerous forecasting errors for nominal GNP growth. However, the proposal under discussion emphasizes deviations of the *level* of actual from target nominal GNP. Thus, even though the four-quarter-ahead forecast *change* in nominal GNP in 1982–83 missed the recession, these forecast changes were calculated from a starting point for the *level* of actual nominal GNP that was dropping farther and farther below target as 1982 progressed. Thus the forecast level of nominal GNP for 1983 was pulled below target, and the suggested procedure would have called for the Fed to reduce interest rates in response.

SUMMARY

1. A set of banks in a closed economy—one with no transfers of funds to the outside—can "create money" by a multiple of each dollar of cash that is initially received. This is true for a single bank on a desert island or for all banks in the United States taken together.

2. Among the assumptions necessary for money creation to occur are that only a fraction of the initial cash receipt is held as reserves by banks or as pocket cash by depositors and that banks lend out excess reserves to willing borrowers.

3. The deposit-creation multiplier is 1.0 divided by the fraction of an initial cash receipt that is held as bank reserves or currency. The money-creation multiplier is then the deposit-creation multiplier times 1.0 plus the currency-holding fraction. The money supply is equal to high-powered money times the money-creation multiplier.

4. There are five sources of lags between an initial change in the economy and the minimum interval before which monetary or fiscal policy can influence spending. The total length of the five lags taken together is about thirteen months for monetary policy in the United States.

5. Rules that make the money supply or nominal GNP the target of monetary policy may make interest rates more volatile than with an interest rate target, particularly if *IS* shifts are more important than money demand disturbances.

6. In implementing a monetary target in the 1979–82 period, the Federal Reserve set target zones for the money supply. But when money-demand shifts occurred, the Fed allowed the money supply to move outside the target zones. Also, the Fed allowed the zones for successive years to drift away from the path for the money supply that had originally been intended.

7. Between 1957 and 1982 the Fed destablized the economy by reducing the real money supply when the economy was weak and by accelerating monetary growth when the economy was strong.

8. During 1982–89, and possibly beyond, the economy experienced its longest peacetime expansion. Skillful management of monetary policy helped prolong the expansion by pushing down interest rates and allowing very rapid monetary growth in 1985–86, when the economy was weak, and by pushing up interest rates in 1987–89 and achieving slower monetary growth, when the economy became so strong that inflation began to accelerate.

9. The main limitations on the use of fiscal policy for stabilization purposes are (1) a legislative lag that has been very long in some historical episodes, (2) the likelihood that temporary income tax changes will be ineffective, and (3) the inefficiency of starting and stopping work on public construction projects.

10. A policy that moves the money supply and interest rates to keep the level of nominal GNP on a preannounced target combines the advantages of controlling the long-run rate of inflation and of offsetting swings in velocity. The main disadvantage is that lags in monetary policy make nominal GNP targets difficult to implement, since major swings in nominal GNP must be forecast in advance.

CONCEPTS

high-powered money
open-market operations
rediscount rate
required reserves

reserve requirements
target zone
nonborrowed reserves

QUESTIONS AND PROBLEMS

Questions

1. What factors have tended to increase the dominance of monetary policy for use as a stabilization policy in the United States in the 1980s and 1990s?

2. At one point in the chapter it is argued that an activist countercyclical monetary policy may do more harm than good. The final conclusion, however, is that activist monetary policy is desirable. What are the major limitations of monetary policy and how might they be overcome?

3. What is high-powered money? Explain why *both* bank reserves and cash held by the public are considered to be high-powered money.

4. What are the required conditions for money creation? In the Great Depression of the 1930s, many bank failures occurred in part because one or more of these conditions was no longer met. Which are the most likely candidates to explain the failure of the banking system to operate properly in the depths of the Depression?

5. Explain what happens when the Fed conducts an

open market purchase of $200 million in bonds. How do the banks get involved? What is the ultimate effect on the level of high-powered money and on the money supply?

6. Explain how the money creation multiplier is similar to the income determination multiplier in Chapters 3–6.

7. Explain why the demand for high-powered money is upward sloping in Figure 17–1. Why is it not downward sloping in a manner similar to normal demand curves?

8. What are the major ways in which the supply of money can change? If it is that simple, why couldn't the Fed effectively control the money supply in the past?

9. What are the two main objections to counter-cyclical activism? Which of these objections has been of primary concern for the monetarists?

10. Will targeting nominal GNP cause more or less interest rate volatility than money-supply targeting?

11. In the 1980s, the growth of $M1$ proceeded at a faster rate than in the inflationary periods of the 1970s. What happened to the inflation rate in the 1980s? Does this result support or rebut the monetarist case?

12. What are the major limitations on the use of fiscal policy for stabilization purposes? Are these the reasons that many economists feel that fiscal policy activism is no longer a viable stabilization tool?

Problems

1. If the ratio of deposits that banks hold in the form of reserves is 7 percent, and people want to hold 8 percent of their deposits in the form of cash, what is the necessary level of high powered reserves if the Fed wants to set the money supply at $800 billion?

2. Assume an economy in which the reserve ratio is 15 percent and people hold 10 percent of their deposits in the form of cash (and there are no other leakages).
   (a) If the current level of higher-powered money (H) if $100 billion, what is the money supply in this economy?
   (b) If the Fed set a target money supply of $560 billion, what would it have to do to achieve that target?

SELF-TEST ANSWERS

p. 518 (1) $D = H/(e+c) = 500/0.4 = 1250$.
$M = (1+c)D = (1.25)1250 = 1562.5$.
(2) $D = 500/0.5 = 1000$.
$M = (1.35)1000 = 1350$.
(3) $D = 500/0.5 = 1000$. $M = (1.25)1000 = 1250$.

p. 522 The short answer is that the Fed sells bonds when it wants to reduce high-powered money (and hence the money supply through equation 17.6), and it buys bonds when it wants to raise the money supply. The easy way to remember this is that the Fed makes high-powered money larger when it increases the size of its assets and liabilities, which it accomplishes by buying government securities (bonds). Why? When the Fed buys bonds, it obtains an extra amount of government securities as an asset and pays for the bond by issuing bank reserves, a liability of the Fed. When it sells bonds, it reduces the quantity of government securities on the asset side of its balance sheet, and the purchase by banks or the public reduces bank reserves on the liability side of its balance sheet.

p. 531 Remaining within the original target zone for 1985–86 would have required much slower $M1$ growth than actually occurred. To restrain $M1$ growth, the Fed would have been required substantially to increase short-term interest rates. The LM curve would have moved to the right much less than actually occurred, and the higher level of interest rates would have reduced investment, prevented the dollar from falling as much as it did, and reduced net exports. Similarly, in 1987 the achievement of faster $M2$ growth would have required lower interest rates, which would have caused the dollar to appreciate more and net exports to improve even more than actually occurred.

PART VII
Sources of Instability in the Private Economy

CHAPTER EIGHTEEN

Instability in the Private Economy: Consumption Behavior

Economists become upset when they learn that we aren't spending money as they've planned for us.

—*Eliot Marshall*

18-1 Consumption and Economic Stability

In Part VI (Chapters 15–17), we studied the role of stabilization policy, which consists of monetary and fiscal policy. The most basic question about stabilization policy is whether "activist" policy intervention should be attempted, and the case against it is made in the monetarist platform of Chapter 15. The objection of the monetarists to stabilization policy is based on four beliefs: (1) in the stability of private spending, (2) in the stability of the demand for money, (3) in the likelihood that policy activism will do more harm than good, and (4) in the flexibility of prices over the time horizon relevant for policy discussions.

Thus far we have examined factors 2 to 4. We discussed the demand for money in Chapter 16, monetary policy mistakes in past historical episodes in Chapter 17, and the sources of price inflexibility in Chapters 8 and 9. Now we turn to factor 1, the stability of private spending. Consumption spending is the subject of this chapter, and the following chapter is devoted to investment spending. We start with consumption spending for the simple reason that it is by far the largest component of total spending and constituted 66.3 percent of GNP in 1988.

Consumption Spending and Shifts in the *IS* Curve

How did consumption spending enter into the basic theory of income determination earlier in the book? Chapter 3 introduced the simple Keynesian consumption function, which makes the level of consumption expenditures depend on disposable income and on an "autonomous" component. Shifts in this autonomous component, due to changes in consumer confidence or optimism, were cited as one of the factors that could shift the economy's *IS* curve (in addition to shifts in business confidence, government spending, tax rates, or autonomous net exports). Further, the Keynesian consumption function determines the size of the economy's multiplier, which states how much the *IS* curve will shift in response to shifts in consumer or business confidence, government spending, tax rates or autonomous net exports. In turn, these shifts in the *IS* curve cause fluctuations in real GNP as long as the *LM* curve is not completely vertical and the aggregate price level is not perfectly flexible.

Forward-Looking Theories of Consumer Behavior

In this chapter we examine the determinants of consumption spending. The focus is a theory of consumer behavior that strongly qualifies the Keynesian theory of Chapter 3. It states that consumers have **forward-looking expectations** and behave quite differently in response to a change in disposable income that is expected to be temporary than in response to a change in disposable income that is expected to be permanent.

Introducing the PIH and LCH. The hypothesis of forward-looking expectations (a concept introduced in Chapter 7) was developed in the 1950s by two economists who have since won the Nobel Prize, Milton Friedman and Franco Modigliani. Friedman's version is usually called the **permanent-income hypothesis** (PIH). It predicts that consumption responds only to permanent changes in income but not to transitory changes in income. It cuts the multiplier for the economy's response to temporary changes in autonomous spending well below the values calculated in Chapter 3, thus implying that the economy is relatively well insulated from destabilizing shocks. In short, the PIH helps to bolster plank 1 of the monetarist platform and supports the monetarist case that the economy can be trusted to stabilize itself.

Modigliani's version is called the **life-cycle hypothesis** (LCH) and shares a forward-looking orientation. It holds that consumers attempt to smooth out their consumption spending over their lifetimes. This implies that transitory blips of income will cause only a small response of consumption. The LCH also implies that consumption spending depends not just on disposable income but on the assets and liabilities of consumers as well. It implies, for instance, that major movements in stock market prices should affect consumption.

Forward-looking expectations attempt to predict the future behavior of an economic variable using an economic model that specifies the interrelationship of that variable with other variables.

The permanent-income hypothesis (PIH) holds that consumption spending depends on the long-run average (permanent) income that people expect to receive.

The life-cycle hypothesis (LCH) holds that people try to stabilize their consumption over their entire lifetime.

18-2   *CASE STUDY:*   Main Features of the U.S. Consumption Data

Before we examine these two forward-looking theories of consumption behavior, we should make an acquaintance with the behavior of data on aggregate consumption in the United States. Plotted in Figure 18-1 are total real consumer expenditures over the period 1950–88, as well as the behavior of the three main components of consumption: durable goods, nondurable goods, and services.

The first evident fact is that the growth of total consumption spending, shown by the top line, has not been smooth. Particularly noticeable slow-

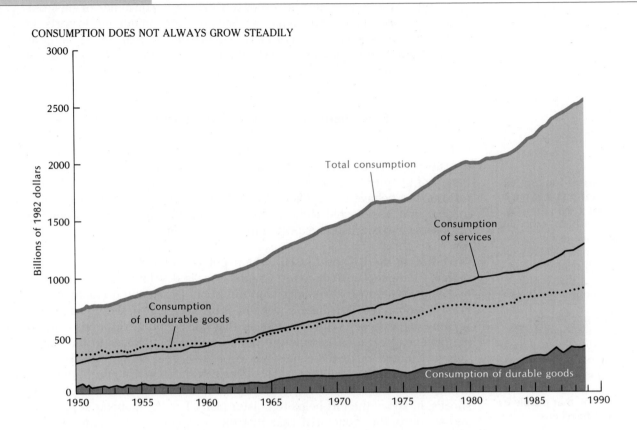

Figure 18-1 **Real Consumer Expenditure and its Three Components, 1950–1988**

The top line plots consumer expenditures and shows a marked pause in growth in 1974–75 and 1980–82. Consumption of durable goods is both the most volatile and fastest growing component. Consumption of services also has grown rapidly and is much less volatile than expenditures on durable goods. Consumption of nondurable goods is the slowest-growing component and has medium volatility.

downs in the growth of total consumption spending took place in 1974–75 and in 1980–82. The forward-looking theories emphasize that consumers should look ahead to their permanent or lifetime income, and should react to temporary declines in income (such as occur in a recession) by reducing saving rather than consumption. Clearly, not all consumers manage to avoid cutting their consumption during recessions, both because they do not have enough saving to absorb the blow of losing a job, and because banks will not lend to unemployed people even though they may have good prospects of regaining jobs and making an impressive total lifetime income.

Of the three components, consumption of durable goods is by far the most volatile. Consumer durable expenditures, like the fixed investment expenditures studied in the next chapter, are often "big-ticket" items that can be postponed. Many households buy new automobiles or TV sets simply because they want improved quality or new features, and they can postpone such purchases if their incomes decline temporarily. Consumption of nondurable goods displays an intermediate cyclical volatility, while consumption of services tends to grow smoothly. Some nondurable goods purchases, particularly of clothing and household articles like draperies and carpeting, can be postponed and respond to fluctuations of income. Another reason for fluctuations in some types of durable and nondurable goods spending is that in cases like appliances, furniture, draperies, and carpeting, the demand corresponds to the amount of new housing construction, which has been highly volatile in several past recessions.

It is clear from Figure 18-1 that the three components of consumption spending do not all grow at the same rate. Both durable goods and services spending have grown much faster than spending on nondurable goods. Percentages of total consumption for the beginning and end of the period depicted are:

	1950:Q1	1988:Q4
Durable goods	10.3	15.7
Nondurable goods	49.0	34.6
Services	40.8	49.5

The basic reason for the slow growth in nondurable goods purchases is that many such goods, particularly food and clothing, are necessities. Many types of durable goods (such as stereo equipment) and services (airline trips to Florida) are luxuries that experience a disproportionate growth in demand when incomes rise.

Have these trends made total consumption more or less stable? The shrinking segment, nondurable goods, has a medium cyclical volatility. The growth in high-volatility durable goods spending and low-volatility services spending roughly cancel out, implying that the overall volatility of total competition did not change appreciably between 1950 and 1988.

18-3 Background: The Conflict Between the Time-Series and Cross-Section Evidence

One of the major innovations in Keynes's *General Theory* was the multiplier, which followed directly from the assumption that consumption behaved passively. Keynes's description of consumption behavior begins with the idea that there is a positive marginal propensity to consume that is less than unity: "The fundamental psychological law . . . is that men are disposed, as a rule and on the average, to increase their consumption as their income increases, but not by as much as the increase in their income."[1]

---

[1] See John Maynard Keynes, *The General Theory of Employment, Interest and Money* (New York: Macmillan, 1936), Book III. The idea of the multiplier was first introduced by R. F. Kahn, "The Relation of Home Investment to Unemployment," *Economic Journal* (June 1931), but Keynes was the first to fit the multiplier into a general economic model of commodity and money markets.

Keynes's second main idea was that there is a specific amount that individuals will consume independent of their income, so that it is possible for saving to be negative if disposable income is very low. Denoting consumption as C and disposable income as Q_D, the Keynesian consumption function can be written:

$$C = a + cQ_D \qquad (18.1)$$

The hypothetical Keynesian consumption function and saving ratio are plotted in the top two frames of Figure 18-2. In the top frame, consumption (C) rises less rapidly than disposable income (Q_D), since the marginal propensity to consume (c) is less than 1.0. Consumption starts out greater than Q_D, equals Q_D at the income level Q_{D0}, and then is less than Q_D. Everywhere to the right of Q_{D0} the shortfall of consumption below disposable income allows room for a positive amount of saving. For instance, the income level Q_{D1} is divided into the consumption level C_1 an the saving level S_1.

Moving down to the middle frame of Figure 18-2, we find plotted the saving/income ratio, S/Q_D. To the left of the income level Q_{D0}, saving is negative; to the right of Q_{D0}, saving is positive. As people become richer, according to the hypothetical Keynesian relation in the middle frame, they save a larger share of their disposable income.

A cross-section consists of data for numerous units (for instance, households, firms, cities, or states) observed at the same moment of time.

The actual data plotted in the bottom frame of Figure 18-2 confirm Keynes's hypothesis for a **cross section** of Americans who were polled in 1986 on their income, saving, and consumption behavior. Most people with low incomes do not save at all but instead "dissave," consuming more than they earn by borrowing or by drawing on accumulated assets in savings accounts. As we move rightward from the poor to the rich, we find that the saving/income ratio increases, just as in the hypothetical relationship of the middle frame.

The Amazing Stability of the Saving Rate

Figure 18-2 depicts a potentially serious problem for the economy. If people save more as they become richer, then one presumes that society will save more as economic growth raises average incomes. If the economy were to

---

Figure 18-2 **The Relation between Disposable Income (Q_D), Consumption Spending (C), and the Ratio of Saving to Income (S/Q_D)**

The top frame repeats the consumption function introduced in Chapter 3. At levels of disposable income below (to the left of) point Q_{D0}, people consume more than their income. To the right of Q_{D0} consumption is less than income, and the shaded pink difference between income and consumption, the amount of saving, is a steadily growing fraction of disposable income. In the middle frame the share of saving in disposable income is plotted, a negative fraction to the left of point Q_{D0} and a positive and growing fraction to the right. The bottom frame plots actual data on the relation of saving to disposable income from a survey of consumers. Notice the close correspondence between the theoretical diagram in the middle frame and the actual data in the bottom frame. (Source for bottom frame: U.S. Bureau of Labor Statistics, *Consumer Expenditure Survey: Results from 1986,* Washington, April 1988, Table 2. *Saving ratio is income after taxes minus average annual expenditures expressed as a percent of income after taxes. Income after taxes converted from 1986 to 1989 prices by taking the ratio of the estimated 1989 CPI to the actual 1986 CPI.*)

THE PERCENTAGE OF INCOME THAT IS SAVED RISES AS INCOME GOES UP

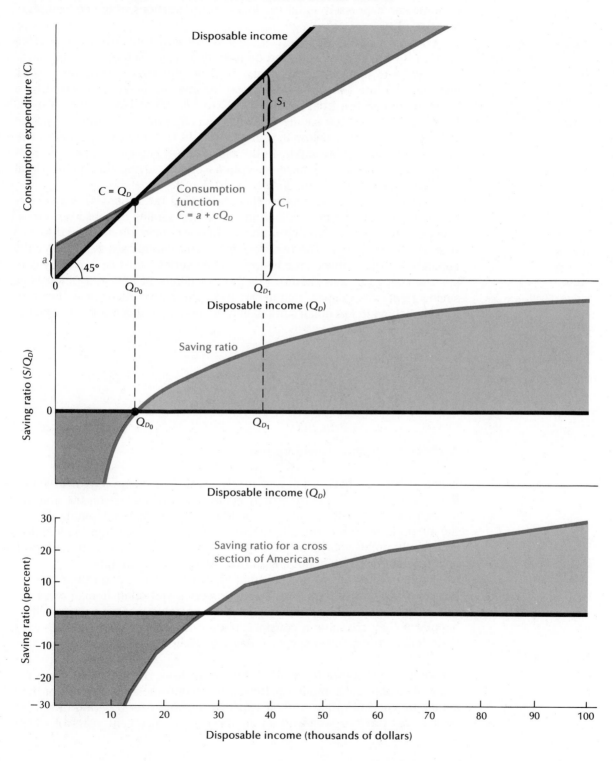

save a larger and larger share of GNP as people became richer, and if there were no corresponding increase in the share of investment in GNP, then the economy could slump into a recession or depression. This explains the concern Keynes expressed about the long-run implications of the consumption function (18.1).

A **time series** consists of data covering a span of time for one or more series (for instance, disposable income or consumption spending).

Look now at Figure 18-3, which plots the actual historical **time-series** data on the saving rate achieved on average during each of the major business cycles of this century. Between 1898–99, the first observation plotted, and 1981–89, the last observation, real income per person increased by a factor of almost five from roughly $4200 to $20,000 at 1988 prices.[2] Yet the feared increase in the saving ratio has not occurred. The saving ratio in 1981–88 was actually below that in 1898–99. In fact, the saving ratio in Figure 18-3 was amazingly stable, in the range of 5–8 percent during the 1910–85 period, with the two main exceptions of low saving during the Great Depression and high saving during World War II.

Clearly Keynes's assumption that the saving ratio increases as society becomes richer must be modified in a way that retains the observed cross-section increase in the saving ratio when poor people are compared to rich people at a given time. The two most important hypotheses that resolve the apparent conflict between the historical time-series evidence of a fairly constant saving ratio and the cross-section evidence of a steadily increasing saving ratio with higher income are two alternative theories of forward-looking behavior: Friedman's permanent-income hypothesis and Modigliani's life-cycle hypothesis.

18-4 Forward-Looking Behavior: The Permanent-Income Hypothesis

A Theory of Stable Consumption

Imagine that you have a job and receive your take-home pay of $1000 on the first day of each month. Strictly speaking, your income on the first day of each month is $1000, and your income on each of the remaining days of the month is zero. According to the simple Keynesian consumption function, you should do all your consumption spending on the first day of the month and consume absolutely nothing during the rest of the month!

Of course people do not consume their entire income on their payday, but set aside part of their pay to buy groceries and other items during the rest of the month. Individuals who have an unstable income pattern will be happier if they consume a constant amount each day rather than allowing their consumption to change each day with their changing income.

A farmer uses saving to even out consumption. People can achieve the desirable stable consumption pattern if they consume a fraction not of their actual income but rather of their expected income over a period of time. A farmer may have experienced an annual income in recent years of $3000,

---

[2]*Source:* Data underlying Figure 12-1.

Figure 18-3

Ratio of Personal Saving to Disposable Income (S/Q_D), Averages over Business Cycles, 1898–1988

The low level of saving during the Great Depression is consistent with our theory (compare Figure 3-3). The high level of saving during World War II was a special event caused by the unavailability of consumer goods. Leaving out these two extreme periods, the ratio of saving to disposable income was fairly constant. Notice that the ratio in 1975–79 was very close to its value in 1910. Observations plotted are averages over complete business cycles, except for 1981–85. (*Sources: 1898–1929 and 1949–69: Paul A. David and John L. Scadding, "Private Savings: Ultrarationality, Aggregation, and 'Denison's Law',"* Journal of Political Economy, *vol. 82 (March/April 1974), Table 4; 1930–48 and 1970–88, Bureau of Economic Analysis, U.S. Department of Commerce.*)

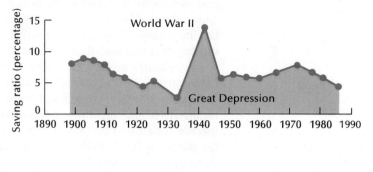

AMERICANS HAVE NOT SAVED A GREATER SHARE OF THEIR INCOME AS THEY HAVE GROWN RICHER

$17,000, $9000, and $11,000. Because his income averaged out at $10,000, his best guess for expected income next year is $10,000. Let us assume on average that he wants to spend 90 percent of his expected income and save the remaining 10 percent. Then his planned consumption will be $9000 and saving $1000. If the harvest turns out to be bad and actual realized income falls to a paltry $5000, achieving the $9000 consumption plan would require withdrawing $4000 from savings, to be returned in years of good harvests.

Milton Friedman first proposed the hypothesis that individuals consume a constant fraction (k) of their expected income, which Friedman called **permanent income (Q^P):**[3]

Permanent income is the average income that people expect to receive over a period of years in the future.

General Form   Numerical Example for the Farmer

$$C = kQ^P \qquad C = 0.9(\$10,000) = \$9000 \qquad (18.2)$$

The individual marginal propensity to consume out of permanent income (k) depends on individual tastes and on the variability of income (farmers and others with variable income need higher saving to support them during bad years). In addition k depends on the interest rate, since people should be willing to save more on average if they receive a higher rate of interest on their saving.[4]

---

[3]Milton Friedman, *A Theory of the Consumption Function* (Princeton, N.J.: Princeton University Press, 1957), especially Chapters 1–3, 6, and 9.

[4]Because of the limitations of the alphabet we are once again forced to duplicate the use of letters. The k here is completely unrelated to the k used in Chapters 3 through 5 to represent the multiplier.

Revising the estimate of permanent income. The permanent-income hypothesis summarized in equation (18.2) does not say that individuals consume exactly the same amount year after year. Every year new events occur that are likely to change each individual's guess about his permanent income. For instance, an individual might find that in good years her income has increased. Gradually she will revise her estimate of average expected income and will find that she can increase her stable consumption level.

Friedman's permanent-income hypothesis consists of the assumption in equation (18.2) that individuals consume a constant portion of their permanent income. But this is not enough, because an additional assumption is required to indicate how individuals estimate the size of their permanent income. Friedman proposed that individual estimates of permanent income for this year (Q^P) be revised from last year's estimate (Q^P_{-1}) by some fraction (j) of the amount by which actual income (Q) differs from Q^P_{-1}:

General Form $\qquad\qquad\qquad$ Numerical Example

$$Q^P = Q^P_{-1} + j(Q - Q^P_{-1}) \qquad Q^P = 10{,}000 + 0.2(15{,}000 - 10{,}000)$$
$$= 11{,}000 \qquad\qquad (18.3)$$

Adaptive expectations. The behavior described in equation (18.3) is sometimes called the "error-learning" or "adaptive" hypothesis of expectation formation. This hypothesis implies that individuals will allow their consumption to respond modestly to changes in actual income because consumption depends on permanent income, and in turn permanent income in equation (18.3) depends only in part on this period's actual income. When we substitute (18.3) into (18.2), we obtain the following relationship between an individual's current consumption (C), this period's actual income (Q), and last period's estimate of permanent income (Q^P_{-1}):

$\qquad\qquad$ General Form $\qquad\qquad\qquad\qquad$ Numerical Example

$$C = kQ^P_{-1} + kj(Q - Q^P_{-1}) \qquad C = 0.9 + 0.18(Q - Q^P_{-1}) \quad (18.4)$$

Exactly the same hypothesis for the formation of expectations was introduced in Chapter 9 in the discussion of inflation expectations (see equation [9.4]). Equation (18.3) can be rewritten in the form used in Chapter 9:

$$Q^P = jQ + (1 - j)Q^P_{-1}$$

This says that permanent income in this period is a weighted average of actual income and last period's permanent income.

Two marginal propensities to consume. Equation (18.4) helps us see that Friedman's theory is based on a distinction between the two concepts of the marginal propensity to consume (MPC). The *long-run* MPC is simply the coefficient (k) on permanent income in the original consumption function (18.2), and indeed k is the coefficient on the first term in (18.4). In our numerical example, the long-term MPC (k) is 0.9. The *short-run* MPC is the coefficient on a change in actual income, the coefficient kj (or $0.18 = 0.2$ times 0.9) on the second term in (18.4). When today's actual income (Q) increases, the second term in (18.4) shows that today's consumption goes up by the short-run MPC $(kj$, or 0.18).

The portion of today's income change that is not expected to be permanent is called **transitory income** in Friedman's theory. Transitory income (Q^t) is simply actual income minus permanent income:

| General Form | Numerical Example |

$$C = Q - Q^P \qquad\qquad C = Q - Q^P$$
$$= Q - Q^P_{-1} - j(Q - Q^P_{-1}) \qquad = 0.8(Q - Q^P_{-1}) \qquad (18.5)$$
$$= (1 - j)(Q - Q^P_{-1})$$

Friedman achieves his sharp distinction between the long-run and short-run MPC by assuming that the MPC out of transitory income is zero. Thus his consumption function (18.2) could be rewritten:

$$C = 0Q^t + kQ^P \qquad\qquad\qquad (18.6)$$

Reconciling the Conflict Between Cross-Section and Time-Series Data

The motivation for Friedman's PIH was the apparent conflict between the cross-section data in Figure 18-2, where rich people have a higher saving ratio than poor people, and the historical constancy of the saving ratio over the past century in Figure 18-3. The PIH creates a reconciliation by interpreting the high saving of rich people *as due to the transitory nature of much income earned by the rich* (executives enjoying a large bonus after a good year, as does a movie star after a popular film or this year's champion used-car salesperson).

Similarly, poor people are interpreted as dissaving (as in Figure 18-2) in response to an actual income that is temporarily below their permanent income. (Examples of people with such negative transitory income include farmers with diseased crops, executives who have just been fired, and movie stars whose popularity has waned.) In each generation there are people with large transitory incomes saving a lot and people with negative transitory incomes saving little or dissaving, but on average, over history, society has tended to save about the same fraction of income.

The two consumption functions illustrated. Figure 18-4 illustrates the distinction between the long-run and short-run consumption functions. The solid red line running through points *A* and *F* is the long-run consumption function; its slope is the long-run MPC (*k,* or 0.9). It is called the long-run consumption function because it indicates the level of consumption only when actual income has remained at a particular level long enough for individuals to have adjusted fully their estimated permanent income to the actual level.

What happens in the short run, when actual income can differ from permanent income? The flatter dashed red schedule running between *A* and *B* is the short-run schedule and plots equation (18.4). When current income (Q) is exactly equal to last period's permanent income (Q^P_{-1}), the short-run schedule intersects the long-run schedule at point *A*. But during a good year when an individual's income is at the high level Q_0, the current estimate of permanent income (Q^P) rises above last period's estimate (Q^P_{-1}) by a fraction (j) of the excess of actual income over last period's estimate. And the higher value of Q^P raises consumption by k times the increase in permanent income.

Figure 18-4
The Permanent-Income Hypothesis of Consumption and Saving

The long-run schedule shows that consumption is a fixed fraction of income in the long run, when actual and permanent income are equal. But short-run gains in actual income, as at point B, are not fully incorporated into permanent income. Thus consumption increases only a small amount (compare points B and A) and at B most of the short-run increase in income is saved. When the same gain in income is maintained permanently, the short-run schedule shifts upward, following the arrows along the long-run schedule to point F.

THE LONG-RUN CONSUMPTION FUNCTION IS MUCH STEEPER THAN THE SHORT-RUN FUNCTION

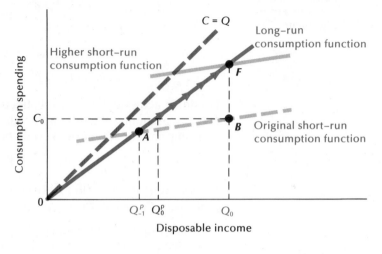

Thus consumption at point B lies vertically above point A by the fraction kj (18 percent in the numerical example) times the horizontal distance between Q^P_{-1} and Q_0. With the short-run marginal propensity to consume (kj) so far below the long-run propensity (k), any short-run increase in income goes disproportionately into saving.

To summarize, estimates of permanent income are continually raised as actual income outstrips previous levels, causing the relationship between consumption and income to follow the long-run schedule, as marked by the arrows in Figure 18-4. Thus in the long run the saving ratio is roughly constant. But in the short run a temporary increase in income raises the saving ratio and a temporary decrease in income reduces the saving ratio, because permanent income does not adjust completely to changes in actual income.

SELF-TEST   Would Friedman's theory predict a higher or lower than average MPC in the following situations? (1) a pro basketball player enjoying his best season; (2) a pro basketball player who has just retired from active play; (3) a North Dakota wheat farmer suffering from the summer drought of 1988; (4) the U.S. economy in a recession; (5) the U.S. economy in a period of unusually high real GNP.

18-5   Forward-Looking Behavior: The Life-Cycle Hypothesis

About the same time that Friedman wrote his book on the permanent-income hypothesis, Franco Modigliani of MIT and collaborators devised a somewhat different way of reconciling the positive relation between the saving ratio and income observed in cross-section data and the constancy of the saving ratio observed over long periods in the historical time-series

Franco Modigliani (1918–   ), 1985 Nobel Prize winner, is best known for the life-cycle model of consumption behavior and for his articulate advocacy of policy activism.

data.[5] Modigliani and Friedman both began from the argument that individuals prefer to maintain a stable consumption pattern rather than allow consumption to rise or fall with every transitory oscillation of their income. But Modigliani carried the stable-consumption argument further than Friedman and suggested that people *would try to stabilize their consumption over their entire lifetimes.*

Because of its emphasis on the lifetime horizon of consumers, the Modigliani theory is called the life-cycle hypothesis (LCH). Since it stresses the way consumers smooth consumption over their lifetimes and save in preparation for their retirement years, the LCH falls into the category of theories based on *forward-looking expectations.* It shares with Friedman's theory the ability to reconcile a low short-run MPC with a high and stable long-run MPC. But the LCH adds to Friedman's theory a "lifetime budget constraint," which is the condition that the consumption of households over their lifetimes equals their income plus their holdings of assets coming from sources other than work (for example, gifts from parents). This feature of the LCH provides a rigorous connection between consumption expenditures and the value of the assets held by consumers and *predicts that a stock market crash, like that of 1987, will tend to cut consumption expenditures.*

Lifetime Asset Holding: "Modigliani's Pyramid" Illustrated

We now examine Figure 18-5, which shows how a simple version of Modigliani's theory predicts how income, consumption, saving, and asset accumulation will behave over the lifetime of the typical consumer. The horizontal axis shows various ages, with the age at retirement marked by R and the age at death marked by L. An individual is assumed to maintain a constant level of consumption (C_0) throughout life. Income, however, is earned only during the R working years. If there are no assets initially, as shown by the zero level of initial assets (A_0) in the bottom frame, then the only way individuals can manage to consume without any income during their retirement is to save during their working years. The amount saved, income minus consumption, is shown by the gray shading during the period up to time R, and then the dissaving that occurs when consumption exceeds income during retirement is shown by the pink shading from time R through time L. In the bottom frame the accumulation of assets occurs steadily during the working years through time R, at which point assets reach their maximum level A_R, after which point assets fall back to zero at time L.

No initial assets.   How are consumption and income related when there are no initial assets? Total lifetime consumption of C_0 per year for L years is constrained to equal total income Q_0 per year for R years:

$$C_0 L = Q_0 R \quad or \quad C_0 = \left(\frac{R}{L}\right) Q_0 \qquad (18.7)$$

---

[5]Franco Modigliani and R. E. Brumberg, "Utility Analysis and the Consumption Function," in K. K. Kurihara, ed., *Post-Keynesian Economics* (New Brunswick, N.J.: Rutgers University Press, 1954). Also A. Ando and F. Modigliani, "The 'Life Cycle' Hypothesis of Saving: Aggregate Implications and Tests," *American Economic Review,* vol. 53 (March 1963), pp. 55–84.

Figure 18-5

The Behavior of Consumption, Saving, and Assets under the Life-Cycle Hypothesis

Under the life-cycle hypothesis particular attention is paid to the relation between the length of the lifetime (L) and an individual's age at retirement (R). The length of the retirement period is $L - R$. In the upper frame a constant amount (C_0) is consumed every year of one's life, as indicated by the red line. A constant amount of income Q_0 is earned each year until retirement. During the working years until R, income exceeds consumption, as shown by the saving that occurs in the pink area. Then consumption exceeds the zero income during retirement and is financed by dissaving, as shown by the gray area. In the bottom frame the black line shows the growth of assets from the initial level (A_0) to the maximum level at retirement (A_R), followed by a decline in assets back to zero at death.

THE YOUNG SAVE DURING THEIR WORKING YEARS, BUT THE OLD DISSAVE DURING RETIREMENT

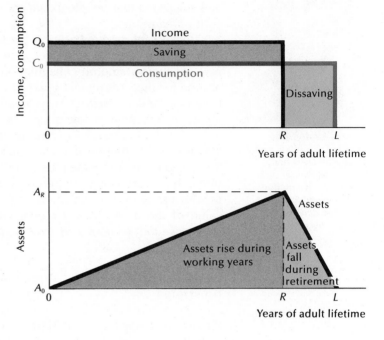

As Figure 18-5 is drawn, R is four fifths of L, so consumption per year is limited to four fifths of Q_0.[6]

The simple version of the life-cycle hypothesis can explain the positive association of saving and income, since those of working age have higher values of both saving and income than those who are retired. But at the same time the time-series constancy of the saving ratio can be explained by the fact that if each historical era is divided into the same proportions of working and retired people, and each age group has the same saving behavior in generation after generation, then the saving ratio should be unchanged as time passes.

---

[6]There are several simplifications in Figure 18-5 and equation (18.7) involving the treatment of interest income. Assuming that interest is earned on asset holdings at rate i, then total income is equal to wage income in real terms (W) plus real interest income (rA). Then (18.7) becomes

$$C_0L = W_0R + \sum_{t=0}^{L} rA_t$$

Thus total income increases gradually through time R and then decreases to zero but is nevertheless positive during the retirement period. To reflect the fact that consumption depends on total income, including both wage income and earnings from the holding of assets, the symbol Q (for total real income) rather than W is used in (18.7) in the text. The official definition of income overstates Q, since it includes the entire income from assets, including that portion of the nominal return ($i - r$) needed to maintain intact the real value of assets.

The life-cycle hypothesis shares with Friedman's permanent-income hypothesis the implication that the saving ratio should rise in economic boom years and fall in recession years. A temporary increase in income today will be consumed over one's entire lifetime. For instance, imagine a person who believes he has forty years left to live and receives an unexpected increase in income this year of $4000 that he does not expect to receive again. His total lifetime consumption goes up by the $4000 and his actual consumption this year goes up by only 1/40 of that amount, a mere $100. In each succeeding year an additional $100 would be spent, for a total of $4000 over the remaining forty years of life.

Thus, in an economic boom widely expected to be temporary, an unexpected bonus of $4000 would lead to only $100 extra of current consumption and $3900 extra of saving. The short-run propensity to consume would be just 0.025, or 100/4000. On the other hand, if the $4000 income increase is expected to be repeated for each of the next forty years, then $4000 extra can be consumed this year and again in each of the next thirty-nine years and the saving ratio will not rise.

The role of assets. The Modigliani theory provides an important role for assets as a determinant of consumption behavior. Let us assume that initially a person has an endowment of assets of A_1, but she plans to use these assets to raise her consumption through her lifetime rather than to leave the assets to her heirs. Then, as shown in Figure 18-6, consumption can be higher for a given level of income (Q_0), and saving can be lower, since the initial asset endowment provides more spending power. Now total lifetime consumption equals total lifetime income from work plus the available assets:

$$C_1 L = A_1 + Q_1 R \quad \text{or} \quad C_1 = \frac{A_1}{L} + \frac{R}{L} Q_1 \qquad (18.8)$$

The right-hand expression shows that consumption per year (C_1) depends not just on income (Q_1) but on the ratio of available assets per year of life.

Figure 18-6 is oversimplified by assuming that the initial endowment of assets is received at the beginning of the working life. In reality, however, increases in the value of assets occur throughout one's life, so one would expect the response of annual consumption to a change in asset value to be larger than is assumed in equation 18.8. Modigliani's empirical research has estimated that a $1 increase in real asset values raises real consumption this year by about $.06, which would indicate that people use a fifteen-year horizon over which to spend an increase in real assets.

We learned in Chapter 7 that the economy's self-correcting forces are enhanced when real consumption spending depends on real assets or real wealth. If a drop in spending cuts the price level, the level of real wealth is raised, which helps arrest the decline in spending.[7] In the other direction, if an increase in spending raises the price level, the level of real wealth declines, which helps dampen the original stimulus to spending.

---

[7]Review the Pigou, or real balance effect discussed in Section 7-2.

Figure 18-6

Consumption, Saving, and Assets under the Life-Cycle Hypothesis When There Is an Initial Stock of Assets

This diagram is identical to Figure 18-5, but here there is an initial stock of assets A_1, in contrast to the initial stock of zero in the previous diagram. If we continue to assume that dissaving during retirement runs the stock of assets down to zero, then the existence of A_1 makes more total consumption possible with a smaller amount of saving. This is shown by an upward shift from the previous level of consumption (C_0) to a new higher level (C_1). The pink saving area is now smaller, as is the pink area in the bottom frame showing the increase in assets due to saving.

AN INITIAL ENDOWMENT OF ASSETS RAISES CONSUMPTION AND REDUCES SAVING

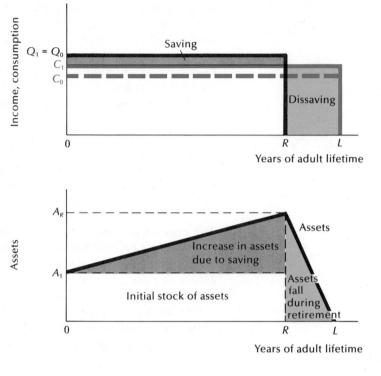

Thus, ironically, Modigliani's life-cycle hypothesis supports plank 1 of the monetarist platform of Chapter 15, even though Modigliani is a prominent activist and a critic of monetarism. Private spending is stabilized because transitory increases in disposable income that are not expected to last a lifetime have only a modest influence on current consumption. In addition, the real-asset effect stabilizes the economy through the effect of higher prices in cutting real assets and dampening spending. Overall, the life-cycle hypothesis helps reduce the current marginal propensity to consume, cut the multiplier, and insulate the economy from unexpected changes in investment, net exports, or other types of spending.

SELF-TEST Assume that an adult is making a consumption plan and anticipates a life of 40 more years, 30 of which will be spent in work and 10 in retirement. If income during the working years is $50,000, and the endowment of initial assets is zero, what will be consumption expenditures per year during the working years? During the retirement years? What will be the average propensity to consume (C/Q) during working years? Now, assume instead that initial assets are $200,000. What will be consumption expenditures per year during the working years? During the retirement years? What will be the average propensity to consume during the working years?

18-6 Rational Expectations and Other Modern Amendments to the Simple Forward-Looking Theories

In recent years consumption behavior has been one of the most active areas of research in macroeconomics. Rational expectations has been applied to the permanent-income hypothesis, and the contrast between the predictions of the resulting theory and the actual cyclical behavior of consumption has highlighted the role of several additional factors that are not part of the pure PIH or LCH theories: liquidity constraints, consumer durables, bequests, and uncertainty.

Rational Expectations

Rational expectations need not be correct but make the best use of available information, avoiding errors that could have been avoided by knowledge of history.

In Chapter 7 we introduced the hypothesis of **rational expectations** as one of the key assumptions of new classical macroeconomics. Recently the study of consumption behavior has focused on the implications of combining rational expectations with the permanent-income hypothesis (PIH). Recall from equation (18.3) that in its original Friedman formulation, the PIH is combined with the adaptive or error-learning method of calculating permanent income. Thus when actual income increases, people only *gradually* revise upward their estimate of permanent income.

The rational expectations version of the PIH continues to assume that consumption depends only on permanent income (as in equation 18.2). The difference is in how people estimate their permanent income. Rational expectations assumes that expectations of future events are formed using the best available information. When combined with the PIH, rational expectations implies that any information contained in *past* values of income relevant for the estimation of permanent income have already been taken into account. Thus only *new* information on actual income can cause any change in estimated permanent income, which in turn means (since $C = kQ^p$ as in equation 18.2) that changes in consumption depend only on current changes in income that were previously *unanticipated* and not on past values of income.

Is consumption too volatile or too smooth? A controversy has developed over the empirical implementation of the rational expectations version of the PIH. Everything depends on how consumers view the nature of new information on income. If a change in current income provides no information about the behavior of income in the future, then estimates of permanent income change very little, and the marginal propensity to consume out of this change in current income should be close to zero.[8] Under this assumption that changes in current income provide no information about changes in permanent income, consumption should be almost completely unrespon-

---

[8]In this case it can be shown in a specific mathematical model that the MPC would be $r/(1 + r)$, where r is the real rate of interest. Thus, depending on the asset used to measure r, the MPC would be between about zero and 0.07. This result is developed in the excellent but mathematically advanced survey by Andrew B. Abel, "Consumption and Investment," NBER Working Paper 2580, May 1988, forthcoming in B. M. Friedman and F. Hahn, eds., *Handbook of Monetary Economics*.

sive to changes in current income. However, our case study (Section 18-2) showed that consumption displayed visible responses to the decline of income in the 1974–75 and 1981–82 recesssions. This approach, then, leads to the conclusion that actual consumption is *excessively volatile* relative to the prediction of the theory.[9]

However, another possibility is that changes in current income provide a good prediction of changes in future income. For instance, a person who loses a high-paying job may have very good reason to predict that future income will be lower, perhaps for many years. In the extreme case, if it were true that estimates of permanent income always responded by one dollar to any change in current income of one dollar, then the marginal propensity to consume out of current income would be unity (simply because the marginal propensity to consume out of permanent income is unity). But the data show clearly that consumption is smoother than current income. So by this contrasting approach, actual consumption is *too smooth* relative to the prediction of the theory.[10]

Thus far the debate over the cyclical behavior of consumption has not been settled. However, the initial conclusion that consumption was too volatile led to the realization that the simple versions of the PIH and LCH reviewed above, as well as the rational expectations updating of these theories, omit several important aspects of consumption behavior. Until these issues are adequately integrated into the theory, it is unlikely that the question of whether consumption is too volatile or too smooth will be resolved.

Consumer Durables

Both the PIH and LCH are based on the desirability of maintaining a roughly constant level of enjoyment from consumption goods and services. For consumer services and nondurable goods, such as haircuts and doughnuts, the enjoyment and the consumer spending occur at about the same time. Consumer durable goods are different. A television set is purchased at a single instant in time but produces enjoyment for many years thereafter. Thus the PIH and LCH suggest that it is not purchases of consumer durable goods that are kept equal to a fixed fraction of permanent income, but rather the services (enjoyment) received from consumer durables.

If there is an increase in permanent income, people will not only want to increase their expenditures on services and nondurable goods, but will also want to increase their enjoyment of the services of durable goods. To do so they need to buy new consumer durables. As a result of the upsurge in purchases of consumer durables, total consumption expenditures may *rise* as a fraction of income when actual income rises, even though the PIH and LCH predict that consumption should *fall* as a fraction of income when actual income rises. Both the PIH and LCH predict that the saving ratio *falls*

---

[9]The rational expectations approach to the study of consumption behavior was introduced in Robert E. Hall, "Stochastic Implications of the Life Cycle-Permanent Income Hypothesis: Theory and Evidence," *Journal of Political Economy,* vol. 86 (December 1978), pp. 971–987. The excess volatility argument is usually credited to Marjorie Flavin, "The Adjustment of Consumption to Changing Expectations about Future Income," *Journal of Political Economy,* vol. 89 (October 1981), pp. 974–1009.

[10]See Angus Deaton, "Life-Cycle Models of Consumption: Is the Evidence Consistent with the Theory?" in T. F. Bewley, ed., *Advances in Econometrics Fifth World Congress.* New York: Cambridge University Press, 1987, pp. 121–148.

with higher income when consumer durables are counted as consumption expenditure but *rises* with higher income when consumer durables are counted as saving. Realization of the procyclical nature of consumer durable expenditures has led all recent investigators to limit their research on the validity of the PIH and LCH to consumer expenditures *excluding* durables— that is, including just services (haircuts) and nondurables (doughnuts).

Behavior of consumer durable expenditures in postwar recessions. Both the PIH and LCH predict that in a recession, when income exhibits a transitory decline, households should maintain their consumption expenditures *by cutting back on the ratio of saving to personal income* (S/Q_P). Yet the data for the postwar period indicate only a very small reduction in the saving ratio, unless an adjustment is made for the procyclical nature of expenditures on consumer durables. In the following table the ratio to personal income of consumer durables expenditure declines more than the saving ratio in recessions, and the ratio to personal income of the sum of saving and consumer durables expenditure ($S + C^D)/Q_P$ declines more than either component separately:

Seven Postwar Recessions, 1953–54 to 1981–82

Ratio to personal income	Peak	Trough	Peak to trough change
Personal saving	6.5	6.2	−0.3
Consumer durable expenditures	10.6	10.0	−0.6
Sum of personal saving and consumer durable expenditures	17.1	16.2	−0.9

Liquidity Constraints

The simple version of the LCH in Figure 18-5 assumes that consumption is constant over the lifetime and that labor income is constant until the date of retirement. Actually, however, labor income tends to rise with age and peaks around age fifty. To achieve a constant level of consumption throughout their lifetimes, young people would need to borrow during their low-income years and repay the loans later in high-income years. But banks generally will not allow young people to borrow all they would like, which implies that the consumption of young people is subject to a **liquidity constraint.** Such constraints are features of "imperfect credit markets." Another feature of such markets is that most people pay much higher rates to borrow money than they receive on their savings. A liquidity constraint may afflict people of all ages who are suffering from a transitory loss of income; for instance banks may be unwilling to lend to a farmer who is close to bankruptcy after a year of poor growing weather, even though the weather can be expected to be better in the future.

Anyone whose consumption can go no higher than their *current income* because of the unavailability of loans will have a much higher marginal propensity to consume in response to temporary changes in income than is predicted by the PIH or LCH theories. Economists have recently attempted to measure the importance of this so-called "excess sensitivity" of consumption to current changes in income. The consensus is that the income of roughly 15 percent of households is subject to liquidity constraints, with an MPC out of transitory income close to unity, while the remaining households

A liquidity constraint occurs when financial institutions do not allow households to borrow as much as they wish now, even though there is sufficient expected future income to repay the loans.

behave roughly as predicted by the LCH and have a negligible MPC out of transitory income.[11] Thus the existence of liquidity constraints only slightly weakens the implication of the LCH (and PIH) that the short-run MPC will be much lower than the long-run MPC.

Interest Rate Effects

Considerable controversy has arisen regarding the effect of interest rates on consumption and saving behavior. A high degree of sensitivity of saving to the after-tax real interest rate would give policymakers two instruments with which to influence the household saving rate—income tax rates and monetary policy. The high real interest rates of the 1980s (illustrated at the beginning of the book in Figure 1-10 on p. 20) provide a good test of the influence of interest rates, because the U.S. saving rate should have risen *both* because of the higher real interest rates *and* because President Reagan's tax cuts boosted the fraction of the interest income that savers could retain after paying income taxes.

However, as we shall see in Figure 18-7, the household saving rate in the 1980s did not rise in response to higher after-tax real interest rates. A recent study confirmed that there was no positive effect of interest rates on saving but that there was a substantial positive impact of inflation.[12] When inflation is high, people cut back on consumption and raise their saving rate, perhaps because they expect the Federal Reserve to react with a tight monetary policy that creates a recession and threatens them with a higher risk of job loss. In terms of our analysis of supply shocks in Chapter 10, this finding implies that an adverse oil price shock would not only boost the inflation rate, but would also reduce aggregate demand.

18-7 Bequests and Uncertainty

In both of our diagrams of the LCH, Figures 18-5 and 18-6, individuals are assumed to *consume all of their lifetime savings during retirement.* Their assets plummet to zero on the date of death, and nothing is left in the form of bequests to their heirs. Realistically, however, we know that people do leave bequests. In fact, a recent study claims that about 80 percent of asset accumulation by U.S. households is transmitted to heirs rather than used for consumption during retirement.[13] This evidence seems to deny that the appropriate horizon to describe consumer behavior is the lifetime.

The Role of Bequests

As we learned in Section 13-10, the existence of bequests has been interpreted as implying a radical theory of fiscal policy, often called the "Barro–

---

[11]The best recent evaluation of scholarly research on liquidity constraints is Fumio Hayashi, "Tests for Liquidity Constraints: A Critical Survey and Some New Observations," in T. F. Bewley, ed., *Advances in Econometrics Fifth World Congress.* New York: Cambridge University Press, 1987, pp. 91–120.

[12]Barry Bosworth, "The Changing Impact of Monetary Policy," *Brookings Papers on Economic Activity,* vol. 20, no. 1 (1989), pp. 77–110.

[13]Laurence J. Kotlikoff and Lawrence H. Summers, "The Role of Intergenerational Transfers in Aggregate Capital Accumulation," *Journal of Political Economy,* vol. 89 (August 1981); 706–732.

Ricardo equivalence theorem." People are expected to leave bequests because they care about their children. Any event that leaves their children worse off will lead members of the present generation to increase their saving in order to leave a larger bequest to the children. A prime example of such an event would be a deficit-financed tax cut that raises the taxes that must be paid by future generations (to pay the interest on the bonds issued to finance the debt). According to the Barro–Ricardo theorem, such a tax cut will not stimulate consumption since people will save all of the increase in their per-capita income in order to raise their bequests.

In Chapter 13 we reviewed some of the criticisms of the Barro–Ricardo theorem and noted that the U.S. household saving rate did not increase at all following the Reagan tax cuts of the 1980s, as the theorem would have predicted. Thus it seems likely that the mere existence of bequests does not validate the kind of behavior postulated by the theorem—specifically the refusal of current households to raise their consumption in response to a tax cut.

Motives for Bequests

If parents do not adjust their bequests for every current event that changes the future tax liabilities to be borne by their children and grandchildren, how are we to interpret the large fraction of personal saving that eventually flows to children in the form of bequests? Many observers think that the central issue is the uncertainty of the age of death. Benjamin Franklin's observation that "in this world nothing can be said to be certain, except death and taxes" omits the fact that the *timing* of death is quite uncertain. Contrary to the assumption of Figures 18-5 and 18-6, households do not know in advance the length of their lifetimes. They believe that there is a good chance that at least one spouse will live to an advanced age and may require expensive nursing home and other medical treatment that is not completely covered by insurance. They want to avoid relying on their children for support, and in many cases they want to continue to live in their own homes.

By this interpretation, *much saving is life-cycle in nature but for a part of the lifetime and for medical care that do not occur for everyone.* Many people die before expensive nursing care treatment becomes necessary and have substantial wealth "left over" that goes as bequests to the children. Many of these bequests are houses and small businesses that parents do not want to sell before death. By this interpretation, bequests are primarily involuntary and are made because parents do not want to lose control of their assets and their living conditions prior to death, rather than because they calculate the effect of each dollar of bequest on their children's welfare.

Implications for the LCH theory. The interpretation of bequests as primarily involuntary leaves the main predictions of the LCH intact. The only adjustment to the LCH is that the relevant horizon for most households extends beyond the actual age of death (as assumed in Figures 18-5 and 18-6) to the *oldest conceivable age of death.* For instance a 25-year-old may have a future life expectancy of 50 years, with 75 the most probable age of death, but may base consumption and saving decisions on the outside chance of living until age 90.

This amended version of the LCH would operate just like the version depicted in Figure 18-6, except the extended lifetime (L^*, say 90) replaces the most probable lifetime (L, say 75). Use of L^* instead of the lower L would imply an even lower MPC for temporary changes in income, and would imply that increases in wealth from the stock market would be consumed over the extended period until L^*. If parents are unwilling to move out of their homes (and are also unwilling to sell their homes to their children and pay them rent), then the gains parents make from higher housing prices may not be consumed over the lifetime but may be largely ignored and lead to a larger bequest.

SELF-TEST   Imagine that there is a $1000 increase in the personal income tax paid each year by every household; the revenue collected is used to reduce the federal budget deficit. The tax increase is announced to be permanent. What would the following theories predict to be the effects on consumption? (1) Permanent-income hypothesis; (2) life-cycle hypothesis with certain lifetime; (3) life-cycle hypothesis that explains bequests as resulting from uncertain lifetimes; (4) Barro-Ricardo equivalence theory.

18-8   *CASE STUDY:*   Tax Changes and the Saving Ratio

According to the permanent-income hypothesis, a drop in this month's actual income does not cut consumption unless people believe that the decline in actual income will persist, in which case permanent income declines. In the life-cycle hypothesis such a drop in current income does not cut consumption unless a person has some reason to conclude that his or her lifetime income has declined. For this reason a change in actual current disposable income caused by a tax change announced by the government as *permanent* should cause a bigger change in consumption than a tax increase announced as *temporary*.

What would happen to consumption and to the saving ratio if individuals assumed a temporary tax surcharge were a short-lived event with no effect at all on permanent income? Then consumption spending (C) would stay the same because, according to the PIH, consumption depends only on permanent income. People would pay for the temporary tax surcharge entirely by saving less, and the ratio of saving to personal income (S/Q_P) would fall by exactly the increase in the ratio of taxes to personal income (T/Q_P).

Temporary Tax Changes in the Postwar United States

We can begin to understand several puzzling episodes of saving behavior if we compare the movements of the ratio of saving to personal income (S/Q_P) and personal tax revenue to personal income (T_P/Q_P), as in Figure 18-7. Several episodes plotted there illustrate sharp movements in the tax ratio T_P/Q_P that are almost totally offset by movements of the saving ratio (S/Q_P).

THE SAVING RATE IS ALMOST A MIRROR IMAGE OF THE
SHARE OF INCOME COLLECTED AS PERSONAL TAXES

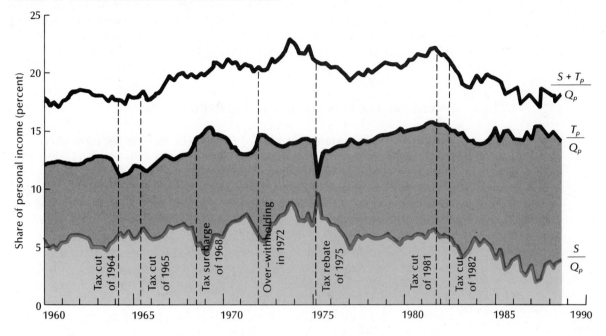

Figure 18-7   **The Relation of Saving (S) and Personal Tax Payments (T_P) to Personal
Income (Q_P), 1963–88**
The lower line shaded in pink is identical to that in the previous figure, the ratio of
saving to personal income (S/Q_P). The middle line is the ratio of personal tax
payments to personal income (T_P/Q_P). Notice how the movements of the S/Q_P ratio
are almost a mirror image of T/Q_P, at least before 1980. *(Source:* Survey of Current
Business, *various issues.)*

The two most important examples occured in mid-1968, when Congress
passed the temporary tax surcharge proposed by President Johnson to finance Vietnam War spending, and in mid-1975, when a temporary tax rebate
was declared to help revive the economy. Individuals must have been led
by the term *temporary surcharge* in 1968 to hold unchanged their estimates
of their permanent income. Thus the mid-1968 increase in the T_P/Q_P ratio in
Figure 18-7 is completely offset by a drop in the S/Q_P ratio. Because the sum
of the saving and tax ratios remained constant, we can conclude that the
tax surcharge totally failed to achieve its aim of dampening consumption. In
fact there was very little further movement in the sum of the saving and tax
ratios (the top line in Figure 18-7) during the ten quarters following the
imposition of the surcharge. The saving ratio fell suddenly in 1968 and then
gradually rose in the next two years as the surcharge was removed.

Another dramatic example of the effect of a temporary tax change occurred in early 1975, when individuals received a rebate of up to $200 per
family on their income tax liability. Much of the rebate went into saving, at

least initially, as indicated by the upward blip in the S/Q_P ratio in 1975:Q2, the same quarter as the downward blip in the T_P/Q_P ratio. The 1975 tax changes also included some permanent elements, which individuals may have treated as calling for an adjustment in their permanent income rather than in their saving ratio. In the last half of 1975 the saving ratio returned to the average level of 1973 and 1974, so that the permanent portion of the 1975 tax cut appears to have succeeded in stimulating consumption.[14]

Permanent Tax Cuts and the Saving Ratio

The two most important episodes of permanent income tax reductions in the postwar United States occurred in 1964–65 and 1981–84. According to both the PIH and LCH, the increase in disposable income caused by a permanent tax cut should be reflected in higher consumption with no change in the saving rate. However, in the 1964–65 episode, the saving rate did not remain unaffected. An increase in saving almost completely offset the tax cuts when they occurred (in 1964:Q2 and 1965:Q3), and there was only a minor subsequent decline in the saving ratio. This suggests that people may not have believed that the tax cuts would be permanent.

The Reagan tax cuts were enacted in August 1981 and were carried out in three stages during 1982–84. The drop in the T_P/Q_P ratio in 1983–84 is clearly visible in Figure 18-7. Also evident is the absence of any upsurge of saving, which indicates that people believed the tax cuts would be permanent.

Bracket Creep and the Disappearing Tax Cut

However, a careful inspection of Figure 18-7 will reveal a startling fact about the Reagan tax cuts. While the tax ratio T_P/Q_P did decline between 1981 and 1984, it rose again in 1985–87. Should we conclude then that the Reagan tax cuts were only temporary? To assess this question, we can use the data underlying Figure 18-7 to calculate the tax ratio (T_P/Q_P) in each year after 1976:

1977	14.4	1983	14.5
1978	15.0	1984	14.2
1979	15.1	1985	14.6
1980	15.1	1986	14.5
1981	15.6	1987	15.1
1982	15.3	1988	14.5

Over the full period 1977–88, there was no change in the tax ratio T_P/Q_P. The ratio rose from 1977 to 1981, fell from 1981 to 1984, rose from 1984 to 1987, and then fell in 1988.

---

[14]The most recent and careful scholarly investigation of the effect of temporary tax changes on saving behavior is Blinder and Deaton, "Time Series Consumption Function Revisited," *Brookings Papers on Economic Activity,* vol. 16, no. 2 (1985), pp. 465–521. This paper reaches the conclusion that temporary tax changes have no effect on consumption and are totally offset by increases in saving.

Average versus marginal tax rates. To understand why tax rates began to rise after 1984, despite the Reagan tax cuts, we need to distinguish between average and marginal tax rates. The figures shown here are *average* tax rates, simply the average of tax revenues collected to personal income. What the Reagan program reduced were *marginal* tax rates, the tax schedule that states the percentage tax on an extra dollar of income at different income levels. For instance, in 1988 a household with $50,000 of income making an extra dollar faced a marginal tax rate of 28 percent. This schedule of marginal tax rates was substantially lower than in 1981, when a household with $50,000 of income faced a marginal tax rate of 49 percent.[15]

Bracket creep. How can we reconcile the sharp decline in marginal tax rates in the 1980s with the insignificant drop in the average tax rate (T_P/Q_P)? The answer is that growth in real GNP, as well as inflation, raises the income of the average household and pushes some households into higher tax-rate "brackets," thus raising their marginal tax rate even though the *schedule* of tax-rate brackets is fixed. This "bracket creep" as households are pushed into higher tax brackets explains the high elasticity of tax revenues to economic growth (a 1 percent increase in personal income usually raises federal personal income tax revenue by 1.3 to 1.4 percent). Thus as the 1980s progressed and U.S. personal income per person increased from $10,950 in 1981 to $16,510 in 1988, many households found that their higher incomes pushed them into a higher tax-rate bracket that left their tax payments as a percentage of personal income little different than had occurred before the Reagan reductions of the marginal tax rates in each bracket.

Bracket creep is nothing new, and in fact has been a feature of the tax system throughout the full 1960–88 period described in Figure 18-7.[16] We note in the figure that each previous tax reduction in marginal tax rates, including that of 1964–65 as well as of 1981–84, was followed by a period of an increasing average tax rate (T_P/Q_P). Thus we should describe such tax cuts as achieving permanent declines in marginal tax rates but only temporary decreases in average tax rates. The permanent income hypothesis predicts that a tax cut having no last effect on average tax rates would have no effect on permanent income, and would cause no change in saving behavior. Correspondingly, in past episodes like 1964–65 and 1975, the average tax rates fell for a short period and then recovered, and the saving rate rose briefly and then returned to roughly its previous value.

One major puzzle remains in Figure 18-7. While the average tax rate in 1987–88 was little different than a decade earlier, in 1977–78, the saving rate was much lower. Clearly, some factor in addition to tax rate changes must have an important impact on the saving rate. One candidate to explain the puzzle is the behavior of the stock market, the subject of the next section.

---

[15]These tax rates are from the tax tables for 1981 and 1988 and apply to married couples filing jointly. At higher income levels the marginal tax rate fell even more. In 1981 a rate of 70 percent applied above $215,500, whereas in 1988 the marginal rate above $30,000 was just 28 percent (except for a quirk in the tax system that applied a 33 percent rate for each extra dollar of income earned between $71,900 and $149,250).

[16]In fact, bracket creep has been less important since the 1986 tax reform, which "indexes" the boundaries between the tax brackets each year to the rate of inflation. Thus a household having an increase in income equal to the inflation rate, with no change in real income, is not pushed into a higher tax bracket under this new indexed system.

18-9 The Stock Market and Consumption Behavior

The previous case study left one puzzle unresolved. We still need to explain why the U.S. saving rate was so low in the mid-1980s. Many economists believe that the explanation lies in the relationship between the stock market and consumption behavior.

The Stock Market and the LCH

The LCH predicts that changes in stock prices substantially affect consumption. Why? Because the LCH in its pure version (without consideration of bequests) assumes that households consume their stock of assets over their lifetimes. Thus if stock prices go up and stocks increase in value, stockholders can gradually sell off shares of the higher-priced stocks and consume more over their lifetime.

Clearly, the exact interpretation of the LCH depends on whether we allow for bequests. The Barro-Ricardo approach assumes that parents care about the utility of future generations; an increase in stock prices today will be shared by current and by future generations, so that current consumption should rise. An alternative approach, outlined earlier, stresses that many bequests are a "residual" that people leave because they do not sell their houses before death, and because they save up for medical and other retirement expenses that may never occur. In such an approach, an increase in stock market prices just increases the residual, without any effect on current consumption.

The standard life-cycle analysis predicts that a $1 increase in consumer assets, for example, the value of stocks, leads to an increase in consumption expenditures over the next twelve months of between $0.03 and $0.06. Thus a 25 percent increase in stock prices, which would raise wealth by about $1 trillion, would cause an increase in consumption of $30 to $60 billion, or between 0.6 and 1.2 percent of nominal GNP. Added to this would be the multiplier effect of the increase in consumption, and any direct or indirect effects on investment.

Evidence on Stock Prices and the Saving Rate

Figure 18-8 displays quarterly data since 1954 on the U.S. saving rate and the real value of stock prices.[17] While the relationship is not perfect, there clearly are inverse movements of the two measures. When stock prices plunged in 1973–75, after the first oil shock, the saving rate reached its post-1954 high. And when stock prices soared in 1985–87, the saving rate fell to its postwar low. Interestingly, the two quarters with the lowest saving rates were 1987:Q2 and 1987:Q3, just before the stock market crash of October 19, 1987.

---

[17]The saving rate in Figure 18-8 is the conventional measure, defined as saving divided by personal disposable income (after payment of personal taxes). The saving rate in Figure 18-7 divides saving by personal income (before payment of personal taxes).

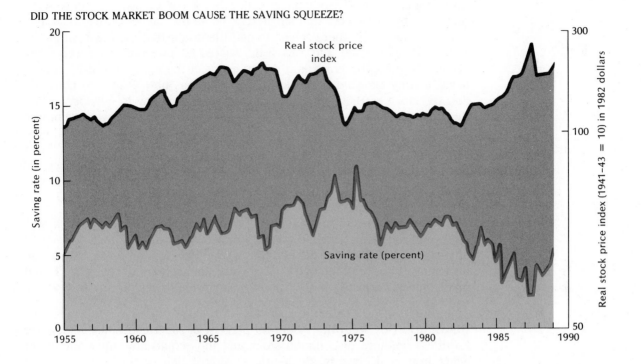

Figure 18-8   **The Saving Rate and the Real Stock Price Index, 1954–89**
The red line displays the personal saving rate, expressed as a percent of personal
disposable income. The black line is the real stock price index, calculated as the
nominal Standard & Poors 500-stock average (1941–43 = 100) divided by the GNP
deflator (1982 = 100). While the correlation is by no means perfect, the decline in
the stock price index in 1974–75 seems to be related to the high saving rate at that
time, and the stock market boom of 1985–87 to the low saving rate of that period.

Barry Bosworth of the Brookings Institution has found strong econometric evidence of the inverse relationship plotted in Figure 18-8.[18] According
to his estimates, a 1 percent change in stock prices sustained over the three
previous quarters changes the saving rate in the opposite direction by 0.12
to 0.14 percentage points. This evidence leads to an interesting interpretation of a boom in stock market prices. By inducing households to consume
more and save less, higher stock market prices may make people worse off
in the future. Why? Because a lower saving rate, just like a higher government deficit, leads to higher interest rates and either lower investment or
an additional buildup of foreign debt. Chapter 13 stressed that the U.S.
budget deficit would not be much of a problem were it not for the very low
saving rate of U.S. households in the 1980s, and we learn here that the stock
market is responsible for a substantial part of this low saving rate.

[18]Bosworth, "The Changing Impact of Monetary Policy," Table 4.

The Stock Market Crash of 1987

On October 19, 1987, sometimes called Black (or Bloody) Monday, stock prices fell by 20 percent in a single day. While the causes of the crash may never be agreed on, there seems to be little doubt that the crash surprised almost all concerned and was little related to previous macroeconomic events. As such, the crash is a dream event of the sort beloved by economists, a truly exogenous shock. Enough time has now passed to conclude that the stock market crash did not cause the economy to collapse, unlike the October 1929 crash, which many economists blame for aggravating the decline of spending in the first year of the Great Depression. In fact, economic growth in 1988 exceeded almost all forecasts (see Figure 15-7 on p. 467). If indeed a stock market boom helps explain high consumption and weak saving in the mid-1980s, why did not the stock market crash cause more of a jump in saving and collapse in consumption?

Timing of the previous advance.   While the October 1987 crash was sharp and relatively large, so was the preceding advance. The average level of stock market prices at the end of the year 1987 was no lower than at the beginning of the year. In contrast, previous stock market declines had lasted much longer. Perhaps the 1987 boom was viewed as temporary, and people had not yet begun to spend their capital gains.

Distribution of wealth.   About 80 percent of American households have no direct holdings of common stock and thus could not suffer any direct effect from a decline in stock prices. Almost half of the common stock owned directly is held by those with annual incomes of more than $200,000. Thus when the stock market crashes, sales of yachts and Jaguars may suffer, but damage to the domestic economy from a decline in luxury spending is likely to be minimal.

Pension plans.   While only a small group of wealthy individuals hold stock directly, a much larger share of American households own stocks indirectly through their retirement or pension plans. But for 85 percent of pension plan participants holding "defined benefit" pension plans, a decline in the stock market has no effect on their standard of living during their retirement years. Instead, in these plans retirement benefits are tied to annual earnings in the years prior to retirement and are entirely independent of stock price movements. The entire brunt of the stock market crash is felt by shareholders in the firm sponsoring the pension plan.

Conclusion on the Stock Market

The evidence of Bosworth on strong effects of the stock market seems to conflict with the weak effects of the 1987 crash, and the explanations based on the distribution of wealth and the role of pension plans minimize the direct consequences of a loss in stock market wealth on the consumption expenditures of most U.S. households. To provide a reconciliation, some have suggested that the main effect of the stock market on the consumer is not through *direct wealth effects* but rather is *indirect,* through the influence of the stock market on consumer confidence and optimism.

The advocates of the indirect channel of influence contend that in past periods when stock market price declines have preceded recessions, the underlying cause of *both* the stock market decline and the recession may have been a preceding period of tight money. As tight monetary policy drove up interest rates, people shifted some of their assets from stocks to high-yielding bonds and short-term Treasury bills, causing stock prices to fall. Thus declines in stock market prices may be as much a symptom of tight money as an independent cause of a decline in consumption spending. By this interpretation, the 1987 crash had little effect on consumption because monetary policy was not particularly tight during 1987, and policy was eased in the months after the crash. In the previous episodes that form much of the basis for Bosworth's work, in contrast, consumer confidence was eroded by tight money, and this was reflected in *both* a decline in the stock market and a cutback in consumer expenditures.

18-10 Consumption and the Case For and Against Activism

If all consumption spending consisted of nondurable goods and services, the permanent-income hypothesis and life-cycle hypothesis both would strengthen the case of monetarists that the private economy is basically stable if left alone by the government. Consumption would respond only partially to temporary bursts of nonconsumption spending, so that the economy's true short-run multipliers would be smaller than those calculated in Chapters 3–5. Both the PIH and LCH predict that consumers dampen the decline of the economy in a recession by cutting their saving rate and dampen the subsequent expansion by raising their saving rate. Both the PIH and LCH are able to reconcile the observed cross-section increase in the saving ratio that occurs with higher incomes with the long-run historical constancy of the aggregate saving ratio.

On the other hand, the nonmonetarist case for policy activism is strengthened by the procyclical fluctuations in consumer durable purchases, because this source of instability in the private economy may need to be offset by countercyclical government policy. The importance of erratic fluctuations in consumer spending is summarized by movements in the ratio to personal income of personal saving plus consumer durable expenditures plus personal tax payments. This ratio fluctuated over a wide range during the postwar years. Part of these swings may reflect movements in consumer confidence, which were an important source of shifts in the *IS* curve in our income determination theory of Chapters 4 and 5. If a sustained improvement in consumer confidence cuts saving and boosts consumption, then an activist tightening of monetary and/or fiscal policy may be warranted, and a sustained decline in consumer confidence may warrant an easing of policy in order to stabilize real GNP.

SUMMARY

1. A major area of dispute between monetarists and nonmonetarists is the stability of private spending decisions. Friedman's permanent-income hypothesis (PIH) and Modigliani's life-cycle hypothesis (LCH) are based on the assumption that individuals achieve a higher level of total utility (well-being) when they maintain a stable consumption pattern than when they allow consumption to rise or fall with every transitory fluctuation in their actual income. Individuals can achieve the desirable stable consumption pattern by consuming a stable fraction of their permanent or lifetime income.

2. If all consumption consisted of nondurable goods and services, both the PIH and the LCH would strengthen the case of monetarists that the private economy is basically stable if left alone by the government. Consumption would respond only partially to temporary fluctuations of nonconsumption spending, so that the economy's short-run multipliers would be smaller than the simple theoretical multipliers of Chapters 3–5. Consumers would dampen the decline of the economy in a recession by reducing their saving rate, and they would similarly moderate the subsequent economic expansion by raising their saving rate.

3. Both hypotheses can reconcile the observed cross-section increase in the saving ratio that occurs for higher incomes with the observed long-run historical constancy of the aggregate saving ratio.

4. Both hypotheses have important implications for fiscal policy. For example, a tax change announced as permanent should cause a bigger change in permanent income, and hence in consumption expenditures, than another equal-sized tax change announced as temporary. Thus temporary tax changes introduced to implement an activist fiscal policy may be rendered ineffective by offsetting movements in the saving ratio.

5. Numerous criticisms of the PIH and LCH have emerged in recent years. A large share of saving seems to be used not for consumption during retirement, but for bequests to children. Households may save more than they need, because they are uncertain about the date of death. Liquidity constraints imply that for perhaps 15 percent of the population the short-run marginal propensity to consume is much higher than implied by the PIH or LCH. And when expectations are formed rationally, the PIH implies that only unanticipated changes in income affect consumption.

6. An additional consideration in explaining observed consumption and saving behavior is that consumer durable expenditures should be treated as a form of saving, not as current consumption. Sharp increases in income tend to go mainly into saving, which means that consumer durable expenditures treated as a form of saving may be very responsive to transitory income changes. Thus the PIH and LCH may be valid, but still consumer durable purchases are a source of instability in the private economy.

7. Increases in stock market prices tend to raise consumption and to reduce the saving rate. Stock market behavior helps explain why the personal saving rate was so high in the mid-1970s and so low in 1985–87.

CONCEPTS

forward-looking expectations
permanent-income hypothesis of consumption (PIH)
life-cycle hypothesis of consumption (LCH)
time-series versus cross-section evidence

rational expectations
transitory versus permanent income
liquidity constraint

QUESTIONS AND PROBLEMS

Questions

1. The saving ratio has been remarkably stable over the long period since 1900. Yet, when we examine cross-section data we find that the saving ratio tends to rise as incomes rise. How can these two observations be reconciled?

2. Why is a distinction made between a short-run marginal propensity to consume and a long-run marginal propensity to consume in the permanent income hypothesis?

3. Is permanent income permanent? If not, what causes it to change?

4. How does the existence of assets affect consumption and income in the life cycle hypothesis?

5. In what ways does Modigliani's life cycle hypothesis support the monetarist platform?

6. Does the fact that many individuals leave bequests for their heirs (i.e., do not consume their entire income over their lifetimes) invalidate the life cycle hypothesis?

7. Both the life cycle hypothesis and the permanent income hypothesis predict that the marginal propensity to consume out of transitory income will be quite small (perhaps, even equal to

zero). Yet, we observe many younger families who seem to spend a fairly large percentage of their transitory income. Is this observation consistent with the two hypotheses?

8. The PIH and LCH suggest that consumer durable expenditures should be considered separately from expenditures on nondurables and services. Why? How does this distinction alter the appearance of saving and consumption behavior? Why do some economists argue that consumer durables expenditures should be treated as saving rather than consumption?

9. Both the permanent income hypothesis and the life cycle hypothesis suggest that consumers will react differently to tax changes which are perceived to be permanent rather than temporary. Explain why this is so. Has the empirical record of the past twenty years supported this hypothesis?

10. In late 1987 stock prices fell precipitously. According to the LCH what effect, if any, should this event have on the saving ratio? Did the saving ratio behave as hypothesized? Explain your answer.

Problems

1. Assume that permanent income and consumption are derived as shown in equations 18.2 and 18.3 in the text, with $j = 0.5$ and $k = 0.8$. In 1989 actual income which is $30,000 is equal to permanent income.

   (a) What would be the permanent income for 1990, 1991 and 1992 if actual income for those three years equals $36,000, $45,000, and $30,000?

   (b) What is the level of consumption in those three years?

   (c) What is the short-run marginal propensity to consume in each of those three years?

   (d) Using the distinction between permanent income and transitory income, explain why the short-run marginal propensity to consume differs from the long-run marginal propensity to consume in 1990.

2. Assume that Gina's consumption decisions are consistent with the life cycle hypothesis. In 1989, Gina is 25 years old, expects to continue to earn income until she is 65, and is expecting to consume until she dies at age 85.

   (a) If Gina earns $30,000 per year and wishes to consume an equal amount each year, how much will she consume each year?

   (b) What is the ratio of consumption to income for Gina? What is the saving rate?

   (c) Assume that Gina had assets equal to $120,000 in 1989. Recalculate your answers for (a) and (b).

   (d) Assume that in 2009, Gina inherits $40,000. Now what are your answers to (c)?

SELF-TEST ANSWERS

p. 558 A pro basketball player enjoying his best season has a transitory income above permanent income and will (or should) have a low MPC; a pro basketball player who has just retired probably suffers a sharp reduction in income to a level below permanent income and will have a high MPC; a wheat farmer suffering from a drought will have a below-permanent income and will have a high MPC; the U.S. economy in a recession has an unusually large number of people experiencing below-permanent levels of income and should have a high MPC; in a period of unusually high real GNP the U.S. economy should have a low MPC.

p. 562 Use the right-hand part of equation (18.8). If $A_1 = 0$, and $R/L = 30/40$, then consumption expenditures per year will be 30/40 times $50,000, or $37,500 during both the working and retirement years. C/Q during working years will be ($37,500)/50,000, or 0.75, which of course equals R/L. With initial assets of 200,000, $A_1/L = 200,000/40 = 5,000$. Consumption expenditures by equation (18.8) will then be $5000 plus $37,500 = $42,500 during both the working and retirement years, and C/Q during working years will be $(42,500)/(50,000) = 0.85$.

p. 568 (1) Since the tax increase is assumed to be permanent, it will reduce permanent income by $1000. Consumption will fall by k times $1000 per year. (2) According to the life-cycle hypothesis as set forth in equation (18.8), Q per year will fall by $1000 per year, and consumption per year will fall by R/L times $1000. (3) According to the life-cycle hypothesis, with an uncertain lifetime L, consumption per year will fall by R/L^* times $1000. (4) According to the Barro-Ricardo equivalence theorem, consumption will not change at all, since saving will decline by the full amount of the tax increase (reflecting the lower anticipated tax liabilities).

CHAPTER NINETEEN

Instability in the Private Economy: Investment

The economy is always straining to get to the full employment limit, but by the mere fact of being there for a time, it is projected downward again.

—*Richard M. Goodwin*[1]

If consumers purchased only nondurable goods and services, the PIH and LCH theories predict that consumer behavior would stabilize the economy. An offsetting factor is the procyclical movement of consumer durable purchases. Although this is consistent with the PIH and LCH, such movement tends to aggravate booms and recessions. In this chapter we find that business fixed investment also fluctuates procyclically. Both durable purchases by consumers and investment purchases by businesses thus introduce instability into the private economy, leading nonmonetarists to claim that an activist stabilization policy is justified.

19-1 Investment and Economic Stability

We found in Chapter 18 that the permanent-income and life-cycle hypotheses of individual consumption behavior explain the partial insulation in the short run of aggregate consumption spending from changes in other types of spending. But what are the sources of changes in these other types of spending? Nominal GNP in 1988 was divided among the major types of real expenditures as follows:

Personal consumption expenditures	66.4%
Gross private domestic investment	15.6
Government purchases of goods and services	19.8
Net exports	−2.0
	100.0

---

[1]"A Model of Cyclical Growth" in E. Lundberg, ed., *The Business Cycles in the Post War World* (London: Macmillan, 1955).

In addition to consumption, the major types of expenditures are investment, government spending, and net exports. Having already considered government spending and other aspects of fiscal policy in Chapter 13, and net exports in Chapter 14, we concentrate here on private investment.

We will review a very simple theory that explains why investment spending is more likely to exhibit pronounced fluctuations than to remain constant. In so doing, we confirm an important criticism of the monetarist platform by advocates of policy activism. Aggregate private spending, although partially insulated by the permanent-income hypothesis of consumption, exhibits marked and persistent fluctuations as a result of the instability of private investment.

According to the permanent-income hypothesis, households try to maintain a constant ratio of their consumer durable stock to permanent income. This creates sudden bursts of durable purchases when an upward revision of permanent income causes the desired durable stock to increase. In this chapter the same idea is extended to investment in plant, equipment, inventories, and housing.[2]

---

[2]Examples of plant and equipment investment are these:

Nonresidential plant (structures)	Equipment
Factories	Electronic computers
Oil refineries	Jet airplanes
Office buildings	Typewriters
Shopping centers	Cash registers
Private hospitals	Telephone switchboards
Private universities	Tractors

The principles developed in this chapter apply also to investment in residential housing, both single-family homes and multifamily apartment buildings.

19-2 CASE STUDY: The Historical Instability of Investment

The High Volatility of Total Investment

We begin by examining the historical record of investment behavior for the postwar years since 1950. Figure 19-1 clearly shows that investment spending is much more unstable than consumption spending (compare with Figure 18-1). The top line in the figure represents the total of all forms of gross private domestic investment (GPDI). By any standard, the fluctuations in total investment are huge. In the 1973–75 recession GPDI fell by more than one third.

The following table shows how GPDI behaved in postwar business cycles.

Quarters			Percentage change	
Peak	Trough	Peak	Peak to trough	Trough to peak
1948:Q3	1949:Q2	1953:Q2	− 27.8	34.0
1953:Q2	1954:Q2	1957:Q3	− 8.7	18.8
1957:Q3	1958:Q2	1960:Q1	− 18.9	33.7
1960:Q1	1961:Q1	1969:Q4	− 19.2	48.5
1969:Q4	1970:Q4	1973:Q4	− 2.0	34.2
1973:Q4	1975:Q1	1980:Q1	− 36.6	40.7
1980:Q1	1980:Q3	1981:Q3	− 17.4	18.1
1981:Q3	1982:Q4	—	− 31.6	—

Shown in the left part of the table are the dates of each successive peak and trough. We can see, for instance, that in the 1973–75 recession, which began at the peak of 1973:Q4 and extended to the trough of 1975:Q1, GPDI fell by 36.6 percent. Then GPDI bounced right back, growing by 40.7 percent by the next peak in 1980:Q1. In the 1981–82 recession, GPDI fell by almost as much as in 1973–75.

Behavior of the Components of GPDI

GPDI is divided into two main parts, fixed investment and inventory changes. Fixed investment is further divided into residential and nonresidential, and in turn nonresidential is divided into nonresidential structures and producers' durable equipment. For simplicity, Figure 19-1 distinguishes only fixed residential, fixed nonresidential, and inventory investment. Clearly all three of the major components contribute to the high volatility of GPDI. All three components have exhibited rises or declines of $50 billion or more at least on one occasion within the brief interval of one to two years. Examining the three components more carefully, we note several differences among them:

1. Residential investment turns early.   Comparing the plotted lines for residential and nonresidential investment, we note that in almost every business cycle the downturn begins earlier for residential investment, as does the subsequent upturn. For instance, fixed residential investment peaked a year or more before fixed nonresidential investment in 1972–73 and 1979–80. The slide of residential investment was startling in magnitude, fully − 50.4 percent in 1973–75 and − 53.4 percent in 1978–82. This component of investment responded promptly to the influence of tight monetary policies in these two episodes; we discussed in Chapters 16 and 17 the likelihood that financial deregulation in the 1980s may make residential construction less vulnerable to the next episode of tight money, with the possible adverse consequence of prolonging the lags of monetary policy and decreasing the Fed's ability to control the economy.

2. Inventory change exhibits sharp but short-lived swings.   The plotted line for inventory change appears as a series of small jagged mountain peaks, with an occasional deep valley. The sharpest drop in inventory investment occurred in 1981–82, when there was a decline of $95 billion in

ALL TYPES OF INVESTMENT ARE VOLATILE OVER THE BUSINESS CYCLE

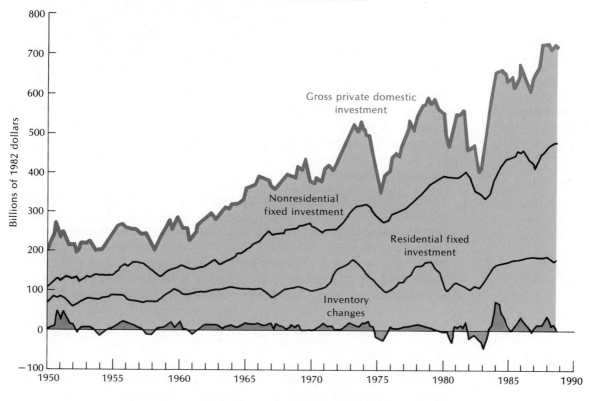

Figure 19-1 **Real Gross Private Domestic Investment and Its Three Components, 1950–1988**

The top line plots real gross private domestic investment and shows substantial volatility in all postwar business cycles, and especially in 1974–75 and 1980–83. All three components contribute to this volatility, but their timing is different. There is a marked tendency for residential investment to turn down earlier than nonresidential investment and to recover earlier. Fluctuations in inventory investment are shorter-lived than either of the other two components.

five quarters followed by a rebound of $143 billion in the next five quarters. These sharp turns of inventory change help explain why forecasters did so poorly in 1982 (see Figure 15-7). But they also suggest that, since changes in inventory investment are usually short-lived, the Federal Reserve Board should not try too hard to offset them. Given the lags in the operation of monetary policy, it is likely that the inventory swings will reverse before a change in monetary policy can take effect.

Because nonresidential fixed investment is by far the largest single component of GPDI, this chapter concentrates primarily on this component.

19-3 The Accelerator Hypothesis of Net Investment

Business firms must continually evaluate the size of their factories and the numbers of their machines. Will they have too little capacity to produce the output that they expect to be able to sell in the forthcoming year, causing lost sales and dissatisfied customers? Or, perhaps, will capacity be excessive in relation to expected sales, causing a wasteful burden of costs to pay maintenance workers and interest expense on the unneeded plant and equipment? The **accelerator hypothesis** of investment relies on the simple idea that firms attempt to maintain a fixed relation between their stock of capital (plants and equipment) and their expected sales.

The **accelerator hypothesis** states that the level of net investment depends on the *change* in expected output.

Estimating Expected Sales

Clearly the first key ingredient in a business firm's decision about plant investment is an educated guess about the likely level of sales. Table 19-1 provides an example of how a hypothetical firm, the Mammoth Electric Company, estimates expected output and determines its desired stock of electric generating stations. The estimate of expected sales (Q^e) is revised from the estimate of the previous year (Q^e_{-1}) by some proportion, j, of any difference between last year's actual sales outcome (Q_{-1}) and what was expected:

$$Q^e = Q^e_{-1} + j(Q_{-1} - Q^e_{-1})$$
$$= jQ_{-1} + (1 - j)Q^e_{-1} \tag{19.1}$$

This so-called adaptive or error-learning method of estimating sales expectations is exactly the same as we previously encountered in the formation of expectations of inflation and of permanent income.[3]

---

[3] The formation of expectations of inflation was the subject of Section 9-6. The calculation of permanent income was discussed in Section 18-4.

Table 19-1 **Workings of the Accelerator Hypothesis of Investment for the Hypothetical Mammoth Electric Company (All Figures in $ Billions)**

Variable	Periods					
	0	**1**	**2**	**3**	**4**	**5**
1. Actual sales (Q)	10.0	12.0	12.0	12.0	12.0	12.0
2. Expected sales $(Q^e = 0.5Q^e_{-1} + 0.5Q_{-1})$	10.0	10.0	11.0	11.5	11.75	11.87
3. Desired stock of electric generating stations $(K^* = 4Q^e)$	40.0	40.0	44.0	46.0	47.0	47.5
4. Net investment in electric generating stations $(I^n = K^* - K^*_{-1})$	0.0	0.0	4.0	2.0	1.0	0.5
5. Replacement investment $(D = 0.10K_{-1})$	4.0	4.0	4.0	4.4	4.6	4.7
6. Gross investment $(I = I^n + D)$	4.0	4.0	8.0	6.4	5.6	5.2

The error-learning method is illustrated in Table 19-1, where j is assumed equal to 0.5. In period 2 the previous period's sales (Q^e_{-1}) were expected to be $10 billion but turned out actually to be 12 billion (Q_{-1}). The revision of expected sales can be calculated from equation (19.1):

$$Q^e = 0.5(Q_{-1}) + 0.5(Q^e_{-1})$$

$$= 0.5(12) + 0.5(10)$$

$$= 11$$

Thus in period 2 expected sales are $11 billion, as recorded on line 2. But then another mistake is made, because in period 2 actual sales turn out to be $12 billion again instead of the expected $11 billion. Once again expectations for the next period are revised.

The Level of Investment Depends on the Change in Output

The next step in the accelerator hypothesis is the assumption that the stock of capital—that is, plant and equipment—that a firm desires (K^*) is a multiple of its expected sales:

General Form	Numerical Example	
$K^* = v^* Q^e$	$K^* = 4.0 Q^e$	(19.2)

For example, Mammoth Electric in Table 19-1 wants a capital stock that is always four times as large as its expected sales. Notice that the desired capital stock on line 3 of the table is always exactly 4.0 times the level of expected sales on line 2. What determines the multiple v^*, which relates desired capital to expected sales? As we will see, in calculating v^* firms pay attention to the interest rate and tax rates. Their chosen value of the multiple v^* reflects all available knowledge about government policies and the likely profitability of investment.

Net investment (I^n) is the change in the capital stock (ΔK) that occurs each period:[4]

$$I^n = \Delta K = K - K_{-1} \tag{19.3}$$

In the example in Table 19-1, we assume that Mammoth Electric always manages to acquire new capital quickly enough to keep its actual capital stock (K) equal to its desired capital stock (K^*) in each period:

$$I^n = K - K_{-1} = K^* - K^*_{-1} \tag{19.4}$$

Line 4 in the table shows that net investment (I^n) is always equal to the change in the desired capital stock in each period, which in turn from equation (19.2) is 4.0 times the change in expected sales:

$$I^n = K^* - K^*_{-1}$$
$$= v^*(Q^e - Q^e_{-1}) = v^* \Delta Q^e \tag{19.5}$$

The accelerator hypothesis says that the *level* of net investment (I^n) depends on the *change* in expected output (ΔQ^e). When there is an accelera-

---

[4]This is an alternative definition to that we learned in Chapter 2, where net investment was defined as gross investment minus capital consumption allowances.

tion in business and expected output increases, net investment is positive, but when business decelerates and expected output stops increasing, net investment actually falls. And if expected output were ever to decline, net investment would become negative.

Adding replacement investment. Total business spending on plant and equipment includes not only net investment—purchases that raise the capital stock—but also replacement purchases that simply replace old decaying plant and equipment or plant and equipment that has become obsolete. Line 5 of Table 19-1 assumes that each year 10 percent of the previous year's capital stock needs to be replaced. The total or gross investment (I) of Mammoth Electric, the amount recorded in the national income accounts of Chapter 2, is the sum of net investment (I^n) and replacement investment (D), and is written on line 6 of the table.

Figure 19-2 illustrates the Mammoth Electric example from Table 19-1. The level of actual sales is plotted as the top red line. Underneath, total gross investment is shown as the zigzag line that rises from \$4 billion to \$8 billion, only to fall in period 3 and afterward back toward the original level.

Figure 19-2
The Behavior of Actual Sales, Expected Sales, Gross Investment, Net Investment, and Replacement Investment for the Mammoth Electric Company Described in Table 19-1

In period 1 actual sales increase, but expected sales do not begin to respond until period 2. Net investment shoots up in period 2, as Mammoth Edison purchases equipment needed to service the higher expected level of sales. Expected sales continue to grow in periods 3, 4, and 5, but more slowly. Thus net investment actually declines from its peak in period 2.

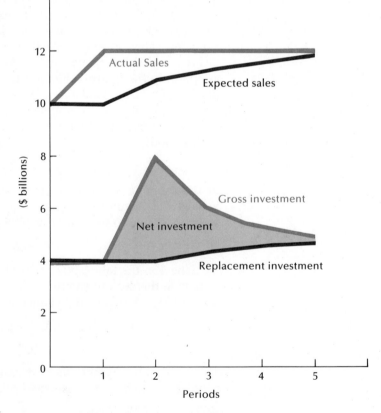

THE ACCELERATOR THEORY SHOWS HOW A PERMANENT INCREASE IN SALES CAN CAUSE A TEMPORARY BURST OF INVESTMENT

Replacement investment is initially at the level of $4 billion, rising gradually as the capital stock increases. Net investment is the pink shaded area, which first increases in size and then shrinks. Overall, the accelerator theory explains why a firm's gross investment is so unstable, at first rising and then falling even when actual sales increase permanently.

SELF-TEST   Which is likely to be more stable from year to year, gross investment, net investment, or replacement investment? Least stable? Would gross investment in long-lived types of capital (like office buildings) be more or less stable than for short-lived capital (like computers)?

19-4   ## CASE STUDY: The Simple Accelerator and the Postwar U.S. Economy

The relation between gross investment (I) and GNP (Q) for the economy as a whole is, according to the accelerator hypothesis, the same as for an individual firm. In the special case when expected sales are always set exactly equal to last period's actual sales, $Q^e = Q_{-1}$, so that $\Delta Q^e = \Delta Q_{-1}$. This allows us to rewrite (19.5) as

$$I^n = v^* \Delta Q_{-1} \tag{19.6}$$

Net investment (I^n) equals a multiple of last period's change in sales (ΔQ_{-1}). Equation (19.6) is the simplest form of the accelerator theory and was invented when J. M. Clark in 1917 noticed a regular relationship between the level of boxcar production and the previous change in railroad traffic.[5]

> *This equation summarizes succinctly the inherent instability of the private economy. Any random event—an export boom, an irregularity in the timing of government spending, or an upward revision of consumer estimates of permanent income—can change the growth of real sales and alter the level of net investment in the same direction.*

Assessing the simple accelerator.   Figure 19-3 compares real net investment (I^n) with the change in real output (ΔQ) in the U.S. economy since 1954.[6] Unfortunately, equation (19.3) is much too simple a theory to explain completely all historical movements in net investment in the United States. True, most peak years in net investment coincided with (or followed by one year) peak years in real GNP growth—1956, 1960, 1966, 1973, 1979, and 1985. And trough years in net investment coincided with

---

[5]J. M. Clark, "Business Acceleration and the Law of Demand," *Journal of Political Economy,* vol. 25 (March 1917), pp. 217–235.

[6]To adjust for the steady growth in the size of the economy, both I^n and ΔQ are divided by real GNP (Q). Thus the actual variables plotted are the share of real net investment in real GNP (I^n/Q) and the percentage growth rate of real GNP ($\Delta Q/Q$). The data plotted in Figure 19-3 are four-quarter moving averages of quarterly data, and all text references refer to these moving averages.

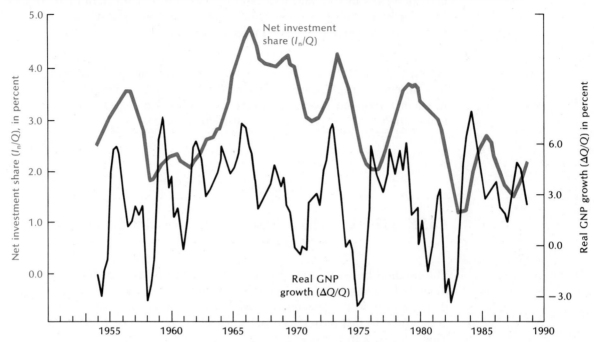

Figure 19-3 **The Relation of the Net Investment Share (I_n/Q) to the Growth Rate of Real GNP ($\Delta Q/Q$) in the U.S. Economy, 1954–88.**

The net investment share does not have a perfect or simple relationship with the growth rate of real GNP. But the period when the net investment share was high, during 1965–74, followed a long period of relatively rapid real GNP growth (1962–73). And the periods when the net investment ratio was low (1958–63, 1975–76, and 1980–83) also followed periods of relatively slow growth. The failure of the net investment ratio to recover after 1984 is puzzling, in view of relatively rapid real GNP growth in 1984–88. *(Source: Net investment share (I_n/Q) is real nonresidential fixed investment divided by real GNP, minus capital consumption allowances including capital consumption adjustment divided by nominal GNP. All figures are from National Income and Product Accounts.)*

(or followed by one year) trough years in real GNP growth—1954, 1958, 1961, 1971, 1976, 1983. Furthermore, ten years of high net investment (1965–74) followed thirteen years (1961–73) in which real GNP growth dipped below average only twice.[7] Also, four years of low net investment (1980–83) followed four years (1979–82) during which real GNP growth fell well below average. Overall, however, Figure 19-3 reveals quite an imperfect relationship.

---

[7]Average real GNP growth over the 1954–88 period plotted in Figure 19-3 is 3.05 percent.

There appear to be three main problems with the simple accelerator theory of equation (19.6), judging from the historical U.S. data plotted in Figure 19-3:

1. Net investment does not respond instantaneously to changes in output growth, as in equation (19.6), but rather displays noticeable lags in response. These lags can be seen clearly in several episodes. Notice, for instance, that the sharp decline in net investment in 1974–76 follows by a year the sharp decline in output growth in 1973–75. Similarly, the sharp increase in net investment in 1983–85 follows by a year the rebound in output growth in 1982–84.

2. The lag, however, is not of uniform length, nor does net investment respond to accelerations and decelerations in real GNP growth with uniform speed. For instance, the response of net investment in 1974–76 and 1983–85 was quite prompt, yet net investment took longer to react to the years of rapid real GNP growth in 1962–64. It is as if an automobile's engine responded in a split second to some movements of the accelerator but took minutes to respond to other movements.

3. The overall level of net investment relative to real GNP (I^n/Q) does not have a consistent historical relationship to real GNP growth ($\Delta Q/Q$). As the accelerator hypothesis predicts, the net investment ratio tends to be higher in a decade like 1964–73, when real GNP growth was high, than in other decades when real GNP growth was lower. However, the relationship is not perfect, and real GNP growth was considerably slower in the last period than the first period although the net investment ratio was almost exactly the same:

Average over period	$\Delta Q/Q$	I^n/Q
1954–63	3.11	2.68
1964–73	3.82	3.90
1974–88	2.50	2.57
Average, 1954–88	3.05	2.98

Prominent features of postwar investment behavior. Figure 19-3 allows us to reach some general conclusions about the behavior of investment spending beyond its relationship with the change in output. What do we learn from a visual inspection of the net investment ratio (I^n/Q), the red line in Figure 19-3? Two main facts stand out in the figure:

1. *Volatility.* As we saw earlier, total GPDI is highly volatile, as is the net investment ratio. The past three decades have shown that the net investment ratio is capable of shifting by three percentage points of GNP within as short a period as two years (as in 1974–76 and 1983–85). This represents a large potential shock for the economy, since three percentage points of GNP was $150 billion in 1989. The potential for fluctuations in investment is even greater than this, however, as indicated by the experience of the Great Depression when the net investment ratio fell from +3.6 percent to −7.9 percent between 1929 and 1933.

2. *Persistence.* The net investment ratio does not zigzag up and down each year but displays periods in which the ratio is relatively high or relatively low for several years in a row. The period of high net investment between 1965 and 1974 is a good example of this tendency, for in no year of that decade did the net investment ratio ever fall even to the 1954–88 average. The persistence of low investment in the Depression decade is even more pronounced, with the net investment ratio *negative for the entire decade 1931–40.*

19-5 The Flexible Accelerator

Defects of the Simple Accelerator

The **flexible accelerator** is the theory that the desired ratio of capital to expected output may be affected by the user cost of capital.

The simple accelerator theory of equation (19.6) depends on several restrictive and unrealistic assumptions. A more realistic version of the theory, called the **flexible accelerator,** can be obtained if we loosen several of these restrictive assumptions.

1. The simple accelerator assumed that this period's expected output was always set equal to last period's actual output. But the error-learning or adaptive hypothesis states that in general only a fraction of expected output is based on last period's output, and the rest conservatively carries over whatever was expected last period.

2. The simple accelerator assumes that the desired capital stock (K^*) is set equal to a constant (v^*) times expected output (Q^e). But actually the desired capital-output ratio (v^*) may vary substantially, depending on the cost of borrowing, the taxation of capital, and other factors; we will postpone until the next section a detailed consideration of the factors that change v^*.

3. The simple accelerator also assumes that firms can instantly put in place any desired amount of investment in plant and equipment needed to make actual capital this period (K) equal to desired capital (K^*). Actually, some kinds of capital take a substantial period to construct. Buildings sometimes take two or three years between conception and completion. Some types of electric utility generating stations can take as long as eight years to complete.[8] Further, installing too much new investment at one time would be excessively costly because firms supplying capital goods might raise their prices and the installation activity might disrupt the flow of production.

Thus net investment in the real world does not always close the whole gap between desired capital and last year's capital stock, but only a fraction of it.

---

[8]At the other extreme, a shop that opens for business today in a large city could probably obtain delivery of needed equipment—cash register, calculating machine, typewriter, postage meter, furniture—in a day or two.

Determinants of Gross Investment

To summarize, the relationship between economywide gross investment and output depends on at least four major factors.

1. *The fraction of the gap between desired capital and last period's actual capital that can be closed in a single period.* The higher this fraction, the more current investment responds to an acceleration in last period's output.

2. *The response of expected output to last period's error in estimating actual output.* The higher this response, the more expected output and hence investment responds to any unexpected acceleration in last period's actual output.

3. *The proportion of the capital stock that is replaced each year.* For long-lived types of capital, such as office buildings, only a fraction of buildings is replaced each year, and so total investment in office buildings is very sensitive to changes in output.

   A further complication is that the proportion of the capital stock replaced may not remain the same from year to year. The assumption that the replacement fraction is constant has been used in much econometric research.[9] But more recent studies have confirmed the obvious fact that firms are not forced to replace old capital on a fixed schedule.[10]

4. *The desired ratio of capital to expected output* (v^*). Investment responds more to changes in expected output in capital-intensive industries (those with a high v^*, such as electric utilities, oil refining, and chemicals) than in labor-intensive industries (those with a low v^*, such as textiles, apparel, and barber shops).

In the next section we investigate the determinants of the desired capital-output ratio and the policy instruments with which the government can affect the size of v^*.

19-6 The Neoclassical Theory of Investment Behavior

One of the most important contributions to the theory of investment behavior was made by Dale Jorgenson, now of Harvard University, in the early 1960s.[11] Jorgenson's insight was to show that the user cost of capital could be derived from neoclassical microeconomic theory by examining the decision of a profit-maximizing firm. Jorgenson pioneered the establishment of the connection between the firm's investment decision and the effects of government tax policy on the incentives to invest.

---

[9]See especially the work of Dale Jorgenson, beginning with his "Capital Theory and Investment Behavior," *American Economic Review,* vol. 53 (May 1963), pp. 247–257.

[10]A study that confirms the procyclical behavior of replacement investment is Martin S. Feldstein and David Foot, "The Other Half of Gross Investment: Replacement and Modernization Expenditures," *The Review of Economics and Statistics,* vol. 53, no. 1 (February 1971), pp. 49–58.

[11]See the source cited in footnote 9.

The User Cost of Capital

The **marginal product of capital** is the extra output that a firm can produce by adding an extra unit of capital.

The **user cost of capital** is the cost to the firm of using a piece of capital for a specified period.

Jorgenson's theory begins by assuming that a business firm is willing to undertake an investment project only when it expects that a profit can be made. Chapter 6 showed that an extra unit of labor will not be hired unless its marginal product—the extra output it produces—equals or exceeds its real wage. Similarly, an extra unit of capital will not be purchased unless the expected **marginal product of capital** (MPK) is at least equal to the real **user cost of capital** (u):

General Form   Numerical Example

$$\text{MPK} \geq u \qquad\qquad \text{MPK} \geq 14 \qquad\qquad (19.7)$$

Both the marginal product and the real user cost can be expressed as percentages. The marginal product of capital consists of the dollars of extra output each year produced by an extra piece of plant or equipment, divided by the cost of the plant or equipment. If the purchase of an extra machine costing $100,000 allows a firm to produce $14,000 extra output each year, then MPK would be 14 percent.[12]

The user cost of capital is the cost to the business firm of using a piece of capital for a period of time, expressed as a fraction of the machine's purchase price. The user cost might be 14 percent, consisting perhaps of a 4 percent annual real interest rate and a 10 percent depreciation rate.[13]

What does equation (19.7) have to do with the profitability of a business firm? When MPK is 15 percent and user cost is only 14 percent, then the extra revenue generated by a new machine exceeds its cost, and the firm's profits are increased. On the other hand, when MPK is only 13 percent and user cost is the same 14 percent, the extra revenue is insufficient to pay the costs of the new machine, and profits go down if the machine is purchased. Only if policymakers can find some way of reducing user cost to 13 percent will the new machine be purchased.

The effect of a reduction in user cost on the desired capital-output ratio is illustrated in Figure 19.4. Initially the user cost is u_0; the capital-output ratio v_0^* will be chosen. Why? A smaller amount of capital, to the left of E_0, would mean giving up some of the profits indicated by the dark gray area that measures the difference between the marginal product of capital and the user cost. But to purchase a larger amount of capital, to the right of E_0, would cause losses. The pink and red areas indicate the loss made by purchasing extra units of capital that have an insufficient MPK to pay for their user cost.

Tax Incentives and Investment Behavior

The user cost of capital depends not only on the depreciation rate of capital and the real interest rate that must be paid on the funds borrowed to pur-

---

[12]As is always true in economics, the marginal product of a single input measures the extra output produced by an extra unit of that input if the quantity of other inputs is held constant.

[13]Depreciation is part of user cost, because the portion of the machine wearing out must be replaced if MPK is to remain unaffected.

Figure 19-4
The Effect of a Drop in the User Cost of Capital (u) on the Desired Capital-Output Ratio (v*)

Initially the economy is at point E_0. Firms are making a profit on their capital stock indicated by the dark gray area. Any further investment will not be undertaken, because it would create losses indicated by the pink and red areas. But if the user cost can be reduced from u_0 to u_1, the economy will move from point E_0 to E_1. The initial pink area of potential losses is eliminated, and the light gray area of added profit is gained.

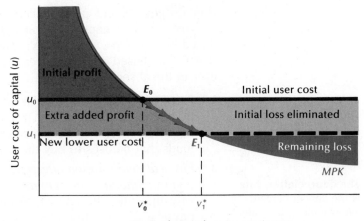

chase the equipment. The user cost as derived by Jorgenson also depends on three aspects of the tax system discussed in the next section. Thus both monetary and fiscal policy can influence the user cost, monetary policy by changing the real interest rate, and fiscal policy by altering the rates and rules of the tax system.

We can use Figure 19-4 to illustrate the effect of a change in government tax policy designed to stimulate investment. Let us assume that the government changes tax rates or rules in order to cut the user cost. For instance, the tax rate paid by corporations on their profits might be cut in half. Additional units of capital will now be purchased to bring the capital-output ratio rightward to v_1^*. The reduction in user cost has made available extra profits, indicated by the light gray area, and it has eliminated the losses indicated by the pink area. Only if the capital-output ratio exceeds v_1^* will the marginal product of capital (MPK) be insufficient to balance the new lower user cost.

By using monetary and fiscal policy instruments, the user cost of capital can be cut. Firms can thus be induced to adopt more capital-intensive methods of production, and the opposite is true as well. Just as an increase in the wage rate can cause firms to replace marginal workers with extra machines, an increase in capital's user cost can cause firms to substitute away from elaborate machines toward more labor-intensive techniques of production.[14]

---

[14]For instance, textile firms in the United States typically use more productive machines and fewer workers to produce given products than those in less developed countries where the wage rate is lower and the user cost of capital is higher.

19-7 User Cost and the Role of Monetary and Fiscal Policy

How do government policymakers determine the user cost of capital (u)? The user cost of capital depends on several factors, which can be introduced in two steps. First, let us neglect the effect of taxation. A capital good that is purchased at a given real price imposes three types of cost on its user in the absence of taxation.

1. *An interest cost is involved in buying a capital good.* Either money must be borrowed at the nominal interest rate (i) or else an investor loses the interest (i) he would receive by investing in a savings account the funds that he uses to buy the investment good.

The **depreciation rate** is the annual percentage decline in the value of a capital good due to physical deterioration and obsolescence.

2. *Physical deterioration affects the ability of every capital good to produce, and in addition some capital goods become obsolete.* The **depreciation rate** indicates the annual decline in value of the capital good due to physical deterioration plus obsolescence.

3. The interest and depreciation cost is adjusted by price changes for capital goods. Rapid price increases mean that used capital goods can often be resold for more than their cost when new. These price changes reduce the user cost and imply that it is the *real* interest rate that matters (the nominal interest rate minus the rate of price changes for capital goods).

Policymakers cannot alter the relative price of capital goods, which depends on the technical factors that influence innovations and productivity change in capital goods industries compared to the economy as a whole. Similarly, they cannot change the rate of physical decay and economic obsolescence summarized in the depreciation rate. But the real interest rate can be influenced by policymakers. As we learned in Chapter 5, a fiscal policy stimulus raises the real interest rate and hence crowds out investment. A monetary policy stimulus, on the other hand, reduces the real interest rate and raises investment. A change in the monetary-fiscal policy mix toward easier monetary policy and tighter fiscal policy cuts the real interest rate and user cost, thus raising investment.

Taxation and Investment Behavior

So far taxation has been ignored. But fiscal policy can have a major effect on investment by altering the user cost. Three basic fiscal tools are available:

1. *The U.S. government levies a corporation income tax on corporate profits.* Firms make investment decisions by equating the marginal product of capital with the real user cost of capital *before* taxes. But savers care about the level of their income *after* taxes. Thus to provide savers with a given market return, an investment project must pay a higher before-tax interest rate (and hence incur a higher user cost) when the corporation tax is high than when it is low.

2. *Firms can cut their corporation tax by deducting the value of depreciation of plant and equipment.* The amount of depreciation they can deduct depends on rules set out by the U.S. Treasury Department. When-

ever the Treasury depreciation rules are liberalized, as occurred in 1954, 1962, 1964, and 1981, more of corporate profits are protected from tax, thus cutting the user cost of capital. The reverse happened in 1986 when the rules were tightened.

3. *During most of the period 1962–86, a substantial part of investment in the United States was eligible for an investment tax credit.* In 1985, for instance, business firms could take 10 percent of the value of the equipment investment and deduct that amount from their corporation income tax. Naturally this reduced the user cost of capital as long as the firm was making profits and was subject to tax. The tax credit was rescinded in 1986 but could be reinstated in the future as a tool if the government desired to stimulate investment.

These three fiscal instruments provide much more flexibility in conducting stabilization policy than would be available if the government were limited to controlling the economy by varying the level of government spending and the personal income tax rate. For instance, government spending can be restrained and the personal income tax rate raised to slow down an economy that is experiencing too much aggregate demand. At the same time any of the investment-related fiscal instruments can be liberalized if it is believed that the economy has too little investment and too much consumption.

SELF-TEST How many tools of fiscal policy can potentially affect the user cost of capital? If the government wants to stimulate investment, how should it change these tools? Does monetary policy also have an effect on the user cost?

The Debate About the Efficacy of Tax Incentives

There has been much discussion by economists of investment behavior in the period after the trough of the 1981–82 recession. Between 1982:Q4 and 1985:Q4, real fixed nonresidential investment increased by 26.9 percent. Then, between 1985:Q4 and 1988:Q4, there was a further increase of just 6.2 percent. The assumption made in many studies is that the behavior of investment was surprisingly strong during 1982–85 and that this strength requires an explanation. One popular explanation was the tax incentives for investment introduced as part of the Reagan administration's tax legislation in 1981 and 1982.[15] Correspondingly, the reversal of tax incentives in 1986 may help explain slow investment growth in 1986–88.

A prominent advocate of the view that tax incentives have a strong effect on investment behavior is Martin Feldstein of Harvard University, who was Chairman of the President's Council of Economic Advisers during 1982–84. Feldstein and a coauthor concluded that each percentage point increase in the real net after-tax return on investment raises the net investment share (I^n/Q) by 0.4 percentage points.[16] By Feldstein's calculations, the

---

[15]For a readable introduction to the recent behavior of investment, and further references, see George A. Kahn, "Investment in Recession and Recovery: Lessons from the 1980s," *Economic Review*, Federal Reserve Bank of Kansas City (November 1985), pp. 25–39.

[16]Martin Feldstein and Joosung Jun, "The Effects of Tax Rules on Nonresidential Fixed Investment: Some Preliminary Evidence from the 1980s," in Martin S. Feldstein, ed., *The Effects of Taxation on Capital Accumulation.* University of Chicago Press, 1987, pp. 101–161.

tax incentives in place in 1983–84 (as contrasted with 1978–80) accounted for an increase in the net investment share of about 0.7 percentage points.

A more recent study by Charles W. Bischoff and coauthors at the State University of New York at Binghampton, covering the decade of the 1980s, concludes that the tax incentives of 1981–82, followed by their partial reversal in 1986, on balance canceled out. The stock of equipment capital was lifted about 8 percent between 1982 and early 1987 by the tax incentives of 1981–82, as compared to the level that would have been attained if there had been no tax changes in the 1980s. But then this temporary stimulus to the stock of equipment evaporated as a result of the tax reversal of 1986, so that by 1989 the stock of equipment capital was almost exactly the same as if there had been no tax changes at all in the 1980s. Overall, this study attributes about one third of the rapid growth of investment during 1982–85 to the initial Reagan tax incentives, and much of the slower growth in 1985–88 to the 1986 tax reversal.[17]

These studies suggest that changes in tax incentives probably have at least a modest effect on investment. However, such changes have numerous limitations and are not a promising instrument for an activist fiscal policy. First, changes in tax incentives are almost always subject to lengthy debate in Congress, and during the debate there may be perverse effects. Second, there is a substantial time lag between the passage of tax legislation and the resulting investment spending. We are far from being able to estimate in advance the quantitative effects of a change in tax incentives and the estimates in the studies summarized above are subject to many qualifications by both the authors and their critics.

19-8 Business Confidence, Speculation, and Overbuilding

Confidence and the Flexible Accelerator

In Chapters 3 and 4 the terms *business* and *consumer confidence* were used as a convenient shorthand to refer to factors that could push output in an undesired direction when government spending and the money supply were fixed at a given level. In the flexible accelerator theory of investment summarized here, the confidence of business firms may influence investment spending in three ways:

1. Investment depends on the fraction of an increase in last period's actual output that is incorporated into expected output and hence into desired capital and investment. When business people lack confidence in the future, they may refuse to extrapolate a quarter or a year of increasing output, believing instead that any increase in output is bound to be temporary.

---

[17]Charles W. Bischoff, Edward C. Kokkelenberg, and Ralph A. Terregrossa, "Tax Policy and Business Fixed Investment During the Reagan Era," State University of New York at Binghampton, working paper, June 1989.

2. The user cost of capital (u) includes the borrowing costs that business firms expect to have to pay if they undertake an investment project. If businesses are pessimistic, they may overestimate the true borrowing cost that they are likely to face, making their estimate of u too high and their desired capital stock too low.

3. Perhaps most important, business firms can only guess the likely marginal product of new investment projects. It is the expected marginal product that matters. If business has recently been bad, a condition experienced by many business firms in 1930–33, or as recently as 1981–82, firms may currently have more capital than they may need. Some present capital may presently be underutilized, and future capital investments may be unprofitable, having close to a zero marginal product for the foreseeable future.

Investment and the Great Depression

Any event, whether political or economic, that causes a drop in business confidence can cause a sharp drop in the level of investment. In the extreme case, the Great Depression of the 1930s, a collapse in business confidence dropped the desired capital stock far below the actual inherited capital stock. Not only did businesses refuse to add to their capital stock, but they allowed net investment to become negative by refusing to replace worn-out and obsolete equipment. Gross domestic private investment plummeted from $139.2 billion in 1929 to $22.7 billion in 1933 (both in 1982 prices), but despite the low levels of gross investment in the 1930s, much capital remained underutilized. The overhang of too much inherited capital depressed investment for a full decade.

Cycles of Overbuilding

Periods of business overoptimism in U.S. history have periodically been followed by overbuilding, underutilized capital, and extensive pessimism. The cycle repeated itself in the late 1960s and early 1970s, and again in the mid-1980s, leaving the United States with a substantial underutilization of some types of capital.

In the 1970s there was an overbuilding of apartments. In the 1980s the problem was an overbuilding of commercial office buildings, condominiums, and hotels. In 1985, *Time* magazine reported:

> During the past five years, U.S. developers have constructed a breathtaking surplus of office towers, condominium complexes and hotels. In Los Angeles, a rusting, 17-story framework of steel girders on Wilshire Boulevard has stood idle for three years because of collapsed condo prices. Denver's tallest building, the 56-story Republic Plaza office tower, is only half rented despite such amenities as a concierge, an Italian-marble lobby, a car wash, and computerized climate control. Florida's $197 million Le Pavillion hotel, part of a posh development called Miami Center, is usually only 15 percent full.[18]

---

[18]"Building a Hollow Skyline," *Time,* August 26, 1985, pp. 42ff.

Tobin's q Theory of Investment and Its Empirical Shortcomings

Both the accelerator theory of Sections 19-3 and 19-5, as well as the neoclassical theory of Section 19-6, define a desired level of the capital stock (K^*), and then assume a gradual adjustment of the actual capital stock toward the desired capital stock. The alternative q theory has been developed by Nobel Prize-winner James Tobin (who also did path-breaking work on the demand for money and whose picture appears in Section 16-7). Tobin's q theory, instead of positing a desired level of capital and a *separate* process of adjustment, merges adjustment costs directly into the firm's single calculation of the desired rate of investment at each moment of time.

Tobin's theory develops an idea of Keynes that the attractiveness of purchasing new capital equipment depends on the market value of capital in the stock market as compared with the cost of purchasing the capital. For instance, if purchasing a new 757 airplane would raise the market value of American Airlines stock by $50 million, while the cost of the plane is $40 million, then the plane should be purchased. But if the new plane would raise the market value of American Airlines stock by only $30 million, then the plane should not be purchased. To create a quantitative measure that reflects changes in market value relative to the purchase cost, Tobin defined his variable q as the ratio of the market value of a firm on the stock and bond markets to the replacement cost of its capital stock. Investment, then, is an increasing function of the q ratio.

An example of an investment equation in the q theory would be the following relation between gross investment relative to the capital stock (I/K), the q ratio (q), the average price of capital goods

(P), and the ratio of replacement investment to the capital stock (d):

$$\frac{I}{K} = j[(q - 1)] + d \qquad (19.8)$$

In words, this says that the I/K ratio is equal to d when Tobin's q ratio is unity. If $d = 0.1$, and $j = 0.2$, then I/K would be 0.1 when q equals unity, I/K would rise to 0.2 when q equals 1.5, and I/K would fall to zero when q equals 0.5.

Because the most important source of movement in q is the change in stock market prices, Tobin's theory creates an additional channel by which changes in the stock market may influence the economy through its effect on the attractiveness of investment. We have already studied the connection between the stock market and consumption spending in Section 18-9. Also, Tobin's theory makes a major breakthrough in the theory of investment behavior. Instead of having to guess how business firms calculated their expectations of future profits, and how those expectations respond to economic events, economists can simply look to the stock and bond markets for the necessary valuation of the firm's future stream of profits.

A notable feature of the Tobin approach in equation (19.8) is that there are no lags in the equation. Thus, if the stock market drops 20 percent, the I/K ratio should drop immediately by an amount that depends on the size of j. Statistical studies of Tobin's theory have shown that investment depends not just on the current value of the stock market (in the numerator of q), but also several lagged values as well. In addition, other variables, especially change in output, the key variable

By 1988 more than 15 percent of U.S. office space was empty, as contrasted with 3.5 percent in 1980, and the vacancy percentage reached 25 percent or more in Denver, Houston, and some other cities. One reason for the building boom was the U.S. tax structure, which until 1986 provided substantial incentives for large and small investors to pour money into real estate.

One would expect that the overbuilding of office buildings and hotels would lead to a slump in construction, and indeed this occurred. Despite the long business cycle expansion that occurred from 1982 to 1989, there

in the accelerator theory, enter significantly into the explanation of I/K, thus contradicting the Tobin theory of (19.8), which states that all information relevant to the investment decision is summed up by the market value of the firm.

Economists have struggled in recent years to isolate the factors that make the Tobin q theory, which is theoretically appealing, so unsuccessful in empirical studies. Some of the most fruitful suggestions have been these:

(1) Tobin's theory posits that an investment should be made when the *change* that it creates in the firm's market value exceeds its cost. The *change* in market value relative to capital cost is called "marginal q" and can differ from the *level* of the market-value-to-cost ratio, called "average q," which is the only data series available for use in statistical tests. The possibility of differences between the theoretical concept of marginal q and data available on average q is especially important in the real world, where there are many different types of capital. For instance, an oil shock could lower the market value of American Airlines while

stimulating it to buy new, more fuel-efficient airplanes. In this example, the average q of the airline (which at that moment has old fuel-guzzling aircraft) declines but the marginal q of fuel-efficient aircraft increases.

(2) There is an ordering and delivery lag that intervenes between the time a firm decides that a new investment expenditure is profitable, and the time the investment good is delivered and is counted in the national income accounts as investment spending. In Section 19-5 on the flexible accelerator we have already discussed ordering and delivery lags, which can range from one day for a standard office filing cabinet to ten years for a nuclear-power generating station.

(3) There can be imperfections in capital markets. Not every firm can or does raise the capital to finance its investment in the stock or bond markets. Some borrow from banks, and others, such as airlines, lease much of their equipment from other firms, implying that aircraft investment may be more related to the stock market value of the leasing firms than of the airlines.

Overall, the attempt to reconcile real-world data with the prediction of Tobin's q theory is an active area of current macroeconomic research.[a]

[a]Most of the references on Tobin's q theory are quite technical. For the original presentation, see James Tobin, "A General Equilibrium Approach to Monetary Theory," *Journal of Money, Credit, and Banking*, vol. 1 (February 1969), pp. 15–29. More recent interpretations are Fumio Hayashi, "Tobin's Marginal and Average q: A Neoclassical Interpretation," *Econometrica*, vol. 50 (January 1982), pp. 213–224, and Andrew B. Abel, "A Stochastic Model of Investment, Marginal q, and the Market Value of the Firm," *International Economic Review*, vol. 26 (June 1985), pp. 305–322. Empirical evidence is provided in Lawrence H. Summers, "Taxation and Corporate Investment: A q-Theory Approach," *Brookings Papers on Economic Activity*, vol. 12 (1981, no. 1), p. 67–127.

was no recovery in the share of nonresidential structures investment in GNP (as had occurred in previous business expansions):

Share of nonresidential structures investment in GNP (percent)

1981	4.6	1985	4.1
1982	4.5	1986	3.1
1983	3.9	1987	3.3
1984	4.1	1988	3.1

Thus by 1988 the share of investment in nonresidential structures had fallen by fully one third from its value in 1981. Taken by itself, such a sustained decline in investment would depress aggregate demand in the economy and require a monetary or fiscal stimulus to keep the unemployment rate from rising. In 1987–88 other components of spending, particularly net exports, were strong, and so a policy stimulus was not necessary, but in some previous episodes, especially the 1930s, sustained slumps in investment occurred that were not balanced out by other components of expenditure.

Keynes placed major emphasis on the role of business confidence in determining the level of investment. In the following passage he stresses that investment decisions are based on estimates of the future "yield" (or marginal product) of extra capital, which may be little better than a guess. Faced with identical information and uncertainty, business people may go ahead with an investment project when they feel optimistic but postpone the same project when they feel pessimistic:

> The outstanding fact is the extreme precariousness of the basis of knowledge on which our estimates of prospective yield have to be made. Our knowledge of the factors which will govern the yield of an investment some years hence is usually very slight and often negligible. If we speak frankly, we have to admit that our basis of knowledge for estimating the yield ten years hence of a railway, a copper mine, a textile factory, the goodwill of a patent medicine, an Atlantic liner, a building in the City of London amounts to little and sometimes to nothing; or even five years hence. In fact, those who seriously attempt to make any such estimates are often so much in the minority that their behavior does not govern the market.[19]

19-9 Investment as a Source of Instability of Output and Interest Rates

The accelerator theory creates a favorite paradox of macroeconomics teachers. We became accustomed in Chapters 4 and 5 to associating low interest rates with high investment and high interest rates with low investment. This inverse relationship between investment and interest rates has been confirmed in this chapter because a low level of the real interest rate reduces the user cost of capital, which in turn raises the desired capital stock and hence the level of gross investment.

Yet a predominant feature of business cycles in almost every nation is a positive correlation between business investment and interest rates. U.S. business investment fluctuates procyclically, reaching peaks in years of high output and troughs during recessions or soon after the business-cycle trough. But at the same time, interest rates also fluctuate procyclically, so that years of low interest rates are usually associated with low investment, not high investment.

How can the positive relationship between investment and interest rates be explained? The accelerator theory provides the answer. Figure 19-5 repeats the *IS-LM* analysis of Chapters 4 and 5. The *LM* curve maintains an

---

[19]Keynes, *General Theory*, pp. 149–150.

Figure 19-5
Effect on Output and the Interest Rate of a Shift in the Level of Investment Relative to the Interest Rate

Shifts in business confidence or in user cost can shift the red *IS* curve back and forth between IS_0 and IS_1. As a result, the interest rate will be high when investment is high, and vice versa. This conclusion assumes that the real money supply, which fixes the position of the *LM* curve, remains unchanged.

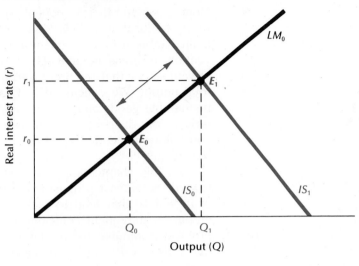

WHY THE INTEREST RATE AND INVESTMENT OFTEN MOVE IN THE SAME DIRECTION

unchanged position whenever the real money supply (M/P) and real demand for money function are fixed. The *IS* curve fluctuates whenever there is a change in the investment purchases that business firms choose to make at a constant real interest rate.

Causes of *IS* Shifts

A long list of factors can make the level of gross investment, and hence the *IS* curve, shift for a given interest rate. Included are (1) an increase in actual output due to some factor unconnected with the investment process, (2) a change in the extent to which a current output change is predicted to continue in the future, (3) a previous episode of overbuilding that makes the actual capital stock high relative to the current desired stock, (4) a shift in demand toward shorter-lived equipment, (5) a change in the relative price of capital goods, and, finally, (6) an alteration in fiscal incentives that alters the before-tax user cost of capital. A change in any of these elements shifts the level of investment that occurs at a given interest rate and, through the multiplier, shifts the level of total output.

Figure 19-5 illustrates two *IS* curves, IS_0 and IS_1. The shifts back and forth between the two *IS* curves reflect any of the elements in the previous paragraph that cause an increase or decrease in gross investment. The positive relationship between investment and interest rates is explained in Figure 19-5 by the constant level of the real money supply, which keeps the *LM* curve fixed at LM_0. That positive relationship suggests that the depressing effect of low output on investment, working through the accelerator, dominates the stimulative effect of low interest rates on investment, at least in the short run.

19-10 Conclusion: Investment and the Case for and Against Activism

Monetarists and their opponents disagree strongly over the need for an activist stabilization policy. Monetarists argue that the private economy remains stable if freed from the destabilizing influence of government intervention, whereas nonmonetarists emphasize sources of instability in the private sector that require government intervention to maintain stability in total output. We concluded in Chapter 18 that consumption spending on nondurable goods and services appeared to bolster the case of the monetarists. Both the permanent-income and life-cycle hypotheses suggested that consumption spending on those items tends to fluctuate less than disposable income.

But this chapter appears to swing the case in the opposite direction, toward the activist proposition that the private economy contains sources of instability that tend to make any equality between actual and natural output an infrequent coincidence rather than a frequent occurrence. The problem is summarized by the accelerator theory of investment. Any event that causes a *permanent* increase in the desired capital stock—whether an increase in expected output or a reduction in the user cost of capital—causes only a *temporary* burst of investment spending. After the temporary burst, when net investment falls, economic instability is aggravated by the multiplier effect of Chapter 3.

Until the past decade, the tendency for fixed investment to be prone to multi-year booms and slumps formed the core of the activist case. In the 1980s, however, it became apparent that net exports can be an equally important source of fluctuations in aggregate demand, as we learned in Chapters 5 and 14. Thus, while investment was extremely volatile in both the 1974–75 and 1981–82 recessions, the greatest challenge to the Fed in the 1980s was to keep the expansion going in 1984–86 when the strength of the dollar caused a prolonged period of slump in U.S. net exports.

The multi-year cycles in fixed investment (and more recently in net exports) support the activist case that policymakers cannot always count on private spending to remain stable, as is assumed in plank 1 of the monetarist platform. However, this by itself does not settle the issue. Monetarists and other opponents of activism might counter that an activist policy could still do more harm than good (monetarist plank 3). The mere fact of fluctuations in private spending does not guarantee that policymakers can forecast such changes far enough in advance to offset the lags in the operation of monetary policy. Nor does this fact address the substantial uncertainty that exists about the multiplier effects of monetary and fiscal policy. Multiplier uncertainty, which we examined initially in Chapter 15, has become even greater in the 1980s as financial deregulation and flexible exchange rates have changed the way monetary policy operates.

Thus both the proponents and opponents of activism have a good case. The activists are correct that investment and net exports can create a source of persistent fluctuations. And the opponents of activism are correct that forecasting is highly imperfect, that stabilization policy operates with long and variable lags, and that policy multipliers are highly uncertain. The best case the activists can make is to point at the success of the Fed in achieving during 1982–89 the longest peacetime business expansion in U.S.

history by a flexible approach to policy activism, and the best case for the opponents of activism is that their numerous objections to activism are valid in principle, were correct in many episodes before 1982, and may be correct again in the future.

SUMMARY

1. The major source of instability in consumption spending is contributed by consumer expenditures on durables, which can exhibit large fluctuations in response to income changes. This chapter adds private investment spending as an additional source of instability, with the potential of causing major changes in GNP in response to small shocks.

2. The simple accelerator theory of investment relies on the idea that firms attempt to maintain a fixed relation between their stock of capital and their expected sales. Thus the level of net investment—the change in the capital stock—depends on the change in expected output. The accelerator theory explains why the gross investment of most firms is relatively unstable, at first rising and then falling in response to a permanent increase in actual sales.

3. The flexible accelerator theory recognizes that net investment in the real world usually closes only a portion of any gap between the desired and actual capital stocks. Furthermore, the desired capital-output ratio may change, altering investment with a powerful accelerator effect.

4. The accelerator theory suggests that any event that causes a permanent increase in the desired capital stock, whether arising from an increase in expected output or from a reduction in the user cost of capital, causes only a temporary rise in investment spending. Thus investment spending may experience sustained booms or slumps lasting several years, resulting from fluctuations in business confidence and lags between the conception and completion of investment projects.

5. Government policymakers can directly alter the user cost of capital. Fiscal and monetary policy can change the real interest-rate component of user cost. Taxation can affect the user cost of capital through changes in the corporation income tax, depreciation deductions, and the investment tax credit. But the use of these policy instruments cannot eliminate all fluctuations in investment expenditures, because most policy measures operate only with lagged effects.

CONCEPTS

accelerator hypothesis
flexible accelerator
marginal product of capital

user cost of capital
depreciation deductions

QUESTIONS AND PROBLEMS

Questions

1. Differentiate between gross investment and net investment. Can gross investment ever be negative? Can net investment ever be negative?

2. Assume that the level of output in the economy is growing. Does the simple accelerator model predict that investment will also be growing?

3. Discuss the role of lags in the accelerator theory. How does the existence of lags change the results of the simple accelerator model?

4. In summarizing the behavior of investment spending, the net investment ratio (I^n/Q) was described as volatile and persistent. Explain what is meant by these terms.

5. Business and consumer confidence are often cited as playing a key role in the investment decision. How does business confidence enter into the flexible accelerator analysis?

6. A capital good that is purchased at a given real price imposes three types of costs on its user. What are these costs? Which of these costs are subject to manipulation by policymakers?

7. What are the three tools of fiscal policy that can be used to influence the level of investment? According to the accelerator theory, are changes in these tools likely to lead to a permanent increase in the rate of investment?

8. What are the limitations to using tax incentives as a tool of activist fiscal policy?

9. What are the major factors that determine the relationship between the level of gross investment and the level of output in the economy? Briefly summarize the relationship involved.

10. According to the theory first presented in Chapter 4 and developed further in this chapter, the interest rate and the level of investment are negatively related. Yet, both business investment and interest rates tend to fluctuate procyclically, i.e., are at their highest levels when the economy is at a high output level. Can you explain this paradox?

Problems

1. This problem uses the example in Table 19-1.
   (a) The economy will reach an equilibrium when the level of expected sales no longer increases. What will be the level of net investment at that point? What will be the level of gross investment?
   (b) Assume that because of a new investment tax credit, the desired capital-stock ratio changes to 5. What is the level of net investment in periods 1–5?
   (c) When the economy reaches its new equilibrium, what will be the ultimate effect on investment of the tax credits?

2. This problem also uses the data in Table 19-1.
   (a) What would the level of expected sales have to be in periods 3–5 in order for net investment to be constant at 4.0?
   (b) What would the level of actual sales have to be in periods 3–5 in order to achieve the constant level of net investment?
   (c) What would the level of actual sales have to be in periods 2–4 in order to achieve a steady 20 percent increase in gross investment in each of the periods 3 through 5?
   (d) At what rate does the level of actual sales increase in (c)?

SELF-TEST ANSWERS

p. 585 Assuming as in this section that replacement investment is a fixed fraction of the previous year's capital stock, replacement investment is the most stable. Net investment, which depends on the *change* in expected output, is the least stable. Gross investment, the sum of net investment and replacement investment, is in between. The longer lived is capital, the smaller is the fraction of the previous year's capital stock that needs to be replaced, hence the smaller is stable replacement investment relative to unstable net investment. Thus we would expect gross investment in office buildings to be less stable than gross investment in computers.

p. 593 The three potential tools are the corporation income tax, the value of depreciation deductions, and the investment tax credit. If the government wants to stimulate investment, it can reduce the corporation income tax rate, or raise the value of depreciation deductions (by allowing business firms to take depreciation deductions earlier), or raise the percentage rate of the investment tax credit. If there is no investment tax credit, as in the United States after 1986, the government can introduce such a credit. Monetary policy affects the user cost through its ability to change the real interest rate.

Appendixes

Time Series Data for the U.S. Economy: 1875–1988

Table A-1   Annual Data, 1875–1988

	Nominal GNP (Y) (B $)	GNP Deflator (P) (1982 = 100)	Real GNP (Q) (B 1982$)	Natural Real GNP (Q^N) (B 1982$)	Unemploy-ment Rate (U) (percent)	Natural Unempl. Rate (U^N) (percent)	Money Supply (M1) (B $)	Money Supply (M2) (B $)	Labor Produc-tivity (Q/N) (1977 = 100)	Nominal Interest Rate (r) (percent)	S&P Stock Price Index (1941-43 = 10)
1875	8.9	8.9	100.8	105.5	—	—	—	2.4	15.6	6.5	—
1876	8.7	8.5	102.0	110.3	—	—	—	2.3	15.9	6.2	—
1877	8.8	8.4	105.2	115.4	—	—	—	2.3	16.2	6.3	—
1878	8.6	7.9	109.7	120.7	—	—	—	2.2	16.5	6.2	—
1879	9.4	7.6	123.1	126.3	—	—	—	2.3	16.9	5.9	—
1880	11.1	8.0	137.7	132.1	—	—	—	2.8	16.9	5.7	—
1881	11.4	8.0	142.6	138.2	—	—	—	3.4	17.0	5.4	—
1882	12.4	8.2	151.6	144.6	—	—	—	3.6	17.1	5.5	—
1883	12.2	7.9	155.4	151.2	—	—	—	3.9	17.2	5.5	—
1884	11.9	7.5	158.2	158.2	—	—	—	3.8	17.3	5.4	—
1885	11.7	7.4	159.4	162.4	—	—	—	4.0	17.4	5.3	—
1886	12.1	7.3	164.2	166.7	—	—	—	4.3	17.5	5.0	—
1887	12.6	7.4	171.6	171.1	—	—	—	4.6	17.6	5.1	—
1888	12.8	7.5	170.7	175.6	—	—	—	4.7	17.6	5.0	—
1889	13.6	7.5	181.4	180.2	—	—	—	5.0	17.7	4.9	—
1890	13.4	7.3	183.9	185.0	4.0	4.1	—	5.4	17.3	5.0	—
1891	13.9	7.3	189.9	189.9	5.4	4.1	—	5.6	17.5	5.2	—
1892	14.3	7.2	198.9	197.1	3.0	4.1	—	6.1	17.7	5.1	—
1893	14.4	7.2	198.8	204.6	11.7	4.1	—	5.9	17.9	5.1	—
1894	13.2	6.8	193.0	212.3	18.4	4.1	—	5.9	18.0	5.0	—
1895	14.5	6.7	215.6	220.4	13.7	4.1	—	6.1	19.0	4.9	—
1896	14.3	6.8	210.6	228.7	14.4	4.1	—	6.0	18.5	4.9	—
1897	15.2	6.7	227.8	237.4	14.5	4.1	—	6.4	19.4	4.7	—
1898	15.7	6.7	233.3	246.4	12.4	4.1	—	7.2	19.8	4.7	—
1899	17.9	6.9	260.3	255.7	6.5	4.1	—	8.4	20.6	4.6	—
1900	18.6	7.0	265.4	265.4	5.0	4.1	—	9.1	20.8	4.6	6.1
1901	21.0	7.0	297.9	275.4	4.0	4.1	—	10.3	22.3	4.6	7.8
1902	21.7	7.1	303.0	285.7	3.7	4.1	—	11.3	21.8	4.7	8.4
1903	22.9	7.3	311.7	296.5	3.9	4.1	—	12.0	21.8	4.9	7.2
1904	23.9	7.4	323.6	307.6	5.4	4.1	—	12.7	22.9	4.9	7.1

A1

	Nominal GNP (Y) (B $)	GNP Deflator (P) (1982 = 100)	Real GNP (Q) (B 1982$)	Natural Real GNP (Q^N) (B 1982$)	Unemployment Rate (U) (percent)	Natural Unempl. Rate (U^N) (percent)	Money Supply (M1) (B $)	Money Supply (M2) (B $)	Labor Productivity (Q/N) (1977 = 100)	Nominal Interest Rate (r) (percent)	S&P Stock Price Index (1941-43 = 10)
1905	26.1	7.4	353.2	319.2	4.3	4.2	—	14.1	23.9	4.9	9.0
1906	28.1	7.6	367.7	331.2	1.7	4.2	—	15.3	23.9	4.9	9.6
1907	28.9	8.0	362.1	343.6	2.8	4.2	—	16.0	23.0	5.1	8.1
1908	26.7	7.8	342.2	356.5	8.0	4.2	—	15.7	22.7	5.1	7.8
1909	29.9	7.8	382.2	369.9	5.1	4.2	—	17.5	24.0	5.0	9.7
1910	31.2	8.1	383.8	383.8	5.9	4.2	—	18.3	23.5	5.1	9.4
1911	32.2	8.1	396.0	396.3	6.7	4.2	—	19.4	23.8	5.2	9.2
1912	34.9	8.3	418.9	409.2	4.6	4.2	—	20.8	24.5	5.2	9.5
1913	36.6	8.4	435.4	422.5	4.3	4.2	—	21.6	25.2	5.3	8.5
1914	34.3	8.5	402.5	436.2	7.9	4.2	—	22.6	23.7	2.7	4.1
1915	36.4	8.7	417.4	450.4	8.5	4.2	12.2	24.3	24.9	5.4	8.3
1916	46.0	9.5	485.1	465.0	5.1	4.2	14.4	28.8	26.9	5.3	9.5
1917	55.1	11.4	484.9	480.1	4.6	4.2	16.7	33.6	26.4	5.5	8.5
1918	69.7	13.3	522.3	495.7	1.4	4.4	18.6	36.8	28.6	5.8	7.5
1919	77.2	15.2	507.2	511.8	1.4	4.4	21.3	42.7	28.7	5.9	9.2
1920	87.3	17.6	496.4	528.4	5.2	4.4	23.2	48.0	27.7	6.6	8.3
1921	73.3	15.3	478.9	545.6	11.7	4.4	21.0	45.2	29.7	6.9	7.2
1922	73.0	14.2	513.2	563.4	6.7	4.4	21.2	46.4	29.6	5.8	8.7
1923	85.6	14.6	585.1	581.7	2.4	4.4	22.4	50.4	31.3	5.9	8.9
1924	87.9	14.6	600.6	600.6	5.0	4.4	23.2	43.2	32.9	5.6	9.4
1925	91.5	14.9	614.1	616.0	3.2	4.4	25.1	57.9	32.5	5.2	11.6
1926	97.5	15.0	651.0	631.8	1.8	4.5	25.6	60.2	33.3	4.8	13.0
1927	96.4	14.7	654.7	648.0	3.3	4.5	25.5	61.6	33.7	4.5	15.3
1928	97.3	14.6	666.7	664.7	4.2	4.5	25.8	63.9	34.0	4.5	19.4
1929	103.9	14.6	709.6	681.8	3.2	4.5	26.0	64.2	35.5	4.8	24.7
1930	91.2	14.2	642.8	699.3	8.9	4.5	25.2	63.0	34.5	4.8	19.4
1931	76.4	13.0	588.1	717.2	16.3	4.5	23.5	58.8	34.4	6.0	12.2
1932	58.5	11.5	509.2	735.7	24.1	4.6	20.6	49.6	33.7	7.8	6.3
1933	56.0	11.2	498.5	754.6	25.2	4.6	19.4	44.4	33.3	6.4	8.2
1934	65.6	12.2	536.7	773.9	22.0	4.6	21.4	47.4	36.4	5.2	9.4
1935	72.8	12.6	580.2	793.8	20.3	4.6	25.3	53.9	37.4	4.8	10.2
1936	83.1	12.6	662.2	814.2	17.0	4.6	28.8	59.9	39.7	3.9	14.4
1937	91.3	13.1	695.3	835.1	14.3	4.7	30.2	63.0	39.2	4.0	14.4
1938	85.4	12.9	664.2	856.6	19.1	4.7	29.8	62.7	41.0	4.8	10.8
1939	91.3	12.7	716.6	878.6	17.2	4.7	33.4	67.9	42.0	4.1	11.6
1940	100.4	13.0	772.9	901.2	14.6	4.7	38.8	76.1	43.4	3.9	10.8
1941	125.5	13.8	909.4	924.3	9.9	4.7	45.4	86.1	46.9	3.5	9.8
1942	159.0	14.7	1080.3	948.1	4.7	4.7	54.1	98.1	51.7	3.5	8.7
1943	192.7	15.1	1276.2	972.4	1.9	4.9	70.5	123.9	58.9	3.2	11.5
1944	211.4	15.3	1380.6	997.4	1.2	4.9	83.3	147.2	64.7	3.0	12.5
1945	213.4	15.8	1354.8	1023.0	1.9	4.9	96.9	174.5	67.1	2.7	15.2
1946	212.4	19.4	1096.9	1049.3	3.9	4.9	104.1	191.1	53.9	2.5	17.1
1947	235.3	22.1	1066.7	1076.3	3.9	4.9	109.2	201.2	51.3	2.6	15.2
1948	261.7	23.6	1108.7	1103.9	3.8	5.0	109.7	204.1	52.8	2.9	15.5
1949	260.4	23.5	1109.0	1132.3	5.9	5.0	108.6	203.2	54.0	2.6	15.2
1950	288.3	23.9	1203.7	1186.7	5.3	5.0	111.5	207.8	57.4	2.6	18.4
1951	333.4	25.1	1328.2	1243.8	3.3	5.0	116.5	215.6	59.3	3.0	22.3
1952	351.6	25.5	1380.0	1303.6	3.0	5.1	122.4	227.3	60.5	3.1	24.5
1953	371.6	25.9	1435.3	1366.2	2.9	5.1	125.4	235.9	62.0	3.4	24.7
1954	372.5	26.3	1416.2	1422.7	5.5	5.1	127.3	244.2	62.9	2.9	29.7

	Nominal GNP (Y) (B $)	GNP Deflator (P) (1982 = 100)	Real GNP (Q) (B 1982$)	Natural Real GNP (Q^N) (B 1982$)	Unemployment Rate (U) (percent)	Natural Unempl. Rate (U^N) (percent)	Money Supply (M1) (B $)	Money Supply (M2) (B $)	Labor Productivity (Q/N) (1977 = 100)	Nominal Interest Rate (r) (percent)	S&P Stock Price Index (1941-43 = 10)
1955	405.9	27.2	1494.9	1465.7	4.4	5.1	131.4	253.2	64.8	3.2	40.5
1956	428.2	28.1	1525.7	1510.1	4.1	5.1	132.9	257.5	65.2	3.7	46.6
1957	451.0	29.1	1551.1	1556.0	4.3	5.1	133.6	264.4	66.4	4.5	44.4
1958	456.8	29.7	1539.3	1606.0	6.8	5.0	135.2	277.2	68.0	4.0	46.2
1959	495.8	30.4	1629.1	1658.3	5.5	5.1	140.4	293.3	70.2	4.9	57.4
1960	515.3	30.9	1665.2	1712.2	5.5	5.2	140.3	304.3	70.9	4.9	55.8
1961	533.8	31.2	1708.7	1768.0	6.7	5.2	143.1	324.9	73.2	4.6	66.3
1962	574.7	31.9	1799.4	1825.6	5.5	5.3	146.5	350.2	75.6	4.4	62.4
1963	606.9	32.4	1873.3	1885.4	5.7	5.4	151.0	379.7	78.3	4.3	69.9
1964	649.8	32.9	1973.3	1952.5	5.2	5.5	156.8	409.4	81.4	4.5	81.4
1965	705.1	33.8	2087.6	2023.2	4.5	5.6	163.5	442.5	83.4	4.6	88.2
1966	772.0	35.0	2208.4	2096.5	3.8	5.6	171.0	471.4	85.2	5.7	85.3
1967	816.4	35.9	2271.3	2172.5	3.8	5.6	177.8	503.7	87.1	6.1	91.9
1968	892.7	37.7	2365.6	2251.2	3.6	5.6	190.2	545.4	89.4	6.8	98.7
1969	964.0	39.8	2423.3	2332.8	3.5	5.6	201.5	579.1	89.0	8.1	97.8
1970	1015.5	42.0	2416.2	2416.5	4.9	5.6	209.2	603.2	89.2	9.1	83.2
1971	1102.7	44.4	2484.8	2500.0	5.9	5.8	223.2	676.4	91.9	7.8	98.3
1972	1212.8	46.5	2608.5	2586.0	5.6	5.8	239.1	760.9	94.7	7.6	109.2
1973	1359.3	49.5	2744.0	2675.0	4.9	5.8	256.4	836.3	96.4	7.9	107.4
1974	1472.8	54.0	2729.3	2764.4	5.6	5.9	269.3	887.2	94.3	9.4	82.8
1975	1598.4	59.3	2695.0	2846.5	8.5	6.0	281.8	970.1	96.0	9.5	86.2
1976	1782.8	63.1	2826.7	2930.1	7.7	5.9	297.3	1095.7	98.4	8.7	102.0
1977	1990.5	67.3	2958.7	3016.2	7.1	6.0	320.1	1234.4	100.0	8.2	98.2
1978	2249.7	72.2	3115.2	3104.7	6.1	5.9	346.4	1339.6	100.8	9.0	96.0
1979	2508.2	78.6	3192.3	3194.8	5.8	5.9	373.0	1450.3	99.2	10.1	103.0
1980	2732.0	85.7	3187.2	3273.6	7.1	5.9	396.0	1566.7	98.8	12.8	118.8
1981	3052.6	94.0	3248.7	3350.8	7.6	6.0	425.1	1714.3	99.7	15.5	128.0
1982	3166.0	100.0	3166.0	3429.9	9.7	6.0	453.1	1874.3	99.2	14.7	119.7
1983	3405.7	103.9	3279.1	3510.8	9.6	6.0	503.2	2108.7	102.4	12.3	160.4
1984	3772.2	107.7	3501.4	3593.7	7.5	6.0	538.6	2274.4	104.5	13.4	160.5
1985	4014.9	110.9	3618.7	3678.5	7.2	6.0	586.9	2477.9	106.0	11.8	186.8
1986	4231.7	113.8	3717.9	3765.3	7.0	6.0	666.7	2686.9	108.2	9.2	236.3
1987	4524.3	117.4	3853.7	3854.1	6.2	6.0	744.0	2861.6	109.0	9.7	286.8
1988	4880.6	121.3	4024.4	3945.1	5.5	6.0	776.0	3009.4	110.6	9.9	265.6

Table A-2   Quarterly Data, 1947–88

	Nominal GNP (Y) (B $)	GMP Deflator (P) (1982 = 100)	Real GNP (Q) (B 1982$)	Natural Real GNP (Q^N) (B 1982$)	Unempl. Rate (U) (percent)	Natural Unempl. Rate (U^N) (percent)	Money Supply (M1) (B $)	Money Supply (M2) (B $)	Nominal Interest Rate (r) (percent)	Weighted Exchange Rate (1980 = 100)	Real Actual Federal Surplus (B 1982$)	Real Natural Federal Surplus (B 1982$)
1947.Q1	227.5	21.5	1056.5	1058.1	3.9	4.9	107.3	197.6	2.5	—	68.8	69.3
1947.Q2	231.5	21.8	1063.2	1064.7	3.9	4.9	109.1	200.5	2.5	—	62.4	62.8
1947.Q3	235.9	22.1	1067.1	1071.4	3.9	4.9	110.0	202.7	2.6	—	45.2	46.5
1947.Q4	246.1	22.8	1080.0	1078.1	3.9	5.0	110.5	204.5	2.8	—	66.7	66.2
1948.Q1	252.4	23.2	1086.8	1084.9	3.7	5.0	110.5	205.0	2.9	—	58.6	58.1
1948.Q2	259.7	23.5	1106.1	1091.7	3.7	5.0	109.6	203.9	2.9	—	44.7	41.0
1948.Q3	266.6	23.9	1116.3	1098.6	3.8	5.0	109.7	204.2	2.8	—	24.3	19.6
1948.Q4	267.9	23.8	1125.5	1105.5	3.8	5.0	109.3	203.8	3.0	—	13.9	8.6
1949.Q1	262.7	23.6	1112.4	1112.4	4.7	5.0	108.7	203.1	2.7	—	2.1	1.7
1949.Q2	259.2	23.4	1105.9	1125.5	5.9	5.0	108.9	203.6	2.7	—	−13.2	−9.0
1949.Q3	260.9	23.4	1114.3	1138.8	6.7	5.0	108.5	203.2	2.6	—	−17.5	−10.9
1949.Q4	258.6	23.4	1103.3	1152.3	7.0	5.0	108.5	203.2	2.5	—	−17.5	−5.8
1950.Q1	269.3	23.5	1148.2	1165.9	6.4	5.0	109.5	204.9	2.6	—	−20.0	−14.4
1950.Q2	278.9	23.6	1181.0	1179.7	5.6	5.0	111.1	207.5	2.5	—	33.1	33.1
1950.Q3	296.7	24.2	1225.3	1193.6	4.6	5.0	112.3	209.0	2.6	—	68.6	60.1
1950.Q4	308.1	24.5	1260.2	1207.7	4.2	5.0	113.3	210.2	2.7	—	70.6	55.7
1951.Q1	322.9	25.1	1286.6	1221.9	3.5	5.0	114.4	212.0	2.8	—	72.9	52.0
1951.Q2	330.9	25.1	1320.4	1236.4	3.1	5.0	115.5	213.7	3.1	—	33.5	7.7
1951.Q3	337.7	25.0	1349.8	1251.0	3.2	5.0	117.0	216.6	3.0	—	4.0	−25.8
1951.Q4	342.1	25.2	1356.0	1265.7	3.4	5.1	119.1	220.4	3.2	—	−7.1	−36.6
1952.Q1	345.2	25.2	1369.2	1280.7	3.1	5.1	120.7	223.6	3.1	—	0.4	−27.9
1952.Q2	345.7	25.3	1365.9	1295.8	3.0	5.1	121.7	225.8	3.1	—	−15.0	−38.5
1952.Q3	351.6	25.5	1378.2	1311.1	3.2	5.1	122.9	228.6	3.1	—	−29.4	−51.9
1952.Q4	364.0	25.9	1406.8	1326.6	2.8	5.1	124.2	231.5	3.1	—	−14.7	−40.5
1953.Q1	370.7	25.9	1431.4	1342.3	2.7	5.1	124.7	233.3	3.3	—	−17.8	−46.9
1953.Q2	374.1	25.9	1444.9	1358.1	2.6	5.1	125.5	235.5	3.7	—	−24.3	−53.0
1953.Q3	373.3	26.0	1438.2	1374.2	2.7	5.1	125.7	236.9	3.6	—	−22.7	−44.2
1953.Q4	368.2	25.8	1426.6	1390.4	3.7	5.1	125.8	238.4	3.2	—	−45.7	−58.2
1954.Q1	367.9	26.2	1406.8	1406.8	5.3	5.1	126.2	240.3	2.9	—	−40.5	−41.1
1954.Q2	368.1	26.3	1401.2	1417.3	5.8	5.1	126.5	242.5	2.9	—	−25.5	−21.2
1954.Q3	372.8	26.3	1418.0	1427.9	6.0	5.1	127.6	245.8	3.0	—	−19.4	−16.7
1954.Q4	381.2	26.5	1438.8	1438.6	5.3	5.1	129.0	248.4	2.9	—	−7.2	−7.3
1955.Q1	394.0	26.8	1469.6	1449.4	4.7	5.1	130.5	251.2	3.1	—	6.7	1.2
1955.Q2	402.3	27.1	1485.7	1460.2	4.4	5.1	131.3	252.8	3.1	—	18.1	10.6
1955.Q3	410.5	27.3	1505.5	1471.1	4.1	5.1	131.8	254.1	3.3	—	17.2	7.1
1955.Q4	416.9	27.4	1518.7	1482.1	4.2	5.1	132.0	255.1	3.2	—	23.4	12.7
1956.Q1	419.5	27.7	1515.7	1493.2	4.0	5.1	132.5	255.7	3.2	—	23.8	16.3
1956.Q2	425.1	27.9	1522.6	1504.4	4.2	5.1	132.8	257.0	3.5	—	21.1	15.5
1956.Q3	429.9	28.2	1523.7	1515.6	4.1	5.1	132.9	258.1	3.9	—	18.8	16.1
1956.Q4	438.3	28.5	1540.6	1527.0	4.1	5.1	133.5	259.7	4.2	—	22.5	18.4
1957.Q1	447.3	28.8	1553.3	1538.4	3.9	5.1	133.8	261.9	4.2	—	16.3	11.7
1957.Q2	449.4	28.9	1552.4	1549.9	4.1	5.1	133.8	263.9	4.5	—	9.7	8.6
1957.Q3	456.5	29.2	1561.5	1561.5	4.2	5.1	133.9	265.7	4.7	—	9.6	9.5
1957.Q4	450.9	29.3	1537.3	1574.1	4.9	5.1	133.1	266.4	4.4	—	−4.4	5.7
1958.Q1	443.9	29.5	1506.1	1586.7	6.3	5.0	133.0	269.1	3.7	—	−25.1	−2.4
1958.Q2	447.9	29.6	1514.2	1599.5	7.4	5.0	134.5	275.7	3.7	—	−39.9	−15.1
1958.Q3	461.0	29.7	1550.0	1612.3	7.3	5.0	135.8	280.6	4.3	—	−40.4	−21.0
1958.Q4	474.2	29.9	1586.7	1625.3	6.4	5.1	137.5	283.9	4.4	—	−33.1	−20.7

	Nominal GNP (Y) (B $)	GMP Deflator (P) (1982 = 100)	Real GNP (Q) (B 1982$)	Natural Real GNP (Q^N) (B 1982$)	Unempl. Rate (U) (percent)	Natural Unempl. Rate (U^N) (percent)	Money Supply (M1) (B $)	Money Supply (M2) (B $)	Nominal Interest Rate (r) (percent)	Weighted Exchange Rate (1980 = 100)	Real Actual Federal Surplus (B 1982$)	Real Natural Federal Surplus (B 1982$)
1959.Q1	485.1	30.2	1606.4	1638.4	5.8	5.1	139.4	287.9	4.6	—	−9.6	0.1
1959.Q2	497.8	30.4	1637.0	1651.6	5.1	5.1	140.5	292.2	4.8	—	5.3	10.3
1959.Q3	498.0	30.6	1629.5	1664.8	5.3	5.1	141.5	296.1	5.0	—	−5.6	4.4
1959.Q4	502.4	30.6	1643.4	1678.2	5.6	5.2	140.3	297.2	5.3	—	−4.9	5.8
1960.Q1	516.1	30.9	1671.6	1691.7	5.1	5.2	139.9	298.7	5.2	—	24.6	18.8
1960.Q2	514.5	30.9	1666.8	1705.3	5.2	5.2	139.6	301.1	4.9	—	13.6	12.6
1960.Q3	517.7	31.0	1668.4	1719.1	5.5	5.2	140.9	306.5	4.7	—	4.5	8.7
1960.Q4	513.0	31.0	1654.1	1732.9	6.3	5.2	140.9	311.0	4.8	—	−3.5	9.6
1961.Q1	517.4	31.0	1671.3	1746.8	6.8	5.2	141.5	316.3	4.5	135.1	−13.9	−.4
1961.Q2	527.9	31.2	1692.1	1760.9	7.0	5.2	142.6	322.2	4.7	134.7	−16.3	−4.3
1961.Q3	538.5	31.4	1716.3	1775.0	6.8	5.2	143.4	327.6	4.8	135.8	−12.4	−3.4
1961.Q4	551.5	31.4	1754.9	1789.3	6.2	5.3	144.7	333.4	4.6	135.9	−7.0	−5.9
1962.Q1	564.4	31.7	1777.9	1803.7	5.6	5.3	145.7	340.3	4.5	136.1	−18.0	−20.1
1962.Q2	572.2	31.8	1796.4	1818.2	5.5	5.3	146.6	347.5	4.3	136.8	−12.9	−16.9
1962.Q3	579.2	31.9	1813.1	1832.8	5.6	5.3	146.5	352.9	4.4	136.9	−10.0	−14.5
1962.Q4	582.8	32.2	1810.1	1847.6	5.5	5.4	147.3	360.0	4.3	136.7	−12.4	−12.2
1963.Q1	592.1	32.3	1834.6	1862.4	5.8	5.4	148.8	368.0	4.3	136.7	−5.9	−7.0
1963.Q2	600.3	32.3	1860.0	1877.4	5.7	5.4	150.2	375.9	4.3	137.0	6.2	2.9
1963.Q3	613.1	32.4	1892.5	1892.5	5.5	5.4	151.7	383.6	4.4	137.1	3.7	−4.5
1963.Q4	622.1	32.6	1906.1	1909.4	5.6	5.5	153.2	391.2	4.4	137.0	−.6	−7.6
1964.Q1	636.9	32.7	1948.7	1926.5	5.5	5.5	154.2	397.6	4.5	137.1	−9.2	−22.5
1964.Q2	645.6	32.8	1965.4	1943.7	5.2	5.5	155.3	404.3	4.5	137.1	−20.4	−33.7
1964.Q3	656.0	33.0	1985.2	1961.1	5.0	5.5	157.9	413.4	4.5	137.1	−7.3	−22.0
1964.Q4	660.6	33.1	1993.7	1978.6	5.0	5.6	159.9	422.1	4.5	136.8	−3.0	−15.1
1965.Q1	682.7	33.5	2036.9	1996.3	4.9	5.8	161.1	430.5	4.5	136.8	13.7	−5.1
1965.Q2	695.0	33.6	2066.4	2014.1	4.7	5.6	162.1	437.6	4.5	137.1	11.9	−10.5
1965.Q3	710.7	33.9	2099.3	2032.1	4.4	5.6	163.9	446.0	4.7	137.2	−9.1	−34.8
1965.Q4	732.0	34.1	2147.6	2050.3	4.1	5.6	166.9	456.1	4.8	137.0	−10.0	−44.1
1966.Q1	754.8	34.5	2190.1	2068.6	3.9	5.6	169.8	464.7	5.1	137.1	1.7	−39.7
1966.Q2	764.6	34.8	2195.8	2087.1	3.8	5.6	171.6	470.2	5.5	137.2	3.7	−35.2
1966.Q3	777.7	35.1	2218.3	2105.8	3.8	5.6	171.1	473.0	6.0	137.1	−9.1	−49.2
1966.Q4	790.9	35.5	2229.2	2124.6	3.7	5.6	171.6	477.9	6.0	137.3	−16.6	−54.7
1967.Q1	799.7	35.7	2241.8	2143.6	3.8	5.6	173.3	485.4	5.5	137.3	−36.1	−71.5
1967.Q2	805.9	35.7	2255.2	2162.8	3.8	5.6	175.7	497.1	5.9	137.1	−37.0	−70.7
1967.Q3	822.9	36.0	2287.7	2182.1	3.8	5.6	179.6	510.8	6.2	137.1	−37.8	−74.9
1967.Q4	837.1	36.4	2300.6	2201.6	3.9	5.6	182.5	521.4	6.8	138.2	−35.7	−70.9
1968.Q1	862.9	37.1	2327.3	2221.3	3.7	5.6	184.9	530.2	6.7	139.6	−26.4	−64.1
1968.Q2	886.7	37.5	2366.9	2241.1	3.6	5.6	188.1	539.2	6.9	139.5	−32.3	−76.3
1968.Q3	903.6	37.9	2385.3	2261.2	3.5	5.6	191.8	549.9	6.7	139.3	−6.9	−52.0
1968.Q4	917.4	38.5	2383.0	2281.4	3.4	5.6	195.9	562.2	7.1	139.1	0.8	−38.9
1969.Q1	943.8	39.0	2422.8	2301.8	3.4	5.6	199.4	571.7	7.5	139.3	29.2	−14.7
1969.Q2	957.6	39.5	2424.6	2322.3	3.4	5.6	201.0	577.1	7.7	139.5	29.1	−9.6
1969.Q3	976.4	40.1	2435.7	2343.1	3.6	5.6	201.9	580.9	8.2	140.4	16.2	−18.4
1969.Q4	978.0	40.6	2409.9	2364.0	3.6	5.6	203.5	586.8	8.9	139.5	10.6	−13.6
1970.Q1	994.2	41.3	2408.6	2385.2	4.2	5.6	205.8	589.7	8.9	139.2	−3.1	−12.4
1970.Q2	1008.9	41.9	2406.5	2406.5	4.8	5.6	207.2	594.1	9.4	138.7	−31.3	−33.1
1970.Q3	1027.9	42.2	2435.8	2426.9	5.2	5.7	210.0	606.3	9.1	138.1	−35.3	−38.0
1970.Q4	1030.9	42.7	2413.8	2447.6	5.8	5.7	213.7	622.7	8.8	138.0	−47.8	−36.9

	Nominal GNP (Y) (B $)	GMP Deflator (P) (1982 = 100)	Real GNP (Q) (B 1982$)	Natural Real GNP (Q^N) (B 1982$)	Unempl. Rate (U) (percent)	Natural Unempl. Rate (U^N) (percent)	Money Supply (M1) (B $)	Money Supply (M2) (B $)	Nominal Interest Rate (r) (percent)	Weighted Exchange Rate (1980 = 100)	Real Actual Federal Surplus (B 1982$)	Real Natural Federal Surplus (B 1982$)
1971.Q1	1075.2	43.4	2478.6	2468.3	5.9	5.7	217.4	642.7	7.6	137.6	−42.6	−42.1
1971.Q2	1094.3	44.2	2478.4	2489.3	5.9	5.8	221.9	668.4	8.1	136.9	−53.4	−47.4
1971.Q3	1113.9	44.7	2491.1	2510.4	6.0	5.8	225.7	687.8	8.1	134.4	−53.2	−44.4
1971.Q4	1127.3	45.3	2491.0	2531.8	5.9	5.8	227.8	706.7	7.6	130.2	−49.0	−35.4
1972.Q1	1166.5	45.8	2545.6	2553.3	5.8	5.8	232.4	727.9	7.5	124.9	−27.9	−21.3
1972.Q2	1197.2	46.1	2595.1	2575.0	5.7	5.8	236.1	747.0	7.7	124.0	−44.7	−44.8
1972.Q3	1223.9	46.7	2622.1	2596.8	5.6	5.8	241.0	771.7	7.7	124.6	−21.8	−24.2
1972.Q4	1263.5	47.3	2671.3	2618.9	5,4	5.8	246.9	797.2	7.5	125.7	−50.1	−61.4
1973.Q1	1311.6	48.0	2734.0	2641.1	4.9	5.8	251.9	816.8	7.7	119.9	−18.3	−42.1
1973.Q2	1342.9	49.0	2741.0	2663.6	4.9	5.8	254.8	830.5	7.7	113.5	−18.0	−39.3
1973.Q3	1369.4	50.0	2738.3	2686.2	4.8	5.8	257.8	843.1	8.2	107.9	−5.8	−23.4
1973.Q4	1413.3	51.2	2762.8	2709.0	4.8	5.9	261.1	854.6	8.0	112.4	−3.5	−23.8
1974.Q1	1426.2	51.9	2747.4	2732.0	5.1	5.9	265.4	870.8	8.4	119.4	−8.5	−21.0
1974.Q2	1459.1	53.0	2755.2	2755.2	5.2	5.9	267.8	881.8	9.3	113.8	−20.0	−25.3
1974.Q3	1489.1	54.8	2719.3	2775.2	5.6	5.9	270.3	891.5	10.3	116.4	−14.4	−6.2
1974.Q4	1516.8	56.3	2695.4	2795.4	6.6	6.0	273.5	904.7	9.7	114.6	−41.6	−19.9
1975.Q1	1524.6	57.7	2642.7	2815.7	8.3	6.0	276.3	921.3	9.2	108.8	−81.5	−32.8
1975.Q2	1563.5	58.6	2669.6	2836.1	8.9	6.0	279.2	955.1	9.6	108.6	−170.8	−124.2
1975.Q3	1627.4	59.9	2714.9	2856.7	8.5	6.0	284.6	989.8	9.7	115.7	−108.0	−64.3
1975.Q4	1678.2	61.0	2752.7	2877.5	8.3	6.0	286.9	1014.2	9.5	117.7	−107.9	−68.0
1976.Q1	1730.9	61.7	2804.4	2898.4	7.7	5.9	290.8	1046.2	8.8	118.9	−87.2	−56.7
1976.Q2	1761.8	62.5	2816.9	2919.4	7.6	5.9	295.4	1078.9	8.9	121.9	−77.8	−46.9
1976.Q3	1794.7	63.4	2828.6	2940.6	7.7	5.9	298.6	1108.4	8.6	121.6	−86.6	−52.8
1976.Q4	1843.7	64.5	2856.8	2962.0	7.8	6.0	304.4	1149.4	8.4	120.9	−88.1	−56.1
1977.Q1	1899.1	65.6	2896.0	2983.5	7.5	6.0	311.5	1188.2	8.2	120.5	−59.8	−33.1
1977.Q2	1968.9	66.9	2942.7	3005.2	7.1	6.0	317.0	1220.8	8.3	119.5	−62.8	−44.1
1977.Q3	2031.6	67.7	3001.8	3027.0	6.9	6.0	322.5	1250.3	8.1	118.1	−76.7	−68.2
1977.Q4	2062.4	68.9	2994.1	3049.0	6.7	6.0	329.4	1278.2	8.3	114.9	−74.0	−60.1
1978.Q1	2111.4	69.9	3020.5	3071.1	6.3	5.9	335.8	1302.0	8.7	109.7	−68.0	−57.2
1978.Q2	2230.3	71.6	3115.9	3093.4	6.0	5.9	343.2	1324.9	9.0	108.9	−35.3	−44.0
1978.Q3	2289.5	72.9	3142.6	3115.9	6.0	5.9	350.2	1351.3	9.0	103.7	−33.2	−42.9
1978.Q4	2367.6	74.4	3181.6	3138.5	5.9	5.9	356.4	1380.3	9.3	100.5	−27.4	−41.7
1979.Q1	2420.5	76.1	3181.7	3161.3	5.9	5.9	360.7	1402.8	9.6	100.8	−12.9	−22.3
1979.Q2	2474.5	77.8	3178.7	3184.3	5.7	5.9	367.3	1433.1	9.7	102.8	−7.7	−12.3
1979.Q3	2546.1	79.4	3207.4	3207.4	5.8	5.9	379.9	1471.8	9.6	99.5	−25.2	−30.6
1979.Q4	2591.5	81.0	3201.3	3226.2	6.0	5.9	384.0	1493.6	11.3	100.0	−35.4	−33.5
1980.Q1	2673.0	82.7	3233.4	3245.0	6.3	5.9	388.1	1517.8	13.0	100.0	−45.7	−43.5
1980.Q2	2672.2	84.6	3157.0	3264.0	7.3	5.9	382.3	1532.3	12.0	100.5	−76.2	−45.4
1980.Q3	2734.0	86.5	3159.1	3283.1	7.7	5.9	400.9	1589.6	12.1	97.7	−86.7	−45.8
1980.Q4	2848.6	89.0	3199.2	3302.3	7.4	6.0	412.7	1627.1	13.9	101.8	−76.4	−39.8
1981.Q1	2978.8	91.3	3261.1	3321.6	7.4	6.0	415.0	1653.1	14.4	108.2	−51.9	−22.6
1981.Q2	3017.7	92.8	3250.2	3341.0	7.4	6.0	422.1	1693.0	15.2	118.0	−53.0	−16.9
1981.Q3	3099.6	94.9	3264.6	3360.6	7.4	6.0	429.1	1733.2	16.3	125.9	−65.9	−27.4
1981.Q4	3114.4	96.7	3219.0	3380.2	8.2	6.0	434.3	1777.8	16.0	120.5	−99.3	−44.0
1982.Q1	3112.6	98.2	3170.4	3400.0	8.8	6.0	442.2	1817.2	16.1	125.8	−111.2	−35.1
1982.Q2	3159.5	99.4	3179.9	3419.9	9.4	6.0	444.4	1848.0	15.7	130.5	−113.6	−31.1
1982.Q3	3179.4	100.8	3154.5	3439.8	9.9	6.0	453.9	1893.0	14.7	137.1	−157.5	−63.0
1982.Q4	3212.5	101.7	3159.3	3460.0	10.7	6.0	471.9	1939.0	12.2	139.8	−199.2	−97.1

	Nominal GNP (Y) (B $)	GMP Deflator (P) (1982 = 100)	Real GNP (Q) (B 1982$)	Natural Real GNP (Q^N) (B 1982$)	Unempl. Rate (U) (percent)	Natural Unempl. Rate (U^N) (percent)	Money Supply (M1) (B $)	Money Supply (M2) (B $)	Nominal Interest Rate (r) (percent)	Weighted Exchange Rate (1980 = 100)	Real Actual Federal Surplus (B 1982$)	Real Natural Federal Surplus (B 1982$)
1983.Q1	3265.8	102.4	3186.6	3480.2	10.4	6.0	483.4	2037.7	12.0	136.6	−181.8	−83.8
1983.Q2	3367.4	103.2	3258.3	3500.5	10.1	6.0	497.4	2091.7	11.6	140.8	−166.1	−80.3
1983.Q3	3443.9	104.4	3306.4	3521.0	9.4	6.0	511.9	2131.2	12.7	147.2	−169.8	−96.6
1983.Q4	3545.8	105.4	3365.1	3541.6	8.5	6.0	520.1	2174.2	12.8	148.9	−160.5	−100.0
1984.Q1	3674.9	106.5	3451.7	3562.3	7.9	6.0	528.0	2214.6	12.9	150.6	−145.2	−104.4
1984.Q2	3754.2	107.3	3498.0	3583.1	7.4	6.0	536.3	2254.0	14.2	151.9	−152.3	−121.0
1984.Q3	3807.9	108.2	3520.6	3604.1	7.4	6.0	542.5	2289.5	13.7	162.1	−159.7	−129.5
1984.Q4	3851.8	109.0	3535.2	3625.2	7.3	6.0	547.5	2339.3	12.6	168.5	−172.0	−141.9
1985.Q1	3925.6	109.7	3577.5	3646.4	7.3	6.0	561.7	2410.0	12.6	179.0	−147.3	−121.7
1985.Q2	3979.0	110.6	3599.2	3667.7	7.3	6.0	576.0	2448.7	11.9	170.5	−190.9	−167.5
1985.Q3	4047.0	111.3	3635.8	3689.1	7.2	6.0	596.7	2506.3	11.5	159.2	−182.1	−161.9
1985.Q4	4107.9	112.2	3662.4	3710.7	7.0	6.0	613.2	2546.4	11.0	146.6	−189.1	−171.4
1986.Q1	4181.3	112.4	3721.1	3732.4	7.0	6.0	627.0	2585.9	9.7	136.7	−174.1	−168.5
1986.Q2	4194.7	113.2	3704.6	3754.2	7.1	6.0	651.4	2652.4	9.1	130.7	−208.5	−190.5
1986.Q3	4253.3	114.6	3712.4	3776.2	7.0	6.0	679.6	2724.0	9.1	124.0	−180.5	−161.3
1986.Q4	4297.3	115.1	3733.6	3798.3	6.8	6.0	708.9	2785.4	9.1	122.4	−164.2	−139.4
1987.Q1	4388.8	116.0	3783.0	3820.5	6.7	6.0	732.3	2830.3	8.6	114.3	−171.9	−149.5
1987.Q2	4475.9	117.1	3823.5	3842.8	6.2	6.0	744.4	2849.2	9.7	110.9	−117.5	−118.8
1987.Q3	4566.6	117.9	3872.8	3865.3	6.0	6.0	746.0	2870.9	10.1	112.9	−122.1	−119.9
1987.Q4	4665.8	118.6	3935.6	3887.9	5.9	6.0	754.7	2905.8	10.4	105.6	−138.5	−148.4
1988.Q1	4739.8	119.2	3974.8	3910.6	5.7	6.0	760.8	2950.2	9.6	103.0	−127.3	−145.6
1988.Q2	4838.5	120.6	4010.7	3933.5	5.5	6.0	772.9	3001.1	10.1	103.5	−117.3	−127.4
1988.Q3	4926.9	121.9	4042.7	3956.5	5.5	6.0	782.9	3029.5	10.1	111.6	−100.5	−129.5
1988.Q4	5017.3	123.3	4069.4	3979.6	5.3	6.0	787.4	3056.9	9.7	106.4	−135.8	−166.5
1989.Q1	5113.1	124.5	4106.8	4002.9	5.2	6.0	786.7	3072.3	10.1	108.6	−118.5	−154.2
1989.Q2	5194.9	126.0	4123.9	4026.3	5.3	6.0	775.8	3081.0	9.8	112.1	−108.7	−143.0

International Annual Time Series Data for Selected Countries, 1960–88

Table B-1　**Canada**

	Nominal GNP (Y) (B C$)	GNP Deflator (P) (1982 = 100)	Real GNP (Q) (B 1982C$)	Labor Productivity (Q/N) (C$/Hr)	Unemployment Rate (U) (percent)	Money Supply (M1) (B C$)	Money Supply (M2) (B C$)	Consumer Price Index (CPI) (1982 = 100)	Long-Term Interest Rates (r) (percent)	Labor Share (w N/Y) (percent)
1960	39.2	27.4	143.2	11.3	7.0	8.4	12.3	28.3	5.2	51.4
1961	40.6	27.5	147.7	11.7	7.1	9.4	13.4	28.6	5.1	52.2
1962	44.1	27.9	158.3	12.2	5.9	9.9	14.0	28.9	5.1	51.7
1963	47.4	28.5	166.5	12.6	5.5	10.6	15.7	29.4	5.1	51.4
1964	51.9	29.2	177.6	13.0	4.3	11.6	17.3	29.9	5.2	51.3
1965	57.2	30.2	189.4	13.5	3.6	13.2	19.0	30.7	5.2	51.8
1966	64.0	31.6	202.3	14.0	3.3	14.2	20.6	31.8	5.7	52.5
1967	68.6	33.0	208.2	14.1	3.8	16.4	22.3	32.9	5.9	54.1
1968	74.8	34.1	219.2	14.8	4.4	17.4	30.2	34.3	6.8	54.0
1969	82.4	35.7	231.1	15.3	4.4	16.7	32.5	35.9	7.6	54.8
1970	88.5	37.3	237.0	15.7	5.6	17.0	35.6	37.1	7.9	55.3
1971	96.6	38.5	250.7	16.3	6.1	19.2	38.8	38.1	7.0	55.7
1972	107.8	40.7	265.0	16.8	6.2	21.6	44.6	39.9	7.2	56.0
1973	126.4	44.3	285.4	17.3	5.5	23.5	53.8	43.0	7.6	55.0
1974	151.0	50.7	297.9	17.5	5.3	23.8	64.1	47.6	8.9	54.9
1975	170.1	55.7	305.6	17.8	6.9	28.4	74.0	52.8	9.0	56.8
1976	196.3	60.5	324.4	18.6	7.1	28.8	88.2	56.7	9.2	57.0
1977	216.1	64.3	336.0	19.3	8.0	31.8	100.6	61.3	8.7	57.4
1978	239.6	68.2	351.4	19.3	8.3	34.0	117.6	66.8	9.3	56.3
1979	274.1	75.1	365.1	19.4	7.4	34.5	138.4	72.9	10.2	55.4
1980	307.7	83.1	370.5	19.3	7.4	38.0	151.5	80.3	12.5	55.7
1981	353.5	92.0	384.2	19.6	7.5	37.8	183.2	90.3	15.2	56.0
1982	371.8	100.0	371.8	20.0	10.9	38.9	186.4	100.0	14.3	56.9
1983	402.2	104.8	383.7	20.5	11.8	43.7	185.4	105.8	11.8	55.1
1984	441.3	108.1	408.1	21.2	11.2	52.4	195.6	110.4	12.8	54.1
1985	475.1	111.3	426.7	21.4	10.4	69.8	206.9	114.8	11.0	54.2
1986	502.2	114.1	440.1	21.3	9.5	80.1	222.2	119.5	9.5	54.7
1987	544.9	119.1	457.7	21.6	8.8	85.1	241.5	124.8	10.0	54.3
1988	593.5	124.1	478.2	21.7	7.8	88.7	265.7	129.9	10.2	54.4

Table B-2 Japan

	Nominal GNP (Y) (Tr Y)	GNP Deflator (P) (1982 = 100)	Real GNP (Q) (Tr 1982Y)	Labor Produc-tivity (Q/N) (Th Y/Hr)	Unem-ployment Rate (U) (percent)	Money Supply (M1) (Tr Y)	Money Supply (M2) (Tr Y)	Consumer Price Index (CPI) (1982 = 100)	Long-Term Interest Rates (r) (percent)	Labor Share (w N/Y) (percent)
1960	16.0	27.0	59.3	0.6	1.6	4.1	10.3	22.4	7.5	40.3
1961	19.3	29.1	66.5	0.6	1.4	4.9	12.3	23.7	7.3	39.5
1962	21.9	30.3	72.4	0.7	1.3	5.7	14.7	25.3	7.5	41.6
1963	25.1	32.0	78.5	0.7	1.3	7.7	18.7	27.2	7.1	42.4
1964	29.5	33.7	87.7	0.8	1.1	8.7	21.5	28.2	7.2	42.1
1965	32.9	35.4	92.8	0.8	1.2	10.3	25.4	30.1	7.2	44.1
1966	38.2	37.2	102.7	0.9	1.3	11.7	29.5	31.6	6.9	44.0
1967	44.7	39.2	114.1	1.0	1.3	13.4	34.1	32.9	6.9	43.1
1968	53.0	41.1	128.8	1.1	1.2	15.2	39.2	34.7	7.0	42.4
1969	62.2	43.0	144.8	1.3	1.1	18.3	46.4	36.5	7.1	42.5
1970	73.3	45.7	160.3	1.4	1.1	21.4	54.2	39.3	7.2	43.5
1971	80.7	48.3	167.2	1.5	1.2	27.7	67.4	41.7	7.3	46.9
1972	92.4	51.0	181.3	1.6	1.4	34.5	84.0	43.5	6.7	47.6
1973	112.5	57.5	195.5	1.7	1.3	40.3	98.2	48.7	7.3	49.0
1974	134.2	69.5	193.1	1.7	1.4	45.0	109.5	60.6	9.3	52.2
1975	148.3	74.8	198.2	1.8	1.9	49.9	125.3	67.7	9.2	55.0
1976	166.6	80.2	207.6	1.9	2.0	56.2	142.2	74.0	8.7	55.2
1977	185.6	84.9	218.6	2.0	2.0	60.8	158.0	80.0	7.3	55.4
1978	204.4	89.0	229.8	2.0	2.2	68.9	178.7	83.0	6.1	54.3
1979	221.5	91.7	241.7	2.1	2.1	71.0	193.7	86.0	7.7	54.2
1980	240.2	95.1	252.4	2.2	2.0	69.6	207.0	92.9	9.2	54.3
1981	257.4	98.2	262.2	2.2	2.2	76.5	229.2	97.5	8.7	54.8
1982	269.6	100.0	269.6	2.3	2.4	80.9	246.6	100.0	8.1	55.3
1983	280.3	100.8	278.1	2.3	2.6	80.8	263.6	101.8	7.4	56.0
1984	297.9	102.0	292.1	2.4	2.7	86.4	281.8	104.1	6.8	55.5
1985	316.3	103.4	305.8	2.5	2.6	89.0	306.8	106.3	6.3	54.7
1986	330.1	105.4	313.2	2.5	2.8	98.2	335.3	106.9	4.9	55.0
1987	343.7	105.2	326.6	2.6	2.8	103.0	372.7	107.0	4.2	55.0
1988	365.3	105.6	345.8	2.7	2.5	113.5	411.4	107.7	4.3	56.2

Table B-3   France

	Nominal GNP (Y) (B Fr)	GNP Deflator (P) (1982 = 100)	Real GNP (Q) (B 1982Fr)	Labor Productivity (Q/N) (Fr/Hr)	Unemployment Rate (U) (percent)	Money Supply (M1) (B Fr)	Money Supply (M2) (B Fr)	Consumer Price Index (CPI) (1982 = 100)	Long-Term Interest Rates (r) (percent)	Labor Share (w N/Y) (percent)
1960	300.7	20.5	1468.8	38.3	1.4	109.2	112.0	21.2	5.1	44.5
1961	328.0	21.2	1549.7	40.3	1.2	126.4	131.1	21.7	5.1	45.6
1962	366.2	22.2	1653.1	42.8	1.4	149.4	155.4	22.8	5.0	46.2
1963	410.6	23.6	1741.5	44.7	1.5	170.1	177.6	23.9	5.0	46.9
1964	455.4	24.6	1855.0	47.1	1.4	185.0	194.5	24.7	5.1	47.2
1965	490.3	25.2	1943.7	49.7	1.5	202.3	215.6	25.4	5.3	47.3
1966	530.7	26.0	2045.0	53.4	1.8	217.2	239.9	26.0	5.4	47.1
1967	573.3	26.8	2140.9	56.1	1.9	227.6	270.6	26.8	5.7	47.1
1968	623.1	27.9	2232.1	60.5	2.6	246.0	301.2	28.0	5.9	48.4
1969	710.5	29.8	2388.1	61.9	2.3	240.4	322.8	29.7	7.6	48.6
1970	793.5	31.4	2525.0	65.1	2.4	265.5	370.1	31.4	8.1	49.3
1971	884.2	33.4	2645.7	68.5	2.6	297.6	437.9	33.1	7.7	49.9
1972	987.9	35.8	2763.0	70.5	2.7	342.2	520.7	35.1	7.4	50.0
1973	1129.8	38.8	2913.3	75.5	2.6	375.4	597.1	37.7	8.3	50.1
1974	1303.0	43.4	3003.8	78.2	2.8	432.7	703.6	42.8	10.5	52.1
1975	1467.9	49.0	2995.5	80.9	4.0	486.4	814.4	47.8	9.5	54.6
1976	1700.6	54.5	3122.6	83.6	4.4	523.1	914.5	52.4	9.2	54.9
1977	1917.8	59.5	3223.1	87.0	4.9	588.0	1054.0	57.4	9.6	55.3
1978	2182.6	65.5	3331.1	90.6	5.2	644.0	1173.0	62.7	9.0	55.1
1979	2481.1	72.1	3439.0	94.2	5.9	711.0	1325.0	69.4	9.5	54.9
1980	2808.3	80.4	3494.9	95.8	6.3	751.0	1427.0	78.8	13.0	56.1
1981	3164.8	89.5	3536.0	98.8	7.4	858.0	1577.0	89.3	15.8	56.6
1982	3626.0	100.0	3626.0	105.9	8.1	942.0	1747.0	100.0	15.7	56.7
1983	4006.5	109.7	3651.2	107.8	8.3	1050.0	1937.0	109.5	13.6	56.4
1984	4361.9	117.9	3699.2	110.3	9.7	1149.0	2096.0	117.9	12.5	55.6
1985	4695.0	124.8	3760.5	113.9	10.2	1186.0	2226.0	124.7	10.9	55.0
1986	5034.9	131.2	3838.8	116.4	10.4	1258.0	2365.0	127.9	8.4	53.5
1987	5288.7	134.8	3922.4	118.8	10.6	1317.0	2730.0	131.9	9.4	53.0
1988	5641.1	139.0	4058.3	120.4	10.3	1359.0	2926.0	135.4	9.1	52.4

Table B-4   Germany

	Nominal GNP (Y) (B DM)	GNP Deflator (P) (1982 = 100)	Real GNP (Q) (B 1982DM)	Labor Productivity (Q/N) (DM/Hr)	Unemployment Rate (U) (percent)	Money Supply (M1) (B DM)	Money Supply (M2) (B DM)	Consumer Price Index (CPI) (1982 = 100)	Long-Term Interest Rates (r) (percent)	Labor Share (w N/Y) (percent)
1960	302.7	38.3	791.4	14.0	1.3	49.6	108.9	42.3	6.4	47.3
1961	331.7	40.1	828.1	14.6	0.8	56.8	123.2	43.3	5.9	48.7
1962	360.8	41.6	867.3	15.5	0.7	60.7	138.3	44.6	5.9	49.6
1963	382.4	42.9	891.3	16.2	0.8	65.1	153.5	45.9	6.1	50.2
1964	420.2	44.2	950.7	17.1	0.4	70.6	172.7	46.7	6.2	50.0
1965	459.2	45.8	1002.8	18.1	0.3	76.0	193.5	48.5	7.1	50.7
1966	488.2	47.3	1032.3	18.9	0.2	77.5	214.6	50.2	8.1	51.4
1967	494.4	47.9	1031.1	19.9	1.3	85.2	243.2	51.0	7.0	50.6
1968	533.3	49.0	1088.4	21.1	1.5	90.8	280.3	51.9	6.5	50.4
1969	597.0	51.0	1169.6	22.5	0.9	95.6	309.3	52.8	6.8	50.7
1970	675.3	54.9	1229.9	23.6	0.8	103.9	336.7	54.6	8.3	53.2
1971	750.6	59.3	1265.5	24.4	0.9	117.1	381.9	57.5	8.0	54.3
1972	823.7	62.5	1318.8	25.9	0.8	133.6	435.5	60.7	7.9	54.5
1973	917.3	66.4	1380.6	27.3	0.8	135.9	473.8	64.9	9.3	55.6
1974	984.6	71.1	1384.3	28.3	1.6	150.5	508.1	69.4	10.4	57.1
1975	1026.9	75.4	1362.3	29.2	3.6	172.0	566.3	73.5	8.5	57.1
1976	1121.7	78.1	1436.1	30.5	3.7	177.6	609.0	76.7	7.8	56.2
1977	1197.8	81.0	1478.5	32.0	3.6	198.9	611.3	79.5	6.2	56.3
1978	1285.3	84.5	1520.9	32.2	3.5	227.9	741.0	81.7	5.8	56.0
1979	1392.3	87.9	1584.0	34.4	3.2	234.5	779.2	85.1	7.4	55.8
1980	1478.9	92.1	1605.6	34.8	3.0	243.8	814.6	89.7	8.5	57.0
1981	1540.9	95.8	1608.3	35.5	4.4	240.0	844.6	95.0	10.4	57.2
1982	1597.9	100.0	1597.9	35.7	6.1	257.1	902.8	100.0	9.0	56.3
1983	1674.8	103.3	1621.9	37.0	8.0	278.7	954.3	103.3	7.9	54.8
1984	1755.8	105.3	1667.6	38.1	8.0	295.3	1007.8	1105.8	7.8	54.1
1985	1830.5	107.6	1700.7	39.1	8.1	314.5	1074.4	108.1	6.9	53.9
1986	1931.2	111.0	1740.4	39.8	7.2	340.2	1144.4	107.8	5.9	53.7
1987	2009.1	113.2	1774.3	40.3	7.0	365.7	1212.8	108.0	5.8	53.6
1988	2109.7	114.9	1836.1	40.8	7.0	405.5	1307.9	109.3	6.1	54.2

Table B-5   Italy

	Nominal GNP (Y) (Tr L)	GNP Deflator (P) (1982 = 100)	Real GNP (Q) (Tr 1982L)	Labor Productivity (Q/N) (Th L/Hr)	Unemployment Rate (U) (percent)	Money Supply (M1) (Tr L)	Money Supply (M2) (Tr L)	Consumer Price Index (CPI) (1982 = 100)	Long-Term Interest Rates (r) (percent)	Labor Share (w N/Y) (percent)
1960	26.7	11.8	226.8	5.2	5.6	7.4	13.0	13.6	5.0	36.9
1961	29.7	12.1	245.4	5.6	5.1	8.6	15.1	13.8	5.2	36.8
1962	33.4	12.8	260.7	6.2	4.6	10.1	17.8	14.5	5.8	38.1
1963	38.3	13.9	275.3	6.6	3.9	11.5	20.2	15.6	6.1	40.5
1964	41.9	14.8	283.0	6.9	4.3	12.4	21.9	16.5	7.4	41.4
1965	45.1	15.4	292.2	7.5	5.3	14.4	25.4	17.2	6.9	40.6
1966	48.9	15.8	309.7	8.0	5.7	16.3	29.1	17.6	6.5	40.1
1967	53.8	16.2	332.0	8.4	5.3	18.9	33.2	18.3	6.6	40.3
1968	58.3	16.5	353.7	8.9	5.6	21.1	37.2	18.5	6.7	40.4
1969	64.4	17.2	375.3	9.6	5.6	24.5	41.7	19.0	6.9	40.3
1970	72.5	18.3	395.2	10.2	5.3	31.2	47.9	20.0	9.0	41.9
1971	79.0	19.7	401.7	10.6	5.3	37.1	55.8	20.9	8.3	44.0
1972	86.6	20.9	414.5	11.2	6.3	43.5	65.8	22.1	7.5	44.8
1973	103.4	23.3	443.7	12.0	6.2	54.1	81.2	24.5	7.4	45.5
1974	127.6	27.6	462.1	12.4	5.3	59.2	94.0	29.2	9.9	45.9
1975	144.5	32.5	445.3	12.0	5.8	67.1	117.0	34.2	11.5	49.3
1976	180.6	38.3	471.4	12.7	6.6	79.8	141.6	39.7	13.1	48.2
1977	219.1	45.6	480.4	13.0	7.0	96.9	173.1	46.7	14.6	48.6
1978	256.2	51.9	493.3	13.4	7.1	122.7	212.9	52.4	13.7	48.5
1979	311.4	60.2	517.5	13.9	7.6	151.8	251.0	60.1	14.1	47.8
1980	390.4	72.6	537.7	14.4	7.5	171.3	285.2	72.9	16.1	47.2
1981	468.0	86.1	543.8	14.6	7.8	188.1	314.3	85.9	20.6	47.9
1982	545.1	100.0	545.1	14.7	8.4	219.6	369.7	100.0	20.9	47.9
1983	633.6	115.0	550.9	14.9	9.3	248.7	420.4	114.7	18.0	47.4
1984	727.8	128.1	568.3	15.5	9.9	279.5	465.7	127.0	15.0	46.0
1985	815.6	139.5	584.7	16.0	10.1	308.6	514.2	138.7	13.0	45.9
1986	902.2	150.0	601.6	16.6	10.9	342.5	556.1	146.8	10.5	44.8
1987	982.6	158.4	620.3	17.1	11.8	368.3	593.3	153.6	9.7	44.8
1988	1087.0	168.5	645.0	17.4	11.8	397.0	643.3	161.2	10.2	44.4

Table B-6 United Kingdom

	Nominal GNP (Y) (B £)	GNP Deflator (P) (1982 = 100)	Real GNP (Q) (B 1982£)	Labor Productivity (Q/N) (£/Hr)	Unemployment Rate (U) (percent)	Money Supply (M1) (B £)	Money Supply (M2) (B £)	Consumer Price Index (CPI) (1982 = 100)	Long-Term Interest Rates (r) (percent)	Labor Share (w N/Y) (percent)
1960	25.7	14.9	172.6	3.8	1.5	6.4	10.2	15.3	5.8	59.1
1961	27.5	15.4	178.2	4.0	1.5	6.6	10.5	15.9	6.3	59.9
1962	28.8	16.0	180.1	4.0	1.8	6.2	10.3	16.5	5.9	60.3
1963	30.6	16.4	187.1	4.2	2.2	7.1	11.2	16.9	5.4	59.6
1964	33.4	16.9	197.1	4.3	2.5	7.3	11.8	17.4	6.0	59.3
1965	35.8	17.8	201.3	4.5	2.2	7.6	12.7	18.3	6.6	59.6
1966	38.2	18.6	205.3	4.7	2.2	7.6	13.1	19.0	6.9	59.9
1967	40.4	19.2	210.9	4.9	3.3	8.2	14.5	19.4	6.8	59.0
1968	43.9	20.0	219.7	5.1	3.1	8.5	15.6	20.4	7.6	58.2
1969	46.8	21.0	222.6	5.2	2.9	8.6	16.0	21.4	9.0	58.3
1970	51.4	22.6	227.7	5.4	3.0	9.4	17.6	22.8	9.2	59.5
1971	57.8	24.7	233.6	5.8	3.6	10.8	19.9	25.0	8.9	58.1
1972	64.0	26.8	239.0	6.0	4.0	12.3	25.4	26.7	8.9	59.3
1973	73.8	28.5	258.3	6.2	3.0	12.9	32.4	29.2	10.7	59.6
1974	84.0	32.9	255.7	6.2	2.9	14.3	36.6	33.9	14.8	62.5
1975	106.1	41.8	254.0	6.2	4.3	17.1	38.4	42.1	14.4	64.7
1976	126.5	48.0	263.3	6.5	5.6	19.1	42.9	49.1	14.4	61.8
1977	145.6	54.7	266.1	6.7	6.0	23.1	47.0	56.8	12.7	59.6
1978	168.1	60.9	275.9	6.9	5.9	26.8	53.8	61.5	12.5	58.9
1979	196.8	69.7	282.1	7.0	5.0	29.3	60.5	69.8	13.0	59.0
1980	230.7	83.4	276.6	7.1	6.4	30.4	71.7	82.4	13.8	59.8
1981	254.2	93.0	273.5	7.5	9.8	36.3	94.5	92.1	14.7	58.9
1982	276.8	100.0	276.8	7.7	11.3	40.4	105.2	100.0	12.9	57.4
1983	302.3	105.2	287.5	8.1	12.5	45.2	120.0	104.6	10.8	56.2
1984	322.3	110.1	292.7	8.0	12.7	52.2	134.9	109.8	10.7	56.0
1985	352.6	116.3	303.2	8.2	12.2	61.6	150.2	116.5	10.6	55.3
1986	376.5	120.5	312.5	8.5	12.2	75.2	184.0	120.5	9.9	55.8
1987	409.9	126.4	324.3	8.6	11.2	92.4	222.6	125.4	9.5	55.3
1988	448.6	134.8	332.8	8.6	9.3	105.7	273.8	131.7	9.4	57.0

APPENDIX C

Data Sources and Methods

C-1 ANNUAL VARIABLES (Sources and Methods for Table A-1)

1. Nominal GNP (Y):
1875–1928: Data from Nathan S. Balke and Robert J. Gordon, "The Estimation of Prewar GNP: Methodology and New Results," *Journal of Political Economy,* vol. 97 (February 1989), pp. 38–92, Table 10, linked in 1929 to
1929–88: Data from U.S. Department of Commerce, current through March 1989, from *Survey of Current Business,* table 1-1.

2. Implicit GNP deflator (P):
Same as Nominal GNP (Y), except table 7-4 for 1929–88.

3. Real GNP (Q):
Same as Nominal GNP (Y), except table 1-2 for 1930–88.

4. Natural real GNP (Q^N):
1875–1946: Q^N is the geometric interpolation between the real GNP for the benchmark years 1869, 1873, 1884, 1891, 1900, 1910, 1924, and 1949.
1947–88: Q^N is the annual average of the quarterly series explained in section B-2.

5. Unemployment rate *(U):*
1890–1899: Lebergott's series, copied from Christina Romer, "Spurious Volatility in Historical Unemployment Data", *Journal of Political Economy,* vol. 94 (February 1986).
1900–38: Series B1 in *Long-Term Economic Growth, 1860–1970,* (Washington D.C.: U.S. Department of Commerce, 1973).
1939–88: *Economic Report of the President, 1989,* (Washington D.C.: U.S. Government Printing Office, 1989), table B-39.

6. Natural unemployment rate:
1890–1901: Assumed to be the same level as in 1902, 4.1 percent.
1902–56: U^N is calculated as the linear interpolation between the U^N values of the benchmark years of 1902, 1907, 1913, 1929, 1949, and 1954. U^N for the benchmark years of 1902, 1907, 1913, 1929, and 1949 is calculated as $U^N = 6.0 \times (U/UA)$ where UA is the published unemployment rate that adjusts for self-employment. UA equals the number of unemployed divided by the civilian labor force net of self-employed persons. The assumed 6.0 rate for UA, assumed to be consistent with long-run

equilibrium, reflects the value of UA observed in late 1954, when the economy was operating at its natural rate of unemployment. Changes in U^N before 1954 reflect only changes in the U/UA ratio.
1954–80: Robert J. Gordon, "Inflation, Flexible Exchange Rates, and the Natural Rate of Unemployment," in Martin N. Baily (ed.), *Workers, Jobs, and Inflation* (Washington: Brookings, 1982), table 11, p. 152.
1981–88: Assumed to remain constant at the same rate as 1980, 6.0 percent. The case for maintaining the U^N series at 6.0 percent is discussed in Robert J. Gordon, "U.S. Inflation, Labor's Share, and the Natural Rate of Unemployment," in Heinz Konig, ed., *Contributions to the Economics of Wage Determination, 1989.* NBER working paper 2585, May 1988.

7. Money supply ($M1$):
1915–46: *Historical Statistics of the United States, Colonial Times to 1970,* (Washington D.C.: U.S. Department of Commerce, 1975), series 414. Linked in 1947 to
1947–58: *Federal Reserve Bulletin,* (Washington D.C.: Board of Governors of the Federal Reserve System), various issues. Linked in 1959 to
1959–88: Data obtained from the Federal Reserve Bank of St. Louis.

8. Money supply ($M2$):
1875–1907: Milton Friedman and Anna J. Schwartz, *Monetary Statistics of the United States* (New York: National Bureau of Economic Research, 1970), 61–65. Linked in 1907 to
1908–46: *Historical Statistics,* series 415. Linked in 1947 to
1947–58: *Federal Reserve Bulletin,* various issues. Linked in 1959 to
1959–88: Data obtained from the Federal Reserve Bank of St. Louis.

9. Labor Productivity (Q/N):
1875–1946: Data computed by dividing real output, from line 3 above, by series A173 from *Long-term Economic Growth, 1860–1870.* Linked in 1947 to
1947–1988: Series 358 from *Business Conditions Digest.*

10. Nominal Interest Rate (r):

1875–1983: The yield on corporate bonds from Gordon, *The American Business Cycle,* Appendix B, 781–783.

1984–1988: Series 116 from *Business Conditions Digest.*

11. S&P's Stock Price Index:

1875–1983: Index of all common stocks from Gordon, *The American Business Cycle,* Appendix B, 781–783.

1984–1988: Series 19 from *Business Conditions Digest.*

C-2 QUARTERLY VARIABLES (Sources and Methods for Table A-2)

1. Nominal GNP (Y):

1947:Q1–1989:Q2: U.S. Department of Commerce, as published in *Survey of Current Business,* table 1-1.

2. GNP implicit price deflator (P):

1947:Q1–1989:Q2: U.S. Department of Commerce, as published in *Survey of Current Business,* table 7-4.

3. Real GNP (Q):

1947:Q1–1989:Q2: U.S. Department of Commerce, as published in *Survey of Current Business,* table 1-2.

4. Natural real GNP (Q^N):

1947:Q1–1987:Q3: Q^N is calculated as the geometric interpolation between the real GNP for the benchmark year 1929 and quarters 1949:Q1, 1954:Q1, 1957:Q3, 1963:Q3, 1970:Q2, 1974:Q2, 1979:Q3, and 1987:Q3. Thus, between benchmark quarters 1954:Q1 and 1957:Q3, the one-quarter growth rate of Q^N (q^N) is calculated as

$$q^N = \left[\frac{Q^N \; 1957{:}Q3}{Q^N \; 1954{:}Q1} \right]^{\frac{1}{14}} - 1.0$$

1987:Q4–1989:Q2: Extrapolated from 1987 value assuming an annual growth rate of 2.3 percent.

5. Unemployment rate (U):

1947:Q1–1989:Q2: *Business Conditions Digest,* February 1988 and various issues, series 43.

6. Natural unemployment rate (U^N):

1947:Q1–1989:Q2: The quarterly values are derived by a linear interpolation between the annual values of natural unemployment, described in section C-1.

7. Money supply ($M1$):

1947:Q1–1958:Q4: *Federal Reserve Bulletin,* various issues.

1959:Q1–1989:Q2: Data obtained from the Federal Reserve Bank of St. Louis.

8. Money supply ($M2$):

1947:Q1–1958:Q4: *Federal Reserve Bulletin,* various issues.

1959:Q1–1989:Q2: Data obtained from the Federal Reserve Bank of St. Louis.

9. Nominal interest rate (r):

1875:Q1–1983:Q4: The yield on corporate bonds, from Gordon, *The American Business Cycle,* Appendix B, 781–783.

1984:Q1–1989:Q2: Series 116 from *Business Conditions Digest.*

10. Weighted Exchange Rate:

1961:Q1–1969:Q4: The Effective Exchange Rate (MERM) from various issues of International Financial Statistics, (Washington D.C.: International Monetary Fund), various issues, series am x. Linked in 1970 to

1970:Q1–1988:Q4: Multilateral Trade Weighted Nominal Exchange Rate, provided by the Council Of Economic Advisers. Linked in 1988:4 to

1989:Q1–1989:Q2: The Effective Exchange Rate (MERM).

11. Actual federal government surplus in 1982 dollars:

1947:Q1–1989:Q2: Calculated by taking the nominal federal government surplus from U.S. Department of Commerce, published in *Survey of Current Business,* table 3-2, and then dividing by the implicit GNP deflator.

12. Natural employment surplus in 1982 dollars:

This series was calculated using data from Charles Holloway, "The Cyclically Adjusted Federal Budget and Federal Debt: Revised and Updated Estimates," *Survey of Current Business,* March 1986, and "Reconciliation and Other Special Tables," *SCB,* August 1988.

1947:Q1–1959:Q4: This was estimated using the Cyclically Adjusted Federal Receipts (CAFR) and Expenditures (CAFE) for 1960:Q1 to 1988:Q2 from the above mentioned *Survey of Current Business* sources. The following method was used:

Let LREV = 100 * Log(Real Actual Federal Receipts/CAFR)

LEXP = 100 * Log(Real Actual Federal Expenditures/CAFE)

QQN = 100 * Log(Q/Q^N)

Real Actual Federal Receipts were calculated by dividing nominal federal government receipts, taken from *Survey of Current Business,* table 3-2, by the implicit GNP deflator. Real Actual Federal Expenditures were calculated in the same way. Nominal federal government receipts and expenditures from U.S. Department of Commerce include the 1989 revisions.

The estimated values of CAFR and CAFE were calculated by first using Ordinary Least Squares to determine the coefficients of the equations:

$$LREV_t = A_0 + A_1 * QQN_t + e_t$$
$$LEXP_t = B_0 + B_1 * QQN_t + B_2 * QQN_{t-1} + e_t$$

Then estimates of CAFR and CAFE were determined according to:

$$CAFR = Exp\{Log(\text{Real Actual Federal Receipts}) - (A_1 * QQN_t)/100\}$$

$$CAFE = Exp\{Log(\text{Real Actual Federal Expenditures}) - (B_1 * QQN_t + B_2 * QQN_{t-1})/100\}$$

The estimated Cyclically Adjusted Federal Surplus = CAFR − CAFE

1960:Q1–1974:Q4: Cyclically Adjusted Federal Surplus from Holloway, *SCB*, Table 3, March 1986. Linked in 1974:Q4 to

1975:Q1–1980:Q4: Cyclically Adjusted Federal Surplus from Holloway, *SCB*, Table 6, March 1986. Linked in 1980:4 to

1981:Q4–1988:Q2: Cyclically Adjusted Federal Surplus from "Reconciliation and Other Special Tables," *SCB*, August 1988. Linked in 1988:Q2 to 1988:Q3–1989:Q2: The same method as was used for 1947:Q1 to 1959:Q4

C-3 INTERNATIONAL VARIABLES (Sources and Methods for Table B)

1. Nominal GDP (*Y*):
Nominal gross domestic product from *OECD Statistics Paris: 1989.* Updated to 1988 using data from OECD *Main Economic Indicators,* May 1989.

2. Implicit GDP deflator (*P*):
Calculated by dividing nominal GDP (*Y*) by real GDP (*Q*).

3. Real GDP (*Q*):
Real gross domestic product from *OECD Statistics Paris: 1989.* Updated to 1988 using data from OECD *Main Economic Indicators,* May 1989.

4. Labor productivity (*Q/N*):
Real Output (*Q*) is real GDP, and total work hours (*N*) are calculated by multiplying total employment (E) and hours worked per employee per year (*H*), or $N = EH$. Total employment is taken from *Labour Force Statistics, 1963–83* (OECD). It was updated to 1987 using data from *Quarterly Labour Force Statistics,* No. 4, 1988 (OECD) country pages, and to 1988 using *OECD Economic Outlook,* June 1989, Table 37. Series for aggregate hours worked per employee per year are from the OECD. Italy and the United Kingdom were updated to 1986 using data from the EEC provided by Charles Schultze. Hours for 1986 for Japan were assumed to be the same as in 1985. The hours for all countries for 1987 and 1988 were assumed to be the same as in 1986.

5. Unemployment rate (*U*):
Standardized unemployment rate, from the OECD Economic Outlook, old table R12 and new table R17. Broken series in table R17 were linked using table R18, reported unemployment rates, keeping the 1979 levels intact. Series for Italy were updated for 1986 through 1988 using table R18.

6. Money Supply (*M*1) and Money Supply (*M*2 − quasi-money):
*M*1 is the money supply taken from the *International Financial Statistics Yearbook 1988,* series 34. *M*2 is "money plus quasi-money," series 351 = 34 + 35, from the same source. The breaks in the series reported in the above source were linked using *OECD Historical Statistics 1960–81* and *1960–85*, tables 10-1 and 10-3. The break for Canada for *M*2 in 1967 was linked using the *M*1 growth rate for 1967. The data were updated to 1988 using *OECD Main Economic Indicators,* April 1989.

7. Consumer Price Index (CPI):
CPI taken from *International Financial Statistics,* various issues, series 64.

8. Long-term interest rates (*r*):
Interest rates were taken from the series for long-term government bond yields or series 61 in *International Financial Statistics Yearbook 1988.* They were updated to 1988 using the *IFS* for March 1989.

9. Labor share (*WN/Y*):
Labor share is the percentage of GDP received by labor in labor compensation. This is equal

to the "productivity gap," which is the ratio of real wages to labor productivity, since labor share $= (WN)/(PQ) = (W/P)/(Q/N) =$ the productivity gap. It was constructed by dividing total compensation received by labor by total GDP, both from *OECD Statistics Paris: 1989.* For 1988, wages were taken from *OECD Economic Outlook,* June 1989, Table 51, and employment and outlook from above sources.

C-4 VARIABLES USED IN FIGURES BUT NOT LISTED IN APPENDIX A OR B

Figures 1-10, 5-12. The real interest rate is derived from the nominal interest rate by subtracting the inflation rate, which was calculated as an annualized four-quarter rate of change in the fixed-weight GNP deflator.

Figure 2-6. Table numbers refer to *Survey of Current Business,* March 1989, pp. 3–9.

C, I, G, X, E: Table 1-1.
Q, S_D, NNP, Q_N, Q_P: Table 1-9.
R_B: NNP $- Q_N$.
R_C, R_S, R_P, government deficit: Table 3-2 plus Table 3-3.
F_G: $R_B + R_C + R_S + R_P - G +$ government deficit.
Q_D, S_P, F_P: Table 2-1.
S_B: $I + X -$ government deficit $- S_P - S_D$.

Personal income created from production:

$$Q_N - S_B - R_C - R_S = Q_P - F_G - F_P.$$

Figure 5-1. Real government revenues and expenditures include federal, state and local revenues and expenditures. 1790 to 1965 data were taken from *The Statistical History of the United States from Colonial Times to the Present* (Stamford, CT: Fairfield Publishers, Inc.), series Y 254, 255, 517, and 536. From 1966 to present *Economic Report of the President, 1989,* table B-79.

Figures 5-11, 5-12. The multilateral real exchange rate was computed and obtained for 1970–88 from the *Economic Report of the President,* 1989. It was linked to the effective exchange rate (MERM) in 1970:Q1 and 1988:Q4. From 1955 to 1960 the 1961:1 value of the effective exchange rate was used.

Table 7-1. The long-term interest rate is series B-72 in *Long-Term Economic Growth.* The average annual earnings was taken from *Historical Statistics,* p. 95, series 696—Average Annual Earnings per Full-Time Employee.

Table 10-1. Figures for oil price per barrel for 1970–85 are taken from *Statistical Abstract of the United States,* (U.S. Department of Commerce), table 1352 from 1980, table 1291 from 1982–83, and table 780 from 1986. Data for 1986–88 is from *Monthly Energy Review,* (Energy Information Administration), December 1988.

Figure 12-1. The calculations start with 1970 U.S. per capita GNP in 1982 prices, calculated from the *Economic Report of the President, 1989.* The real income per capita comparison for 1970 is based on a careful study which collected data on the prices for goods identical in quality to those in each other nation. Adjustments were made for services provided free by the government in some countries but not in others, e.g., free national health care in the United Kingdom. See Irving B. Kravis, Alan W. Heston, and Robert Summers, "Real GNP *Per Capita* for More Than One Hundred Countries," *Economic Journal,* vol. 88 (June 1978), Table 4, column (5), pp. 232–237. Figures for other years were obtained as follows: For 1960–86 the 1970 dollar figures were extrapolated forward and back by GNP per capita data obtained from *OECD Statistics,* Paris 1987. 1987–88 figures were obtained from *Main Economic Indicators,* OECD, Department of Economics and Statistics, December 1988. The postwar figures were linked in 1960 to those compiled for 1870–1979 in Angus Maddison, *Phases of Capitalist Development* (Oxford, England: Oxford University Press, 1982), tables A6, A7, A8 and B2, B3, B4.

Figure 13-2. Calculated with data received from Steve Morrel, constructed for J. Barth and S. Morrell, "A Primer on Budget Deficits," *Economic Review,* Federal Reserve Bank of Atlanta, Vol. 67, August 1982.

Figure 19-2. Net investment share for 1954–84 was calculated with data from John Musgrave, "Fixed Reproducible Tangible Wealth," table 4, *Survey of Current Business,* January 1986. Net investment share was computed by taking the first difference of nonresidential fixed capital and dividing by real output. For 1985–88, the values were forecast by regressing the sample of net investment share computed above on the current value and one period lag of net investment share, computed as real nonresidential fixed investment divided by real GNP, minus capital consumption allowances including capital consumption adjustment divided by nominal GNP. These figures were taken from the *Economic Report of the President,* January 1989.

Glossary

Note: Numbers in parentheses indicate the chapter and section where each term is first introduced. Words and phrases in the text set in boldface type are those defined in this list. These glossary definitions correspond to definitions given in the text margin next to each boldface term, but the definitions here are longer and more complete.

Accelerator hypothesis (19-3). The theory that the level of net investment depends on the change in expected output, because firms are assumed to maintain a fixed ratio of desired capital to expected output.

Accommodating policy (10-5). Following an adverse **supply shock,** a stimulus from **monetary** or **fiscal policy** that raises the rate of **nominal GNP growth** and offsets the reduction in the **output ratio** caused by the shock.

Activism. *See* **Policy activism.**

Adaptive expectations (9-6). A hypothesis that claims economic units base their expectations for next period's values on an average of actual values during previous periods.

Adjustable-rate mortgage (ARM) (16-9). Has an interest rate that can change frequently in response to changes in financial-market conditions, in contrast to a fixed-interest mortgage.

Aggregate (1-2). The total amount of an economic magnitude for the economy as a whole. Example: **GNP** is an economic aggregate.

Aggregate demand curve (6-1). The schedule that indicates the combinations of the price level and output at which the money and commodity markets are simultaneously in equilibrium.

Aggregate supply curve (6-1). The schedule that shows the amount of output that business firms are willing to produce at different price levels.

Appreciation (5-6). A rise in the value of one nation's currency relative to another nation's currency. Example: The appreciation of the American dollar relative to the German mark during 1980–85 meant that $1 bought more German marks than before.

Auction market (8-2). A centralized location where professional traders buy and sell a commodity or financial security.

Automatic stabilization (3-7, 5-4, 15-2). A feature of any economy in which tax receipts depend on income; the economy is stabilized by the **leakage** of tax revenues from the spending stream when income rises or falls.

Autonomous (3-2). A magnitude which is independent of the level of income. Example: Autonomous consumption spending.

Backward-looking expectations (9-6). The formation of expectations based only on information about the past values of economic variables. **Adaptive expectations** is one example of backward-looking expectations.

Bretton Woods System (14-6). This system, established at the end of World War II, maintained fixed exchange rates among nations until 1971.

Budget deficit (1-1, 5-2). *See* **Government budget deficit.**

Budget line (5-4). A positively sloped schedule relating the **government budget surplus** on the vertical axis to the **output ratio** on the horizontal axis; the positive slope occurs because a higher output ratio raises government tax revenues and thus boosts the government budget surplus.

Budget surplus (5-2). *See* **Government budget surplus.**

Business cycles (1-4). Fluctuations in output relative to its long-run trend (i.e., in the output ratio) that typically have a duration of three to five years. They are distinguished by broad dispersion across the economy of the sectors and industry groups experiencing a slump in sales followed by a sustained expansion. Business cycles are said to reach their **peak** when **real GNP** reaches a maximum level and then declines, and to reach their **trough** when **real GNP** reaches a minimum level and then rises. The period between peak and trough is called a **recession.** The movements in the **output ratio** during **business cycles** are almost always accompanied by movements in the unemployment rate in the opposite direction. *See* **Okun's law.**

Capital account (14-2). The portion of the balance of payments that includes direct investment and trade in both long-term and short-term securities.

Capital consumption allowances (2-9). Amount of capital stock used up in the process of production due to obsolescence and physical wear. *See* **Depreciation.**

Capital gain (11-9). Any increase in the value of a physical or financial asset. If you buy a share of stock for $20 and sell it six months later for $25, your capital gain is $5.

Capital-market instruments (16-2). Assets sold on financial markets that have relatively long maturities, can experience large fluctuations in price, and expose investors to the risk of capital loss.

Closed economy (1-8). Has no trade in goods, services, or financial assets with any other nation.

Cold turkey (9-8). This approach to disinflation operates by implementing a sudden and permanent slowdown in **nominal GNP** and growth.

Comparative statics (6-4). A technique of economic analysis in which a comparison is made between two equilibrium positions, ignoring the behavior of the economy between the two equilibrium positions, either the length of time required or the route followed during the transition between the initial and final positions.

Constant-growth-rate rule (CGRR) (15-2). A policy (recommended by many monetarists) that advocates a constant percentage rate of change of the **money supply** in order to prevent the Federal Reserve from destabilizing the economy.

Consumer expenditures (2-2). Purchases of goods and services by households for their own use.

Coordination failure (8-2). Occurs when there is no private incentive for firms to act together to avoid actions that impose social costs on society.

Cost-of-living agreements (COLA clauses) (8-3). Provisions in wage contracts for an automatic increase in the wage rate in response to an increase in a price index, usually the Consumer Price Index.

Countercyclical (6-7). An adjective describing any economic variable that fluctuates in the opposite direction as real output over the **business cycle.** *See* **Procyclical.**

Cross section (18-2). Data that cover numerous units each at the same point in time. Example: Cross-section studies of the income-consumption relation often gather consumption data for the various income classes during a single year.

Crowding out effect (4-10). The decrease in one component of spending when another component of spending rises. Example: When government expendi-

ture rises, the interest rate rises, depressing investment spending. This fall in investment is the amount that has been crowded out.

Current account (14-2). The portion of the balance of payments that includes **exports** and **imports** of goods and services, as well as **transfers** and gifts.

Cyclical deficit (5-4). The amount by which the actual **government budget deficit** exceeds the **structural deficit,** which in turn is defined as what the deficit *would be* if the economy were operating at **natural real GNP.**

Cyclical unemployment (11-1). The component of unemployment that rises and falls during **business cycles.** The remaining unemployment, which tends to remain even at the **peak** of the **business cycle,** is often called **structural unemployment.**

Deflation impotence (7-2). The failure of **real GNP** to respond to an increase in the real **money supply** caused by falling prices. *Keynes*

Deflator (1-3, 2-10). *See* **Implicit GNP deflator.**

Demand disturbances (15-1). Changes in business and consumer optimism, changes in net exports, and changes in government spending or tax rates (e.g., in wartime) not related to **stabilization policy.**

Demand inflation (10-1). Inflation caused by a continuous rightward shift of the **aggregate demand curve.**

Depreciation (2-9). Same as **capital consumption allowances.**

Depreciation (5-6). A decline in the value of one nation's currency relative to another nation's currency. Example: The depreciation of the American dollar relative to the German mark in 1985–88 means $1 bought fewer marks in 1988 than in 1985.

Depreciation rate (19-7). The annual percentage decline in the *value* of a piece of capital due to physical deterioration and obsolescence. Example: If your new car purchased for $5000 is worth only $4000 after one year, then its depreciation rate over that year is 20 percent.

Discretionary fiscal policy (5-4). A deliberate policy that alters tax rates and/or government expenditure in an attempt to influence real output and unemployment.

Discretionary policy (15-8). Treats each macroeconomic episode as a unique event, without any attempt to respond in the same way from one episode to another.

Disinflation (9-8). A marked deceleration in the **inflation rate.**

Disintermediation (16-9). The shift of funds out of savings banks when the interest rate on Treasury bills and bonds increased in the era before 1985 when there were **Regulation Q** ceilings, which prevented savings banks from raising their interest rate on deposits to compete with the higher returns available on Treasury bills and bonds.

Dynamic multipliers (15-7). The amount by which output is raised during each of several time periods after a $1 increase in autonomous spending. Example: The econometric models discussed in Section 15-7 have dynamic multipliers for a change in government spending, which generally rise through the first year, peak in the second year, and decline steadily thereafter.

Econometric models (15-6). A group of equations, each one representing a different relation in the economy, in which the parameters are estimated by the statistical study of past historical episodes. All the equations of an econometric model can be solved simultaneously to determine the levels of inflation, unemployment, other variables of interest, and what changes would occur with differing economic policies.

Economic growth (12-1). The study in economics of the causes and consequences of sustained growth in **natural real GNP.** Different rates of economic growth, maintained over long periods of time, can drastically change the order of nations' standings in the league table of living standards, as in Table 12-1.

Endogenous (3-1). An adjective describing a variable whose value is determined within an economic model rather than assumed as given from outside the model. Opposite of **exogenous.**

Equilibrium (3-4). A state in which there exists no pressure for change. Example: The commodity market is in equilibrium when the demand for commodities equals the supply of commodities.

Equilibrium real exchange rate (14-6). The exchange rate that would be consistent with a balanced current account after all lags of adjustment are completed.

Equilibrium real wage rate (6-6). The level of the real wage rate at which there is no pressure for change. This is the level determined by the crossing point of the labor demand and labor supply curves.

Eurosclerosis (10-10). An alleged European illness involving the effects of excessive government regulation and the encroachment of the welfare state in impeding the efficient operation of the labor market.

Excess reserves (17-2). The amount of reserves held by a bank in excess of its **required reserves.**

Exogenous (3-1). An adjective describing a variable whose value is assumed as given from outside an economic model rather than determined within the model. Opposite of **endogenous.**

Expansion (1-4). The period in the **business cycle** between the time **real GNP** reaches the level achieved at the **peak** of the last cycle and the peak of the current cycle.

Expectations-augmented Phillips curve (9-2). Same as the SP curve; it shifts its position whenever there is a change in the **expected rate of inflation.**

Expectations effect (7-2). The decline in commodity demand during a price deflation due to the expectation that future prices will be lower, leading to a postponement of purchases to take advantage of lower prices in the future.

Expected rate of inflation (9-2). The rate of inflation that is expected to occur in the future. The length of time into the future over which expectations are set depends on the decision maker. A union negotiator might look forward three years in setting a three-year union wage contract, but an investor might look over thirty years when investing in a bond with a thirty-year maturity.

Expected real interest rate (11-8). The real rate of return people expect to pay on their borrowings or earn on their savings after deduction of the **expected rate of inflation** from the **nominal interest rate.** Example: If people receive a 10 percent nominal return on their savings and expect a 7 percent inflation rate, the expected real interest rate is 3 percent. *See* **Real interest rate.**

Exports (2-5). Goods and services produced in country A and shipped to residents of another country. *See* **Imports.**

Extinguishing policy (10-5). Following an adverse **supply shock,** a restrictive **monetary** or **fiscal policy** that reduces the rate of **nominal GNP** growth in order to offset the extra inflation caused by the shock.

Extra convenience services (11-10). The convenience of money compared to bonds and other assets for conducting transactions. Money is immediately and universally accepted for purchases and payments, whereas bonds and other interest-bearing financial investments are not, forcing bondholders to convert their bonds into money before making transactions.

Factor inputs (12-3). The economic elements that directly produce **real GNP,** especially labor and capital (structures and equipment). Other types of factor input are research and development, education, and specialized training. The relation of output to factor inputs is given by the **production function.**

Feedback rule (7-6, 15-8). Sets **stabilization policy** to respond in a regular way to a macroeconomic event, like an increase in unemployment or inflation.

Final good (2-3). Part of **final product.** *See* **Intermediate good.**

Final product (2-3). All currently produced goods and services that are sold through the market but are not resold. Same as **gross national product.**

Financial deregulation (16-4). Occurred in the United States in the late 1970s and early 1980s, allowing financial institutions to offer many new types of assets offering both interest payments and check-writing privileges.

Financial intermediaries (16-2). Make loans to borrowers and obtain funds from savers, usually by accepting deposits.

Financial markets (16-1).   Organized exchanges where securities and financial instruments are bought and sold.

Fiscal policy (1-7).   Government policy that attempts to influence **target variables** by manipulating government expenditures and tax rates.

Fixed exchange rate system (5-6).   A system in which the **foreign exchange rate** is fixed for long periods of time.

Fixed investment (2-4).   All **final goods** purchased by business that are not intended for resale. Example: Buildings, machinery, office equipment.

Flexible accelerator (19-4).   The theory that the desired ratio of capital to expected output may be affected by the **user cost of capital.** The flexible accelerator hypothesis usually maintains that only a portion of any gap between the actual and desired capital stock will be made up in any one period.

Flexible exchange rate system (5-6).   A system in which the **foreign exchange rate** is free to change every day.

Flow magnitude (2-2).   Economic magnitude that moves from one economic unit to another at a specified rate per unit of time. Examples: **GNP, personal income.**

Foreign exchange rate (1-6, 5-1).   The amount of another nation's money that residents of a country can obtain in exchange for a unit of their own money. For instance, in July 1989, residents of the United States could obtain 1.85 deutsche marks for one U.S. dollar.

Foreign trade deficit (1-1, 5-6).   The excess of the nation's **imports** of goods and services over its **exports** of goods and services.

Foreign trade surplus (5-6).   The same as **net exports,** that is, **exports** minus **imports.**

Forward-looking expectations (9-6, 18-1).   A method of forming expectations that attempts to predict the future behavior of an economic variable using an economic model that specifies the interrelationship of that variable with other variables.

Frictional unemployment (11-1).   Occurs in the normal process of job search by individuals who have voluntarily quit their jobs, are entering the labor force for the first time, or are reentering the labor force.

General equilibrium (4-8).   A situation of simultaneous equilibrium in all the markets of the economy.

GNP.   *See* **Gross national product.**

GNP deflator (1-3).   *See* **Implicit GNP deflator.**

GNP gap (7-2).   The difference between **natural real GNP** and actual **real GNP.**

Government budget constraint (13-4).   Relates government spending to the three sources available to finance that spending: tax revenue, creation of bonds, and creation of money.

Government budget deficit (1-1, 5-2).   Excess of government expenditures (on goods, services, and **transfer payments**) over government tax revenues.

Government budget surplus (5-2).   Excess of government tax revenues over government expenditures. Equal to the **government budget deficit** with its sign reversed.

Gradualism (9-8).   This approach to **disinflation** operates by implementing a slow and gradual reduction in **nominal GNP** growth. *Opposite of Cold Turkey*

Gross (2-9).   An adjective that usually refers to magnitudes that include **capital consumption allowance.** Example: **Gross national product.** *See* **Net.**

Gross national product (GNP) (1-3).   The market value of all currently produced goods and services during a particular time interval that are sold through the market but are not resold.

High-powered money (17-2).   The sum of currency held by the nonbank public and bank reserves. This money is capable of supporting bank deposits equal to a multiple of itself.

Hyperinflation (11-10).   An extremely rapid inflation, reaching 100 percent or more *per month.*

Hysteresis hypothesis (10-10).   Holds that the **natural rate of unemployment** follows automatically in the path of the actual unemployment rate; if the actual rate were lowered by stimulative policy, the natural rate would automatically decline as well.

Implicit GNP deflator (1-3).   The economy's aggregate price index. Defined as the ratio of **nominal GNP** to **real GNP.**

Imports (2-5, 19-2).   Goods and services consumed in country A but produced elsewhere. *See* **Exports.**

Indexed bond (11-11).   A bond that pays a fixed **real interest rate** to its holder. Its **nominal interest rate** is equal to the fixed real interest rate plus the actual inflation rate.

Indirect business taxes (2-9).   Taxes on business levied as a cost of operation. Examples: Sales, excise, and property taxes.

Induced consumption (3-2).   The portion of consumption that responds to changes in income $(= cQ)$.

Induced saving (3-2).   The portion of saving that responds to changes in income $(= sQ)$.

Inflation (9-1).   A sustained upward movement in the aggregate price level that is shared by most products.

Inflation rate (1-1).   The percentage rate of increase in the economy's average level of prices.

Inflation tax (13-4).   The revenue the government receives from inflation; the same as **seignorage,** but viewed from the perspective of households.

Injection (2-6).   That part of income which is spent on nonconsumption goods. Example: Private investment, government spending. *See* **Leakage.**

Interest rate (1-1). Percentage rate paid by borrowers to lenders.

Interest rate differential (5-7). The average U.S. interest rate minus the average foreign interest rate.

Intermediate good (2-3). Any good that is resold by its purchaser either in its present or in altered form. *See* **Final good.**

International crowding out effect (5-6). Occurs when an expansionary **fiscal policy** reduces net exports by raising interest rates and the **foreign exchange rate.** Higher domestic interest rates attract capital inflows from abroad, which indirectly help finance the budget deficit created by the expansionary fiscal policy.

International reserves (14-1). The internationally acceptable assets each nation maintains to pay for any deficit in its balance of payments. The main types of international reserves are gold, the U.S. dollar, and special drawing rights.

Inventory investment (2-4). Changes in the stock of raw materials, parts, and finished goods held by business.

Investment (2-4). The portion of **final product** that adds to the nation's stock of income-yielding assets (inventories, structures, and business equipment) or that replaces old, worn-out assets.

IS curve (4-4). The schedule that identifies the combinations of income and the interest rate at which the commodity market is in equilibrium; everywhere along the *IS* curve the demand for commodities equals the supply of commodities.

J-curve phenomenon (14-5). The tendency for a nation to run a larger excess of **imports** over **exports** in the short run following a **depreciation** of its exchange rate, followed later by reduced **trade deficit.**

Labor-force participation rate (10-3). The ratio of the labor force (the total of the employed plus the unemployed) to the population of working age. In the United States the population of working age includes all individuals sixteen or older.

Lag of monetary policy (15-6). The time delay between policy changes by the Fed and the resulting response of private spending.

Leakage (2-6). That part of income which leaks out of the spending stream to taxes, saving, or imports rather than being spent on consumption goods. *See* **Injection.**

Life-cycle hypothesis (18-1). The theory that people try to stabilize their consumption over their entire lifetime. The life-cycle hypothesis predicts that young and old households will consume in excess of their income and that those in the middle-aged groups will save to support themselves during their retirement.

Liquidity constraint (18-6). Occurs when financial institutions do not allow households to borrow as much as they wish now, even though there is sufficient expected future income to repay the loans.

Liquidity trap (4-9). A situation in which the interest rate is believed by all to be at its minimum possible value and the price of bonds is as high as it is likely to go. Because people uniformly expect that bond prices will fall, they hold no bonds and there is no one from whom the Federal Reserve can purchase bonds in order to lower the interest rate and stimulate the economy.

LM curve (4-6). The schedule that identifies the combinations of income and the interest rate at which the money market is in equilibrium; everywhere along the *LM* curve the demand for money equals the supply of money.

Long-run equilibrium (6-7). A situation in which aggregate demand equals aggregate supply, and in addition, expectations turn out to be correct. *See* **Short-run equilibrium.**

Long-term labor contracts (8-3). Agreements between firms and workers that set the level of nominal wage rates for a year or more.

M1 (16-4). The narrowly defined **money supply;** the public's holding of currency and transaction accounts, that is, accounts at financial institutions against which checks may be written.

M2 (16-4). The broadly defined **money supply;** the sum of currency and checking accounts held by the public (*M*1) plus savings deposits and certificates held at commercial banks and **thrift institutions** plus accounts at money-market mutual funds.

Macroeconomic externality (8-2). One economic unit creates a macroeconomic externality when it imposes costs on other economic units without having to pay the bill.

Macroeconomics (1-1). The study of the major economic totals or aggregates.

Managed floating (14-6). A system intermediate between fixed and flexible exchange rates, in which the exchange rate is allowed to respond to movements in the long-run equilibrium exchange rate but not deviations from that equilibrium rate.

Marginal leakage rate (3-7). The fraction of income that is not spent on consumption; the fraction of income that flows into savings, income tax payments, and import purchases.

Marginal product of capital (19-5). The dollars of extra output in constant prices that a firm can produce over a specified period by adding an extra unit of capital, divided by the total cost of that capital. The marginal product, like the user cost of capital, is expressed as a percent. Example: If an extra $1000 machine produces an extra $150 worth of output in a year when no additional labor is hired, the marginal product of that piece of capital is 15 percent.

Marginal product of labor (6-5). The extra real output a firm can produce by adding an extra hour of labor.

Marginal propensity to consume (3-2). The change in **consumption expenditures** that results from an extra dollar of income; the fraction of an extra dollar of **personal disposable income** that households spend on consumption goods and services.

Marginal propensity to save (3-2). The change in **personal saving** induced by a $1 change in **personal disposable income.**

Market-clearing (7-2). A market-clearing model or theory holds that the economy is always in equilibrium at the intersection of supply and demand curves, particularly in the labor market.

Markup pricing (8-6). With markup pricing the price is set at the level of the average cost of labor and materials inputs, times a certain fraction, called a "markup," to cover capital cost and profits.

Medium of exchange (16-3). Used for buying and selling goods and services and is a universal alternative to the barter system.

Menu cost (8-1). Any expense associated with changing prices, including costs of printing menus or distributing new catalogs.

Mismatch unemployment (11-4). Another name for **structural unemployment,** it is one of the two components of the **natural rate of unemployment.**

Monetarism (15-1). A school of thought that opposes activist government policy intervention aimed at stabilizing aggregate demand.

Monetary impotence (7-2). Describes the failure of **real GNP** to respond to an increase in the real **money supply.**

Monetary policy (1-7). Government policy conducted in the United States by the Federal Reserve Board that attempts to influence **target variables** by changing the **money supply** and/or interest rates. *See* **Fiscal policy.**

Money-market instruments (16-2). Assets sold on financial markets that have short maturities, usually less than one year, small fluctuations in price, and minimal risk.

Money supply (4-6). The main policy instrument of **monetary policy.** The money-supply concept **M1** consists of currency held by the public and all checking accounts (demand deposits). See also **M2.**

Multifactor productivity (12-5). The growth rate of output per hour of work, minus the contribution to output of the growth in the quantity of other factors of production per hour of work, notably capital, but sometimes including energy, raw materials, or other factors of production. *See* **Total factor productivity.**

Multiplier uncertainty (15-7). The uncertainty about the exact numerical values and timing of spending multipliers; used as an argument against an activist **stabilization policy.** Example: Since each **econometric model** produces different estimates of policy multipliers, policymakers are uncertain as to the time value of each multiplier and therefore of the actual effect of policy changes.

National income (2-9). The income that originates in the production of goods and services; **net national product** less **indirect business taxes.**

Natural employment deficit (NED) (5-4, 15-2). The difference between tax revenue and government expenditure which would be generated if the economy were operating at the natural rate of output.

Natural rate hypothesis (NRH) (7-4). A model obeys the natural rate hypothesis when shifts in aggregate demand have no long-run effect on **real GNP.**

Natural rate of unemployment (1-4). The minimum sustainable level of unemployment below which inflation tends to accelerate. At this rate of unemployment, there is no tendency for inflation to accelerate or decelerate.

Natural real GNP (1-4). Estimate of the amount the economy can produce when actual unemployment is equal to the **natural rate of unemployment.** In this situation, there is no tendency for inflation to accelerate or decelerate.

Net (2-9). An adjective that usually refers to magnitudes that exclude the **capital consumption allowance. Net investment** is the amount by which the capital stock changes over a specified period. *See* **Gross.**

Net exports (2-5, 14-2). Excess of **exports** over **imports.**

Net foreign investment (2-5). Excess of **exports** over **imports** or **net exports.**

Net national product (2-9). Net market value of goods and services produced per unit of time; **GNP** less **capital consumption allowances.**

Neutral policy (10-5). Following any supply shock, a monetary or fiscal policy that maintains the previous growth rate of **nominal GNP.** Any impact of the shock on the inflation rate thus will cause an equal impact on **real GNP** growth in the opposite direction.

New classical macroeconomics (7-5, 15-1). The Lucas version of the new classical model is based on the three assumptions of **market clearing,** imperfect information, and **rational expectations. The real business cycle** model is another type of new classical model.

New Keynesian economics (8-1). Explains rigidity in prices and wages as consistent with the self-interest of firms and workers, all of which are assumed to have **rational expectations.**

Nominal (1-3). An adjective that modifies any economic magnitude measured in current prices. Example: **Nominal GNP** is the current dollar value of **GNP.**

Nominal GNP (1-3). The value of **gross national product** in current (actual) prices.

Nominal interest rate (1-6, 11-8). The interest rate actually charged by banks and earned by bondholders;

the market interest rate. Example: When a customer pays 12 percent interest on an auto loan, the nominal interest rate is 12 percent.

Nominal rigidity (8-1). A factor that inhibits the flexibility of the nominal price level due to some factor, such as **menu costs** and **staggered contracts,** which makes it costly for firms to change the nominal price or wage level.

Nonborrowed reserves (17-9). Total bank reserves minus bank borrowings from the Fed.

Nonmarket clearing (7-2, 8-1). A model in which workers and firms are not continuously on their demand and supply schedules, but rather are pushed off these schedules by the gradual adjustment of prices.

Normative economics (1-7). An individual's recommendations regarding an optimal or desirable state of affairs. *See* **Positive economics.**

Official reserve transactions (ORT) **balance** (14-2). The balance-of-payments surplus or deficit concept that includes all trade in goods and securities; any such deficit must be offset by an outflow of international reserves.

Okun's law (11-2). The name given to the close relationship in the postwar United States between the unemployment rate (U) and the ratio of actual to natural real output (Q/Q^N). According to the original version of Okun's law, a 1 percentage point rise (drop) in the unemployment rate is associated with roughly a 3 percent decrease (increase) in Q/Q^N. Now, however, it appears that there is a 2 rather than a 3 percent decrease (increase) in Q/Q^N.

OPEC (10-1). An abbreviation for the Organization of Petroleum Exporting Countries, the "oil cartel" that raised oil prices in 1973–74 and in 1979–80, thus administering a **supply shock** to the rest of the world. In 1985–86 a worldwide surplus of oil, resulting in part from the excessive previous price increases, caused OPEC to lose its power to control oil prices, and as a result oil prices fell by more than half.

Open economy (1-8). An economy in which there are flows of labor, goods, bonds, and/or money between nations.

Open-market operations (17-4). Purchases and sales of government bonds by the Federal Reserve, used to change the supply of **high-powered money,** the **money supply,** and interest rates. When the Federal Reserve wishes to raise the money supply, it buys bonds, paying with high-powered money, resulting in a higher money supply.

Output ratio (Q/Q^N) (9-7). The ratio of actual to **natural real GNP.** Movements in the output ratio are closely related to changes in unemployment. Its movements are determined by the interaction of the *IS-LM* model and aggregate supply behavior. Several concepts in the book are defined by setting the output ratio equal to 100 percent, including the **natural**

unemployment rate and the **natural employment deficit.**

Parameter (3-4, 5-appendix). Something taken as given or known within a particular analysis. Example: In the consumption function $(C = a + Q_D)$, autonomous consumption *(a)* and the **marginal propensity to consume** *(c)* are parameters. Many exercises in economics involve examining the effects of a change in a single parameter.

Peak (1-4). The highest point reached by **real GNP** in each **business cycle.**

Permanent income (18-3). The average income people expect to receive over a period of years, in the future often estimated as a weighted average of past actual income.

Permanent income hypothesis (PIH) (15-3, 18-1). The theory that consumption spending depends on the long-run average (permanent) income people expect to receive. Example: If people's incomes rise and fall with the **business cycle,** then their actual incomes will be above their permanent income in booms and below in recessions. Their saving will rise and fall with their actual income.

Persistent unemployment (7-2). A situation in which a high level of unemployment can last for many years, as in the United States from 1929–41 and 1980–85.

Personal consumption deflator (2-10). The price deflator for the personal consumption expenditures component of GNP.

Personal disposable income (2-9). The income available to households for consumption and saving; **personal income** less **personal income tax payments.**

Personal income (2-9). The income received by households from all sources (interest, wages, **transfers);** national income less corporate undistributed profits, corporate income taxes and social security taxes, plus **transfer payments.**

Personal saving (2-4). That part of **personal income** which is neither consumed nor paid out in taxes.

Pigou effect (7-2). The direct stimulus to autonomous consumption spending that occurs when a price deflation raises the real **money supply** and thus wealth. Also called the **real balance effect.**

Policy activism (15-1). Uses the instruments of **monetary** and **fiscal policy** actively to offset changes in private spending. An approach to policy that is criticized and opposed by **monetarism.**

Policy credibility (15-8). The belief by the public that the policymakers will actually carry out an announced policy.

Policy ineffectiveness proposition (7-6). Asserts that predictable changes in monetary policy cannot affect real output. One of the major contributions of the Lucas version of **new classical macroeconomics.**

Policy instruments (1-7, 15-2). Elements that government policymakers can manipulate directly to influence **target variables.** Examples: Personal income tax rate, **money supply.**

Positive economics (1-7). The attempt to describe and explain scientifically the behavior of the economy.

Price index (2-10). A weighted average of prices in the economy at any given time, divided by the prices of the same goods in a base year. Example: The Consumer Price Index is the ratio of an average of the prices of consumer goods in each month to the average prices of the same goods in 1982–84, the base years.

Procyclical (13-5). An adjective describing any economic variable that fluctuates in the same direction as real output, rising during a boom and declining during a recession. *See* **Countercyclical.**

Production function (6-5, 12-3). A relationship, usually written in algebra, that shows how much output can be produced by a given quantity of **factor inputs.**

Productivity (1-1). A general term that most often means the average amount of output (real GNP) produced per employee or per hour. New machines and inventions tend to raise the productivity of labor by helping workers to produce more.

Protectionist (5-2). A protectionist measure raises tariffs and/or quotas on foreign goods in an attempt to reduce **imports.**

Purchasing-power-parity (PPP) theory (14-4). The theory that the prices of identical goods should be the same in all countries, differing only by the cost of transport and any import duties.

Quantity theory of money (16-5). The theory that money is demanded to conduct transactions and that to facilitate these transactions people hold a constant fraction of their nominal income in the form of money. The strong version of the theory assumes also that real output is fixed, so price changes are proportional to changes in the **money supply.**

Rate of return (4-3). The annual earnings of an investment good divided by its total cost.

Rate of time preference (13-2). The extra amount a consumer would be willing to pay to be able to obtain a given quantity of consumption goods now rather than one year from now.

Rational expectations (7-5, 18-6). Such expectations need not be correct but rather are based on the best use of available information, avoiding errors that could have been foreseen by knowledge of past history.

Real balance effect (7-2). *See* **Pigou effect.**

Real business cycle (7-7). A cycle in actual **real GNP** due to fluctuations in **natural real GNP** (Q^N).

Real business cycle approach (7-7). Explains **business cycles** in output and employment as caused by technology or **supply shocks.**

Real exchange rate (5-6, 14-4). Equal to the average nominal **foreign exchange rate** between a country and its trading partners, with an adjustment for the difference in **inflation rates** between that country and its trading partners.

Real GNP (1-3). The value of **gross national product** in constant prices.

Real interest rate (1-6). The interest rate people actually pay on their borrowings or receive on their savings after allowing for the **inflation rate.** This equals the **nominal interest rate** minus the actual inflation rate. Example: When the nominal interest rate is 12 percent and actual inflation is 10 percent, the real interest rate is 2 percent.

Real money balances (7-2). The total **money supply** divided by the price level.

Real rigidity (8-1). A factor that makes firms reluctant to change the real wage (that is, the wage relative to the price) or the relative wage (the wage relative to other wages).

Recession (1-4). A period of declining real economic activity, often defined as a period during which **real GNP** falls for two quarters or more. A recession begins after the preceding expansion has reached its **peak** and continues until the economy reaches its **trough,** after which a ''recovery'' begins.

Rediscount rate (17-4). The interest rate the Federal Reserve charges banks when they borrow funds.

Redistribution effect (7-2). The effect on commodity demand caused by the redistribution of income from debtors to creditors during a price deflation. If debtors cut their consumption more than creditors raise theirs, then aggregate consumption falls.

Regulation Q (16-9). Until 1985 the Federal Reserve Board requirement that set an upper limit on the **nominal interest rate** commercial banks could pay to holders of time deposits. A similar regulation limited the allowable interest rates payable on deposits by savings and loan institutions. Resulted in **disintermediation** when market interest rates increased relative to the Regulation Q ceiling interest rate.

Required reserves (17-4). The reserves banks must hold according to Federal Reserve regulations; banks' deposits times the reserve ratio. Example: A bank with $100 million in deposits has required reserves of $10 million when the reserve ratio is 10 percent. In the United States, reserves can be held either as cash in the vault or as reserve deposits at the Federal Reserve.

Reserve requirements (17-4). The rules that stipulate the minimum fraction of deposits that banks must maintain as required reserves.

Residual (12-5). The amount that remains after subtracting from the rate of real GNP growth all of the identifiable sources of economic growth, including growth in the labor force and capital stock, as well as the contribution of education, research, and other factors.

Rigid rule (15-8). Sets a key **policy instrument** at a fixed value, as in a **constant-growth-rate rule** for the **money supply.**

Rigid wages (7-2). Refers to the failure of the nominal wage rate to adjust by the amount needed to maintain equilibrium in the labor market.

Sacrifice ratio (9-8). The cumulative loss of output incurred during a **disinflation** divided by the permanent reduction in the **inflation rate.**

Saving. *See* **Personal saving.**

Saving function. *See* **Consumption function.**

Seasonal unemployment (11-4). Occurs as the result of seasonal fluctuations in employment opportunities.

Seignorage (13-4). The revenue that government receives from inflation, equal to the inflation rate times real high-powered money.

Self-correcting forces (7-1). Inherent forces in the economy, particularly price flexibility, that propel it toward the natural output level without any government intervention. *Classical.*

Short-run equilibrium (6-7). A situation in which aggregate demand equals short-run aggregate supply, given the current state of expectations (expectations do not have to be realized in short-run equilibrium, as is required for long-run equilibrium).

Short-run Phillips curve (9-2). The schedule relating unemployment to the **inflation rate** achievable given a fixed **expected rate of inflation.**

Spending responsiveness (4-5). The dollar change in planned autonomous spending divided by the percentage point change in the interest rate that causes it.

Stabilization policy (1-7). A general term for **monetary** and **fiscal policies.** Any policy that seeks to influence the level of aggregate demand.

Stagflation (1-7, 9-7). A situation that combines stagnation (zero or negative output growth) with inflation.

Staggered contracts (8-1). Contracts setting the price of the wage level that have differing expiration dates for different groups of firms or workers.

Steady state (12-4). A situation in which output and capital input grow at the same rates, implying a fixed ratio of output to capital input.

Stock (2-2). An economic magnitude in the possession of a given unit or aggregate at a particular point in time. Examples: The **capital stock,** the **money supply.**

Store of value (16-3). A method of storing purchasing power when receipts and expenditures are not perfectly synchronized.

Structuralist hypothesis (10-10). Holds that the **natural rate of unemployment** is high because of specific impediments in the operation of the economy, particularly the labor market, including excessive real wages, high unemployment benefits, excessive government spending and regulation, high marginal tax rates, regional imbalances, and others.

Non-mon.

Structural unemployment (11-1). The component of unemployment that remains even when the economy is operating at or below its **natural rate of unemployment.** Structural unemployment consists of **mismatch unemployment** due to the imbalance between the skill and location requirements of jobs contrasted with the available skills and existing location of the unemployed.

Supply disturbance (10-1). *See* **Supply shock.**

Supply inflation (10-1). An increase in prices that stems from an increase in business costs not directly related to a prior acceleration of **nominal GNP** growth.

Supply shock (10-1). A change in the amount of output firms are willing to produce at a given price level. Examples: Crop failures caused by droughts and the 1973–74 and 1979–80 increases in oil prices.

Supply-side economics (13-9). The school of thought that predicts a substantial increase in **natural real GNP** as a result of reductions in marginal tax rates. Such tax reductions are predicted to reduce the disincentives for individuals to work and to save and to spur a large increase in work effort and in saving as a percentage of income. The influence of supply-side advocates was important in achieving the passage in Congress of President Reagan's 1981 tax-reduction proposals, which had the effect of pushing the natural-employment federal budget from balance to a large deficit during the period after 1981.

Target variables (1-7, 15-2). Aggregates whose values society cares about; society's economic goals. Examples: **Inflation, unemployment.**

Target zone (or range) (17-7). The level of a target variable like **M1** implied by the allowable range of growth rates under current policy.

Target zones (14-6). The **target zones** proposal specifies intervention by central banks whenever exchange rates move outside a specified band or zone.

Tax indexation (15-2). A proposal adopted in the United States in 1985 to raise nominal boundaries between tax brackets, as well as tax exemptions and the standard deduction, in proportion to changes in the Consumer Price Index. This eliminated one of the real effects of inflation, its tendency to push people into higher tax brackets and to reduce the real value of their exemptions and standard deductions, thus raising both their average and marginal tax rates.

Thrift institutions (16-2). Includes two types of **financial intermediaries,** savings and loan institutions and mutual savings banks. They formerly obtained most of their funds from savings deposits and made almost all of their loans in the form of mortgages, but in recent years have been allowed to become more like commercial banks.

Time inconsistency (15-8). Describes the temptation

of policymakers to deviate from a credible policy once it is announced.

Time series (18-2). Data that cover a span of time. Example: The behavior of consumption and income since 1900 constitutes time-series evidence that income and consumption are related.

Total factor productivity (12-5). The ratio of real output to a weighted average of factor inputs, especially labor and capital. The weights used to combine labor, capital, and sometimes other inputs (like energy) correspond to the shares of the income of each factor in total national income.

Total labor force (11-3). The total number of those employed and unemployed. Excludes those not working who do not seek work, but includes members of the armed forces.

Trade deficit (1-1, 5-6). *See* **Foreign trade deficit.**

Trade surplus (5-6). *See* **Foreign trade surplus.**

Transfer payments (2-3). Payments made for which no goods or services are produced in return. Examples: Welfare and social security.

Transitory income (18-3). The difference between actual and **permanent income;** not expected to recur.

Trough (1-4). The lowest point reached by **real GNP** in each **business cycle.** The calendar quarter when real GNP reaches its lowest point is sometimes called the "trough quarter."

Turnover unemployment (11-4). Another name for **frictional unemployment,** it is one of the two components of the **natural rate of unemployment.**

Unanticipated inflation (11-9). That portion of actual inflation which people did not expect; actual inflation minus expected inflation. Example: If people expect inflation to be 10 percent per year, but the actual rate is 12 percent, the unanticipated inflation rate is 2 percent.

Unemployment rate (1-1). The number of jobless individuals who are actively looking for work (or are on temporary layoff), divided by total employment plus unemployment.

Unintended inventory investment (3-4). The amount by which businesses are forced to accumulate inventories above their plans when the economy's planned expenditures fall short of production and income.

Unit of account (16-3). A way of recording receipts, expenditures, assets, and liabilities.

User cost of capital (19-5). The cost to the firm of using a piece of capital for a specified period, expressed as a percent of the total cost of the capital. The user cost is influenced by the interest and depreciation rates and by the tax treatment of investment, depreciation, and corporate profits.

Value added (2-3). The value of labor and capital services that occur at a particular stage of the production process. Thus value added in the retailing sector includes wages of workers in retail stores and capital income (interest, profits, and depreciation) of persons and firms owning retail establishments, but does not include any of the costs of manufacturing the products sold in the retail stores.

Velocity (4-7). The ratio of nominal income *(PQ)* to the **money supply** *(M);* the average number of times per year that the money stock is used in making payments for final goods and services. The inverse of velocity *(M/PQ)* is the amount of money held relative to nominal income.

Index

Symbol	Chapter where introduced	Definition
m^s	15	Growth rate of money supply
M	4	Nominal money supply
MC	6	Marginal cost
MLR	5-appendix	Marginal leakage rate
MPC	3,18	Marginal propensity to consume
MPK	19	Marginal product of capital
MPN	6	Marginal product of labor
MR	8	Marginal revenue
n	12	Rate of population growth
N	6	Level of employment
NED	5	Natural employment deficit
NNP	2	Net national product: $NNP = GNP - S_D$
NOW	16	Negotiable order of withdrawal
OPEC	10	Organization of Petroleum Exporting Countries
p	9	Actual inflation rate
p^e	9	Expected inflation rate
p^f	14	Growth rate of foreign or world price level
P	1	Implicit price deflator for gross national product
P^e	7	Expected price level
P^f	5,14	Foreign or world price level
PIH	15,18	Permanent income hypothesis
PIP	7	Policy ineffectiveness proposition
PPI	2	Producers' Price Index
PPP	14	Purchasing power parity
q	9,12	Growth rate of real income or real GNP
q^N	10-appendix	Growth rate of natural real GNP
Q	1	Real income or real GNP
$\hat{Q}$	10-appendix	Output ratio $(100(Q/Q^N) - 100)$
Q_D	2	Real disposable personal income
Q_N	2	Real national income: $Q_N = NNP - R_B$
Q_P	2	Real personal income: $Q_P = Q_N - S_B - R_C - R_S + F_G$
Q^e	19	Real expected sales
Q^N	7	Natural real GNP
Q^P	18	Real permanent income
Q^t	18	Transitory income: $Q^t = Q - Q^p$
QQ	6	Natural real GNP line
r	4	Real interest rate
r^e	11	Expected real rate of return